Copyright © historyofwrestling.info 2014. All Rights Reserved.

Published by lulu.com

All rights reserved. This book may not be reproduced, in whole or in any part, in any form, without written permission from the publisher or author.

This book is set in Rockwell Extra Bold, Impact and Arial.

10 9 8 7 6 5 4 3 2 1

This book was printed and bound in the United Kingdom.

ISBN 978-1-291-75779-8

THE RAW FILES 1997

James Dixon
Arnold Furious
Lee Maughan
Rick Ashley
Bob Dahlstrom

THE RAW FILES 1997

MEET THE TEAM

All of the contributors in this book have been wrestling fans for a long time, probably longer than we would care to admit. Some of our favourite memories of our early wrestling fandom involved renting video tapes and watching them repeatedly. However, there had never been one truly all encompassing guide to those tapes, and what turns up on them. Yes, there are some great sites on the internet here and there, but nothing ever published. No guide book. Here at *History of Wrestling*, we decided that *we* would write that book, and we did! With a century of combined viewing between us, we have lived through all of this many times over. We decided to bring that knowledge and love of wrestling, to you. While the opinions you will read are often controversial, off-the-wall or just plain moronic, they are from likeminded people who put wrestling before almost anything else. Disagree with them if you wish, certainly the office has seen its fair share of furniture thrown and occasional bloodshed (there was an unpleasant incident with a stapler that was later resolved with a pint). After the success of our ongoing *Complete WWF Video Guide* series, and the fun we had doing it, we have decided to branch out further and cover *everything* the WWF has ever produced. It might take a while. This is the fifth in our series of books covering WWF flagship show Monday Night Raw. Look out for other TV shows and books about other wrestling promotions, coming soon.

THE TEAM AT WWW.HISTORYOFWRESTLING.INFO:

ARNOLD FURIOUS
Arnold Furious likes… Mitsuharu Misawa, Jushin Liger, Eddy Guerrero, Bret Hart, Raven, Toshiaki Kawada, Vader, Samoa Joe, Bryan Danielson, Kenta Kobashi, Star Wars, Martin Scorsese, Arnold Schwarzenegger, Bill Hicks, Wall-E, Akira Kurosawa, Johnny Cash, Scott Pilgrim, Tintin, The Wire, Firefly, The Simpsons, Jackie Chan, AC/DC, Rocky, Simon Furman, Danny Wallace, Aerosmith, The British Red Cross, Garth Ennis, Batman, Kiss, Asterix, Alan Moore's Top Ten, Astor City, Christopher Waken, Juliette and the Licks, Quentin Tarantino, Goodfellas, Kurt Busiek, Watchmen (the book, not the film), White Out (the book, not the film), Super Troopers, Swingers, Death's Head, Iron Maiden, Will Ferrell, Clint Eastwood, Trish Stratus, Everton FC, Tom Hanks, The Blues Brothers, Simon Pegg, Clerks, Terry Pratchett, Richard Pryor, Viz, Mutemath, Joe Bonamassa, How to Train Your Dragon, Stevie Ray Vaughan, Dexter, Jimi Hendrix, Alien, Aliens, Predator, Frankie Boyle, Secret Wars, Woody Allen, True Romance, Lethal Weapon, Takashi Miike, Graham Linehan, Big Bang Theory, Darren Aronofsky, John Woo, Charlie Chaplin, films with ridiculous shoot-out sequences in them, Douglas Adams, Chow Yun Fat, 12 Angry Men, Wilson Pickett, Studio Ghibli, Pixar, The Avengers, Fable II, history, Bill Bailey, Skyrim, Stephen Fry, Top Gear, kung fu movies, Alan Wake, Meet the Feebles, Die Hard, Sin City (the books and the film), zombies, Red Dwarf, Peter Sellers, Peter Cook, Michael Caine, Planet of the Apes, conspiracies, steak, The Princess Bride, Grimlock, Mel Brooks, top fives, 30 Rock, Preacher, Pringles, Pirates of the Caribbean, Back to the Future, Klaus Kinski, The Sopranos, boxing, Casablanca, Stephen King, Hunter S. Thompson, Mike Leigh's Naked, Captain America, Hawkeye, Spaced, Flight of the Conchords, Monty Python, Pearl Jam, Carol Danvers, 100 Bullets, Indiana Jones, The Goon, Thorntons, Jack Nicholson, Jim Beam, real ale, cartoons, novelty underwear, the Joker, Frank Miller, Robert Brockway, The Breakfast Club, Far Cry 3, Freddy Krueger, Alec Baldwin's speech in Glengarry Glen Ross, John Carpenter, Bill & Ted, MMA, John Wayne, Terrence Howard, The Terminator, Guy Forsyth, nudity, coffee, crazy Japanese films that make no sense, crazy Japanese wrestling that makes no sense, crazy Japanese people that make no sense, Greg Benson, Tony Cottam, Bernard Rage, Redje Harris, Ezet Samalca…and forever Maria.

JAMES DIXON
James Dixon has been watching wrestling for over 20 years. Inspired by the likes of Davey Boy Smith, Bret Hart and The Undertaker, Dixon was drawn to the business like any other fan, for reasons that are difficult to explain. A hobby quickly became an obsession, and Dixon was determined to get involved in wrestling by utilising the one thing he could do: write about it. In previous books James wrote alongside his "writing partner" Evil Ste. The truth is, the Evil Ste character was merely an extension of Dixon's own personality, his way of sharing his Jekyll and Hyde opinions on things. The writing choice worked fairly well at first, but the team all feel it has perhaps become more gimmicky that was hoped, so Dixon has reverted to just writing as himself. Well, we say himself. In reality James is a former British professional wrestler, but he has adopted the pseudonym to retain relative anonymity and to distance himself from his past career in the industry. However, that past experience does give him a unique and more inside perspective on things than the others, though he is still a "mark" at heart. James has limited patience for anything in wrestling post-2002, and much prefers 80s and 90s grappling. Curious really, because as you will see in these pages, he spends a lot of time complaining about it. James currently lives in the North of England, where it rains the majority if the time.

LEE MAUGHAN
Lee Maughan has been a fan of the professional wrestling industry for as long has he can remember, dating back to an embryonic memory of sitting on his grandparent's living room floor, his eyes transfixed to British household names Big Daddy and Giant Haystacks belly-busting their way through ITV's *World of Sport*. Somehow this wasn't enough to deter him, and young Lee was rewarded with having the incredibly good fortune to be within the WWF's target demographic just in time its early 90s UK boom period. He was hooked, his bedroom quickly becoming a wall-to-wall palace of video tapes, action figures, magazines, posters and any piece of tat all stamped with the WWF insignia. His thirst for the quasi-sport was ravenous but unfortunately, his family were too cheap to subscribe to Sky television, home of the WWF. His quencher? WCW *International Pro*, broadcast well past his bedtime on regional terrestrial station Tyne-Tees. Those WWF magazines soon found themselves piled up alongside copies of *Pro Wrestling Illustrated* and *Superstars of Wrestling*, making Lee possibly the most clued-up eight year old wrestling superfan in the entire TS14 postcode. It's possible, nay probable thanks to a further 20 years of research, that Lee is still the most clued-up wrestling superfan in the entire TS14 postcode. A trader of tapes, a distributor of DVDs and a purveyor of pixels, Lee keeps up with everything from New Japan to CHIKARA whilst continuing to catch up with the classics of pro wrestling's territorial days. Away from the grapple game, Lee likes to watch sitcoms, rock out in punk bands, and play video games with a strong preference for old school platformers and kart racers. Despite this, he even found the time to graduate from the University of Teesside in 2005 with a degree in media production, and after much soul searching and stints making Christmas cards for a living and working as a producer and on-air talent for a community radio station, is now taking the tentative first steps into the world of film video editing. He also tweets with a reverently dry sense of humour **@atomicbombs**, but reserves the right to ignore you entirely unless you want to pay him to write about wrestling, guitar bands or 80s pop culture for your book, website or magazine.

BOB DAHLSTROM
Bob Dahlstrom is many things. A son, a brother, an uncle; but also is a dude who likes to draw. And more importantly than that, a lifelong wrestling fan. It all started back at WrestleMania III, which hooked young Bob. He would then go onto rent every wrestling tape from every video rental place around, and watch them over and over. He's never looked back. All the artwork in this book has been loving crafted exclusively by Bob, specially for this publication. He lives in Illinois with his girlfriend and pet guinea pig. His wrestling artwork and autobiographical webcomic *Egomaniac* can be found at www.robertpfd.com.

Follow us on Facebook:
www.facebook.com/historyofwrestling.info

Follow us on Twitter:
@WWFVideoGuide

THE SCORING SYSTEM

We have used the popular star system in order to rate the matches that appear in this book. For those who are unaware of it, here is the key:

*****	Perfect
****½	Very close to perfect
****	Superb
***½	Very good
***	Good
**½	Decent
**	Average
*½	Nothing to it
*	Bad
½*	Terrible
DUD	Utterly worthless
SQUASH	Not rated (too short)
N/R	Not rated (for various reasons)
Negatives	Any match that goes into negative stars is one of the worst you will ever see

Sometimes things will be so bad, that we go into negative stars. These are matches that will make you want to stop watching wrestling and find a new hobby. We also dabble frequently in quarter stars, just when we cannot quite decide which of the above criteria a match falls under, and decide that it is somewhere in between.

It is important to remember that all star ratings are entirely subjective to the person awarding them. One man's **** bout could be another man's **. There is no set judging system for these things, this is not gymnastics or synchronised diving. That is the uniqueness of wrestling; everyone likes it for different reasons. There have been a few times in the past that the writers have reviewed the same matches and given different ratings. This is an example of how different people perceive things. So if your favourite match is not rated as highly as you might have hoped, don't worry, it shouldn't change your enjoyment of it. In fact, many a good natured argument has occurred in our offices about whether a match is "*****" or "****¾", that is just the nature of the business and one of the things that makes it so unique and fun to watch.

Some may also be wondering how we reached the scores that each show receives at the end of a review. Rest assured, it is not just a figure plucked out of the sky, like in some video games magazines. Rather, we have created a complex algorithm that takes into account various factors and data. These include: length of the show, the ratings of the matches (and segments) broken down into weighted points that are awarded to the show, the number of matches, historical relevance, and many other factors. Unfortunately this is top secret, and we cannot go into a full explanation here. However, we can guarantee that many hours have been spent on this in order to make it the fairest and most consistent overall review scoring system you will ever find. Of course, you can still get the opinion of the writers about whether it is worth seeing, regardless of the score, in the verdict section of the review.

The score it produces is not so much an overall rating for the show, but rather a "watchability" rating. Basically, how easy it is to sit through in one sitting and enjoy. Some shows have genuine, all-time classic matches, on long cards full of dull wrestling otherwise. While that match will improve the score of the show, it alone is not enough to make the whole show watchable on its own. The match yes, the show no.

Some tapes, shows and events inevitably end up with very high scores, and can even surpass the 100 point limit that we set. Our cap is 100, so that is the highest score a card can get. Similarly, a show can drop below zero if it is so bad, but we cap the minimum at zero so it cannot. If something receives a full 100 score, it does not necessarily mean that all of the content is perfect. Rather, as a whole, it is generally so good and consistent and in places outstanding, that it is entirely watchable and the time flies by when viewing it. These scores crop up now and again, but not too frequently. The score is the overall equivalent of a 5* match. In our eyes at least, anyway.

A complete list of the shows in order of score is available at the back of the book.

We have made attempts to be a little more generous with the ratings we awarded to matches in this book, as compared to say a pay-per-view event or home video release. This is because the content offered here was available for free on TV, and thus you are not paying to watch the bout. That in itself can sometimes be enough to turn a ** match on PPV into a *** match on TV.

CONTENTS

JANUARY

10 01.06.97
11 01.13.97
12 01.20.97
13 01.27.97

FEBRUARY

14 02.03.97
17 02.13.97 - "Thursday Raw Thursday"
20 02.17.97
23 02.24.97

MARCH

25 03.03.97
27 03.10.97
29 03.17.97
32 03.24.97
34 03.31.97

APRIL

36 04.07.97
38 04.14.97
41 04.21.97
44 04.28.97

MAY

46 05.05.97
48 05.12.97
51 05.19.97
53 05.26.97

JUNE

55 06.02.97
58 06.09.97
61 06.16.97
65 06.23.97
68 06.30.97

JULY

70 07.07.97
73 07.14.97
75 07.21.97
77 07.28.97

AUGUST

79 08.04.97
82 08.11.97
85 08.18.97
87 08.29.97 - "Friday Night's Main Event"

SEPTEMBER

90 09.05.97 - "Friday Night's Main Event"
92 09.08.97
94 09.15.97
96 09.22.97
98 09.29.97

OCTOBER

100 10.06.97
104 10.13.97
108 10.20.97
111 10.27.97

NOVEMBER

114 11.03.97
116 11.10.97
118 11.17.97
121 11.24.97

DECEMBER

122 12.01.97
125 12.08.97
128 12.15.97
130 12.22.97
133 12.29.97

137 Raw Recap Summary
138 The Story So Far...

139 **The Shotgun Files**
140 01.04.97
141 01.11.97
142 01.18.97
144 01.25.97
145 02.01.97
146 02.08.97
147 03.08.97

149 **The Flashback Files**
150 WWF Summer Flashback
151 WWF Flashback: Survivor Series

154 Coliseum Classics - What the World was Watching
155 Hall of Shame - The Worst Matches of the Year
156 The Best Matches so far...
157 The Worst Matches so far...
158 The Raw Awards
166 Show Rank Index

01.06.97 by Arnold Furious

Venue: Albany, NY
Taped: 12.30.96
Raw Rating: 2.1
Nitro Rating: 3.4

This was technically taped in 1996 but I'm beginning to get used to sitting down to a new month of *Raw* and discovering a taped show. Hosts are Vince McMahon and Jerry Lawler. Video Control opens with Vader threatening Bret Hart. That's tonight's main event. Vince talks about *Shotgun Saturday Night* where Marlena got her tits out and Ahmed hit the Pearl River Plunge on a car.

Owen Hart vs. Mankind
To refresh your memory; Owen is one half of the tag champs with Bulldog. He's part of Camp Clarence. Mankind has Paul Bearer as a manager. Both guys are heel, but the WWF were doing more heel-heel and face-face matches. Owen outwrestles Mankind in the early going and almost gets the Sharpshooter. Mankind is more interested in mauling Owen and trying to get the Mandible Claw. Owen counters that by biting the fingers of Mankind. The psychology is really strong as both guys have a good understanding of both their character and their opponent. Owen is in a particularly creative mood and uses his tag belt ahead of a seated version of the spin kick. Foley brings super selling and drops through the ropes to sell the enzuigiri. Not the dazed, staggering fall of Shawn Michaels. He just dropped, deadweight. These guys mesh surprisingly well. You'd think Owen's purist and flying style would clash with Mankind, but as he showed against Shawn Michaels, Foley likes wrestling guys with that style. They show skill again as Owen counter out of a neckbreaker into a DDT and then escapes the Mandible Claw by wrestling out. Owen takes a header into the buckles and gets nailed with a quick piledriver for the pin. Terrific stuff from both men. A hard fought contest with some of the slickest countering you'll see.
Final Rating: ***

Backstage: In Jose Lothario's locker room HBK's trainer gets words on his recovery. His son is there too; Pete Lothario. You can tell he's from Texas because he's got a cowboy hat on.

Video Control gives us more clips from *Shotgun Saturday Night*. It took place in a night club in New York. The Flying Nuns debut (one called Mother Smucker). We get that Ahmed Pearl River Plunge on the car again.

Razor Ramon II & Diesel II vs. Doug Furnas & Phil LaFon
Honky Tonk Man joins commentary. He's scouting talent. I pity Phil, having to try and get something useful out of the Fake Outsiders. Vince seems to have been informed that Furnas and LaFon are good because he suddenly puts them over like crazy. He seems more enamoured with Furnas for his raw power, especially so when he throws Razor Rick over his head with a belly to belly. Honky makes reference to not wanting any jobbers. No scrubs, if you will. The fakes work protracted heat on Furnas. The fans in Albany are not interested. LaFon gets a hot tag and messes Diesel up with kicks. His back kick is fantastic. Razor Rick comes in to get suplexed around and Furnas comes back in, right back into more heat. The match breaks down and Diesel takes a horrible spot where he lands head first on the apron. Razor Rick is left alone and double teamed into the pin. The Fakes dragged this down. Furnas & LaFon needed quality to work with. It should have been a wake up call for a bad tag team division.
Final Rating: *¼

Video Control gives us more footage from *Shotgun Saturday Night* with Marlena exposing herself to both freak out Bob Backlund and cause the Sultan to lose to Goldust.

Backstage: Bret questions Shawn's integrity but his interview is cut off by the arrival of Sycho Sid in the ring for another interview. Bret looks pretty pissed off.

Promo Time: Sycho Sid
Sid gets mic time, Bret's by the look of it, during an in-ring interview conducted by Jim Ross. Sid has a definite heel edge to him. Sid says he's "not intimidated by nothing", which is a double negative. Technically everything intimidates him. He tells us he has a policy of striking first, as if Jose Lothario might have hit him with a camera. Although the odds are against him Sid claims he'll leave San Antonio still "the man". The interview wasn't too thrilling and came off as cookie cutter from the champ. Shawn Michaels shows up before Sid is done, which pisses him off and Sid warns he's "not responsible" for what he'll do next.

Bret Hart vs. Vader
For those who like hidden highlights Shawn Michaels comes out without a shirt on. See, last time he commentated on a Bret match the Hitman pulled Shawn's shirt over his head and gave him a hockey style beating. Shawn wastes no time getting his shots in on Bret, pointing out he's been out here defending the WWF title while Bret sat at home and criticised him. This match made it onto Bret Hart's tape released about a week later. We clip away to show Jim Cornette getting a Tombstone on *Superstars*. Shawn continues the abuse calling Bret an "oil spot on the mat". He then moves on to fashion; "Vader hits you so hard when you wake up your clothes are out of style. Of course that's not a problem for Bret". He then rounds on Lawler for stealing his jokes and Vince for the whole "The Man They Call Vader" thing. Who are "they"? He wonders. The shoot-ish commentary is very entertaining but hugely distracting. Luckily Vader and Bret don't have much of a plan. Bret works the arm a bit to slow Vader up. It doesn't. Vader dominates after a sluggish opening period, using his size and power. Shawn continues to rail on Bret by calling him "no angel" before adding he can't mention specifics or Bret will punch him again, obviously referencing Bret's extramarital affairs on the road. Next up is Shawn calling all Bret's matches the same, which is rich coming from a guy who finishes every single match with the same three moves. Bret's criticisms of Shawn at least had some basis in fact, whereas Shawn comes off as bitter for retaliating. The idea was for Bret to be the heel in their feud. Sid comes out to acquire a cameraman and Steve Austin runs out here at the same time to clock Bret with a Stunner. Vader rolls the Hitman back inside and finishes with the Vaderbomb. I like that Vader got himself a big win, but poor Bret got screwed again. Considering what a hot property he was in early 1997 the WWF jobbed him out over and over again. When I watched this for Bret's tape it seemed a bit better thanks to the opening 3-minutes of nothing happening being clipped off.
Final Rating: **½

Backstage: Sid's cameraman captures Sid powerbombing poor Pete Lothario onto a table. Screw you, Pete!

THE RAW RECAP

Most Entertaining: Owen Hart. I thought he was superb

against Mankind, incorporating wrestling and his own high spots into Foley's normal match. A longer PPV match would have been great.

Least Entertaining: Razor Rick. Another year, same shit.

Quote of the Night: "Those nuns have terrible habits McMahon" – Honky Tonk Man makes the "funny".

Match of the Night: Owen Hart vs. Mankind

Verdict: The petty bickering between Bret Hart and Shawn Michaels was already affecting the show. They'd both have better nights in wrestling than this. Instead it was left to Owen Hart and Mick Foley to steal the show and they did so easily. Their encounter showed tremendous promise and I'm surprised the WWF didn't consider a longer program but I guess the heel/heel nature of their alignments prevented that.
Rating: 50

01.13.97 by Arnold Furious

Venue: Albany, NY
Taped: 12.30.96
Raw Rating: 2.3
Nitro Rating: 3.4

We're still in Albany, New York and this is the same taping as last week, from the end of 1996. Hosts are Vince McMahon and the Honky Tonk Man.

Hunter Hearst Helmsley & Jerry Lawler vs. Marc Mero & Goldust

Mero is half asleep and forgets to attack Lawler at the bell. He just stands there watching Goldust attack Hunter. A typical Jerry Lawler match, in the WWF at least, was considered a night off for most guys because he could draw ridiculous heat without doing anything. Apart from poor Jackie Doan, as Lawler takes a massive back bump onto his leg. Not easy being an official in the WWF. The storyline in this match is that Goldust is incredibly pissed off with Hunter, so Helmsley avoids tagging in and tries to get Mero isolated. Which is a case of formula being designed very deliberately as the hot tag will eventually see Goldust get his hands on Hunter and that's what the fans want to see. It's all very clever and orchestrated but unfortunately until that happens the fans just sit around bored. Goldust even sneaks around on the floor to take a run at Helmsley on the outside. Honky tries to keep the tone light by mentioning Vince is on his hit list because "you can sing". Someone's been watching the '*Stand Back*' music video again Goldust jumps in without a tag and Hunter bails on King Jerry. The heels have miscues at every opportunity, as if Lawler has it in his contract that every time he works a tag his partner must accidentally punch him at least twice. Hot tag to Goldust and finally Hunter takes his beating, after 10-minutes of hanging around on the apron. Goldust gets Hunter tied up in the ropes and chokes him out until Jack Doan has seen enough and calls it a DQ. Goldust punches Lawler off him, and Mero, causing babyface dissention. Mero is stupid enough to not fight back thus killing the angle dead. The match was based on Goldust finally getting a measure of revenge on chickenshit heel Helmsley, but then when he did it lasted all of 30 seconds.
Final Rating: *

Video Control takes us to tape of Sid talking about slaying monsters and how you may become a monster yourself. The best part of Sid's analogy is he considers Shawn the monster, not him. The tape comes from the Alamodome in San Antonio and Sid's yelling and screaming echoes around the empty building. It's a good promo.

Video Control takes us live to San Antonio where Shawn Michaels is at Park Place. Vince shows him footage of Sid messing with the Lothario family, culminating with the powerbomb on Lil' Petey Lothario last week. Shawn tries to respond to Sid's points but the live interview doesn't help him. He says Texans can be nice or kick you in the teeth. Shawn makes wild claims about knowing everyone in San Antonio. Vince suggests the pressure of all those fans might be too much for Shawn. It's weird how they totally skewed this after Shawn was booed out of the building in MSG when he lost the title. Shawn ends up running out of things to say and reminds us he'll kick Sid in the teeth a few times.

More from Video Control as Steve Austin jumps Bret Hart on *Superstars* and Pillmanizes the ankle. Bret hobbles out here, probably confusing the fans who've not yet seen the *Superstars* angle, to do commentary on the next match. The idea being that British Bulldog had Bret's back the first time Austin tried to attack Bret. So now Bret is watching out for Austin.

The British Bulldog vs. Rocky Maivia

Bret puts Rocky over big time, and indeed rated him from the beginning. Vince throws to clips of Rocky saving Sable on *Shotgun Saturday Night*. That might have been an interesting angle. Vince tries to sell the *Royal Rumble* and throws to Bret for help, only for Bret to go on an anti-Austin rant to get his own angle over. It makes sense. The next question relates to Bret and Honky Tonk and Bret skims over it, thankfully thinking about his past association with Honky under the Jimmy Hart banner. Rocky gets to throw Bulldog around a bit and Davey makes the rookie look solid. Slammy Award winner Owen Hart comes out as Bret preaches harmony and says if Owen leaves him alone he'll leave Owen alone. Owen's idea is to keep an eye on Bret so he can't interfere in Bulldog's match. Owen's character was somewhat blinkered wasn't he? Surely he should be watching out for Steve Austin. The shenanigans allow the wrestlers to take a backseat. They run through basics and Davey controls the pace nicely. There's not much actually happening but they don't do anything wrong, which was a trademark of early Rocky matches. He might not do anything complicated but he'd always do it all right. To give Rocky a bit of flair, he's adopted Rocky Johnson's punches. Austin takes an opportunity to run out and chopblock Bulldog. Stunner! Bret goes to get him but Owen blocks his path, not realising what's happening. Rocky rolls back inside and Davey loses on count out. Rocky continues to showcase his confidence and strength at the basics of pro-wrestling. His learning curve was quite remarkable and he's better here than he was just two months earlier.
Final Rating: **

Backstage: Nation member Crush rants a bit, trying to look intimidating with his smudged head "tattoo".

The Undertaker vs. Crush

The Nation get to come out second, which allows Taker the chance to storm the entire group in the aisle. Taker-Crush is about as good as you'd expect. They could do with adding an extra layer of booking to this one, much like in the last match. Faarooq does his best to interfere, crotching the Dead Man as he tries for the Old School ropewalk. The match is a brawl until

Crush hits a piledriver. He doesn't like being called a "jailbird" says Vince. "Here's your jailbird right here" shouts Crush as he elbows Taker in the match. Which would be fine… if anyone was chanting anything. Which they're not. It's just the WWF's way to try and get heat on something that has no heat. Oh, he doesn't like it when you people chant "tamponbrain" at him. Crowd dutifully start "tamponbrain" chant. Hey, look, he's over now! Except nobody cares about Crush because he's been around for years and he's been worthless for years. Crush plods through a heat segment as Honky makes fun of Ahmed Johnson for his incoherent promos. Crush escapes a Tombstone into a belly to belly in the only decent piece of wrestling in the match. Taker counters the Heart Punch into the chokeslam. That was NOT good wrestling. Crush didn't bother jumping on the chokeslam at all. The Nation run in for the nWo-style DQ. Vader joins in, presumably because of his belief in black power, and gives Taker a few Vaderbombs. Ahmed Johnson runs in with a 2x4 for the save but Vader stops that in a hurry and Faarooq nails Ahmed in the kidneys with the 2x4 as we go off the air.
Final Rating: ½*

THE RAW RECAP

Most Entertaining: Given the total lack of entertainment on this show I'll go with Sid. At least he tried.

Least Entertaining: Crush. Given his past, he really shouldn't be pushed as a wrestler anymore.

Quote of the Night: "Sable was on your list last Saturday night at Shotgun Saturday Night, Saturday night" – Vince McMahon gets slightly carried away.

Match of the Night: Rocky Maivia vs. The British Bulldog

Verdict: A pretty dull *Raw* on the whole. The long taping session had worn the crowd down and Taker vs. Crush wasn't going to wake them up. Davey's decent match with the young Maivia showed he was in the mood to have a good year. He'll be popping up in the awards section more than once, I suspect. 1997 is a year of huge change. We start out with new stars, all manner of conflict with the existing stars and no sense of direction at all. If you were watching this show; who is the WWF's top guy? Bret? Shawn? Taker? Austin? Vader? Ask that question again a year later and it's Austin. All the way. That sense of the unknown made it great to watch at the time but in retrospective, it's not so much fun.
Rating: 30

01.19.97 - Royal Rumble 1997
(James Dixon)
[Alamodome, San Antonio, Texas]

- Hunter Hearst Helmsley def. Goldust (-*)
- Ahmed Johnson def. Faarooq (*½)
- Vader def. The Undertaker (**)
- Perro Aguayo, Canek & Hector Garza def. Fuerza Guerrera, Heavy Metal & Jerry Estrada (-*)
- Steve Austin won the Royal Rumble (**½)
- Shawn Michaels def. Sycho Sid (**¼)

Rating: 27

01.20.97 by Arnold Furious

Venue: Beaumont, TX
Taped: 01.20.97
Raw Rating: 2.2
Nitro Rating: 3.7

We're in Beaumont, Texas, the night after the 1997 *Royal Rumble*. Hosts are Vince McMahon, Jim Ross and Jerry Lawler. The former loves mentioning the 60,000 fans in San Antonio last night and JR refers to Shawn Michaels as "San Antonio's favourite son". Vince promises Gorilla Monsoon will confirm exactly who faces Shawn at *WrestleMania* tonight. The announcers are in the process of shilling the line up when Bret Hart comes out...

Promo Time: Bret Hart
He singles out Vince for a word (not for the last time). He says he was promised a title opportunity when signed his deal. He beat Steve Austin to get a title shot but blames Shawn Michaels for his title loss to Sid, calling it convenient. "Don't worry about it, you can go in the *Royal Rumble* and fight 29 other guys". Bret points out he won the *Royal Rumble*, as he was the last legal man in the ring, and wonders where his title shot is. "Where is my opportunity?" Bret complains of a lack of opportunities and quits. He shakes a few hands and leaves through the crowd as Vince looks to proffer a very late apology. The crowd chants "We want Bret". The promo was just a touch too whiny but made a few important points.

Promo Time: Steve Austin
He runs right out here to bitch about Bret. "Ever since you came back, you ain't done nothing but cry". Austin isn't pleased with his cheers. He tells Bret to go back to Canada because the only person he could beat is Stu. Austin points out he was due a match with Sid tonight but he's been screwed for seven years and it's still happening tonight. He stops off to call Sid a coward and Gorilla a monkey. He calls out the Undertaker, given the absence of everyone else, and threatens to kick his dead ass. Brilliant and aggressive counterpoint promo from Austin. Both Bret and Austin got their characters over perfectly in the opening 10-minutes of the show. Vince McMahon heads off to sort out this situation.

**The British Bulldog & Owen Hart
vs. Doug Furnas & Phil LaFon**
The tag champs don't put their straps on the line here. Owen put Bulldog out of the Rumble last night so they're having issues. LaFon vs. Owen is a bit of a dream match and they work some tidy counters. Both men are technically able but also fast. LaFon opts for more deliberate pacing than usual, perhaps to offset Owen's speed, but it also makes Furnas look electric when he tags in. Furnas pops off power spots at speed before Owen clocks him with a spin kick. Davey tags in, to a decent pop, and eats a rana off the excitable Furnas. He's on fire tonight. LaFon tags back in and finds himself taking heat but he's really not interested. He's more interested in kneeing Bulldog in the ribs repeatedly. To hell with heat! Balls to it! Owen gets in a sensational blind tag before clocking Furnas with a sniper missile dropkick. They insert the heat during the ad break, which I approve of, although I'd rather not miss any of this action. The tag champs continue to kick Furnas' ass but Doug loads up the hope spots. A double clothesline included. Owen clocks him with the enzuigiri before Davey tags in to show Furnas who's boss with the power and the suplexes. Owen allows a hot tag and LaFon brings the ass-kickery. I'm

particularly stricken with a senton right into a pin. Bulldog gets a bit confused on an armbar takedown and headspikes it. Owen trips Phil up and bashes him in the face with his Slammy to set up Bulldog's powerslam. That's the pin. Great match. I just wish it had gone on longer and that LaFon had been a bit sharper. This is probably the best Furnas & LaFon match of their WWF run.
Final Rating: ***¾

Faarooq vs. Bart Gunn
Poor Bart, still running his old gimmick from the Smoking Gunns. Time has passed him by and he doesn't even realise it. He's an okay wrestler, who'd get better after a stint with All Japan, but doesn't click with Ron Simmons at all. Totally different styles. Every spot looks a bit awkward, as if they don't clearly hear the spots they're calling. Faarooq decides a spinebuster is enough complexity and goes to a chinlock with his feet on the ropes. The hour long *Raw* doesn't have time for lengthy rest holds. At least it gives the director time to focus on D'Lo Brown's goofy haircut. It's like someone dumped a stack of hair onto the very top of his head. JC Ice and Wolfie D's continued yelling and jabbering pisses Bart off enough for him to go and beat up some rappers. It's country music vs. rap music. Again. Crush levels him and Faarooq finishes with an almightily sloppy Dominator where Bart almost lands on his head. These guys had no chemistry whatsoever.
Final Rating: ¼*

Promo Time: Gorilla Monsoon
The president says Steve Austin won the *Royal Rumble* because the officials' decision is final, but he calls the victory tainted and says Austin won't get a title shot at *WrestleMania*. Gorilla instead announces the Final Four match for a title shot at the big show. The participants are Undertaker and Vader (both illegally eliminated by Austin), Bret Hart (also illegally dumped by Austin) and Steve Austin himself. Steve Austin is NOT pleased with this turn of events. He tells Gorilla that Bret just quit and there's no instant replay rule anyway. Austin calls Gorilla a "jackass" and he'll do the four-way and when he's done with the other three "I'll toss your carcass around the arena". Vince tries to break things up but Austin gets in his face too, only for Bret Hart to come back down and accept the match before attacking Austin in the aisle. Oh, man, this has been a fun episode of *Raw* and the main event is still to come!

Steve Austin vs. The Undertaker
Taker comes out and Bret starts brawling with him too! This gives Austin an opening to jump the Dead Man from behind and they brawl around ringside. Taker is the aggressor and is clearly pissed off by the whole situation he finds himself in. I love Austin here though. When Taker does his zombie sit up Austin kicks him square in the face. He's not intimidated; he's practical. Jerry Lawler gets so upset with Austin not being aware that Taker has hurt ribs that he jumps around at ringside yelling about it. Taker shows a dark side here by hoofing Austin in the balls. Stunner! Austin stays down holding his nutsack, but this one was over. We clip away to backstage where Bret has decided to go after Vader as well. Hey, why not? Austin heads up top and Taker dumps him on his groin again. Apparently Vader got a bit pissed off by the backstage assault and runs in to attack Taker. He eats a chokeslam and Bret Hart runs in here too. The Final Four battle it out to sell the next PPV. This was half a great match with Austin and Taker showing their willingness to take shortcuts to win. If it had another 10-minutes it might have erupted into one hell of a contest. As it stands it was a teaser. All four guys continue to brawl all over the place until the show goes off the air.

Final Rating: **½

THE RAW RECAP

Most Entertaining: Steve Austin. He had a hand in everything that was fun, bar the opening match.

Least Entertaining: Bart Gunn.

Quote of the Night: "I've been screwed by Shawn Michaels, the boy toy, I've been screwed by Stone Cold Steve Austin, I've been screwed by the World Wrestling Federation and I've been screwed by you (aimed at Vince)". – Bret Hart makes his feelings known.

Match of the Night: The British Bulldog & Owen Hart vs. Doug Furnas & Phil LaFon.

Verdict: What a superb episode of *Raw* this was. It had star power, good storytelling, great promos and in Davey & Owen vs. Furnas & LaFon, a great match. You can't ask for any more than that. This show really did deliver. After a few mediocre taped shows, this episode of *Raw* shows the value of a live broadcast. The atmosphere alone was worth it being live, not to mention the shocks. Vince McMahon leaving commentary made Bret's decision to quit seem like a shoot. This is how I remembered 1997; a madcap brawl between all the biggest guns in the company for dominance, both out front and backstage.
Rating: 96

01.27.97 by Arnold Furious

Venue: Beaumont, TX
Taped: 01.20.97
Raw Rating: 2.2
Nitro Rating: 3.6

Video Control opens with Bret Hart's opening rant last week and Austin's rebuttal, plus the announcement of the Final Four main event. Hosts are Vince McMahon and Jerry Lawler.

Ahmed Johnson vs. Crush
Crush again? Come on, guys. Savio Vega just turned heel and joined the Nation thus completing their original line up. Crush has everyone bar Faarooq and Savio out here, which is sufficient to distract Johnson. This match is not one of my dream contests. More like a nightmare. Ahmed is sloppy but at least he's exciting, compared to the boring Crush. Ahmed brings a number of crazy looking kicks, as if he hasn't decided what he's going to do before he does it. Crush hasn't got a clue what's coming and has to improvise his bumps. As a result he's badly out of position several times. But then, communication was never Ahmed's strong point. Crush opts for an ugly body scissors, which is so bad that he has to stop doing it. They botch Ahmed's comeback spot and need the ropes to support Ahmed powering out of a chinlock. Ahmed doesn't bother jumping for a backbreaker so that's another ugly looking spot. Ahmed has the temerity to insert a spot where he dropkicks Crush coming off the top. Why on Earth did Ahmed think he could do stuff like that? Faarooq runs down to assault Ahmed on the floor as the match rumbles on. Crush nails Ahmed with the Heart Punch and wins? Holy shit, they put Crush over Ahmed! "That's unbelievable" says Vince. No kidding!
Final Rating: DUD

Video Control shills *Thursday Raw Thursday*; a two hour long special, which James gets to recap. It's been labelled "Titan Strikes Back" by some as it was the point where the WWF finally kicked it into higher gear and fought back against the might of WCW.

Promo Time: Shawn Michaels
Considering he's on the brink of losing his smile and forfeiting the WWF Title, he seems to be moving around just fine. I've had knee problems, if his were serious he wouldn't be able to walk without a limp. Vince McMahon hops in the ring for an interview and tries to build to *WrestleMania*, by way of *Thursday Raw Thursday*, which was supposed to be the final Shawn vs. Sid match with Shawn finally putting the monster to bed. Vince speculates what will happen IF Shawn retains past Sid and asks about a potential *WrestleMania* opponent. Shawn weighs up his opponents and points out Bret isn't happy with him. He says the title brings out the worst in WWF superstars. Vince decides to stir the pot by bringing out Bret Hart. Bret says he'll walk out of *Final Four* as the man and he prophetically demands Shawn at 100% at *WrestleMania*. Vince reminds us of Sid, which Bret ignores. He wants Shawn at 'Mania. Bret has no doubts Shawn will be facing him IF he gets by Sid. Vince brings out the Undertaker too, as if to not skip over his legitimate threat. Taker gives us a history lesson, saying he respects Bret after last year's *Royal Rumble*, but reminds us he's been screwed time and time again so the title is rightfully his. Taker is also prophetic by telling Shawn to give his "soul to the lord" because his body and the belt belong to him. Next up is Steve Austin, who brings Jim Ross as his own interviewer. He calls this an ambush. "From where I sit, I see three cry-babies and little boy blue" – of Bret, Shawn, Taker and Vince. He reminds Bret and Taker that he eliminated them from the Rumble. Austin stops off to argue with Vader on his way out. This segment continued to build everyone up as close to equal. The idea being that the title picture was wide open.

The British Bulldog vs. Doug Furnas
The battle of the powerhouses. Owen and LaFon corner their respective partners. Davey and Furnas know their strengths because they're almost identical. Furnas takes a wicked header over the top and almost wipes out Owen in the process. Bulldog takes a few shortcuts and uses the ring steps. We cut away to see Ahmed breaking into the Nation's locker room but it's empty. This powerhouse brawl doesn't seem to get over, with the fans not sure who to root for. Furnas is the face but has no charisma but Davey is leaning face, compared to Owen, himself. Given their similarities, the fans are left confused. If either LaFon or Furnas could talk it would have helped their team. "I hate him, he gives Canada a bad name" – Owen has words for LaFon. Furnas opts to punch rather than suplex, which is a pity. WWF style is done better by big lugs. He really gets the reactions with suplexes and slams and stuff. All done at speed. He tries for a rana but it's blocked into a powerbomb. Owen accidentally waffles Bulldog with the Slammy but he still kicks out. Furnas tries for a sunset flip and Bulldog lifts his victory pin from *SummerSlam '92* to go over. The match made Furnas look like a chump. After the match Bulldog is hot about the Slammy miscue. They teased Bulldog turning face for weeks and the fans want him to, but the formation of the Hart Foundation faction after *WrestleMania* would kill the angle. All of course to the detriment of Furnas & LaFon, who couldn't get a decent match out of anyone bar Bulldog & Owen and weren't really suited to the WWF environment. A pity, as they were both terrific wrestlers.
Final Rating: **¼

Video Control takes us to last Saturday's MSG house show where Ahmed tagged with Savio Vega against Faarooq and Crush, and Savio turned on his partner to join the Nation. On *Shotgun Saturday Night*, Savio blames his "hot Puerto Rican temper" for his actions, before officially joining the Nation in a 3-on-1 beat down of Rocky Maivia.

Vader & Mankind vs. The Godwinns
We quickly skip to a press conference where the WWF announce the signing of Tiger Ali Singh. That's one of the signs of a forthcoming apocalypse isn't it? Hopefully all his matches will fall in James' months. Mankind decides to give the Godwinns a lengthy opening shine before sitting in the corner and rocking. He's unlikely to ever get either one of them over though. Vader keeps screaming "TAG" at him. Mankind looks totally freaked out. Maybe he's remembering his matches with Vader earlier in the decade; facial bludgeoning, powerbomb on the floor, etc. Vader tags himself in and beats the hell out of Phineas. Mandible Claw for Phineas, but his caring brother Hank comes in and shoves them both over the top rope. Save the match, break your cousin's neck! Phineas seems game for taking silly bumps and gets slingshot out to the floor where Hank stomps all over him to get at Vader. This has not been the most caring performance from Henry Godwinn. Vader is still being booked as a beast so Henry gets big pops for knocking him over. Mankind miscues with a chair shot on Vader, which didn't even look close to being an accident and indeed Mankind seems to find it funny. Vader gets counted out. "I think he had time to stop" says Lawler. Henry moved WAY before the chair shot.
Final Rating: *½

Backstage: Ahmed finds the Nation leaving and throws Wolfie D into the boot of their car, but the Nation drive off in tact.

THE RAW RECAP

Most Entertaining: Steve Austin. Of all the chatty main eventers he not only got his point over but also made it funny.

Least Entertaining: Crush.

Quote of the Night: "This isn't a dream anymore, this is reality" – Shawn Michaels boyhood dream comes into focus.

Match of the Night: The British Bulldog vs. Doug Furnas.

Verdict: After last week's live *Raw* this one was a bit of a comedown, though the WWF's insistence at creating mayhem around the main event scene makes for interesting viewing. At the time it was never really clear who they were going with; Bret, Shawn, Sid, Taker, Austin, Vader? Having six legitimate main event stars allowed them to create intrigue before Vader faded away and Sid dropped off the face of the planet, leaving just four big names. The wrestling on this show is a little bit weak but it's nice to see another decent singles match from Bulldog. People don't give him enough credit for his work in 1997; his last great year in the wrestling business.
Rating: 44

02.03.97 by James Dixon

Venue: Toronto, Ontario, Canada
Taped: 01.31.97
Raw Rating: 2.6
Nitro Rating: 3.0

Raw this week is dubbed "Royal Rumble Raw" and comes from the cavernous Toronto SkyDome, home of *WrestleMania VI*. The building holds 60,000+ but there are 25,000 in tonight, which is still a very impressive number for a television taping. They must have been getting a good deal on the rent there or something, because it still seems like an overly lavish setting. Not only that, but *Raw* is now two hours each week instead of one. Things sure have come a long way since the Manhattan Center.

Vader vs. Steve Austin
Well, lavish the setting may be but it looks absolutely phenomenal on camera. The lighting is superb too, and this harks back to the company's hot streak in the 80s and the kind of crowds they used to draw back then. Clearly this along with the *Royal Rumble* taking place at the massive AlamoDome were an attempt by Vince to make the WWF seem like it was doing well and was a prospering, thriving company. What a shame that *WrestleMania* ended up being in the much smaller Rosemont Horizon, giving it a significantly smaller time feel than ever before. What a strange company. This match takes time to get going thanks to interference from Bret Hart, who comes out and brawls with Austin. Once they do go at it the crowd is unsure what to do, because both are positioned as heels. From a match structure point of view it is hard to put together, as there is nothing to base things on. They settle for exchanging control and brawling, which is usually a lazy shortcut, but these two happen to be among the best in the business at it. They eventually give up on the pretence of having a wrestling match and just start fighting hammer and tongs in the corner, until the referee gets too close to Austin and eats a Stunner. That is a DQ, but Austin and Vader couldn't care less and continue to fight up the aisle, setting the stage nicely for the upcoming *In Your House: Final Four* pay-per-view. Not as good as their rip-roaring and more chaotic battle late last year on the show, but still a pleasing enough start.
Final Rating: **

Flash Funk vs. Savio Vega
Just over a week ago, Savio turned heel on Ahmed Johnson during a tag match and joined the Nation, marking the end of his usefulness to the WWF. He was fairly popular and lively as a babyface, and capable of tearing it up with the right opponent. As a heel, he sucked in similar ways to Tatanka when he turned a few years back. Because the turn is so fresh, Vega is still sporting his babyface gear. Speaking of gear, Funk is brighter than the sun in his yellow and orange ensemble, which stands out even more than usual against the backdrop of a blackened crowd. Now, Funk would have been a perfect candidate to join the Nation. If anyone needed a character makeover, it was him. He had only been with the company for three months, but it was already crystal clear that he wasn't going to progress beyond the lower midcard while stuck with this gimmick. Savio does exactly what I expect from him as a heel: nothing. Funk mounts a sloppy head of steam and throws himself wildly at Savio with a bizarre ensemble of flippy moves, before taking a break to dive onto the Nation and then takes out D'Lo Brown with a spinning kick. D'Lo, on the outside no less, takes the best bump of the show. Flash goes to the well once too often though, as he tends to do, and misses a moonsault and stays down off the subsequent pin. I bet around this point Funk wished he had never left ECW. Jobbing clean to Savio Vega; can you get any lower?
Final Rating: *¼

In a USA Network tie-in (and boy, how we have loved those down the years), Vince McMahon interviews Peta Wilson, star of *La Femme Nikita*. The show is notorious for its raunchy nature (and shitty acting), which Vince asks about: "What about the sexuality, if you would? It seems to me there's a, well, there's a certain degree of sex that everyone appreciates". You have never seen a man look as uncomfortable as Vince when saying the word "sex". He is like a child. Peta lies and calls it a "prim and proper show" and one that you can "sit and watch quietly at home". Yeah, with a box of tissues in one hand and a bottle of lubricant in the other...

Promo Time: Sycho Sid
This is a complete waste of air time, given that its sole purpose is to hype a Shawn Michaels-Sid match on *Thursday Raw Thursday* next week, which doesn't happen due to Shawn losing his smile. Not only that, but this is one of Sid's less entertaining promos, because he doesn't flub any lines and he also has nothing much to say. One thing I have noticed though is that Sid always does his promos while his music is playing in the background and the lights are dimmed. I don't recall this treatment for anyone else, so why Sid?

WWF Tag Team Champions Owen Hart and the British Bulldog are backstage, and tensions are high between the two following the Rumble, as Owen threw Davey out "accidentally" and Bulldog was livid, calling Owen an "idiot". Vince, as he always does, tries to stir the pot. Owen calls him on it and expresses again that it was an accident, but Davey doesn't buy it and is not impressed with his brother-in-law.

WWF Tag Team Championship
Owen Hart & The British Bulldog (c)
vs. Doug Furnas & Phil LaFon
Owen amuses me right away by looking into the camera and declaring: "I don't see what's so good about Canada!". His tune will change in a couple of weeks. LaFon and Davey start and their exchanges are smooth and flow nicely, and Owen's work with the underrated LaFon is much the same. According to JR, Furnas has a bad case of the flu, but he doesn't show any signs of that here and gets the better of Owen, prompting Hart to tag Davey. Michael Hayes, with years or tag wrestling experience to back him up, says it is interesting that Davey tagged out when the match was in hand, yet Owen tagged out when he was in trouble. Analysis! From a WWF announcer on Raw! Furnas and Davey exchange power, but Owen tags in blind and hits a spin kick to give the champs the advantage. Poor Furnas, having to take the heat when he has the flu! I guess it makes selling easier and it makes sense given the announcers have mentioned him having the illness, but still. Davey stomps away as I notice how oddly the ring is mic'ed for the first time. Each time Bulldog delivers one of the blows, it sounds like someone banging on a steel drum. The heat from the champions isn't quite as exciting as their usual Brain Busters-esque delivery, and features more clubbing and grinding than I wish to see, but that is probably down to Furnas not feeling up to doing a great deal. Other than a visual win when the ref is distracted, he doesn't do much in the way of hope spots either. Furnas finally manages an overhead belly-to-belly on Owen and makes the hot tag to the explosive LaFon, but the response is fairly muted due to the sound being lost in the cavernous arena. LaFon throws both guys around like he is Kurt Angle in his pomp, and seems to have the belts won when he pins Owen, but Hart has his foot on the bottom rope so it doesn't count. The match continues as Vince ludicrously states: "Furnas and LaFon have been all over Owen Hart and the British Bulldog". Could have fooled me, what with that 10-

minute heat section I have just sat through. The finish of this is smart, with Owen whipping LaFon into Davey for a backdrop over the ropes, only for LaFon to switch it and Davey accidentally hit the move on Owen, where he lands badly and asks for a timeout because he is hurt. Davey hits his powerslam on LaFon, but Owen is the legal man and can't beat the count and thus Furnas & LaFon win it. Owen and Davey argue a little after the result, but they retained the titles so what is the problem? This started really well, trailed off a bit and then picked up again for the finish. It was very reminiscent of a tag match from a bygone era, which given the strength of tag wrestling in years gone by, is a compliment. The two teams will do it all again at the pay-per-view in a few weeks time.
Final Rating: ***

Backstage, Ahmed Johnson cuts a promo, and the most intelligible close approximation to what he said went something like: "SAVIO! YOU WANNA TOY HIM? TOY HIM! BUT I'M NOT A JEW! YOU. WILL PLAY. WITH ALL. THE RATS!" Love that guy.

Crush vs. Goldust
Oh, come on. Please don't do this! I have made my feelings on Crush perfectly clear over the course of these books, and while I was a big fan of Goldust as a creepy heel in 1996, he is the pits as a babyface in 1997. His character is completely neutered by being a fan favourite and it takes away all his superb character nuances. He is left with boring holds and little else. You know a match is the shits when the announcers ignore it and hype forthcoming house shows as well as *SummerSlam*, which is six *months* away. It's hard to blame them too much when Goldust is just sat casually with an armbar on. Hunter Hearst Helmsley shows his face to distract Goldust, but thankfully he disappears again before he can bore anyone to tears. Crush and Goldust are doing a perfectly good job of that themselves, dammit! The other reason you can tell Vince isn't watching this match is the fact that he happily ran this again on pay-per-view four months later, putting it on *King of the Ring*. It was the shits there too. Crush is an embarrassment to pro wrestling with his gurning "angry man" facials and his sloppy yawn-inducing offence, though at least he is not doing anymore of his "martial arts" like he did during his ten minutes as a Japanese sympathiser. Crush goes for a piledriver, but that would be too interesting so Goldust blocks it. As this match approaches the one hour mark (ok, I admit to not actually accurately timing this, but I have an internal clock that reads 60-minutes for this snoozefest), Goldust finally comes back with a DDT and bulldog, before setting up the Curtain Call. He holds it for an age while the Nation dick around getting into position, and Savio Vega runs in to hit a spin kick to the back of Goldust's head. A Crush heart punch follows and this is mercifully over. What an absolute stinker.
Final Rating: DUD

A video airs seemingly hyping the return of the Blackjacks, though Mulligan and Lanza would have been well past it in 1997 at 54 and 61 years old respectively. The vignette is actually for the impending arrival of the New Blackjacks, Barry Windham and Bradshaw, though that is not made in any way clear here. Some long-time fans must have seen this at the time and dreaded the arrival of two near-pensioners to the mix. Mind you, they would have still been a far more preferable option than the Godwinns.

Promo Time: Shawn Michaels
Michaels responds to Sid's comments earlier that the WWF Title brings the "evil" out of people, and he agrees. Michaels says the belt brings the worst out of him and others who wear it. Well, that's a shoot right there folks. Michaels compares himself to Muhammad Ali, saying how he was hated while he was champion but is now considered the greatest of all time. Actually, that is a pretty damn accurate parallel to draw. Shawn was despised by most of his peers when he was on top on account of him becoming an egocentric asshole, but nowadays many, myself included, would consider him the greatest ever. Bret Hart has heard enough and comes out to mock the Ali claims, then rips into Michaels viciously. Just as things are getting interesting, Steve Austin comes out and attacks Bret as retribution for earlier on. Sid decides he wants to be involved so strolls out, and we cut to commercial. When the dust settles and we come back, Austin and Sid have been ejected and Michaels and Hart stand face-to-face in a stare-down. Michaels puts the belt on the floor between them, but when he goes to pick it back up, Hart stands on it. The rising "ooooohhhh" from Toronto is brilliant and really captures the tension between the two. Bret picks up the belt and throws it down to Michaels before walking off, as Toronto shreds Shawn. This was a fantastic segment and Bret came across as a real badass, but again it is sadly a waste of airtime. The purpose was clearly to create tension leading into *WrestleMania* where the two were set to collide, and if anyone ever doubted that was the direction the WWF were going, then they need to see this. If it doesn't scream "future match build-up" then I don't know what does.

Earlier today the WWF signed Tiger Ali Singh to a contract, who promised to "carry the Canadian flag to even newer and greater heights". He did not. In fact, he is one of the worst wrestlers that the WWF ever had.

WWF Intercontinental Championship
Hunter Hearst Helmsley (c) vs. Marc Mero
Wow, is this show peaks and valleys or what? Every time something good happens it is followed by something tedious, and Hunter Hearst Helmsley falls directly into that category. After the horror show of boring wrestling that was Helmsley in 1995 and 1996, I think as 1997 unfolds he is perhaps my least favourite performer on the entire roster to watch. Unless he is against Mick Foley later in the year as an exception. Before the match starts, Vince goes off on a tirade against WCW''s business practices: "And how about it we err... bait and switch there, and say we were gonna have a championship match and not have it and all that kind of crap, and tease you with stuff that we're not gonna present. Cos what we *are* gonna present is what we *said* we are gonna present...". Subtle, isn't he? These guys have actually been feuding for an age, going all the way back to Mero's debut at *WrestleMania XII* in fact, which was a year ago. I can barely believe that this Mero is the same one as the punch-happy, sluggish, out-of-shape bloated mess that he became at the end of the year. This drags on for twelve boring minutes, explaining why the WWF was getting creamed by WCW in the ratings each week. Hell, if I turned over and saw this, I would tune back in to *Nitro* too. Mero tries to drag Hunter to something watchable by bumping big, but it is a lost cause because Helmsley has nothing that warrants overselling. It's another bout that goes on way past what anyone actually wanted to see, until finally Hunter knocks Mero out using brass knucks. Incredibly boring, like 99% of Helmsley's matches.
Final Rating: ¼*

No Holds Barred
Mankind & Faarooq vs. Ahmed Johnson & The Undertaker
Anyone else sick of the Nation of Domination yet? The WWF needs to realise that less is more. If you force something down people's throats, they will soon tire of it and will no longer want

to see it. Isn't that just simple logic? Mankind is not a good fit to be teaming with the Nation at all, it just doesn't make any sense that he would align with them, or indeed that they would align with him. Mankind tries to fit in, bless him, by throwing out black power first salutes. Cute. Ahmed comes out with a 2x4 because of the No Holds Barred nature of the match, as Vince once again goes off on a tirade about how the WWF gives you exactly what they promise, and don't pull bait and switch crap after spending the whole show building something up. Oh really? I could probably think of a dozen instances of EXACTLY that happening without even really trying. I am sure most WWF/E fans could as well. Hypocrisy is a dirty thing. Hell, there is a WWF Title match promised for next week on the *Thursday Raw Thursday* special, which doesn't happen... This is just two long-running feuds blending into one, which is a perfectly acceptable booking practice and from that perspective I guess the two teams do make sense. It might as well be two singles matches taking place at the same time though, because Undertaker pairs off with Mankind and brawls around the ring, while Faarooq and Ahmed tussle in the ring. Taker sees Ahmed in trouble so jumps in to battle Faarooq, so Ahmed rolls to the outside for a donnybrook with Mankind. It is very reminiscent of the chaotic six-man tag street fight at *WrestleMania XIII* pitting the Nation against Ahmed and the LOD, only with less guys and less weaponry. With Faarooq and Mankind taking a beating, Crush and Savio come out to make their 23rd appearance of the night, just as Mankind locks the Mandible Claw on Taker. Ahmed spots it and hits the Pearl River Plunge, but Faarooq breaks it up and has a go with his finisher, the Dominator. I guess the Tombstone is next? No, as it turns out, because Mankind kicks Taker right on the knob-end, but then runs at him with a chair and ends up eating it back in his face thanks to a big boot. Ahmed brawls with the Nation on the outside as Taker hits a chokeslam on Mankind, and the director can't keep up and doesn't know what to follow. They settle on Ahmed chasing the Nation to the back with a 2x4, but back in the ring the Undertaker is in peril. Ahmed soon rectifies that with his big wooden stick, and beats Faarooq with it to the back. We are left with Undertaker and Mankind, and the latter tries to use wrestling powder but gets it thrown back into his eyes. Cue the interference, as one of Undertaker's *Final Four* opponents Vader comes out and splashes the Dead Man, but misses with a chair and hits Mankind, aping a similar situation that occurred between the tag partners last week. Vader tries again and connects, but Taker just stares at him and chases him off, before finishing Mankind with a Tombstone. Well this was certainly wild, but almost too much because it was hard to keep up with everything going on. Despite that, it was entertaining and a fun main event with the right conclusion, so I have no qualms with it.
Final Rating: **

THE RAW RECAP

Most Entertaining: Phil LaFon. Doesn't often get the credit he deserves for his work in North America, which is a shame. If LaFon had arrived in 2000 when workrate was in vogue, he would have been considered alongside the super-workers of the day such as Angle, Guerrero, Malenko, Benoit and Jericho. I enjoyed him tonight and he deserves the plaudits.

Least Entertaining: Hunter Hearst Helmsley. He is perhaps my least favourite wrestler to watch of all time from 1995-1997. Hey, Hunter, wrestling is supposed to be *entertaining*. Duller than IRS? Tough call...

Quote of the Night: "He's not in his mid 40s, he's not bald and he's not making promises that he can't keep. Shawn Michaels is promising you, that on *Thursday Raw Thursday,* he is gonna put it all on the line and the WWF Title is going to be decided in the rubber match" - Jim Ross. Hilariously and ironically, it wasn't. Read on to the next episode to find out why.

Match of the Night: Owen Hart & The British Bulldog vs. Doug Furnas & Phil LaFon. Was it ever likely to be anything else when Bret and Shawn were on promo rather than in-ring duty?

Verdict: A reasonable start from my perspective, with plenty of good stuff dotted throughout. Unfortunately there was also two tedious matches to ruin the flow, making me think how much better this would have been if it had been an hour like it used to be. The WWF doesn't yet have the roster or the personalities to fill two hours, but they will start making moves to rectify that over the coming weeks. A unique episode given the unique setting, and if you are going back over and watching these things again, you will be fairly entertained by this one. Just fast forward through Crush and Helmsley so you don't fall asleep.
Rating: 49

02.13.97 - "Thursday Raw Thursday" By James Dixon

Venue: Lowell, MA
Taped: 02.13.97
Raw Rating: 2.7
Nitro Rating: 3.8

This is a special episode of *Raw*, taking place on a Thursday due to pre-emption on Monday. The WWF couldn't afford to not run an episode of the show with a pay-per-view coming up and with them being in the middle of a heated war with WCW, so we have *Thursday Raw Thursday*. What a stupid name. The show opens with a voiceover from Vince McMahon, announcing that Shawn Michaels will be forfeiting the WWF Championship tonight. More on that later. After the show took place in the immense SkyDome last week, we are back to the usual half-arenas for this taping.

WWF Intercontinental Championship
Hunter Hearst Helmsley (c) vs. Rocky Maivia

Oh goodie, we start with Helmsley. This match is obviously a much bigger deal years later, but here we have the tiresome blueblood Helmsley against the greener than grass Maivia, and the crowd couldn't care less about either guy. It still seems amazing watching things like this back, that in just 18-months they would be contesting a classic ladder match at *SummerSlam '98* and just a few months after that, Rocky would be WWF Champion and one of the most over guys in the business. Ever. Being the more experienced guy, Helmsley controls the majority of this, but as noted last week his offence is not conducive of a good match, and once again it is slow and laboured. Helmsley focuses on the arm, which means lots of armbar. Thrilling stuff. Nearly 10-minutes in, former Intercontinental Champion the Honky Tonk Man randomly turns up to observe, then joins the announce table. Honky is currently in the middle of a search for a new protégé, but he says he isn't impressed with Rocky. He ended up picking Billy Gunn. What a fine judge of talent. In an interesting side note, Honky's headset is barely working here, which is something he discussed years later in a Kayfabe Commentaries shoot interview. Now take this with a pinch of salt because Honky is often full of shit, but he reckons he was purposely sabotaged by his cousin Jerry Lawler, who didn't want him horning in on

his "spot". In the ring Rocky mounts a generic babyface comeback, but Hunter rolls through a top rope crossbody for a near fall. Hunter uses the knee, for a change, then a neckbreaker gets another close count. The crowd are starting to react a little more to this now, but they are hardly rabid. Hunter hits an AWFUL piledriver than he flat back bumps because he can't sit out properly, and Rocky kicks out again. Good, if he had stayed down from that horrible looking mess, it would have ruined his credibility. Hunter slaps Rocky around on the top rope and eventually hits a superplex, but Maivia again kicks out, which Vince is stunned by. Finally Hunter hooks up the Pedigree, and they run the old Diesel-Hart spot from *Survivor Series '95* with Rocky out on his feet, and Rock catches him with a cradle for the win and the title. The crowd pops, but they will soon turn on him for getting too much too soon. And it *is* too soon, because Rocky has barely been with the WWF for three months and he is not ready for what is supposed to be such a prestigious spot. A title is something to be worked towards, it shouldn't be something won on a fluke. This picked up at the end, but they went 15-minutes and it dragged on and on and on until the final stages. And to think, in three years they have a 60-minute Iron Man Match which is an absolute blinder. Furious actually really enjoyed this match in Volume #4 of our Complete WWF Video Guide series, but I found it an absolute chore.
Final Rating: *½

Footage is shown from the nightmare inducing *Prime Time Country*, which was *Prime Time Wrestling* meets country and western music. It is as bad as it sounds, just horrid. Some skinny guy with a TV show wrestled alongside Jesse Jammes against the Godwinns, and actually did some moves. Wait a minute, didn't the WWF heavily criticise WCW for doing the same thing with Jay Leno a few years later?

The Headbangers vs. Bob Holly & Aldo Montoya
Sunny is the ring announcer, and she is dreadful at it, as usual. She was a decent manager and a good talker, but her voice doesn't suit announcing at all. As the WWF keeps changing, Bob Holly is starting to look more and more out of place in that dumb racing attire. Of course, Aldo has always looked dumb so there is no change there. Vince and JR spend the match talking about Shawn Michaels, with Vince calling the Iron Man Match with Bret Hart from the previous year "nothing short of extraordinary". Yeah, extraordinarily boring! Vince is almost in tears discussing Michaels, and for the first time tonight his supposed knee injury is brought up. Vince says he feels partly responsible for what's happened to Shawn "given the schedule". Well, that's the first time he has admitted that one. Why didn't he DO something about it then? Oh of course, money is more important than anything. There is a match going on as well, but let's face it, no-one cares. Literally, no-one in the entire world cares about this completely pointless and overly long match, which the Headbangers win after a double team. Next.
Final Rating: ½*

Promo Time: Shawn Michaels
You all know this one, believe me. Shawn comes out wearing a suit but unshaven so he looks scruffy and unkempt, which I believe is by design to generate sympathy for the guy. If he came out looking flash and top of the world like he usually does, this wouldn't have generated anywhere near as much sympathy. The gist is that Shawn is forfeiting the WWF Title due to a knee injury, and his doctors have told him he needs major reconstructive surgery and may well never wrestle again. Allegedly. My understanding of what followed is that Shawn sought a second opinion who told him it was bad for a normal person, but no worse than you would expect for a wrestler. Seems he jumped the gun just a tad. Suddenly, not long after *WrestleMania 13* coincidentally, he was fine to wrestle again. This of course resulted in Bret Hart, who Shawn was supposed to put over on the big show, deciding that Shawn was ducking a job to him. That led to tension between the two even further than what already existed, which spilled over into a catfight backstage at *Raw* in June. Shawn quit the WWF for the second time in 1997 thanks to that, but once again he returned. Of course, Michaels didn't help matters when he started skipping around the ring and jumping off the ropes a few weeks after he had delivered this moving soliloquy. Mind you, even nearly two decades later, Shawn still insists that the injury was legitimate and he was only risking damaging it further with his prancing around as a big "fuck you" to the boys in the back who doubted him. It's a vicious circle. As powerful and dramatic as the knee talk is, it pales in comparison to the reason this promo is so famous; it's the one where Shawn lost his smile. Shawn fights back crocodile tears as he says he has lost a lot of things over the years, and one of them is his smile, but he will go home and find it along with fixing his body. As insincere as this all may seem given what happened down the line with HBK, this was still captivating television and will always be remembered. Hell, "lost his smile" is now a part of wrestling vernacular, folklore and legend. As for the WWF Title? It will now be awarded to the winner of the four way match between Bret Hart, Steve Austin, the Undertaker and Vader at the *Final Four* pay-per-view this coming weekend. Sid, who was due a title shot against Michaels tonight, will face the winner on *Raw* in a few days time.

Savio Vega vs. The Undertaker
Just in case you didn't get enough of the Nation from the triple dose on the last episode, here they are again! Like I said during that episode, they forced it too much. Savio has only just turned heel and started coming out with the Nation, but already the novelty of it is wearing off and he is becoming tiresome. Vega is not even in the same sport as Taker, never mind his league, and he gets a hammering here. Taker just casually takes him apart, running effortlessly through his offence until a desperate Vega low blow slows him down. For about a second. Then Taker takes Vega's head off with a clothesline. Vega finally gets some offence in when he connects with his nice spinning heel kick, but there is not much he can do to Taker outside of clubbing away and choking. When that doesn't work, Savio throws on a chinlock, as this match joins the others tonight in going on for longer than it needs to. It is becoming a problem for *Raw* now that it is two hours every week, and the snappy feel of the show has gone. At least in the early days of *Raw* the pointless or unappealing matches would be brief, but now everything goes 10-15 minutes. Taker gets bored of selling for pint-sized Savio and finishes him off with a chokeslam, then the Nation hit the ring and gang up on Taker. Ahmed Johnson comes out for the save, but he too gets outnumbered, but Taker sits up and tears through the Nation, and he and Ahmed clean house. A hot ending to another dull match.
Final Rating: ¾*

Steve Austin vs. Sycho Sid
I have no idea how this one is going to go. It could be excellent or it could be a complete train wreck. Such is the unpredictability of Sid. The crowd gets right behind Austin as they have a brawl on the outside, and you have to think the WWF was aiming for that reaction even prior to the *WrestleMania* double turn with Bret Hart, because they keep

programming him against heels, and much bigger ones at that. This is a brawl, and a fairly decent one, but is truncated before it properly gets going thanks to interference from Austin's nemesis Bret Hart. The two brawl, but Sid is not exactly thrilled to see Hart either and they have a pull-apart too, as referees (including Earl Hebner bizarrely clad in a leather jacket) try and separate them.
Final Rating: *¾

Vince gets a word with Vader, who is backstage. He simultaneously shows why Jim Cornette was so important to him and why he never became a true headliner in the WWF, when he delivers a garbled, horrible interview. He stumbles over his words, kills his aura and gets Thursday and Monday confused in one big disaster.

WWF Tag Team Championship
Owen Hart & The British Bulldog (c) vs. Faarooq & Crush

I can't say I quite fathom why this is taking place either, given that once again both teams are heel. Nor can I explain another appearance from the Nation, especially after they were bitched out by Ahmed and Taker earlier on. If anything, shouldn't Furnas and LaFon be due a title rematch after their count out victory last week? Crush is so bad that he can't even manage a back body drop on Owen, and instead just dumps him on his face. Bulldog against both Crush and Faarooq are matches that may have appealed five years ago, but not in 1997. I don't know why, but Kona Crush against British Bulldog circa 1992 has a fascinating intrigue to it. Similarly WCW champion Ron Simmons against Bulldog from the same era. The match valleys enough for a Bret Hart split-screen promo, which is preferable to the Crush nerve pinch currently going on. Bret talks about Shawn Michaels, saying how he hopes Shawn comes back because he wants to wrestle him again and that he hopes things work out for him. His tune has changed from last week and indeed will again, considerably, as the year progresses. Back to the ring and the Nation are still slowly grinding away at Davey, and the match follows the others on the card in going on and on beyond entertainment and into tedium. Wow, I didn't realise what an absolute slog some of the stuff on *Raw* was. It is heatless, passionless and lacking in excitement. Again, you can't blame the crowd too much for their lack of reaction, as the WWF is asking them to cheer for guys they have always booed, and when Owen gets the hot tag, no-one reacts. Crush eventually dumps Owen to the outside, where he once again injures his knee and gets counted out. Faarooq gives Davey a woeful looking Dominator after the match, with Owen unable to get back in the ring and save his partner due to the dodgy wheel. Tedious match, crap finish. Worthless.
Final Rating: ½*

Vader vs. Bret Hart
Before we start, Undertaker comes out and apologises for interrupting, then complains about the lack of respect he has been shown recently and promises the guys in the Final Four will suffer for it. His Texas twang is especially noticeable tonight. Vader jumps Bret while he is distracted and pounds away, then during commercial Steve Austin comes out to stomp away at the Hitman. Vader continues the assault in a smoke-covered ring, which is amateur from the WWF. Bret catches Vader with a powerslam off the top and goes into some of his Five Moves of Doom, but also throws in an effortless bodyslam. Not long after, he follows up with a back suplex! Who is this, Bret Hart of the friggin' Ultimate Warrior!? Bret gets the Sharpshooter, but Vader is right next to the ropes and immediately grabs them. Steve Austin turns up in the crowd to distract Bret, allowing Vader to hit and short arm clothesline, but he misses the Vadersault and gets covered for the pin. Even though Bret was getting the WWF Title at the pay-per-view, I don't think he should have gone over here. Bret wasn't getting pushed as the next long-term WWF Champion and he was beginning an angle where he complained about anything and everything, so a loss here because of Steve Austin would have fit the bill and helped build up Vader as a realistic contender going into *Final Four*. This had the potential to be really good and a long match between the two would have been a fine encounter, but it was too brief to be much more than a few highlights and then the finish. Shame really, given that almost every other match tonight went on for far longer than anyone would realistically have wanted to see.
Final Rating: **

THE RAW RECAP

Most Entertaining: Shawn Michaels. His sincerity may be questionable, but the emotional delivery of his famous "smile" speech was superb. Genuinely captivating, heart-wrenching television.

Least Entertaining: Oh, I am spoilt for choice this week. Despite such a plethora of options, Crush still comes out on top for his incredible ability to make both Owen Hart and Davey Boy Smith boring. Quite the feat.

Quote of the Night: "Well, it seems like we've done this before. And this time, unfortunately for me, it's much more serious than last time. I've never had a doctor look at me in the face and say that I may never be able to wrestle again. And I was, I was told that the other day. Of course, you know I, it's not something that I believe. But the fact is it's something that I have to deal with. Time has taken its toll on, on my body... Well there's one thing about me is I can't do anything halfway and I, and I come here and I hear the people and they chant Sid's name or they chant Bret's name or they chant a lot of peoples' names, and one thing's for sure, you're going to have all of that in the future, and that's what I want for the World Wrestling Federation fans. In spite of what people may think about me, what I've always wanted for all these people is, is for them to have a good time and to enjoy themselves. I've always tried to be the one to provide it, whether it was on the good side or the bad side. But what was always important to me was the performance, was the performance so that these people, each time they reached in their pocket, they paid to get a WWF ticket, they didn't regret it because they knew that if they saw my name on the card they could yell, they could come and they could cheer and they could boo and they could do whatever they wanted as long as they had a good time. Over the last couple of months there's been a lot of talk of people having bad attitudes and a lot revolving around this belt. All I know today is that one thing that's not going to revolve around this belt, for a long time, is going to be Shawn Michaels. I don't know where I'm at right now. I have to, I have to have everything checked. I may be... I may be beyond reconstructive surgery. I may, or may not be able to fix it. But if I can't come back and perform at the level I performed at, before... I can't, I can't perform. I can't come out here and just go half-ass. I have to come out here and I have to romp and stomp and I have to get tossed around. I have to toss people around and I have to have fun. The schedule over the last year I took on because I didn't feel like I could say no. I wanted to do everything. I wanted to enjoy my life as the WWF Champion. I wanted to, I wanted to ride in leer jets and ride in limousines and I wanted to be on TV shows and I wanted to do autograph sessions and I got to do every bit of that. If nothing else, I have all of that to take with me. Again, and I know right now we're in the middle of a time where toughness is real big here in the World Wrestling Federation, and unfortunately all I've got right now for you is a lot of sorrow, a lot of tears, and a lot of emotion. I don't have any toughness for anybody, so I guess, here you go, here's your belt. (hands the belt to Vince) What I'm going to do is go back home and see what's left for me; whether it'll be in this ring... whether it'll be out of this ring. I know that over the, the last several months I've lost a lot of things and one of them has been my smile. And, and I know it doesn't mean a whole lot to everybody else, but it means a lot to me. So I have to go back and fix myself, and take care of myself, and I have to go back and I have to find my smile because somewhere along the line I lost it and I don't care, really, I don't care if it's unpopular, and I don't care if people want to make fun of me because I'm an emotional guy. But this is all I've ever wanted to do and over the last year I got to do it and whether you like me or not, I just want to tell you that last year was the most wonderful year of my life. And if I never do get to do it again, it'll be okay because I got to live one full year as being the number one guy in this business and it was the single greatest year of my life. And I have you to thank, and I have everybody here to thank, and it means a lot to me and I'm gonna go home now. Okay?" - Shawn Michaels

Match of the Night: Bret Hart vs. Vader. It was brief, but there were signs that the two had great chemistry. They do get the chance to have a longer match later in the year.

Verdict: Another difficult episode to sit through from an in-ring perspective, because the matches were given far longer than they should have been when they didn't warrant the time, apart from the main event which should have been at least twice as long. What a maddening company. The show does remain notable for the first ever title win for the Rock, and the legendary "lost my smile" promo, but the title change is not worth sitting through, and neither is this show as a whole. Track down the Michaels interview but don't bother hunting down the rest.
Rating: 42

02.16.97 - Final Four
(Lee Maughan)
[UTC Arena, Chattanooga, Tennessee]

- Marc Mero def. Leif Cassidy (*½)
- Faarooq, Crush & Savio Vega def. Bart Gunn, Goldust & Flash Funk (**)
- Rocky Maivia def. Hunter Hearst Helmsley (*½)
- Doug Furnas & Phil LaFon def. Owen Hart & The British Bulldog (***½)
- Bret Hart def. Steve Austin, Vader and The Undertaker in a four corners elimination match (****½)

Rating: 81

02.17.97 by James Dixon

Venue: Nashville, TN
Taped: 02.17.97
Raw Rating: 2.45
Nitro Rating: 2.9

This comes from the night after *Final Four*, a show that saw Bret Hart win his fourth WWF Championship in a tremendous elimination match over the Undertaker, Steve Austin and Vader. He has to defend the belt tonight, right away no less!

WWF Championship
Bret Hart (c) vs. Sycho Sid
This is quite the way to start. This very well could have been Steve Austin defending the title, as at one point he was scheduled to win the *Final Four* match and lift the belt, but the WWF changed their mind. It is a good job too, because Austin winning his first title and then quickly losing it would have damaged him and reduced the impact when he did win it in 1998. Speaking of Austin, he interjects himself before we even get going, jumping Hart before the bell. Sid is not amused and goes after Austin himself, but Stone Cold takes out his leg. "Dammit! Dammit! Dammit!" screams Sid as he writhes around on the canvas, doing a better sell job than at any other time I can remember. Discussions between the two combatants and a number of referees takes place, as they try and decide if the match can go ahead or not. It would be ironic if they cancelled it given the constant barrage of reminders on recent broadcasts that the WWF delivers on its promises and scheduled bouts. I do enjoy a bit of irony. As things get ironed out, we see highlights of Shawn Michaels forfeiting the title a few days ago, and then the *Final Four* last night, including close-up shots of Vader's sickeningly gory busted eye. When we cut back to live pictures, Sid is in the locker-room, for some reason wearing his ring jacket again, and says he would wrestle even if he had a broken leg. There's that whole irony thing again. So, this match will now take place later on, as the WWF doesn't quite deliver what it promises...

Marc Mero vs. Savio Vega
Sable appears to think she is Catwoman tonight. The talk is of the newfound aggression shown by Sable recently, as we see footage of her foolish decision to kick the Undertaker in the ribs, and then her involvement in Mero's win over Leif Cassidy last night. How utterly horrid that the first proper match, some 15-minutes in now no less, involves the Nation of Domination! Remember what I said about overkill the other week? This is now the third week running that Savio Vega has wrestled on *Raw*. Seeing Sable stood at ringside in Mero's corner when Savio has a whole gang with him, does lead to questions. Why don't they target Sable, which would surely throw Mero off his game in a big way? They are a street gang, it would fit their characters to do something like that. Well, it would if they weren't an utterly spineless Disney-like set of thugs. Mero again comes out of this with credit, as he tries to throw himself around to get a good match out of Savio, including hitting some tremendous armdrags and a flip plancha to the outside. You can almost understand him giving up later in the year, because all the flashy big-bumping was doing nothing for his career expect shortening it. The Nation show why they are little bitches when they let Sable kick the shit out of them and fail to retort. Just slap the bitch, she started it! Finally the Nation do go after Sable, who jumps in the ring and hides behind Mero for protection. Things are looking bad for the Meros, but Ahmed Johnson, clad in the most incredible orange tracksuit you have ever seen, comes out with a 2x4 to clear them out. This was pretty good actually due to the lively action brought about by Mero.
Final Rating: **

Backstage, Bret Hart says after he beats Sid tonight he will fight anyone. Jim Ross throws out the possibility of a Hart-Undertaker match for the belt at *WrestleMania*, but Bret is not afraid.

WWF Intercontinental Championship
Rocky Maivia (c) vs. Leif Cassidy
Big night on Raw for title matches. Back in 1993 when the show started, title matches would be a rarity and a special selling point for the show, but they happen seemingly every week in 1997. Before the match starts, Sunny comes out for no other reason than to give her something to do, and in this case it is the perfunctory role of guest timekeeper. The WWF really were baffled when it came to Sunny, because they wanted her on screen on account of her attainable girl-next-door face, tight little body and perfectly formed (fake) tits, but she couldn't actually do anything useful. As a manager she had proven herself to be pretty much a curse who offered nothing to her charges, and she couldn't wrestle. What else could she do? Come out and pout of course. She was a decent talker though and understood the business better than a lot of WWF women down the years, and she was actually well positioned as host of Livewire!, but that was a Saturday morning throwaway show and not prime-time, which is where they wanted her. This match is like every other Rocky Maivia match: crap. After exchanging punches, Rocky goes to the staple of every exciting babyface; a long and pointless armbar. And by long, I mean many minutes long, until Cassidy just casually shrugs it off and escapes. Smooth! They try a little sequence, but everything they do looks like they purposely pull it and prevent it connecting. Cassidy decides to up the excitement levels... with an armbar of his own. I guess there is a modicum of psychology in that because Hunter worked over Rocky's arm last week, but I can't possibly give them credit for that in good faith because I am not convinced it is in any way intentional. Like Rock's match with Helmsley last week, this has now gone on far longer than it should, and watching it really does feel like the visual equivalent of wading through treacle. No-one buys Cassidy as anything but a total joke, so if the WWF wanted to build the credibility of Rocky then they should have had him tear through Leif with ease. But Rocky was not that kind of wrestler, he was merely a punching bag for the heels with a few generic stilted-motion comebacks. He is not smart either, and when he hits a crossbody from the top to seemingly win it, he gets off and hits a shoulder breaker, his finisher at the time, and then pins him. This was 10-minutes that felt like 20-minutes, which is obviously the mark of a horrible match.
Final Rating: ¼*

Jerry Lawler grabs some fans' signs from the crowd that say "ECW Rules", and goes off on a tirade against the promotion. He compares it to a prison and says it is a place where anyone who couldn't make it in the WWF goes. He says he is sick and tired of fans turning up with ECW signs and waving them in his face, and then challenges anyone from ECW to come to Raw next week and prove themselves. This is probably the best Jerry Lawler rant on Raw to date, partly because everything he did before this was pretty terrible, but also because he was venomous, serious and not making lame jokes. This is the Jerry Lawler that I like. The response from the ECW crew, as you will see next week, is pretty phenomenal.

Promo Time: Goldust & Marlena
The point of discussion is Hunter Hearst Helmsley, as the two are involved in a bitter dispute over Marlena. Goldust says things are personal and that the only way Hunter will get Marlena is over his dead body. Marlena dismisses the couple's past histrionics as "a lot of games" and calls Goldust "all man", finally putting to bed any talk of him being gay. The fans still don't really bite on the character, with the majority clearly uncomfortable cheering him. Hunter comes out and does some pointing, a trait he has retained throughout his entire career. He loves a good point and an angry facial. Hunter throws a drink in Goldust's face and hits a Pedigree, then the currently still unnamed Chyna comes in and destroys Marlena, rag-dolling her around in a tremendous visual. JR and Lawler claim she is a fan, and the fact she gets dragged away by event staff enforces that to the audience. I have said this in other books too, but I find this a very dangerous way to introduce new characters. All it takes is one nutcase thinking that this is a way to get into the business, to jump the barrier and legitimately hurt someone. The WWF are lucky it has never happened. Considering the participants, this was remarkably entertaining.

The Headbangers vs. The Hardy Boys
Don't get too excited, the Hardys are still just jobbers, though they now have matching tights with their names on them, and actually get a little offence. They have moved up in the world from television enhancement talent to named jobbers on the absolute bottom rung. It's a long ride to the top. The WWF thinks this match is a suitable place to insert a Faarooq promo, and he rails on Ahmed Johnson before challenging him to a Chicago Street Fight at WrestleMania. JR is seemingly familiar with gang fights: "Oh those, those are so, so, talk about violent!". Is anyone else now picturing JR as a real-life version of Marlon Brando's character in the Godfather? No? Must just be me then... The Headbangers run through their, erm, "unique" offence, as JR shows his ignorance by saying he doesn't know who Marilyn Manson is, and displays his fuddy-duddy nature in an hilarious exchange regarding mosh-pits. See the Raw Recap for that little gem. Jeff Hardy takes a clothesline upside-down on his head and then the Bangers finish the future WWE Champion off with their double-team legdrop/powerbomb combo. The Hardy's actually did a great job in making the Headbangers look like an entertaining team here, which is quite a feat.
Final Rating: *½

WWF Championship
Bret Hart (c) vs. Sycho Sid
Ok, let's try this again then. The fact that the show is only half-way through suggests more shenanigans, and indeed Steve Austin attacks Bret from behind backstage on his way to the ring, as Sid, referees, officials and even Vince McMahon try and break things up. It is chaos! When we return from commercial, President Monsoon gets in on the WCW-bashing and says that the WWF are not like anyone else, and they will deliver what they promise, and he guarantees that Sid-Hart will take place tonight. Don't lower yourself to that Gorilla, it's beneath you.

Flash Funk vs. Owen Hart
The existence of this match prompts the question: was this match scheduled anyway or was it quickly made because of the postponement of Sid-Hart? If it was already booked, what on earth was it doing going on after the obvious main event that is the WWF Championship match? I can accept the title match opening the show, but realistically why would it be in the middle of the card? I am purposely being petty and pedantic, yes, but these things keep me awake! I have no complaints about the choice of match though, because both guys are tremendously talented and this could be a real mini-classic. That is if the WWF gives it time, because when they have a good match on paper it usually gets shafted on time, whereas as you have seen, they will happily give the lesser workers 10-15 minutes. Owen comes out with both tag title belts and his Slammys, and also curiously enough Clarence Mason. Now, Mason has managed Hart on and off for a few months, but surely given Mason's Nation of Domination association, that

creates a conflict of interest? Again, I am being overly analytical perhaps, but little things matter! The opening two minutes don't disappoint, with both guys exchanging holds, switches and counter-switches at speed, including some excellent knock-down / nip-up trades, and then end the sequence by both going for a dropkick and then having a stand -off. There was more movement and action in that opening sequence than on the rest of the show so far. Sadly the WWF use this match as a backdrop for Paul Heyman to call in an accept Jerry Lawler's challenge for next week on *Raw*. I am usually happy to hear from Heyman, one of the greatest orators the business has ever known, but why during this superb contest? Why not during the Rocky match? Heyman makes allusions to Lawler's questionable past in a very cheeky insider shot, which just adds to the realism of things. The way this has been presented is brilliant, and the fact it has all come about in one night (along with the wild Hart-Austin-Sid situation) really helps give *Raw* and the WWF that "anything can happen" feel that they have long championed, but rarely delivered on. When the match returns to focus, Clarence Mason nearly costs Owen the match, which results in an argument between the two and Flash catching Owen with a big dive. Was Mason distracting Owen on purpose to try and help Funk, with designs on inducting him into the Nation? It is something I talked about two weeks ago as something that would have made a lot of sense and helped Flash/Scorpio in the WWF, but alas it never happened and the thing with Mason goes no-where. Owen's tag partner the British Bulldog comes out and tells Mason to clear off, and sticks around for the remainder. The action is consistent and fluid, but the WWF are determined to ruin it, and insert a split-screen with Steve Austin to further take away from the bout. How frustrating! After another few minutes of top-notch combat, Davey clocks Funk with a Slammy and then holds his leg while Owen pins him for the win. A really energetic and exciting match, that would have got an even higher rating if it wasn't for the copious unwelcomed distractions. Rarely have I been so annoyed to see both a Paul Heyman and a Steve Austin promo.

Final Rating: ***¼

Hunter Hearst Helmsley vs. Bart Gunn

Oh come on now, we have seen this monotonous tosspot once tonight already, and that was quite enough. His angle with Goldust was pretty decent, don't ruin it by having him wrestle. And boy, what a thrilling opponent for him. Honky Tonk Man joins the commentary team as he continues his search for a protégé, but surely he was never considering Bart Gunn. Mind you, he did pick his "brother", so hell, who knows what goes on in his head. Before the match starts, JR gets a word with Hunter, who claims to have no idea who Chyna is. Tonight's episode of *Raw* is sponsored by the armbar, which Bart Gunn uses to work his scrappy offence out of. It's like being back in the 80s. Gunn continues to focus on Hunter's arm, but as soon as Hunter mounts some offence Goldust charges the ring and Hunter hightails it out of here and gets counted out. Yes! Thank you Goldust! I have never been so happy to see him!

Final Rating: ½*

We get a quick update from Dr. James Andrews regarding Shawn Michaels' knee injury. Andrews says they won't proceed with surgery but instead will rehab Shawn at home, then reassess in 4-6 weeks. Andrews says he is confident that Shawn will be able to resume his "wrasslin'" career once the rehab is complete. Jump the gun a bit, Shawn?

WWF Championship
Bret Hart (c) vs. Sycho Sid

Third time's a charm. This time the match does get underway, and they exchange shots in the corner, with Sid getting the bigger reaction from the crowd. Remember that Bret has not turned heel yet, whereas Sid has been positioned as a villain, so that is somewhat surprising. Times were indeed a changing. Sid uses his power and clubs away at Hart, who responds with a backbreaker and a headbutt to the knackers. Bret is going into his Five Moves of Doom real early, and follows those up with the middle rope elbow, before Sid cuts him off with more clubbing blows to the back. Sid's punches are so strange; he looks like a farmer cutting corn with a machete. Bret remembers the leg injury from earlier, not that he needs much prompting to target that particular extremity, and he zones in on it. Bret wraps Sid's leg around the post and then locks on the tremendous ringpost figure four, possibly for the first time ever given Ross' reaction to it. It's strange, because that move is so strongly linked and associated with Hart, yet he only started using it in the last six months of his WWF tenure. Sid finds the answer in thwarting Hart to be more corn cutting blows, and he levels Hart with a clothesline before following with a legdrop and a lazy slam, as he almost completely forgets about the knee injury. Sid goes up top, which always makes me cringe, and hits a really dangerous and ugly looking legdrop. Bret escapes the chokeslam but misses a clothesline over the top, only to recover and clothesline Sid out. Steve Austin appears, but Sid sees him coming and takes him out, then he tries and just about hits a sunset flip back into the ring (!), but Bret rolls through and locks on the Sharpshooter. He would win it, because Sid is miles from the ropes, but Austin recovers on the outside and waffles Hart with a chair, which useless Earl Hebner fails to see. Both guys make it to their feet and Sid hits the powerbomb to win the match and the WWF Championship, to a healthy pop. This marks the first time ever that the WWF Championship has changed hands on *Raw*, making it a momentous occasion. So, Sid is two-time WWF Champion and he will meet the Undertaker at *WrestleMania 13*. The Dead Man comes out and has a stare-down with Sid as the show goes off the air. Good match thanks to Bret's aggression and usual strong psychology, even if Sid was a bit all over the place with his selling and execution.

Final Rating: ***

THE RAW RECAP

Most Entertaining: Bret Hart. There were a lot of very good performers tonight. Jeff Hardy for his wild bumping, Marc Mero for desperately trying with Savio Vega, Owen Hart and Flash Funk for putting on a strong wrestling match and even Jerry Lawler for his superb work in hyping a feud with ECW. But credit must be given to Bret Hart for being involved in some fun angles, dragging a *** match out of Sid the night after working for 30-minutes in a brutal PPV main event, and for debuting the genius ringpost figure four.

Least Entertaining: Rocky Maivia. His opponent Leif Cassidy was just a rotten, but at least he wasn't being pushed far too quickly into a spot he wasn't ready for, and thus isn't completely intolerable.

Quote of the Night: Jerry Lawler - "Have you ever seen a mosh pit?". Jim Ross - "Err, a couple of times on the news. I've never experienced it." Jerry Lawler - " On the *news*?" Jim Ross - "Yeah, I watch the news". Jerry Lawler - "On the news!? What would a mosh pit be doing on the news!? You might see one on MTV, I don't think you'll see one on the news, Ross."

Match of the Night: Flash Funk vs. Owen Hart. I actually had a choice tonight! The younger Hart brother pips it because the smooth, technical excellence of the Funk-Owen match was slightly more entertaining than the storyline bout between Bret and Sid. Shame the WWF seemed determined to ruin it with countless distractions.

Verdict: This was a much better effort than the last two weeks, with two *** matches and plenty going on to keep the broadcast flowing at a brisk pace. As well as a couple of good matches, there was also some good outside of the ring stuff, with Steve Austin making a general nuisance of himself and Paul Heyman cutting his first reality-laced promo on WWF television. Future multiple time WWF/E Champions The Rock and Triple H dragged the show down though, and neither is currently worth watching in the slightest under their current guises. Still, this is much more like what *Raw* should be at its peak, and with better time management the show will begin to excel.
Rating: 58

02.24.97 by James Dixon

Venue: Manhattan, NY
Taped: 02.24.97
Raw Rating: 2.5
Nitro Rating: 3.0

The WWF is back at the Manhattan Center, *Raw*'s original home, for the first time in years. I am thrilled to see the group return to the building, and wish they had done that again in the future. This is a very special episode of *Raw*, because half of the regular crew are currently on tour in Germany, so the WWF has agreed a deal with ECW for a number of their guys to appear on the show. It is a mutually beneficial agreement for both, with the WWF generating interest in their show from working with another promotion that is currently red hot, whereas ECW gets national exposure as they promote their inaugural pay-per-view *Barely Legal*, taking place in April. Naturally the union is presented as an angle, with the ECW crew having accepted Jerry Lawler's challenge from last week to turn up and prove themselves.

The Godwinns vs. The New Blackjacks
Unfortunately we don't start with a killer ECW angle, but instead with the Godwinns. And their opponents? Why, the equally stereotypical southern folk gimmick of the New Blackjacks. So yes folks, just months away from the WWF going full-on into Attitude, they were still presenting hillbillies against cowboys. Both of these teams are purveyors of clubbering, though the Blackjacks are by far the better at it. Neither team can decide who is heel or face, so they take turns playing both. It's hard to know who we are supposed to cheer for. Midway through we cut to the crowd and see Ken Shamrock sat in the audience, making his first onscreen WWF appearance. The Godwinns eventually decide that they are babyfaces, so HOG can make the hot tag to Phineas, only for him to get belted with Bradshaw's Clothesline From Hell while he has a sleeper applied. Windham gets the win, but only after moving Phineas' leg off the ropes after the fall. Speaking of falls, the referee takes a slopping and then thrashes around like a fool afterwards. Horrible.
Final Rating: ½*

And now for something completely different, as the Eliminators from ECW invade the ring and take out a petrified ring attendant with Total Elimination. Paul Heyman jumps in the ring and accepts Lawler's challenge and introduces the next match, which is an ECW invitational bout. The WWF have done this kind of thing once or twice on *Raw* before, with Jim Cornette's SMW and Mexican group AAA, but never has it been presented in such a hostile manner. That kind of thing was popular in the late 90s thanks to the nWo, and fans loved watching something with a real edge to it after years of saying their prayers and taking their vitamins. The irony of them rebelling against the same man they were then supporting to lead the revolution tickles me.

Little Guido vs. Big Stevie Cool
So ECW's big splash on *Raw* comes in the form of pint-sized grappler Little Guido and nWo parody act the Blue World Order, whose numbers tonight include one Rob Feinstein, who is playing Syxx/Sean Waltman parody "7-11", but all he does is film the stars of the group. Poor Sean. Lawler mocks Guido for being such a short-arse, while Vince looks on slightly bewildered and perplexed by it all, but amused nonetheless. He had never seen any of these guys before, and Lawler's disparaging "freak show" comments are almost justified in this case. Of course, the WWF/E would go on to hire all of these guys (and indeed pretty much all of the ECW representatives on the show) as the years rolled on. "I guess your answer has been challenged" says Vince to Lawler. Flustered, are we? No, actually, Vince is remarkably unflappable about everything going on, which is not what you would expect at all. Paul Heyman does manage to cross a line though, responding to Jerry Lawler's comment of the bWo being a rip-off, by asking who exactly they are ripping off? Lawler and Vince obviously can't say the nWo on air, so they say nothing. Stevie hits a few cool and rarely seen on *Raw* moves, but Raven comes out to distract him, giving Guido a near fall. Stevie is getting pushed to the ECW Title match at *Barely Legal* though, and he wins this one with the Steviekick, which Lawler dismisses because Shawn Michaels has done it "thousands of times". Paul Heyman immediately and viciously responds by saying the difference is Stevie Richards never lost his smile. Burn!
Final Rating: *½

Arm Wrestling Match
Sunny vs. Marlena
Finally, they have found something for Sunny to do that has "wrestling" in the title, though we are pushing it a bit. Sunny gets a huge pop from the rowdy Manhattan crowd and then she sets about trashing them, directly ripping off Rick Rude's pre-match spiel before disrobing and revealing her tight butt. Video Control shows us clips of Chyna battering Marlena and injuring her ribs, so Sunny offers her an out in the form of a forfeit. Marlena rejects and it is on, with the Honky Tonk Man refereeing. Well, letching over younger women runs in the family... Sunny dicks around with heel stall tactics, and then Marlena tries it herself, but Honky threatens to DQ her if she does it again. The actual contest is your standard arm wrestling match, with the addition of Sunny gyrating wildly in a less than PG manner, as the camera focuses on her bouncing ass. Marlena starts to win so Sunny throws her coke stash in her face and shoves the table on her. For no conceivable reason this brings out Savio Vega, who has finally shed his babyface gear and is now decked in all-black. He moves menacingly towards Marlena, which of course brings out Goldust and that leads to a match...

Savio Vega vs. Goldust
These guys had a match on the show less than a year ago that made it to the back of the book, but both guys have switched alignment (and in both cases it is for the worse) and now neither is over. This match isn't a patch on that excellent

contest. It's shit. Just complete and utter shit. Savio spends the majority of the bout either choking or using a nerve hold, and when they do try anything they make a complete mess of it, with both missing elbows and Savio missing a leg lariat by approximately 50-feet. Goldust sells it anyway, sort of. To make matters worse, Miguel Perez, perhaps the blandest wrestler of all time, is on commentary. Where did he suddenly appear from? This is yet another *Raw* match that suffers from being given far too much time, and it just drags on beyond belief until Crush saves the day and causes the DQ. I can't believe I am about to say this, but thank God for Crush! Miguel Perez sticks his oar in afterwards on the side of Goldust, but in a few months he will be part of Los Boricuas with Savio. Fickle bunch, these WWF wrestlers. What a mess this was.

Final Rating: DUD

At ringside, Jerry Lawler gets an interview with his "close personal friend" Ken Shamrock, asking him to tell the world about how he showed Ken his submission moves and helped train him. Shamrock, with all the charisma of an IRS chinlock, dismisses Lawler's claims and reveals he doesn't even know him.

Mikey Whipwreck vs. Taz
This whole ECW invades *Raw* situation almost didn't happen because of Taz. When the crew arrived at the Manhattan Center and found out that their locker rooms were basically two glorified closets, many were pissed off. Taz was the ringleader in telling Paul Heyman to just forget the whole thing and go home, due to the perceived lack of respect being shown. Heyman obviously values money ahead of pride, and he saw the immense value in ECW being associated with the WWF product, and calmer, cooler heads prevailed. To make up for it, he took all of his boys out for pizza after the show, as his own way of saying thank you. Can you imagine Vinny Mac doing that for his boys? Picture *that* scene! It would be like something from a Tarantino film. Whipwreck is just fodder for Taz and his multiple suplexes here, though the head-dropping is broken up briefly by the arrival of Sabu. In typical Sabu style, he manages to botch his big moment when he falls off the "R" of the RAW entrance rather than jumping off it onto Team Taz, and then Taz and Whipwreck complete the amateur hour feel of the whole thing when Taz tries to throw Whipwreck out of the ring onto Sabu, only for them to end up stuck in the ropes. Sabu does what he always does and just pretends it didn't happen, then catches Whipwreck when he awkwardly falls onto him. Sabu, botch machine that he is, really was terrible. Taz finishes Mikey off with the Tazmission, as Vince starts to struggle with remembering everyone's name (see the Raw Recap). Good fun, yet disjointed and brief.

Final Rating: *¾

The Headbangers vs. The Legion of Doom
All show long Vince has been harping on about a surprise, and here it is: the return of the Legion of Doom. The pop they get when the "Oh, what a rush!" line of their entrance music hits is spine-tingling. Everyone rises in unison and there is a real "Holy shit" feel to it, because it wasn't expected at all. New York is glad to have them back, and so am I. This is actually the Legion of Doom's *Raw* debut, because they had left the company before the show first started, and in fact it is over four years since they last competed for the WWF. What a shame then, that the match doesn't come anywhere near to matching the response to their return. In one sense that is down to the booking, because the Headbangers were in the midst of a fairly strong push as they had just arrived in the company and thus couldn't lose. Obviously the LOD can't be losing on their return either, but they needed a win here and a comprehensive and quick one, to establish that they were still the same maulers that they always were. Sadly what we get instead is a plodding, clubbing affair, with Hawk showing that he hasn't changed as a worker at all in the years away from the company, and he still does his no-selling shtick and missed shoulder charge into the post as the cut-off. The undoubted highlight of the match is Jerry Lawler, surprisingly enough, when he starts discussing bands that the Headbangers might be into. He drops in the Butthole Surfers, which prompts an immediate shocked "I beg your pardon!?" from Vince that absolutely cracks me up. His taken-aback delivery of the line which clearly caught him off guard, is just wonderful. So anyway, to counter both teams not being able to job, the WWF treats us to a lame double-count out finish, killing all of the LOD's momentum in one fell swoop. They hit the Doomsday Device on Mosh afterwards to pop the crowd, but this was badly booked and boring.

Final Rating: ½*

Shawn Michaels' pandering, wimpy and slightly overrated 'Tell Me A Lie' music video airs, showing Shawn touching the hearts of his fans, and doing an awful lot of dancing, showboating and hot-dogging. Why do people love this thing so much?

D-Von Dudley vs. Tommy Dreamer
Given that Dreamer is entirely weapons based in his offence, this match features a fair bit of plunder. On the outside, Dreamer starts taking weapons from fans, which concerns Vince: "I think we need to be drawing some lines here, ladies and gentlemen!" The steel steps come into play as Vince then claims anyone can get extreme, and says that Faarooq-Undertaker coming up next will do just that. Lawler and Heyman start to argue, and Lawler goes on a tirade about how he has never been ashamed to be a wrestler, but when he sees "this crap in the ring", he is embarrassed to be associated with it. "Chill out!" says Vince to both, but they don't, they continue viciously barbing at each other, with Lawler calling Heyman a "jock sniffer". "Stop telling me to "wait a minute", I've had it" says Heyman to Vince, calling him on one of his frequent sayings. This is a riot. As ever the WWF like to focus on everything but the in-ring, and the Undertaker gets a split-screen interview. He looks thoroughly appalled by what he sees in the ring, then cuts a promo about *WrestleMania 13* as Beulah gives D-Von a low blow and Dreamer hits his DDT to win it. Bubba Dudley comes in immediately afterwards and the Dudleys hit 3D, a move that would become very familiar to WWF fans in a couple of years. The Sandman comes out, not to Metallica, as Vince asks: "The who!?" Damn right, fuck that guy. Sandman is probably the all-time worst wrestler to ever achieve the level of success that he has. Never has a man with so little talent done so much in wrestling. He has had runs, inexplicably, in the WWE, WCW and obviously ECW, and I don't recall him hitting a single wrestling move in any of them. I know his character, I understand why he gets cheered, but once you have seen his act once it should be enough to last you a lifetime. Once you meet him and wrestle him, as I have, you will realise that he is the worst thing to ever happen to the business. I would take IRS over the Sandman any day of the week.

Final Rating: **¼

After the match, Lawler and Heyman argue, which results in the ECW guys coming to Heyman's aid as Vince gets caught in the middle of it all. Following that, Jim Ross talks us through the WWF Championship situation and what happened last week with Bret Hart and Sid, and then Jim Cornette does the voiceover as Bret loses his temper backstage on *Superstars* exclusive footage from after the title loss. Back to Ken Shamrock, as Toad tries to get a real interview with him. Shamrock introduces his wife and father, but it is the wrong crowd for this. Shamrock predicts the Undertaker will beat Sid at *WrestleMania* but can't decide between Bret and Austin. New York can, and they loudly boo Hart and chant "Bret Hart sucks", showing their unanimous support for Steve Austin.

Faarooq vs. The Undertaker

More Nation... What a horrid juxtaposition this show is. Faarooq has words with Shamrock before the match, and Shamrock finally shows some fire and charisma, calling Faarooq out for hiding behind his goons and then challenging him to a match. More pressing for Faarooq is this match with Undertaker, but given recent form from the WWF, how do you think it goes? If you guessed "overly-long", "boring" and "sloppy", you get a gold star. Faarooq takes Undertaker's offence for a while, but once he gets on top it is laboured, and he uses a chinlock for an age. Faarooq dicks around after a powerslam and makes himself look stupid, just completely lacking in ring savvy. Taker gets lowbridged after a comeback but kicks the steel steps into Faarooq's face, sending him down. The problems with that are two-fold: 1. Dreamer and D-Von just did that, and did it FAR better. 2. Taker barely touched the steps, which in turn barely touched Faarooq, and the slow tree fall sell made things seem completely hokey. So hokey in fact, that a few guys in the front row start hyena laughing at Faarooq for being so naff. Obviously we don't get a finish in a Nation match, and the gang run in to beat on Taker, before the LOD make the popular save. Boring, but not to IRS, Hunter Hearst Helmsley or the Godwinns levels.
Final Rating: *¼

THE RAW RECAP

Most Entertaining: Vince McMahon. For having the balls to abandon his usual "ignore everyone else" policy and try something as bold and brash as this. Then the fact that he sits there all night and remains nonplussed by the very un-WWF like action on display, speaks volumes about him.

Least Entertaining: Savio Vega. What a difference a year makes. Last year he was tearing it up with Steve Austin and had a tremendously entertaining match with Goldust on *Raw*. This year, he is a nerve-pinch using, over-exposed waste of time, and had a shoddy outing with the same opponent.

Quote of the Night: "You need to watch the tapes that Bruce Prichard leaves on your desk" - Paul Heyman to Vince McMahon when he mispronounces "Mikey" Whipwreck as "Mickey". Gotta love those insider references.

Match of the Night: D Von Dudley vs Tommy Dreamer. Tonight wasn't about the in-ring stuff, but Dreamer and D-Von still brought weapons, violence and chaos to proceedings, doing a match unlike anything ever seen on *Raw* before this.

Verdict: This is must-see television from the WWF, though purely because of the novelty factor and the superb stick-work from Heyman, and yes, Lawler, rather than the in-ring stuff, which was secondary to everything else going on. The ECW guys provided the best wrestling action, with the WWF guys rather letting the side down. But on the Federation side the LOD return was tremendous, and Undertaker-Faarooq could have been worse, I guess. Ultimately this was a highly commendable and groundbreaking display of unity from both promotions, and is definitely a show worth getting hold of.

Rating: 79

03.03.97 by Arnold Furious

Venue: Berlin, Germany
Taped: 02.26.97
Raw Rating: 1.9
Nitro Rating: 3.4

We're in Berlin, Germany. Vince McMahon starts out by detailing the recent history of the reunited Germany and segueing into the Bulldog-Owen feud/friendship and the first ever European Championship title match tonight. Hosts are Vince McMahon, Jim Ross and the Honky Tonk Man. Ring announcer is Carsten Schaefer, which gives the whole situation a totally different vibe. Apparently Vince was pissed off with how flat the show came across on TV, but to me it feels exciting. Hearing the ring entrances in German on an American show, combined with the focus on the in-ring makes this show rather unique.

Hunter Hearst Helmsley vs. Bret Hart

This being Germany, Bret is ridiculously over. The WWF never quite understood Bret's popularity in the country, but he was head and shoulders above everybody else. Even a headlock takeover gets a huge pop. Seeing as this show is taped, it's barely a week after Bret lost his title to Sid. He's still considered the company's top guy by the German fans. Due to the reactions, Bret and Hunter are able to take it easy. The camera work makes this feel a bit like a taped house show, which is probably why Vince hated it so much. The angles feel a lot like ROH's earlier stuff, albeit in a much larger venue. Bret was apparently a bit disgruntled by Hunter's position in the company, given his relative lack of experience, as he'd ridden Shawn's coattails onto the booking committee, so Bret isn't prepared to make him look good. Hunter isn't advanced enough to make himself look good either, so the result is decidedly mediocre. Bret sleepwalks through Hunter's heat before launching into the Five Moves of Doom. Hunter tries to beg off during it, but that's like Sarah Connor trying to beg off from the Terminator. Hunter tries for the Pedigree in line with the ring post, which is so obvious a spot to counter it contends with Scott Hall's Razor's Edge by the ropes. After the reversal Hunter gets tied up in the ropes, Bret won't stop kicking him and that's a disappointing DQ. The as yet unnamed Chyna runs in to prevent further damage. The sense that both guys were going through the motions here was palpable.
Final Rating: *½

Video Control takes us to the studios in Stamford where Steve Austin isn't available to comment as he's busy taking a shit. Yep, that's the gag.

WWF Intercontinental Championship
Rocky Maivia (c) vs. Vader

JR claims that the Final Four match reinvigorated Vader, which is true, but the WWF having rediscovered Vader's awesomeness, rather forgot about him again. Vader just OWNED Final Four. Obviously Vader is way above the IC belt, having just dropped out of the WWF Title picture. We get a clip of Vader beating Rock in the European Title tournament 11 days beforehand to demonstrate his superiority. Given that Vader used to work extensively in the country as "Bull Power" and was CWA champion, he's got a reputation outside of the WWF. He mangles Rocky from the offset and leaves Maivia as a plucky underdog. Rocky doesn't let himself be intimidated

and hits a few aggressive moves before Vader crushes him again. If they wanted to avoid Rocky being hated they should have just switched the belt here. Cut that run short and have Vader as the unstoppable champion and strengthen the IC belt in the process. Of course that didn't happen, but it would have been an interesting switch in the booking. Rocky gets a sweet near fall by countering Vader off the top into a "powerslam", which was more like a hip toss. He does come flying back with a belly-to-belly and a floatover DDT though, and the fans really respond to his dominance against big Vader. Mankind runs out, for no apparent reason, to knock Rocky out with the urn and that's a DQ. Vader is somewhat confused as to why his tag team partner at *WrestleMania* just "saved" him. Before the dumb finish, used to protect both guys, it was a humdinger. Rocky's youthful exuberance versus Vader's full-bore destruction. I think they missed the boat on Rocky by having him continue on as IC champion too long, but it led to the fans resenting him and a subsequent heel turn, which set the world on fire.
Final Rating: **½

Video Control takes us to clips of ECW's insanity from last week. Including Sandman bashing a beer on his head, Total Elimination, Sabu diving off the RAW sign, an instrumental version of "Man in a Box" and Lawler going off on an long rant about how much he hates hardcore wrestling. I really enjoyed the ECW invasion. It launched my love of the company back in 1997 and opened up a lot of wrestling doors. Ever since then I've been open to different wrestling experiences. The WWF learned from ECW's wild approach to wrestling, stole the concept and turned it into Attitude. Even using many of the same workers (Steve Austin, Mick Foley, Dudleys, Taz, etc)

The Sultan vs. Flash Funk
This matchup made it onto the *Revenge of the Taker* free for all next month so the WWF must have enjoyed this bout. Or forgot it had happened. One or the other. The problem with loading *Raw* with big matches is it limits what is then available for the PPV market, thus watering down the product. Both guys are good wrestlers, albeit with goofy gimmicks. Vince gets words with Jerry Lawler, who runs down ECW, and Paul Heyman who doesn't care for Lawler's comments, shills the ECW PPV and threatens to show up next week on *Raw*. Sultan lands on his head off a rana, which sets up a moonsault. Sultan manages to kick out of that and dumps Flash on the his face to block a head scissor takedown. Camel clutch finishes as they try to keep Sultan strong for *WrestleMania* and his IC title shot. I feel bad for Flash as he'd have been a better guy to work Rocky at 'Mania, even if he'd have helped to turn Rock heel a lot quicker. The match had some exciting high spots, but it was too short to mean anything.
Final Rating: *

Video Control shows us clips of Steve Austin horsing around last time he was interviewed live on *Raw* back in October. Next up is a Sid interview backstage where he screams nonsense into the camera, paraphrases *Mad Max: Beyond Thunderdome* and gets all symbolic about winning tonight. You see, Mankind is towards the dark side so he's taking that journey toward the Undertaker. We get more clips of Bulldog and Owen having issues, this time at *Final Four* during their tag title defence where Davey clotheslined Owen after a Hart miscue.

Promo Time: Ahmed Johnson
This is Ahmed's chance to confirm whether he'll accept Faarooq's challenge to a Chicago Street Fight at *WrestleMania*. Carsten conducts the interview meaning the at home audience can't understand either guy. Ahmed accepts but says he won't come alone before starting another fascinating "YO GO DAH" chant with the Germans chanting "You're going down" with perfect diction. This didn't work at all, as Carsten had to translate everything before the pops kicked in. Video Control then takes us to an LOD promo from *Shotgun Saturday Night*. They basically put over Chicago and say they hope to take part in *WrestleMania* there, thus giving us the connection between Ahmed's statement and the actual 'Mania card.

WWF Championship
Sycho Sid (c) vs. Mankind
We get pre-recorded comments from Mankind in German, which are also insanely in character. There are times when Mick Foley is nothing short of brilliant. To bring that level of weirdness to the plate leaves the usually crazy Sid somewhat confused. Foley, despite a prior PPV title shot against Shawn last year, isn't seriously considered for the belt here, which shows you what a terrific job he did of humanising his character and making him into a sympathetic Rocky Balboa-like star over the following two years. Sid grinds away at an armbar so Vince McMahon cuts to an interview with Steve Austin, who says Bret is a whiner and a quitter and it makes him sick. JR hauls us back to the match, bemoaning a lack of attention for a WWF Title bout. Quite right too. Mick's approach to this one is a bit weird and he tries to work Sid's throat but can't convince him into buying that psychology. Sid just bumps everything normally and mounts a comeback. Sid wasn't only limited in the ring, he was limited in the brain. So poor Mick Foley is left to take a few silly bumps to get the match over while Sid's contribution is yelling and being muscular. Mankind continues to work the throat and still can't get Sid to sell it. It's all an attempt to disrupt Sid's breathing, which assists with the Mandible Claw, so when it's hooked, in the middle of the ring it should be over, but Sid just shrugs it off and powers out. Considering the Undertaker couldn't do that, Sid shouldn't be able to either. I guess it gives the serious viewer thought as to Sid being stronger than Taker, but to the casual fan it just destroys Mankind's finish. Silly spot. Having seen his A-game come up short Mankind resorts to a sleeper, which also doesn't work. Sid mounts another comeback with those horrible punches of his before an obvious heel miscue with Paul Bearer, as Sid constantly looks over his shoulder for Mankind. Sid wins with a powerbomb after Mankind sets early on a backdrop. At least the finish was good. The whole finishing sequence was pretty hot, albeit stilted. I feel bad for Mick here because he brought all the bumps and the psychology and Sid had no idea how to deal with it, so the match was pretty poor but it was all Sid's fault. His run in the sun was nearing an end.
Final Rating: *¾

Video Control gives us footage of Davey Boy Smith losing to Crush on *Shotgun Saturday Night* and his manager Clarence Mason having a conflict of interest by ignoring Nation of Domination cheating. Davey fires him. We get live footage of Davey and Owen, with the latter doing push ups while staring at his tag team title. How he did this with a straight face is amazing. Owen was such a ribber.

Promo Time: Steve Austin
We finally get Austin for a sit down live from Stamford. We see footage of Austin costing Bret the WWF Title two weeks ago. Austin rants about Shawn Michaels getting tribute videos when he's got a cold, but when Steve was sick at *Final Four* with one leg, he went 25-minutes. Bitter about Shawn's knee injury, eh? Not the only one. Austin says he's got no quit in him so he can't

lose the submission match at *WrestleMania*.

WWF European Championship (Vacant)
Owen Hart vs. The British Bulldog

These guys are tag team champions as well as brothers-in-law, but they've spent the last month or so getting increasingly frustrated with each other. This is the blow-off for the storyline as the Hart Foundation reunion is right around the corner. Seeing as the title was created specifically for Davey, it's pretty obvious who will win. They start off with arm ringer counters where both guys wrestle out in the most complicated way possible. They bring counters at the kind of speed and consistency that you'd expect from an Indy main event circa 2003. Not only is it technically excellent, but it looks like a legitimate struggle too. That is until Owen uses the ropes to set up a rana and Davey plants him with a powerbomb. I guess that is realistic though as the flippy nonsense basically didn't get the job done. Owen tries for another flip to escape a hammerlock but Davey just drops him on the arm in mid move, which is a fantastic counter. The psychology behind that is amazing, as it's Davey's understanding of Owen's abilities and mentality combined with his own ingenuity. It follows again moments later as Owen goes for the enzuigiri and Bulldog avoids it easily. Davey switches his moves up to make himself unpredictable, being fully aware of Owen's own understanding of his moves. So he breaks out stuff like the surfboard and stays on top with his power. Owen gets totally into the spirit of it by taking a series of terrific bumps. Owen shows good sportsmanship by holding the ropes for Davey after Bulldog takes a tumble to the floor, which shows that while Owen is a heel he likes Bulldog. Not enough to play totally fair though as he fakes a knee injury to enormous heat. He tries for the Sharpshooter but Davey powers out and tempers begin to get frayed.

Owen clocks Davey with a sensational spinning heel kick. It looked botched to begin with but he just planted an unsuspecting Davey across the face with his calf. Owen takes over from there but Davey continues to score flash pins for near falls. Owen litters his own heat with high impact moves including a belly-to-belly suplex at speed. The urge to win a belt gets the better of Owen and he starts to cheat, using the ropes on a pin. The counters in this match are sharp, sudden almost, like Davey countering a superplex into a crossbody. He does it so fast that Owen can barely even get him up. They sneak in some nice tributes to Warrior-Savage with Owen lifting the Savage Elbow and Davey hitting the multiple clotheslines. Owen brings the German suplex… because we're in Germany! It doesn't get a big pop, surprisingly. Davey goes after his powerslam but Owen counters in mid air into an inside cradle before he clocks Davey with the enzuigiri. This time Davey was confused by Owen switching gears. Sharpshooter follows but Davey powers into the ropes. They go back into the counters with Owen attempting a Tombstone only for Davey to counter right into the powerslam… for 2! Owen kicks out! How? Because Davey hooked the wrong leg. Yes, they even have some tidy psychology on a finisher kick out. Owen goes after a victory roll but Davey blocks it into the pin to echo the *WrestleMania X* finish between Owen and Bret, this time with Owen on the wrong end of it. The selling near the end gets a wee bit suspect and there are a few rest holds in the middle section, but apart from that this match is awesome. One of the best of the decade and one of the best to ever feature on *Monday Night Raw*. Everyone suspects that Owen will sucker punch Davey in the back, but instead they shake hands. For one night at least Owen accepts that Davey is the better man.
Final Rating: ****¾

THE RAW RECAP

Most Entertaining: Davey Boy Smith and Owen Hart. An absolute clinic and one of the best matches of both men's careers. A shoe-in for best match of the year come the awards section.

Least Entertaining: There are a few candidates, but when the show finishes like this one did it's hard to remember anything negative about it.

Quote of the Night: "One of the truly great World Wrestling Federation champions" – Vince McMahon brings praise for Sid. Not sure I agree. Nor would Vince just a few months later.

Match of the Night: Davey Boy Smith vs. Owen Hart.

Verdict: The final match is obviously what the show is remembered for, and rightly so, but the entire undercard is pleasantly watchable. Sometimes the WWF go out of their way to push one match as a massive *Raw* main event and all their hype just added to the excitement generated by two excellent wrestlers having a wonderful match against each other. Easily in the top five for both men's respective careers (#3 for Owen, #2 for Bulldog, I'd wager) and one of the finest Raw matches, ever. What more can you ask for? If you've never seen it, this one is well worth tracking down. If it had happened in ECW at the same time people would be calling it the greatest match of all time. The match is on the *Best of Raw - 15th Anniversary* DVD and it also appears on the *Hart and Soul* DVD.
Rating: 73

03.10.97 by Arnold Furious

Venue: Worcester, MA
Taped: 03.10.97
Raw Rating: 2.3
Nitro Rating: 3.5

This was a big change for the WWF as they switched to Marilyn Manson's *'Beautiful People'* as the theme music and started referring to the second hour as "Raw is War" (and later "War Zone"). This is also the first time they used a load of fireworks to start the show. We're in Worcester, Massachusetts. Hosts are Vince McMahon, Jim Ross and Jerry Lawler. They shill the card, Ken Shamrock's announcement and ECW's Paul Heyman is in the house.

Promo Time; Sycho Sid

The famous opening promo to set up the main event! It begins! JR hops into the ring to talk to the champ. Sid is reluctant to tag with Undertaker this evening. He implies the number one contender is in cahoots with Paul Bearer still and the main event is basically a 3-on-1. It's a clever assumption from the champ, even if he bludgeons his delivery of the sentiment. Undertaker answers the accusations in person to point out that it's in his interest to see Sid healthy after tonight so he can take the title from him at *WrestleMania*. Taker declines Sid's partnership and offers to go solo tonight. "I don't need a plot to beat you" sayeth the Dead Man. Paul Bearer interrupts with his team, of Vader and Mankind, to accuse both title contenders of being cowards. A ruck ensues. The whole segment was laboured and forced. The WWF really started to push this opening talk segment as *Raw* moved forward. The idea being to hype the main event with a load of yakking. Sometimes it worked, here it didn't.

Rocky Maivia vs. Tony Roy
This match just exists for Iron Sheik, Bob Backlund and the Sultan to interject and set up the *WrestleMania* IC title match. I like Backlund calling Rocky "Mr. Johnson". Vince has a mental block with jobbers again and refers to Roy as "Rua" throughout. Sheik and Backlund rant over the entire match, which Rocky takes with a high crossbody. The Sultan runs in after the bell and Rocky kicks his ass too, thus eliminating any intrigue they were attempting to build to at 'Mania. Tony Atlas is shown in the crowd, Rocky Johnson's tag team partner, and he jumps the rail to watch Rock's back. Not that Rocky needed it, having already dealt with the three clowns by himself.
Final Rating: SQUASH (Not rated)

Heavy Metal, Pentagon II & Pierroth vs. Latin Lover, Octagon & Hector Garza
I've added the rider of "II" on Pentagon as the original Pentagon retired in 1996 and Antonio Pena (boss of lucha firm AAA) merely put the mask on someone else. A little like Vince's assertion that anyone could play his characters. But while Pentagon was a masked luchadore, relatively easy to clone, Vince tried it with Razor Ramon. Octagon was one of AAA's biggest stars and Pentagon is the evil clone version of him. Both guys dress the same as Great Sasuke, if that helps your visualisation of them; like ninjas. Octagon and his good looking teammates are the "technicos" or babyfaces. Pierroth and company are the "rudos" or heels. The crowd are not conditioned to Mexican wrestling, to this point mainly associated with ECW and WCW, so these six wrestle to silence. The announcers give up on calling it and talk about other things instead. JR contributes a spot of knowledge while Lawler questions why all these outside scrubs are being used. There's no characterisation from the Mexican cohorts so instead they just run spots one after another. Most of them silly lucha spots that require massive cooperation. Vince gets so bored they concentrate on the as yet unnamed Chyna being escorted out by security. As Pierroth launches into a load of chops they cut away again to talk to Brian Pillman. This causes the dives segment to get ignored entirely, which is for the best as it's a convoluted mess. It's so bad they might as well put a flashing message in big letters onscreen saying "WRESTLING IS FAKE". They make a royal mess of the finish where Garza is supposed to miss a dive, only Heavy Metal moves out of the way at least five seconds too early before winning with La Majistral. When lucha libre is bad, it is the worst of all bad wrestling. This was an abortion. Luckily nobody in the WWF cared.
Final Rating: DUD

Ahmed Johnson vs. Roy Raymond
Ahmed is wearing a quart of baby oil this evening. The match is all of one move in when the Nation of Domination show up. Ahmed botches throwing Roy out of the ring in horrific fashion. I'm surprised he didn't injure the poor jobber. The Nation stand around doing nothing as Ahmed runs through his spots and finishes with the Pearl River Plunge. Faarooq rants at Ahmed, reminding him what the streets are about, and accuses Ahmed of turning up "stupid and alone" as always. Ahmed points out not only is he not scared but he's got back up; the Legion of Doom. "I'm bringing the whole city of Chicago with me". One of the best promo duels these two had on TV. Jim Ross gets back in there to get words. "All of a sudden you're all turning white, even the black boys" – Ahmed of the Nation. That brings a wonderfully racist little chuckle from Vince McMahon.
Final Rating: SQUASH (Not rated)

The British Bulldog & Owen Hart vs. The New Blackjacks
JR tries to get words with the tag champs pre-match but can't stir up any trouble. The New Blackjacks might not have been such a bad idea if they'd let Windham look like Barry Windham instead of dying his hair and moustache black. Bradshaw gets to quote *Deliverance* by telling Owen he has "purdy lips, boy". How many of Vince's Southern teams have used that phrase? Most of them I'd wager. I seem to recall the Godwinns using it on Hawk from LOD the following year. Vince can't stay with this either and goes quickly to an interview with Vader and Mankind. The show is two hours long! You can't fit that in after the match? Davey and Owen show good continuity despite their increasing discomfort in teaming together. At least until the Harts reunion. The Blackjacks haven't really got any team stuff as they're both just big hosses. Vince cuts away again to tell us about Bret Hart getting a title shot at Sid next week! We cut away AGAIN, and this time it's ECW's Taz who seems a touch upset with Lawler. The match rumbles on with the Blackjacks showing a lack of anything interesting. Bradshaw was too good for this rehash. Owen has it won with a Sharpshooter only for Bulldog to rush in to attack Windham and get his team disqualified. Owen isn't pleased.
Final Rating: *½

Post Match: Taz runs out to get in Jerry Lawler's face. Sabu runs into the ring, attempting to kill someone, but ends up going through a table with his triple jump plancha. It's weird that I'm more excited to see Taz vs. Sabu than anything at *WrestleMania 13*, though the Bret-Austin match obviously delivered.

Leif Cassidy vs. Miguel Perez
Believe it or not, Cassidy is STILL the jobber here as this was a brief period where Perez was being pushed. The idea being he came in to show Savio Vega the error of his ways in forgetting his roots. Perez would end up in Savio's Boricuas stable but here he's just a vanilla babyface. No wonder he never took off. They blow one spot with Perez going for a leapfrog and Leif just standing there looking confused. Cassidy dumps Perez on his head with a German suplex as we get words from Paul Heyman. He's super pissed off with Jerry Lawler and challenges him to meet his friends in the ring later. The match is a few loosely connected spots finishing with Perez reversing a powerbomb into a roll up. Poor Leif; jobbed to hell.
Final Rating: ½*

Backstage: Sid gets an interview, again. How many interviews are on this show? Sid says he doesn't react, he reacts with action. Uh? He doesn't seem that concerned that he has to defend his title next week against Bret Hart. "Reason why?" yells Sid. Um?

Promo Time: Ken Shamrock
Ken Shamrock, from the Ultimate Fighting world, joins us for another interview. Jim Ross does most of the talking and announces that Ken will be the referee for the Bret-Austin submission match, which if Bret wins next week could be a WWF Title match. Ken talks about submission wrestling and his experience thereof, so he's prepared for *WrestleMania*. He adds he won't be intimidated and will be a fair referee. He's a bit dull so Steve Austin interrupts from the Titantron, threatening to stomp Ken's guts in. He calls Bret's title match next week "BS" but hopes Bret will win before adding he's never quit at nothing (a double negative, surely). He claims once he's done with Bret Hart he'll wipe the ring with Ken Shamrock too. That brings Bret Hart to the ring, with a

confused Austin leaving the 'Tron. Bret says it's his first chance to talk in three weeks. He puts himself over for winning a fourth WWF title but calls Austin's interference a day later a rip off. He launches into Sid; "You're not as good as me, you'll never be as good as me" and says he'll become a five time champion next week. He whines about being screwed by everyone, including referees (just wait on that one, Bret). He respects Shamrock, though if Shamrock screws with him at 'Mania it'll be the biggest mistake of his life. That sentiment causes Steve Austin's arrival but in a switch in character he decides not to run down and attack both men. Keep in mind he was still a heel and technically Bret and Shamrock were faces.

Billy Gunn vs. Aldo Montoya
Billy is still dressed as a Smoking Gunn, but the presence of the Honky Tonk Man at ringside shows where his career is going. HTM has a shortlist of three guys now that he wants to manage. These guys decide to have a competitive match with Aldo getting fluke flash pins to offset Billy's power. This includes a very poorly executed enzuigiri where Billy slowly kiels over sideways before remembering to flip bump and almost landing on his head. We cut away to talk to Sunny about *Shotgun Saturday Night* only to miss the finish where Billy takes it with a leg jam.
Final Rating: ¼*

Backstage: Mankind gets an interview as the WWF runs through the entire roster in interviews. Mankind throws the urn away saying he doesn't need it and he's smarter than people give him credit, as the WWF disrespectfully play him out by going to commercial.

Goldust vs. Tim McNeedy
Before they even lock-up, Hunter Hearst Helmsley shows up on the ramp with Chyna, who had been arrested earlier. Goldust hits a few spots and finishes with the Curtain Call. Post Match: Chyna distracts to allow Hunter to jump Goldust from behind. Marlena jumps on Chyna's back to show a little fight and officials come down to break it up.
Final Rating: SQUASH (Not rated)

The Great Debate: Jerry Lawler vs. Paul Heyman
JR hosts as these two argue about the intricacies of Extreme. Lawler barracks ECW for running shows in a bingo hall and having a bunch of scrubs that couldn't get a job anywhere else. That's probably true of John Kronus. Lawler points out the show is all violent crap and people in Philadelphia are idiots. Heyman retorts by saying they earn the respect of anyone that watches the show. Whether it be 1,100 people, more or less. Sandman runs in to threaten violence. Lawler runs Heyman into the ground with numbers, causing Heyman to get personal. Tommy Dreamer jumps in and threatens a war. Sandman busts himself open with a beer can in the process as Lawler asks for support from the locker room and gets none. Funny to think everyone in the ECW party, Kronus aside, actually worked for the WWF later in their career.

Vader & Mankind vs. Sycho Sid & The Undertaker
Sid and Undertaker are set to face each other at *WrestleMania* while the unorthodox team of Vader and Mankind will get a tag title shot. You'd think the heels would go over to stress the issues between the two championship participants, and thankfully that's exactly what happens. The heels start by double-teaming Sid as Taker takes forever to get to the ring. When Taker finally shows up he chokeslams Vader. Mankind Cactus Clotheslines Taker to the floor, but badly positioned ring steps almost cripple the poor guy. Vince warns of TV time running out but they still find time to show Marlena going after Chyna again from earlier. The match follows formula with Sid taking heat until a hot tag to Taker. Chokeslam for Mankind, but as Sid comes back in Taker accidentally punches him. Sid takes umbrage so Taker chokeslams him and hits a crazy outta control zombie plancha on the heels. Luchataker! Sid grabs him though and hits the powerbomb. This leaves Taker as easy pickings for Vader. It also gives the fans food for thought as the fan favourite Undertaker was beaten by big Sid's finishing move. It implied the possibility of him not winning at *WrestleMania*. The match was a decent TV affair, with Taker busting out his A-game.
Final Rating: **¼

THE RAW RECAP

Most Entertaining: Steve Austin. In a night of talking the most entertaining man on the stick was the company's future main guy.

Least Entertaining: Everyone in the Mexican tag was culpable for such a poor showing, but I'll go with Heavy Metal for botching the finish.

Quote of the Night: "The streets is having your mother die when you're eight years old. Having your father leave to who knows where. And guess who turns up in the living room then? An Uncle Tom black man that every time I look at you reminds me of your black ass" – Faarooq lays a verbal smackdown on Ahmed Johnson.

Match of the Night: Vader & Mankind vs. Sid & Undertaker.

Verdict: The first ever *Raw is War* show was a mixed bag of crazy crap. The WWF threw so much stuff at the wall during the 90-minutes of airtime that eventually something would stick. This was Vince's response to the "dry" nature of *Raw* the week before. There were a few good segments including the ECW debate, Austin and Bret meeting Shamrock and the main event. However the sheer amount of crap on this show makes you wonder if all the positive was just accidental. Did the show really need four squashes? Was Miguel Perez vs. Leif Cassidy really Raw material? Also the habit of cutting away from matches for interviews was frustrating. Interviews set up conflict, not divert away from it. This show was definitely guilty of having too much stuff going on. They need to scale that back and focus on the product. Although, that's something a lot of purists have been arguing since the start of the Attitude Era.
Rating: 43

03.17.97 by Arnold Furious

Venue: Syracuse, NY
Taped: 03.17.97
Raw Rating: 2.4
Nitro Rating: 3.6

We're in Syracuse, New York. Hosts are Vince McMahon, Jim Ross and Jerry Lawler. And for the second week running we're LIVE! Taking *Raw* to two hours certainly allowed the WWF freedom to run live shows more frequently.

The Legion of Doom vs. Savio Vega & Crush
This was set up last week when Ahmed announced the LOD would join him in the Chicago Street Fight at *WrestleMania*, so they play loose with the rules here, which helps with the

limitations of the weaker members of the respective teams. Crush, especially, who's a bore in normal matches. We cut away to hear from Ahmed who, clear as mud, tells us he doesn't know what will happen at *WrestleMania* as street fights are so unpredictable. Vince, not content with that, interviews Faarooq too as Hawk no-sells a piledriver. He switches to ebonics so Ahmed can understand him. "Ahmed Johnson took a whupping last night in Madison Square Garden" says Vince without a hint of irony. Back in the match the Nation work over Hawk but Vince cuts away again to speak to Faarooq, who's not there, before talking to Ahmed again as Faarooq jumps him from behind. It's one of those ghetto beat downs I've been hearing so much about. During that Animal got a hot tag. Not that the WWF seems to care about wrestling anymore. I'll cut them some slack with this match though, which has been decidedly uninteresting. Faarooq runs down to break up the Doomsday Device and that's a DQ. It's also a notice of intent concerning the Chicago Street Fight. Ahmed runs in with a 2x4 for the save and poor D'Lo takes the Doomsday Device. The match was nothing but the hints of violence at *WrestleMania* were tempting.
Final Rating: *

The announce team talk about the main event tonight and JR suggests it might not be for the WWF title. Lawler claims he's heard Shawn Michaels is on his way to the arena too. Ah, live TV! Vince Russo's playground.

Hunter Hearst Helmsley vs. Flash Funk
Hunter is now officially accompanied by Chyna, which means she's now got a name and indeed a highlights package of her WWF career so far. Flash is accompanied by the Funkettes. I love the Funkettes, but unfortunately the whole gimmick somewhat slowed Scorpio down, while it was a positive boon for the 'Funkasaurus' years later. Flash and Hunter have some interesting near miss stuff lined up and it makes for an exciting opening few minutes. Hunter almost botches an electric chair, but they pull through with a nice kneeling improvisation from the future Game. Both guys seem eager to showcase their skills; Funk his flying and Hunter his ability to *deal* with Flash's flying. Chyna saves Hunter after a funky legdrop off the top. Hunter rather botches the follow-up German suplex. Weak bridge. He's certainly operating outside his comfort zone during this match. Chyna distracts to set up the Pedigree and that's it for a lively five minute contest. I really enjoyed it! Hunter did make mistakes here, but it is nice to see him try different things. This is the first time I'd really seen Hunter show potential as a big star, outside of matches with Shawn Michaels or other bigger stars.
Final Rating: **½

Mini Mankind & Mini Vader vs. Mini Goldust & Mascarita Sagrada Jr.
Vince cuts away immediately to get footage of Christine Todd Whitman bringing wrestling back to New Jersey. They even invited her to a PPV to get this over. Naturally Whitman is a Republican. MSJ went on to become Max Mini. He's a proper tiny midget. Everyone else is a bit of a freak. Mini Goldust at least has the theatrics down. Many, many armdrags occur in this match. Vader makes me laugh by kicking MSJ in the back of the head. Full bore. MSJ takes it by hitting Mini Mankind with a victory roll. The match was nothing but they have an awesome spot afterwards with Mini Vader tumbling off the stage and MSJ hitting an insane dive after him. It's so cool it merits a replay.
Final Rating: ½*

Backstage: Gorilla Monsoon joins us to discuss the main event. He confirms it will be a WWF Title match, which makes you wonder where the "rumours" came from or what the point of them even occurring was. Vince accuses Gorilla of bowing to Bret's pressure, but Monsoon says Bret deserves a rematch for the belt.

Promo Time: Bret Hart
Kevin Kelly gets interview duties with JR remaining at ringside. Bret's out to discuss his title match this evening. Bret points out he won the Rumble, the Final Four and he's a former 4-time champion so he deserves some respect. This draws a chorus of boos. The mention of Austin draws a noticeable pop. The double turn was the right move. Bret cuts an ambling promo saying he'll win the title, give Taker a shot down the line, beat Steve Austin at *WrestleMania* and become the man, once again. The response to Bret's promo and his catchphrase is decidedly mixed. To some people he remained a hero figure despite the whining.

The Sultan vs. Mike Bell
Rocky Maivia, the IC champion, joins commentary for this bout to scout his *WrestleMania* opponent. He doesn't have much to go on as Sultan treats the chunky Bell with disdain. Sultan just gets his moves in (savat kick, piledriver, top rope splash, camel clutch) and goes home. It leaves Rocky with absolutely nothing to talk about. Tony Atlas runs out to make sure Rock doesn't get into a fight with the Sultan and both of his managers.
Final Rating: SQUASH (Not rated)

Promo Time: Shawn Michaels.
HBK hadn't been seen since losing his smile on *Thursday Raw Thursday* and forfeiting the WWF title with a suspect knee injury. It's also known as jobbingitis (or fear of counting lights). Shawn starts out by saying he found his smile back in San Antonio but he's brought it with him. He thanks the fans for their patience as he's the "world's most emotional wrestler". Shawn gets around to his knee injury, which Doc Andrews has pretty much cleared already, and he'll be back in a few months. Shawn bemoans a lack of invitation to *WrestleMania* and the Slammys. A touch underwhelming considering the big '*Tell Me A Lie*' send off he got. Maybe they weren't sure when he'd be back in the ring and didn't want to set up anything solid.

Tangent: Shawn's knee injury has been the source of much consternation on the internet over the years. Basically Shawn went to his doctor, who isn't used to seeing wrestling injuries, and the doctor saw how knackered Shawn's knee was and told him he couldn't do anything anymore. Shawn, being heavily into drugs at the time and severely paranoid, believed him and that's why he dropped the belt. As soon as Vince sent him to see Doctor Andrews, the guy who could sew a detached head back on and have his guy back wrestling in a week, they discovered that by wrestling standards the knee injury wasn't that bad at all. At the time both Steve Austin and Bret Hart were working with knees that were in worse condition. All of this, capped off by Shawn's behaviour, created ill feeling towards him. The feeling that he dodged *WrestleMania* to avoid jobbing to Bret Hart. He'd already strategically derailed Vader's push to maintain his main event status for longer and was keen to not take high profile losses. He'll tell you that wasn't the case but everyone else had Bret-Shawn pencilled in at 'Mania with a submission finish and Bret getting his win back. Shawn used the knee as an excuse to dodge that bullet and make himself look like a bigger star. Which is one of many reasons why people don't like Shawn. I personally missed him during the first half of 1997. His in-ring was better than anyone in the company at the time. When you lose your best worker the shows will suffer.

Vader vs. The British Bulldog
Bulldog is leaning face alongside the heel-ish Owen, against the very heel Vader and his equally heel partner on the floor; Mankind. This is to set up the tag title match at *WrestleMania* between these two teams. JR continues to mention how great Vader has been over the past few months, but doesn't mention how awesome Davey Boy has been in early '97. Possibly in the form of his life making this a potential dream match with both guys at their peak. Bulldog uses his power to jack Vader up on a stalling suplex, which freaks out everybody. Davey marries his power with speed and is able to avoid a lot of Vader's trademark weight throwing around. However Davey's attempted crucifix sets up a Samoan drop. While Davey had incredible tools in the ring, his brain wasn't one of them. Vader is game for selling too and throws himself into several Davey clotheslines before launching himself into a Davey powerslam. Davey even considers the running powerslam and has Vader up for it, but Mankind interjects and Owen jumps on the apron too drawing a DQ. Owen gets his ass handed to him for that and Davey makes the save with the urn. Another good TV match from Davey in a string of them and a teaser of what a potentially excellent PPV match they could have had. Of course the Hart Foundation storyline stopped any potential babyface matches Davey had lined up.
Final Rating: **¾

Billy Gunn vs. Aaron Ferguson
Ken Shamrock is here to do guest commentary and hand Billy Gunn's ass to him. Ferguson is a fat mess and one of the sloppiest conditioned jobbers the WWF have used on *Raw*. Billy decides to show Ken a few submission holds and grabs a leg grapevine and an abdominal stretch. I never had Billy pegged as a submissions specialist. Billy takes it with an armbar as Shamrock puts the hold over before accusing Gunn of being able to do it with "someone of little experience". Oh, you've been burned Ferguson! Billy challenges Ken into the ring afterwards. Shamrock says he's never backed down from anything in his life so hops in there. Billy gets slapped in a Fujiwara from a lock up and taps out. Billy thinks Ken was lucky and demands another go so Shamrock taps him with his patented anklelock instead. That'll do for Billy and he walks. The match was a squash, but the antics with Shamrock were really entertaining. Shamrock posed an interesting threat to the WWF roster with his submission skills, and indeed his tap-outs changed the way wrestling was delivered to the public during the era that followed. Tapping out gave submission holds a visual connection to the crowd that hadn't been enjoyed beforehand.
Final Rating: SQUASH (Not rated)

Backstage: Steve Austin calls Ken Shamrock "overrated and a big piece of trash". Ken can see all this from ringside. "If he sticks his nose in, I'll punch his lights out". Austin's logic for being here, when not booked, is brilliant. "I'm the King of the Ring. You set the ring up, I'm here. It's my job". Austin proceeds to rant about how he's the best wrestler in the company and Bret "on his best day" couldn't lace his boots. Superb.

Elsewhere: Sid rants about powerbombing Bret through the floor. This is all to kill time while the cage is set up. Back at ringside the three commentators debate the outcome of the match with both Undertaker and Austin in the arena.

Cage Match
WWF Championship
Sycho Sid (c) vs. Bret Hart
I wanted Bret to win this match so bad in 1997, but I guess they didn't want the title to overshadow the double turn at 'Mania nor have a champion switch from face to heel with the title. Although they did that with Randy Savage. JR implies that Sid has Bret's number as he's beaten him twice in recent months. Albeit with heavy interference in both matches. Sid brings a lot of clubberin', which is executed quite slowly. A little worrying for an 8 minute TV match. No wonder they got shot of Sid after he dropped the belt to Taker. He was in the right place at the right time in '96 to early '97 but that time was brief. Sid tries to escape but Austin comes down to blockade the doorway. Bret gets caught with a powerbomb, this time clean as a whistle. Sid tries to climb out so Austin climbs the cage to stop him once again. This leads to Austin and Bret double teaming Sid to further their own gains of a WWF title match at *WrestleMania*. The Undertaker has seen enough of that and comes down to eliminate Austin and return this to a one-on-one contest. Bret still has a minor advantage and hits a superplex. Austin opens the door for Bret but Taker slams it in his face allowing Sid time to climb out and retain. The match was more about the storyline between Austin and Bret than Sid and Bret. As if the WWF would ever completely re-jig *WrestleMania* six days before the biggest PPV of the year.
Final Rating: **

Post Match: Bret Hart is fuming. Vince McMahon makes the decision to go in there and interview him. Not his greatest idea. Bret shoves Vince over and calls the finish "bullshit". Bret goes off on an almighty rant about how he was screwed, again, and nobody cares about it. He pops off his catchphrase; "If you don't like it, tough shit". Austin gets on the Titantron to say he tried to help Bret but the Hitman is a loser. Bret calls him gutless for talking from the Titantron and that brings out Sid as Bret proclaims himself to be the true champion. "I don't know shit" says Sid. Ain't that the truth. That brings out Undertaker and Bret hits him with a tope, incensed about the finish and Austin, ever the opportunist, runs down to kick Bret's ass. Taker and Sid end up brawling in the ring while Bret and Austin brawl on the floor. Bret even angers Vince in the brawl by knocking out Hall of Famer Pat Patterson. "That dirty son of a..." With everyone brawling around, Shawn Michaels comes out for a better look. I'm not sure what he's supposed to be doing out there but he seems to be perfectly mobile.

THE RAW RECAP

Most Entertaining: Steve Austin. Whether he's wrestling or not Steve is the best thing about *Raw* in 1997. His character and personality are really coming to the forefront. For me he edged out everyone else with his promo skills. Looking back he was just on fire until that neck injury.

Least Entertaining: Crush. He was so dull, the WWF pretty much cut all his in-ring.

Quote of the Night: "Frustrated isn't the goddamn word for it, this is bullshit" – Bret Hart gets upset with his failure to reclaim the WWF Title.

Match of the Night: Vader vs. The British Bulldog. Both men were at the top of their game in early 1997. Vader had bowled Vince McMahon over with his performances in a Shawn-free WWF. Meanwhile Bulldog was having a run of matches in 1997 that proved to be his best run in wrestling.

Verdict: Although the star ratings may not reflect it, this was a fun episode of Raw. They brought an interesting mix of personalities and action. Vader-Bulldog and Hunter-Flash were solid TV matches and the stuff with Austin, Bret, Shawn and Shamrock delivered. The only downside to things was Undertaker's angles and his refusal to change with the times. When he eventually did enter into a different state of being it was perhaps a little late. Everything else on the show is about violence, gangs and hatred. Taker's dedication to his "creatures of the night" was from a simpler time. Both at the time and looking back I much preferred Austin, Bret and Shawn. Not to mention Vader, Owen and Bulldog. For me Undertaker shouldn't have been positioned for a title run in 1997 because he was such a relic.
Rating: 64

03.23.97 - WrestleMania 13
(James Dixon)
[Rosemont Horizon, Rosemont, Illinois]

- The Headbangers def. The New Blackjacks, Doug Furnas & Phil LaFon and the Godwinns in a four way elimination match (¼*)
- Rocky Maivia def. The Sultan (½*)
- Hunter Hearst Helmsley def. Goldust (*)
- Owen Hart & The British Bulldog vs. Mankind & Vader ended in a double count out (**)
- Bret Hart def. Steve Austin (****¾)
- The Legion of Doom & Ahmed Johnson def. Faarooq, Crush & Savio Vega (***)
- The Undertaker def. Sycho Sid (¾*)

Rating: 48

03.24.97 by Arnold Furious

Venue: Rockford, IL
Taped: 03.24.97
Raw Rating: 2.5
Nitro Rating: 3.0

Hosts are Vince McMahon, Jim Ross and Jerry Lawler. JR announces Mankind is the number one contender for the WWF title. Because of what exactly? Surely Bret Hart with his big win over Steve Austin at 'Mania would be top contender. Mankind hasn't beaten anyone for ages. The only thing in his favour is a good record against Taker.

WWF Tag Team Championship
The British Bulldog & Owen Hart (c) vs. The Headbangers
Owen is behaving like a jerk now and he stands directly in front of Bulldog during their entrance. The friendly rivalry has an edge to it. The Headbangers won this title shot at WrestleMania in a four team match. The WWF had already quit on Furnas & LaFon unfortunately, denying us a potential classic here. Davey and Owen's team, despite issues with each other, has been a highlight of 1996 and 1997 on Raw. Owen gets in the wrong place for the old Survivor Series '93 spot and Davey knocks him off the apron. But Davey kicks out, unlike Owen four years earlier. The Headbangers work Davey over with some fairly creative double teams, but the crowd boo them, thus proving Davey's face turn is pretty much cemented. Owen gets a hot tag, which isn't that hot because of the weird dynamic, but clears house with an assortment of cool stuff. Owen's petulance is amusing as he quickly tags out and then gets pissy about being tagged back in. His move set is wonderfully creative for a heel. Thrasher gets trapped in the Sharpshooter but Mosh saves, so Bulldog runs in and powerslams Thrasher. Owen gets all pissed off about that claiming he can do it himself, so Davey shoves the ref over for the DQ. A solid TV match though the tag champs brought the majority of the psychology and spots. Owen's bitching after the bell causes Davey to lay him out as they finally stage a break up. Owen grabs the mic to say he's sick and tired of carrying Bulldog before demanding a European Title match. Owen's punctuation is calling Davey a "gutless coward". Davey gives him the match, but says it'll be the only shot he'll get.
Final Rating: **½

Backstage: Mankind is quietly rocking in a corner muttering "he's gone". When quizzed about it, Mankind says Uncle Paul (Bearer) has left him. Elsewhere Bret Hart appears on the Titantron. He says he wants time to talk later. Vince agrees providing Bret doesn't use any profanity.

Bart Gunn vs. Hunter Hearst Helmsley
Chyna mangled Marlena last night at WrestleMania so the focus is on her. The camera frequently appears over her shoulder, getting her view of the action, which is probably for the best as Hunter-Bart isn't a particularly good bout. Both guys are solid and have the basics down but the match is fairly uninteresting. We cut away for words from a distraught Goldust, who makes several movie references including Silence of the Lambs. He seems pretty angry. For Hunter it's just business as usual. He got his win already, he's moved on. Hunter shows elements of his love for Ric Flair here, taking a load of bumps including the face bump. Bart runs the usual NWA babyface offence against Hunter to try and recreate a classic match from the late 80s. Not sure who Chyna is… Arn Anderson? As Bart is getting some momentum Chyna low bridges him and slams Gunn on the floor. Bart turns the other cheek so Chyna runs him into the ring post too. Some babyfaces are so dumb they deserve to lose. Bart is easy pickings for the Pedigree after the antics on the floor. Another win for the Tripper. The match had the bare bones of a good encounter, but a lack of passion rather scuppered it.
Final Rating: *¾

Video Control takes us to the Slammy Awards. Rocky Maivia won "New Sensation of the Squared Circle". Sable wins "Dressed to Kill". Owen announces himself as Slammy winner. Taker wins "Best Tattoos". The Funkettes, Tracy and Nadine, dance. Shawn and Bret win "Match of the Year". HHH gets "Best Hair". Mankind is "Loose Screw". Sable roams around in her bikini. Austin wins "Freedom of Speech". Arnie Skaaland gets the lifetime achievement award and "Miss Slammy" is Sable. Lots of love for Sable! This was the way to showcase the '97 Slammys; in about 30 seconds flat. Poor Lee had to review the whole shebang for The Complete WWF Video Guide Volume #IV. Shame Mankind's line about Aldo Montoya wasn't retained, but I guess they want him serious again now as he's in line for a title shot.

El Mosco, Hysteria & Abismo Negro vs. Venum, Super Nova & Discovery
Oh, not another one of these. The last AAA six man tag was total garbage. You may know Mosco better as Mosco de la Merced, his name in ECW. You definitely know Hysteria by another name; Super Crazy. Negro you may know from TNA. The trio, with others, were known in AAA as Los Rudos del la Galaxia (translated means "Villains of the Galaxy"). So, they're the bad guys. Super Nova is so small he started out in the

mini's division. He's not the same guy as in ECW. That's Mike Bucci. He's also not the same guy that works the gimmick nowadays. The face trio are known as the Space Cadets. That should give you an adequate idea of their style. They start with some sloppy, awful stuff, so the WWF cut to Bret Hart who once again demands time to talk. Hysteria and Venum get some wacky Rey Jr. style stuff in that slightly interests the crowd. More so than the sloppy mess around it. Hysteria takes a silly bump to the floor and he's pretty much stolen this match. As per usual there are flashes of brilliance and insane high spots, but no transitions and horrible technical stuff. If you like that sort of thing you'd probably get a kick out of this match. More so than the previous six man. This is more thrills but with no structure whatsoever. Nova hits the worst rana of the year because they're just firing off one spot after another. Nova takes it with a flying rana, which makes no sense to me as he's the worst wrestler in the ring. The faces go over but honestly, I don't think the fans could tell the difference anyway. Hysteria showed moments of quality but they were lost in the sloppy shuffle.

Final Rating: *

Video Control takes us to Rocky Maivia and Rocky Johnson earlier tonight in the empty arena. Rocky Senior claims he flew himself to *WrestleMania* and promises he'll never interfere in Maivia's matches again.

Flash Funk vs. The Brooklyn Brawler
Honky Tonk Man joins commentary again as his never ending search for a protégé continues. Lawler and Honky start into the Memphis nonsense. They should not be allowed in the same place. Brawler has trouble getting into Flash's move set so Funk throws him with a half nelson suplex. Flash's flying gets less interest from the fans than usual as the last match absolutely burned them out on high spots. Bringing in guys from AAA was definitely counterproductive as they never let anyone get over, and just had a bunch of spotfests with no personalities involved. Flash finishes this squash with a 450 splash, which again doesn't get a big pop because of all the high spots in the last match.
Final Rating: ½*

Backstage: Ken Shamrock gets asked about calling the submission match last night. Shamrock says because Austin had passed out he decided to call it to protect the unconscious man, as he could not protect himself. He also defends his decision to put Bret down after the match as he was attacking a man that was down. Ken puts Austin over for having no quit. That dull robotic monotone is already Shamrock's Achilles heel, and he's not even debuted properly yet.

Promo Time: Bret Hart
The fans have been waiting for this; Bret's reasoning for being a jackass at *WrestleMania*. Bret apologises to his fans in Germany, Great Britain, all over Europe, Japan, the Far East, Middle East, South Africa and Canada. "To you, my fans right here across the USA, to you I apologise for nothing". Even when he wins Bret feels like he lost. Bret gets upset that the American fans cheered Austin to the back last night like he won. He goes back to *WrestleMania XII* and the fans cheering a "pretty boy like Shawn Michaels". So Bret went home and watched TV in Canada while Shawn posed for "gay magazines". He felt the WWF needed a hero so he came back. He recounts everything that's happened since including the various times he was screwed out of the WWF Title. He takes another shot at Michaels, claiming the knee injury was "potentially life ending". It's weird how Lawler changes horses halfway though the promo, deciding Bret is actually telling it like it is after weeks of calling him a cry-baby. The heel-face dynamic in action! Bret accuses the American fans of abandoning him and cheering Austin last night. He claims Americans don't understand dignity, prestige and class. He says American heroes are Charles Manson and OJ Simpson. "It's obvious to me that all you American wrestling fans, coast to coast, you don't respect me. Well, the fact is, I don't respect you. You don't deserve it. So from here on in, the American wrestling fans from coast to coast can kiss my ass". Having gotten that off his chest, Bret stops talking and Shawn Michaels comes out to defend America. Shawn suggests only God could get the belt off Bret (falling short of calling him a belt mark). Shawn says he's aware of his faults, but he lives his life differently. He moves on to Austin and says Steve never quit. Shawn carries on, this time calling Bret a mark, saying the fans have the right to do whatever they want (unless it's boo *him* when he's a babyface, ahem). Shawn finishes with "America, love it or leave it". Bret offers him a chance to "get the hell out of my face" so Shawn gets right in there and suggests Bret reads gay magazines and checked out his pictorial, which is suitable provocation for Bret to wipe out Shawn's knee and strap him in the ring post figure four. Fantastic angle, great work on the stick from both men. It cemented Bret as a bona fide heel and gave them a reason for Shawn to take a little extra time off to rehab his knee. Bret's promo was killer and Shawn's retort was great fun too. A pity these guys were legitimately hating each other, but that just poured fuel on the fire of their feud.

Rocky Maivia vs. Leif Cassidy
Leif doesn't get an IC title shot despite this match having no finish. As soon as they're underway, out comes Bret Hart to join commentary. Thus begins a stunning six month run for the greatest heel in wrestling. When asked what happened to him, Bret says "I opened my eyes". He heels on the American fans some more but stops to put over every other country he's worked in. Rocky runs through his spots and poor Leif lies down for the crossbody. Bret promises to show us "wickedly bad" and takes out Maivia's knee too. I enjoy Leif giving Bret a thumbs up as he leaves the ring.
Final Rating: ½*

Ahmed Johnson vs. Savio Vega
A bit of a lame duck finish after all the excellent Bret stuff over the previous two segments. Faarooq is absent after injuring his shoulder and puncturing a lung in the Chicago Street Fight last night. Ahmed misses his opening charge, forgoing the shine and Savio goes right into the heat. Ahmed's comeback is righteously sloppy. He makes a mess of everything. I feel bad for Savio as he's genuinely in danger of getting hurt. So is Ahmed, but he's putting himself at risk. There are no fewer than nine Nation members on the stage backing Savio up. You'd think they'd just rush in and kick Ahmed's ass. Johnson mounts a second comeback with a urinage and a spinebuster, then down come the Nation. Crush saves Savio from the Pearl River Plunge and that's a DQ. Ahmed grabs the mic and says this has gone too far, with Faarooq in hospital. He offers a challenge. If he beats any one member of the Nation they have to disband and leave the WWF. There's no reply nor is there any reason for the Nation to accept as Ahmed puts nothing on the line. The angle promptly went nowhere, suggesting Ahmed may have gone into business for himself with that promo.
Final Rating: ¼*

Promo Time: The Undertaker
Undertaker, wearing a pimp leather cowboy hat (not as gay

looking as it sounds), says he's won the most prestigious title in all of sports. He thanks Sid for his courage and for not shitting his pants during it, presumably. Vince mentions Mankind as Taker claims he won't lose his edge like he did during his first title reign. "He makes me a better gladiator" claims the Dead Man. This brings out Paul Bearer to beg for Taker's forgiveness. With time running out, Mankind appears on the Titantron to scream "I need you, Uncle Paul. Don't make me come find you". The show goes off the air with nothing said and nothing resolved.

THE RAW RECAP

Most Entertaining: Bret Hart. Killer mic work from the Canadian hero. This was his night and his alone.

Least Entertaining: Ahmed Johnson. Sloppy as ever and a horrible main event match with Savio Vega. Also a promo that made no kind of sense and wasn't well thought out.

Quote of the Night: "To you, my fans right here across the United States of America, to you I apologise for nothing". – Bret Hart sticks it to the US.

Match of the Night: The British Bulldog & Owen Hart vs. The Headbangers. Easily the best match on a night of forgettable contests.

Verdict: The wrestling wasn't up to much, but this show really kicked off the summer of 1997. Bret Hart's heel turn shocked many as he'd been a clean-cut, hand slapping babyface for years and certainly for his entire singles run dating back to 1991. His promo detailed all the perfectly valid reasons for the turn as well as assaults on the characters of Steve Austin and Shawn Michaels. The attacks on Shawn and Rocky Maivia rounded the night out and showed us who would be the top heel in the business for the remainder of the year. His insistence of thanking fans in other countries made for a swerve though. Bret, while a heel in America, would remain a babyface in other countries; especially Canada. This was a great start to a memorable angle. A pity Bret, Shawn and Austin couldn't stay healthy during this year.
Rating: 49

03.31.97 by Arnold Furious

Venue: Peoria, IL
Taped: 03.25.97
Raw Rating: 2.7
Nitro Rating: 3.4

The opening is Bret's promo from last week, which should show you how important it was. Hosts are Vince McMahon, Jim Ross and Jerry Lawler. Vince shows his colours by saying Bret has flushed his legacy down the toilet. Only an American would see it that way.

WWF European Championship
The British Bulldog (c) vs. Owen Hart
They've been clever with this angle as Bulldog and Owen were coexisting fine, even after Davey won the European Title, but the announcers kept needling them to fight until they did. Which is exactly the point Bret Hart will make later. These two had the Raw MOTY in Germany at the start of the month so there is an air of excitement for this rematch. Owen starts fast and assaults Davey on the floor, perhaps thinking his lack of aggression hurt his chances in Germany. It really shows when Davey mounts a comeback and Owen punts him in the groin. While Davey is lacking in the aggression department he's still got his power and uses that to escape most of Owen's submission attempts. Like in Germany, they have some excellent counters based on knowledge of each other's move set, but they don't go into the same depth. Bulldog in particular gets some terrific flash pins. Owen scores a pin after a piledriver and the Savage Elbow, but discovers Davey's foot was on the rope. Davey goes for a Sharpshooter and botches it a bit, but that does make sense as it's not his move and Owen slips out into the enzuigiri. Great psychology behind that. Owen knowing the hold better than Davey, who was ill advised to try and apply it. Compared to Germany the match is a little rough around the edges, with Davey missing a catch on the floor, but it's still an excellent contest between two great wrestlers. Davey murders Earl Hebner by mistake and Owen bails for a chair. Another cracking ref bump from Earl. Davey grabs the chair and Bret runs in for the save, which confuses everyone including both wrestlers. Bret plays peacemaker as Vince calls him selfish. Skewed view of reality there. The match is superb but the lack of finish and the angle rather detract from it.
Final Rating: ***¾

Post Match: Bret Hart grabs the mic and says Americans want them to fight. He says Americans know nothing of family values. "I need you" he says to Owen and Davey. Bret reminds us of Davey's win over Bret at Wembley and how the American fans turned them against each other. And especially Bret and Owen. Owen listens to Bret and seems to take it onboard. As if he's finally talking in a language Owen understands. Owen's acting is amazing. Bret asks for Owen and Davey's help. "I don't care about these people. Not anymore. Owen, I love yak". That breaks Owen into tears and they hug. The crowd, on seeing two brothers hug it out after a three year feud, boo. And thus the 1997 version of the Hart Foundation is born. Great opening to *Raw* as Bret really started to change the landscape of the WWF. Reconciling with Owen was a wonderfully emotional moment. A pity it couldn't take place in Canada.

El Mosco vs. Super Nova
Sunny joins commentary because they've got nothing else for her to do, but she's too over to cut loose. No doubt WCW would have been all over that action. Following two messy six men tags we finally get a chance to see a singles match between two AAA guys. I'm not sure they picked the right ones. Mosco is okay but tends to do better against more talented men and Nova is a spotty little fell. Sunny breaks out a little Spanish, thus earning her coin. Well, that and the dress she's wearing. Nova blows a flying head scissors, which irks Vince. Sunny joins the Spanish team and starts calling the lucha spots. "Muy bueno tope". Mosco takes it with a mid rope Arabian press. The match is a sloppy mess with a bunch of high spots. It's the kind of thing I'd have enjoyed when I was young (and stupid), but I could live without it now. I'd completely forgotten how much Vince actually tried to follow in the lucha footsteps of WCW during 1997. They just didn't hit on the right talent. Although, Nova could have been their Rey Jr. if he wasn't so slapdash.
Final Rating: ¾*

Promo Time: The Legion of Doom
JR reminds the LOD that until the opening segment tonight Owen and Davey looked like easy pickings. Animal rants about America and sports teams. Hawk threatens to "kick the doggie dumplings" out of Bulldog. I'm not sure these comments were really worth bringing the team to the ring to make.

Jesse Jammes vs. Jerry Fox
The Real Double J has a six year old guest manager that he has to babysit into the ring. He's still singing that balls awful song too. Honky Tonk Man has his eye on the Roadie, which would have made way more sense than Billy Gunn. Especially as his face run was nothing special. Mainly because his biggest feud was with Jeff Jarrett… who was in WCW at the time. Fox sets early on a backdrop and Jammes hits his pump handle slam right out of that for the duke.
Final Rating: SQUASH (Not rated)

Post Match: Honky Tonk Man jumps in the ring to offer Jesse the spot as his protégé, but only if he can play the guitar. Jesse opts to smash the guitar to bits and stay face. Luckily they abandoned Gunn's push as Rockabilly and turned them into a tag team; the New Age Outlaws. All because Honky Tonk Man couldn't carry an angle and Billy can't sing and dance.

Savio Vega & Crush vs. Adam O'Brien & Rod Bell
This is a total squash so Vince takes a phone call from Shawn Michaels instead of paying attention. He says he'll be here on *Raw* next week to confront Bret Hart about last week's attack on his knee. Crush has fun mangling his jobber, but Savio looks bored. They opt for a misguided Demolition Decapitation, with Crush jumping off the ropes (whose idea was that?) for the finish. I appreciate Crush used to be in Demolition, but surely Savio is the more aerially talented of the duo?
Final Rating: ¼*

Video Control gives us footage of Ken Shamrock running through Billy Gunn and murdering the heck out of people in the Octagon. A lot of takedowns, mounted strikes and a rare appearance on WWF TV of "Big" John McCarthy. Shamrock will be doing a no holds barred exhibition next week.

Vince tries yelling slogans in time with the explosions from the fireworks that go off to signal the start of "Raw is War" (one of which is "contusions", I think). It really doesn't work.

Promo Time: Paul Bearer
As we went off the air last week, Bearer came out to discuss something with Undertaker but TV time expired. Apparently he begged for forgiveness and wanted to "walk again on the dark side". Paul claims he did everything during his heel turn for the Undertaker to let him discover himself and win the WWF Title. Bearer apologises for his failures as a manager and for holding Taker back. "Undertaker, I want to come home!" The Dead Man comes down personally to answer. He says he can never forget betrayal but he may be able to forgive. The fans don't care much for that viewpoint. Especially not as Taker hands the WWF Title over to Bearer. But then Taker sucker punches his former manager, who was blatantly just scheming, as was evidenced by a sly wink to camera in between belt and punch. Taker stalks Bearer with the urn only for Mankind to sneak in blindside and throw a fireball at the champ. Sid runs in for the save as Taker rolls around on the floor holding his face. This was a tidy little angle to both get more heat on the Mankind PPV match and to tie it into Taker's previous relationship with Bearer. The two would remain intertwined for the remainder of the year, and indeed through most of 1998 with the Kane angle.

Backstage: Sid joins us to rant about fire and people messing with him. The coherency and urgency disappeared from his promos around this time and it's amazing how quickly his usefulness to the company diminished.

Hunter Hearst Helmsley vs. Goldust
Goldust is pissed off about Hunter and Chyna's mistreatment of Marlena. Hunter doesn't seem all that bothered so Goldust has his way with the Greenwich native in an aggressive opening shine. Until he misses with an ill advised crossbody and falls to the floor. This serves as stimulus for the sleepy Hunter and he clocks Goldust on the floor. Hunter's approach around this time was to antagonise a fiery opponent into making mistakes and then picking up the pieces. Much like Ric Flair, a man he admired greatly. When Hunter is in charge he just runs through his spots; suplex, knee drop, curtsey, chinlock. Goldust's attempted comebacks are routinely cut off. For some reason these two never really clicked. I think it's a combination of Hunter's inexperience in big matches and the Goldust character not really working as a face. The angle where he turned was over but the matches afterwards were a bit of a drag. Oddly enough later in his career, when the character became more comedic, it worked just fine. Curtain Call for Hunter but Chyna runs down and punts him to cause the DQ. The match just existed to further the angle and establish Chyna as being able to beat the crap out of a man. Hunter continues the assault only for Pat Patterson to make the save in his role as official. Why was Pat making a comeback on Hunter? Chyna gives him a kicking too and Goldust makes the save.
Final Rating: *¼

Promo Time: Steve Austin
This is Steve's first big interview since turning face at *WrestleMania*, so this will show what kind of babyface he'll be, which is crucial to the character. Many face turns have cut the legs off great heel characters. Austin immediately points out he never quit at *WrestleMania*. Austin moves on to Bret, saying he "beat Steve to a bloody pulp" and that a guardrail bust him open, not Hart. "My head was pumping out more blood than my heart could handle". He calls Bret's hero campaign "BS". Austin points out he won't change for anybody and he doesn't care if he wrestles a good guy or a bad guy. He doesn't care if he's booed or cheered. "When the bell rings I just whup somebody's ass". He calls Bret out right now, if he isn't "in the back crying". Bret appears on the Titantron and points out that *he* won and *he* threw Austin into the rail, so he did bust him open. He says he's finished with Austin. "You'll have to kill me to be finished with me". Austin swears to bloody Bret ten times worse than what Hart did to him at 'Mania. Austin bottom lines it by saying Bret's grave will read "the reason he's here is because Steve Austin whupped his pink and black ass". This confirmed Austin's character would remain the edgy antihero regardless of what the fans thought of him. A face turn without the face behaviour, which is exactly what Attitude needed; a badass antihero figurehead.

WWF Intercontinental Championship
Rocky Maivia (c) vs. Bret Hart
Something of a dream match would be Rock and Bret at their respective peaks. For Rock it's about three years early. For Bret probably three years late. Although Bret's 1997 matches were excellent considering his physical condition. Tony Atlas is sitting at ringside, presumably in case the newly formed Hart Foundation decide to beat up Rocky. Bret works the match smartly by having Rock hit flash babyface stuff while he stalls and keeps the heat on. He's slow and methodical. It gives Rocky plenty of time to take a beating off Bret's strikes. I sometimes get the feeling that the office weren't too hot on Bret's work in '97, but taking Rocky outside his comfort zone would have been a mistake. He makes sure Rock gets plenty of sympathy heat for taking a beating from an experienced pro.

Rocky gets very little, which is quite right. His inexperience was better suited to fluke pins and ballsy comebacks. Bret treats him like Flair treated muscle heads in the late 80's NWA. Rocky rather botches his floatover DDT to set up the high crossbody. Bret rolls through it with JR claiming Bret's shoulders were down. Bret has had enough and hooks the ringpost figure four, which Earl Hebner isn't best pleased with so it's a DQ. Bret didn't really care about the title. He just wanted to put a young punk in his place. Steve Austin runs in for the save, not because he likes Maivia but because he hates Bret, but Bulldog and Owen save for Bret. Austin takes a 3-on-1 but the Legion of Doom, American Originals, make the actual save. Welcome to the babyface club Stone Cold!
Final Rating: **

THE RAW RECAP

Most Entertaining: Steve Austin. His assertion that Bret would have to kill him to finish their feud cemented his babyface status, but his attitude remained that of a bad guy.

Least Entertaining: Savio Vega. Didn't give a rat's ass about his squash match.

Quote of the Night: "I don't care about these people. Not anymore. Owen, I love yak". – Bret Hart reconciles his differences with his wrestling family.

Match of the Night: The British Bulldog vs. Owen Hart. Not a patch on their European title match in Germany a few weeks beforehand, but an excellent contest nevertheless.

Verdict: A belting opener combined with several solid storyline developments made this a good episode of *Raw*. The fallout from *WrestleMania* was evident in the directions both Bret Hart and Steve Austin took on this show. Bret's heel turn was fully cemented by his insistence at teaming with his hated brother Owen at the expense of the American fans. Meanwhile Austin's face turn showed real edge and his personality was not crushed by it here. That attitude would define the Attitude Era. A time when a bad guy was cheered for his resilience and hatred of authority. An everyman antihero that would be cool to kids of all ages and could connect to a jaded generation, angry at the world. Austin was a full-on representation of youth culture at its purest. His personality may have taken off after *King of the Ring '96*, but even at this point the fans remained divided on a guy who was tenacious but didn't particularly care about them.
Rating: 77

04.07.97 by James Dixon

Venue: Muncie, IN
Taped: 04.07.97
Raw Rating: 2.8
Nitro Rating: 3.65

Tonight, Mankind promises to give the Undertaker a present! I hope it's not just an empty box, because that gimmick belongs to Doink the Clown, dammit. Honky Tonk Man is on commentary, but we can barely hear him again. Hmm, maybe there is something to his wild claims of sabotage.

Owen Hart & The British Bulldog vs. The Godwinns
Owen gets on the stick before the bout and thanks his brother Bret for reuniting the family last week, then warns Shawn Michaels that if he says a single negative word about Bret, the Hart Foundation will destroy him. The Godwinns are about the worst possible choice of opponents for the champs, and they are even more annoying tonight than usual as they are being accompanied by a fat little inbred looking kid sporting a pro-farming banner. Why is this on the screen? Why are the Godwinns always on the screen!? At least the belts aren't on the line. Henry shows his technical acumen right away by powering Owen down from a lock-up, as Vince wonders if Owen "perhaps" (his favourite word) landed on the back of his head. No, Vince, I would wager he landed on his back. As would EVERYONE ELSE watching it. Why say dumb things that entirely contradict what has just happened? No-one would ever think Owen landed on his head from being pushed down off a tie-up, it's just a silly thing to claim. How I long for the end of the year so I don't have to listen to Vince talking nonsense every week ever again. Well, from behind the announce desk at least. Owen and Davey try to make Phineas into something resembling a wrestler, but they are severely limited by how friggin' awful he is. At one point he loses his temper and starts wildly flailing elbows at both of the champs, then acts like a complete fucking loon, doing a headstand and kicking his legs around like a bucking mule. This guy needs to be put down. Phineas even gets a visual win on Owen from a backslide but Davey distracts the referee, then Owen knocks Phineas goofier with an enzuigiri. Almost as annoying as Phineas is Honky's commentary. He just shouts, rants and raves in his bitter, snarling voice. It's awful. The Godwinns get another visual win from a Slop Drop, but an LOD split-screen promo causes the finish to be completely missed. The replay shows Owen came off the top with an elbow to the back of Henry's head to score the duke. Fab. The LOD turn up on the ramp as Owen and Davey are leaving, and the Godwinns block their return to the ring on the other side of the aisle. The horrible hillbillies try and slop the champs, but they duck and LOD end up taking the slopping. Naturally that results in a brawl. Now see, that is why you shouldn't throw that shit at people, you dirty hillbilly pigs.
Final Rating: *

Backstage, Owen and Davey are delighted with what went down and watch the replay over and over. Steve Austin shows his face, looking for a fight as ever, but officials keep him away.

Steve Austin vs. Billy Gunn
Billy is accompanied by the Honky Tonk Man, with the assumption being that he is Honky's new protégé. It turns out he isn't, but then in a few weeks, he is. Some real solid storytelling there. Billy is still donning his Smoking Gunns attire, which instantly makes this match less appealing. Austin just beats the hell out of him, but then another unwelcome split screen promo breaks up the action, this time from Owen and Davey. They warn Austin that if he pokes his nose in their business, they will do the same to him. I hope that doesn't mean a long match and a lame DQ finish, because Billy Gunn does not need protecting. He needs help here though because Austin is relentless in his attack, with his primary focus being the arm. JR promotes "Sunday Night Heat", but it is nothing to do with the WWF, rather a horrible looking USA Network line-up for Sunday evenings. Billy gets some offence as things start to get more exciting as the match becomes back-and-forth, but then Austin hits the Stunner and wins it. At least it wasn't a non-finish. Honky, impressed with Gunn getting hammered and then losing, offers him the chance to be his protégé. Honky lays his proposal on the table, but Billy punches him in the mouth. Gratitude.
Final Rating: *

Hands up who remembers The Commandant, the original manager of the Truth Commission? You might know him better as actor Robin B. Smith, who starred in *Invictus*. He comes out and informs the crowd that *Raw* next week will come from South Africa. He then proceeds to rant for 5-minutes and runs down America before handing over to Bret Hart, currently in South Africa, on the video screen, who has his own rant about Steve Austin and the US.

Promo Time: Shawn Michaels
Vince is positively gleeful at seeing Shawn. Michaels refuses to say when he is coming back from his "career ending" knee injury, then goes off on a tirade about his favourite subject: Bret Hart. He says the two loathe each other in the ring and backstage, and they hate each other's guts. Gee, tell me something I don't know. Shawn says Bret has always been a bad guy and derides his family values, claiming the WWF has exploited Hart's family because Bret let them and it made him money. He delves behind the scenes, saying how he played second fiddle to Hart for years in the early 90s but did it "with a smile on my face". Oh man, there are pages and pages that could be written to counter that zinger! Shawn criticises Bret for having to be dragged "kicking and screaming" into supporting him (read. put him over) and then has the gall to complain about Bret taking time off! Shawn reckons Bret did it so he could watch the WWF fall flat on its face without him, then claims the company did its best business "in six years" with him on top. He even asks Vince to clarify that, which he does!

Well, let's compare, shall we? *SummerSlam 1996* headlined by Shawn and Vader drew easily the lowest buyrate in the show's history, coming in *significantly* lower than 1995's 0.9 with a disastrous 0.58. Bret co-headlined the 1992 and 1994 shows, which pulled 1.5 and 1.3 buyrates respectively. How about *King of the Ring 1996*, which was main-evented by Shawn Michaels and the British Bulldog? A shoddy 0.6, lower than any other KOTR show prior to that. More? *Royal Rumble 1997* headlined by Michaels and Sid pulled a 0.7, compared to the 1.1 that Bret and the Undertaker managed a year earlier. Shawn's box office performance on the *In Your House* shows failed to shatter the earth either, but then no-one really made a difference to those numbers until 1998. Hell, the *Raw* ratings dropped considerably when Shawn was champion and *Nitro* began its winning streak during that run. And yet, there is Vince happily making himself look like he doesn't even know his own business's performance for the sake of a Michaels rant.

While Shawn may be completely wrong about the business side of things, but his response to Bret's numerous criticisms of his persona (the dancing, long hair, pierced naval, etc) is right on the money: "They liked it you idiot!". Fair point, what else needs to be said? Oh, plenty more yet. Jim Cornette said in an interview that on a taped show the writers would often just let Shawn go out and vent and get his feelings out, then cut things down to the few useable points he made. No such chance to do that tonight though, because we are live. Shawn says Hart is all about the money and lays into him for pitting WCW against Vince in order to get a better contract. Not that he is jealous about earning half as much per year, or anything. Shawn essentially calls out Bret for being a mark for himself and says he is unable to separate real life from his Hitman persona, which is a criticism often levelled at Hart by his detractors. He follows up by telling everyone he is not a role model, but he appreciates how much people pay to come to see the WWF, and he respects that and thus works his ass off for them. That is one thing no-one can criticise Shawn Michaels for, because more than anyone else he always worked hard, be it on television or pay-per-view. I wonder if that genuinely was the reason why, or if he just wanted to prove to everyone that he was the best each and every time out. Shawn wraps things up with the hauntingly prophetic words: "Your obsession with the WWF Championship will be your destruction!". Indeed it was. This was a brilliant promo, laced with real feelings and a venom that was rarely seen in Michaels the year before. The exchanges between Bret and Shawn were some of the finest things on *Raw* in 1997, and this is another corker. And, we are still just getting warmed up with that issue.

Not everyone was impressed though, and Bret, who was in Kuwait at the time, was livid when he found out what Shawn had said from Davey and Owen. He took issue with the personal criticisms directed at him, claiming he had only ever insulted the Shawn Michaels character, not the man behind it. In particular Bret took umbrage to Shawn's claims of him being greedy, shocked that Vince would stand there and allow Michaels to run him down when he knew the truth, that he had rejected an offer from WCW of almost double what Vince was paying him in order to stay with the company. It was yet another example of Shawn letting his mouth run away with him, and added to the already intense friction between the two.

After the segment, a pissed off Owen and Davey come out to give Shawn a kicking, but he uses a chair to fend them off, then does some handstands on it to rub his lack of injury in everyone's faces.

The Headbangers vs. Barry Horowitz & Freddie Joe Floyd
Remember when Barry Horowitz was booked as a star, albeit an undercard one? He was even slightly over. Well, all of that might as well have not happened, because he is back to enhancement duty here. Though with two hours to fill on *Raw* these days, we have the joy of these squashes being extended. With the right guys, the additional time is welcomed, but the Headbangers are not the right guys and the result of this is never in any doubt. Both Freddie Joe and Horowitz would be cast adrift within a few months, with neither offering anything to the WWF's new Attitude movement.
Final Rating: ½*

No Holds Barred Exhibition
Ken Shamrock vs. Vernon White
The WWF actually advertises the upcoming UFC pay-per-view on a graphic at the bottom of the screen, and Vince discusses some of the fighters that Shamrock has beaten and then talks about the different styles on display in the Octagon (though "jujitso" is not a thing, Vince). Vince even defends UFC as being misunderstood. Wow, talk about different times! White actually is a legitimate fighter with an extensive background, and he has a history with Shamrock, though they never fought, but rather Ken brought him into Japanese MMA group Pancrase. He did have a fight with Ken's adopted brother Frank Shamrock in 1995 though, which he lost. White was a regular for Pancrase for years and didn't actually make his UFC debut until June 2003, drawing with British fighter Ian 'The Machine' Freeman. His only other UFC appearance came in a knockout defeat to the legendary Chuck Liddell a year later at *UFC 49*. This might have been a fairly good fight at the time, but with it taking place in the WWF it is obviously worked. It does feel ahead of its time though, almost like a blueprint for the style of Indy wrestling that the likes of Ring of Honor would later present in the early 2000s. They go for some submissions then White belts Shamrock with a kick to the chest which thrills Vince. "I think he just surprised him!". Indeed he did. "You won't like him when he's angry!" bellows Vince. Yes, because he is

the Hulk. I am actually surprised Vince didn't paint him green. Five years ago he would have for sure. Shamrock gets annoyed and mounts White, punching the hell out of him and causing the match to be stopped. The crowd boos the display of aggression and White bleeds all over. Vince complains that it was supposed to be an exhibition and White "turned it into something it wasn't supposed to be". Hey, you wanted a shoot pal, punches and kicks are legal. "It must be quite an adrenaline rush to be pounding on someone like that" salivates Jim Ross in a post-match interview. Envious much? Vader comes out afterwards for a stare-down with Shamrock, setting up the newcomer's first programme. I can't really rate this because it wasn't a wrestling match as such, but it was certainly different and entertaining.

Vader vs. Frank Stiletto
East Coast wrestling mainstay Frank Stiletto is no match for Vader, who puts on an exhibition of his own. I wonder if upon seeing the board backstage with his name next to Vader's, Frank shed a few tears and considered leaving like a host of WCW enhancement guys used to earlier in the decade. Seriously, Vader was so feared at the time, even amongst his peers, that he genuinely provoked that kind of a reaction. If you have only ever seen his WWF work, you will probably find that hard to believe. Here he demolishes hapless Frank with German suplexes, Vaderbombs and powerbombs. Tough night to be Frank Stiletto.
Final Rating: SQUASH (Not rated)

Backstage, Gorilla Monsoon tells us that Sycho Sid hasn't arrived and thus won't be in his scheduled match with Mankind tonight. I hope everyone reading is revelling in the hypocrisy after the numerous rants against WCW a few weeks back for not delivering what they promise. Gorilla says the only suitable choice of opponent for Mankind is Steve Austin, which is a ridiculous thing to say. Don't get me wrong I am happy about it because it will be a better match, but Austin has already wrestled and there are countless guys on the roster who haven't. Calling him the "best choice" is thus ludicrous. Austin expresses the same sentiments to Gorilla, and blackmails him into letting him wrestle Bret Hart at the upcoming PPV instead of Sid. Monsoon acquiesces. Good call. The reality behind the match switch was that McMahon worried about the show bombing, and despite Hart needing knee surgery he asked him to work with Austin on the PPV and then again the following night on *Raw*, before taking time off for the operation. The carrot dangled in front of Hart was the promise of a match at *King of the Ring* with Shawn Michaels, who Vince claimed would put him over...

Promo Time: Mankind
Mankind gets the Sycho Sid treatment, with his music playing in the background and a spotlight on him, but it takes the production team an age to turn the house lights down. Shoddy stuff from the crew. That doesn't take away from Foley's usual excellent delivery, as he justifies burning the Undertaker and then keeps in with tonight's trend of shooting, bemoaning the road schedule and then secretly burying Marc Mero: "...wrestling in main events for half the money of jumped up pretty boys in the opening match". Foley throws in some reverse psychology, telling fans not to order the PPV because he can't be responsible for his actions. Just as things are about to meander into the realms of being too long, the Undertaker's music hits and he cuts a disembodied promo over the house mic. Not a patch on Mankind's reality-laced quasi-shoot, Taker instead stays true to form and offers up promises of "eternal damnation". Good segment overall though, it made me want to see them wrestle again despite having watched them contest dozens of matches already.

Mankind vs. Steve Austin
This is a brawl from start to finish, which may come as a surprise to some of you... Hmm, perhaps not. While both are among the best in the field at fisticuffs, there are too many distractions for it to be anything other than a decent television match. The main culprits are Owen Hart and the British Bulldog, who first cut one of those pesky split screen promos and then turn up in the crowd. They are annoyed that Austin has bartered his way into a match with Bret, you see. Foley takes his usual unnecessary bumps, including a suplex on the ramp, and at one point he pulls up the ringside mats to expose the concrete, just so he can make his Cactus Elbow that more painful... for himself. What a stupid and nonsensical thing to do. I don't understand the logic of that at all. I also can't decide whether to respect or deride the guy who paid for tickets to be in the front row, but is too cheap to buy an official nWo shirt, and instead sports a cruddy knockoff. The unstructured brawling occasionally gives way to chinlocks, which you wouldn't really expect from either guy. It's not a bad match, but it doesn't come close to their tremendously fun outings in 1998. Owen and Davey eventually make their way to ringside, so LOD run out to cut them off. Vader gets involved as well, but accidentally hits his stablemate Mankind, drawing the DQ. All storyline, not enough action.
Final Rating: *¾

THE RAW RECAP:

Most Entertaining: Shawn Michaels. A blistering promo from the Heartbreak Kid. He is often the frontrunner for this award on any show he is part of, but usually for his in-ring performances rather than behind the stick. This Bret Hart war brought the best out of him as a talker.

Least Entertaining: Phineas Godwinn. While Shawn Michaels might well lead the way when it comes to the most entertaining award, Phineas inevitably tops the list of worst performer. Another rotten showing from the hillbilly, despite the best efforts of Owen and Bulldog.

Quote of the Night: "We didn't fall face flat, anywhere" - Shawn Michaels. Apart from with that sentence, huh Shawn?

Match of the Night: Ken Shamrock vs. Vernon White. Something completely different and thus refreshing. It certainly made a change from the usual half-assed *Raw* matches.

Verdict: Entertaining when the wrestling took a backseat to the interviews and "shoot" fighting. *Raw* in 1997 became far less about what happened in the ring and far more about what happened behind the mic, and this show exemplifies that. The talking is tremendous, with both Shawn Michaels and Mick Foley delivering some corking verbiage, but the best in-ring action on the show belongs to two MMA fighters. Go figure...
Rating: 56

04.14.97 by James Dixon

Venue: Muncie, IN / Johannesburg, South Africa
Taped: 04.07.97 / 04.09.97
Raw Rating: 2.2
Nitro Rating: 3.45

Man, I never get tired of the *'Thorn In Your Eye'* opening for *Raw*, it creates such a buzz and is so much more exciting than the likes of Papa Roach or Lee's favourite band, the horrific Nickelback. Tonight's show is unique, with half of the matches taped last week in Muncie, IN and the rest in Johannesburg, South Africa five days ago. Vince McMahon and Jim Cornette host from Muncie, with JR and the Honky Tonk Man in South Africa.

The Legion of Doom vs. The Godwinns
The sheer amount of television time awarded to the Godwinns is frankly beyond a joke now. It was bad in 1996, and it remains unfathomable in 1997. At least there is a reason for this to happen, following last week's inadvertent slopping. Practically the first move in the match is a piledriver from Phineas on Hawk, which he naturally no-sells completely. What an idiotic and business-killing spot that is. If being dropped on your head with a move banned in many territories (include modern day WWE) doesn't keep you down, then how are the people supposed to buy anything else. Hawk has always done that spot, much to the chagrin of Jerry Lawler and other proponents of the manoeuvre, but it is stupid. Jim Cornette claims that the last time the LOD lost on television it was in black and white. They are about to get a sharp shock in that regard this year. "Here comes the big man" says Vince of Godwinn, which Cornette immediately jumps all over him for given that all four guys are beasts. Hawk shows how little things have changed in the world of the LOD since 1991, taking the heat after charging shoulder-first into the post. At least Hank has enough ring savvy to hit a shoulder breaker to try and capitalise, but Phineas as usual is the weak link and allows Hawk to make a tag after some uninspired heat. Animal comes in and cleans house, even though the Godwinns are still technically faces at the moment by the way, but Owen Hart and the British Bulldog come out and deck Animal with a tag title belt, and wrestling fans the world over throw up all over themselves as the Godwinns beat the Road Warriors. Horrid. It would have been acceptable if the LOD had then won the titles from the incumbents at the upcoming PPV, but the WWF instead cut the LOD's legs off by running a Dusty Finish and a lame DQ.
Final Rating: ½*

Hunter Hearst Helmsley vs. Jesse Jammes
We go to South Africa for this one, which in a year's time would have been far more interesting given that both guys were part of D-Generation X, but here they are just a lame country singer and a tiresome blueblood bore. Literally nothing happens, but because it comes from a glorified house show in South Africa, it gets 15-MINUTES! Honky Tonk Man is almost Pete Doherty levels of annoying on commentary, with his snarly, bitter, vindictive voice grating on me right away. "You are a bitter man" says JR, and he is right. Anyone who has ever seen a Honky shoot - and there are many because he loves the sound of his own voice - can attest to that. The commentary goes back-and-forth between Africa and the States, with Vince and JR chiming in here and there. Given that the shows are thousands of miles apart and neither took place live, and indeed were on different days, it is a fairly impressive feat. And it is seamless too. I realise I have shredded Hunter so far in this book, and indeed in others, so I think my feelings on his character and ability from this era are fairly clear, and thus I won't go over it again. All I will offer is a repeat of something I have said once before: wrestling is supposed to be entertaining. Hunter, is not. This match certainly is not. Repetitive, basic, full of rest holds and duller than dirt, this is an absolute chore. Hunter wins it with the Pedigree after interference from Honky, which occurs to set up Jammes against Honky's much anticipated mystery protégé on Sunday at the PPV. And then it was Rockabilly... "We are having some audio problems... Well, we are in South Africa you know!!!" defends JR. But, surely the commentary, or at least some of it, was done in post, making it intentional!? Thus that means it is:

Instances in 1997 that the WWF used technical incompetence of their own people as a plot point:
One!

Honky and Jammes get into a tiff after the bout, but it goes nowhere.
Final Rating: DUD

- - -

LPW Score: Hunter Hearst Helmsley

Look: Given that this is for Hunter Hearst Helmsley and not Triple H, which are two different characters in my eyes, I would score Hunter low here. As post-99 Triple H he looks great, if occasionally slightly bloated, but in 1997 he is a strange shape. Not particularly muscle-bound or impressive, and his gear is boring and his hair very feminine. No one in a million years would have pegged him as a future top guy based on how he looks here.
3/10

Personality: Almost non-existent. He improves significantly once DX comes along (then meanders into long-winded and with a vastly inflated sense of worth as the years roll on), but as the snobby blueblood he is horrible. The plumy voice comes in for constant criticism within these pages, as it should, and outside of looking down on hillbillies and treating women like objects (only to then emasculate himself by pairing up with a woman more muscled than he), he has nothing.
2/10

Wrestling Skill: Distinctly average at best when against genuinely world class opponents, but utterly IRS levels of boring with nearly everyone else. Fundamentally Hunter has always been sound, and once again he comes on incredible leaps in a short space of time, but the blueblood Helmsley was tiresome, and remains my least favourite performer to watch from the era.
3/10

Overall: A terrible score for a man who would go on to be a multiple time WWE Champion, one of the top guys in the business (though not the industry changing business mover he pegs himself as) and eventually one of the chief operators behind the scenes of the company and the man given the real-life task of leading WWE for a new post-Vince generation. But all that is the future, and this LPW score focuses on Hunter Hearst Helmsley, who as you can see was a great steaming pile of shit.
8/30

- - -

Loads going on tonight on *Raw*, including Bret Hart ranting about America from Kuwait. They are going a grand job of giving the WWF a global and "big" feel with tonight's broadcast. Shame the wrestling is all terrible.

Rocky Maivia vs. Savio Vega
JR calls Rocky the "Tiger Woods of the WWF". Pardon!? How

prophetic though, I guess, because he certainly could be considered a sport surpassing star on that level in the future. Now though? No. This is another match that would have been more interesting in a year's time with... Oh, who am I kidding? Savio Vega was never interesting in 1998. Rocky is the reigning IC Champion, but the title is not on the line here because Vega is such a scrub. Vince and Cornette chime in again, with Vince asking Honky if he has met Nelson Mandela yet. Honky shows his true demeanour by referring to Apartheid as "the hair parting thing", causing a flustered Jim Cornette to correct him and call him an idiot. Ahmed Johnson appears on the split screen and cuts a promo so incoherent that it sounds like a foreign language. There is an amusing moment, when JR tells Ahmed the South African fans love him, and Ahmed mishears and says "I love you too" to Ross. Hmm. Honky and Cornette mock Ahmed afterwards for being so incomprehensible. You know what is a good thing to follow an overly long rest-hold filled yawner with? If you guessed an even LONGER rest-hold filled yawner, then welcome to the WWF booking team. This match, inexplicably, is given 17-minutes. A lot of it is a chinlock. Savio Vega is NOT the guy to be giving this much time to, especially as a heel. A chinlock turns to a bizarre "hold", which is actually just a pleasant shoulder massage, so JR gives up and shills his $99 a minute (ish) hotline, promising to reveal which WWF superstars is stuck in Kuwait. Let me save you some money: it's Vader. He got all pissy with a Kuwait television host asking if wrestling is fake, and shoved him over. For that he was detained and had to pay a (paltry) fine when they finally did release him. Meanwhile, this match is STILL going on, until Savio finally puts Rocky away with a tights assisted roll-up. One of the most boring matches I have ever seen. The match was so bad, they ran it again on pay-per-view six days later, and it was a disaster then too. We are at the halfway stage, and this show is absolutely terrible so far!

Final Rating: DUD

For the record, if *Raw* was still only an hour and the show had ended after the last match, it would have scored something like 3/100. This second half MUST be better.

Promo Time: Steve Austin
Back in America, and here comes Steve Austin to save the show! Hey, the first hour didn't feature a single in-ring promo! I challenge you to find another occurrence of that happening since! Vince conducts the interview, and Austin says how he is sick of being held down so it's about time he got what he wanted, namely the match with Bret Hart on Sunday that he bartered with Gorilla for. "With all due respect, Mr. Austin, talent can never be held down. It always rises to the top" sayeth Vinnie Mac. Oh really? What about Chris Jericho? Rob Van Dam? Chris Benoit? Daniel Bryan? CM Punk? Dolph Ziggler? Sure, all of those guys were over and eventually had WWF/E title runs, but in all cases it was AFTER they were hot and after the company had already tried everything it could to stop the wave of fan support for them. WWE didn't want any of them to get over because they were not the ones picked by the powers that be to get over. What a ridiculous business. These comments mark the second week in a row that Vince has said something relating to the business that is not only ludicrous, but also rather exposes him as being pretty damn clueless about absolutely everything. Is he really a genius after all? You decide. Austin comments on Bret Hart's recent complaints about being screwed, before offering: "You ain't been screwed yet Bret". Foreshadowing words indeed. A lot of this kind of talk pertaining to Bret occurred prior to Montreal and the real life screwjob. It makes you wonder, fleetingly at least, whether there is any credibility to the Montreal Theory. Austin is his usual cursing self, but doesn't have much insightful to say outside of the usual wrestler threats loaded with expletives. Jim Cornette clarifies for viewers at home that the previous promo was not a test of the emergency broadcast system, on account of the frequent bleeping out of the swears. Meaning it was really just a constant tone.

Goldust vs. The Sultan
We return to South Africa, which almost certainly means more laborious in-ring action. Goldust tonight, has his face painted like a leopard. This causes Vince McMahon to declare: "Gentlemen, I'm not so certain if that E-Coli virus isn't running rampant down there". WHAT? I mean... WHAT? Where the hell did that come from? What does that have to do with anything!? Is Vince, with whatever his own crazy ass self-justification, trying to imply that Goldust has his face painted like a leopard because of the E-Coli virus!? Nothing about that makes any sense at all and indeed, is perhaps the most nonsensical thing he could have said. Maybe, just maybe, it is because he is in AFRICA! Hell, perhaps he was just feeling whimsical. E-Coli... what an absolute tool. Sultan bails after a big Goldust right hand to confab with his manager the Iron Sheik, who Jim Ross erroneously refers to as a former WWWF Champion. Actually, the WWWF "got the W out" in 1979, and Sheik won the title in 1983, some four years later. Given that Sheik then dropped the title to Hulk Hogan in one of the most famous title switches in the history of the business, and Hogan became the face of the WWF, not the WWWF, JR should really know that. Back in the ring, Sultan hits a piledriver, which Goldust naturally sells as he should. But because Hawk no-sold one earlier, it just makes him seem like a pussy. Hunter Hearst Helmsley runs in and causes the DQ, then combines with Sultan to hit a spike piledriver as the never ending Helmsley-Goldust rivalry plods on. This is easily the best match of the night so far, but it doesn't even crack a single star.

Final Rating: ¾*

Meanwhile in Kuwait, Bret Hart does his bit for American-Middle East relations by encouraging them to boo the United States because of their support for Steve Austin and their attitudes towards him.

The Headbangers vs. Mankind & Vader
Over to America, and we have the Headbangers. Thankfully the US fans won't be quite so tolerant of a dry 15-minute match featuring the 'Bangers, so this one should be fairly brief. The most interesting thing about the match is that while this was airing to audiences worldwide, Vader was sat under house arrest in Kuwait for his aforementioned publicity stunt gone wrong with the unwitting Good Morning Kuwait host Bassan al-Othman. Vader sells for the Headbangers far too much, and makes them look more competitive than they have any right to. I didn't realise until watching these shows back for this book just how protected the 'Bangers were! Why is Mankind even in this, what with his WWF Title match against Undertaker just a few days away? Because he just wrestled earlier in the taping against Steve Austin, Mankind doesn't do a great deal in this, letting Vader do the majority of the work. The show, which has been absolutely filled to the brim with plugs and shills, drops all pretences and just turns into a WWF advertising spot that happens to feature a smattering of wrestling, as Vince and Corny put over the WWF Magazine and JR chimes in from South Africa about the newest Raw Magazine. Mosh spits "some sort of liquid" in Mankind's eyes, which is obviously water, but if he was Japanese would be "white mist". The bell rings for another DQ, and a blind Mankind accidentally locks

the Mandible Claw on Vader, debilitating him.
Final Rating: ½*

Now, courtesy of Coliseum Video, we see highlights of the swimsuit competition from the 1997 Slammy Awards. Make no mistake, this is just an excuse for the WWF to show footage of the soon to be Divas exposing their side-boobs and flashing their dinners. Worthless, unless you are a horny teenager with no access to internet porn.

Back in South Africa, the Commandant gets into the ring to once again promise the arrival of the Truth Commission. Well, aren't these fans just being treated to a humdinger of a show.

Ahmed Johnson vs. Crush
And it is about to get so much WORSE! This, quite remarkably, is the main event! So to sum up: no Undertaker, Steve Austin, Bret Hart, Owen Hart or British Bulldog wrestling on this show, but we do get Crush, Savio, the Godwinns and the Headbangers. Wow, they sure knew how to best utilise their TV time. At least this has potential... potential to be so very bad that it comes right back around to good again. I do love watching car crash wrestling. This is the blind leading the blind. When people talk about bad feuds and matches, and bring up powerhouse brawls like Warrior vs. Hercules, it just shows that they have never seen Crush wrestle. This, is a million times worse than any of their matches. At least they were exciting, solid and at times good fun, whereas this is rotten. Occasionally at HoW we have been criticised for perhaps being overly negative, but believe me, we try not to be. It is just near impossible to say anything positive about Crush, especially when he hits that awful legdrop of his where he has to hold his own leg because he can't sit out properly. To make things worse, he does it three times. Sluggish is not the word for this. What moves slower than a slug? Crush sticks with the Nation's proud tradition of expert masseurs when he gives Ahmed's shoulder a good rub, before Ahmed responds with a horrible scissor kick. Ahmed follows up with an elbow drop so bad, that it is actually a back senton onto Crush's face. There is sloppy, and there is Ahmed. But he is fascinating, because you just want to see what he will do next. Crush decides that taking Ahmed's moves is too much of a health risk and responds with the move of the evening, the piledriver, before going to a sleeper. Why doesn't anyone cover after a piledriver!? Jesus, it is not a set-up move for a rest hold! Crush uses a temporary lack of concentration from the referee to choke out Ahmed illegally, then puts on the worlds lamest body scissors, but Ahmed fights up. Crush takes him back down with a knee to the gut as this trickles past 10-minutes. This timing for these South African matches is a rib right? More eye-wateringly ugly "wrestling" occurs briefly before Ahmed flings himself at Crush into a cradle for the win. South Africa is delighted. They are less pleased, as am I, with Faarooq cutting a promo afterwards. The Nation leader challenges Ahmed to face all three members of the faction at *A Cold Day In Hell*, and if he wins then the Nation will disband. We haven't even got *Revenge of the Taker* out of the way yet. What if Savio had beaten Rocky for the IC belt? For the record, this match would have looked out of place on a low-budget Indy show featuring the British Bullfrog, Bulk Slogan, the Penultimate Warrior and Screwz. No structure, no cohesion, no logic to anything, botches, rest holds and sloppier than Joe's. No good.
Final Rating: -*

THE RAW RECAP:

Most Entertaining: I'm sorry I can't, I just can't. Not tonight.

Least Entertaining: Henry Godwinn. Phineas Godwinn. Hawk. Animal. Hunter Hearst Helmsley. Jesse Jammes. Savio Vega. Rocky Maivia. Ahmed Johnson. Crush... All of them deserve it.

Quote of the Night: "Ahmed, Ahmed... You're going down" - Honky Tonk Man cheekily mocks Ahmed's now infamous "YO GO DA" promo with a little insider wink. He was full of it all night, talking about JR's praise of Jesse Jammes as "putting him over" and saying Vince was "blown up" from the interview with Austin. What a cad.

Match of the Night: Get real.

Verdict: It is a contender for the worst episode of *Raw* ever. While I enjoyed the global feel of the presentation and I thought they did the simulcast thing brilliantly, the actual content on offer was dire. The wrestling was amongst the worst I have ever seen on the show and the only proper segment, Steve Austin's interview, was mediocre at best. Moving *Raw* to two hours to compete with *Nitro* might have seemed like a good idea at the time, but it would take a good few months before the roster was firmly in place to be able to do that. This was just utter garbage.
Rating: 6

04.20.97 - Revenge of the 'Taker
(James Dixon)
[War Memorial Auditorium, Rochester, New York]
- The Legion of Doom def. Owen Hart & The British Bulldog (*½)
- Savio Vega def. Rocky Maivia (DUD)
- Jesse Jammes def. Rockabilly (DUD)
- The Undertaker def. Mankind (***)
- Steve Austin def. Bret Hart (***)

Rating: 38

04.21.97 by James Dixon

Venue: Binghamton, NY
Taped: 04.21.97
Raw Rating: 2.8
Nitro Rating: 3.4

After the horror show that was last week's taped show, we are back live tonight. JR and Jerry Lawler welcome us to the show, with Vince in the ring already for the opening segment.

Promo Time: Steve Austin
By virtue of his DQ victory over Bret Hart at *Revenge of the 'Taker* last night, Austin is the number one contender to the WWF Title and will face Undertaker at *A Cold Day in Hell* in just a couple of weeks time. Austin says he isn't done with Bret and he never will be, then challenges Bret to a street fight right now, giving him a minute to respond. Bret doesn't show so Austin says he will go and find him, but Bret appears on the Titantron and lambasts Stone Cold, accepting the challenge and calling him a "hyena". Bret goes off on his usual tirade about the US fans and then complains about Austin getting a title match with the Undertaker, before promising to send him to hell. As far as show opening promos to set up a match later on go, this one felt pretty organic. It wasn't just two guys going out there and then getting put into a match, it was two guys who hate each other who wanted to fight, but under their own terms

and with mind games thrown in.

The Sultan vs. Ahmed Johnson
Neither of these guys showered themselves in glory last week. Ahmed brings his usual wild and dangerous offence, kicking Sultan directly in the face and then running around like a headless chicken before a savat kick takes him out. The Hart Foundation's stirring of the xenophobic pot spills into this contest, as the crowd chant "USA" rather than "YO GO DA" to encourage Johnson. The piledriver continues its frequenting of the show, as Sultan drills Ahmed with a good one. Much like last week, that is followed up with a chinlock rather than a pinfall. The piledriver, like the DDT, should *always* be a finish. Ahmed's big comeback is to simply block a suplex and hit a front variation of his own, then a spinebuster sets up the Pearl River Plunge, but before he can hit it the Nation of Domination turn up for the distraction. Sultan throws Ahmed into the ring post to slow him down as the Nation head to the ring, but Ahmed finds a 2x4 under the ring and the Nation retreat. Ahmed belts Sultan with it instead, drawing the DQ. He doesn't care, and continues to whale away on the Sultan with the timber after the match, until referees, One Eyed Jack and Honest Earl drag him away. Considering how bad it could have been, this was just about bearable.
Final Rating: ¾*

Sunny comes out advertising the Undertaker's latest shirt as Michael Hayes sells his soul and acts like a flea market shill over the mic. What a fantastic use of talent. The raping of *Raw's* integrity as it descends into an extended shopping channel pitch continues...

Backstage, Steve Austin beats up the Hart Foundation's locker room door with a chair, as Bret complains and demands respect.

At ringside, Ken Shamrock joins the announce team as Vince discusses Vader being detained in Kuwait. Vince actually uses the term "asking if wrestling is fake", which shouldn't seem that strange, but for some reason it is. The WWF are clearly delighted about the publicity generated from this, and play some jaunty music over the top of a picture of Vader behind bars. Jerry Lawler gets in on the act, showing off a cartoon of Vader cleaning up camel shit and then his action figure with prison bars drawn on the box. Compassionate bunch over in Stamford. Shamrock says he cannot abide bullies and that Vader is a bully. Conveniently enough, he is wrestling him in a couple of weeks at the PPV. That match is phenomenal, and often overlooked. It is one of the best "shoot" style matches the WWF have ever put on. Up until Lesnar-Cena in 2012 at least. Shamrock then makes himself look silly by throwing out a grandstand challenge to Mike Tyson, which was rightfully dismissed by observers as nothing more than a publicity stunt. A Shamrock-Tyson match would have drawn some monster money, but it never would have happened.

Street Fight
Bret Hart vs. Steve Austin
Austin is dressed in jeans and a t-shirt for this, as is Bret. It gives a fresh feel to a match that the WWF have now ran on PPV three times (five if you include the *Royal Rumble* match and the *Final Four*). As noted already, the two wrestled just last night on PPV too. Bret is tentative, but only to distract Austin so Owen Hart and the British Bulldog can jump him. With the numbers advantage the Harts pound on Austin, but Shawn Michaels comes in from the crowd with a chair and runs off Davey and Owen, but misses Bret. Despite that, Hart remains the aggressor and unloads with punches, and then we get another piledriver! Bret's is a beauty, one of the best in the business, but that is two matches running and after last week's excess, I am sick of the move. Bret tries to Pillmanize Austin's ankle, but Austin moves and leathers Bret's knee with the chair, relentlessly beating the hell out of it. Bret in reality did have a knee injury sustained from a match with Undertaker in Kuwait, so this whole thing is just a way of establishing that in the storyline as well, and justifying him taking a few weeks off from in ring activity. Bret underwent knee surgery two days later, and didn't return to the ring until the back end of June, though he remained all over the television show. He and the WWF hardly had a choice, given how over the Hart Foundation were getting. After dismantling Bret's leg, Steve Austin puts on the Sharpshooter and keeps it on for an age, refusing to break it as referees and officials surround him. Not that he should break in mind you, as Bret hasn't given up and technically the match should just continue. Bret can have few complaints about Austin's action, because he pulled the same trick to Jerry Lawler four years prior at *SummerSlam '93*. When we return from commercial, Bret is still out on the mat, unable to move because of the knee. Bret was not someone to take time off for injuries and would frequently work through niggles and bumps, so for him to have to go under the knife, it must have been pretty serious. All of which just serves to make Shawn Michaels look like even more of a coward and a tool for handing over the WWF Title instead of doing the job when he had his injury two months earlier, when Bret was willing to work a match and get his leg battered in the process. Not much of a match, certainly by the lofty standards set by these guys, but the angle was good and Bret sold it like a champ.
Final Rating: *½

Backstage, Steve Austin and President Monsoon get into a tremendous argument, with the usually reserved Monsoon shouting down Austin and calling him "out of control", to which Austin responds "You're damn right!". Gorilla throws Austin out of the building, as Austin continues to rant at him as he exits, telling Monsoon he has cut him a break by not kicking his ass.

Tiger Ali Singh vs. Salvatore Sincere
These guys don't even get entrances, which is a surprise given that Tiger is making his television debut, hot off an unexpected and frankly unfathomable victory in the second (and last) annual Kuwait Cup. In that tournament, Tiger beat Leif Cassidy, Billy Gunn, Mankind and Owen Hart on route to victory. Every single one of those guys is a multi-time champion both in singles and tag competition, and all are pretty highly regarded by fans who grew up watching them. Tiger Ali Singh, is not. Even though he has been hyped far beyond his talents and earmarked as a future star by someone in the company, this ends up being his last match for four months, either on television or house shows. Hell, if he was that bad, you would think they would at least put him on the house show loop to hone his craft. It is a tried and tested method of tightening up guys' work. It worked wonders, to a degree, for the likes of the Ultimate Warrior and other rough around the edges talent. Then again, Tiger is not just rough around the edges, he is just rough to watch full stop. Singh just looks like a fatter and less mobile version of Leif Cassidy, though with an even worse mullet. The crowd couldn't care less. Vince couldn't either, and after putting up with a few minutes of Tiger's dreadful offence and Sal's questionable selling, we cut backstage to Bret Hart on a gurney, and Owen Hart arguing with referees. "Boring" chant three or four people in the crowd, who are as quiet as I have ever heard a *Raw* audience. We go back to Bret at any opportunity, as the match inexplicably

continues. Tiger finally puts it out of its misery following a spinning heel kick, which was more Ahmed Johnson than Owen Hart. He certainly laboured to that one.
Final Rating: DUD

Backstage, Bret gets wheeled to an ambulance by incompetent staff who keep knocking and jarring his knee by driving over electric cables. Bulldog is apoplectic about what Austin has done, and Owen is furious with the unsympathetic officials. "WATCH HIS KNEE YOU IDIOT!" he screams. Bret gets put in the ambulance only for the camera to pan to the driver and reveal Steve Austin! In a segment that has been replayed over and over since, Austin tells Bret he promised him he would take him straight to hell, and jumps in the back and pounds on him again. Davey, Owen and officials eventually get him off, as Bret finally gets taken for medical attention. Great, legendary segment that opened up the backstage area in a way that had never really been done before. Anyone watching with jaded eyes might see it as a good segment, but not really get what the big deal is, but this really was groundbreaking behind the curtain type stuff.

Jesse Jammes vs. Rockabilly
Because their match last night was so good they just had to run it again on free television so more people could see it? If anyone is unsure, that is sarcasm. Their match last night was rotten. You know what the best thing about Rockabilly is? It keeps Honky Tonk Man off commentary. Vince mentions that the ring is smoky, which it is from the pyro, and then ludicrously claims that "bombs have been going off both figuratively and literally". Shouldn't they evacuate? Oh right, the show must go on... Despite the Austin-Hart angle having just happened, JR is already plugging his hotline as having more information on the story. What, more than the live television show!? This match is just as bad as last night, and the crowd just as silent as in the previous one. The talent roster was really bizarre in 1997, because you had great workers who mainly talked, charismatic guys stuck in career killing gimmicks and horrible workers getting excessive television time as well as being protected. I guess the problem was that the booking team consisted of a few people with diametrically opposed ideals, and thus there were many clashes in opinion, resulting in some of the team just biting their tongues and letting things slide rather than argue every point. There *are* good things on display in places, great things actually, but this match is not one of them. In fact, it is a disaster. Billy Gunn responds to the bored silent crowd by putting on a chinlock, boring and silencing them even further. Swell. This goes 10-minutes, with Billy just pounding and pounding and pounding at Jammes until Gunn gets bored and hits the Shake, Rattle and Roll to win it. Jammes doesn't even get any hope spots, never mind a comeback before the finish. Vince, despite creating the character, doesn't even get that Gunn just used Honky Tonk Man's old finisher, and simply calls it a "spinning neckbreaker". JR is there to correct him, as ever. After the match, Honky MURDERS Jammes with a guitar shot to the back of the head and then another one for good measure. I sure hope that was a gimmicked guitar, because that looked like it sucked. If I was Jammes and the notoriously swing-happy Honky had hit me with a guitar like that, I would have some choice words for him backstage for sure. Clearly, Honky either learned nothing from screwing up Jake Roberts' neck, or he just didn't care. Probably both.
Final Rating: DUD

In the locker room, Steve Austin turns his attentions to Shawn Michaels, arguing with him for saving him, because he is Stone Cold and doesn't need any help. Michaels says he wasn't helping Austin, he was attacking the Harts. Gorilla gets in the middle of the two and tries to calm the situation down, but he doesn't succeed. The tension here is superb.

The Undertaker vs. Hunter Hearst Helmsley
Before the match, Mankind cuts a promo from in a boiler room about how brave Paul Bearer was at the hospital last night, following the Undertaker burning his face. That angle was a farce. It was supposed to be Mankind accidentally burning Bearer, but the lighter they were using completely no sold them and Foley couldn't get the thing to spark. Undertaker, like an annoyed dad, took over and changed things on the fly, lighting the fireball himself. With the Undertaker's typical slow working style and Hunter bringing all the less than thrilling qualities outlined last week, this is a slog. Incredible really, when you consider the tremendous matches that the two contested at *WrestleMania X-Seven, XXVII* a decade later *and XXVIII* the following year. This goes on and on, until Mankind decides he has seen enough of the horrible action and gets so worked up about it that he brings a blowtorch out with him to set Undertaker on fire. Or maybe it is because of the Paul Bearer thing... Mankind tries to light the blowtorch and struggles, and Mick Foley vs. Fire continues (dating back to his ECW and indeed IWA days). When he does get it going, Taker sits up and grabs Mankind and chases him off. Let's not forget Helmsley and Chyna, who are still at ringside. Suddenly, they are attacked by seemingly two members of the crowd, but it turns out to be Goldust and Marlena in disguise. Fan attack angles, again! I really hate them. They encourage and abate so much potential trouble. Like the majority of the wrestling tonight, and last week, the match was balls. At least Steve Austin has been on fire tonight to keep things ticking along though...
Final Rating: ½*

Promo Time: Steve Austin
...So on fire it seems, that he gets a second in ring promo of the night. It is a good job Austin was so creative, interesting and generally excellent, because the usual WWF ham-fisted shove down the throat approach was in full flow here, and with anyone else (hello, Nation of Domination), it could have gotten stale much quicker than it should have. That never happened with Austin though, fans just lapped him up. Austin makes threats towards Vince, then calls Bret Hart "finished". Austin's attention turns to the Undertaker, and he tells the Dead Man to shine up his belt real nice, which is a phrase the Rock made pretty famous. He then lifts from Sid, calling himself the "ruler of the world" before Owen and Davey take umbrage to the promo theft and jump Austin. Vince takes a tumble amidst the chaos, with the audible "ooohhh" from the crowd showing how quickly everything is changing in the WWF, with that kind of thing involving officials uncommon. Shawn Michaels comes out with a chair again and saves Stone Cold, as Vince demands medical attention for Austin, though it never arrives. I guess they are reluctant to help him given he kicked their asses while beating up Bret earlier. Things get even wilder as Austin's former tag partner Brian Pillman turns up from the crowd after months out injured thanks to Stone Cold's famous assault on his leg. Pillman belts him with a chair and then goes to repay the favour for the ankle break, but Michaels again makes the save. A wild end to *Raw!*

THE RAW RECAP:

Most Entertaining: Steve Austin. He was involved in everything that was good tonight.

Least Entertaining: Rockabilly. Just horrible.

Quote of the Night: "He (Ahmed Johnson) galvanised a whole nation. Something even Nelson Mandela has not been able to do." - First the E-Coli comment last week and now this? Do you ever get the impression that Vince is an absolute imbecile?

Match of the Night: Bret Hart vs. Steve Austin. More angle than match, but it was still the best of a bad bunch. *Raw* was not about the in ring stuff tonight, though it was slightly, ever so slightly, better than last week.

Verdict: The actual wrestling was near enough useless again, but tonight it didn't really matter because Steve Austin was on fire. The angles with Bret were tremendous, as were his interactions with Shawn Michaels, Gorilla Monsoon and Brian Pillman. WWF risked over egging the pudding, but Austin was just so good that they got away with it, and it resulted in some captivating television. Losing Bret and with Shawn Michaels still out, the in-ring stuff is going to continue to suffer, but if Austin carries on like this, it won't be a problem.
Rating: 60

04.28.97 by James Dixon

Venue: Omaha, NE
Taped: 04.28.97
Raw Rating: 2.7
Nitro Rating: 3.4

Once again tonight we are live, and indeed will remain that was for the next couple of months. The live *Raw* shows are always better than the taped ones, with an extra energy and oomph to them, so that bodes well. We open with highlights of Steve Austin crippling Bret Hart last week and his various other antics throughout the show.

Promo Time: Brian Pillman
This should be good. Pillman refutes suggestions that he is crazy and says he has a sensitive side, and is in fact deeply religious. The rebel Nebraska crowd boo. God bless 'em. Pillman says he went back and studied last week's carnage, and since then he has prayed. He asks the crowd to join him in prayer, and they get *really* pissed off with him and chant for Austin. I bet God is livid. Pillman wants everyone to pray for Bret Hart's speedy recovery and the complete annihilation and destruction of Steve Austin. Pillman gets on his knees and starts to raise his voice, as his wonderful personality is given the chance to shine through for the first time in a long time. Steve Austin turns up on the Titantron and says the only thing Pillman needs to pray for is that he doesn't kick his ass. "I'm not afraid of the Devil!" states Pillman, and then shows Austin his ability to turn the other cheek, as he bends over and points his ass to the screen. This brings out Austin, to a rowdy ovation, but as Vince states in his best Admiral Akbar impression: "It's a trap! IT'S A TRAP!", with the British Bulldog and Owen Hart trying to jump him. Austin is smart to it after last week's assaults on him, and escapes through the crowd without incident. Pillman, not to be interrupted, returns to his prayer, this time with Owen and Davey alongside him. They all drop to their knees and ask everyone to pray for Bret. Meanwhile, Austin has found his way backstage and he rummages for a weapon, eventually deciding on a big wooden stick. It reminds me of the scene in *Pulp Fiction* where Bruce Willis' character acquires a chainsaw. Suffice to say, the Hart Foundation bail. What a fun opening segment this was, with Brian Pillman absolutely excelling and his demented personality shining through. A great opening segment.

Flash Funk vs. Rockabilly
TAFKA Billy Gunn is now sporting a dodgy dyed hairdo a'la Greg Valentine when he was forced into the role of Honky Tonk Man #2 in the late 80s. He still wears jeans though, albeit black ones, making him a bizarre hybrid of Elvis and Clint Eastwood, but without the charisma or ability of either. I like Billy Gunn, but this horrible gimmick engulfed him. Flash flings himself around the ring with his usual reckless abandon until Billy cuts him off with a clothesline on the apron and a delayed suplex back in. Jim Ross stops off to plug "hot and steamy action" coming up on the USA Network, which I didn't need to hear. Rockabilly hits the Fameasser, but it isn't his finish yet so doesn't get the job done. Funk cuts Billy off on the ropes but gets caught with a tornado DDT, as Billy dances in celebration. Perhaps pin the guy first!? Honky gets on the apron for absolutely no reason at all other than to be in position for a spot where Billy accidentally gets sent crashing in to him by Funk. Jesus, talk about a blatantly obvious spot. Anyone who has ever seen a single minute of wrestling could see that one coming. I detest unnatural and contrived spots. The miscue allows Funk a roll up for the win, but he eats a guitar shot from Billy after the decision. A far safer guitar shot than the wild swings that Honky does mind. Not bad thanks to Funk's willingness to hurl himself around, but why they kept jobbing out Rockabilly after only just establishing him as a character is baffling. If you have so little faith in a gimmick that you have it lose over and over, why even bother with it in the first place?
Final Rating: *½

Promo Time: Bret Hart
We see Bret Hart arriving in a wheelchair and then some footage of his knee surgery, before Vince introduces him. Davey Boy and Owen wheel him into the aisle and then stand guard while Bret cuts his promo from the stage. Bret throws out the metaphors, calling Steve Austin a hyena who got a lucky kill on a lion, which is him. He decides that all of the crowd are hyenas and American scumbags. In keeping with his character as of late, Bret whines about not deserving the assault from Austin and calls the American audience a "sick, depraved society". He gets in his catchphrase and gets serious heat, so immediately lures them in, asking them if they are sick of him saying he is the best. Naturally, they respond in the affirmative, and Bret jumps all over them, saying that is exactly how the rest of the world views America. Zing! Bret wraps it up by warning Steve Austin his days are numbered and that "you people make me sick" before demanding to be taken away. Vitriolic and aggressive, with no playing to the crowd for pops, this was a good heel promo from the Hitman.

The Legion of Doom vs. Doug Furnas & Phil LaFon
Man, if this had taken place anywhere other than in the WWF it could have been a real belter, especially in Japan. Unfortunately, it is nothing more than a sub 4-minute TV bout. In an insert promo, LaFon alludes to the fact they haven't been pushed and utilised fully because of their different ring style. That is to say, they can actually wrestle. JR cannot understand why they haven't gotten over and Vince says their style is "more European". What he means is, they are all steak and no sizzle. Personally, I would choose steak over sizzle, but Vince is all about the sizzle. Hell, most of the time he doesn't even need the steak. It's a shame this is short, because what they do in there is pretty good, with Furnas throwing Hawk around and LaFon completely flummoxing him with his technical expertise. Before we even really get going, LaFon misses a spin kick and

a double clothesline leads to the hot tag to Animal, who runs through his usual tired routine. At one point everyone collides and it ends up being an LOD double clothesline, though Hawk is unsure and stands there for a moment debating whether to sell or celebrate, before plumping for the latter. The Doomsday Device is countered by a dropkick to the back, but Hawk comes off with a flying clothesline on Furnas and Animal covers him for the clean win. JR jumps in the ring after the match to find out what Furnas and LaFon have to say for themselves, and they blame the officiating and illegal LOD tactics. That would be fine if they had used any. "Rematch. SOON!" says the ever verbose LaFon.
Final Rating: *½

Next up we have a repeat of last week's Michael Hayes and Sunny super shill, this time for the "Austin 3:16" shirt, which surely of all the shirts, doesn't need any plugging.

Promo Time: Ahmed Johnson
Yes! Ahmed is backstage in the locker room, with Vince conducting the interview from the safety of the announce desk. It turns out that Ahmed injured the Sultan last week and he ended up in hospital. Well, fancy that. Vince wants an explanation or an apology from Ahmed:

"Well, you know, football... I'd like to apologise for my actions from last week. But I know I don't know wh-wh-wh-wh-wh-wh-what you expec' from me, Vince. I don't know what ANYBODY expec' from me anymore. YOU GOT MEAT. ONE OF YOUR GOOD GUYS. DOING THE GAY FIGHT. BY MYSELF. (*throws over a table in rage*) I AINT FUCKING GAY! YOU WANT A GAY FIGHT!? You got it Faarooq. Does anybody want me? I'm right here. You want it? You got it. If you wanna get crazy, I'll get crazy. Sit here apologisin'... FOR WHAAAAAAAAAT!? Because I had to fight three guys? Three guys gonna kill me!? I'm a gang member baby, remember that!!!"

"Alright, I think we have heard enough of this" says Vince. No Vince, we can NEVER hear enough of this!

WWF Intercontinental Championship
Rocky Maivia (c) vs. Owen Hart
Backstage, Brian Pillman prays with the Slammys for Owen to win the gold, and Owen cuts a promo pre-match, promising Bret he will win this one for him. The Rocky experiment had thus far been an unmitigated disaster, with the fans not buying him in the elevated role at all. That much is clear by the complete silence and smattering of boos he receives when on offence. His work tonight is actually much tighter than usual, which is a lot to do with Owen, but Rocky was an incredibly quick learner (just look at how good he became in such a short time over the next year or two) so must take credit for that. Owen makes his usual generic babyface flash look crisp and smooth, and guides him through a fairly basic but consistently solid encounter. It doesn't quite develop into anything past that thanks to an overreliance on methodical holds, but Owen can hardly bring his slick and complex countering with the green Maivia. He would get lost and it would make him look bad. Owen was selfless like that in the ring, often putting his opponent and their particular needs in a match ahead of his own. Very few showed proverbial ass like Owen Hart. After being worked over by Owen for a while, Rocky mounts a comeback and hits the future Rock Bottom, but it is not his finish yet and Owen responds with a sweet spinning heel kick, right on the button. Owen climbs the ropes but gets caught with a back suplex from Rocky, but doesn't hook the leg so Owen gets out, and hits his double leg O'Connor roll variant for the win and his first WWF singles gold. And long overdue to.
Final Rating: **¾

Backstage, someone has seemingly let Steve Austin loose in a medical supply closet, and now he gleefully rolls around a corridor in a wheelchair, having the time of his life... What a random interlude.

Promo Time: Steve Austin
Fresh from his game of one man Wacky Races, Austin comes out through the crowd, brining his new toy with him. He cuts his promo from in the chair and asks the crowd: "Who wants to see a wheelchair match?" before challenging Bret tongue-in-cheek to come down for said encounter. Austin dismisses Bret's early talk of the American fans being "his people", and that he looks in the mirror every day and sees "his people". Austin says he is going to be the next WWF Champion, then Bret Hart appears on the Titantron like the Emperor from *Star Wars*, and promises Austin that he will be leaving in an ambulance tonight.

Backstage, Vader warms up as Vince helpfully points out that he is back in the States following being detained in Kuwait, and criticises him for not representing the WWF or America very well. Hmm, yeah, but if it was *really* embarrassing then they wouldn't show it on TV would they? Isn't it convenient that the whole thing ties in quite nicely with the Shamrock match and storyline too? The whole thing was pre-orchestrated, there is no way Vader simply "lost his cool". He was clearly just being worked by the office though, who didn't tell him that the host had no idea what was going to happen. Ultimately it didn't matter, but a stunt like that could have gone horribly wrong. Some countries treat crime very differently to the US or the majority of western nations. Who knows what potentially could have happened.

A video package airs for Ken Shamrock, with comments from Shammy and a voiceover from Todd Pettengill. It is really good at establishing the man rather than just a generic character, and makes you interested in Shamrock as a performer. These kind of real life videos are sorely missing from wrestling. People long since stopped buying silly cartoon performers as anything other than just an act.

Jesse Jammes vs. Vader
Speaking of which... Not Vader, of course. JR calls Vader "an embarrassment" for his actions in Kuwait before declaring that he would be "the favourite" if he competed at the forthcoming UFC PPV. Vince then plugs the show! Watching that back in 2014, it is shocking to hear. Vader never had a recognised MMA match, though he did compete in the UWFi, which was a shoot style promotion, and held their version of the World Title. Then again, he also got knocked silly by a sandals-wearing Paul Orndorff, so who knows how he might have done. He certainly gets the job done with minimal fuss here, demolishing the hapless Jammes in under two minutes. As he should!
Final Rating: SQUASH (Not rated)

Jim Ross jumps in the ring and barrages Vader with questions about the Kuwait situation, asking him quite aggressively if he has any remorse for his actions. Vader gets annoyed and says he was doing his job and he apologises for nothing. They are all very stubborn, this roster. JR probes Vader too far, dismissing the legitimacy of the "is wrestling fake" question but asking if Vader went too far with his reaction. Vader starts getting pissed off and loses his cool with JR, telling him he will finish the interview from Kuwait right now. He asks JR is he is "some sort of Oklahoma tough guy" and knocks off his hat and glasses, then backs him into a corner. Ken Shamrock comes out for the save just as Ross is about to get splattered, and takes Vader down with a belly-to-back suplex that gets a great reaction from the crowd. "When we meet, it's not gonna be Vader time, it's gonna be hard time!" says Robo-Ken. Hey, Shamrock; the Big Bossman called and he wants his catchphrase back!

Hunter Hearst Helmsley vs. Goldust
No! Why is this feud still happening four months after it started, when they have had a match at *WrestleMania* no less! That should have been the end of it. Goldust is at least animated at first and charges to the ring to get this started, with Hunter taking the Flair flip in the corner to get his homage in early. Chyna makes the difference for Hunter, so Marlena comes out against Goldust's wishes to support her man. What is she gonna do exactly? She is a chocolate fireguard and a hindrance, not a help. Selfish cow. Goldust mounts a comeback after a thankfully short heat, and Marlena throws Sunny's stash in Chyna's eyes, blinding her. Much silliness ensues as Chyna accidentally chokes Helmsley, thinking it is Marlena or Goldust and gets him counted out. Far better than their other matches, but only because it was over sooner.
Final Rating: *¼

The Undertaker talks nonsense on the Titantron before promising to make Austin rest in peace. Fresh! Then, Sable comes out for another one of those terrible Michael Hayes plugs, which Vince thinks is great.

The Undertaker vs. The British Bulldog
This is non title, which it should be really because it is *Raw*. Having the title defended too frequently against anyone and everyone just cheapens the championship. Mind you, if anyone deserves it for performances this year, then it is the Bulldog. I bet an Undertaker-Bulldog title match in the UK could have done pretty fantastic business. Davey, much like Owen, gets on the mic before the match to thank "his inspiration" Bret Hart. For once Davey doesn't have a power advantage, and Taker throws him around from the off before we cut to commercial and subsequently miss most of the match. When we return Davey hits a suplex, but Taker sits up and hits the chokeslam, causing an Owen run in. Steve Austin breaks up the double team and assists his upcoming PPV opponent, for his own interests naturally (he doesn't want Undertaker to be unable to compete) and then grabs the WWF Title and raises it over his head, before giving a livid Undertaker a Stunner. Taker practically no sells it and hits Austin with a chokeslam, who responds with a no sell in turn. Austin spots a prone Bret Hart still in his wheelchair on the ramp, seemingly with nowhere to go and no one to help him, so he goes after him. Bret gets out of the chair, so Austin throws it over, but then from nowhere, Jim Neidhart makes his shock return and pounds on Austin, before Bret belts Stone Cold with a crutch and knocks him off the stage. It seems Bret's earlier promise was accurate. Not much of a match, but the post match frolics were a lot of fun. A maniacally laughing Brian Pillman closes us out.
Final Rating: N/R

THE RAW RECAP:

Most Entertaining: The Hart Foundation. Yes, all five of them. This was their collective night, with the group fully forming with all of its members, and each of them playing a pivotal role in the show. Great stuff.

Least Entertaining: See last week: Rockabilly. Just horrible. Though as an addendum, he was more tolerable tonight than last week thanks to Flash Funk, though his hair was a bad idea.

Quote of the Night: " I AINT FUCKING GAY!" - But, nobody said you were Ahmed... Any line from his promo could have been included here, the whole thing is a treat. If you love bad promos that is!

Match of the Night: Rocky Maivia vs. Owen Hart. Chalk up another stellar performance for the Rocket, and a much improved outing from a much sharper looking Maivia too. He is getting there.

Verdict: In keeping with the rest of the month, the wrestling itself was not too hot, but we are starting to go beyond a time where that matters now, with talking taking over. Tonight, there was a lot, but thankfully the guys out there delivering it happened to be excellent at it. While there were no killer homerun promos, everything was entertaining and the show had a snappy, engaging and unpredictable feel to it. The Hart Foundation were all over this, and it made for a refreshing and welcome change of pace from the earlier April shows, which were jammed full of turgid crap. I would always choose good wrestling over good talking, but I would always choose talking over a 10-minute plus Crush match.
Rating: 68

05.05.97 by Arnold Furious

Venue: Green Bay, WI
Taped: 05.05.97
Raw Rating: 2.8
Nitro Rating: 3.2

We open the show with clips from last week with the Harts praying for Bret's speedy recovery until Steve Austin shows up. As the evening develops Bret rants at the fans for their depravity. Later still Owen Hart wins the IC title from Rocky Maivia. Finally Austin goes after Bret Hart on the stage only for the surprise return of Jim Neidhart to allow Bret time to smash a crutch over Austin's head.

We're in Green Bay, Wisconsin. Hosts are Vince McMahon, Jim Ross and Jerry Lawler.

Promo Time: The Hart Foundation
The entire Hart Foundation, now complete, comes out for the opening talk. Bret opens by thanking his fans around the world for their support during this difficult time before rounding on the Americans again. He runs through the achievements of the Harts last week until saying that Austin doesn't have the guts to show up this week. Bret points out the group have all the belts apart from the WWF Title. "Do unto others and enjoy it" says Brian Pillman. Bret calls them the "Excellence of Execution dream team". He accuses Shawn Michaels of hiding with his fake knee injury and calls HBK out. The "opening talky bit" was already starting to wear thin. Here Bret made points he's made many times before and even flubbed his lines. Not a great start to the show.

Ahmed Johnson vs. Rockabilly
These two guys feel like they're from different worlds. Ahmed's street feud with the Nation shouldn't exist in the same ring as

Honky Tonk Man's throwback protégé. Vince tries like hell to get this all over by yelling Rockabilly's name and laughing at his ineptitude. We get a split screen to allow Faarooq time to rant about the gauntlet match at *A Cold Day in Hell* and claim Crush will run a gauntlet of ghetto bad men (his words, not mine) this evening. Meanwhile, in the battle of Memphis vs. the ghetto, Rockabilly grinds away at a sleeper. Honky jumps on the apron to distract and allow the acoustic equaliser, but Ahmed steals it and uses the guitar himself. This allows Rockabilly to score a DQ victory. I can't say I really understand why this match even exists, let alone the finish. Of course at this point they were actually serious about pushing Billy as Honky's protégé, but the gimmick was total death.
Final Rating: ½*

Video Control gives us footage of Ken Shamrock. He talks about focusing his rage into sporting pursuits. They take the edge clear off it by talking about Shamrock's wife and four kids. If UFC was like wrestling Tito Ortiz would have stolen Shamrock's wife and then had one of his kids call him "dad" in the Octagon. This fluff piece doesn't help Shamrock at all. He almost crosses the line from lacking in charisma to full-on boring. They shouldn't have tried to humanise Shamrock at all. Just leave him as a human wrecking machine. Humanising monsters only works when they're sympathetic; like Mick Foley.

Vader vs. Goldust
This is to hype Shamrock's debut match against Vader, which is an excellent mesh of shoot-style, striking and submissions. It is brutal. One of the most brutal matches in WWF history. I'm not sure why Goldust was selected for this mauling as they were in the process of trying to humanise him too. Perhaps it's purely for sympathy purposes? Shamrock joins commentary to further bore the audience. He talks at length about his zone. Goldust's histrionics rather show why Shamrock was so out of place in the WWF. That said, the WWF should have changed more dramatically during Attitude and I persist they should have shed the sillier stuff, like everything the Undertaker did, to make Attitude more realistic. It should be Goldust's weirdness that's out of place, not Shamrock's intensity. "I dislike this guy, very much" – Shamrock. When pressed, Shamrock debates submission over KO and wants to tap out the bully to further embarrass him. Meanwhile Vader just clubs away at Goldust. The storyline is overriding the action. Goldust probably gets too much and the lustre has come off Vader somewhat since his efforts earlier in the year. Goldust gets slammed and the Vaderbomb finishes. Shamrock's witty retorts during this match included telling Jerry Lawler to shut up twice and Vader to shut up once. Vader calls Shamrock out so Ken jumps in there with a double leg and Mankind makes the bizarre save, attempting to claw Shamrock only for Goldust to save. A weird mixture of sports and entertainment there. It should not exist. An ongoing theme for this evening.
Final Rating: *½

Video Control takes us to Jim Ross' sit-down chat with Dustin Runnels and Terri (aka Goldust and Marlena). JR narrates some stuff about family and Dusty Rhodes. Dustin talks about trying to escape his father's shadow. JR says Dustin never stood a chance of escaping the American's Dream "sizeable shadow" (JR's words). They talk about Goldust being Dustin's only shot at escaping the Rhodes legacy. Dustin talks about the abuse he received from fans and how frustrating it would be when people refused to work with him. Scott Hall in particular gets singled out for it, and named and shamed on TV for homophobia. Sure, stick the knife into a guy who can't defend himself and works for your rivals. Dustin talks about understanding the gay community based on the abuse he received and puts them over. "They said it couldn't be done, but I did it and I proved them wrong". Dustin adds that he's not spoken to his Dad in years but he loves him and hopes he's proud. This is less effective than the forthcoming Mankind interviews, but it gave Goldust some much needed heart and realism. It explained the gimmick and why he did it, which happened at a time when the character was getting a bit played out.

Gauntlet Match
Crush vs. Three Jobbers
The first ham and egger runs in and takes a whirl backbreaker before the press gutbuster finishes him off. The second jobber tries to get the fans going. It doesn't work. Faarooq says he got these guys "from the ghetto", but this guy is a scrawny white kid. Crush throws him around a bit and finishes with the heart punch. Jobber number three is sporting a hoodie and a mask to disguise himself. One Pearl River Plunge later and Crush is counting lights for the sneaky Ahmed Johnson. Given this whole thing lasted 3-minutes and had all of Crush's high spots in it, I'd say it's one of his best matches. Apparently it was a victory "on the part of Ahmed Johnson's part" according to Vince. Part.
Final Rating: **

Post Match: Sable comes out to model the Austin 3:16 t-shirt, thus proving herself somewhat useful to the WWF's merchandising division.

Promo Time: Shawn Michaels
Hour two begins with another promo. This one makes sense as the Hart Foundation had spent the entire first hour hunting for Shawn backstage only for Shawn to casually stroll out here for a chat with Vince McMahon. Vince is more interested in Steve Austin after the Rattlesnake decked him two weeks ago. Shawn claims Austin needs support battling the Hart Foundation. He has Austin's back, not to help Steve but to hurt the Harts. Shawn talks about the trend of everyone barracking the fans so he's going to suck up to them "because somebody's gotta do it". Shawn says the Clique is the most powerful faction in wrestling today, perhaps referencing the nWo. Vince asks when Shawn will wrestle again and Michaels says he'll compete at *King of the Ring*. Shawn is incredibly twitchy here. He can't stop moving around and keeps messing with his hair. Drugs, much? We move on to Bret Hart and Shawn mentions that Bret likes the American dollar just fine, alluding to Bret's enormous contract. HBK throws in a nice reference towards American attitude saying it made Homer Simpson an icon. He'll bring up *The Simpsons* again in a few weeks by wearing a Homer shirt on *Raw*. Shawn keeps glancing towards the Titantron during the promo as well, which is either another nervous tick or a genuine concern that someone might run down here and kick his ass. It doesn't happen and Shawn mentions he'll go through all the Harts if he has to. As Shawn walks around the ring slapping hands, Bret Hart gets on the Titantron. "I don't mind you making fun of me, but don't make fun of the Simpsons". Bret goes on to say that Shawn's knee is fine so he should accept a challenge from Jim Neidhart right now. The Anvil is swiftly followed by the rest of the Harts and Shawn gets mugged. The Legion of Doom, "American Originals", make the save.

Doug Furnas & Phil LaFon vs. The Legion of Doom
Furnas gets a pre-match promo saying the fans should have rooted for them last week as they're the most exciting tag team in the WWF. Hawk has no idea how to sell LaFon's stuff. No

wait, that should read "Hawk has no idea how to sell". We cut away to see Shawn Michaels going after the Harts backstage. LOD rather dominate considering they're the babyfaces. Poor Jack Doan nearly gets crippled by a double suplex on Animal, which hits him in the knee. Animal comes firing back on a repeat by blocking a double suplex into his own. Hawk gets a hot tag and hits a chokeslam! British Bulldog runs down to distract while Owen botches interference on Hawk to allow LaFon a pin. The match was a hot mess with LOD all over the place. Furnas & LaFon deserved better. At least they went over here.

Final Rating: *

Promo Time: The Undertaker
He feels the need to remind us he's the WWF Champion, seeing as Austin, Shawn and Bret have been all over this show so far. He's mighty pissed off because someone has stolen the WWF Title. He doesn't really say anything of note. He's quite boring compared to the other big three WWF stars of the time.

Sunny has a crack at modelling the Austin 3:16 t-shirt. She whores it up like an absolute tramp, as if she wanted to out-whore Sable in some sort of whore-off.

The British Bulldog vs. Steve Austin
This is naturally an extension of Austin's feud with Bret, but also harks back to a feud the two had as a placeholder while Bret moved into title contendership a few months back. After an opening scuffle, Davey takes over with power. Austin comes battling back and tries for a Sharpshooter, to stick it to Bret, only for Davey to power out and take charge again. Austin escapes the running powerslam and for some reason Austin's gut kick *doesn't* set up the Stunner. That just looked weird considering how many times I've seen him use that set up. Davey sets early for a backdrop right afterwards and Austin clocks him with the Stunner for the win. The Harts immediately run in to give him a kicking, this time leaving Brian Pillman to protect Bret. Owen uses the WWF Title belt as a weapon, showing us who stole Taker's strap, though he's the worst one to use it as he already has two titles so the crowd don't get it. LOD run in for the save, again, only for Furnas & LaFon to help out the Harts. Shawn Michaels runs down to try and sway things in favour of the Americans. The brawl continues like a dead spot in the *Royal Rumble* until the Undertaker makes his presence felt. This sets Taker firmly against the Hart Foundation as he lays out Owen for stealing his belt. I think that's lost on the audience somewhat because of belt similarity. When everyone clears out it's left with Taker and Austin, the latter of who happened to pick up the WWF Title and use it as a weapon. Austin practically tells Taker to stop being a mark, and tries to be the bigger man by walking off, only for Taker to jump him from behind. Seeing as Taker and Austin were facing each other for the belt at *A Cold Day in Hell*, the focus is in on them with a big one-on-one brawl to conclude the show.

Final Rating: **

THE RAW RECAP:

Most Entertaining: Goldust. His sit down interview was a refreshing change of pace compared to the verbal barbs of Bret, Shawn, Austin and Taker that dominated the rest of the show.

Least Entertaining: Rockabilly. Why did they even bother with this?

Quote of the Night: "I knew this was going to shock the heck out of people" – Dustin Runnels talks about the fear of becoming Goldust.

Match of the Night: Steve Austin vs. The British Bulldog. It wasn't a great match, but I can't give an award to Crush.

Verdict: The one thing about *Raw* in 1997 is that they were rarely boring. The idea being that they kept switching gears and changing characters around to develop wrestlers and alter the product. It was part of an enormous overhaul that blurred the lines between good and evil. I like the idea of cheering whoever you want, because that's what I've always done, but the lack of structure ultimately hurt the reactions that matches would get. Although something needed to be done as traditional match styles (like tag team formula) were very much dying off with the widespread wrestling knowledge that was available to smarter fans on the internet. Everyone knew the terminology now; heels, faces, blade jobs. It forced wrestling to change, some say for the worst, and 1997 was the first real tumultuous year for change. Mainly because Vince wasn't just battling against an army of smart fans, but also WCW. It forced the company into some interesting decisions. The Dustin Runnels interview here is a good example, but the Mankind one later is even better. They wanted fans to see there was a real person behind these crazy gimmicks and the reasoning behind the gimmicks was there too. So they could carry on promoting crazy characters while also giving the smart fan a reasoning for their existence, thus promoting to kids *and* adults with the product.
Rating: 48

05.11.97 - A Cold Day in Hell
(James Dixon)
[Richmond Coliseum, Richmond, Virginia]
- Hunter Hearst Helmsley def. Flash Funk (*½)
- Mankind def. Rocky Maivia (*½)
- The Nation of Domination def. Ahmed Johnson (DUD)
- Ken Shamrock def. Vader (***¾)
- The Undertaker def. Steve Austin (**)

Rating: 40

05.12.97 by Arnold Furious

Venue: Newark, DE
Taped: 05.12.97
Raw Rating: 2.8
Nitro Rating: 3.2

Hosts are Jim Ross and Jerry Lawler. This episode of *Raw* is dedicated to the memory of Rose Anderson, who was a close friend of the McMahon family. Jim Ross actually mentions her during *A Cold Day in Hell* too, which was the night before this.

Promo Time: The Hart Foundation
As per usual *Raw* starts out with a recap of past events followed immediately by a bunch of heels coming out to talk. Bret being out with a knee injury in 1997 was unfortunate timing, but it allowed him time to get seriously despised as a heel. Bret once again puts over the Harts as the best group in wrestling before accusing the crowd of being the heels, not him. The crowd rapidly get bored of Bret running down Stone Cold, yet again, and chant for "Austin". Bret finally gets around to his point; when he's fit and able he'll be coming after Undertaker's WWF Title. After that Bret promises a big

surprise, but the crowd upset him with chants of "go home" so the Harts get pissed off and leave. As much as I generally love Bret's heel promo work in 1997, it was better when he had someone in front of him who he hated. Here, he just rambled.

King of the Ring Quarter Final
Hunter Hearst Helmsley vs. Ahmed Johnson
We begin this year's KotR with the Quarter Finals, as the tournament has only eight possible winners due to a thin roster. Here's the bracket:

Hunter Heart Helmsley vs. Ahmed Johnson
Vader vs. Crush
Goldust vs. Jerry Lawler
Savio Vega vs. Mankind

Honestly, from that bracket you'd book Vader vs. Mankind as a tag team imploding and Foley bringing his babyface style against the insurmountable odds of Vader. It would have been a good story. Especially with Vader eager to get his mojo back after being tapped out by Shamrock. Instead the WWF went in a completely different direction with the top end of the bracket. Jim Ross mentions over and over again that this is a "single elimination tournament". Keep that one in mind. Ahmed brings his usual sloppy stuff, which is popular but not good. When a bad wrestler meets a dull one it's hard to know who to root for. For what Hunter wins in competence, he loses in move set, whereas Ahmed is incompetent yet entertaining. JR mentions, once again, that Hunter had a wrestling tutor at the age of three. Who has a wrestling tutor at three? I always felt that was a ridiculous and unnecessary addition to the character's backstory. Chyna jumps in the ring with Ahmed in charge and chair shots him for the DQ. Therefore Ahmed wins and Hunter is out of this "single elimination tournament". Not how you remember *King of the Ring '97* going down? Don't worry, something suitably Russorific is forthcoming.
Final Rating: ½*

Video Control takes us to Sunny, who's shilling for Super Soaker, one of the WWF's sponsors. The Headbangers do a lousy sell on being drenched. "Wetter is better" says Sunny.

Promo Time: Steve Austin
Vince McMahon gets in the ring for an interview. Austin threatens to knock Vince's head off his neck. He goes off on a rant about how he'll be WWF Champion sooner or later regardless of the Hart Foundation. Austin compares the Hart Foundation to a snake and says the only way you kill a snake is by chopping the head off. But Steve doesn't want to do that; he wants to start with the snake's ass. The snake's ass is Brian Pillman so he's coming for him first. And that's the bottom line, folks.

Scott Putski vs. Leif Cassidy
Putski was a second generation wrestler, son of Hall of Famer and muscle head Ivan Putski. Just being a second generation guy isn't enough, as David Sammartino proved conclusively, and many other second gen workers have struggled to escape their father's shadow. Much as Dustin Runnels alluded to last week. Unfortunately Putski is a muscular flier, which is a weird combo. Cassidy tries to walk him through a match and introduces some reasonable counters on the mat. He doesn't look terribly happy to be out here jobbing to a guy with half his ability though. It's Cassidy who pops the crowd with a sit out powerbomb, a move way cooler than anything Scott has in his locker. It's a pity they opt to use so many flippy moves that require an overabundance of cooperation. They run a few embarrassing near miss spots, which look dreadful. Scott does have a decent overhead belly-to-belly, but twice goes to it as an escape after a spot goes wrong. Poor Leif gets dumped on his head off a release German suplex and thankfully that ends the match. The WWF would try to market Putski as a flier, which didn't really suit him, until an injury in September permanently derailed his push and he left. Most careers that last four months would be considered unsuccessful, so Putski is a footnote player, even in 1997, in the WWF. This match showed why.
Final Rating: ½*

Post Match: Cassidy gets pissed off and takes out the rookie sensation, only to get laid out again to make his performance doubly embarrassing. No wonder Leif starting talking to a plastic mannequin head in ECW. His character here was improving and he seemed unhinged, but without a major change he'd have been forever enhancement. The ECW run helped establish his personality, which would allow him as Al Snow to get booked in the WWF during the peak of their late 90s popularity.

The Legion of Doom vs. PG-13
Hawk's pre-match rant about "slaughtering defenceless domestic animals" is amazing and one of the best of his career. JC Ice and Wolfie D are perfect cannon fodder for the LOD as they can take sensational bumps, but they have heat from the Nation rappers gimmick. This was billed as LOD vs. Nation of Domination but the other guys bully JC Ice and Wolfie D into the match. The result is one of the most hilarious squashes on *Raw* since the Steiner Brothers were killing jobbers back in 1993. Highlights include Wolfie D getting bielled clean across the ring, JC Ice bringing the kung fu before being lariated, Hawk totally no selling a double team piledriver and Wolfie getting the Doomsday Device on top of JC Ice. PG-13 end up with nothing at all and this loss saw them booted out of the Nation and indeed the WWF. Thanks for coming, fellas.
Final Rating: **

Promo Time: Mankind
He reminds us that he brought to the Undertaker "a great wall of flame", hoping to scar him. "I was not entirely successful". He calls Taker a coward for going after Uncle Paul as an act of revenge. Mankind brings out Bearer and tries to get him to reveal his horrible secret. Paul has wrapping around his face after Taker burned him. Once again he demands that Taker come back to him or face the consequences. The whole Bearer-Taker-Kane thing just went on forever. The entire of 1997 was filled with vague promos like this one. A pity, as Mick's promo was going great until Bearer turned up.

Promo Time: Faarooq
He talks about a long line of number one contenders to come out here, but there has never been a black champion. Faarooq implies that the WWF are racist and plays the affirmative action card. Faarooq's promo hits incredible points, but his delivery isn't the best. "Your white saviour, the Undertaker, will be a dead man". Vince calls Faarooq a racist, which makes me laugh out loud. This would have been a stunning promo if Faarooq had hit all the beats, but the inconsistency of it all was disappointing. Perhaps scripting certain promos was the right move, because this would have been absolutely killer given some practice.

The Undertaker vs. Savio Vega
This was due to Faarooq being next in line for a WWF title shot. Taker's run as champion sure was a meandering mess.

They had to shoehorn him into the various other ideas, concepts and feuds while continuing the spiritual feud with Paul Bearer and eventually Kane. It's all a bit distracting. They should have just kept the nonsense on the undercard and left the title to the wrestlers. This match is non-title, which is an interesting concept. Savio isn't good enough to have a title shot so he doesn't get one. Compared to WCW, for example, who actually gave Scott Putski a shot at the WCW Title. He lost to Goldberg in under a minute. Much like Savio there was no point in him getting a title match. Savio, boring heel, grinds away at Taker's leg for the whole match. Austin spent most of his title shot doing the same only more creatively, obviously. JR points out he's probably just setting the table for Faarooq, like Arn Anderson did for Ric Flair so many times. Rough up the opponent before a big match. Like Double A, Savio is doomed to defeat. A chokeslam would be enough to finish, but Crush jumps on the apron. Taker hits the Tombstone anyway and the Nation jump in for the DQ. Faarooq goes after the champ with a belt, making me wish they turned the title match into a "country whippin' match". Again, that's the kind of thing WCW would have done. Faarooq poses with the belt for bit but sadly doesn't scream "BLACK RAGE" while doing so.
Final Rating: ½*

Rob Van Dam vs. Jeff Hardy
Do not adjust your book, readers! RVD did indeed make his *Raw* debut back in 1997. Jerry Lawler quickly jumps into the ring to talk about how bad ECW is. "Extremely Crappy Wrestling, that's what it stands for". Lawler puts RVD over as being the only good wrestler in ECW. Rob got enormous heat for going on *Raw* and running down the company that employed him and Lawler christens him "Mr. Monday Night". His career took off after that. Hardy is just a jobber for RVD to kick around the ring. Even so Rob manages to land on his head with a plancha to the floor. He lands leg first on the rail and head first on the floor. The fans barrack him with "you sold out" chants. On *Raw*! What planet is this match from? RVD hits the Five Star Frogsplash but that's just a set up for the split legged moonsault, which finishes. One of my favourite squash matches of all time. I remember reading about Rob Van Dam long before I saw him wrestle, and this was a real eye-opener.
Final Rating: **¼

Video Control takes us to part two of the Dustin Runnels interview. This time he talks about entertaining the people and having fun, ultimately to make sure his family is happy. Jim Ross mentions similarities between Dustin and Dusty, and Dakota and Dustin, as Dustin talks about how he looked up to Dusty and Dakota mimics him sometimes. The crux of the interview is that Dustin still wants Dusty Rhodes' approval. They probably didn't need to run this as well as the interview from last week. It hit most of the same topics and had much the same sentiment.

Promo Time: The Undertaker
JR interviews him via the Titantron as the arena sits in darkness. Taker cautions Paul Bearer to keep his secrets that way before giving the generic "vault of souls", "rest in peace" promo to Faarooq. No mention of the racism card from the champ.

Owen Hart & The British Bulldog vs. Doug Furnas & Phil LaFon vs. The New Blackjacks vs. The Headbangers
Owen and Bulldog are the tag champs but there's no mention of the belts being on the line. It's an elimination match. I hate the WWF for turning Furnas & LaFon into the pair of bumbling morons that work here. LaFon miscues on Furnas before Bradshaw clotheslines him to hell for the first elimination. The WWF should have built a tag team division around good teams instead of pushing Furnas & LaFon to the sidelines because they couldn't cut an interview. Anyway, they hold Bradshaw down from the floor for them to get booted and that leaves Owen & Bulldog vs. the Headbangers. Which is what they pretty much booked anyway, given how quickly the other two teams got dumped. Owen gets double teamed into a pin but gets his foot on the ropes when Mosh scores the three count. Jerry Lawler keeps referencing the one-time only *Raw Bowl* as the rules are the same. At least he provides some interesting continuity. The Headbangers insist on working heat on both Owen and Davey despite the champs being the heels. The crowd do not care one iota. Owen gets the Sharpshooter but Thrasher saves. A malfunction at the junction allows Davey to powerslam Thrasher for the win. "Neither one of them was legal" points out JR. Logic doesn't exist here, Jim. Move along.
Final Rating: *

Promo Time: Bret Hart
He sends the Foundation to the back in order to call out Shawn Michaels. The idea being that he rants at and dismantles Shawn verbally until HBK has had enough and hits the superkick. But Bret either went into business for himself and went over time or he accidentally overran, because the TV time runs out before Shawn hits the kick. This is something that pissed Shawn off for years afterwards and he was still bitter about it when WWE released the *Greatest Rivalries* DVD about their feud a decade and a half later. Whenever Bret had Shawn in front of his face he really unleashed his best venomous material. "Go ahead, take your jacket off, make yourself at home. It symbolises something, taking your jacket off. You're hot, you're cold, you're hot, you're cold; that's the story of your whole career". Burn! Bret doesn't like Shawn's dancing or his cockiness and accuses him for being a symbol for Americans everywhere. "You think you're better than everybody else". Bret compares America to ancient Rome in an interesting allegory that kind of rings true. That greed will corrupt and eventually destroy. Bret accuses Shawn of screwing Bret out of the title at *WrestleMania XII*. "You didn't have the guts to face me like a man" says Bret before accusing Shawn of being a degenerate. "You didn't have the guts to face me this year at *WrestleMania*". The last line that makes the air is Bret calling Shawn "a piece of crap". That's all, folks. Shawn spent the entire promo trying to look tough and intimidating by standing over Bret. It didn't really put the Hitman off his stride. Bret dragged out what he was saying here, stretching his points out, leading one to suspect that he did it on purpose so he could bury Shawn and avoid taking a superkick live on the air. I know mostly the internet and smart fans take Bret's side against Shawn, but this instance is one time where Bret seemed to be out of line. It wasn't like him to not hit his marks and his behaviour here scuppered an otherwise excellent segment.

THE RAW RECAP:

Most Entertaining: Rob Van Dam. A breath of fresh air. Everyone else was in holding patterns.

Least Entertaining: Savio Vega.

Quote of the Night: "I crippled your sorry carcass once before and in the bush leagues I carried you in my back pocket". – Steve Austin runs down Brian Pillman and WCW.

Match of the Night: Rob Van Dam vs. Jeff Hardy

Verdict: A thoroughly uneven night for wrestling. Certainly the in-ring was lacking, but the storylines didn't take any dramatic twists and turns either. Bret and Austin just did their usual. Even the different pacing of Goldust's "shoot" interview repeated all his points from last time. I remember RVD's *Raw* debut with great fondness, significantly more so than Scott Putski's. Had they got the timing right on the main event interview it may have been memorable for all the right reasons. In the end it just contributed to the ongoing backstage feud between Bret and Shawn, and did nothing for the actual show.
Rating: 47

05.19.97 by Arnold Furious

Venue: Mobile, AL
Taped: 05.19.97
Raw Rating: 3.1
Nitro Rating: 3.6

We're live in Mobile, Alabama. Hosts are Vince McMahon, Jim Ross and Jerry Lawler.

Promo Time: Steve Austin
The WWF had begun a serious habit of opening *Raw* with their biggest draw to make sure everyone stayed tuned and didn't skip over to see what was on *Nitro*, so out comes Austin to be interviewed by Jim Ross to kick-start the show. "I don't give a rat's ass about Shawn Michaels". He claims he didn't save Shawn, he came out to cheap shot the Harts. This brings out Shawn to a decidedly mixed reaction, compared to the massive pop for Austin. They basically agree that they don't care about each other but bond over hatred of the Hart Foundation. Shawn makes a point of calling Austin "son". "You might as well take your little bandana and go backstage before I kick your damn teeth down your throat" says the Texas Rattlesnake. Shawn takes offence at Austin stealing his line so he threatens to "stomp your guts in", which pisses Austin off and the two have a pull-apart brawl. Interesting to see how pro-Austin this crowd was considering Shawn starting sucking up to the fans just last week. Owen and Bulldog join us from the Titantron to mock the Americans for fighting each other instead of the Harts. Owen challenges Shawn and Austin with the tag belts on the line next week. Shawn calls them "nimrods" before refusing to team with Austin. "You ain't cleaning nothing up but the toilet" rants Austin. "I'll find some piece of crap that weighs 75lbs or 75 years old" says Austin, refusing Shawn's help and they get into it again. The uneasy alliance between Austin and Shawn made for great television and a stunning match at *King of the Ring '97*. Not to mention the great tag match next week.

King of the Ring Quarter Final
Crush vs. Vader
Jerry Lawler mentions Vader is injured and can't compete in the *King of the Ring* qualifiers. Vader had his nose broken by Ken Shamrock at *A Cold Day in Hell* just over a week before this. The worst case scenario is that the untalented Crush gets a bye, but bizarrely enough Vader is instead replaced by a sub: Hunter Hearst Helmsley.

King of the Ring Quarter Final
Crush vs. Hunter Hearst Helmsley
Hunter claimed he'd not had the rules adequately explained to him last week on his DQ loss to Ahmed Johnson, which means he's an idiot who doesn't watch wrestling. "The Game", ladies and gents. Gerry Brisco joins us to explain that Hunter was told by Timmy White that Hunter could only win or lose by pinfall or submission. He threatened a lawsuit so the WWF gave him another shot. It's a lame, lame storyline. It also gives us an all-heel match between two very boring wrestlers. Crush actually works heat on Hunter, which should tell you everything you need to know about his psychology. You can't work heat on Hunter! Nobody likes him. Hunter tries like hell to work like Ric Flair and treat Crush as a big lummox. Crush is so bad he can't even fill the broomstick role. Not that Hunter can actually wrestle like Flair, just mimic him. Both Savio Vega and Chyna try to get involved, but Savio's interference backfires and Hunter pins Crush after a Savio kick. The bumbling Nation began to fall apart here. Faarooq has to come down to play peacemaker.
Final Rating: ¾*

Owen Hart vs. Bob Holly
This is not for Owen's IC title. He's accompanied by Jim Neidhart and the British Bulldog. Seeing as we're in Alabama, Holly is over big time. Jerry Lawler takes a moment to mock a few locals. The WWF frequently misjudges homecomings as they look at the bigger picture, but the reactions of fans are always important; which is why CM Punk is over in Chicago and Bret Hart was over so big in Canada. Holly brings a rana from the start and aims for a quick and entertaining pace. Holly was always a solid hand and a better worker when he was carrying less muscle around. But obviously bulking up allowed him greater longevity in the WWF. "These people think the Gaza Strip is a topless club" – Lawler continues to berate the locals. Not a big Alabama fan, clearly. Owen goes after a Sharpshooter but Holly rolls him up for the cheeky upset pin. This was a tidy little match but they could have done better if they'd had more time.
Final Rating: **¼

Backstage: Shawn Michaels and Ken Shamrock are hanging out. Shawn claims he can trust Ken so he'll be teaming with him next week for a shot at the tag belts. Shamrock was about to feud with Bulldog, so that would have made sense.

Video Control takes us to Jim Ross' interview with Mankind. JR points out this is "not like Dustin Runnels' interview". Damn skippy. JR's introduction alone is superb. "The journey of Mick Foley. A boyhood dream turned living hell". Mankind opens up by saying he's not a bad person. He goes off on a rant about cowboys and Indians, and how he was always an Indian. "Standing up for what I believe in. If that makes me a bad person, you've got me bang to rights". We see the infamous dive off the garage roof before Foley talks about his childhood. He talks about his first experience of pain, having his lip split by another kid's shoe, and how he was good at being hurt. He could take the pain. Foley goes on to talk about his love of wrestling growing up and how he broke his brother's nose by backdropping him into the wall. In high school he was a bit different and ate worms. "I'm a good kisser but I never had the chance to show it". JR teases next week, which will be an extension of the story, not a repeat like the Goldust one. Next week Mick will talk about Dude Love and Cactus Jack. This was incredible viewing as Mick stayed in character but layered in truth and story to enhance his character. These interviews helped change perception of Mankind and indeed Mick Foley, and turned him into a hero for the masses and eventually WWF Champion. Quite the conclusion to a remarkable story.

Scott Taylor vs. Leif Cassidy
Leif is out here as enhancement yet again. They won't even put him over Scotty. Jerry Lawler goes off on a rant about how RVD is under contract to ECW and therefore can't work on

Raw. Taylor was originally due to be pushed as a cruiserweight, with the division just around the corner. The ECW connection is there as Leif is beginning to work on his character and personality before being loaned out to Philadelphia to become Al Snow. Taylor's babyface offence is horribly generic. Lazy looking dropkicks ahoy. Leif gets himself over a bit by beating the piss out of Taylor, who comes off as a punk rather than plucky. Taylor scores the duke with an inside cradle, much like Holly did earlier. Leif going nuts after the match is the only highlight.
Final Rating: ½*

Backstage: Steve Austin walks in on Sable and asks if she'll be his tag team partner, before changing his mind. Funny little segment as Austin comes across as a bit of a pervert but in a comical manner.

Elsewhere: Bret Hart shows up, rather late, and he's promising a big surprise. But, we won't hear it until later.

Video Control gives us the end of last week's *Raw* where Bret ranted at Shawn Michaels until the show went off the air. We pick up the footage as Bret stands up at 10.01pm and Shawn superkicks him. Sensational sell from Bret on the superkick. Absolutely brilliant. The Harts come out to attack Shawn but he somehow avoids them and fends them off with a crutch as the crowd chant for "Austin". Eventually Shawn gets picked up by Bulldog, threatening to throw him off the stage, and Steve Austin makes the save. That's how *Raw* *should* have finished.

Promo Time: Bret Hart
He's out to reveal his "big surprise" as Vince McMahon speculates Bret will name a new member of the Hart Foundation. Bret somehow blames Shawn for last week and calls the crowd both rednecks and scum. Bret makes fun of Shawn's knee injury and his return at *King of the Ring*. Bret's surprise is that he'll also return at *King of the Ring* from his legitimate knee injury. Bret challenges Shawn to a match and promises if he can't beat Shawn in less than 10 minutes he'll never work in America again. Shawn pops onto the Titantron to respond. "You couldn't beat me in 60 minutes, what in the world makes you think you can beat me in 10 minutes". Shawn orders a stipulation where each Hart member will be handcuffed to a ring post. "You couldn't go 10 minutes in any situation, if you know what I mean". That's before hinting that Bret has shagged Sunny (See: Raw Recap). This whole thing is riddled with inside stuff, which led to Bret getting pissed off with Shawn for the whole "Sunny days" comment. The match ended up being cancelled as Bret felt Shawn couldn't be trusted with his bad knee. Shawn ended up having a blinding match with Austin instead and Bret and Shawn's eventual showdown was postponed until *Survivor Series*.

Goldust vs. Rockabilly
Goldust introduces two Marlenas; Terri and Dakota. Lawler pretty much nails it by saying "this is the Warzone". It ends up as family play time with Vince calling it "cute". I can see what they were getting at with humanising Goldust, but they went too damn far here. He shouldn't be a family man in the ring, he should be a wrestler. Lawler continues to rant; "No wonder his dad hates him". "I bet Dusty Rhodes is turning over in his grave". Vince's "he's not actually dead" correction makes me smile. Goldust and Billy have a reasonable if heatless match, until a flub leads to the finish with Billy missing his spot before getting trapped in the ropes. Honky Tonk Man jumps in the ring for the DQ and Goldust bashes him with El Kabong. Somehow Goldust is disqualified. I don't know how they figured that one out. Presumably for using the guitar, but the other guys manager is in the ring, that's an instant DQ. He didn't even hit Billy with it.
Final Rating: ½*

Backstage: Ahmed Johnson gets time to talk about Faarooq playing the race card last week. Ahmed calls Faarooq a sell out, a racist and a cheat, but goes on to point out there's never been a black WWF Champion. Ahmed hints that he agrees with Faarooq before comparing himself to Hank Aaron and claiming he'll be the first black WWF Champion. A total mess from Ahmed. He was all over the place.

Backstage: Steve Austin's hunt for a tag team partner continues as he's not allowed to wrestle alone. He's picked Harvey Wippleman, so the Brooklyn Brawler comes in to offer his services and Austin kicks his ass. "You suck".

Video Control takes us to another fluff Sunny piece shilling Super Soaker, this time drenching Jim Cornette.

Rocky Maivia vs. Faarooq
This was an actual feud few year down the line, but Rocky is on a de-push after mixed reactions to his IC title run and Faarooq is in line for a WWF title match, so this one is a no-brainer. Faarooq tries to invite Rock into the group only for Maivia to respond with attitude. Why was he not turned heel earlier? He was so perfect as a bad guy. He brings the generic babyface spots like a powerslam and a crossbody as the crowd dislike him, mildly. Rock Bottom but Faarooq kicks out as that's not Rock's finish yet. Floatover DDT and Rocky nips up. It's surprising how much offence he gets in against the number one contender for the WWF Title. Faarooq crotches Rock up top and finishes with the Dominator. Rocky bossed this match, which came as a surprise. After the match, in a show of race solidarity, Faarooq stops Crush and Savio from jumping future black champion Maivia. Perhaps he'd already planned to bring Rock in at this point. Interesting.
Final Rating: **

Backstage: The Harts get a receipt out of Bob Holly's ass for that earlier fluke win.

Promo Time: The Undertaker
I guess we have to get the WWF Champion out here, so Vince hops in the ring for the interview. Taker opts to talk about Faarooq over Paul Bearer. Taker claims to not recognise colour because he's "the reaper of wayward souls". Vince drags him back to the Bearer secret. "This is not the time" barks Taker, only for Bearer to show up and threaten to reveal his secret unless the Undertaker rejoins him. Taker asks for more time so Bearer gives him "seven sunsets" to decide or he'll open Pandora's Box. Bearer's choice of words made this moderately more entertaining than most Taker promos from 1997.

Steve Austin vs. Jim Neidhart
This is Raw's main event, kicking off at 9.55pm. In future years USA allowed over runs but this one is just a short match. It's also very one-sided with Austin wearing out his boot leather on Anvil's rear end. Brian Pillman joins commentary, but Austin goes after him to stop that. That should give Anvil an opening but instead Pillman runs in with one of Bret's crutches to nail Austin for the DQ. The Harts put a gang beating on Austin, so Shawn Michaels runs in for the save with chair shots. Vince announces that Austin and Shawn will be forced to team with

each other for the tag title shot. Jim Ross jumps in there to make sure they both know about it. This leads to yet another Austin and Michaels brawl as we go off the air.
Final Rating: ¾*

THE RAW RECAP:

Most Entertaining: Mick Foley. On a show that relied heavily on character development, his made the biggest moves. The sit down interviews with JR were wonderful business for Foley and changed public perception of him.

Least Entertaining: Scott Taylor. A tame showing where he was easily outshone by Leif Cassidy.

Quote of the Night: "I know you've had a lot of Sunny days lately" – Shawn Michaels irritates Bret Hart live on the air.

Match of the Night: Owen Hart vs. Bob Holly. A solid little encounter putting over the hometown guy.

Verdict: 1997 in the WWF felt a lot like the radical 60s in California. Anything could happen at any time. Everyone was so energised and motivated to move up the card, at a time where that was possible, and *Raw* felt lively. The stuff on this show between Austin and Shawn is superb and Mick Foley's interview just added to it. Plus Faarooq's character was finally showing a bit of subtlety while he was trying to show he belonged at the top end. Even Leif Cassidy and Bob Holly tried to steal this show. There was a feeling a fire could break out under anyone at any time. Steve Austin had exploded out of the midcard and now everyone felt it was possible for them to dream that dream. After all, someone has to be champion. Someone has to challenge them. In 1997 a whole load of guys were looking in the mirror and saying "why not me?" Compare that to 1998 where everyone was suddenly subservient to Steve Austin and it feels like a different company. I get that the WWF needed Steve Austin to be an icon they could build the company around, like Hulkamania bossed the mid 80s, but the period of uncertainty in 1997 is very refreshing to watch.
Rating: 68

05.26.97 by Arnold Furious

Venue: Evansville, IN
Taped: 05.26.97
Raw Rating: 2.7
Nitro Rating: 3.2

I think they've turned the opening pyro up a notch. It seems louder than before. Hosts are Vince McMahon and Jim Ross. They plug the tag title match that headlines tonight's show.

Promo Time: Steve Austin vs. Shawn Michaels
As I've mentioned before; in the WWF's continued ratings battle with WCW their most common tactic was to open the show with their biggest draw. With him being as hot as he was, that means Stone Cold. I love that they pan in to a Shawn Michaels sign that a young kid is holding up only to discover it reads "Shawn Michaels can die". Shawn sports a Homer Simpson t-shirt to win me over, and reference back a few weeks to him putting Homer over in a promo. They immediately bicker over who's the captain of their tag team. After Shawn's assertion that they're the "two meanest SOBs in the WWF" the LOD come down to argue tag team superiority. Apparently Hawk and Animal are pissed about the tag team division. The mikes pick up Shawn telling Hawk that "when" they win the tag titles they'll defend them against the LOD. Austin doesn't seem to care one way or another. This brings out the entire Hart Foundation. Nothing actually happens as an ad break interrupts. An 8-man tag would have been pretty sweet.

The Legion of Doom vs. Jim Neidhart & Brian Pillman
The Harts send out the B-team to deal with the LOD, which is unfortunate as Pillman is more bluster than talent at this stage of his career and Anvil is worse in the ring that he is. At least Pillman can muster a few half hearted bumps in his *Raw* debut. Anvil just throws himself into the air or flops embarrassingly over sideways. As great as the Harts were as a unit, this is the worst possible combination they could have sent out. Even the explosiveness of the LOD can't rescue the match. It just flat out sucks. A brief heat segment on Animal is ended by two awful bumps from the Harts and Pillman is set up for the Doomsday Device so the other Harts run in for the DQ. Steve Austin and Shawn Michaels run in for the save only for HBK to miscue on Stone Cold and the two end up brawling around ringside.
Final Rating: DUD

Video Control gives us another of Sunny's Super Soaker adventures, this time drenching the Honky Tonk Man. Next up is Paul Bearer, with scabby facial injuries, who tells us his secret is hidden in his attorney's safe, in case the Undertaker kills him tonight. Bearer promises Undertaker will be back with him or the secret will be revealed tonight.

D'Lo Brown vs. Bob Holly
Total filler but at least both guys are talented. D'Lo has the entire Nation in his corner, thus giving him a significant edge. Holly is hopelessly outdated, but he did sneak an upset win over poor Owen Hart last week in his home town. So this is the WWF putting him back in his jobber place. Holly blows an early slide through Brown's legs. Faarooq joins commentary to accuse Vince of racism, to which Vince responds "you haven't been one of my favourites over the years". Holly hits a few babyface spots like dropkicks and such. Nobody cares. We're not in Alabama anymore, Bob. Faarooq goes off on a massive rant about slavery only for Vince to shoot it all down, which continues until D'Lo hits the Sky High for the squeaky clean win. The match was secondary to the angle, but after an early flub both guys settled into a pleasing rhythm. There was talent there.
Final Rating: *

Video Control takes us to the Undertaker only for audio problems to disrupt his promo. They are forced to do it again only for Taker to say next to nothing. Worthless. Jerry Lawler joins us after that to call Goldust a "sissy" and suggest he rename Dakota "Target" as all the boys had a shot at being her daddy. When Uncle Jerry was at his vicious best he was truly entertaining. Superb and vile promo from him here.

King of the Ring Quarter Final
Goldust vs. Jerry Lawler
'Dust already dislikes Lawler after Jerry called him a queer live on *Raw* at the back end of last year, but that pre-match promo should establish him as a definite heel. But we're in USWA country so the crowd cheer every single Lawler spot and the set up for the piledriver is met with a raucous reaction. Goldust doesn't stay down for it as Lawler spends time mocking Marlena. Goldust responds with his own piledriver, which draws a chorus of boos. I love it when crowds just blatantly ignore what they're supposed to do. It also shows a weakness behind Dustin Runnels' face turn. At the end of the day, how

many people enjoyed him as a face? A few months later they went ahead and turned him into a different heel, having blown this face run. Unlike the vast majority of Lawler matches from the WWF, they keep a good pace and throw in plenty of bumps. It's the opposite of what you'd expect from either Lawler or Goldust. Marlena, described as "spunky" by both Ross and Vince, slaps Lawler, but Jerry gets a win with his feet on the ropes. Not at all what you'd expect from these two and they worked their asses off out there. My only complaint is that the match is too short! James Dixon would be shocked by this match and how good it is.

Final Rating: **½

Backstage: Steve Austin gets more interview time, but it's interrupted by Brian Pillman and the rest of the Harts attacking him. Afterwards Austin goes looking for Shawn Michaels to discover he's been jumped too. Both men blame each other.

Flash Funk vs. Rocky Maivia

The Headbangers show up through the audience with inflatable chairs to sit at ringside. This somewhat distracts from Flash throwing funky kicks. Rocky slips out of a hold to hit the Rock Bottom, back when he was using it as a transition. The Headbangers make some interesting points about illegal punches before yelling "he missed, hahaha" on a missed dropkick. Puerile. Rock blows a fall to the floor before Flash hits a crazy dive. This brings the Headbangers over to kick both guys' asses and Flash gets clocked with a boom box. Rocky finishes off the injured Funk with a high crossbody. It's weird to see Rocky in this post-IC title, pre-heel turn phase. He looks so directionless.

Final Rating: ¾*

Video Control takes us to Part II of the Mick Foley interview. Mick talks about pain and how much he loved lacrosse and being a goalie without protection. "Testicle the size of a grapefruit" is not a phrase you hear too often. Mick talks about spending all his money on going to MSG to see Jimmy Snuka. More later in the show.

Backstage: Bret Hart compares the forthcoming match at King of the Ring to a lion ripping apart an antelope. He says 10-minutes is enough time for him to punch Shawn's face in. All the Harts take turns to bitch about Steve Austin as the first hour of Raw comes to an end, hyping the main event in the process.

Vader vs. Ahmed Johnson

Ken Shamrock joins commentary as he'd just defeated Vader in his debut. That's why this match is happening. Originally Vader was in the King of the Ring tournament but his injuries sustained working Shamrock kept him out of his qualifier. So now Vader has a shot at Ahmed's King of the Ring berth. If he wins, he's in and Ahmed is out. Got that? Good. Ahmed's sloppiness rather hurts the opening exchanges. As does his insistence on wearing white gloves, like he's some sort of shoot fighter, which segues nicely into JR plugging the next UFC PPV. As Ahmed bobs and weaves, displaying tactics he's never used before, or since, the match tries like hell to ape Shamrock-Vader. As if to emphasise the shoot style Vader starts laying in kicks to the inner thigh. What the hell am I watching? Vader then runs into a spinebuster and it's all over. They tried to make this feel shootish and while I appreciate the attempt, it really wasn't Ahmed's forte. The finish plays into UFC lore nicely as it would count as a flash knock out, rather than a finishing move.

Final Rating: *¼

Backstage: Paul Bearer continues his rambling from earlier about Taker's secret.

Hunter Hearst Helmsley vs. Rockabilly

Hunter using 'Ode to Joy' as entrance music makes me happy because I get all nostalgic for Die Hard. Billy is still trying to get this stupid gimmick over, bless him, but it doesn't suit him at all. Billy actually has this won with a Rocker Dropper only for Chyna to drag him off the cover, thus proving herself to be a far superior manager to the Honky Tonk Man. Honky tries for a guitar shot but Chyna stops him and slams him. That leaves Billy distracted and prone for the Pedigree. Score one for Chyna's Manager of the Year award!

Final Rating: ½*

Backstage: The Undertaker talks about being forced into making decisions and cryptically states he'll do what he has to do.

Video Control takes us to the next instalment of the Mankind interview. This time he slants towards wrestling, saying he didn't care about anything but blood and guts, so he hitchhiked for 17 hours to Madison Square Garden to see Jimmy Snuka vs. Don Muraco in a cage. He claims the moment changed his life and he wanted to do the same thing. He envisaged himself as a hero. When he was 18 he made a movie about his wrestling persona. Mankind talks about how he saw himself as a tattooed good guy who gets the fame and the girls. Clips of his home movie follow with the first shots of Dude Love as he performs moves on his friends and jumps off the roof of the garage, in a famous shot. Mankind talks about not being ready to be Dude Love yet, but he'd get the look and the girls later when he was ready. "Cactus Jack was supposed to be around for three months but he stayed for eleven years". JR plugs the rest of the interview next week with barbed wire rings. "Mrs. Foley's little boy is finally home!" squeals Mankind. This was brilliant. The humanisation of Mankind has to be one of the most amazing character builds any wrestling company has ever achieved.

WWF Tag Team Championship
Owen Hart & The British Bulldog (c)
vs. Steve Austin & Shawn Michaels

"Steve Austin is just about ready to, if you'll excuse me, open a can of whupass" – Vince McMahon. He sure knows how to swear. Hell of a way to main event Raw; four of the best workers in the world tagging up. Austin and Owen start at a fast pace with the crowd loving everything Steve hits. He goes after the Sharpshooter to mess with Bret, but Bulldog jumps in to stop it. Shawn gets a surprising early tag, which allows him to take an amazing bump off Davey. He landed on his neck and then rolled backwards into the ropes like Rock selling a Stunner. He runs through stuff with Davey at breakneck speed as if to show Austin he is still boss. The match becomes a game of one-upmanship between Steve and Shawn. They have a quick contest to see who can tag out the fastest to demonstrate that famous tag team continuity. The Hart Foundation come down to distract Shawn while Austin gets picked off for heat as the Harts use the numbers game. Austin gets a jawbreaker to escape a sleeper and Shawn gets an electric hot tag. Shawn always tried to be on his A-game, but he sometimes found another gear above top. This is one of those matches. Bulldog dumps him on the ropes crotch-first as Vince debates whether the Harts are aiming for the DQ. JR reminds us this is Shawn's first match in months as Davey hits the running powerslam, but Austin saves. This leads to heat on Michaels but Austin is in and out of the ring as often as Earl

Hebner will allow, never stopping moving. When this many good workers get motivated in the same place it is a thing of beauty. The heat involves a sneaky missed tag as the champs run fantastic formula. Shawn litters his heat with hope spots but he's constantly cut down by Davey lariats and Owen kicks. Hot tag to Austin takes the roof off and the champs are so tired they can't even come charging at Steve. He has to drag them into beatings. Superkick for Davey and Austin gets the pin. New champions! This match is sensational. It's only 13-minutes long, but the sheer effort of all involved is incredible. Owen and Davey blew themselves up giving Shawn a kicking, like the famous Ali Rope-A-Dope. Shawn knackered them both out, then tagged Steve in.
Final Rating: ****½

Post Match: the Harts run in to demolish Shawn so Austin goes after Bret Hart and reinjures his knee to cancel the *King of the Ring* match. Shawn Michaels is left unconscious in the ring while Austin is getting his cheap shots in.

Backstage: Steve Austin gets interviewed and he's blown up, sucking down air. He claims he won the match by himself only for Shawn Michaels to show up and point out his part in the win. Amazing to see Shawn Michaels barely tired after that performance, even if he's soaked in sweat. Some people are not affected by life the same way as the rest of us. Shawn Michaels did not have the cardio of a human being, he was like a genetically engineered superhuman.

Promo Time: Paul Bearer
Bearer comes down to the ring for his big reveal. Vince McMahon gets to interview him. Bearer points out Taker had seven sunsets and the sun has gone down. Bearer also points out he's known Undertaker for many years and when the Taker's parents died there were three graves, not two. This brings the Undertaker down, as quickly as I've seen him move not on a motorcycle, to put a stop to this. Taker says he hates Bearer with all that he is and briefly teases destroying Paul, referring to the fans as "the ones who loved me in the past". He grabs Bearer by the throat but stops and drops to a knee, subservient to his former manager. Jim Ross gets in a tidy "Oh no, what's he doing? Oh my Gawd" as the crowd scream "noooo" and we fade to black.

THE RAW RECAP:

Most Entertaining: Mick Foley. I could have gone with anyone involved in the main event, but this interview was life-changing for Foley's Mankind character and gave him fresh impetus in the WWF.

Least Entertaining: Brian Pillman. Made a comeback after a lengthy stint out, but looked in horrible condition. Wrecked the opener singlehandedly.

Quote of the Night: "I know Dusty Rhodes and he told me why he doesn't like you. It's because you married the biggest gold-digger in Georgia, then you put on a woman's wig and you went around the ring kissing men like a flaming fag" – Jerry Lawler gives Goldust an earful.

Match of the Night: Steve Austin & Shawn Michaels vs. Owen Hart & British Bulldog. Sensational stuff.

Verdict: Some episodes of *Raw* just plain deliver. This is one of them. The final third, with Mankind's interview, the main event and Taker's decision, was tight TV. Fantastic viewing all round. I'm not a fan of Taker's storylines in general but this promo with Bearer was perfect. Bearer had a secret to hold over him so Taker had to do as he was told. Until the actual arrival of Kane at *Badd Blood,* this was one of the best moments of their feud. The tag match is obviously terrific, one of the best matches of the year and one of the best *Raw* matches you'll ever see. Constant action, despite a reliance on formula, and a wonderful showcase for four of the best workers in the business. All legitimate Hall of Famers. The match has found its way onto several DVD's including *The Monday Night War* and is well worth checking out. Finally, the Mankind interview was great business and over the course of the interviews, changed public perception of Mick Foley as a wrestler and as a human being. The later interviews stressed the Cactus Jack persona and Mick's hardcore history, but the stuff here with Dude Love was what the public loved at the time. It was Mick's dream. Mankind was his dream gone sour. People were eager to see Mick as a fun-loving babyface because it was such a contrast to Mankind. In short, this was quality television.
Rating: 89

06.02.97 by James Dixon

Venue: Huntington, WV
Taped: 06.02.97
Raw Rating: 2.5
Nitro Rating: 3.3

Promo Time: The Undertaker
After the bedlam of last week, we need a video recap and voiceover from Vince McMahon to get us up to speed. One man involved in shenanigans was the Undertaker, who was forced to bow to and reunite with former manager Paul Bearer, doing so against his wishes and better judgment because of blackmail. He is out here now to explain himself: "It's very simple, but it's very complicated". Right, thanks for clearing that up. Taker says it would have felt great to have broken Bearer's neck last week, but it wouldn't have helped his situation. I disagree. Killing the person blackmailing you surely removes the threat of blackmail does it not? "I know full well that nobody will understand why" says Taker of his reluctant reunion with Bearer. But how could we not when you explain it with such clarity!? Taker apologises to his creatures of the night, but says he has no choice and he is currently living in Hell. Bearer comes out and chastises Undertaker for going behind his back and doing this interview, telling him he does what he is told no matter what. Bearer talks down to Taker like no one ever has, and says he is going to be the ruler of the world. Poor choice of words, because Sid takes exception to his catchphrase being pilfered and makes his way out to a HUGE pop. Why did they ever cut this guy loose? Ok, he shouldn't have been on top in 1997 given the roster they had full of guys like Austin, Hart, Michaels and Taker who were better suited, but he could have offered something. I guess with someone like Sid, you either have them on top or not at all, because of the sheer intensity of the character. Sid bollocks Bearer for the catchphrase theft and then demands his rematch from *WrestleMania*. Taker tells Sid not to mistake the situation for weakness on his part, and accepts the chance to drop Sid on his head again. This cues yet another arrival, with Faarooq turning up on the stage and dismissing everything going on because he is going to be the first black WWF Champion after Sunday's *King of the Ring* pay-per-view. Crikey, what a hectic, but entertaining, opening!

Ahmed Johnson cuts a promo next to a bunch of barrels,

aimed at Faarooq. This may not be verbatim, but he appeared to be telling him to cancel his plans for the evening and demanding a date with him. Hmm. Like I said, that might not be entirely accurate.

Ahmed Johnson vs. Faarooq
These guys have now been embroiled in a bitter feud for nearly a year, and thus Ahmed is pumped up, shiny and volatile for this, and he starts strong. He leathers Faarooq with a belt behind the referee's back and takes him down with a wild scissor kick. JR tries to bring his usual sporting references, discussing Ron Simmons' football background, which Vince McMahon ignores completely. As usual we have a brawl, with the Nation coming out to surround the ring, bringing out the Undertaker, who fends them off. In the ensuing melee Taker accidentally whips Faarooq into Ahmed, and Faarooq scores the pinfall. Ahmed is less than thrilled with Taker's involvement and gets in his face, which results in a chokeslam. Man, I can't explain it because I know it would be rotten, but I would love to see that match. It was actually supposed to happen too, and was scheduled for *Canadian Stampede* in July, but Ahmed managed to once again get himself injured and missed out on another title opportunity. He wouldn't get another.
Final Rating: *

Promo Time: The Hart Foundation vs. Steve Austin vs. Shawn Michaels
Vince conducts the interview with the Harts in the ring, while Shawn Michaels and Steve Austin watch from the Titantron. Vince wants to know if Bret will be competing at *King of the Ring* on Sunday, but Bret cries off because of Steve Austin and other American wrestlers pounding away at his leg while he has been recovering. Austin beams a smile, but Bret's proposed KotR opponent Shawn Michaels is pissed off. Shawn dismisses Bret's excuses and turns his attentions to Austin, his tag team partner and title co-holder no less. Michaels accuses Austin of not getting the job done when he left him getting beaten up by the Harts last week while Austin targeted Bret, and Austin gets annoyed with him. They argue back-and-forth before Shawn storms to Austin's locker room and they exchange barbs some more. They decide to get the job done in their match later tonight first, and then kick seven bells out of each other. Back in the ring, the Hart Foundation are amused. The group have a private confab and Brian Pillman offers to give up his scheduled match with Austin at *King of the Ring* so Shawn Michaels can step in and the two can iron out their differences. Naturally, Austin is never going to back down from a challenge because he is the wrestling equivalent of Barney Stinson, and Michaels is all about the bold and bluster, so what the Harts have smartly done is take the two egos of their biggest rivals and play them against each other. It's incredibly brilliant characterisation booking, and gets over the cerebral nature of the group. They are not just street thugs like the rest of the slugs who turn up in the Gang Warz, they are the thinking man's stable.

WWF Intercontinental Championship
Owen Hart (c) vs. Bob Holly
Bob Holly getting an IC Title shot in 1997? Ooookay. You could be forgiven for forgetting that Bob was even around this year, so little did he fit into the newfound Attitude Era, still peddling a gimmick that was lame and past its sell by date years ago. It would be another couple of years before he finally "found" himself as Hardcore Holly, and it is amazing he retained a job as long as he did, when fellow undercard guys like Aldo Montoya, Freddie Joe Floyd, Duke Droese and countless other relics from a simpler time were cut loose. The match actually comes by virtue of a shock win for Holly a few weeks ago over Owen in a non-title match in his hometown, and going back even further he scored a win over Hart in a six-man tag in 1995. Jim Ross gets his facts muddled not for the first time this year, claiming Holly had a "cup of coffee" with the IC title in the past, implying he briefly held the belt. He didn't. While it is true that he defeating then reigning IC Champion Jeff Jarrett on an episode of *Action Zone* from May 1995, the pin was declared illegal due to Jarrett's feet being on the ropes, and the belt was vacated. Holly was never recognised as the title holder. So close, JR, but no cigar. This could actually be a really good match if given time, but they only get a couple of minutes to showcase what they can do. Owen is among the best at sub 5-minute matches, but while this is perfectly fine, it is not up there with his belting encounters against 1-2-3 Kid from 1994. The pace they cut here is pretty impressive and never slows up, but nor should it in 4-minutes given their conditioning. Hart blocks a rana attempt from Holly into the Sharpshooter, and that is the end for our Bob. Good TV match, plenty happening, but not long enough to be memorable.
Final Rating: **½

Backstage, Shawn Michaels accepts the match against Steve Austin at *King of the Ring*, but makes it clear that he is not doing it as a favour to Pillman. In hindsight I am delighted that the Pillman-Austin match was nixed, even though it was a bout many wanted to see. The Michaels-Austin bout ended up being a forgotten classic, whereas the Austin-Pillman match coming up on *Raw* is average at best.

We get a recap of last week's tremendous sit down talk with Mick Foley, as he adds flesh to the bones of the Mankind character as part of a remarkable series of interviews. There will be more coming up later, and frankly I cannot wait. I think they are some of the finest work in Foley's storied career.

Hunter Hearst Helmsley vs. Goldust
AGAIN! "Shattered Dreams Productions... YEAH!!!" bellows Vince as Goldust charges to the ring. Too much coffee. Things start fast and furious and the crowd is into it, making it far better already than any of their PPV matches. Vince matches JR on the title facts errors, discussing an upcoming European Title match and saying it is the first time the belt has ever been defended on *Raw*. No. Davey won the title on *Raw*, which counts in my book, but even if it doesn't, he defended it against Owen Hart a few weeks later in the match that ended up with the formation of the Hart Foundation. If he is not paying attention to the product, how can he expect anyone else to? This match goes downhill when Hunter goes on offence, as ever, and Chyna chokes Goldust out when she gets the chance. Marlena has seen enough and tries to pull Chyna off, and in the melee Hunter accidentally knees Chyna and gets caught with a roll up by Goldust, which is met by a massive pop. Much better than their usual matches thanks to the brevity and the hot crowd.
Final Rating: **

WWF Tag Team Championship
Steve Austin & Shawn Michaels (c) vs. Legion of Doom
This is quite the marquee match to be taking place on *Raw*, and is another really strong outing from the odd-couple duo. Given how hot both men are in 1997, that probably shouldn't be a surprise. The Legion of Doom don't get enough credit for their role in this year either, and I think they added a lot to a previously struggling tag division, and they proved a number of times that they could still very much go when properly motivated. Fast forward a year and the same cannot be said,

but here they more than match the immensely talented champions. There are shenanigans of course, because God forbid we get too many clean finishes on Raw in 1997, as Animal accidentally wipes out the referee and thus there is no-one to count after Austin waffles Hawk with the title belt. Cue the Hart Foundation, who Michaels wants to fight, but is prevented from doing so by another referee. Austin comes out to drag Michaels away and make him focus, because he realises that distraction tactics are exactly what the Foundation are trying to employ. They have been booked brilliantly tonight. Austin and Michaels end up getting counted out and a helpful graphic on-screen informs us that LOD have won the match but not the belts. Well, duh. As is customary for them, Michaels and Austin brawl after the decision.
Final Rating: ***

Promo Time: Mankind
This is another instalment from the aforementioned interviews with Jim Ross, and the subject matter today is Cactus Jack. You know what, these things are so good, that I feel the need to transcribe the entire thing. For your reading pleasure:

Jim Ross: "The evolution of Mankind... What fuels the insanity? So far we've explored the tormented youth of Mick Foley, and we've seen his bizarre underground home video. Tonight we'll explore the formative years of his wrestling career, one that began with a brief stint in the WWF as the unheralded Jack Foley in 1986. But despite performing before several organisations, success wasn't achieved until Mick Foley unveiled his dark alter ego: the sadistic Cactus Jack."

Mankind: "What made Cactus Jack different was he just wanted it a little bit more. He was willing to go the extra length. He was willing to sleep in a filthy car. In order to achieve his dream, he was willing to forego bonds and romantic relationships to be the best. He was somebody in an era of bodybuilder physiques, who carved out his own niche and said "I'm going to make it on my own style." He said "no one else is going to tell me what to do. I'm not going to dye my hair. I'm going to be exactly who I am, and I'm going to do it my way!""

Jim Ross: "As the legend of Cactus Jack grew, so too did his affinity for pain. Concerned independent promoters soon asked him to tame his increasingly brutal behaviour, but Mick Foley always did things his way. Instead of compromise, he left the United States to seek satisfaction in a bizarre, sadistic wrestling subculture in Japan."

Mankind: "And I'd heard rumour about these horrible matches that took place, and I didn't care! As far as I was concerned, this was my destiny. And I walked out the first time I saw barbed-wire strung up in place of ring ropes, and I said: "I'M FINALLY HOME! Mrs. Foley's little boy is FINALLY HOME!" And Jimmy, I kid you not when I say it didn't matter the match. I wrestled on beds of nails, I wrestled on ten thousand thumbtacks, I wrestled on C-4 explosives. And the funny thing was it didn't matter how mutilated I was... physically, I healed myself spiritually. Because for the first time I was respected. I'll go so far as say I was loved. People lined up and chanted my name: "Cactus Jack! Cactus Jack!" They sure as hell didn't line up, as they do here, to spit on me! To pee in a paper cup and pour it on me! I had my dignity, and I'm not sure I got it anymore!"

Jim Ross: "Obviously these matches in Japan were bizarre, they were dangerous, career threatening. If I'm not mistaken you, I see you've been rubbing your arm there a lot while we've been talking, very significant scars there. Those occurred in one of those matches in Japan?"

Mankind: ""He shall strip his sleeves and show his scars and say these wounds I had at St. Crispin's Day. And the good story shall be told from, father to his son, for we shall be remembered. We few, we happy few, we brothers. For he who sheds his blood with me today, shall be my brother." It's kind of touching, isn't it?"

Jim Ross: "Well, it's a little Shakespeare. You're very well read, aren't you?"

Mankind: "You see Jimmy, it shows me that I'm not alone. There's nothing freaky about being proud. When I look in the mirror, you know what I see?"

Jim Ross: "I'd be afraid to guess. I don't really know."

Mankind: "I see a life fulfilled! I see a road map of everywhere I've been. I just have to look and say (points to scars): Tokyo, Japan, Munich, Germany, Louisville, Kentucky... and everywhere in between."

Jim Ross: "The nomadic reign of Cactus Jack lasted nearly eleven years, but his fondest memory occurred aboard a commercial airline, where his battle-ravaged body made an indelible impression on a fellow passenger."

Mankind: "I'm a "coach class" person, but they took one look at my wounded face, my scarred, battered arm, my stitched head, my stitched hand, my stitched ear, and they bumped me up. The woman sitting next to me didn't quite understand that. She spent double her money, and ended up moving back to coach, to get away from me. She felt that much of me, that she couldn't stand to be around me! Not a day goes by when I don't think of her face, drifting to the back, and I stretched out in her seat... and I had the ride of my life! I was a deathmatch champion, and I had the ability to make people sick!"

King of the Ring Quarter Final
Savio Vega vs. Mankind
From that tremendous interview, we go to a match against Savio Vega. Talk about peaks and valleys. The crowd pops Mankind, which stuns Vince and JR, but the fans can appreciate someone who is good at what they do, and this was the start of a rollercoaster ride to the top for Foley. He takes his usual unnecessary bumps on the outside, which is just a waste against a scrub like Savio. Vega throws Mankind around for a minute or two, connecting with various kicks but missing a charge in the corner and eating a back suplex. Foley busts out the Cactus Clothesline over the top as Jerry Lawler rags on him, so he grabs the King and threatens to belt him one. Back in the ring, Crush makes a mess of his interference and "accidentally" hits Savio (in the most blatantly obviously way possible, he practically moved Mankind out of the way) and Mankind wins and advances to the semis to face Jerry Lawler at the PPV. Crush and Savio argue after the match and it turns into fisticuffs.
Final Rating: *

In a worthwhile segment, Sable dances and grinds around an inflatable King of the Ring chair. What a twat she looks doing that.

The Undertaker vs. Sycho Sid
Even though this is Sid's rematch from the woeful main event

at *WrestleMania 13,* it is suddenly a non title match. I guess Sid got his promo wrong earlier. With a significantly reduced running time and the lack of pressure, it is a much better match than at the "granddaddy of them all". Instead of being filled with rest holds, there are actual moves, and indeed move*ment*, and even a clean finish to boot as Taker polishes off the former champion with the Tombstone, just like at *WrestleMania*. The Nation of Domination hit the ring afterwards for yet *another* post match brawl. Gang overkill in the WWF means the majority of matches on *Raw* won't have clean finishes from now on, and if they do they are followed by things like this. WCW is just as bad, if not worse, and you are lucky to ever get a main event on *Nitro* that has a conclusion. There is no rhyme or reason to the Nation attacking Sid, he just happens to be in the wrong place at the wrong time, which I actually like because it makes sense. At one point Sid hits a chokeslam on Crush in the chaos. Man, just imagine a singles match between *those* two guys...
Final Rating: *½

THE RAW RECAP:

Most Entertaining: Mankind. Some good work all around from a lot of others, Shawn Michaels and Steve Austin especially, but Mankind steals the show with his interview.

Least Entertaining: Sable. None of the real performers deserve it tonight, as everyone was "on". Sable just danced around a chair looking all the world like a lost stripper.

Quote of the Night: "I'll kick your little crippled, raspy, horse-voiced ass on Monday night" - Steve Austin; not a PC guy.

Match of the Night: Shawn Michaels & Steve Austin vs. The Legion of Doom. The Owen-Holly match was decent too, but this was a few shades better.

Verdict: Excellent. From the brilliant character work from the Harts to the legendary Foley interviews, as well as a *** match thrown in there for good measure, this is one of the best shows of the year. When even Hunter Hearst Helmsley and Bob Holly are making worthwhile contributions in an era where they usually made none, you know you are on to a winner.
Rating: 77

06.08.97 - King of the Ring 1997
(Arnold Furious)
[Providence Civic Center, Providence, Rhode Island]

- KotR Semi Final: Hunter Hearst Helmsley def. Ahmed Johnson (*½)
- KotR Semi Final: Mankind def. Jerry Lawler (*)
- Goldust def. Crush (¼*)
- Owen Hart, The British Bulldog & Jim Neidhart def. Sycho Sid & the Legion of Doom (*)
- KotR Final: Hunter Hearst Helmsley def. Mankind (**)
- Shawn Michaels vs. Steve Austin went to a double disqualification (****½)
- The Undertaker def. Faarooq (*¼)

Rating: 49

06.09.97 by James Dixon

Venue: Hartford, CT
Taped: 06.09.97

Raw Rating: 2.2
Nitro Rating: 3.4

This is a very famous episode of *Raw*, though the notoriety of the show relates to something that happened outside of the ring rather than in it, with the venue being the scene of the legitimate shoot between Bret Hart and Shawn Michaels backstage, in a catfight that saw Michaels lose a chunk of his hair. The story goes that the two had an altercation in a bathroom while Jerry Lawler was sat minding his own business taking a dump. It started with Shawn going off on a tirade against Bret after Hart had said hello to him, with Shawn berating him for not having talked to him in a month. Bret lost his cool and shoved Shawn, asking him "Have you got something to say to me!?" Michaels threw a punch, but Bret countered with one of his own and they had a pull-apart, with Lawler and Pat Patterson trying to separate them as Davey Boy Smith and Crush looked on, refusing to help the disliked Heartbreak Kid. Things escalated to the point that Hart ripped a clump of hair from Michaels head in the struggle, and Shawn took the chunk of hair and slammed it down on Vince's desk before demanding his contract release so he could go and play with his buddies in Atlanta. Vince, obviously realising he couldn't afford to lose Shawn, balked at this. Both guys were sent home from the show for their "very unprofessional conduct" (Vince) and their relationship remained frosty at best for the remaining five months of Bret's WWF career. It will be interesting to see how it affects the broadcast...

The Legion of Doom & Ahmed Johnson vs. Faarooq, Crush & Savio Vega
We open with a rematch from *WrestleMania*, though without the street fight rules. Faarooq failed in his quest to become WWF Champion last night at *King of the Ring '97*, and thus begins his descent back into the midcard. There is dissent within the Nation, and they struggle for unity during their entrance. The crowd are rowdy for this and are into the LOD in a big way. Hawk and Savio start out, with the former selling very little as ever, before Crush pairs up with Animal. There is history here, with Crush having had countless matches against the LOD in 1990-91 as part of Demolition. That isn't mentioned here, of course. Crush takes a messy spill to the outside and then decides to do an hilarious judo roll back to his corner to tag in Faarooq. Watching him do stuff like that is like watching a fat guy doing ballet. Ahmed comes in with a reluctant Faarooq and the crowd goes crazy at the prospect, making Ahmed's imminent heel turn in a few weeks all the more foolish/brilliant depending on your perspective. Do you go with the flow or pull the trigger when the impact will be the greatest? The babyfaces dominate, as they should given the issues within the Nation, with Crush and Savio refusing to tag Faarooq when he is in peril. Faarooq catches a breather on the outside and argues with his teammates, and LOD send them all into each other to cause further friction. Ahmed drills Faarooq with the Pearl River Plunge as the rest of the NOD walk off, giving the babyfaces a decisive and popular win. This was just a mauling, but it was an exciting one.
Final Rating: **¼

Promo Time: Hunter Hearst Helmsley
Oh great, they are letting him talk. Vince recaps Hunter's battering of Mankind in their underwhelming match last night, and Hunter responds by claiming he was making up for last year's "politics", and that he should have been the *King of the Ring* last year. What he is referring to of course is the fact that he was originally scheduled to win the 1996 tournament, not Steve Austin, but because of his participation in the "fuck you"

to the business Curtain Call, he was scapegoated and buried. It was the best thing that could have ever happened to the WWF, given how things turned out with Austin. Of course this was hardly common knowledge amongst casual fans at the time, so his comments go right above the heads of pretty much everyone in the crowd. Mankind turns up on the Titantron and says he wants a rematch, but Hunter leaves the decision to Chyna. Oh God, now they are letting her speak! She tells Mankind to come down here and kiss her ass, which is the wrong thing to say because Mankind is "a good kisser". He comes out, but Hunter cuts him off with a crown shot, but it doesn't keep the resilient Foley down for long. This is the start of a summer-long feud between the two which transformed Hunter from a laborious bore into a viable performer who actually offered something to the company and became, get this, entertaining. This was probably Hunter's best interview up to this point, but that isn't actually saying much.

WWF European Championship
The British Bulldog (c) vs. Goldust
They are hyping this pretty well, and show a highlight package of Davey winning the title prior to the bout, but the angle they are pushing of this being the first defence of the belt on *Raw* is wrong, as I outlined last week. Bulldog has been one of the MVPs of *Raw* so far this year, but stylistically Goldust is not really the best opponent for him. Thus the opening exchanges are decent enough, but never anything more. The pace is fairly swift at first, and then all of a sudden it is over following a Goldust DDT... Only it isn't, because Bulldog had his foot on the ropes and the match has to continue. What follows is a chinlock, then lots and lots of chinlock and a horrible double count out finish. The bout is all about the post-match angle, with Davey ramming Goldust into the steps and getting slapped by Marlena for his troubles. All that does is piss him off, and he brings a chair into play and threatens to whack Goldust with it, whether Marlena is in the way or not. Ken Shamrock comes out to be the moral police, and takes Davey out with a belly-to-back suplex, and Bulldog bails. You know, something struck me while watching this regarding Marlena and the cigar that she smokes at ringside. Now, granted she very rarely actually takes a drag, but I wonder if that character nuance was suggested by her or creative. If it was her, does she buy the cigars each time? Where does she get such massive ones from? If it was creative, then doesn't forcing your employee to smoke violate all manner of employer codes? Things like this keep me up at night.
Final Rating: *½

Backstage, super-shill Michael 'Dok Hendrix' Hayes is outside of the Nation of Domination's locker room, and all hell is breaking loose. Faarooq storms out and says he is going to the ring, so Dok sneaks in and grabs a word with Savio and Crush. Savio rants at him in Spanish and Crush bollocks him for coming in uninvited, then says the Nation are fine. Denial.

Promo Time: Faarooq
Faarooq says the Nation was set up to watch his back and they were supposed to die for him if necessary, but they failed. He rags on Savio and Crush for floundering prior to joining the Nation, so he fires them both. He then loses his temper and rashly decides to fire all of the hangers on (which in reality was surely a WWF cost-cutting measure), and then Clarence Mason too. The only person retained is D'Lo Brown. Smart choice; he is a better worker than all of them. Faarooq wants Ahmed Johnson and the Undertaker, the two people he hates the most, to be the first two victims of the new Nation next week. A fun, fairly memorable segment. Cutting loose the deadwood was the best thing Faarooq could have done for the group, though that it spawned the Gang Warz was an unfortunate aside.

Paul Heyman and Tommy Dreamer appear in the crowd, with Rob Van Dam scheduled for action later on.

Doug Furnas & Phil LaFon vs. The Headbangers
Furnas and LaFon come out sans music, pyro, robes, or indeed anything other than robotic movement. It is one of those bizarre anti-booking decisions from the WWF, trying to make them get over by being boring. How will that ever work? When has it EVER worked? It is counterproductive and dumb. JR does at least put Furnas and LaFon over as wrestling machines, but this charisma black hole gimmick is killing them. It is not the first time this year that I have wrote that about a WWF performer, with countless guys with genuine talent struggling to get over because of the way they are utilised. The match plays out in front of a silent crowd, which isn't a surprise given the gimmick but is a shame because Furnas and LaFon bust out some cracking moves. The Headbangers offer nothing and are vastly inferior, but they are a dumb gimmick so in the world of the WWF, they get to go over. Why do the Headbangers never lose!?
Final Rating: *½

Backstage, a hoarse Jerry Lawler is with 'Mr. Monday Night' Rob Van Dam, who doesn't speak. Lawler has a few choice words for Heyman, but nothing he hasn't said plenty of times before and better.

Promo Time: Steve Austin
Austin refuses to apologise for flushing Brian Pillman's head down the lav last night at *King of the Ring*, saying the only thing he is sorry for is that there wasn't any shit in the toilet at the time. Austin tells Pillman that he is going to tear through him tonight, and will beat him with the Stunner when he sees fit. Vince turns the conversation towards Bret Hart, and Austin volunteers his place on Team USA for the epic 5-vs-5 match at *Canadian Stampede*. Austin would be happy enough to do it by himself, but says Gorilla Monsoon won't authorise it, just like how he was forced to team with Shawn Michaels. Austin says he will do more than just beat up the five guys in the Hart Foundation, but rather everyone in the Hart family. Not the most memorable Austin promo, and that is not a criticism given how many great ones he has, but it hit the marks and made the required points.

Rob Van Dam vs. Flash Funk
This fantastic cross-promotional union continues, with ECW's Rob Van Dam becoming something of a regular feature on *Raw*. It was a unique situation for the WWF, because despite Rob being an ECW contracted guy, they put him over on a regular basis. Not against anyone of particular note, sure, but as the subsequent WCW/ECW bodged invasion proved in 2001, the WWF were reluctant to let anyone from the outside go over their own established talent. Video Control shows us footage of Jerry Lawler turning up in ECW this past week, and the suffering King joins the commentary team, though his throat is so bad he can barely speak. In a pleasing piece of kayfabe continuity, Lawler blames Mankind's Mandible Claw last night. Van Dam's opponent here is of course ECW alumni, though the former Scorpio is almost unrecognisable under this silly gimmick. Flash is on a road to nowhere in the WWF whereas RVD is the hottest rising star in the industry, despite not being a WWF guy, and he dominates proceedings. It doesn't seem all that strange to see RVD wrestle on *Raw* when watched years

later, given he ended up working with the company for the better part of a decade, but this was a remarkable occurrence at the time. RVD pops the crowd with his "unorthodox" style, including his impressive flip plancha, but Flash fires back and nearly finishes with his trademark flying. They go back-and-forth with RVD landing kicks and a powerbomb into a floatover bridge pin, but Flash comes back with a Ghetto Blaster only to get caught coming into the corner and an RVD slam is followed with a split leg moonsault for the win. Fun little TV match, made all the more entertaining due to its uniqueness. After the match, Paul Heyman and Tommy Dreamer jump the barricade and brawl with Van Dam and Lawler, as ECW angles and storylines continue to feature and get promoted on WWF broadcasts. Many questioned why at the time, but when it later transpired that Paul Heyman was on the WWF payroll, suddenly it made perfect sense.

Final Rating: **½

Sycho Sid vs. Owen Hart
This is the final match on *Raw* for Sid for some 15-years, when he was brought back as part of the build-up to the *Raw 2000* show, smashing through the hapless Heath Slater while looking not much different to how he did here. Given that, the outcome in this is a surprise, with Sid getting the clean win following a chokeslam. Prior to that Owen bosses much of it, smartly targeting the leg as he had done in previous outings between the two, at one point loudly exclaiming: "I'll break his knee off, I'll snap it off." With the benefit of hindsight, that comment brings up the queasy memories of Sid's horrific leg break in WCW in 2001, which remains probably the worst injury I have ever seen in a match. Well, that or Vader's eye getting smashed up and coming out of the socket in the semi-shoot match he had with Stan Hansen on an AJPW/NJPW super-show in Japan. Ken Shamrock is on commentary for this, for whatever reason, and has various issues with Owen cheating and using the post as a weapon in his leg assault, and with Jim Neidhart interfering. The Anvil gets involved one time too many for Shamrock's liking, so he belts him with a suplex on the outside, leading to Sid's victory. Poor Owen.

Final Rating: **

Another Sable t-shirt spot follows, but this one gets a very subtle allusion to a bigger picture situation, as Marc Mero, up until then a clean cut and popular babyface, wanders out and tells her that's enough, and leads her backstage...

Promo Time: Mankind
To the final instalment of this celebrated interview series, and once again it is so good that I am going to transcribe the lot:

Jim Ross: *(Voice Over)* "Mick Foley. Cactus Jack. Mankind. Three bizarre, yet distinct personalities. Each one scarred by trauma and suffering. Each one still haunted by the pain." (To Mankind): "Why didn't Cactus Jack ever come to the WWF?"

Mankind: "Because he wasn't welcome. I would have set the WWF on its ear! So when you look at Mankind, you're saying to somebody, every time I put on the Mandible Claw, in my mind, that's Vince McMahon, and I'm saying: "Why didn't you take me when I was good?! Why didn't you take me when I was young?!" That's where the Mandible Claw comes from: it's power, tempered with mercy, just like me."

Jim Ross: "Earlier you mentioned Shawn Michaels, and how you'd like to see Shawn Michaels end his career handing out change in an arcade. Why the venom?"

Mankind: "Shawn Michaels... Remember at one point they were saying: "Shawn Michaels: a boy and his dream"? I wonder, Jimmy, why didn't they ever say: "Mick Foley: a boy and his dream?" We had the same dream, so why does he look like he does, and why do I look like this? Do you think that's unfair to want me to wish him a lifetime of misery? I don't think that's unfair at all. I think it's a perfectly logical thing to ask. And I'm not ashamed. I wish him and a lot of the WWF Superstars nothing but personal trauma and tragedy in their personal and professional lives. Does that make me a bad person? I want the suffering to be on the other side, and I'd like to cause it, because that to me is a nice day!"

Jim Ross: "Have you ever been treated or have you ever been diagnosed with a multiple personality disorder?"

Mankind: "You know, I thought we talked about this when I said I don't believe in doctors. I believe in the body's ability to heal itself. If there's something wrong with my mind, I'd think I'd be the first one to know."

Jim Ross: "Don't you think that it's about time in your life where you looked squarely in the mirror and accepted the personal responsibility for who you are? Don't you believe that you, yourself, have caused and brought on all these problems?"

Mankind: "I think it's time for you to maybe start doing your damn job. I think it's time for you to end this facade of journalistic integrity. You know what you tell the people week in and week out? You say: "Look at Mankind; I don't even know if he feels pain, or maybe he likes pain!" You see, you're a powerful man, Jimmy. You have got the ability to reach a lot of people, to spread the truth, and you neglect to do it. Let me ask you a couple of questions: what is it about pain that I love? You see, I feel pain just like every other person... (hits himself in the head). YOU SEE THAT!? IT HURTS! Is it when I can't get up when my little boy wants to play ball, and I can't do it? Is that where the fun starts? Is it where a doctor injects a twelve inch needle into the discs of my spine so that I can wrestle one more day? Whoopee! Let the party begin! I can't believe you sit here and ask me those questions; do I bring it on to myself? I haven't done a DAMN THING TO YOU! ALL YOU'VE DONE TO PEOPLE IS MISLEAD THEM, AND LET THEM THINK THAT I'M HAVING THE TIME OF MY GODDAMN LIFE, WHEN I'M IN PAIN! DON'T YOU LOOK AT ME WITH THAT SMUG LOOK! YOU MAKE ME SICK... A MAN OF INTEGRITY? I OUGHT TO SMACK YOU ... "

Foley plays all of this with such incredible conviction, that you do believe the man in the backyard videos and stories told, is the same man here who has just let the pressures of the world and desire to succeed morph him into this maniacal beast. Mankind completely loses his cool at JR's lack of "journalistic integrity" and disables him with the Mandible Claw. JR's sell of the hold is superb and the production team's reaction to this "shoot" is tremendous (remember, this is from a time when things like this didn't used to happen to non-wrestlers anywhere near as often, though as soon as Vince Russo saw it work once here, it happened every week), but the best part is Mankind letting go and instantly trying to sooth Ross then calling for help as he assesses what he has done and backs away. These interviews are one of the finest things that the WWF did in the entire Attitude Era and a definite highlight of Mick Foley's superb career. Absolutely must-see viewing.

Rockabilly vs. Bart Gunn
The Smoking Gunns Explode! Of course, they never had a proper blow-off following their split thanks to the silly neck injury angle with Billy that went no-where. That happened in a sub 3-minute match which was well on the way to sucking, so my anticipation is hardly at a high for this. Billy clotheslines Bart to the outside early on and goes to work on the outside, with Bart's attempted comebacks cut off by the superior Billy. Wow, calling Rockabilly superior to *anything* sure feels dirty. Bart does get an uninspiring comeback, which might as well be taking place inside of an empty auditorium. The Attitude fans have no interest in the anachronistic Bart. Billy ends things out of nowhere with the Shake, Rattle and Roll, with apathy the order of the day.
Final Rating: ½*

Brian Pillman vs. Steve Austin
The WWF adds yet another feather to its hypocritical hat by reneging on the promised main event just seconds before it is due to start, with the Hart Foundation jumping Austin in the aisle. How can they can have the gall to hype something all night then not deliver? You know, like WCW did, and just like they complained about WCW doing in numerous tirades. They are such colossal hypocrites sometimes that it is almost comical. Mankind gets involved in the melee and all of a sudden, the match is changed...

Brian Pillman vs. Mankind
Mankind is a decent replacement because he has started to get over as a babyface already thanks to those interviews. Vince is unable to hide his kayfabed disappointment at the scheduled Austin battle not occurring, but Mankind tries to change his mind by taking his usual over-the-top bumps, including a nasty back suplex on the ramp. Geez Mick, come on, it's only *Raw*! This is a mess, a scrappy bitty brawl with little going for it. Pillman's main offensive moves are forcing Mankind to eat his own hair and trying to rip off his mask. At one point Pillman delivers a headbutt, and then sells it himself. It makes sense in a way, but it does look rather silly. Vince has given up on this and calls it shit in his own words, condescendingly offering: "They are having a go here". Mankind locks on the Mandible Claw, but predictably that leads to the Hart Foundation coming in to deliver a shoeing. Steve Austin has revenge on his mind and appears to be recovered from his earlier beating, and he cleans the Harts' clocks, alongside Ken Shamrock, who is again out here because it is the right thing to do. Who does he think he is, Batman? Actually, wait a minute... he *is* Batman. He certainly fits the bill... After the Harts are successfully dispatched, Austin gives Shamrock a Stunner too, just because he is Steve Austin and he can. This match was horrid.
Final Rating: ¼*

THE RAW RECAP.

Most Entertaining: Mankind. It couldn't be anyone else. Forget the crappy main event, this for the interview. This particular instalment was probably my all-time favourite, with the payoff at the end of Mankind putting the Mandible Claw on JR a suitably fitting and apt one. It got over the character and his nuances, because Ross pushed him too far. Rather than just berating Ross because of the myriad cruel reasons for which he came in for abuse over the years, this was done to advance the development of a persona, and it was delivered perfectly.

Least Entertaining: The Headbangers. For going over the vastly superior Furnas & LaFon. How horrid.

Quote of the Night: Despite a stellar show on the mic from Hunter for the first time in his WWF run, this cannot go to anyone except Mankind. Take your pick from the transcription which part you prefer. It could be literally any of it.

Match of the Night: The Legion of Doom & Ahmed Johnson vs. The Nation of Domination. I might have rated the RVD-Funk match higher, but this takes the award due to surpassing my expectations and being important to a fun storyline/promo later on too. In short, it meant more than the throwaway spotty fun of the Van Dam encounter.

Verdict: This was another top show, as *Raw* really starts to get into its stride and become must-see. The unpredictable nature of things might get tiresome as the years wear on (and ironically enough right back around to mind-meltingly predictable in the John Cena era), but here it was a thrill ride and the show never stopped long enough to get boring. Even the middling matches were kept brief, with a few decent television encounters in there and some superb mic work from the surprise performers Faarooq and Hunter, as well as the legendary Mankind series. No ***+ match to tip this over the edge, but this was still a fun-filled two hours of WWF television, and it flew by.
Rating: 72

06.16.97 by James Dixon

Venue: Lake Placid, NY
Taped: 06.16.97
Raw Rating: 2.4
Nitro Rating: 3.3

We start out with Vince and JR discussing the backstage fight between Bret Hart and Shawn Michaels in Hartford last week. Vince calls the conduct of both "unprofessional", but calls Bret the aggressor, which he was, and then brings up the injuries both suffered in the melee. Shawn losing a chunk of his flowing locks is never mentioned. Because Shawn is now "injured", and a co-holder of the tag titles, a tournament will take place to rectify the situation, with the winners facing Steve Austin and a partner of his choice to crown the champions.

Promo Time: Steve Austin
Stone Cold couldn't care less about the tag title situation because he was forced to team with Shawn Michaels in the first place. Mankind pops up on the 'tron and offers his services, but Austin is unreceptive to say the least: "I don't need no freak watching my back... You ain't got no ears!". Excellent. They have a comical argument about Mankind's ass (honestly) and the now babyface Mankind tells Austin to think on it. We change tact to Brian Pillman, with Vince recapping the footage from last week that resulted in the heavily pushed match not taking place. Austin brags about laying out Ken Shamrock with a Stunner last week, which of course brings the World's Most Dangerous Man to the ring. Shamrock tries to cut a promo, bless him, but it is dreadful. Just LOTS and LOTS of RANDOM shouting FOR NO particular REASON! Shamrock challenges Austin to a match tonight, which Austin accepts once he has dealt with Pillman. Plenty happening in the opening promo this week, but Shamrock rather dragged it down with his horrible delivery.

Video Control once again shows us the footage of Brian

Pillman getting a swirly from Steve Austin at *King of the Ring*. The match with Austin will take place tonight, with the Hart Foundation handcuffed to the ring. With that in mind, we cut to Pillman backstage:

"You know, you're really funny, McMahon; you're a real... laugh. Right when the Hart Foundation severs the shackles of oppression and censorship and lets the world know what we really think, you've got the audacity to handcuff my comrades like common thieves? Well, you made one mistake: you didn't put the cuffs on the convicted felon, the one with the rap sheet. So, Stone Cold's gonna pay. So Shamrock, you've got nothing to worry about. You can stay being the world's most dangerous referee and working on that three count, son, because Stone Cold is going down the toilet tonight."

Some of the delivery and facial expressions in this make me wonder if the late Heath Ledger was a Brian Pillman fan, and used him as an inspiration when playing Joker in *The Dark Knight*. Probably not, but the similarities between the two are vast. Watching in 2014, you can also see a lot of echoes between this and the tremendous Dean Ambrose, who was clearly a Brian Pillman and/or Heath Ledger fan.

Tag Team Championship Tournament First Round
The New Blackjacks vs. Owen Hart & The British Bulldog
Barry Windham from a decade ago would have meshed wonderfully with Owen Hart, but this podgy, fake-haired version is embarrassing to his rich legacy. His exchanges with Owen are still smooth enough, but quite frankly it is hard to take either of the Blackjacks' offence seriously with the big, gay pornstar 'taches they are sporting. Bradshaw gets a tag in following a cursory TV heat on big Baz, as Vince forgets the fabricated history of his own creation and decides that Bradshaw is related to Blackjack Lanza "somehow". Windham looks to have it won against Davey, but Owen intervenes with a spinning heel kick and Davey floats over into a double leg for the pin.
Final Rating: *

Video Control recaps the Nation of Domination break-up from last week, then we cut to the Undertaker and Paul Bearer backstage, because tonight Taker will be teaming with Ahmed Johnson against Faarooq and a new as yet unknown member of the faction. Taker tries to speak, but Bearer immediately cuts him off: "Hush, rigor mortis!". I liked that. Bearer says Ahmed will do what he wants him to do if he knows what's good for him.

Yet another backstage interview next, this time with Ken Shamrock. "And for that, he will pay for that" about sums up his interview skills. I lose track of what he is saying because I can hear the Godwinns' frigging awful theme music in the background. Oh lord.

Phineas Godwinn vs. Hunter Hearst Helmsley
Oh GOOD lord! Phineas acts like a total clown in front of Chyna, who responds as anyone should to Phineas; with complete and utter disdain. Chyna is so upset with the sight of the fat, useless hillbilly that she attacks a ring attendant. Godwinn sucks the life out of the building with an embarrassing mule kick, and Hunter decides that is quite enough of that nonsense, and takes over. For the first time on *Raw* this year, I am happy that Hunter is on the offensive. Chyna gets some shots in on the outside to once again demonstrate how useful she is in Helmsley's corner, but Phineas slugs away to mount a comeback and Hunter takes some Flair bumps for him. Chyna prevents the Slop Drop by distracting the dumb hick, and Phineas gives her a kiss, but Helmsley drops him with the Pedigree. At least this was short. The previously injured Henry Godwinn turns up to lambast Phineas for his lack of concentration, then bizarrely turns and points to Vince, and shouts to him that "This is all your fault, McMahon!". I'm not sure I quite get that. What is Vince's fault exactly? That Phineas kissed Chyna? Well, in the sense that he booked it sure, but he obviously doesn't mean that. In the sense that he made the useless Dennis Knight into a step above retard with his gimmick? Also true, but again it doesn't seem likely that he means that either. How peculiar.
Final Rating: ½*

LPW Score: Phineas Godwinn

Look: He is just a big out of shape guy, who happens to be fairly tall. The perfect size for a big dumb country boy scufflin' gimmick, but horrid by general standards. His gear is a shambles too (dungarees half buttoned over a sweatshirt) and his hair is horribly greasy. One of the worst looks in the business.
1/10

Personality: Put "devoid of" in front of that, and you got it. Phineas is a hillbilly gimmick, which means he has the personality of a brick. It later turned out that it wasn't just the gimmick engulfing the guy, because he sucked as Mideon too. He gets 2 rather than 1 because now and again he was capable of showing a tiny modicum of fire. And by "now and again", I mean about once a year.
2/10

Wrestling Skill: Gorilla Monsoon's famous wristwatch/wristlock quote pretty much sums it up. I have seen some unbelievably bad things from Phineas, from timing issues to positioning to making things look so blatant that it is embarrassing. Not the worst wrestler ever, but he is in the running for sure.
1/10

Overall: About as close to the bottom of the pile as you can get. Phineas for me is right down there with IRS, most of the Divas, John Cena, Uncle Elmer, Typhoon and all the other horrible workers who have populated the industry down the years. He never had a good match in his career, induced nothing but apathy and far outstayed his welcome. Abysmal.
4/30

To yet another backstage interview, this time with Faarooq. He promises two bigger, better, badder and blacker members of the Nation tonight, and that is all...

Sunny comes out to be the guest ring announcer for the next match, as the WWF continue to desperately try and keep her relevant. Paul Heyman is the guest commentator, which should be mighty interesting.

Inter-Promotional Match
Brian Christopher vs. Chris Candido
Well, what about this then? This is billed as "USWA vs. ECW", taking place on WWF *Raw*! What a time to be a wrestling fan this was. This is not the first time Candido has appeared on *Raw* of course, and hopefully I don't need to insult your intelligence by reminding you of his past life in the WWF as

Bodydonna Skip. This is another one of those happenings that seems so much less monumental now than it did at the time, what with WWE owning every video library going and happily throwing matches from other promotions onto its DVD releases. But prior to 1997, the WWF was an insular place and a world of wrestling outside of the company didn't exist, or at least that is what they would have you believe. For Vince to get into bed with other groups and actually let them use his television time to promote their product, while at the same time giving him the use of new talent and the chance to make *Raw* seem fresh, unpredictable and exciting, was unheard of. 1997 was a banner year in that regard, with the WWF joining forces with ECW, the USWA, AAA and Michinoku Pro, with varying degrees of success.

Lee Maughan: *Vince did actually show other promotions' tapes on his USA Network show before the Hogan boom, and the WWF even reported David Von Erich's death on air, despite him never working there. It was all a ploy, of course: Vince told all the regional promoters to send him their tapes and he'd show their stuff on his TV, because he was the only one who had national coverage thanks to getting the USA Network slot after it binned Joe Blanchard's group. So the devious little monster played a bunch of regional tapes on his show, while at the same time secretly preparing his national expansion. And who did he show? Why, everyone he planned on taking in the raids, of course. So while he didn't technically actually lie to anyone, he still got months of free footage to introduce all his future new talents to his audience before they arrived.*

The pace of this is brisk, and puts the efforts of Phineas Godwinn to shame. The exchanges are slick and they throw in some nice spots, such as a top rope legdrop from Candido and a super rana. Meanwhile, Paul Heyman loses his rag with Vince's persistent questioning and blurts out that Christopher is Jerry Lawler's son. This incenses Lawler, who turns up for an argument, and then throws Candido off the ropes for the DQ (because let's face it, neither guy was going over properly here due to the politics of it all). Rob Van Dam comes out to join the assault on Candido, before Tommy Dreamer makes the save with a chair. All of this, on WWF television! Incredible.
Final Rating: **

Backstage (again), Ahmed Johnson cuts a promo. Unfortunately, it is calm and intelligible, which is not what I want from one of his promos at all! Where are the livid denials of being gay when not even asked? Instead, Ahmed just says he hopes he and Undertaker can do things "the easy way" tonight.

Backstage for the fiftieth time, and Jim Neidhart gets a turn. Wow, they are throwing out the promo big hitters tonight. He cuts an interview straight out of the 80s, which says nothing.

Jim Neidhart vs. Goldust
This has "styles clash" written all over it. "The WWF is not going to censor the fans for expressing themselves" says Jim Ross regarding some of the signs in the crowd. Well, that's a laugh. Less so the WWF, but WWE is absolutely notorious for confiscating signs, often with no reasonable justification. As we saw last week, they are a gloriously hypocritical company. Things go wrong almost instantly as Neidhart just stands there off a Goldust crossbody and then overcompensates trying to make up for it, taking a ridiculous jumping bump from a little tap of a clothesline. It's not quite as impressively absurd as his bump over the top from an Andre the Giant headbutt at *WrestleMania 2*, but it is still a beauty. Jim Ross gets bored and throws in a chunk of Goldust back story, specifically as pertains to his relationship with father Dusty Rhodes. It is interesting stuff, certainly more so than the match. The British Bulldog apparently can't fight his urge to get involved and comes out to confront Marlena, carrying on the issues between Davey and Goldie last week, so Goldust belts him. A 2-on-1 briefly occurs, but Jim still can't get the job done. Goldust hits him, barely, with his uppercut thrust and Neidhart takes another huge jumping bump and then stays down from it! What the hell kind of finish is that!? This is *Raw,* not *Survivor Series.* To add insult to insult, Davey Boy's music plays when Goldust is announced as the winner. Shambolic all around.
Final Rating: ½*

Backstage (yes, again), Steve Austin says he has Brian Pillman where he wants him and that he wants to rock Ken Shamrock's world. Kinky.

Brian Pillman vs. Steve Austin
The stipulation for this is that the Hart Foundation are handcuffed to the ring on the outside, which was something originally pegged for the proposed Shawn Michaels-Bret Hart 10-minute match at *King of the Ring* (which never happened). The Harts surrounding the ring was a way of giving the WWF an "out" for Hart to go over. The stipulation when you think about it, is entirely baffling. I mean, why would they ever even agree to something like that. Was it so important to the faction that Pillman got to wrestle Austin that they complied? Naturally it leaves them all prone for random assaults from Austin when he gets the chance. Pillman gets his nose busted during a fracas on the outside and it bleeds all over, making a mess of his face. He doesn't seem overly concerned and chokes Austin with a camera cable, then works him over. It is all rather messy, with punch-kick brawling the order of the day. Vince and JR offer some interesting commentary, with Vince referencing the infamous gun angle from last year which he promises will "never be shown on USA again" while Ross mentions how these two "fell out of favour politically" in WCW. They brawl and brawl some more, but it is a major disappointment compared to what you would hope from a Hollywood Blondes collision. A highlight sees Austin wipe out the referee as the announcers lose it and question his motives. He doesn't have motives, he is Steve Austin! Somehow the Hart Foundation gain access to a key for the handcuffs, which is absurd. No-one came out and gave them it, meaning they must have had it anyway, which of course begs the question of why they didn't just use it earlier when Austin was pounding on them. A mass brawl follows, with Ken Shamrock and Goldust getting involved to assist Austin. Stone Cold doesn't want any help and goes to belt Shamrock again, like last week, but Shamrock is wise to it and suplexes Austin down, and then they break out into a brawl. The Legion of Doom come out to split them up as bedlam ensues, and there is your Hart Foundation opposition team for *Canadian Stampede*.
Final Rating: *½

BACKSTAGE (man, can't you just tell that Vince Russo has a hand on the pencil? After the success of the Bret Hart-Steve Austin backstage stuff a couple of months ago, now EVERYTHING is taking place behind the curtain), the Hart Foundation dismiss the newly formed quintet that they will face at *Canadian Stampede*. A bloody Brian Pillman loses his rag, saying the battle lines will be drawn in blood and they will take the American team straight to Hell. Vince seems uncomfortable with it all. Hey, you open Pandora's box and allow the product to evolve into something more risqué and violent, you deal with the consequences.

Bobby Fulton vs. Tommy Rogers
Because Sunny did ring announcing earlier, Sable simply has to do it too. Unfortunately, that means hearing her horrible shrill voice. This is billed as a special light heavyweight match by Vince, but more importantly it is the explosion of the Fantastics! Fulton and Rogers were a fairly notable team in the 80s, feuding with Jim Cornette's Midnight Express and having well-received matches across the territories. They have a rich history, and Jim Ross delights in telling it to the world, because he actually called most of it when it happened. The match is taking place on the recommendation of Jim Cornette, with both guys having worked for him previously under the Smoky Mountain Wrestling banner, and in fact Fulton used to promote Big Time Wrestling out of Ohio, which ended up essentially morphing into SMW. According to Fulton, the idea here is that the guys impress Vince so much that he starts a light heavyweight division, but that is nonsense because the division was already scheduled and the announcers discuss the forthcoming tournament. If any one match would have convinced Vince, it wouldn't have been this, it would have been the exceptional Michinoku Pro guest match between the Great Sasuke and Taka Michinoku at *Canadian Stampede*. Vince says that 215lbs is the weight limit for the fledgling division, but looking at the paunch on Fulton, there is no way he is under that. JR spends literally the whole match putting Fulton and Rogers over, with Vince even feigning interest, asking how JR thinks the Fantastics would have fared in the WWF. Vince saying "the Fantastics" is another one of those odd little things that it is strange to hear him say, even though there is no reason for it to be. The crowd shits all over this, chanting "boring" at the two "unknown" grapplers (to the WWF audience at least) before Rogers wins it. I really wanted to give this a chance and for it to be good, but both guys are in their late 30s at this stage and are well past their primes. What they deliver is like an 80s version of a light heavyweight match, and compared to the exceptional stuff going on in WCW, it sucks. What a shame. It's a good job the match didn't exist to sell the division to Vince, because if it did he would have balked at the idea.
Final Rating: ½*

Jim Cornette: The Light Heavyweight Title situation is this: they wanted to establish one, so I went about booking the best light heavyweights I knew outside the company that would come in for a little cash and one or two guaranteed appearances for a tournament which was going to be won by Taka Michinoku. But by the time it came about, Vince's interest had waned, the matches were given little time or build. The only reason I had Bobby wrestle Tommy was since they were the two best workers in the thing, I wanted them to have the best match to see if they could get jobs out of it. But with only four or five minutes to have a match and the WWF crowd or office not giving a shit, it was passable at best and they were gone. This, combined with the time in 1996 when the roster was so thin that I suggested bringing in great working outside talent for a little more cash than job guys to put stars over on TV, and got Tracy Smothers, Dirty White Boy, Bill Irwin, Alex Porteau, etc, only to see them treated like jobbers and given ridiculous gimmicks, soured me on ruining my reputation with guys by trying to get them jobs. So I quit doing it.

Tag Team Championship Tournament First Round
Rob Van Dam & Jerry Lawler vs. The Headbangers
Double exposure tonight for ECW. The crowd are strangely muted for this one too, but that's the Headbangers for you. RVD takes some meaty bumps for them and displays his usual flash and flying, rather showing up the guys in the last match. Lawler is an altogether different prospect, and couldn't be more different to Van Dam in style. Van Dam hits the Five Star Frogsplash, but Thrasher kicks out when Lawler comes in to cover him. There is no structure to speak of here, so when Mosh tags in the crowd continues its apathy towards the bout. It probably deserves a little better than that, because while it is not great, it doesn't suck. As things start getting chaotic, a worse wrestler than Phineas Godwinn shows up!: the Sandman. He blasts Lawler in the crown jewels with his Singapore cane and Jerry eats a Headbangers double team, as the unbeatable moshers progress. Like earlier, a brawl breaks out with Dreamer and RVD, with Paul Heyman having to restrain Sandman from getting further involved.
Final Rating: *½

"Yeah we ready. We was born ready!" says Blade. Sorry, Ahmed Johnson. Tensions are high between Johnson, Taker and Paul Bearer. Trouble is a brewing.

The Undertaker & Ahmed Johnson vs. Faarooq & Kama
"When I make a promise, I eat liver" says Faarooq, as he introduces long-time Undertaker nemesis Kama Mustafa as the new Nation of Domination member. At one point Charles Wright was pencilled in to reprise his Papa Shango role rather than continue on as the new militant variation of Kama, but the impending introduction of Kane put paid to that. Because the Nation have promised another new member, Vince and JR discuss who it could be, throwing out names of any black wrestlers they can think of such as Butch Reed, Abdullah the Butcher and even the Junkyard Dog. Ahmed doesn't even make it into the ring for this, but for good reason as you will read in a minute, and Faarooq and Kama just systematically dismantle the Undertaker. It is complete dominance, and Kama pins Taker cleanly in the middle of the ring following a spinning Rock Bottom, which is a result I certainly never would have predicted given how protected Taker usually is and the fact he is WWF Champion! He lost to friggin' Kama! That win has been some two years in the making for Kama, who could never get the job done against Taker when he was a supreme fighting machine. Post match, the Nation go to continue the beating on the Dead Man, but Ahmed stands over him and they bail up the ramp. Then in a shocking moment, albeit one met by a surprisingly muted response given how over he once was, Ahmed turns on Taker and hits him with the Pearl River Plunge, then joins the Nation on the ramp and gives the black power salute. But, you have been feuding with them for a year!!! Shame the turn lasted all of ten minutes before Ahmed was switched back to a vastly diminished response. Once the trust is gone, you can't get it back. This was supposed to lead to Ahmed-Taker at *Canadian Stampede,* but Ahmed got injured. Again. From there the Undertaker-Nation feud rather fizzled out, and Taker worked with Vader at the PPV instead. Logically, shouldn't he have faced Kama, given that he jobbed clean to him here?
Final Rating: *

THE RAW RECAP:

Most Entertaining: Vince McMahon. There were no particularly outstanding performers tonight, so the award goes to Vince McMahon for starting to think outside the box and expand his mindset when it comes to working with other promotions. Things like this made *Raw* unpredictable and exciting in 1997, two things wrestling fans generally crave the most.

Least Entertaining: Phineas Godwinn. Though, the Fantastics could well have taken this for their half-assed match.

Quote of the Night: "I guess nearly everything's my fault these days" - A perplexed Vince McMahon after Henry Godwinn randomly blamed him for Phineas losing to Triple H. Poor guy, he just needs a hug.

Match of the Night: Brian Christopher vs. Chris Candido. Purely because Austin-Pillman could and should have been much better. This was brief and had a dodgy finish, but it was contested at a brisk pace and featured some nice moves.

Verdict: Not so good this time out. There was plenty going on, but none of it was particularly memorable in the long run. There were far too many backstage segments and all the matches were super short and thus almost pointless. No Bret Hart and Shawn Michaels hurts this show, and it will be nice when they both return. Steve Austin can only do so much, and here carrying the physically demolished Brian Pillman to a quality match, was beyond him. Not a horrible episode, but not a good one.
Rating: 41

06.23.97 by James Dixon

Venue: Detroit, MI
Taped: 06.23.97
Raw Rating: 2.4
Nitro Rating: 3.2

The show opens with an "in memoriam" piece for Stan Stasiak, who died a few days earlier from heart failure aged 60. Back in 1997 the death of a former performer would be rightly treated as the sad occurrence that it is, rather than being swept under the carpet and ignored by a company paranoid about preserving its image, as seen in later years. Stan was not a great worker by any stretch, but he was big and strong, so was an excellent choice to dethrone popular WWWF Champion Pedro Morales, so the company could transition the belt back to Bruno Sammartino little over a week later. Back then the prospect of a babyface match between two guys as loved as they were was simply unheard of. It was probably for the best too, because given the vociferous support from the Italian-American community for Sammartino and the huge swell of support from the Hispanic population for Morales, it may well have turned into all-out war in the stands. The Stasiak name lived on in the WWF, with his son Shawn Stasiak bending bones for the promotion at the end of the decade and into the early 2000s, after a stint with WCW.

Promo Time: The Nation of Domination
The new look Nation of Domination heads to the ring, and credit to Ahmed Johnson, who has immediately shed his babyface gear in favour of an all-black ensemble. Savio Vega, Tatanka and all other babyfaces who turned heel and did nothing different; take note! Ahmed looks like a bad motherfucker, and while I think his turn was a mistake, it does give him a fresh feel and a host of new opponents to work with. I guess I look back on his heel run as an error because it was so brief, but given time it may well have worked. Of course, Ahmed was too injured too often for us to find out. "Why? Ahmed, Why?" pleads Vince. Ahmed's justification is that he was held down for being black, and that he never got a title shot when he returned from his injury. Gee, which one, Ahmed? If you had a title shot every time you got injured, you would be headlining every week! He does have a point though, because on more than one occasion he was set to clash with the WWF Champion, only to crock himself again. The irony of that being the case again is too much. While I think that turning the Nation into a full-on black supremacist group was maybe a line crossed too far, there is no question that the new look quartet are intimidating. They surround Vince and warn him that no one, including him, will hold them back any longer, and Faarooq says that the world fears intelligent black men. I hope for the love of God he is not putting himself and Ahmed into that category! D'Lo Brown is by far the most verbose of the four, but Ahmed is easily the most threatening. He looks like he could genuinely snap and murder someone at any given moment. He even loses his temper with Vince, but rather than shouting and ranting like he usually does in his hilarious way, instead he calmly tells Vince that he will kill him if he carries on disparaging the group (see the Raw Recap). D'Lo rounds things off with the NOD "By any means necessary" catchphrase, which signals the arrival of Crush and three unknowns, wearing leathers and riding bikes. Crush cuts a promo, dismissing the Nation's talk as "a bunch of crap" and then introducing his own faction: the Disciple of Apocalypse, or DOA. They are Chainz (Fake Undertaker), Skull and 8-Ball (the Blu Brothers), so none are new to *Raw*, but they certainly look different to before. Try picturing the DOA as those previous gimmicks alongside Kona Crush, and it almost blows one's mind. A big ass brawl breaks out to signal the official start of the Gang Warz, as officials struggle to break things up. In the chaos, Ahmed Johnson incredibly manages to injure himself AGAIN. You can see him standing in the corner struggling, while everyone else is engaged in fisticuffs. You have to feel bad for the guy, but at the same time I have never known a performer so brittle. This whole thing was a tremendous start to *Raw*, with the Nation coming across as stars and intimidating badasses, and Ahmed in particular looking great. What a frustrating performer he is though. You can see why Vince lost faith in him.

Rockabilly vs. Ken Shamrock
On one hand you have a joke character that makes the WWF look like a company stuck in a bygone era (though at least he has dropped the dodgy dye do), and on the other we have a character ahead of his time in Ken Shamrock, a legitimate fighter and a robotic killing machine. What a strange place the WWF was in 1997. Dan Severn joins the commentary team in his first WWF appearance, and Vince introduces him as "former UFC Champion and current NWA Champion". There's another one of those strange things to hear Vince say. We cut to footage of Shamrock mashing people in UFC and Vince wants comments from Severn, but his headset is broken. Well, so Vince claims, but Severn is so softly spoken and even more robotic in his delivery than Shamrock, that they may well have just heard him speak and turned it off. In a comment that is incredible even today, Vince goes on a tirade against government officials who have criticised UFC and misunderstood it, defending no holds barred fighting as never having had a death, unlike boxing and pro wrestling! What is this!? What an incredible thing for him to say. Naturally a match featuring the useless Rockabilly can't hold a candle to comments like that, especially when suspension of disbelief is ruined by Shamrock actually selling for him. After his immense debut win over Vader, the WWF really dropped the ball on Shamrock. He should have been demolishing everyone in seconds a'la Goldberg, not labouring to wins against scrubs. The WWF were never fully convinced on Ken, pushing him so far and then holding off pulling the trigger and reeling him back in. I think he turned up a few years too early, because against

the super-workers of 2000 (Benoit, Guerrero, Angle, Jericho, Guerrero, etc) he could have had some real belters.
Final Rating: ½*

Backstage, the Godwinns who are apparently heels all of a sudden, promise to make the LOD suffer for breaking Henry's neck a few weeks back. I am sure I have noticed before and blanked it out, but Phineas is shirtless under his dungarees today, and sports a huge "RED NECK" tattoo on his arm. I am about as open as you can get with regards to body art, but my God that is an idiotic tattoo.

**Tag Team Championship Tournament First Round
The Godwinns vs. The Legion of Doom**
With the broken neck issue, there is at least a bit of heat and oomph to this from the start, rather than the sluggish crap you would expect. The Godwinns slop both of LOD in the aisle before the bell, which only serves to piss them off and the Godwinns get a beating. When they take over Henry hits a piledriver on Hawk, which he ignores as usual. The psychology there could have been pretty sound, with Henry looking for neck breaking revenge by doing the same to Hawk, but Hawk kills it. Animal takes the heat, which is a first, but Phineas makes a horrible mess of a spot and displays his usual terrible timing. It looks bush league. Hawk comes in on fire and LOD look to finish with the Doomsday, but Phineas prevents it. Hank gets beaten anyway, taking a flying clothesline from Hawk and taking the bump on Animal's back. What an ugly spot. Immediately following the win, the Hart Foundation jump LOD and lay a beating on them, setting up the upcoming 5-on-5 at the PPV. For a Godwinns-LOD match this wasn't abysmal.
Final Rating: ¾*

Backstage, an extra evil looking Undertaker wraps his hand around the throats of Paul Bearer and Vader, making the latter look completely useless and feeble in the process. Taker is getting annoyed with being subservient to Bearer and is acting out. Bearer says "remember the fire" and Taker instantly lets go and walks off. The plot thickens.

Still backstage, Owen Hart calls tonight's first ever *Raw* triple threat match a "bunch of bullcrap" and quite correctly points out the stupidity of the rules, where the champion can lose his title without even getting beat.

Flash Funk vs. Sabu
Yes, you read that right; Sabu! Wrestling on *Raw*! In 1997! Have you noticed that they always put the ECW guys on with Funk, because he is probably the only one willing to work properly with them due to his own ECW past? Highlights from Sabu in ECW air as he enters, with the majority of the footage shown being his ridiculous chair assisted stunts. Sabu charges low at Funk, but the former Scorpio knows him and meets him with a kick to the head. Even Vince can recognise the fact they have worked together before, and points it out. Sabu brings his insane flying with no regard for his own body, and Funk follows suit with his high octane stuff, making for a very different match than what you usually see on *Raw*. Paul Heyman gets a shot in at current WCW and former ECW stars Public Enemy, as Sabu dicks around on the outside with a table. "Eric Bischoff can tell you that the Public Enemy invented tables on national TV, but I can tell you as the man who discovered the Public Enemy, that they stole the entire deal from that man: Sabu". Sabu is over with the crowd and gets popped for all of his wild moves, such as a springboard super rana. It's an incredible juxtaposition to the Fulton-Rogers match last week, both stylistically and in terms of response. The action is fairly sloppy given who is involved, but you can't fault the effort shown by both. They get a reasonable amount of time by *Raw* standards too, which helps. Funk nearly finishes Sabu off with a big moonsault from the top, but Sabu kicks out. Sabu backdrops Funk to the outside and follows with a rana off the apron, then sets up a table as both get counted out. Sabu couldn't care less, and hits an Asai moonsault onto Funk on the table, but it doesn't sell for him. Undeterred, Sabu does his usual trick of making the botch look even worse by trying to cack-handedly make up for it, this time by simply splashing Funk from a running start. It looks like shit and the table still doesn't budge. Sabu finally wins one of his many wars against the balsawood with a legdrop from the ropes. "I think he killed him" says Vince in a nonplussed and frankly uncaring manner. If you like matches with no psychology that simply bounce from one spot to another, this is the bout for you. I do not, but I will concede that this was exciting and completely different to everything else on *Raw* so far. Watching it directly after the Godwinns and Rockabilly makes it even more enjoyable.
Final Rating: **¾

Mankind vs. The British Bulldog
Mankind comes out wearing a Steve Austin shirt and a sign around his neck saying "Pick me, Steve", as he continues to politic Austin to pick him as his tag partner due to the temporary departure of Shawn Michaels. Austin calls in and refers to Mankind as a "nice man", but he has no interest in teaming with him. Unfortunately the call serves as a distraction to the match, which used to be a frequent problem on *Raw* last year. The WWF ran random extra-curricular frequently, and it was commonly a detriment to the action. That has been the case far less in 1997, with the unnecessary interjections replaced with copious backstage segments, run-ins and non-finishes. I am not sure which is worse, actually. Once Austin hangs up, Davey and Mankind have a brief, solid but unspectacular match. Mankind floats out of a running powerslam attempt into the Mandible Claw, but Davey escapes with a low blow. Bulldog then goes to his increasingly frequent last resort in the shape of a chair, smacking Mankind around with it, including some vicious shots to the head, for the DQ. Hang on, what is Davey's beef with Mankind all of a sudden? Wasn't he trying to do the same thing to Goldust just a few weeks back? And isn't that all leading to a feud with Shamrock? Not to mention the tag tournament and constant rivalries with Steve Austin and Shawn Michaels by virtue of being a Hart Foundation guy. Too many balls in the air, Davey, too many balls.
Final Rating: *½

Backstage, Owen Hart confronts Gorilla Monsoon and the participants in his upcoming match, saying that if they have managers with them, he wants Brian Pillman out with him. Gorilla has no problem with it, but Owen chooses to ignore that and carry on demanding it anyway.

Video Control gives us a highlights package of former Intercontinental Champions, with Vince and JR providing a voiceover. Conspicuous by their absences in this ultra-political time are WCW stars Curt Hennig, Randy Savage, Scott Hall and Roddy Piper, as well as people who left on bad terms like the Ultimate Warrior. Nice idea, but the pettiness instantly reduces it to nonsense. What was even the point of the piece anyway!? Surely not to hype the forthcoming throwaway IC title triple threat? Points for effort and for trying to make it matter, but that kind of thing is better served leading up to a big PPV match really.

WWF Intercontinental Championship
Owen Hart (c) vs. Hunter Hearst Helmsley vs. Goldust
This is the first triple-threat match on *Raw*, and Pat Patterson is the referee for the occasion. They really are trying to make this routine defence seem like a big deal. "It is almost as if the Intercontinental Championship is vacant coming in" says JR when he explains the rules. That's true, which is why multi-man title matches or any bout that removes the champion's advantage are stupid. Goldust looks to have this won when he pins champion Owen following the Curtain Call, after Owen had prevented the Pedigree on Goldie from Hunter with a spin kick. However, Owen had his foot on the ropes and his corner man Brian Pillman remonstrates wildly about it. Gorilla Monsoon comes out to restart the match, robbing the fans of the babyface victory. The same thing happened to Goldust a year earlier when he was champion and Savio Vega beat him thanks to shenanigans, so he can't have too many complaints. Chyna gets involved and throws in a rana, prompting JR to refer to her as a "phenom". I don't think the Undertaker will be too thrilled with that. Owen wins this when Goldust comes off the top to drop an elbow on him, but Owen moves and Goldust hits Helmsley, and Hart scurries on top for the win.
Final Rating: *¾

Promo Time: Bret Hart
This is the first appearance for Bret in a few weeks, other than briefly turning up in the aisle earlier on. He comes out with Jim Neidhart, with the purpose of the interview to build up the 10-man tag at the PPV. He runs down the LOD, saying they are not the greatest team in WWF history, but rather he and Jim Neidhart are. Check out our *Superstar Series: The Hart Foundation* for reviews of every televised match the duo ever had and decide for yourself! Bret calls UFC the "Ultimate Fairy Championship" and gives Goldust and Steve Austin a few choice words as well, all to major heat. Bret turns his attention to professional boxer Thomas "Hitman" Hearns, who is sat in the front row. Bret is livid with him for stealing the "hitman" moniker, and calls him out. "I don't think you're the Hitman, I think you're the chicken-man!" says Bret. Oh, snap! Apparently this childish probe is enough to bring Hearns into the ring, and he and Bret look like they are about to get it on, as the crowd volume rises. Neidhart gets in the way and Hearns lays him out with a few punches to the gut (which Neidhart sells in a similar manner to in his match last week) before a herd of security break things up. The crowd loves it and chant "USA" loudly as Bret scarpers. This was one of those deals where the WWF let themselves be made to look inferior and weak compared to a "legitimate" sporting guy, just as they do every time they wheel out a celebrity or someone from the mainstream. It was only Neidhart I guess, but why let a boxer be made to look stronger? How does it help the WWF?

Backstage, the Nation of Domination are about to cut a promo, when Savio Vega wanders into their locker room, complaining about the lack of respect shown last week. Foolish move; he gets battered by the Nation and whipped by Faarooq with his belt. What a dumbass.

Scott Taylor vs. Brian Christopher
In keeping with the recent spate of tag teams doing battle on *Raw*, we get Too Much/Cool explode, some 12 months before they even first formed as a team. Christopher is polished from nearly a decade on the independent scene, having debuted in 1988. Taylor only came into the business a year later, but his stuff still requires some honing. They have a few timing issues early on but Christopher holds it together and hits a nice German suplex, with Taylor responding by hitting a bizarre flip double legdrop to a bent over Christopher. It probably sounds better than it looked. Sometimes ideas for moves and spots seem good in the planning phase, but don't quite work in execution. Christopher busts out a Rockerdropper, which is almost ironically appropriate with Taylor looking all the world like a member of the Rockers. The future Grandmaster Sexay controls the majority of the pace, then finishes the jobberific Taylor with a reverse DDT and a top rope legdrop. Of note also, is that Jerry Lawler spends the match on commentary, vehemently denying the statement made by Heyman of Christopher being his son. Of course, no one believes him. There's a good reason for that: he is lying. Christopher, as if it wasn't already incredibly obvious from the facial resemblance, is indeed "Jerry's kid".
Final Rating: *¾

Tag Team Championship Tournament First Round
The Undertaker & Vader vs. Faarooq & D'Lo Brown
Vince mentions that Ahmed Johnson was injured in the brawl with the DOA, and he sounds frustrated and annoyed about it. That's his push over and done with then. Too unreliable, despite how incredibly shiny he was. This only exists to further the issue between Taker and substitute PPV opponent Vader, but I have to say that really should have been at least a multi-man involving someone from the Nation based on the television in recent weeks, even if the overall quality would have undoubtedly suffered. Like all NOD matches this just plods along, and then Taker and Bearer have an argument causing Vader to interject, so Taker belts him in the chops and Vader turns in to a Faarooq clothesline and gets pinned. Post match Taker and Vader argue some more, so Taker hits the Tombstone. What an awful way to build a title challenger, sub or not. First he gets pinned from a nothing move as if he is at *Survivor Series* and then the champion wipes him out decisively. It should have been the other way around and Vader should have crushed Taker. Post match, a livid Paul Bearer gets on the mic and tells Taker that he is going to tell the whole world his secret next week, but Taker seems more annoyed than concerned, and gestures that he will kill him.
Final Rating: ½*

THE RAW RECAP:

Most Entertaining: Ahmed Johnson. Yes, really! Ahmed looked and sounded menacing during the opening segment, and almost made it seem like his heel turn was a good idea. It may well have been if not for yet another career killing injury.

Least Entertaining: Rockabilly. On a show filled with shoot fighters, extreme political leanings and various other in-your-face real life based personalities, he stood out like a sore thumb.

Quote of the Night: "You know what? You best straighten your face up. If I see you cross your eyes at one of us one more time, there's no telling what I might do to you. I don't care who you are, I don't care whose cheque you sign. If you cross your eyes at one of us again, you'll wish to GOD you were never born" - Ahmed Johnson to Vince McMahon. Yes, he is a heel now for sure! And, it was intelligible too!

Match of the Night: Sabu vs. Flash Funk. It wasn't my cup of tea, but it was a nice change of pace and felt completely different to everything else on the show.

Verdict: It started tremendously, but rather went downhill from there. The wrestling was never boring, but never went above

average, and nothing else on the show could hold a candle to the intense opening promo. The real question is: where the hell was Steve Austin? Not having the most popular and entertaining act in the company on card really hurt the quality of the show. I can only assume he was injured, as he didn't work the house show loop around this week either, but surely he could have made an appearance? Much like last week, this was far from terrible but certainly not one of the year's better efforts.
Rating: 44

06.30.97 by James Dixon

Venue: Des Moines, IA
Taped: 06.30.97
Raw Rating: 2.5
Nitro Rating: 3.3

We start out with Video Control running down the storied history of the Undertaker and Paul Bearer, including Bearer's heel turn at *SummerSlam '96* and Taker's forced reunion with him due to blackmail. Tonight, Bearer will reveal his secret. Welcome to *Raw is Days of Our Lives!*

Hunter Hearst Helmsley vs. Ken Shamrock
Shamrock gets a monster pop from Des Moines when he comes out, making him look like a star. The accompanying UFC footage makes him seem like a shit-kicking hard case too. But he is not the right guy to make Hunter interesting, and vice versa. At this stage, Hunter needed to be led by someone exciting to have a good match, hence why his matches with Mick Foley were pretty good: he was carried. Shamrock spends much of the match working out of an armbar, which is just riveting stuff. Chyna, still square-jawed and man-like, hurls Shamrock into the steel steps to give Hunter an advantage, but Mankind begins to wander down the ramp. The distraction allows Shamrock to hit a belly-to-belly and he scores the pin. This was a boring way to start the show.
Final Rating: ¾*

Video Control, who are busy tonight already, recap the last few tumultuous weeks of Ahmed Johnson, with JR providing the voiceover again. He reveals that Ahmed tore ligaments in his knee during the brawl with DOA last week. Who injures themselves in a brawl!? Post surgery, an out of it Ahmed has some comments. He is under the impression that the Undertaker sent the DOA to attack him, and warns him that he is "not dead enough".

Backstage, the LOD are with MICHAEL COLE. Oh, shoot me now. Hawk says the Nation will be "small animal excrement" when they get through with them. Or in other words; Michael Cole.

Tag Team Championship Tournament Semi Final
The Legion of Doom vs. Faarooq & D'Lo Brown
This is exactly how you would picture LOD-Nation to be, which means lots of clubbing and little in the way of refinement. After a mercifully short outing, Henry Godwinn interferes with a slop bucket to the head of Hawk, and Faarooq covers for the win. Hawk still kicks out right after the three count, because God forbid he show any signs of weakness. The Nation are on fire at the moment; they have beaten everyone recently!
Final Rating: ½*

Promo Time: The Nation of Domination

Faarooq wants Vince McMahon in the ring after the match, which must thrill Vinny Mac after last week's near miss. Faarooq rightly wants to know why none of the Nation are replacing Ahmed Johnson against the Undertaker at *Canadian Stampede*, which from a purely storyline point of view is a damn good question. Don't get me wrong, I don't want to see Kama vs. The Undertaker for the WWF Title, or indeed ever again in any capacity after their horrid series in 1995, but logically he is probably the number one contender after pinning him a few weeks back. Faarooq thinks he knows why Vader has been given the nod instead: he is white. Vince doges the accusation and changes the subject to Crush. Faarooq says the DOA are disciples of the Undertaker, which may well have been a direction they were intending to go at one point, but nothing ever came of it. Undertaker circa 2000 would have been a perfect fit, given that he was pretty much just a one man version of the then long forgotten group, with his 'American Badass' gimmick. Just for the record, I despised that version of Taker. Savio Vega, clad in all-white, appears at the top of the stage to run down Faarooq for talking too much. Like every jilted former employee, he claims he wasn't fired, he quit. Faarooq brushes it off and challenges him to a fight, and Savio accepts because this week he has back-up. Thus we have the debut of the completely useless Los Boricuas. The fact that they are all dressed in all-white and fighting a bunch of black men, is obviously by design. Revving engines signal the arrival of the DOA, as all hell breaks loose. The Gang Warz, ladies and gentlemen.

Backstage, Los Boricuas take over LOD's interview spot with Michael Cole and rant in Spanish. "In English! In English!" pleads the racist little worm.

In this month's *Raw Magazine:* exclusive photos of a secret liaison between Brian Pillman and Sunny on a beach somewhere. Jesus, there's two people you don't want at the same party! Talk about combustible!

Scott Putski vs. Brian Christopher
This is a second generation match, billed as a light heavyweight contest, though Putski surely is beyond the 215lbs weight limit that Vince claimed was imposed on the division. Putski looks pretty incredible physique wise, and I bet Vince wishes he was 50lbs bigger, because he would have been pushed for sure. Vince once again brings up the Lawler/Christopher father/son stuff, which Lawler dismisses as his business. "If people don't stop sticking their noses into my business, I am going to start sticking my fist in people's noses!" says an annoyed Jerry. I have enjoyed the King much more this year than in previous years, where he was almost intolerable. This is a tidy little match, though you would never consider it as a rival to the explosive WCW cruiserweight division. It is different to most of the matches from the heavyweight roster in the WWF though, in that they actually string sequences together rather than rest and grind. At one point Christopher's braggart nature gets the better of him when he celebrates pre-rana, and gets nailed with a powerbomb. Later on, Putski has it won with a top rope splash, but Jerry Lawler gets on the apron to distract him and prevent the pin. Lawler ends up getting inadvertently knocked off by Christopher to a huge pop, but recovers to trip Putski allowing Christopher to get the win. Putski unloads on Christopher after the match, but Lawler gets involved and the father and son combo unleash a beating on poor Scott, drilling him with a spike piledriver. Hawk would have just stood up, but Scott sells it right and has to be carried to the back. He wins points from me.

Final Rating: **¼

We see footage from the 'Cause Stone Cold Said So VHS tape, and specifically Austin's promos from ECW where he impersonated Hulk Hogan. Vince mentions Hogan by name on air, while JR says he parodies others who are "best remaining nameless". More silly politics.

Backstage, a despairing Undertaker says that Paul Bearer is going to tell a twisted version of a story tonight, and he hopes his fans will let him tell his side. Why doesn't he just tell his side first and get it over with?

We get highlights of the phenomenal Great Sasuke, who is making his WWF debut against "Taka Michinoko" at *Canadian Stampede*. It's a helluva match as well. Sasuke is who the light heavyweight division should have been built around, not character guys like Brian Christopher.

Backstage again, and Brian Pillman gives an insincere apology for his actions on *Shotgun* where he attacked a fan.

Brian Pillman vs. Mankind

Mankind channels Doink the Clown and brings out a wrapped gift with him, and gives it to JR by way of apology for the Mandible Claw attack at the end of their interview a few weeks back. It turns out to be a mannequin hand with a Mandible Claw finger. Pillman takes the opportunity to jump Mankind on the outside and then uses the gift as a weapon, putting the claw on Mankind with it. Cute, innovative spot. Pillman gets all surly and aggressive towards JR, who shouts at him in a direct homage to Bobby Heenan, when he legitimately lost it with Pillman in WCW a few years prior. Only, without the swearing. This match sucked last time they wrestled on *Raw*, but this one is much better, with Pillman taking some big, crisp bumps. We go to a split screen with Steve Austin while Mankind is in control, and he says Mankind is smart for wanting to team with him, but he thinks he sucks and that you don't know which of his personalities you are getting with him. Things are going fairly well, so it has to be ruined by outside interference, this time in the form of Hunter and Chyna in the aisle. Pillman uses the ring bell on the outside and sends Mankind ear-first into the post, then tries to rip off Foley's good ear. Smart tactic. Pillman tries to stab Mankind with a pencil, which Vince is uncomfortable with and clearly thinks is going too far. Mankind comes back, but then misses a charge and runs into the steps headfirst. How have they not been counted out? Back in the ring and Pillman comes over and Mike Tyson and bites at the ear, but gets caught with a kick attempt and has his formerly injured ankle slammed into the post. You know, this has been really good! A million times better than their previous encounter and easily the best solo display from Pillman in the WWF. Hunter and Chyna come down to get physically involved, but Mankind cuts them off at the pass and locks the Mandible Claw on Hunter. Pillman takes his boot off and uses it as a weapon, which doesn't make much sense when you think about it. Why not just kick? Hunter accidentally hits Pillman with the most pathetic chair shot you will ever see, and Mankind chases Hunter and Chyna up the aisle and gets counted out. This was a blast, full of big bumps, smart psychology and innovative spots.
Final Rating: ***

Promo Time: Paul Bearer

Here we go then; the big secret reveal. On his way to the ring, Bearer is jumped in the aisle by an overly excited female fan, who is all gothed up and clearly an Undertaker mark. She believes, dammit! She manages to tackle Bearer and take him off his feet before security drags her away. Bearer shrugs it off and continues with the interview as planned. He gives a longwinded back story about the Undertaker's family, saying Taker's dad was a "mortician of excellence" at their family-owned funeral home, and that there were two kids, one a "red headed punk" who turned out to be the Undertaker, and another called Kane. Bearer says the Undertaker had the "look of the devil", but his brother Kane followed him around and looked up to him anyway. Bearer says he saw them stealing chemicals from the embalming room, smoking cigarettes and one night he came home to see the funeral home reduced to ashes thanks to a fire. Bearer blames the Undertaker, and says he killed his family. "YOU ARE A MURDERER" screams Bearer. With that, the lights flicker and we cut to commercial. The choice of the name "Kane" is an interesting one actually, because the Undertaker was originally known as "Kane the Undertaker" in the WWF for a few weeks, before the first name was dropped. A few TV shows went out that were taped prior to the decision to remove it, with Mean Gene Okerlund referring to "Kane the Undertaker" and Brother Love doing the same in promos. Frankly, I am surprised they didn't go with something stupid like "R. Igor Mortis" for Kane.

Jim Cornette: I believe it was Bruce Prichard's idea for Taker to have an evil brother, and Kane was picked both as an inside rib because Taker used the name briefly right at his start and also because of "Cain and Abel". One of Bruce's kids is actually named Kane. I didn't have much input on Taker's business; he did mostly what he approved at that time, but it ended up getting so far away from the essence of Taker after a while (due to Russo's increasing influence until he left), that Taker began floundering and realised that they finally had to hit reset and bring back the Dead Man, but that took a while. I had a lot of input with Kane though. I thought of him as Michael Myers in Halloween, sitting in a dark room plotting revenge for years. They ended up putting him in a superhero costume, but he still used the same mannerisms.

As for the segment and the big reveal? It was actually pretty good. If you like your wrestling to contain large doses of supernatural soap opera, then you will love it. I have never been a huge fan of Bearer, who often comes across as a cartoon villain and is the kind of character that makes you embarrassed to be a wrestling fan when there are non-fans in the room, but his delivery here was tremendous, especially after the goth girl assault. Kudos to that man.

Tag Team Championship Tournament Semi Final
The Headbangers vs. The British Bulldog & Owen Hart

The winners of this take on Faarooq and D'Lo Brown, and with them being the heels and the Headbangers the babyfaces in this one, you might assume they would win here, but this is 1997, remember. The Headbangers manage some offence early on, but the Bulldog and Owen use their smarts and blind tag to take the advantage. Vince promises Bret Hart on the phone, then reneges and says he won't be here, and then all of a sudden his is. What is going on!? Bret says the fact he is not there has nothing to do with Steve Austin, then discusses *Canadian Stampede*. He promises the fans in Canada will get what they want, but the fans in America won't. Meanwhile, a match is going on, which finishes as Bret gets off the phone with Owen catching a roll up. Throwaway stuff.
Final Rating: *

Post match, Jim Cornette out of the blue makes his first appearance in six months, randomly bringing out the Samoan

Squat Team / Headhunters. Vince acts like he has never seen them before and has no idea who they are, but they were both in the 1996 *Royal Rumble* so he should pay more attention. They brawl with both teams from the previous match, before Bulldog and Owen leave and they just fight with the Headbangers. One of them goes up for a spot off the top way too early, and has to quite obviously be cut off by Thrasher. The Headbangers beat them up for a bit, which is silly considering they have just wrestled a match and are against two 350lbs plus guys making their first appearance. The Squat Team redeem themselves and fight back, then get to do their top rope stuff, with one hitting a diving headbutt and the other a moonsault. Not the best of introductions, truth be told, and obviously the WWF felt the same way because they didn't appear again. This show is utterly wild in 1997. Anyone can show up at any minute!

Jim Cornette: *The Headhunters was a fucked up deal from the start. Someone had recommended them so they were at TV, and suddenly someone came up with the idea to have me go out with them on the spur of the moment. It was a fucked up deal, and Bulldog & Owen decided to have a little "haha" with them, and Davey slammed one of the "giants" like it was nothing. The whole thing was a mess and they were dead as four o'clock after it was over, and never came back.*

Backstage, an almost teary Undertaker says that what Paul Bearer said was true, and that his father, mother and brother all burned to death in the family funeral home. He admits to playing with matches, but says he was reprimanded by his father and left before anything happened. He then says as he was leaving, he saw Kane with the chemicals and he knew what he was going to do, but he did nothing about it. When he returned, it was too late. He says he was prevented from entering the building to save his family by the fire fighters, and he had to watch it burn to the ground with his family inside. He adds that Bearer insisted on dragging him to another funeral home to see the charred remains of his family, and that the image of his burnt mother still scars him for life, and that day changed him forever. That was the day that he found death, and was essentially the Genesis moment for the Undertaker character. Christ, this is strong, dark stuff, unlike anything ever seen in the WWF before. This storyline had the potential to be really ridiculous, and it does become that way eventually when they start busting out the magic tricks, but here it was a deeply emotional and powerful tale, and the Undertaker delivered his side with just as much conviction and passion as Bearer did earlier. Probably his best promo to date.

Rockabilly vs. Vader
And to follow that hard hitting piece? Why, Rockabilly of course. Like I said last week, Rockabilly just does not fit in anywhere in the WWF. Vader should demolish him in seconds like he did to Jesse Jammes the other week, especially with a WWF Title match coming up. Rockabilly realises as much and waffles Vader with his guitar before the bell, but Vader barely acknowledges it, never mind sells it. Within seconds, Undertaker charges down the aisle and unloads on Vader, taking out all of his pent up rage and aggression on him. "Murderer! Murdered!" yells Bearer. Taker confronts him and slaps him around, shouting at him to tell the truth. Bearer does, screaming that his brother Kane is alive. The revelation shocks Taker enough for Vader to hit him from behind, and he and Bearer hightail it to the back.

Steve Austin vs. Jim Neidhart
"And this is not going to be good" says Vince as we start, which about sums it up. Neidhart's offence is not exciting, and he relies on the usual 1997 staples of hitting and resting. Austin fights out of a sleeper with a jawbreaker, which I attest was a baffling choice of move for him. If he had done it like Jeff Hardy and turned around to differentiate it from the Stunner it would have been fine, but it looks almost identical. Austin turns things around and that results in a run-in from nemesis Bret Hart, who it turns out was not at home in Calgary at all! Thus we have another DQ in a year already chocca-block full of them. Bret locks Austin in the ring post figure four as Neidhart holds him in place, so Mankind comes out to make the save with a Mandible Claw. Brian Pillman comes out to try and get him off, but his shots do little to quell Mankind, as the bell rings and we go off the air. I like that Jim Neidhart matches are only used to set up other things featuring better workers, it seems somehow fitting.
Final Rating: ½*

THE RAW RECAP:

Most Entertaining: The Undertaker. I thought his promo work was exceptional, and he turned a potentially very far-fetched angle into a believable and heart-wrenching story.

Least Entertaining: Hunter Hearst Helmsley. Hellishly boring and delivered a chair shot that Lance Storm would be embarrassed about.

Quote of the Night: "Kane is alive! Kane is alive!" - Paul Bearer. And thus begins the next chapter in the epic story that is the Undertaker's career, with the revelation that he has a storyline brother. It will be another three months or so before we see him, and he goes on to become one of the most enduring characters in company history.

Match of the Night: Brian Pillman vs. Mankind. The last good Pillman singles match, and it was great to see the once immense in the ring Pillman doing so well after weeks of mediocre in-ring performances.

Verdict: A great episode, featuring something for everyone. The Undertaker-Bearer drama was exceptionally well done, Brian Pillman pulled one last good solo performance out of his hat, and the Gang Warz got into full swing with warring factions. Elsewhere the wrestling was pretty solid, with only Hunter Hearst Helmsley really letting the side down. This show almost single handedly encapsulated what *Raw* could be at its best in 1997: unpredictable, easy to sit through and mostly entertaining.
Rating: 84

07.06.97 - Canadian Stampede
[Saddledome, Calgary, Alberta, Canada]
(James Dixon)

- Mankind vs. Hunter Hearst Helmsley went to a double count out (***¼)
- The Great Sasuke def. Taka Michinoku (***½)
- The Undertaker def. Vader (**¾)
- The Hart Foundation def. Steve Austin, Ken Shamrock, Goldust & the Legion of Doom (****¾)

Rating: 100

07.07.97 by Arnold Furious

Venue: Edmonton, Alberta, Canada

Taped: 07.07.97
Raw Rating: 2.5
Nitro Rating: 3.4

Video Control gives us highlights from Canadian fans rooting for Bret in Canada, with Vince calling it "blind patriotism", which is hilarious coming from him. As a bonus we're in Edmonton, Alberta, which is very much Hart Foundation territory. The crowd is a sea of signs, showing that the Attitude Era is in full flow.

Promo Time: Bret Hart
The Hitman has an Edmonton Oilers jersey on, not that he needed to suck up to these fans who worship him. His reaction is enormous, just a massive babyface pop. He may have been a mark for himself, but Bret *was* a hero in Canada. That was real. The only place Bret looked like he was enjoying himself in 1997 was in Canada. But hey, that was the angle. Bret seems surprised with how this whole US-Canada thing has escalated but points out he's not so much anti-America as very pro-Canada. Bret talks about Canada being a country to be proud of because they look after their elderly, have gun control and it isn't riddled with racial hatred. He promises not to let his Canadian fans down at *SummerSlam* and will win his fifth WWF Title. Bret promises he'll never wrestle on American soil again if he doesn't win the belt. He brings out "the best technical wrestler in the WWF" Owen Hart to share the moment, followed by the "most powerful man in the WWF today" the British Bulldog. Both men are belt holders, Owen the IC champ and Davey the European champion and both are defending their belts at *SummerSlam*. Bret, disgruntled about how American the WWF is, calls for the Canadian National Anthem. While the Harts are standing to attention Steve Austin runs in with a chair and nails Owen Hart in the back. HEEEL! Enormous heat for that. One final defiant act of evil from one of the company's top faces. Bret gets in a rant during the break accusing the WWF of "walking all over Canada". Vince is so horrified by Austin's jackassery that he offers a solemn apology.

Taka Michinoku vs. The Great Sasuke
This is a rematch from last night where Sasuke went over in a sensational match. Brian Christopher comes down to join commentary. I'm mortified that Sasuke shot himself in the foot by making all sorts of outrageous claims in Japan about what he'd do in the WWF, including refusing to take jobs, thus tanking this division from the start. Sasuke pretty much opens the match with a somersault plancha that almost cripples both men. Beautiful form. Shame about Brian Christopher cackling over it like a hyena. Sasuke goes to the mat by trying to remove Taka's leg with an extreme half crab. When that doesn't work he goes for stiff body kicks before nearly taking Taka's head off. All of this is ruined by the Lawler family claiming none of this hurts. Assholes. Do you know nothing about psychology in wrestling? You build your enemy up so when you cheat and beat them, it makes you look twice as good as you are. Taka blows an Asai moonsault but somehow manages to lay out Sasuke with one leg. Unfortunately they re-do the spot, which is needless and exposes the business. Taka wows the crowd by landing on his feet off a German suplex. Michinoku Driver! Taka wants a moonsault though and Sasuke moves. Sasuke tries an Asai on the inside but Taka dropkicks him in mid air while he's upside down. They kinda botch that spot. Space Flying Tiger Drop! Sasuke botched that too, getting no height over the ropes. Sasuke starts into his A-stuff after that and plants Taka with a Thunderfire powerbomb for the win. Potentially a show stealer, this came up a bit short due to the mistakes but it was a thrill a minute. At five minutes, this rates five thrills or **¾.
Final Rating: **¾

Crush vs. Savio Vega
The Gang Warz recently kicked off so they feel the need to touch on it here. Video Control gives us a quick recap of the Nation imploding, Faarooq firing Savio and Crush and then both forming their own factions. Given the Hispanic roots of Los Boricuas, they're babyfaces to the Spanish announce team. DOA are straight up faces, because they ride motorbikes to the ring. That's pretty badass. Obviously the match is dog awful. It's made to look even worse because it has to follow Sasuke and Taka. The focus is very much on the groups, not the match. Chainz blatantly attacks Savio on the floor and that's a quick DQ. Probably for the best as at least one of Savio's bumps was embarrassingly bad and Crush is Crush. The DOA sure is over though and a loud "DOA" chant breaks out post match.
Final Rating: ¼*

Video Control takes us to an extraordinary shill for *WWF Summer Flashback*, a show I have no memory of whatsoever, that features footage of many persona non grata including Diesel, Mr. Perfect and Randy Savage. The Macho Man! Hulk Hogan and the Ultimate Warrior are also mentioned. How did that ever get past Vince McMahon?

Backstage: Paul Bearer is interviewed by Vince. He rants about Taker admitting the Kane/fire story was true and that Kane is indeed alive. Bearer mentions Kane's "charred body parts". Keep that in mind for later years when Kane was revealed to not be scarred at all. I like how Bearer reiterates Taker is evil because he's a killer, which is a good point.

WWF Tag Team Championship Tournament Final
Faarooq & D'Lo Brown vs. Owen Hart & British Bulldog
The winners get a match with Steve Austin and his partner next week, rather than the belts themselves. This being Canada, Owen and Bulldog are the faces. Anvil and Pillman come out to make sure the Nation don't have a numbers advantage. We get quick words with Austin, who once again points out he doesn't give a crap who his partner is. "I don't care about nobody". We cut away again to shill the *'Cause Stone Cold Said So* VHS (see: *The Complete WWF Video Guide Volume #IV*). He was really on fire during 1997 and it was becoming increasingly evident he was the future of the WWF. The uncrowned champion. D'Lo isn't quite ready for this spot, but his learning curve was steep and by early 1998 he was a decent worker. Faarooq tries to take a few bumps off Davey but looks very awkward in doing so. Jerry Lawler finds himself in a really awkward spot too, having to cheer on the heel Davey because he's wrestling face Shamrock at *SummerSlam*, but thus finding himself actually siding with the entire crowd as Bulldog is a face in Canada, which is contrary to his heel commentator spot. Interesting stuff. 1997 was a veritable minefield for both commentators and the heel/face structure. One thing is for sure; Faarooq tries like hell to carry this for his team but does a horrible job of it. Everything looks either bad or fake. The Nation work formula on Davey until Owen gets a hot tag and it *is* hot, courtesy of Alberta, but then Kama interferes causing the match to turn into a massive ruck on the floor. Everyone gets counted out apart from Owen Hart who never left the ring, so the Harts advance cheaply. Crowd reactions aside, this wasn't particularly good.
Final Rating: *½

Post Match: Mankind, wearing an Austin 3:16 shirt comes down to make a point. That he's not afraid of the Harts. We get another word with Steve Austin, who runs down Hunter and threatens to punch Chyna in the face.

Steve Austin vs. Hunter Hearst Helmsley
Interesting to note that Austin is wrestling against Mankind's current feud opponent, as if to solidify the tag team that Austin claims doesn't exist. Amazingly, despite being booed out of the building at the start of the show, Steve gets a hearty pop when he comes out to wrestle against anyone but the Harts. Testament to his personality. Either that or the Canadians just hate Hunter more. Testament to his heeldom. These two have a pretty decent brawl, an early WWF Main Event Style match. Hunter isn't quite adjusted to that style though and keeps trying to revert to an old school wrasslin' match. Austin's stuff is more exciting and the pace quickens when he's in charge. It took Hunter some time to change when Attitude kicked in. Teaming with Shawn obviously helped a great deal. Chyna gets involved so Mankind runs down to even the numbers. Hunter whacks him with a chair shot but turns into the Stunner. Austin doesn't really give a crap one way or the other. He still won. The match had moments but not enough of them. Basically, Hunter's reliance on a dated style held the match back. A shame as he'd been working good brawls with Mankind for a few weeks.
Final Rating: *¾

Post Match: Austin demands a mic and orders Mankind, "you long haired freak", to get in the ring. "I don't like you one bit but I'll go to war with you if that's what you want". He offers a handshake, Mankind wants a hug instead, which happens but he turns right into a Stunner. Great characterisation from both guys. "DTA you stupid piece of trash. Don't trust anybody. You won't be my partner ever because you're a long haired freak and you suck". Mankind promises "drastic measures will be taken" and next week he'll do something "he thought he'd never have to do again". Wonderful mic work from both men here, hyping a solid angle.

Video Control gives us details on the million dollar *SummerSlam* giveaway, which seems to involve Sable taking a bath. She's in room 2A. That's a clue, apparently. I don't remember it, because there was no wrestling involved.

Eric Shelley vs. Brian Christopher
The Lawler boys kicked Scott Putski's ass last week so Ivan Putski has offered a tag team challenge for next week: Putskis vs. Lawlers. Shelley is a jobber who sucks up to the crowd by "representing all of Canada". He is a passable Indy guy so he knows a few counters and such, but he's not in the same condition as Christopher. Shelley's moves are slightly goofy, with weird looking roll ups and predictable flying. He doesn't move like a wrestler. He almost reminds me of Eugene, except Nick Dinsmore was actually quite talented. Shelley makes a hash of most moves including a horrible nip up. Christopher gets in a few finishers including the Stroke and the Scorpion Death Drop before finishing with the Tennessee Jam. Shelley was out of his depth here. Incidentally, Sunny did guest ring announcing again because they still can't find anything useful for her to do. Sunny was a real predicament for the WWF. They knew if they released her she'd end up in WCW so they kept her around and gave her an assortment of filler jobs. I think this match summed up why the WWF light heavyweight division went south. Christopher had a few flashes of excitement about him but he was better placed opposite a flier who he could ground. Shelley was so rough around the edges he barely even had edges.

Final Rating: *

Video Control gives us more footage from *'Cause Stone Cold Said So* with him barking abuse at authority figures, which includes Todd Pettengill for some reason. It is quite endearing to hear Uncle Gorilla use the word "ass" though.

Promo Time: Steve Austin
Just to stress how thin the WWF's top end roster is, this would be Austin's third trip to the ring this evening. What with Bret main eventing, Taker off somewhere else and Shawn crying about his fight with Bret, that pretty much just leaves Steve. JR suggests that Austin might give Vince a Stunner right now! Vince reminds Austin of his vile behaviour at *Canadian Stampede* before moving on to Steve's tag team partner, as Austin reiterates he'll defend the belts by himself. "Don't flinch, I ain't gonna hit yak". Austin tells us if he can't beat Owen Hart he'll kiss his ass. "I'll kiss his ass if I can't kick it". That could have backfired with the neck injury. Would Owen have had to squat on his face or something? It would have looked like a teabagging.

Bret Hart vs. Goldust
Just to completely cut the legs off the babyface Goldust character, he's shown guest starring on a cookery show before the match. At least Mankind's shoot-ish interview left him with his balls, even if they were the size of grapefruits. Vince's claim that Goldust is probably the third best technician in the company, behind Bret and Owen, is laughable and shows exactly how much he knows about wrestling. He might know the wrestling business, but when it comes to the in-ring... not so much. I'm assuming he was caught up in the moment or trying to sell the match, but come on! Not that the WWF had a load of top technicians in 1997 mind you. Considering he's the country's big hero, Bret works heel and takes an aggressive stance. After a few minutes the DOA come down on motorbikes, for some reason, which brings out the Harts. Bit of a mismatch. Only Anvil is below Crush, the top DOA guy, on the company's totem pole. Anyway, the DOA just sit around on the bikes while the match continues. Bret systematically runs through the Five Moves of Doom as the commentators speculate the point of the DOA being out here. Presumably the aim was to include the Harts, as Canadians, into the ethnic gang war. The issue was that DOA and Boricuas were too poor to match up to the others. As the match continues the LOD and Ken Shamrock show up. That I can understand as they're Americans from the American team at *Canadian Stampede*. As if that wasn't enough, out comes Steve Austin for the fourth time this evening, to stand alone behind the other Americans. A pity as the match probably would have been ok but all the distractions render it an afterthought. Bret gets a nice hook of the leg for the pin, while blocking a sunset flip.
Final Rating: **

THE RAW RECAP:

Most Entertaining: Steve Austin. It's almost on default as Austin was out in the ring for so many different segments that it felt like the Steve Austin Show and everyone else was just the guest.

Least Entertaining: Crush and Savio Vega. NOD outcast faction warfare starts with a bad match between two of the new gangs' leaders.

Quote of the Night: "A few weeks ago I was told America, love it or leave it... I looked forward to loving leaving it" – Bret Hart makes his feelings on the USA known.

Match of the Night: Taka Michinoku vs. Great Sasuke. They blew a few spots but the level of difficulty was a lot, lot higher than anything else on the show. Not a patch on the *Canadian Stampede* match between the same guys but good enough for MOTN on *Raw*.

Verdict: Considering the night before was one of the best WWF PPV's of all time, this *Raw* came up a little short. It had a massive overreliance on Steve Austin, who was dangerously close to being overexposed. He appeared in four segments and his VHS was shilled twice. The attempts at variety elsewhere were appreciated, but the light heavyweight division was split here into two halves; the exciting and the drab in equal measures.
Rating: 55

07.14.97 by Arnold Furious

Venue: San Antonio, TX
Taped: 07.14.97
Raw Rating: 2.6
Nitro Rating: 3.5

Video Control opens with a big shill for the Hart Foundation and Bret's main points from his promo last week.

Promo Time: The Hart Foundation
Not quite the same reaction as last week. This time Bret's arrival is met with a chorus of boos and chants of "USA". It is LOUD. Bret starts on San Antonio, calling it a town full of rats (perhaps alluding to all the ring rats he's boinked in Texas). Vince pulls Bret up on his exact quote when he said if he didn't win the WWF Title at *SummerSlam* he'd never wrestle in America again. Bret agrees and says, as a Canadian, he'll do his best and keep his promises. Vince moves on to Owen and asks him about Steve Austin. Owen says the Harts will get their tag belts back tonight and Austin will kiss his ass at *SummerSlam*. Davey is asked about Shamrock and he adds in a stipulation, that being if he loses to Shamrock, he'll eat a can of dog food. A superb Brian Pillman's promo follows where he says he loves Dusty Rhodes' style and calls his son the "most celebrated drag queen of the century". His stipulation is that if he loses to Goldust he has to wear a dress. Anvil claims he'll shave his goatee off if any of the Harts lose. Bret claims it'll be a Canadian summer. This brings out Steve Austin to face down the entire group. He has backup as Ken Shamrock shows up, followed by a debuting Patriot and SID! I didn't even know Sid was still in the WWF. This is his last appearance on *Raw* until 2012. Vince debates who'll be teaming with Austin tonight. When all the speculation is dying down out dances Shawn Michaels. Damn, that would have been a fun 5-on-5. Shame it'll just be Owen & Davey against Austin and his partner

Jerry Lawler & Brian Christopher vs. Ivan & Scott Putski
This is a father/son contest, though Lawler still denies Christopher is his boy. Ivan hasn't been in a WWF ring in a decade and he wasn't that good then. Jerry is, by some distance, the better worker. Scott Putski finds motivation in the presence of his old man and nails all his spots, including a swank powerbomb on Christopher. If all of Putski's WWF run had been at this level, he'd have been set. Seeing as Ivan is rusty, the Lawler's are able to pick off Scott. Lawler just plants him with a piledriver. Christopher asks to get the pin himself and naturally misses with the Tennessee Jam like a cackling jackass. Christopher then compounds the error by superkicking his old man. Ivan gets the hot tag and cleans house like the crazy old Polish bastard he is. Polish Hammer finishes Lawler off in a fine dose of nostalgia. This may be the best match I've seen from either Putski. It was short, to the point and energetic. Ivan's limited involvement was a perfect use of him.
Final Rating: **¼

Video Control takes us to Mankind taking a chair shot for Steve Austin last week and then being hit with a Stunner. This leads to Mankind swearing to do something he thought he'd never do again. "Mankind will never be the same" he squeals. Indeed. We go to Mankind live, who's in the bowels of the building somewhere. Vince tries to get an interview but a sulky Mankind isn't interested in responding. "Hoo boy" says Vince. We go right into *Shotgun Saturday Night* footage of Owen Hart beating Flash Funk, in what was surely a blinder. Next up is Paul Bearer who gives us a quick history lesson of Kane's last ten years. He "eagerly awaits to confront you" claims Bearer.

Yoshihiro Tajiri vs. Taka Michinoku
This is Tajiri's second WWF appearance, having worked for the group as a jobber briefly last year. This time out he's here to help rebuild Taka. He needs it after jobbing twice to the Great Sasuke. The WWF desperately need to replace Sasuke, so Taka is the man. Honestly though, Tajiri looks phenomenal here and they could easily have gone with him. They run through incredible counters in Mexican fashion before Tajiri blows falling through the ropes and has to redo it. Taka goes flying to capitalise. The match doesn't have the same weight as the Sasuke bouts as it resorts to too much flippy-floppy stuff, but Tajiri does ground it with his moves. A sit out powerbomb sets up the rolling cradle for Tajiri. His diving special is the Asai moonsault. The crowd don't like him much, which is disappointing. I guess they figure he's the heel if Taka is the face. Taka tries to come off top but Tajiri dropkicks him out of the air and goes to his kicks. They are vicious and give this a different feel to the Sasuke matches. They then slap each other so hard it's a DKO. Tajiri pulls out a dragon suplex for 2 so Taka missile dropkicks him in the head and hits the Michinoku Driver for the win. Extremely spotty match up but a hell of a lot of fun. Tajiri looked so good here, albeit stiff, that I'm amazed he wasn't picked up for the light heavyweight division.
Final Rating: ***

Video Control mentions the August issue of WWF Magazine, which focuses on the 'Loose Cannon' Brian Pillman. They needed every dollar in 1997, hence all the shilling.

The Headbangers vs. Miguel Perez & Jose Estrada Jr.
Mosh gets confused and thinks they're wrestling Cheech & Chong. Not only is that slightly racist, but Tommy Chong isn't even Hispanic. Considering the Headbangers are starting to wear out their welcome, they still have a tag team title run to look forward to. Miguel is at least over because of his hairy back. And hairy shoulders. Eww. JR insists we need to "keep the proverbial eye" on Los Boricuas. They're not bad wrestlers, but it's hard to really care about the faction as all they've got going for them is dapper white slacks and a Hispanic background. There's no actual personality there and no style to their approach. Thrasher gets isolated and does well for a while until Miguel catches him in a cheeky roll up for the win. The Headbangers get a shoeing after the match, which brings out DOA. Gang Warz! DOA clear the ring out, as they're miles more popular than Los Boricuas. Even in San Antonio, with its large Hispanic population.
Final Rating: *¼

Backstage: The Patriot says he's not here for Steve Austin but to defend the USA against the "forces trying to destroy her". His whole position in the company is to oppose the evils of the Hart Foundation, who've dared to talk smack about the good ol' USA.

Video Control gives us another plug of Austin's VHS. I love the he's "sick of taking shBEEP" line from the announcer.

Promo Time: Shawn Michaels
He's back after crying foul over a backstage brawl with Bret Hart and threatening to join WCW. San Antonio is the perfect place to bring him back as it's his home town and the crowd won't shit all over him. Vince asks him if he'll team with Austin tonight, which would have been cool if it a repetition. The fans go crazy for the idea, and it does seem a coincidence that he's here. Shawn claims not to be 100% and that wouldn't stop him, but it's up to Steve Austin. Shawn decides to rebuke Bret Hart instead, reminding us of Bret's "never wrestle in America" stipulation. Shawn slyly puts Vince over as the owner of the WWF and maker of decisions. "It's up to you, boss man". He asks to be a part of *SummerSlam* and will do anything from setting up the ring to selling tickets because he wants to see Bret's American career end. Vince doesn't specify what Shawn will be doing, on account of his continued obsession with being portrayed as a lowly announcer, but he'll end up being the ref. Vince does break up Shawn's stripper action and the two horse around like a couple of high school sophomores.

Promo Time: Savio Vega
Savio runs out to get a camera as "a terrible accident has happened in the back". Egad, I hope it's not an impromptu match with Crush. We head backstage and Los Boricuas are smashing up one of the four motorcycles belonging to the DOA. The DOA take exception and show up for a brawl. Egad, it *is* an impromptu match with Crush! Damn you, Savio! As far as brawls go this is uncreative garbage. Boricuas do earn bonus points for dragging the broken bike away behind their pimped out whip. The various car alarms sound like '*Intergalactic*' by the Beastie Boys as they compete with each other for attention. "Swim to Puerto Rico, Savio" yells Crush quite racistly.

Jim Neidhart vs. Ken Shamrock
Anvil has no idea how to deal with Shamrock's innovative shoot-style and just flops around taking it like a gay fish. Unlike some of Shamrock's other opponents, he doesn't even bother trying to mimic the shoot stuff and just throws a bunch of worked punches. Both guys are really obvious with their communication too as Anvil hooks a chinlock and they sit there chatting to each other like a couple of old ladies getting blue rinses. They must have been discussing Anvil tapping out to a sleeper, which is what happens. A sleeper, Jim? That's not even a *Survivor Series* finish. Post match Bulldog runs down to put a beating on the 'World's Most Dangerous Man' and the Patriot makes the save with a pair of Uncle Slams.
Final Rating: ½*

Backstage: Mankind once again refuses to take questions by sitting in silence and rocking back-and-forth. This leads to another recap of Mankind taking a chair shot off Hunter last week and a Stunner from Austin. The commentators debate who Austin's tag team partner will be and Lawler selects Sid due to them both being nuts. Sid would never be seen again. JR goes on to shill the *SummerSlam* million dollar giveaway, which was a massive con as the two winners only had a 1 in 100 shot at winning anyway. This week's clue comes from the Headbangers, playing golf. Mosh lies about his score and gets killed by lightning. The clue, bizarrely, is "life". They should have showed a clip from the Eddie Murphy movie instead, even though it won't actually be a released for another two years. A technicality.

The New Blackjacks vs. The Legion of Doom
The WWF's tag team division sure was a sorry meandering mess in 1997. This isn't even about the New Blackjacks, who are not important in the least. The Godwinns jump LOD in the aisle and give Hawk a Slop Drop on the ramp, which he doesn't sell but it sure busts the back of his head open. Hawk has to see a trainer and the match is a no contest.

Flash Funk vs. Vader
Vader still has Paul Bearer as his mismatched manager. I guess they wanted to keep Bearer on TV for some reason other than teasing the arrival of Kane. Vader is still a big star but the lustre has gone off his push, despite a recent title match with Taker, and he'd soon be fodder for the debuting Kane. He works Funk over in the corner with those awesome forearms but he rather oversells Flash's dropkicking comeback. It doesn't match his reaction to everything else, like stopping Flash dead when he runs into him. A splash draws a familiar "FUHGEDDABOWTIT" from Vince as JR mistakenly calls Flash "Too Cold Scorpio". Moonsault gets 2 for Flash, but he runs in to Vader again and loses to the powerbomb. This was a fun little hard-hitting contest. A pity it was only 5-minutes long.
Final Rating: **½

Backstage: Steve Austin points out that he doesn't care who his partner is and he's not been 100% for a year, thus belittling Shawn Michaels' suggestion that he wasn't fit.

WWF Tag Team Championship (Vacant)
Steve Austin & Mystery Partner
vs. Owen Hart & The British Bulldog
Austin starts the match as a handicap bout, attacking both Harts. Technically Austin was still the tag team champion until this match started, but as soon it was underway the belts were vacated. The Harts use the numbers game and isolate Austin in their corner. They can afford to take it in turns to put a beating on Austin. With Austin down on the floor Vince throws to backstage as music kicks in. "Austin's partner has arrived". We go to commercial and on returning Austin is still getting a beating. Owen takes out the knee with a chop block and it's only a matter of time before Austin is defeated. "If Austin loses he'll have to kiss a certain part of the, uh, anatomy of, uh" – Vince tries hard to avoid saying the word "ass" on TV to describe the *SummerSlam* stipulation against Owen. Austin goes after the Stunner but Owen shoves him off into Davey and both challengers topple to the floor. "OWWWW, Steve-O looks like you need a little help". It's the hippest cat in the land; Dude Love! "OWWWW, have mercy!" The arrival of Dude Love is sold so well by Steve Austin. The wrinkled brow, the "what the hell?" look in his eyes. Austin must surely consider a Stunner as Dude dances by the ropes. Austin tags him in anyway. I remember marking out for the arrival of Dude Love. It was a way for Mick Foley to have a laugh and I was laughing with him. Dude avoids the running powerslam with the Mandible Claw but Owen saves with a missile dropkick. Austin runs in; STUNNER! Owen can't save this time and Dude scores the pin for the belts. Steve Austin and Dude Love are the tag team champions. Dude offers his tag belt to Austin to give him the full credit and is besieged by make-out chicks. He has groupies. Austin caps Dude's night off with a handshake.

The girls must surely have gone early into the ring as Austin's gesture ended up totally overlooked. Otherwise the booking was terrific fun and Dude Love, while a terrible worker, was entertaining. The match isn't a patch on the one with Shawn Michaels from May but holds up better than I remember it.
Final Rating: ***

THE RAW RECAP:

Most Entertaining: Dude Love. The Dude didn't get many great moments during the course of his WWF run but this was one of them. A great debut that even managed to overshadow Steve Austin. During Attitude almost no one else could claim the same.

Least Entertaining: Jim Neidhart. Coasting by on name alone.

Quote of the Night: "I have been waiting a long time to see Bret's sorry ass get the hell out of America" – Shawn sends the love to Bret.

Match of the Night: Taka Michinoku vs. Yoshihiro Tajiri. The WWF's light heavyweight division never quite took off like WCW's cruiserweight division did, but this was a solid match, albeit a touch spotty. It slightly edges out the main event tag for relying on wrestling rather than storyline. Both matches were good though.

Verdict: Despite a noticeable lull in the middle of the show, this is a good episode. I enjoyed the opening interview, which teased a bigger picture of Hart feuds, but it didn't quite deliver on the mass-mayhem it promised. I also enjoyed the Lawlers-Putskis family feud, the light heavyweight contribution, Vader roughing up Scorpio and the debut of Dude Love. The show was bright and breezy, which is considerably different to the rest of 1997 where everyone was miserable and angry. Levity makes this show stand out.
Rating: 66

07.21.97 by Arnold Furious

Venue: Halifax, Nova Scotia, Canada
Taped: 07.21.97
Raw Rating: 4.05
Nitro Rating: N/R

Video Control opens with debate over why Bret Hart is so loved in Canada and yet so hated in America. Tonight Bret has challenged any three Americans to a flag match.

Vader vs. Ken Shamrock
Technically Vader is the heel and he sure hates Canadians, as well as everything else, but Shamrock is feuding with the Harts so you'd think he'd get heat too. But he doesn't. It's very weird how Canadians pop faces unless they're directly against the Harts. These two had a hugely underrated war when Shamrock made his WWF PPV debut, but Ken has toned the intensity down since that match. Shamrock switches gears and comes in looking for kicks. It's interesting that Shamrock's shoot background gives him that mix it up psychology, to keep his opponents guessing. Vader straight-up mangles him with forearm shots. He's no respecter of reputations. Neither is Paul Bearer, who waffles on Shammy with his shoe. The wacky world of pro-wrestling has absorbed the 'World's Most Dangerous Man' and smacked him in the face with a slip-on. Ken flips out of a powerbomb and hits the belly-to-belly in a nice wrestling spot. Shamrock gets a kneebar only for Bearer to rake Ken's eyes. Shamrock roughs him up but that leaves him open for a Vader assault. Shamrock survives the Vader Splash without incurring any of his famous internal injuries. Shamrock tries a rana but Vader dumps him over the top in a nice spot. While Vader is being chastised, the British Bulldog runs down and powerslams Ken on the floor. That'll do it and Vader wins on count out, thus inflicting Shamrock's first defeat on TV. This lacked the same intensity as the original Vader-Shamrock match, as well as importance, but it still had tidy wrestling, decent psychology and great striking. For me Vader was still one of the company's top performers and yet the WWF ignored him from here on out and used him strictly to put over newcomers and wallow in the midcard, constantly being told to lose weight.
Final Rating: **½

Video Control gives us a first look at Brakkus, an extremely muscular German competitor on his way to the WWF. He threatens the Hart Foundation in Germany. The former bodybuilder never really gained enough in-ring skill to make it onto TV and was farmed out to USWA and ECW before eventually making his WWF debut the following year. He is a footnote at best and I don't remember him ever winning a match on TV, but according to the record books I have that to look forward to about a year from now.

Promo Time: The Hart Foundation
The crowd is so loud Bret can barely be heard. As he disparages America the crowd loudly chant "US sucks". Bret claims no one has accepted his flag match challenge before challenging the Undertaker to grow a set. Bulldog cuts a confusing promo about slamming Shamrock through the mat (it was on the floor) and challenges Shamrock to join the match. Owen challenges Austin to join, calling for him to "suck my toes", in a bizarre threat. Steve Austin doesn't give a damn if there are three guys and he storms out here to call Halifax a "living hell". He accepts the flag match challenge and walks off.

Brian Walsh vs. Brian Christopher
Walsh, with his tiny Canadian flags, originally hails from Canada but now lives in Rhode Island so he gets booed. This is officially a match in the light heavyweight division. Christopher doesn't like Canada and doesn't endear himself to the fans by eating one of Walsh's small flags. He proceeds to work with it in his gob. Walsh has no light heavyweight moves so Christopher has to bring the thrills, which he doesn't have either. This may be the weakest light heavyweight match you'll ever see. It's like watching two gigantic meatheads trapped in tiny bodies. There's nothing wrong with the pacing as such, but it's just so awful. At one point Walsh stops and then jumps into Christopher's arms. Christopher thankfully finishes with the Tennessee Jam in short order. The WWF's light heavyweight division, ladies and gentlemen.
Final Rating: ½*

Video Control gives us a look at the forthcoming Truth Commission, the latest and most pointless faction in the 1997 Gang Warz. Maybe it'd have some relevance if Apartheid was current, but it ended in 1994. I guess these guys are supposed to be throwbacks to that time or remnants of the military police or some such. We move on to *SummerSlam '95*, just staying topical as hell this evening WWF, and Todd Pettengill giving away the *In Your House* house to Matt Pomposelli. It's one of these "hey, remember when we did something stupid" moments. Yes. Yes, I do. Sable introduces us to the concept with a million dollar casket. Only one key will open it, out of

100.

Video Control moves back to Mick Foley as we get clips from JR's recent interview. This is to remind us of Dude Love and his origins. Vince does the V/O claiming Mick always saw himself as Dude Love, not Mankind or Cactus Jack. Vince continues as Jack Foley gets dismantled by Dynamite Kid and Cactus Jack gets all disfigured in barbed wire. Finally Mick warps into Mankind but can't get the love. "Less than Herculean physique" is how Vince describes him. We get the build to last week and the match with Dude Love's debut. The WWF must have been thrilled with how the storyline had panned out. JR's call of "Dude Love lives" is wonderful. I like how Foley's transformation into a heartthrob saw him immediately win a title. We finish things off with Steve Austin's pre-recorded thoughts. He's not sure if Mick is crazy or gutsy, but either way he still doesn't want a tag team partner.

#1 Contenders Match
The Godwinns vs. New Blackjacks vs. The Headbangers
The WWF's tag division in a nutshell. Two lummox hillbillies, two rehashes of old gimmicks and two cross-dressing metal fans. The rules for this are triple threat so three men are in at all times. It gives the match a total lack of structure. The Headbangers look really lightweight compared to the two bigger teams, with Bradshaw and Hank particularly dominant. The match is a colossal mess though, just three guys punching each other ad nauseum. Windham takes a bucket to the head and the Godwinns score the win. The match was five minutes of nothing and the worst team went over.
Final Rating: ¼*

Promo Time: Shawn Michaels
HBK doesn't get the same reaction as last week, far from it. Shawn just bathes in the heat. He takes it all in as he dances, strips into the ring, salutes Old Glory and moonsaults off the buckles. The crowd absolutely loathe him. Shawn refers to Jim Ross as "Girth Brooks" before making gay jokes. He says he got some Canadian army men for Christmas one year and they came out surrendering. After he tells Canada it sucks, the crowd rail on him by yelling "FAGGOT" over and over again. The heat is unreal. Shawn teases involvement in tonight's flag match as the camera pans over the crowd. The hate is palpable. He goes on to discuss *SummerSlam* as the crowd chant "you are gay" or possibly "we want Bret". Maybe both. Back to *SummerSlam* then, and Shawn was told there was only one job going at the show: refereeing. "What match?" asks JR. "I only work one match... the main event". Shawn will referee Bret vs. Taker. Shawn's gleeful taunting of Canada by skipping around the ring waving tiny Maple Leafs is hilarious. Shawn does add that if he doesn't call the match down the middle he'll be banned from wrestling in the US. Everything Shawn said and did got volcanic heat here. Not only because he was a total jerk about it, but because the stuff he was saying was hugely detrimental to Canada's hero; Bret Hart.

Video Control gives us the *SummerSlam* million dollar giveaway. The first three clues: "key 2A life". "Of luxury" is added in by far the least inspiring of the four.

Hunter Hearst Helmsley vs. The Patriot
Not terribly clever having a pro-American like the Patriot work up in Canada. He claims to be patriotic towards all countries (what?), but then comes out waving Old Glory. Basically, he's a liar. Hunter gets the biggest face pops of his life by whaling on Del Wilkes. JR claims Patriot is a "top international star". I don't agree. His style is about as far from international as you can get. He works a bland American style with a few big trademarks. Bret Hart comes storming out to get into a spot of verbal with Vince McMahon over the guest referee announcement. "Kick him in the gonads" yells one of the ringside Canucks. Bret slaps Vince's headset off and Vince puts on his biggest angry snarl. Bret comes back for a scuffle with Vince and the crowd goes nuts. Patriot runs out to make the save for the USA so Owen and Davey give him a kicking and the match is over. Should have minded his own damn business. Considering about 20 seconds of the match actually made the air, there's no rating. Bret's fracas with the chairman of the board might have overwhelmed the match, but it was jolly good Sportz Entertainment.
Final Rating: Not Rated

Backstage: Paul Bearer gets more words relating to Kane. JR calls him a liar as Bearer has brought no proof whatsoever. Bearer claims Taker and Kane have two halves of the same statue. Paul has Kane's half of the statue, which he claims is proof of Kane's existence. It's certainly proof that they have two months of stuff like this before Kane actually debuts. They are dragging it out already.

Faarooq vs. Goldust
Vince stops off to say Shawn is the guest ref at *SummerSlam* but "cannot show impartiality". As the match rumbles along Vince leaves, getting word of antics in the backstage area. Faarooq is clearly aware there's no attention on this bout and grinds at a chinlock. Kama trips up Goldust and beats him up on the floor. Mike Chioda looks right at it and somehow doesn't deem it a DQ. Dominator connects but Chioda calls it a DQ for Kama's interference. The booking and execution of this was as weird as it was dreadful. They screwed the pooch something fierce. I don't know what Chioda was doing with his positioning or his timing, but it was a total mess.
Final Rating: DUD.

Backstage: Shawn Michaels has been beaten up by the Harts, which is why Vince went into the back. This being a cheeky storytelling interpretation of the real event that happened in Hartford last month when Bret attacked Shawn backstage.

Flag Match
Bret Hart, Owen Hart & The British Bulldog vs. Steve Austin, Dude Love & The Undertaker
Dude arrives to show support for his tag team partner and the tag champs find themselves outnumbered 3-on-2. Owen dominates the early proceedings but Austin dumps him to the floor when he heads up for the flag. The ad break kicks in just as the Undertaker arrives, which is terrible timing. Taker's arrival changes the match completely and he chokeslams Owen. Bret breaks the pin but everyone suddenly realises there's no pins anyway. This match sort of acts like a minor version of the *Canadian Stampede* 5-on-5 tag, but the lack of pinfalls hurts the flow of the match. Honestly, I don't think I've ever seen a good flag match. The tag champs work in a little heat on Owen until Owen counters Dude's swinging neckbreaker into a DDT. Nice fluid action on that counter. The heat continues on Owen as the Americans cut the ring off. I'm not sure why they insist on tagging because the winner gets the flag down, there's no DQ. Austin tries a Sharpshooter on Owen but gets kicked off and Bret gets the molten hot tag. Dude Love prevents the ringpost figure four, then Bret saves Davey from a Tombstone and the crowd go nuts for Bret scrapping with Undertaker. After a double down Taker sits up and goes after Old Glory, but Brian Pillman stops him and Bret pulls the Maple Leaf down at the same time. The Harts win the

76

flag match in Canada. The matches issues were quite severe (why bother tagging with no DQ, nobody tries for the flag until the end), but it was an entertaining 3-on-3 regardless.
Final Rating: **¼

THE RAW RECAP:

Most Entertaining: Shawn Michaels. 1997 was not a year where Shawn got to enjoy himself all that much, but he was on form here with a vibrant, scathing attack on Canada. He revelled in his role and delivered an excellent interview.

Least Entertaining: Many contenders for in-ring but from a sheer laziness perspective I'll go for Faarooq.

Quote of the Night: "You ever notice the United States is shaped like one big giant toilet bowl… because most Americans are plain full of crap" – Bret Hart takes a few shots at the USA.

Match of the Night: Vader vs. Ken Shamrock

Verdict: This wasn't quite the same vibe as last week. Things got more serious, Shawn Michaels aside, and it took the edge off the fun. Shawn's promo is an undoubted highlight as was a surprisingly good rematch between Shamrock and Vader. The main event was slightly underwhelming and indeed the Hart Foundation's run should have featured more thrilling multiple person tags than it did. *Canadian Stampede* shouldn't have been a one-off. Bret's attack on Vince McMahon did make for great television and it's a wonder they never pulled the trigger on a Vince-Bret feud considering their previous altercations. Ultimately it would have meant Vince acting as a babyface though.
Rating: 56

07.28.97 by Arnold Furious

Venue: Pittsburgh, PA
Taped: 07.28.97
Raw Rating: 2.9
Nitro Rating: 3.4

Promo Time: The Hart Foundation
I like how Vince deflects interview duties to Jim Ross. There was a disciplinary hearing this morning, says JR, where Bret was under pressure for his attack on Vince McMahon. Bret's punishment will be deferred until a new commissioner is appointed. Bret calls it a "kangaroo court" and says there's no justice in America. Look at OJ Simpson. Bret does try to backtrack on his promise to leave America if he doesn't beat the Undertaker, which has now been inserted into his contract. "Fear and hope are the same underneath". A very noticeable "Austin" chant breaks out, even though Bret is talking about Shawn and Undertaker at *SummerSlam*. That should tell you who the future of the company is. Bret demands an apology from Shawn for all the trash he said about Canada. Bret goes on to a memorable quote where he claims if you gave the USA an enema, you'd stick the hose right here in Pittsburgh. Bret finally rounds on the Patriot, but the crowd are already drowning everything out with support for the city of Pittsburgh. It's deafening. A shame as Bret compares Austin and Michaels to "the Unabomber and Richard Simmons" before calling Patriot out for a match. This was one of Bret's most passionate and clever promos as a heel when he didn't have Shawn or Vince standing right in front of him.

Video Control gives us vox pops of idiotic American fans putting over the Undertaker and predicting Bret's demise at *SummerSlam*.

Miguel Perez & Savio Vega vs. The Legion of Doom
I guess this is the Boricuas A-team. Perez isn't a bad talent, he throws a good punch and his timing is decent. In the WWF he never really showed any technical skill, but that's the problem with the Gang Warz; it doesn't really lend itself to technical stuff. When two gangs throw down, they don't usually hook a short arm scissors. Perez does work in a fruity standing moonsault, which gets no reaction. Heel gymnastics are never over. Perez gets picked off for the Doomsday Device but the other two Boricuas jump in there for the DQ. The Godwinns run out to Slop Drop Hawk on the floor, for the second week running, and poor Hawk gets slopped for good measure.
Final Rating: ¾*

Backstage: Hunter Hearst Helmsley is interviewed regarding his forthcoming cage match with Mankind at *SummerSlam*. Vince gives us a recap of their violent feud so far. Hunter continues with his plummy accent claiming Chyna only ever interfered after he'd already "got the job done". When pressed on Vader he calls it "Jenny Craig time". Ah, and now the secondary reason for refusing to push Vader. Having already claimed he was too stiff, it was then decided that he was too fat. That's Vader!!! He's a big fat guy who smashes your face in. The best big man of all time, and yet this petty obsession with body type in the WWF railroaded him.

Hunter Hearst Helmsley vs. Vader
Mankind, dressed as a cameraman, jumps Hunter from behind with Chyna busy staring down Vader. Mankind puts a beating on Hunter until Chyna saves him, contrary to Hunter's backstage assessment of their relationship. Hunter and Mankind end up fighting into the crowd and Vader just ups and leaves, so this match is a no contest.

Video Control gives us a promo from the Commandant, the leader of the Truth Commission. He says very little. Bret Hart recommended him for the job, incidentally, and he was good mouthpiece but the WWF wanted someone who could wrestle to fit in with the four man structure of all their gangs. He was shoved to one side and replaced by the Jackyl. Which eliminated the South African element as the Commandant was the only actual South African in the group. From there we get a promo from another failed foreign hire; Brakkus.

The Truth Commission
vs. Flash Funk, Bob Holly & Jesse Jammes
Gorilla Monsoon joins commentary, under his figurohead president role, to promise a new law in the WWF and that a commissioner will be appointed soon. This is the future JOB Squad plus Jammes in action here. Jammes would have been in the JOB Squad if he'd not taken off with the New Age Outlaws. Because the Truth Commission are debuting they're the ones to go over but it's hard to see what makes them better than Funk, Holly and Jammes, other than matching uniforms. The x-factor is the big man; the Interrogator. As soon as he tags in the midcarders get overrun. Holly can't compete and gets crushed with a side slam. It's a little disappointing to think this is what the WWF think of three of their best midcard talents. All of them are far superior workers to all of the Truth Commission.
Final Rating: ½*

Backstage: The Patriot accepts Bret's challenge for a match tonight. Del Wilkes doesn't like Bret or any of things he's been saying about America. Of course he doesn't. As I'm not American, I always considered the Patriot to be a heel. Much like all Americans would regard someone from another country with a strong patriotic gimmick, which is almost every foreigner in the States over the years, as a heel.

Crush vs. Faarooq
Ahmed Johnson is back in the Nation after missing time with a knee injury, which meant he missed *Canadian Stampede* and his title shot. Both factions come down in full force. Like all other Gang Warz matches, this one sucks. Mainly because Crush is a horrible worker, but Faarooq's deterioration during 1997 kicked in during the second half of the year. Faarooq plods through most of his stuff while Crush is somewhat sloppier than usual. Jim Ross gets in one of his patented insults; "that wasn't pretty but it was effective" to describe a Crush piledriver. The finish is embarrassing as Crush looks dead at Kama then runs into his side of the ropes to get tripped up. A DQ follows. Everyone spills in for a fight apart from Crush who gets pulled out and powerbombed on the floor by the Boricuas. The match was awful, but it was entirely secondary to the Gang War. The only character who I'm interested in is Ahmed, and he's just background noise here.
Final Rating: ¼*

WWF Tag Team Championship
Steve Austin & Dude Love (c) vs. The Godwinns
A tag title defence from Austin & Love that I don't remember happening. I also forgot that Dude Love's original music is just a drum line. The crowd get a "Dude Love" chant going along with it, which is pretty cool. Owen and Bulldog join commentary and Bulldog calls Mick "Dude Loser". He was never the best at insults, was he? Obviously the Godwinns are way below Austin and Foley as singles guys and Mick dominates by himself. He isn't quite sure how to sell the Dude Love gimmick though, and is very tentative. As if he keeps expecting the crowd to shit on it. A double arm DDT even has the match won, only for Phineas to save his cousin/brother/uncle. The Godwinns eventually get a tiny bit of joy against Dude by double-teaming, but Dude quickly tags out and Austin handily beats the crap out of both hillbillies. Phineas eats a Stunner only for Hank to throw Austin to the floor where Owen nails Steve with the IC belt for the count out. Naturally Austin gets pissed off and goes after Owen, only to find himself and Dude outnumbered. LOD run down for the save. Notable that both Dude and the LOD remain on the floor as Austin stands on the buckles ranting at Owen while his music plays. We know who the star is.
Final Rating: **

Ace Darling vs. Devon Storm
This is for the light heavyweight division. Storm came out of Iron Mike Sharpe's tutelage and worked in ECW for most of 1996. He's actually under contract, but had an ignominious run in the WWF consisting of two years jobbing on *Shotgun Saturday Night*. He used to have an Indy tag team with Ace, hence them working each other here in Storm's showcase match. Ace's only claim to fame is training one Mike Quackenbush to wrestle. Quack himself went on to train dozens of workers including Claudio Castagnoli (Antonio Cesaro), Eddie Kingston and a slew of Chikara talent. This is one of the most Indy matches you'll ever see take place in a WWF ring. It's all fast paced stuff with no psychology. Tons of counters though, and as Darling goes for a rana Storm counters into a roll up for the win. Storm would later find fame in WCW by going full-on nuts and becoming Crowbar. A little like how Al Snow's constant jobbing made him go berserk. The match was really short but they had great chemistry, which you'd expect after them teaming for as long as they did. Storm's failed nip up post match shows how rough around the edges he is though, hence why he wasn't pushed. That and he was a total dork.
Final Rating: *½

Arm Wrestling Match
Ken Shamrock vs. The British Bulldog
After comments made by Davey about being the strongest wrestler in the WWF, we get this test of strength. Both guys are muscular with Davey having that freakish strength but Ken has bigger arms. As far as worked arm wrestling contests go this is pretty dull. Not that arm wrestling is much of a spectacular sport outside of Sly Stallone movies and *Raiders of the Lost Ark*. Bulldog is about to lose so he head butts Ken, chair shots him and shoves Pedigree Chum in his kisser. It makes a royal mess of the ring. The more I think about it, the more you can trace Kenny's issues back to this point. Up to this Bulldog feud he'd been booked as invincible, but when he failed to beat Bulldog at *SummerSlam* it took a little shine off his veneer. That was amplified by the failure to beat the Rock in 1998 for the IC belt, but it all begins here. Once you start choking, you're doomed to a life of choking.

Goldust vs. Rockabilly
The Runnels make fun of Pillman's penis size and sexuality to finalise the hype for *SummerSlam,* with the stipulation that if Pillman loses he has to wear a dress. The dress is on a mannequin at ringside, which Billy Gunn hits on. Billy bounces around for 'Dust and generally makes him look like a champ. Billy heads outside to make fun of and then slap IBF World Heavyweight Boxing Champion Michael Moorer. That ends badly for him. He's knocked clean out and Pillman runs in for the DQ. Pillman has a pretty decent match with the mannequin until Terri jumps on his back. Once she gets her teeth in, it's hard to get free. She's like a Rottweiler. Officials break it up and the hype for the PPV is complete. A lot going on there, a match defining the era. As if a guy getting punched out by a boxing world champion wasn't enough, they still had a DQ after that. Moorer would slip off the scale of top guys when he lost his world title the month after this, but for once the WWF was being topical.
Final Rating: *

Video Control gives us a shill for the main event at *SummerSlam*. Bret puts Taker over massively by saying he's a big man, a big star and he desperately wants to perform at the highest level every match. The clips come from the UK shoot-ish interview release *(The Fab 4)* as Bulldog also appears, completely out of place, for talking head stuff.

Promo Time: Shawn Michaels
I'm getting increasingly frustrated at seeing a clearly healthy Shawn dance to the ring every week to talk when I'm being deprived of him as a worker. Vince asks him if he'll apologise for disparaging Canada. "Shawn Michaels doesn't apologise to anybody or anything". Shawn claims to be safer in the ring than backstage because he's not popular in the locker room. Understatement! Shawn decides to join commentary for Bret Hart's match to ensure his safety. Or something. Not Shawn's best work on the stick, but his sentiments were rushed.

Bret Hart vs. The Patriot
Shawn sits right in Vince McMahon's seat and dances away, wearing Vince's glasses, during Bret's entrance music. Bret

demands the Canadian national anthem, which doesn't go over well in the USA. Shawn is overcome by the beauty of it. Sign in the crowd: "I hate *La Femme Nikita*", which, as always, follows *Raw* this week. JR puts over Del Wilkes and his football career as Shawn sarcastically butts in: "How do you know that, he's wearing a mask?" Patriot demands the American national anthem in retaliation. Bret's reaction is superb. You see him leaning on the ropes just stewing, letting all his anti-American anger build up until he jumps Patriot during the anthem. Top heel work. Shawn claims he stands for "truth, justice and the American way", which is hilarious given this whole angle is leading to a heel turn and the formation of DX. Vince announces we will "go beyond the ten o'clock hour". As if we're exploring brave new country by overrunning. Not that USA wants to lift ratings from *Raw* and skew them into *La Femme Nikita*. Bret works in his ringpost figure four during the break. When we return Shawn belittles the refereeing profession. "How hard can it be?" The old Jeremy Clarkson quote. With all the external distractions, the match is an afterthought. They do work in a nice spot where Patriot looks for the Uncle Slam but Bret runs the buckles and falls back to escape. Earl Hebner gets bumped during that denying Bret a victory via piledriver. Shawn Michaels hops into the ring and just pulls Bret off the cover. Impartial. Bret leans out to argue with him and Patriot scores the upset cradle, with a handful of tights no less, for the win. The wrestling was largely secondary to the story but the work was solid enough. Shawn dances on the announce table to mock Bret and the Undertaker turns up just as we head off the air.
Final Rating: **¼

THE RAW RECAP:

Most Entertaining: Bret Hart. He just about edges Shawn Michaels, who was gold on commentary but distracting, by cutting a better promo and actually wrestling.

Least Entertaining: Crush. With heavy Gang Warz booking any number of guys could have gotten this. Crush is supposed to be the only babyface of the Warz however, and yet he's still boring.

Quote of the Night: "If he (Shawn Michaels) doesn't call it down the middle, I still get screwed and he gets to sit at home for ten years looking for his smile" – Bret Hart questions HBK's impartiality as a ref.

Match of the Night: Bret Hart vs. The Patriot

Verdict: This was a very Attitude Era edition of the show. We didn't stay on anything for long and when we did there were other distractions, with multiple angles playing out in every single match or action lasting seconds instead of minutes. That pretty much defines the era. This didn't feel like "Crash TV" though, it just felt like a quickly paced version of a normal *Raw* show. I guess they had a lot to get in.
Rating: 43

08.03.97 - SummerSlam 1997
(Arnold Furious)
[Continental Airlines Arena, East Rutherford, New Jersey]
- Cage Match: Mankind def. Hunter Hearst Helmsley (***¼)
- Goldust def. Brian Pillman (DUD)
- The Legion of Doom def. The Godwinns (¾*)
- The British Bulldog def. Ken Shamrock (*¾)
- Los Boricuas def. DOA (DUD)
- Steve Austin def. Owen Hart (****)
- Bret Hart def. The Undertaker (***¼)

Rating: 56

08.04.97 by James Dixon

Venue: Bethlehem, PA
Taped: 08.04.97
Raw Rating: 2.6
Nitro Rating: 4.36

We are live tonight in Pennsylvania the night after *SummerSlam*, and the crowd is molten hot.

Promo Time: The Hart Foundation
Last night Bret Hart won his 5th and final WWF Championship, defeating the Undertaker thanks to an inadvertent assist from Shawn Michaels. Bret says last night's title win vindicates what he has been saying for months, and that he stuck to his word in regards to the stipulations in last night's match. He adds that Shawn Michaels didn't stick to his, because he showed blatant favouritism. He wants the WWF to do something about it, and for Shawn to be kicked out of the company. We move on to Bret's proposed *Ground Zero* opponent the Patriot, who is in line for the title shot by virtue of a fluke win over Bret last week. Hart dismisses him as a "missile with nothing in it" and refuses to put the belt on the line, then says Ken Shamrock won't be getting any title shots anytime soon either. Hart claims himself to be the new sheriff in town, and regarding Brian Pillman, he goes against what he just said about sticking to stipulations, saying that Pillman won't be wrestling in a dress despite his loss against Goldust in a match with a stip that said he had to. Owen gets some mic time and brags about crippling Steve Austin, then says he regrets showing compassion because it cost him his title. JR brings out new WWF commissioner Sgt. Slaughter, who comes down to the generic Linda McMahon/WrestleMania theme instead of his own. He says that he is the new sheriff in town, not Bret, and he makes the rules so Patriot will in fact be getting a shot at the gold. "Who did he ever beat to get a title shot!?" demands Bret. "You!" fires back Slaughter. Can't argue with that logic. Slaughter turns his attentions to the rest of the clan, telling Bulldog he *will* wrestle Shamrock again, Pillman that he *will* wear a dress tonight and Owen that he will get a rematch with Austin "when Stone Cold says so". This brings Steve Austin out who "says so right now", despite what his doctors might think. He rips on Owen for being stupid and not beating him when he had the chance, and says that he will beat him again. Conspicuous by his absence in this segment is Jim Neidhart, who was supposed to shave his goatee if any of the Hart Foundation lost last night. Anvil was currently battling legal problems, as prior to rejoining the WWF he had signed with a small-time Indy group UCW of New York, and technically shouldn't have been able to sign with the WWF at all.

Ken Shamrock vs. Kama Mustafa
This is interesting, sort of, in that Ken Shamrock was a legitimate MMA fighter and Kama played one on TV for a year or so. Of course, he sucked at it in a big way and was a colossal bore in the ring, but that's neither here nor there. If you expect this to be akin to an MMA fight, you are going to be sorely disappointed. It does start out that way, with the two squaring off with kick exchanges, but Kama is so frigging awful at it that they change tact and just wrestle. Of course, Kama is

terrible at that too, so this sucks. The crowd, who were red hot just 20-minute ago, are now deathly silent to the point that you can hear some smart-ass in the crowd doing Tatanka's war cry. I should point out that prior to the match, Sgt. Slaughter came out and sent all of the Nation to the back, with the black supremacist group quite happily and without protest, kowtowing to the whims of the white man in power. A message from the WWF or just shoddy booking? It could be either. Or both. Kama ends up getting attacked on the outside by two of Los Boricuas, and Shamrock finishes him off with the belly-to-belly suplex. Thankfully brief.
Final Rating: ¾*

A vignette airs for the 'roided to the gills German monster Brakus, with the caption stating "Brakus. Coming soon". Well, as I write this 17-years later, we are still waiting. Outside of a brief appearance on glorified UK house show *Mayhem in Manchester*, he did absolutely nothing of note, despite being around for years.

Taka Michinoku vs. Brian Christopher
Sunny reprises her role of guest ring announcer, with creative still unable to find anything better for her to do. Surely she could have managed someone? She was the kiss of death in many respects, but some guys had careers that couldn't go much lower at the time anyway. Bart Gunn perhaps. Leif Cassidy maybe. Bob Holly even. Jerry Lawler shows that he is a big (read: lot) of a xenophobe when he inexplicably laughs at Taka Michinoku's name being announced. It's Japanese and thus sounds funny, you see. That is pretty pathetic, even for him. These were the two guys whom the light heavyweight division was built around initially, which is half a great idea. Christopher is fine, but he works like a heavyweight in a light heavyweight's body, rather than a human speed ball. The hyena laugh that he insists on doing after every move grates quickly and becomes annoying and then unbearable in swift succession. That aside, they do run some nice spots and sequences, such as Taka landing on his feet from a German suplex and responding with a snap belly-to-belly and a spinning heel kick, and later on a big air Taka springboard dive. Christopher is not without merit either, but that laugh just kills my interest in him stone dead. The finish is a cheeky one, with Christopher hitting a few suplexes, but Taka throwing his legs back and catching Christopher in a cradle to score an sneaky win. It has to be sneaky of course, because this is the WWF and Taka is Japanese. Christopher attacks Taka after the bell and slingshots him out of the ring (which Taka bumps excessively with a flip), as he kisses his unbeaten streak goodbye.
Final Rating: **¼

Backstage, Slaughter continues to impose himself on proceedings by handing Brian Pillman his dress (where did he get it from? Did he skip out and pop to a store?), demanding "put it on". Pillman is not amused and throws in some cock innuendos at Sarge, who is nonplussed and warns Pillman that he has to wear the dress every week until he wins on *Raw*, lest he be suspended.

The WWF continues to surpass itself in the hypocrisy stakes, advertising a Steve Austin vs. Owen Hart match for tonight that they already know for sure won't be happening. Go back and re-read February's shows if you are not clear already on why this is such a hilarious thing for them to be doing.

Hunter Hearst Helmsley vs. Vader
This is a heel-heel match, though Vader's babyface turn is imminent. The problem is he is not there yet, so the apathy levels from the crowd rise. There is no formula as such to go with, so they just take turns being in control and Vader does his usual big bumping. Too much really as it kills his mystique and cheapens his size. This goes on for too long for the ref, before both guys get counted out while brawling on the outside. Why were they so adamant at getting this match on (it was supposed to happen last week), especially when that was the finish?
Final Rating: ½*

The Patriot vs. The Sultan
The Patriot cuts a passionate promo before the bout, telling Bret Hart: "America: love it or leave it... GET OUT!!!" and nicely building the story for his upcoming WWF Championship bout with the Hitman at *Ground Zero*. I never had Del Wilkes pegged as a good interview, but I thought this was tremendous. The match against Sultan? Not so much. It is a styles clash to say the least. The pairing of the two in combat was almost inevitable though, given the WWF's love for on the nose booking. Sultan starts with a back suplex, and the lack of shine for Patriot suggests another quickie TV match, and indeed that is exactly what it is. Patriot quickly polishes off his large foe with the Patriot Missile and the Uncle Slam, then the Hart Foundation immediately appear. They make their way to the ring, but Commissioner Slaughter intervenes and cuts all but Bret off at the pass, only the Hitman doesn't realise he is alone. Hart engages in a shouting match with Patriot from outside the ring and when he turns around he sees his back-up isn't there, giving Patriot chance to jump him from the ring. For a change on *Raw*, a brawl breaks out. This only existed to set up *Ground Zero,* but it was watchable due to its brevity.
Final Rating: *

Promo Time: Shawn Michaels
Shawn comes out doing a stripper dance in the aisle, then does his promo wearing his incredibly camp shorts. Who wears short shorts? Shawn wears short shorts. He gets a very mixed response from the crowd, but that doesn't matter because this is essentially his full heel turn anyway. Shawn reacts to it and says he doesn't care what people think of him and never has, but he is not happy with everyone blaming him for what happened last night (when he swung a chair at Bret Hart, who ducked, and accidentally hit the Undertaker and cost him his WWF Title). He wants people to take responsibility for their own actions rather than dump everything on him. It doesn't make sense really, because he was the one who swung the chair, so who else could be responsible? "Are you in cahoots with Bret Hart?" asks Vince. Oh come on, no one was ever thinking that, it didn't need to be asked. Shawn, unsurprisingly, is aghast at the prospect: "I always knew you were a nimrod, but you have just convinced me that you are the dumbest son of a bitch I have ever met in my life" he growls to a gleaming Vince. Honestly, he is positively beaming. But then suddenly he changes his tune at the drop of a hat (something I am sure many a booking committee is familiar with) and says he doesn't appreciate Shawn talking to him like that. Shawn mocks him and pretends to be scared, but Vince snaps back that he might well be shuddering with fear when he faces the Undertaker at the PPV. Vince decides to bail, leaving Shawn to rant alone. He vehemently denies being in cahoots with Hart before reminding us all that they don't get on at all, but that Bret needs him because Shawn beat him. The logic there doesn't quite add up either. It doesn't matter though, because the heat for Shawn is immense. So much so that it pisses him off and he throws in a shoot, letting the whole locker room know that he has no intention of jobbing to any of them (see Raw Recap).

The more he speaks, the more the crowd rails on him and the more pissed off and entertaining he gets. "Ten years, ten years I've given you, and this is the respect you've given me? Each and every one of you can go to Hell". Cue the Undertaker. Michaels wants no part of it and bails, so Vince returns to the ring. Taker says he has been doing too much talking lately so he isn't going to do that, and simply says Michaels will pay for his crimes and rest in peace. Cue Paul Bearer on the 'tron, who tells Taker he can call him all the names he wants and "make fun of the fat man", but he was with Kane last night and Kane is coming soon. Everything turns red as Taker leaves, as we go from a hard-hitting and intense reality-laced promo to *Phantom of the Opera* in a matter of minutes. Still, the whole thing was a riot, and Michaels' promo was intense, heated and perfectly delivered. Great turn.

Backstage, Sgt. Slaughter talks to a "doctor" who I would best describe as "70's Mark Madden". He is clearly just some fat Canadian randomer that managed to convince Slaughter that he was a doctor. Canadian, eh? Conspiratorial. "No wrestling tonight" says That 70's Mark, and Slaughter buys it. I cannot believe for a second that we were supposed to buy this dude as being an actual doctor. At least put him in a white coat or something.

Ahmed Johnson vs. Chainz
Ahmed comes out to his rarely used NOD remix version of his music, along with two of the biggest knee braces you will ever see. He is back awful soon from torn knee ligaments. Chainz was responsible, allegedly, hence this match. Sgt. Slaughter comes out again to remove the gangs, with the NOD putting up a modicum of resistance this time, but not much. The biker street thugs comply with him as well, obviously, as the nasty gangs get sent to the back like naughty children. Way to make two factions look piss weak in one go. JR calls Slaughter "overzealous", which is right. He has stuck his nose in everything tonight. The fans chant "ECW, ECW" at the former 'Prime Time' Brian Lee. He targets the injured leg and works it over for his shine, which means Ahmed selling! Yippee! Ahmed counters with a deadly looking Michinoku Driver, tells JR and Vince that "everyone is gonna die", then does it again. Amazing. Boricuas come out again, and for all his interfering, Slaughter has done sweet FA to stop them interfering tonight. Savio tries to steal Chainz's bike and the distraction causes him to turn into the Pearl River Plunge for the three. Out come DOA (a little late) to run off Boricuas, and with Ahmed now outnumbered the Nation returns. They do the salute then wham, Faarooq twats Ahmed across the head and the NOD beat him down. And thus, he is a babyface again. Yes, moments after saying "everyone is gonna die". Wha? He won! That's how you kill a career: turn a popular babyface heel and have them go against everything they stood for, then switch them back two months later with all the trust gone. Baffling. Ahmed looks to be Injured, again! From a squash!
Final Rating: ½*

The Godwinns vs. The Headbangers
Kill me. This actually starts surprisingly well, with Hank and Thrasher doing a run spot and some mat work! Honestly. Once the Godwinns take over and go to generic heat, the crowd dies and a few people chant "boring". Vince ignores the match and instead talks about Brian Pillman wearing a dress later, and says he must have "tried on loads", which is silly when we already saw a segment where Slaughter gave the dress to him. Godwinns over, nothing to see here.
Final Rating: ½*

Brian Pillman vs. Bob Holly
Goldust and Marlena pull up in the front row before we get going so they can get a good look at poor Brian in the dress. Marlena is particularly pleased, because she wants to see what kind of woman he makes, as he was not a very "gentlemanly man". Pillman hams it up to the hilt and is reluctant to come down the aisle, and has to be pushed through the curtain. He looks great in a dress actually, it suits him. He tries to retain his manliness with some meaty chops, but the crowd are having none of it and chant "faggot" at him. Holly scores with an atomic drop, which apparently hurts more when you are wearing a dress as opposed to skin-hugging spandex... To add to the gag, Pillman is wearing tighty whities underneath his dress. JR doesn't see the funny side and warns that the WWF might have made a mistake and that a monster could be spawned from this, because Pillman is a dangerous and unhinged man. I would have loved to see how his character progressed into 1998 and beyond, because I think once his ring sharpness came back properly and he honed his style to fit his injury-induced limitations, he would surely have been a viable contender to work against Steve Austin on top. Marlena distracts with a bra, which means she either took hers off or she carries one around with her for moments just like this, and Goldust taunts Pillman, causing him to get counted out without even realising it.. Pillman is furious and the gag continues.
Final Rating: *

Owen Hart vs. Dude Love
Bret Hart joins the commentary team for this. One of the two "Dudettes" in the crowd is Mick Foley's smoking hot wife Colette. She dances to his music as the cameras get a close-up shot of her waps. Considering the guys involved, this no-where near meets expectations. Mick Foley was cursed when he donned the Dude Love tights prior to 1998, because his performances as the Dudester were usually pretty rough. Here he works over Owen for an age, despite being the babyface, with nothing really happening. Entertainment is found from Bret Hart ripping into Dude and America for rule-breaking, and then mockingly shouting: "Stoooopppppiiiid. That's what he is; stupid" when Love misses a running diving elbow on the ramp. What a painful bump to take for such a pointless, nothing match. Foley has just essentially worked a heat, so the last thing I want to see is Owen doing the same, but unfortunately he does. I mean don't be mistaken, this is not a bad match, far from it, I just think they could have had a much better one. The arrival of the British Bulldog at ringside sufficiently distracts the referee enough for Bret Hart to get involved and nail Dude, making me wonder why a Foley-Hart match was never booked on pay-per-view. I guess there wasn't a lot of time due to Hart's 1996 hiatus and 1997 departure, but I think they could have had an incredible series given their collective wrestling brains. Steve Austin, broken neck and all, comes out and belts Owen with his own Slammy and Dude gets the win. Post match, Colette straddles him in the corner and macks off with him. How the hell did Foley manage to score someone so fine!? Pardon the *Red Dwarf* reference, but: "What a guy!"
Final Rating: *¾

THE RAW RECAP:

Most Entertaining: Shawn Michaels. The heel turn was the right decision, and playing the character wasn't a stretch for Shawn. At all. If anything, his onscreen character was *less* obnoxious and arrogant than his real life personality.

Least Entertaining: Phineas Godwinn. As soon as he got in the ring, his match turned to shit.

Quote of the Night: "I wanna tell you people something: Undertaker; the Heartbreak Kid lays down for absolutely no one. I don't do it for Bret Hart, I don't do it for you, I don't do it for the fans of the World Wrestling Federation, I don't do it for anybody".

Match of the Night: Taka Michinoku vs. Brian Christopher. A solid if unspectacular light heavyweight match, which did feature some nice sequences but didn't set the world alight.

Verdict: The highlight of the episode is the vitriolic Shawn Michaels promo, though there are a few other memorable moments such as Brian Pillman in a dress and Ahmed Johnson being excommunicated from the Nation. It won't go down as a classic episode due to the unspectacular matches and an overuse of Sgt. Slaughter in his new commissioner role, but with a quick pace to the show, it never gets dull. Enjoyable enough.
Rating: 54

08.11.97 by James Dixon

Venue: Biloxi, MS
Taped: 08.11.97
Raw Rating: 2.9
Nitro Rating: 3.8

Promo Time: Shawn Michaels
Shawn is dressed slightly better this week, though "slightly better" for him is pretty much a fashion abomination for everyone else. JR takes over from Vince McMahon on interview duties after Shawn tore into Vince last week. We rehash the situation at *SummerSlam* again, and Shawn says he had a job to do and he did it. Shawn changes his tune from last week, saying that if WWF management want to dump everything in his lap, then that is fine because he has had plenty on his lap before. Oo-er. Michaels rails on Vince for not having the guts to call him and tell him he was working with Mankind tonight, and that he had to find out by watching *Superstars*. How awful for him having to watch *Superstars*! "You think I cussed you last week? You ain't seen nothing yet" says Shawn, as the crowd start a loud "Shawn is gay" chant. Jerry Lawler plays his favourite trick of trying to get his co-commentator to repeat something inappropriate, asking Vince: "What are they saying, McMahon?". Vince shows his usual PC side, responding: "I don't think it is complimentary". Yeah, because everyone hates a homo, right Vince? "Why don't you ask your sister and your momma how gay Shawn is?" says HBK to the yokel crowd. Shawn complains, like how he accuses Bret of doing, saying that WWF officials have him on their hit list. Vince shakes his head at this, and when Shawn says he doesn't want people stealing his spotlight because he wants it all for himself, Vince says: "I know that's right!". The tension here is palpable, manufactured or not. Sgt. Slaughter strolls out and shrugs off Shawn's barb about the size of his chin, telling him he is going to put his "big jaw" in his business. Slaughter drawls out a promo, but the content is almost white noise because of Shawn's clarting about, as he gets on his tiptoes to make himself look bigger, constantly wipes Sarge's spittle off his face and then calls him "Commissioner Gordon". I always appreciate a Batman reference. Shawn says he feels his "life is in danger again" and thus has hired an insurance policy, and as his track record in the past can attest, he always delivers in that regard. "And that's an order!" mocks Michaels to

finish the promo, before giving Sarge a crotch chop before that meant anything in a wrestling sense. Another great promo from an invigorated and unleashed Shawn Michaels. The WWF have let a verbal monster run loose, and while he might give Vince and the USA Network officials some headaches and near heart attacks, he is unquestionably fantastic television.

Country Whippin' Match
Road Warrior Hawk vs. Henry Godwinn
Unfortunately this is not some form of sick joke, and the rules state that the winner is the man to whip their opponent out of the ring with a leather strap that is attached to their wrist. That is it, they are the only rules. Remember that. If anyone is curious why Hawk is working the match rather than the generally better suited Animal, it is because when he returned to the WWF it was under the condition that he only worked in tag matches, because he had a Lloyds of London policy that covered his injuries, and if he worked singles bouts it would violate the terms. Hawk is more reckless though, so at least this could be unnecessarily violent. Shame in a sense that it is Henry rather than Phineas, because I would be quite happy to see the useless P.I.G whipped to pieces. There is a kayfabe issue here too of course, with Hawk being the one who broke Henry's neck. To add to an already busy situation, Owen Hart and the British Bulldog join the commentary team, and both discuss wrestling the Patriot, and they have a friendly argument about who gets to kick his ass tonight. As for the match? There is a lot of whipping each other with the leather strap, and not much else. But hey, what do you expect from a match like this? It does what it says it will, which I guess is all you can ask. It is actually far more interesting that you would expect, but the finish is idiotic. First, Phineas gets involved as it is no DQ, which really begs the question why neither he nor Animal got involved earlier. Then Animal uses the Godwinns' slop bucket on Phineas and Henry, knocking Hank out of the ring so Earl Hebner calls the match. But the rules were that you had to whip your opponent out of the ring to win. Literally, they were the only rules and they don't follow that! It is little things like these that people criticise Vince Russo for, because anything that he perceives as unimportant or an unfortunate aside to the story he wants to tell just gets ignored. What the clueless bastard doesn't realise is that these small things all add up and eventually start to unravel. I can't say with absolutely certainty that he booked that finish, but it has his hallmarks all over it.
Final Rating: *¼

Earlier tonight, Sgt. Slaughter gave Brian Pillman his wrestling gear for the evening, which happened to be another gold dress. This was almost a carbon copy repeat of the interaction the two had last week, with Slaughter even delivering the same line about Pillman wearing it until he wins on the show.

Tony Williams vs. Scott Putski
This is another of those underwhelming light heavyweight exhibitions, featuring a guy incorrectly pegged as one of the stars of the division against an unknown who has no chance of getting over. Today it is former WWF enhancement talent Tony Williams, who is also a current USWA mainstay (and tag partner of Brian Christopher). Because everything has to have something else going on, Goldust and Marlena come out to watch the action from ringside, joining the announce team for the bout. Putski and Williams assemble a decent enough match, but the WWF has already lost interest in the division before it has even really started, and they cut to a split screen of Goldust's new "Shattered Dreams Production", which is footage of Brian Pillman in the locker room struggling to get his dress on. "This is the first time we have seen Pillman in his

underwear, which is pretty exciting" says JR out of the blue. Ooookay. "Not for most men!" responds Vince. Chalk up another one of gay rights. I should note that the split screen is far from an even split, which the Pillman footage some three time bigger than the completely irrelevant match. Putski wins with the Polish Hammer, but the Pillman stuff overshadowed this to the point that I can't even rate it. After the match, Sgt. Slaughter comes down and evicts Goldust and Marlena from the announce desk, because Pillman is up next and he is thinking ahead to prevent an incident. Smart from the Sarge.

Brian Pillman vs. Flash Funk
Pillman again gets pushed through the curtain due to his reluctance to come out. I never really realised prior to this just how excellent and terrifying Pillman's music is. It's even better than Sid's on the list of fantastic psychotic themes. Is it better than evil Doink's music though? Hmm, I'm not so sure about that. Because Pillman is all character and no longer much cop in the ring since his broken ankle, the match is not that interesting. In fact, it is sufficiently uninteresting that Lawler, Vince and JR discuss Lawler's upcoming appearance on the ECW *Hardcore Heaven* pay-per-view and namedrop the likes of Tommy Dreamer and Sabu. That doesn't sound particularly interesting now, but at the time it was incredible for the WWF to be promoting another company's pay-per-view. Like last week on *Raw* where Pillman lost to Bob Holly via count out thanks to Goldust and Marlena sat in the front row, the shiny twosome come out and distract Pillman again, this time showing the video of him getting changed from earlier on the Titantron. Flash rolls Pillman up for the upset win, and Pillman is boiling.
Final Rating: ¾*

To promote the Coliseum Video release of *SummerSlam*, the WWF compassionately shows footage of Owen Hart breaking Steve Austin's neck. They are such a caring company to work for.

Promo Time: Dude Love
Busy night for Mick Foley, as he is wrestling Shawn Michaels in tonight's main event under the Mankind guise as well. Vince conducts the interview, and he is wearing a huge smile throughout, enamoured as he clearly is with the Dude Love character. Vince obviously does get personal satisfaction out of letting someone live their dream, and he is also a fan of goofy gimmicks and characters (see: the 80s/early 90s). Dude is one of the goofiest of them all in his own charming way, and he amuses me greatly with his update on "the ice man" ('Stone Cold' Steve Austin). Vince questions whether Dude and Austin can reign as tag champions much longer, what with an imminent fatal four way tag match coming up at *Ground Zero* against the British Bulldog & Owen Hart, the Legion of Doom and the Godwinns. Yes, they were going to put the Godwinns in there with Steve Austin on PPV. Keen observers will be well aware that said match never occurred in that form, with Austin having to pull out because of the injury. The replacement tandem, the Headbangers, were hardly a like-for-like switch were they? But at this point, the original match is still booked so Dude runs down the opposition in his charming manner. First he says of the Legion of Doom: "Owww, what a rush, daddy" before losing his way (intentionally, though that is lost on Lawler), saying the Godwinns "wouldn't know hip if they smoked it" and that he hoped Owen and the British "bow wow wow" Bulldog "have nine lives". Complete gibberish, but that is the gimmick. Vince delves into the popular late 90s phenomenon of self-referentialism, asking Dude who he thinks will win between Shawn Michaels and Mankind. This is all too much for Michaels, who appears on the Titantron and throws

his favourite insult ("nimrod") at the Dude, before railing on him: "You are not me, you are not even you, you idiot! Don't you understand that?" Dude quotes John Lennon and then tells Michaels that Mankind is going to tear him up "koo-koo-ka-chou". As warm inside as the character might make you feel, because Mick Foley truly is a master of making wrestling fun and entertaining, I am not a fan of the gimmick and I don't really enjoy Dude's promos either. It's not bad, but it is not to my tastes. Others will surely enjoy Dude much more, but I for one prefer Mankind and Cactus Jack.

Owen Hart & British Bulldog vs. Patriot & Ken Shamrock
"Things are getting quite political out here" says Vince McMahon as the Patriot makes his way to the ring. "I know that's right" responds JR. While Vince meant due to the Canada vs. USA war, JR was quite clearly referring to the backstage struggles Wilkes had with the Harts, who for whatever reason just didn't like him. In his book, Bret Hart said of his feud with the Patriot:

"It was hard to do anything extraordinary because Wilkes had worked only in Japan and wasn't over by any stretch of the imagination in the United States. What had been a red-hot American versus Canadian angle for the WWF lost its heat when the champion had to fight a cartoon - a hokey, masked marvel in red, white and blue that fans couldn't relate to because, with a mask on, he couldn't express pain or anything"

Shamrock comes out and he is OVER like rover and gets a phenomenal reaction. This is a hot, hot crowd and it gets Vince all pumped up too. Someone needs to get Shamrock a towel to dab himself down with though, because he looks like he just fell into a tub of grease. Bret Hart wanders out during the middle of the bout as JR mentions his "Jim Jones-like influence", which is an absurd thing to say. Jones, for those unaware, was the leader of the Peoples Temple, a cult group who partook in a mass murder/suicide in 1978 of over 900 of its members in Jonestown, Guyana. Jones was a koolaidist who brainwashed people into thinking they were moving on to a better life, which is hardly comparable to the Hart Foundation's hatred of America. Well, Jones was frustrated with America too due to the country's condemnation of communism and the fear of a backlash he would receive for his Marxist views, but that is not quite the same. Wrestling is escapist entertainment, comparing anything that happens in it to one of the biggest mass losses of American life (war aside) in history is never right, off the cuff comment or not. So, history lesson and moral outrage out of the way, what of the match? Well, it's blah, but the crowd makes up for it by reacting to everything. Shamrock and Owen end up on the outside and the referee is distracted by them, and Patriot hits the Uncle Slam on Davey onto a chair for the win. He gets a huge pop for that, and the more I rewatch the Patriot, the more I think that perhaps the WWF missed the boat with him. Though, I guess once the Hart Foundation dispersed at the end of the year and left the company, he would have lost a lot of his appeal. His character was very much the antithesis of everything that was in vogue in the company as we moved in to 1998.
Final Rating: *¾

Video Control gives us footage of the hundreds of fans who gathered at Toronto airport after last week's *Raw* to welcome home new WWF Champion Bret Hart. The fans, who are a mix of ages, mock America for their guy losing and then burst spontaneously into song, singing *'O Canada'*. On top of that, various Canadian newspapers ran front page stories about Hart winning the belt. Bret's popularity in his home country was remarkable, and he really was every bit the Canadian hero he claimed to be.

Backstage, the Patriot (who sounds a lot like a Von Erich when he speaks) tries to cut a promo about deserving his place in the WWF and deserving the title belt, but Bret Hart blindsides him with a chair and lays the boots in.

Faarooq vs. Chainz

I didn't expect this to be good, and indeed it isn't, with timing and communication issues blighting the contest such as Faarooq setting for his increasingly blatant electric chair drop reversal only for Chainz to just casually wander out from under his legs. Another example sees Faarooq fail to roll out of the way fully from an elbow drop, making the whole thing look really ugly. The ref gets bumped and that cues Rocky Maivia, who shockingly lamps Chainz with a Rock Bottom for the Faarooq win. Post match, Rocky, already oozing far more charisma after ten seconds as a heel than in his entire initial babyface run, throws the black power NOD salute. This was a pivotal moment in WWF history, because if Rocky hadn't turned heel and had just stayed as a blue-chipper babyface, he might not have made it much further and could even have been cut. Instead, this turn catapulted him on an unstoppable route to the top. In 14-months he will be at the pinnacle of the profession as WWF Champion.
Final Rating: ¼*

Backstage, an enterprising cameraman attempts to catch a glimpse of a confab between the Nation and new member Rocky Maivia, but Faarooq spots him and locks him out of their locker room. Cue the arrival of DOA, who do the job for the same door. Four big burly bikers, and they can't figure out how to get into a locked door. Hitting it with chairs is not the answer. Try kicking it down maybe? The DOA have the collective IQs of a fish.

Out comes Sable, clad in pleather from head to toe. Jerry Lawler and JR make subtle innuendos about her, with Lawler talking about how much bigger... than Marc Mero she has gotten and JR saying she has a profile more prominent than Sgt. Slaughter. In other words, she has massive fake tits. The Patriot takes over the segment, thankfully, saying he can take on anyone face-to-face, one-on-one, but there is not much he can do when he gets attacked from behind with a chair. He wants Bret to prove himself as a man and come out and face him right now. Bret acquiesces, and a ruckus ensues. Obviously the WWF was never actually going to give away their PPV title match on free TV a few weeks beforehand, and the Hart Foundation quickly come out to lay a gang beating on the Patriot. They wrap him in the Canadian flag and choke him with it as officials try and stop them, but the Harts are relentless. Patriot sells it convincingly and shows out well, but the crowd don't quite bite on it.

Mankind vs. Shawn Michaels

This is Michaels' first match since his tantrum in June and a rematch from their classic a year ago at *Mind Games*. I am glad Mick Foley is back under the mask as Mankind for this rather than Dude Love, because it probably means this match will be better for it. Credit to Foley for getting in the zone for three characters in such a short space of time though. Mankind brings a bin to the ring but Michaels is the one who uses it. They do a fun spot with Michaels clocking Foley while the bin is on his head, and when it comes off he is wearing the bin bag that was inside. You would think that would hamper him, but it doesn't, and he manages to put on the Mandible Claw while

still trapped inside the bag. It makes for a unique visual. Lawler and JR discuss the forthcoming ECW *Hardcore Heaven*, which has Vince scrambling to point out that it is not a WWF show. JR shills it again and Vince gets annoyed at the match getting ignored and asks JR if he is "commentating on it or something", and JR says: "I should be!". Poor Joey. Michaels and Mankind brawl on the outside and Michaels tries a back body drop through the announce table, which fails. Michaels tries again and hits a flying elbow, but the table doesn't sell for him. Ouch. Back in the ring, Michaels hits the Savage Flying Elbow as JR throws in a snide "Nobody delivers that elbow off the top like Shawn Michaels", which is a sly and not so subtle dig at Randy Savage, who for the record does do it way better. Better than anyone in fact. Mankind ducks a Sweet Chin Music attempt and catches the Mandible Claw, which sends them tumbling to the outside again. Michaels ups the aggression by brutalising Mankind's head into the ring steps and the post, then tries a backdrop onto the table, which still refuses to break. Michaels will have a tantrum with it soon and politic for it to lose its spot. To the catering room for you, announce table. Hunter Hearst Helmsley and Chyna come out to watch, though the assumption is that their presence is due to their current ongoing feud with Mick Foley, but in reality it is the first chance for the WWF to pair Michaels and Helmsley together as they begin the formation of D-Generation X. Mankind manages to rally and drives Shawn's head into the mat before hitting his running knee in the corner, but then suddenly 'Ravishing' Rick Rude strolls down the aisle in his first WWF appearance since 1990. He is Shawn's new insurance policy, and a fine choice at that. Rude is in my personal top five. Hunter trips Mankind as the referee struggles to keep track of things, and Rude BELTS poor Mick in the head with a chair, allowing Michaels to hit the Sweet Chin Music for the win. Undertaker comes out as the outsiders involved reaches four, but he is stopped in his tracks by Paul Bearer on the Titantron, saying the waiting is nearly over and Kane is coming. This was a good match, though nowhere near their *Mind Games* classic, obviously. That Rude chair shot though... Jesus.
Final Rating: ***½

THE RAW RECAP:

Most Entertaining: Shawn Michaels. Another great performance from the Heartbreak Kid. Not only did he deliver in the ring in his first match in a couple of months, but he also excelled behind the stick. *Raw* is a much stronger show when HBK is involved.

Least Entertaining: Chainz. He was dire against Faarooq, and while the NOD leader was just as poor, at least he wasn't later defeated by a door like the hapless biker was.

Quote of the Night: "Why don't you ask your sister and your momma how gay Shawn is?" - Shawn Michaels loses his temper with the crowd and resorts to playground level retorts. It would be a good few years before he learned how to "turn the other cheek", so to speak.

Match of the Night: Shawn Michaels vs. Mankind. Not quite as good as some have rated it, because it is fairly brief and basically a significantly lesser version of their PPV classic, but still an excellent *Raw* main event and yet another example of just how much the in-ring on the show improves when Shawn Michaels is wrestling.

Verdict: Everything that Shawn Michaels was involved in on this show was great viewing, but a lot of the other stuff rather

meandered. At times there was just too much going on, which was exciting and great for the pace of the show, but it flat out ruined some things, like the light heavyweight match. Memorable for the Rock heel turn and the return of Rick Rude, but other than that this was very much the Shawn Michaels Show.
Rating: 59

08.18.97 by James Dixon

Venue: Atlantic City, NJ
Taped: 08.18.97
Raw Rating: 3.2
Nitro Rating: 4.0

Promo Time: Rick Rude
Vince McMahon is in the ring for this interview and announces Rude as "one of the all-time World Wrestling Federation greats". This is true, he is, but if Vince agrees then why the reluctance to put him in the Hall of Fame? Rude opens with his classic pre-match promo from the past for the nostalgia pop, but what follows is a disaster. Vince questions Rude's motives and wants to know who paid him off, and Rude doesn't quite know how to answer so goes into a diatribe about being an insurance salesman. Vince needles at him more to try and get him to define his role, and Rude starts to lose his cool, repeating "What I'm trying to tell yak!..." a couple of times as he tries and fails to get his point across. Rude brings an end to things by asking for his music and skulking off, as JR defends the segment by declaring "I'm not sure we got all of our questions answered, but Rick Rude is in the building". As noted, I love Rude and I am delighted he is briefly back, but outside of his well rehearsed pre-match gambit he struggled on the stick.

Owen Hart & The British Bulldog vs. The Legion of Doom
As well as having had a few outings with each other already this year, both tandems are also in the overhyped Ground Zero four way tag match. I firmly believe that you can generate more interest in matches by not having the participants touch prior to the big confrontation, but the WWF/E often feels the opposite way. The worst ever example of that was when they ran the Rock-Hogan dream match on *Raw* in March 2002 a week before *WrestleMania X-8* as part of a handicap match, with Rock teaming with Steve Austin in defeat to the nWo triumvirate of Hogan, Hall and Nash. Not only were a few dream confrontations splurged in one go, but it was also the first match in the WWF for any of the nWo guys in half a decade or more. That kind of behaviour is WCW levels of throwing away PPV calibre matches on free television. This is not quite at the same level, but the point remains the same. This is the standard power versus technical acumen match that we have seen these two teams do with each other before, and as usual the LOD spots don't change a great deal. Yes, Hawk takes the heat after missing a shoulder charge in the corner. He even takes a bump or two during it, including an effortless stalling suplex from the powerful Bulldog. Hawk finds himself in the wrong corner as these two legendary teams decide that formula is the way to go for a throwaway television match, and it is hard to blame them. A double clothesline is a fitting cliché to lead to the hot tag and the finishing sequence is pretty good, with Owen and Animal exchanging fall attempts before Hank Godwinn gets revenge for last week by welting Animal with a slop bucket across the chops, and Owen drops on top for the win. A donnybrook breaks out, but there is no sign of the fourth participants in the match Steve Austin and Dude Love. There wouldn't be of course, because there was no chance Austin would be involved due to his injury, something the WWF knew from probably the night after *SummerSlam*. That didn't stop them advertising it still anyway of course. This was a fine TV formula match but nothing more.
Final Rating: *¾

At *Ground Zero* the Undertaker and Shawn Michaels will meet "for the first time ever" according to the PPV hype man. Other than in tonight's main event of course, where they will also clash... This company is laugh out loud hilarious.

Backstage, Shawn Michaels complains about being painted into a corner by "Caesar" (Vince McMahon) and promises that he will respond in turn.

Brian Christopher vs. Flash Funk
In an hilarious WWF production gaffe, Sunny begins to announce Flash Funk when his music plays, but out comes Brian Christopher. Seems someone wasn't doing their job right. It's funny because it is Kevin Dunn's department. I bet his teeth were chattering with rage ten to the dozen. Christopher dances to the ring wearing that shit-eating grin that makes you want to punch his head off, and cuts a promo complete with hyena laugh that makes one feel the same. Even though his character is annoying beyond simple heat, Christopher can work good matches with the right opponent, and Funk may well be that. Vince refers to Flash as a heavyweight, and while he certainly outweighs Christopher by some 30lbs at least, he is easily the better flyer of the two and far more suited for the style the group wants for its light heavyweight division than 'Too Sexy'. The exchanges between the two are smooth and fairly exciting, with Funk looking good yet again in a match on *Raw* where he is allowed to shine. He even picks up the win, hitting the impressive 450 splash after accidentally crotching Christopher on the top. Jerry Lawler berates Christopher after the result, and presumably grounds him for a week and takes away his toys when they get home too.
Final Rating: **¼

Backstage, the Undertaker says his patience with Shawn Michaels has ran out, and he seems to be under the impression he is on an MTV special, as he says he will "settle the score" with HBK tonight.

The Sultan vs. Ken Shamrock
Sultan has been reduced to the role of JTTS so he has little hope coming into this. Even so, he sticks to his usual game plan rather than aping others and attempting to "shoot" with Shamrock, and it looks to be working when he catches a crossbody, but he ends up getting clotheslined to the outside. Sultan recovers and sends Shamrock into the steel steps and Iron Sheik belts him with the flag, but Sultan remains the aggressor for only a matter of moments before getting slammed and then turned inside out with a clothesline. An overhead belly-to-belly from Shamrock is impressive, and then he drags Sheik in there and gives him one too. A rana to Sultan follows, and the ankle lock taps him out for the win in another breezy and fun match tonight on *Raw*. The crowd in Atlantic City approve and give Shamrock a sustained ovation.
Final Rating: **

Promo Time: The Nation of Domination
The Nation come out uninvited, and Faarooq goes on a 100 mile an hour rant without pausing for breath for about three solid minutes. He covers everything from the ejection of Ahmed Johnson from the group (a white man in a black body,

apparently) and then rips Savio Vega and Crush, who he claims to have taken from the trash heap. He is not far off the truth. Man, he is so angry and passionate, why couldn't he always be like this? Faarooq puts over new Nation member Rocky Maivia, who he says tried to do things the "American way" by slapping hands and smiling, but the fans turned on him. Rocky puts it somewhat better:

"I got three words: "die, Rocky, die". That's the gratitude I get from you pieces of crap for all my blood, my sweat and my tears? This isn't about the colour of my skin, this is about respect! I became the youngest Intercontinental Champion in WWF history, and what did it get me? In arenas across the country I heard chants of "Rocky sucks". Well, Rocky Maivia is a lot of things, but "sucks" isn't one of 'em. Hey, it's not a black thing, it's not a white thing. Hey, let's talk about a racist faction: you wanna talk about a group that's prejudice, let's talk about the DOA. The DOA epitomise racism. But hey, to hell with the DOA. I wanna make one point to all you jackass fans out there: Rocky Maivia and the new Nation of Domination lives, breathes and dies respect, and we will earn respect by any means necessary."

Following that, Crush appears on the screen and follows that now legendary Rocky promo by calling the NOD the "Nation of Constipation". Oh, just get the fuck off my screen you useless lump of shit. Crush wants the Nation to meet the DOA in the parking lot so they can have a ruckus without the overzealous Sgt. Slaughter sticking his massive chin in. Other than Crush, brah, acting like a five year old, this was all gold. Faarooq was as good behind the stick as I have ever seen him and Rocky went from unbearable generic blue-chipper babyface to asshole heel with one beautifully delivered and right on the money promo. Shifting the focus away from "black power" (which Rocky was uncomfortable with) and making it instead about respect, was a smart move. This promo was another integral cog in the future success of the WWF machine, because it established Rocky as someone who could talk and someone with the right Attitude in the new look WWF. His ascent was just beginning, but the journey would be incredible. A true landmark moment, even if it might not have seemed quite as important at the time.

Backstage, Hunter cuts another of his annoying promos, threatening Vince with a war because of being forced to team up with Shawn Michaels. Delightfully, Vince cuts him off so we can go to the parking lot and see a brawl erupting between the DOA and the Nation. As they exchange fisticuffs, Los Boricuas steal their bikes. Great stuff.

Brian Pillman vs. Jesse Jammes
Back to this angle then, as Pillman continues to work in a dress due to his inability to win a match. Jammes seems like a good opponent for him given that he was still a few months away from being the Road Dogg and turning his career around. In other words, he was a jobber. A perverted one at that, as he gets his kicks lifting up Pillman's skirt, which gets him chopped. Pillman is thrilled when Jammes misses off the top with something because it gives him an opening to win the match, but Goldust wanders out and casually drops an elbow on Double J, and of course causes the disqualification. Clever swine. Goldust thinks it is funny, but Pillman is pissed off now, and that is a volatile cocktail. Pillman wants one more match with Goldust and puts his WWF career on the line, but in return Goldust has to stake Marlena's services as Pillman's "personal assistant" for 30 days. Goldust bottles it and Pillman goads him, saying he knows Marlena as "Terri" and that Dustin's daughter Dakota is actually his. Goldust takes the bait and charges the ring, then Terri jumps her cue and accepts the challenge while Pillman is still ranting, meaning everyone misses it. She repeats it three or four times with the most awful wooden delivery I have witnessed from a WWF personality this side of Kaitlyn, and the whole thing almost gets killed stone dead right there. Terri was bad. Really bad. There is a modicum of truth to some of this angle as the lines between reality and storyline blur, because Pillman used to date Terri when they were both in WCW in the early 90s prior to her getting with Dustin. It's a murky road to travel down, especially with the intended payoff being Terri leaving Goldust for Pillman, but that sadly never came to pass due to Pillman's death two months later.
Final Rating: ¾*

Vader vs. The Patriot
The pushes are the wrong way around here really, because a Vader-Hart program would have had far more appeal with the masses than Patriot-Hart. That is, if Vader hadn't been booked like such a loser as of late. Vader starts well when Patriot is distracted by Bret Hart in the aisle, and pounds away like the badass he is. Patriot soon fires back with a flying clothesline, but they make a real mess of a duck spot in the corner when Patriot gets his timing wrong. Vader continues to take a beating, but remembers who he is and drops a big ass splash on Patriot's chest and goes back to his clubbing, getting a two count from a splash. Patriot responds with head butts, but the crowd is really not that into him at all. Vader goes for the Vaderbomb but eats knees, and a sloppy DDT gets a near fall from Patriot. This has been perfectly watchable, worked at a fast pace and with plenty of back-and-forth, but the audience just doesn't believe in the Patriot character as anything more than midcard, which is a shame. Still though, it should be no real surprise that he wins this one clean with the Uncle Slam, what with Vader's current jobbing streak and Patriot being on a missile (hoho) to the top of the card. Vader attacks Patriot after the match and Bret Hart comes to the ring to join the beating, putting the Maple Leaf over Patriot for Vader to hit him with the Vaderbomb, but Vader changes his mind and gets down from the ropes then snaps the flag in half. Naturally this leads to a Vader-Hart brawl, which the crowd does get in to. The Hart Foundation get involved afterwards to break things up, as I continue to wish that Vader and Hart had worked on PPV in a singles bout at least once. Vader breathed new life into his career with this babyface turn, briefly, putting in some splendid performances at *One Night Only* and *Survivor Series*, but then falling down the pecking order again and disappearing.
Final Rating: **½

Backstage, a pissed off Bret Hart rants at the fans for spitting on him and throwing stuff at him, and calls out Vader for a match at any time. The funny thing is, all the American fans were doing by acting like that was further proving Bret's point.

Promo Time: Steve Austin
Prior to this they show a great video package of the *SummerSlam* incident, and the Steve Austin aggrandisement from Vince McMahon in the voice over is a thing of brilliance. If only he put this much passion into making other people into stars. This promo doesn't take place in the ring but rather is conducted by Jim Ross in a shithole of a hotel room in Philly. JR wants to know about *SummerSlam*, what Austin's doctors have said and his future. Austin is "pissed off" about what happened, and that is a shoot. Stone Cold was livid with Owen for trying the move, which he had expressed that he didn't want to take in the first place. I can't quite figure what was going

through Owen's head at the time, because it is such a dangerous move to attempt. He was such a safe worker, so for him to have done that just doesn't make sense. I think he set for the Tombstone, then realised he couldn't do it on the same show as Undertaker, especially when he was WWF Champion and following him in the main event, so switched to the sitout version, and because of the slight split-second indecision, he didn't set Austin right and thus his head was too low and he got injured. Austin in semi-kayfabed world says that Owen is going to pay and get the "shit kicked out of him" when he comes back. Regarding the doctors, he says they can tell him whatever they want, but he will do whatever he wants to do because the decision is his. Austin says he will be at *Ground Zero* but doesn't specify that he will be wrestling, and even admits he might be there to give up his belts. Stone Cold is excellent in this, delivering his lines like a machine gun sprays bullets, coming off as surly, pissed off and ready for a fight, but not without humour. One moment in particular amuses me, with Austin stopping in the middle of a sentence to berate JR for wiping his nose, then continuing only to tell him "don't smile" and returning to his sentence without missing a beat. The guy is a hoot.

Shawn Michaels & Hunter Hearst Helmsley vs. The Undertaker & Mankind
This is the first outing for the yet to be officially formed D-Generation X, with Hunter and Michaels teaming for the first time, whereas Mankind and Undertaker have a long and storied rivalry and thus their alliance is shaky at best. Everyone in this match has had a long history with everyone else in it at some point in their respective careers. All four are of course legendary figures in the WWF/E, with multiple World Championships to their name, and three of the four can be comfortably considered among the great workers of their generation. The fourth merely thinks he is and is positioned as such, even though everyone else knows it to be false. Hey, there are perks to marrying into success... As you would expect, Mankind is on the receiving end of the majority of the offence, with Hunter and Michaels actually very coordinated as a tandem, busting out clever tags and nice double-teams. Mankind eventually avoids Sweet Chin Music and applies the Mandible Claw, only for Hunter to save and go for the Pedigree, which is switched into a slingshot and then switched again into a kick into the buckles, with Mankind falling on Hunter's balls as we go to a triple down. Taker gets the tag and cleans house, so Rick Rude comes over with a chair to belt him, but stops in his tracks when Taker spots him. Good job too, because if he had hit Taker like he hit Foley the other week, he would be in trouble. That prospect doesn't stop Michaels though, who belts Taker in the head with a chair shot so hard it sends him crumbling to the mat and breaks the chair. Obviously, that's a DQ. Michaels stands with Hunter, assessing what he has done, and when Taker sits up they all scarper. Fun match, some nice spots, but a solid TV main event and nothing more. Considering who was involved, it could have been one of the all-time great *Raw* matches.
Final Rating: **¼

THE RAW RECAP:

Most Entertaining: Rocky Maivia. A killer promo from the future Rock changed the course of his WWF career and set him on a one-way upwards trajectory.

Least Entertaining: Crush, brah. "Nation of Constipation"!? What is this, WWF Attitude or Sesame Street? Actually scratch that; Sesame Street would never be so juvenile.

Quote of the Night: "Under all that thick black skin of his is a white man dying to get out. He wants to be pretty like Shawn Michaels, he wants to be like Stone Cold Steve Austin. Well I got news for you Ahmed Johnson: you couldn't be white if they sandblasted your ass twenty times." - Faarooq has a few choice words for Ahmed Johnson.

Match of the Night: Vader vs. The Patriot. Tonight's in-ring was shockingly consistent but never spectacular. Vader against the Patriot might not have been a classic but they cut a helluva pace and tried damn hard to get an uninterested crowd to bite. I appreciated the effort.

Verdict: Another enjoyable effort from the WWF, with everyone feeling in the mood to put on a show rather than run through the motions in the squared circle as is often the case on *Raw*. Rocky Maivia was the surprise star behind the mic, though the show loses points for that horrible meandering Rick Rude interview that opened the show. Outside of Rocky becoming "The Rock" in all but name, nothing was exceptional tonight, but for once the solid wrestling action carried it through and made it well worth a watch.
Rating: 64

08.29.97 - "Friday Night's Main Event" by James Dixon

Venue: Chicago, IL
Taped: 08.23.97
Raw Rating: N/A
Nitro Rating: 5.0

With *Raw* cancelled for the next two weeks due to the USA Network's coverage of the US Open, the WWF realised they could not afford to go two weeks without any programming, so they came up with this replacement broadcast airing on Friday evenings. To make it a big deal, we are taped from the prestige venue the Rosemont Horizon, which also hosted *The Wrestling Classic*, 1/3rd of *WrestleMania 2* and also *WrestleMania 13* earlier in the year. Hey, the two *WrestleMania* shows it hosted were the only ones with no roman numerals... What does Chicago have against Rome? We kick off with a recap of the previous episode of *Raw*, which ended with Shawn Michaels destroying the Undertaker with a chair and busting him wide open. This show then gets its own opening video package entirely different from *Raw*, complete with swank logo. It is pretty cool, and the effort leads me to believe they may well have been considering this as a regular part of the programming schedule. The set is completely different too, with the usual Titantron and ramp combo replaced with an old-school style entranceway. Jim Cornette is the host, with JR already in the ring for the opening promo.

Promo Time: Shawn Michaels
The heat for Michaels is unbelievable. It is no longer just the guys booing him, it is everyone in the building. He says that after having initially tried to dump everything that has happened recently on him, the WWF has suddenly changed its tune since Shawn Michaels reacted to being "painted in a corner" and demolished the Undertaker with a chair. He calls himself reactionary, which is absolutely a personality trait of his, and the cause of many of his backstage problems. Michaels dismisses other guys in the locker room who have been pegged as having "attitude" or who are supposedly "ticking

time bombs" (a not so subtle burial of the two former Hollywood Blondes, Steve Austin and Brian Pillman) and calls himself the original outlaw in the WWF and that he is the same way in real life and not just acting that way on screen. Michaels shows off the chair he used to cave in Taker's skull last week with a sickeningly violent shot, and warns that it is the result of people pushing him and pushing him when he warned otherwise. He goes to the intentional shoot comments aimed at the locker room again, declaring: "There's only one guy that decides what I do and what I don't do, and that guy is me. Nobody, but nobody, tells me what to do. And one thing I'm not gonna do at *Ground Zero* is lay down and die for the Undertaker". Back in kayfabe world, he says that if he is going down, then he is taking Taker with him and going in a blaze of fire. Cornette suggests that fans want to set Shawn on fire. Yeah, along with half of the locker room. This crowd is HOT and the heat for Shawn is just unreal. "Shawn is gay" chants the ENTIRE crowd. "Well about twelve or fourteen thousand of these folks are questioning Shawn Michaels' preferences" says Cornette. Michaels' response is immense, and while it is bleeped out (it's a taped show after all) I THINK he says "If I have told you once, I have told you a thousand times, now don't make me come out there and fuck your mothers just to show yak". If not that exactly, it is certainly a close approximation, and the crowd is fixing to lynch him. Michaels says he is going to make Taker rest in peace permanently even if he has to run him down with a truck and kill him, and then he will dance all over his corpse. Charming to the last. "Come here sweetie, let's show 'em how gay I am" he says to a random ring rat in the crowd, who he then makes out with. What a start. You think the fans hate Cena? Wait until you hear this.

WWF Championship
Bret Hart (c) vs. Vader
This stems from the pull-apart they had last week after Vader snapped the Maple Leaf in half. Vader comes out and cuts the promo that featured on *Beyond the Mat*, as he begins the first major babyface run of his career. Bret cuts a playground promo on Vader by calling him fat, which is a running theme and criticism of Vader in the WWF from here on in. A hard clothesline soon shuts Hart up. Vader snaps the flag again and pounds Hart, but misses a charge on the outside and meets the rails before Bret sends him hard into the steps. It is so refreshing to have JR and Jim Cornette on commentary, because they actually talk about the strengths and weaknesses of the guys involved and add a great deal to things as a contest. Back inside and Bret begins to control and hits a back suplex, which Vader takes like a light heavyweight. When we return from commercial Vader is potatoing Hart with his big paws, and one looks to catch Bret in the ear, so he responds with some shots of his own. Vader's response? A kick right to the jaw and a clothesline. They are working super tight here and it looks great. Bret gets tired of being beaten up and rolls to the outside to get a chair, but gets crotched by Vader coming back in. Vader gets the chair and intends to take Hart's head off, but Owen and Bulldog run out to prevent it and cause the frustrating DQ. What a shame, because that was building into a really solid contest. Bret puts the ring post figure four on after the decision, but the Patriot makes the save. The response to him is lukewarm again, and based on this my theory of a Vader-Hart PPV match being a better option seems vindicated.
Final Rating: **½

After the Harts run away, Del Von Erich cuts another promo on Bret in a last ditch attempt to generate interest in the PPV match with the Hitman. Swing and a miss I'm afraid.

Sunny joins the announce team, causing Jim Cornette to come over all horny and desperately barter with JR for him to switch seats. Amusing stuff. Discussion moves on to the actions of Brian Pillman, which Sunny doesn't approve of, and we get highlights from *Raw* last week with Pillman's claims of being Dakota's father and the challenge to Goldust for his own career versus the services of Marlena. Pillman's delivery here is brilliant and I am happy to see it again. Marlena's wooden drone, not so much. At least Video Control is kind enough to cut it down.

Salvatore Sincere vs. Goldust
Jim Cornette finds the prospect of Pillman winning Marlena for a month hilarious, causing a brilliant squabble between him and an outraged JR. You can't help but smile when listening to their interaction with each other. Just like Gorilla Monsoon and Bobby Heenan, they are clearly good friends in real life and their interplay doesn't feel forced in any way. It is just two guys who are great at their jobs. No fake hyena laughing and stupid scripted terms here. Sal riles Goldust with a slap, so Goldust pounds on him, "If you weel" - JR, and gives him a kiss. JR and Cornette try to put over the skills of Sal, but they don't have much to work with and Goldust finishes him off with little problem following the Curtain Call. Post match, Brian Pillman turns up in the crowd and cuts another promo on Goldust, throwing in the line that Goldust is going to "find out the hard way that the Loose Cannon doesn't shoot blanks". Goldust chases after Pillman through the crowd while Marlena looks on. Hang on... Sunny didn't do any commentary for this!
Final Rating: *

Video Control gives us the Steve Austin promo from last week on *Raw* in its entirety, only this time JR promises it is uncensored. It is, apart from the word "shit", which remains censored. Why have JR even say that? It just serves to make him look foolish. They did it to Cornette earlier after the (censored) Michaels promo too, having him say the show was "late night and uncensored". If the WWF spent half as much time trying to get people over as they did making people look silly or churning out toilet humour, they would be a much bigger and better company.

Rockabilly vs. Dude Love
And things were going so well too... Anyone, anyone but Rockabilly. Apart from Phineas. Or Crush. Or any of Los Boricuas! Hmm, maybe Rockabilly wasn't all that bad. Well, that or the WWF just had a horrible undercard in 1997. In little over six months time these two will be involved in a great little midcard tag feud and have some fun hardcore style matches, incredibly enough. They actually start at a much brisker pace than I was expecting, with Billy showing some of that famous "athletic ability" that JR constantly puts over, and Dude happily taking a beating. Conspicuous by his absence is the Honky Tonk Man, which may well explain why Billy is much more entertaining tonight. He is carrying himself and working much more like Bad Ass Billy Gunn than Rockabilly, which is a good thing. Dude scores the win after a gallant effort from Gunn following the Sweet Shin Music and the double arm DDT, then in his post match promo he says Steve Austin is "his horse", which basically means that if Austin ends up having to give up his title, then he will do the same. He follows up with a corking line so bad it is good: "You could say Stone Cold is like cheap toilet paper; he don't take crap from anybody".
Final Rating: **

Sunny wanders into the Hart Foundation locker room, but quickly gets kicked out so Julie Hart doesn't get pissed off..

Erm, I mean because she is an American.

Promo Time: The Undertaker
We have been here before. Undertaker rambles through a promo saying little and threatening much, as well as giving Shawn Michaels credit for two things: his ability to swing a chair and his ability to run his mouth. Taker says the only reason they haven't touched "in ten years" (it's seven) is because he wanted someone left to tell his story in the future, but now that is ruined. Hasn't he heard of video tape? The internet? Books!? Taker says he will use Hunter Hearst Helmsley as an example of what he is going to do to Shawn when he faces him on *Friday Night's Main Event* next week. "Rest in peace". Urgh. This meandered like a mountain path.

Road Warrior Hawk vs. The British Bulldog
More singles action for Hawk, and this match has a strange appeal for some reason. The start justifies my optimism, with a quick pace and big moves aplenty. Hawk gets the better of the early few minutes, and even lifts a move from Davey's own arsenal when he delivers a stalling suplex. Davey doesn't care for the move theft, and returns with one of his own before rather ruining things with a chinlock. Then the unfortunate sight of the Godwinns appearing in the aisle sours things further, but Hawk takes that as a cue to fight back, only to get cut off coming off the top with a gut shot. Bulldog sends Hawk to the outside where Owen does a number on him, but Hawk gets a foot on the ropes. Cornette rightly points out that Bulldog (and Owen) are much more accustomed to singles matches than the LOD, which is the kind of spot on analysis you just don't get from the likes of Jerry "puppies" Lawler and Michael "download the app" Cole. We cut to commercial and return to Hawk fighting out of a chinlock, but Davey stays on top of him. Bulldog makes a mistake by putting his head down and gets caught with a vicious powerbomb, but Owen prevents Hawk coming off the top with a belt shot and that is another shitty DQ. This is becoming annoying now. A much better match than you would probably think when seeing it on paper, but like with the opener the finish loses it points.
Final Rating: **½

Backstage, Sunny speaks some Spanish as she interviews Los Boricuas. Savio says they returned the DOA's stolen bikes because Sgt. Slaughter told them off. Wow, what dangerous heels! Savio doesn't like Crush because he "always talks about Puerto Ricans". Not that he speaks negative about them or is racist towards them or whatever, just he talks about them. Great promo Savio, just some real top notch work.

Faarooq & Rocky Maivia vs. Crush & Chainz
Despite Rocky's newfound swagger and instant acclimatisation to the heel role, I think this may well bring the quality of the show down significantly. I mean, Crush is involved after all. I honestly can't believe that this Rocky is the same one who was stinking up the arenas just a few months ago, because his mannerisms, selling, movement and general demeanour are exceptional already. Not for the first time tonight, I am stunned by how fast and furious this starts, with Chainz and Crush running roughshod over Rocky and then Faarooq and Crush having probably their best sequence opposite each other, which ends with an emphatic Crush piledriver. Rocky comes back in and nearly gets turned inside out with a clothesline, but he responds with a nicely executed floatover DDT. Faarooq returns and raises my ire by taking the electric chair spot that he does every match, which allows Crush to fire back and then throw Rocky around some more with a suplex and a backbreaker. Three guesses what happens to ruin this shockingly entertaining affair? Yep, Los Boricuas come down and that leads to a DQ and an all-out gang brawl, marking the third time this evening that the WWF have taken the proverbial wind out of the sails and failed to deliver a conclusive ending to a good match. Yes, a good match, involving CRUSH. This is probably the best performance I have seen from him since 1990 (against the Hart Foundation at *SummerSlam '90*). He looked lively, exciting and intense, with not a toss martial arts move in sight. Props for effort, shame again about the finish.
Final Rating: **½

Jerry Lynn vs. Taka Michinoku
The roll-call of former and future ECW Champions continues on *Raw* with Jerry Lynn making his first appearance on the show, against a now WWF regular in Taka. I am a huge fan of Jerry and have always found his work to be incredibly tight and smooth. This, if given the time and respect it deserves, could well be a show stealer on a card full of exciting TV matches. Fortunately, that is exactly what happens as they get the full attention of JR and JC, who provide background information and offer strategy, once again adding a little extra to the match. There is no one to fill in the blanks for the live crowd of course, but pleasingly that is not a problem because Taka and Lynn win them over on their own merits with spectacular flying, lightning counters and high impact moves. They only get 5-minutes or so, but they use them well and even get some pops for near falls, which is all the more impressive when you consider Lynn is an unknown to the WWF audience. Taka is the golden boy of the light heavyweight division so he gets to go over with the Michinoku Driver, but they keep you guessing right until the end. I cannot fathom why the WWF didn't hire Lynn on the spot for the light heavyweight division and title tournament, because he proved here that he could perform at a WWF level. Just another example of Vince not having a clue what made the division entertaining, and just constantly instead trying to plug his "mini-heavyweights" in. Curiously enough, Lynn did win the Light Heavyweight Title years later in 2001, when he was signed by the WWF after leaving the sinking ECW ship, beating Crash Holly to snare the gold. His run was brief and he was treated like a jobber, depriving fans of some potential classics at a time when the roster was probably the best in the world.
Final Rating: ***

Backstage, Sunny tries to get a word with the Truth Commission's leader the Commandant, who starts his promo in a friendly, cordial manner before suddenly snapping at his men "EYES FRONT!" when he clocks them ogling Sunny. "That is exactly the problem with America today! No discipline! Everybody is more concerned with pleasures of the flesh!" Great delivery from the Commandant.

The Headbangers vs. Recon & Sniper
This, remarkably, is your main event. In the 80s *Saturday Night's Main Event* used to run its main event at the start of the show, which I assume is what they are going for here. But this show is more akin to modern *Raw* than SNME in everything but the name, so it is a strange choice. As I have admitted in a different book; I am a fan of the Interrogator and I am not ashamed. I'm not! Unfortunately, he is not in this match, so we have to suffer the tiresome Recon and Sniper instead. This whole thing is immensely boring and a really disappointing way to end the show. Because the WWF doesn't really know what it is doing, they put the hapless Commission over its soon to be tag champs after interference from the Interrogator. Was the intention to build them for a future title shot? Why not put them over a tandem on the way down the ranks rather than one you

are pushing? I think the Headbangers were lame and completely undeserving of a title run anyway, but if that was the direction they were going then they should have at least built them up strong going into the PPV. I can only reason that they didn't because they wanted the title win to be a complete fluke, but those kind of champions *never* get over anyway. A shoddy end to an otherwise excellent show.
Final Rating: *

THE FRIDAY NIGHT'S MAIN EVENT RECAP:

Most Entertaining: Jim Cornette and Jim Ross. While Shawn Michaels was superb behind the mic and there were also stellar performances from a number of other talents, it was all consistently held together by the perfect pairing of Jim Ross and Jim Cornette behind the announce desk. They made all of the matches seem better and caused many a smile at their interaction. A master class in broadcasting and a refreshing change from Vince, Lawler and co.

Least Entertaining: It seems almost harsh to give this to anyone, but Savio Vega can have it for his horrible promo, which reduced the supposedly gritty and real gang warz down to a petty squabble.

Quote of the Night: "Sunny is going to try and score... an interview, with Bret Hart" - Jim Ross. "I'm glad YOU said that!" - Jim Cornette. With this coming not a great deal of time after the infamous "Sunny days" comment directed at Bret from Shawn, this was a cheeky little probe and one that ticked me greatly.

Match of the Night: Jerry Lynn vs. Taka Michinoku. Taka continues to impress in the WWF, and he is barely out of second gear yet as far as what he can do. Jerry Lynn looked fantastic in his first notable WWF match, but the decision not to hire him continues to confound. I can only assume he was getting offered a better deal elsewhere. The WWF was hardly cash rich in 1997 and a light heavyweight would not have commanded much of a sum.

Verdict: This was a real good show from start to finish, though for once the wrestling was more consistent than the mic work. Shawn Michaels was excellent behind the stick in a heated opening promo, but others such as the Undertaker and Savio Vega were pretty bad. In the ring there were some performances that went beyond expectation from Crush, Hawk and Rockabilly, with everyone seeming extra motivated and willing to work hard. As a result this is an easy and fun watch, and an excellent replacement for *Raw*.
Rating: 71

09.05.97 - "Friday Night's Main Event" by Arnold Furious

Venue: Chicago, IL
Taped: 08.23.97
Raw Rating: N/A
Nitro Rating: 4.7

The Patriot vs. Owen Hart
James keeps referring to the Patriot as underrated, which is probably fair. I'd say he fell into the same camp as Sting and Rocky Maivia, only without the personality, in that when he faced better talent he was entertaining. Owen tends to work around the weaknesses of others and can carry lesser lights, so all of the intangibles are in place for them to have a solid match. They both establish a decent pace, avoiding rest holds but with Owen having the better offence. Patriot gives Owen a huge chunk of the match, trusting in his judgement and abilities before timing a comeback. When the comeback does come Owen bumps around like crazy to get Patriot over. The match is well structured but I can't help but feel it lacks a certain x-factor. Both guys are over so it's not that, but Patriot's Americanism doesn't come across as being diametrically opposed to Owen's Canadian hero stature (not like it did with Bret). It just feels like a match. Patriot's comeback reaches its zenith but Bulldog runs in for the DQ. The match was solid but unspectacular and I suspect my dislike of the whole Bret vs. Vader & Patriot angle taints it. It all felt like a step down for the WWF Champion while Shawn and Taker contested the real main events and Steve Austin was the real ace of the company.
Final Rating: **¾

Video Control takes us to Sgt. Slaughter who, like a jackass, lisps his way through an office based promo where he suspends Steve Austin for his own good. The WWF camera crew goes after Steve Austin and finds him in Texas. The interviewer gets short thrift from Austin who says he'll only speak to someone with some authority. The interviewer is not even shown on camera so I don't know who it was. Austin switches gears and decides he wants to speak. Meanwhile, back in the arena, Sunny joins commentary to explain her intentions on interviews this evening. She'll be talking to Rick Rude and Shawn Michaels later. JR takes over and sends us back to Austin in Texas. "I'll wrestle your ass right now" he says to the cameraman, suggesting he's ready to go any time. Austin points out he doesn't want to own the WWF, via lawsuit, because it'd be a headache. Which is funny because Austin would end up taking over part ownership of the company during the Austin-McMahon feud. Austin decides to do some shooting and sets up 8x10 photos of WWF officials. His remarks to camera cause a few chuckles, including telling the cameraman if he falls over he'll kick his ass. JR's 8x10 gets it squarely in the groin courtesy of Austin and his bow. After ranting some more he orders the camera crew off his land. Austin repeated himself a lot here, verbatim from classic promos at times, but he was still very entertaining. Like a "best of" the past month or so.

The British Bulldog vs. Dude Love
Despite Austin's injury, Dude is still one half of the tag champions. Dude is in the process of telling JR how upset he is about Austin's injury when Bulldog jumps him behind. These two haven't worked with each other much outside of Mick's debut match as jobber Jack Foley, where he was murdered by the British Bulldogs tag team, as well as in the final of the WWF Tag Team Title tournament last month and in a bout hidden away on *Shotgun Saturday* Night, but they have good chemistry. Davey bosses with power and Foley bumps around his strengths. Some of Mick's bumps are absolutely sickening considering this is a) a throwaway TV match and b) Foley's using his least crazy character. He takes a full-on ring steps bump knees-first. The extra intensity from Foley makes this one of his better Dude Love matches (although still behind the Triple H match in England or the Austin title match). Sweet Shin Music has this finished, but like in the opener the Harts interfere with Owen causing a DQ. This was pretty good! I know I shouldn't be surprised as Davey was great in 1997 and Foley is terrific most of the time, but the Dude Love name usually rather taints Foley's 1997 matches. That wasn't the case here. Owen decides to break Dude's neck to show Austin a lesson, but the LOD run in for the save.

Final Rating: ***

Video Control gives us a lengthy take on the Pillman-Goldust feud before Sunny goes to interview Pillman backstage. Pillman delivers an innuendo laden promo, which is subtle and clever as any kids watching would totally miss the use of words like "swallow", "hard" and "box" the way Pillman slipped them in. Oh, there's another one!

Promo Time: Bret Hart

JR gets in the ring to interview the WWF Champion Bret Hart. He calls himself "the greatest hero in wrestling history… of all time". Slightly overselling himself. He points out that he won the title anyway, regardless of his treatment by the American wrestling fans. Bret thanks the Patriot for his masked anonymity as it allows him to imagine himself beating everybody in America at the same time. "Patriot, I'm gonna beat you so bad you'll be the only guy in heaven rolling around in a wheelchair".

Backstage: Sunny has caught up with Rick Rude and tries to get him to divulge his role in the WWF. He avoids the questions while hitting on Sunny. Rude points out that anyone who wants protection can pay for his services. Rude turns to Sunny saying she could use a little protection before reaching into his wallet, the implication being he's reaching for a condom, so the WWF cuts away quickly. Sunny interviews quickly degenerate into smut.

Hunter Hearst Helmsley vs. The Undertaker

This was to allow Taker some retribution against Helmsley for his role in Shawn's recent chair assault on the Dead Man. They couldn't let him loose on Michaels because of their clash at the forthcoming PPV, and Hunter isn't yet a big deal so he gets mangled instead. Taker batters Hunter around the ring and chokeslams him over the top, which is not as good as it sounds, but Rick Rude comes down to distract. Hunter gets an opening but Taker just destroys him again. Hard to imagine a time when Taker was so far above Triple H in the pecking order that Hunter had zero chance in a match between them. Especially when that time was 1997, the year before Hunter took over DX. But the gulf is huge. Taker hits everything clean, including the Old School rope walk. Chyna and Rude continue to distract until Shawn Michaels runs in for the DQ. The 4-on-1 sees Chyna fending off officials to allow a beating, but Taker busts free and takes out his frustrations on Gerry Brisco. Shawn flees with his entourage in tow, having lost this particular round in their feud. The match was a squash to set up another gang attack on Taker, which in turn would set up Hell in a Cell.
Final Rating: *

Jesus Castillo & Jose Estrada Jr. vs. The Legion of Doom

If you ever wanted an example of how badly pushed the Headbangers were as tag team champions, it would be this match. The 'Bangers struggled against Jesus & Jose before needing a Godwinns run in to prevent a clean loss. LOD don't even notice the Boricuas B-team. "They hold a lot of victories over a lot of teams" claims Dok Hendrix. Why must you lie, Dok? The LOD flat out mash the Boricuas and when the Godwinns do turn up, Animal hits them both with a suicide dive. Then it takes all four Boricuas and the Godwinns to beat the LOD down. DOA run, or should I say bike, down for the save. The match was nothing and the big brawl is just an extension of 1997's ongoing gang war.
Final Rating: ½*

Video Control gives us a really, really long shill video for the Patriot, which features footage from All Japan. So we get Sabu, and genuine footage of Misawa elbowing people. So the greatest wrestler of the 90s did actually appear on WWF TV after all. And I don't mean Sabu. If that wasn't shockingly weird enough, we see footage of Ahmed Johnson hanging out with LL Cool J.

Ken Shamrock vs. Salvatore Sincere

No intro for Sal. He's waiting politely in the ring to get squashed pre-match. Sal can wrestle a bit and gets in some hold and counter hold stuff, but Shamrock's stuff is slick and clever while Sal's is predictable. In this match Shamrock seems to block everything by going after the ankle lock. It keeps Sal completely off balance as he's constantly fending off the potential pain and loss package that is the hold. Shamrock gets a Fujiwara armbar and Sal's weird 80s selling makes it look like he's tapped out. To be fair to Sal, he makes Shamrock look sensationally dangerous here. Everything Shamrock does looks like a damn finish. Sal can't draw much heat as the fans don't buy him as a winner, but they limit the heat and work around that shortfall before Shammy pops off a rana and finishes with the ankle lock. Bright and breezy little squash for Ken. Sal made for a great jobber as all his best attributes involved selling.
Final Rating: **

Steve Casey vs. Scott Putski

This is part of the light heavyweight division. Putski is on the verge of his PPV debut against Brian Christopher, the one where he tore up his knee and never wrestled for the WWF again. Casey was trained by Les Thatcher and JR puts him over at length while Putski crushes the poor guy. Casey is young and directionless, which doesn't help the match at all as Putski is also young and directionless. Both guys are just eager to get their stuff in. Casey tries for a rana and gets himself powerbombed. Putski continues hitting a powerslam before the Polish Hammer finishes. I don't get people hitting moves like powerbombs and not pinning. As if only one move can possibly finish the match; the patented finishing hold! This was why the light heavyweight division failed. The guys weren't showy enough, weren't fun enough and couldn't work all that well.
Final Rating: ¾*

Backstage: Sunny gets another interview, but this time it's Paul Bearer so the run of innuendo ends. Bearer even refers to Sunny as "Miss Sunny" like he's a driver for an old lady in the deep south. In the '20s.

The Interrogator vs. Sonny Rogers & Jerry Fox

First main event for the Interrogator! I think this match rather sums up why *Friday Night's Main Event* doesn't quite feel like *Raw*. Would *Raw* ever end with this? JR puts over the jobbers by pointing out the Interrogator could beat four men of their calibre. The jobbers get nothing until Interrogator slams Fox on Rogers and pins with one foot.
Final Rating: SQUASH! (Not rated)

THE FRIDAY NIGHT'S MAIN EVENT RECAP:

Most Entertaining: Steve Austin. I don't know if it speaks volumes about Austin or the rest of the WWF that he was more entertaining target shooting with a bow than everyone else was wrestling. A lot of my "Most Entertaining" awards for Austin are a lot more cut and dry though. This was at least quite close.

Least Entertaining: The Truth Commission. As a group they felt remarkably bland. The last five minutes of the show was a slow fade out for me.

Quote of the Night: "You call yourself the voice of the WWF, you're more like the ass of the WWF. Piss off, Vince" – Steve Austin makes his feelings known.

Match of the Night: The British Bulldog vs. Dude Love. This should have been a feud. They clicked extremely well in the ring with Foley bringing the bumping and timing while Davey brought the athleticism and power. It wasn't a million miles off Foley-Michaels, but with the added power element that Davey brings. Sad to say this was a one-off.

Verdict: This does not feel like a *Raw* show. I think that was partly deliberate, choosing Hendrix as a colour guy, and partly because they didn't use Austin in a live setting. Losing Austin off the actual show made a remarkable difference. Plus Shawn and Bret weren't involved in matches. The wrestling was solid enough with the opening two bouts featuring Hart talent being the best. The show had a weird habit of throwing out long shill or recap videos though, which made it feel like halfway to *Raw*, halfway to *Superstars* or some other show with recap footage. Neither one nor the other. It's a fairly easy 90-minute watch, but not on the par with a good episode of *Raw* as it's lacking in that show's spontaneity.
Rating: 51

09.07.97 - Ground Zero
(Arnold Furious)
[Louisville Gardens, Louisville, Kentucky]

- Brian Pillman def. Goldust (**¼)
- Brian Christopher def. Scott Putski (½*)
- Savio Vega def. Crush and Faarooq (DUD)
- Max Mini def. El Torito (***)
- The Headbangers def. The Legion of Doom, Owen Hart & the British Bulldog and The Godwinns in a four way elimination match (¾*)
- Bret Hart def. The Patriot (**¾)
- Shawn Michaels vs. The Undertaker ended in a no contest (***¾)

Rating: 47

09.08.97 by Arnold Furious

Venue: Cincinnati, OH
Taped: 09.08.97
Raw Rating: 2.2
Nitro Rating: 4.3

Vince opens with clips from *Ground Zero*. The event finished with Taker and Shawn in a schmoz to set up Hell in a Cell while Bret Hart retained the title against Patriot. Other business includes the Headbangers winning tag gold and Pillman securing the, uh, services of Marlena for a month. Hosts are Jim Ross and Jerry Lawler in a pleasingly trimmed down two man team, with Vince in the ring...

Promo Time: Sgt. Slaughter vs. Steve Austin
He immediately introduces Sgt. Slaughter, real life GI Joe and fat controller, erm, commissioner. Sarge points out that *Ground Zero* was "chaos" and promises law and order in the WWF, which the fans boo. Sarge barks out orders including a diatribe against Steve Austin for, gosh, interfering in matches. The cad! He suspends Austin until he's medically cleared to wrestle, which draws a deafening "Austin" chant. Sarge promises a tournament for the now vacant IC title, which Austin has been stripped off because of his injured neck. He further orders Austin to forfeit the belt at the next PPV. Having heard enough orders, Steve Austin comes out to respond, which draws another thunderous pop. His first call of order is to call Sarge a "jackass" before promising to deliver, not the IC title, but a "big can of whupass" and dropping Sarge with a Stunner. Vince takes umbrage and Austin considers dropping him too, which draws massive reactions until Vince thinks better of it and slips out of the ring. Austin isn't done yet and steals Vince's headset, taking over his spot on commentary. The reaction for everything Austin did here was red hot. Austin served up a tonne of Attitude and his FU to authority had the fans rabid for more.

We get back to the commentators who condemn Austin for his actions as we get footage of Austin giving JR a Stunner at *Ground Zero*. Ross isn't best pleased with either the Stunner or the replay of it. "He's a Rattlesnake, is what he is" sums up JR. Video Control takes us backstage where Austin has gotten into a scuffle with security. Back at ringside Lawler hopes Vince is the next recipient of a Stunner and questions why McMahon didn't throw a punch at Steve if he dislikes him so much. This was pure Attitude and served to get Austin over huge. The WWF has been bringing their biggest star, or biggest hope, out at the start of the show to try and drill them into the audience, ever since.

No Holds Barred Match
Bret Hart vs. Vader
For some reason Bret's WWF title isn't on the line here as the match only exists to set up a forthcoming flag match. Bret runs cheap heat in an uninspired pre-match promo: your city is notoriously bad, you are all rubbish and your women go to sleep unfulfilled; that sort of thing. Both guys use the WWF title as a weapon, which is surprisingly ineffective. They spend the match brawling around ringside but there's no DQ and nothing the ref can do to restore order. With that being the case, Davey Boy Smith comes out here... and does nothing. It's no DQ Davey, fill your boots! Vader works Bret over with those big forearms of his so Bret punts him in the balls to demonstrate the stipulation. They flub Bret's turnbuckle bump and have to re-do the spot. Was it that important fellas? Bret walks right into a powerbomb afterwards so maybe it was. Bulldog runs in to prevent the Vaderbomb thus setting up a 2-on-1. This brings out the Patriot for the save, further setting up the forthcoming flag match tag contest at *Badd Blood*. Owen Hart isn't keen on a 2-on-2 situation though and runs in to turn the tide again. Bret chair shots both faces and the ref throws this no DQ match out for some reason. Steve Austin runs in to prevent further damage for the faces and chases the Harts to the back. Can't say I understand them booking a no DQ match with no finish, but the fans seemed to enjoy the storytelling. Ideally this would result in a 3-on-3 main event, but Austin is injured so they can't do that.
**Final Rating: ** **

The Godwinns vs. The Headbangers
The Godwinns claim the Headbangers tag title win was a fluke, Henry claiming it wouldn't happen again in "a million damn years", and a non-title impromptu match up occurs. James' favourite team start well, leaving the 'Bangers in trouble. Way to book your new champs strong! Rather predictably the WWF's booking cut the legs off the 'Bangers before they had time to establish themselves and this short reign was their only

tag title run. A pity, as they're certainly a better team than a lot of other options especially the Godwinns. Speaking of the Godwinns, they win when a debuting Uncle Cletus jumps the rail and bonks Thrasher in the head with a lucky horseshoe for the win. The repackaged Tony Anthony must be cursing his luck. First he gets to be a plumber and now they've changed his name to Cletus. Poor Cletus went home to Tennessee after about a month, so if you don't remember him don't feel too badly about it. "Oh great, another Godwinn, just what the WWF needed" moans Vince sarcastically. But, but, but, it's all your fault Vince! You and your hillbilly obsession! Not only was this an awful match but of huge detriment to the new champs and showed the fans right out of the gate that they'd be no-hopers with the belts. There is no attempt at all to push them at all.
Final Rating: ¼*

Promo Time: Sunny
She basically just whores herself out indiscriminately while claiming to be a roving backstage reporter. She'll specifically be covering the men's shower area. No really, she actually said that. She introduces Dude Love. Oh Sunny, they can't think of anything for you to do at all can they?

Intercontinental Championship Tournament Quarter Final
Dude Love vs. Brian Pillman
No bracket or anything, we just jump right into the tournament. Dude introduces his corner man this evening; Goldust. Pillman is from Cincinnati so actually gets popped, until refusing to wrestle because he's stayed at home. He claims, from the Titantron, that the arena isn't a safe working environment (which is a reference to what Shawn Michaels said when quitting the company, briefly, post-Hartford), but he's also really tired from boinking Goldust's wife. Instead of an appearance he brings us video footage from his hotel room last night. The raspy voiced maniac puts over Marlena's bedroom skills. The video smells like sex. Pillman promises more video later. I guess Dude gets a bye in the tournament, which really puts over that prestigious IC title that the incumbent champion is already too good for. In actuality the match was re-done on a later episode of *Raw* because, apparently, if you don't want to work one day you can just take it off and the WWF will be understanding about it.

Piratita Morgan vs. Max Mini
We open with clips of Max jumping onto King's knee last night at *Ground Zero*. They start out with lucha stuff, as they're Mexican, until Max starts into the dives. Lawler starts recycling his gags from last night and Ross picks up on it calling him "Henny" after legendary king of the one-liners Henny Youngman. Max takes it with La Majistral. This was total filler but that's what the midgets were used for, a little change of pace because Vince didn't have a cruiserweight division worth talking about.
Final Rating: *

Video Control gives us a recap of the Shawn-Taker feud and why it's now resulted in something as drastic as the forthcoming Hell in a Cell. Shawn's turn on Taker began his DX run, one of the most sensational heel runs in the history of the business. Which is saying something considering Shawn only worked as part of DX, originally, for six months.

Promo Time: The Undertaker
Vince is on interview duty. Taker informs us that he and Shawn "opened the gates of hell". "I felt his fire" praises the 'Taker in a homoerotic piece of business. He promises to never rest until the flesh rots from Shawn's bones… or his brother turns up.

Vince reiterates that the Hell in a Cell means "no interference". Taker tries to stay in character but keeps mixing his lines up, like an idiot, so Shawn Michaels interrupts via Titantron. He points out he survived last night and he'll survive again. Taker goes to the "rest in peace" and this was a surprisingly poor promo encounter.

Backstage: Sunny, roving reporter, gets a word with the Harts. Bret cracks me up by trying to look at absolutely everything but Sunny. His wife must have been pissed off. Owen makes a few vague threats before we finally get a look at the Intercontinental Championship tournament bracket:

Dude Love vs. Brian Pillman
Goldust vs. Owen Hart
Ken Shamrock vs. Faarooq
Ahmed Johnson vs. Rocky Maivia

The tournament features people at the IC title level. There's no doubt about that. None of these guys would be considered high card talent. Not yet, anyway.

Intercontinental Championship Tournament Quarter Final
Owen Hart vs. Goldust
Goldust is in a bad mood and takes it out on Owen. He is a stable mate of the target of Goldust's ire, Pillman. Guilty by association. Goldust can't really get his personality over on Owen though despite all his rage. Also the numbers are against him as Owen has Bret and Bulldog in his corner. Goldust works the groin to the point where Mike Chioda disqualifies him and the Harts pile in to kick his ass. This provokes Steve Austin into another attack, this time from the crowd where he arrives with a broom. A broom? Did he just walk past it and think "that'll do". I like that it makes the attack seem more unplanned and improvised. Austin gets a few chuckles from sweeping the ring and throwing the broom at Vince. The match was so short Owen didn't even take his jacket off.
Final Rating: *½

Post Match: Brian Pillman joins us again. This time to point out Marlena is in the shower. Oh the humanity!

Backstage: The Hart Foundation, who look steaming mad, join us to watch footage of Steve Austin attacking them five minutes ago. Bret points out Austin is completely out of control and should be barred from wrestling "forever". Bulldog somewhat errs by calling the WWF "crap". He's quickly cut off.

The Patriot vs. British Bulldog vs. Hunter Hearst Helmsley
A strange choice perhaps, but basically you've got the Harts vs. future DX, with another guy who hates both in there for the faces. However Bulldog doesn't make it to the ring as DX jump him and injure his knee to set up *One Night Only* against Shawn. Instead a suitable replacement is provided and wouldn't you know it; it's only Savio Vega! So the new match is…

The Patriot vs. Hunter Hearst Helmsley vs. Savio Vega
The reasoning for Savio is that he won a triple threat match the night before against Faarooq and Crush. Vince calls him the "triple threat champion" like that's a thing. To demonstrate the every man for himself aspect, Hunter gets himself double teamed. Vince quickly gets bored and starts talking about Steve Austin, which makes this somewhat like *Nitro* where they book something, get bored with it and talk about something else practically every week. A triple threat match is extremely

hard to work. It's one of the toughest matches in all of wrestling because normally you've got two guys fighting and one overselling. It's extremely rare to get three guys who know how to mesh together. Shawn Michaels strolls out to enforce the rules, or run people down on commentary. Shawn's commentary makes me laugh as he goes completely overboard and claims he'll be beloved in the UK. In the ring you've got two boring heels working each other over and Patriot well aware he can't carry both of them. This goes on for 17-minutes. 17-minutes! Hunter gets planted with the Uncle Slam but Savio just walks over to break up the pin. They finally get a good idea and run a three-way head scissors, but there's no counter at the end of it. Hunter squirms out and instead of doing something interesting, lies around selling. Hunter continues lying around until Patriot goes for a pin and then miraculously recovers. The crowd really start to get pissed off and chant "boring" because this is. At least at home we get the benefit of Shawn Michaels' commentary where he refers to himself as a "bad guy" and accuses Vince of turning him face when he was champion. The "boring" chants continue until Savio spin kicks the ref. They finally manage a three-way spot where Hunter is catapulted into Patriot, thus crotching him up top. They still sneak in a convoluted spot where Hunter runs the other two together to get the pin. Oh great, and Hunter goes over after all that. Dreadful match. JR stops off to question "what's the relationship between Michaels and Helmsley?" I'd question why Shawn didn't just interfere earlier and save me 17-minutes of agony, but I guess he had to get himself over on commentary first. One of *Raw*'s worst main events, I'd wager.
Final Rating: DUD

THE RAW RECAP:

Most Entertaining: Steve Austin. Nobody else was close. His constant interrupting of the show and assaults on authority figures made the episode worthwhile. The wrestling around him was completely forgettable.

Least Entertaining: Hunter Hearst Helmsley, the Patriot and Savio Vega. Hands up if you're not ready to main event a show? Hi guys.

Quote of the Night: "The only thing you've been ordering is a whole bunch of cheeseburgers" – Steve Austin disparages the condition of Sgt. Slaughter.

Match of the Night: Bret Hart vs. Vader.

Verdict: A poor episode of *Raw* for in-ring, no doubt about that. Bret and Vader's lengthy opening brawl was the only match that was worthwhile. Everything else was just a side salad for the sportz entertainment main course. I could have lived without the dull main event, though it is the only truly offensive thing about the show.
Rating: 39

09.15.97 by Arnold Furious

Venue: Muncie, IN
Taped: 09.09.97
Raw Rating: 2.55
Nitro Rating: 3.85

We're in Muncie, Indiana, and any mention of Muncie immediately reminds me of the *Hudsucker Proxy*. Gooooooo Eagles! Hosts are Jim Ross and Jerry Lawler. Vince McMahon, scared of eating a Stunner in the wake of assaults on JR and Sgt. Slaughter, is "on assignment" elsewhere.

Intercontinental Championship Tournament Quarter Final
Ken Shamrock vs. Faarooq
The WWF's plan all along is for Owen to win the strap back so Austin can beat him for it, but surely a better move would have been putting the belt on Shamrock. Austin was already way above the strap and could have taken it out on Owen without the belt. Shamrock certainly screams "IC title over" at this point in his career and Faarooq is rapidly on a downturn after failing to play the race card on the Undertaker and capture his WWF Title. They go quickly to the big spots with a Shamrock belly-to-belly being followed by a Faarooq spinebuster. Shamrock, who loves a good internal injury, uses it as an opportunity to spit up some blood. Shamrock comes right back with another belly-to-belly and somehow that one is far more devastating and wins the match. Faarooq retorts with a Dominator and the Nation run in to apply a beating, but the Legion of Doom make the save thus setting up Nation vs. LOD & Shamrock at *Badd Blood*, which rather telegraphs that Shamrock won't be in the final.
Final Rating: *

Backstage: Steve Austin gets interviewed, from ringside, as nobody wants to interview him up close. Jerry Lawler points out Owen has a "big surprise" for Steve, but he doesn't care. Lawler points out to JR how cordial Austin is with him.

El Pantera vs. Taka Michinoku
Pantera is from CMLL so he does a load of shitty lucha spots, has a terrible outfit and nothing he does makes sense. Taka decides to resort to a spotfest and getting his shit in. Pantera gets his shit in too. It's a bunch of dives. At least Pantera's topé looks good. He works in a few clumsy headstand spots before getting a moonsault press for like 1 ½. So many spots! Pantera gets 2 off La Majistral. Taka gets a tornado DDT for barely a 2 count. Missile dropkick sets up the Michinoku Driver and the spotfest is over. Non stop action, some of it even worked, zero selling. It's the kind of match WWF workers would see on the Indies and then accuse the guys of not knowing how to work.
Final Rating: *½

Backstage: The Truth Commission is interviewed. The Commandant promises a demonstration of "true military discipline".

The Truth Commission vs. The Legion of Doom
Truth Commission are undefeated. Not that they've faced any team of the calibre of the LOD. TC are a squad of hosses. All big meatheads, well over six feet tall. Interrogator is billed as 7 feet tall. Animal takes a lot of rudimentary heat but unenthusiastically so. LOD basically treat this like any old outing. Hot tag to Hawk and they go for the "Devastation Device" – JR. Not in this company, Jim. Doomsday Device connects and Interrogator jumps in for the DQ. LOD can't budge him so Shamrock runs in for the save. Interrogator no sells him too, showing how hard they pushed this guy at first. The Nation of Domination runs in to co-exist with the white supremacists and put a beating on the faces. That doesn't make a lot of sense. They're only teaming up because they're all heels, which is something Attitude tended to veer away from generally. As for the match, LOD ran through their stuff and it felt quite badly dated.
Final Rating: ½*

Max Mini & Mr. Lucky vs. Piratita Morgan & El Torito

Sunny is wheeled out again to introduce this and she's incredibly over, even if she doesn't do anything. Torito starts out by trying to gore Max before booting him in the face. Those guys have good chemistry. Mr. Lucky is pretty good too and does most of Max's spots without Mini's adorable tininess. They do a lot of silly lucha stuff but at least it's supposed to be silly because they're midgets. The heels decide to throw Max around a bit, which is delightful. Bullying is a perfect fit for heels. They switch to Mr Lucky, which isn't as much fun. Piratita isn't as graceful as the others and tends to lumber into his spots. Max makes up for that by bumping around him. Lots of armdrags follow. Lots. Max follows that with Rey Jr. spots before Torito boots him in the face again. Max scores the win with a flying headbutt after Torito misses off the top. It went a bit too long and got disjointed as the lack of tags hurt it, but it was a decent midget match.
Final Rating: **¼

Intercontinental Championship Tournament Quarter Final
Dude Love vs. Brian Pillman
This is replayed due to Pillman's failure to arrive last week thanks to sexual exhaustion. Surely Dude should win because Pillman no showed? Anyway, Pillman is accompanied by Marlena, who has been Pillmanized (not had her ankle broken by a steel chair, but rather dressed like a female version of Pillman). Dustin Rhodes has been banned from the arena to prevent him ruining this match. Because Dude Love vs. Pillman from 1997 would have been a blinder without interference, eh? Dude inserts a lot of goofy stuff until Marlena goes to leave and Pillman has to bring her back, as if the match is entirely secondary to her. Yet another successful bid to put the IC title over chaps! Top notch work. Dude continues to mix up goofy spots with brawling. Dude hits a neckbreaker and sets up Sweet Shin Music only for Goldust to run in for the DQ and cost Foley the match. Hell of a way to repay Dude for last week, Dustin. The match was not good, as most Dude Love matches suffered from silliness, and Pillman was in rough condition. Anyway, Pillman advances to face Owen Hart in what would be yet another mockery contributing to a disastrous tournament and devaluing the IC title in the process.
Final Rating: ½*

Promo Time: Steve Austin
Jerry Lawler has Steve Austin out for a chat, with Lawler figuring Austin won't drop him with the Stunner as he's a wrestler/commentator, not an authority figure. Lawler sucks up to Stone Cold by laughing at his attacks. Lawler goes as far to say that Vince McMahon deserves a Stunner. Austin points out JR was in the wrong place at the wrong time, but Sarge deserved it for ordering him around. He moves on to Owen Hart and says he could take him out easily. This brings the entire Hart Foundation out onto the stage. Bret's mic time has been diminished of late, with the rise of Austin and Shawn turning heel, but he gets a chance to talk here. He doesn't really say anything of note so Owen serves Austin with a restraining order. Jerry leans over Austin's shoulder to read it and antagonises Austin into hitting him with a Stunner. I love that Austin volleys King's crown up the ramp afterwards.

Owen Hart vs. The Patriot
Jim Cornette joins commentary to replace the Stunnered Lawler. Owen's Hart Foundation jacket always bothered me; they all had their nicknames, apart from Owen. His just read "Owen". Why not "Rocket"? Cornette starts off by getting stuck into Patriot's poor tactical choices in his title shot. Patriot decides to work heat on Owen, perhaps mistaking Muncie for somewhere in Canada, and grabs an assortment of rest holds targeting Owen's arm. Cornette spends a while shilling the importance of the forthcoming PPV Flag Match, as if each country's honour depends on the result. Patriot makes a few technical snafus, which Owen does his best to cover up before going after Patriot's leg. Steve Austin considers interfering but security remind him of the restraining order and he heads back. Owen holds the match together by taking slick bumps and making sure the wrestling makes sense. Shame the crowd doesn't care about Patriot. You can see why the WWF went cold on him when the Harts left. Steve Austin reappears at ringside to tear up the restraining order and Owen gets rolled up for the loss. Owen orders Austin arrested for breaching a legal restraining order so Steve flees into the crowd.
Final Rating: **½

Backstage: the cops go looking for Steve Austin.

Promo Time: Shawn Michaels
Jim Ross interviews Shawn Michaels. HBK comes out wearing tiny shorts and nothing else. Shawn says he's done everything in wrestling apart from being the European Champion, so he jumped Bulldog to set up *One Night Only* so he could become the first ever Grand Slam winner. Ross moves on to Hell in a Cell. "Desperate times call for desperate measures" says Shawn. He forgets the build up to SummerSlam by saying the WWF "begged and pleaded" for him to referee at the show, when the opposite was true. He goes on to claim he had the best match at the last PPV and got rewarded by being trapped in the Hell in a Cell with the Undertaker. Shawn promises to drag the whole WWF down to hell with him, which draws the Undertaker out on the Titantron. He calls Hell in a Cell Shawn's final resting place. Like last time these were two strangely muted promos, as if neither man was all that thrilled to be working the other. Luckily the match was an absolute winner.

WWF Tag Team Championship
The Headbangers (c) vs. Bret Hart & The British Bulldog
Given that the challengers are both singles champions and Bret is the WWF Champion, you'd think they'd win quite easily. Especially against unfavoured champions in the Headbangers. Cornette claims the Headbangers have gained confidence from their new-found celebrity as tag champs. They pick off Bulldog and work his back over and even Bret takes a bunch of armdrags when he comes in. Bret and Bulldog do a lot more for the champs than the Godwinns did last week. No surprises there. Unfortunately the Headbangers can't make the match interesting and tend to work heelish heat. They don't have a good enough move set to pop the crowd. Cornette does a hell of a job putting over the change in attitude of the Headbangers, as if to explain how they're suddenly able to compete on an equal footing with guys who'd have squashed them a month ago. Though when Davey does take over it feels as if it's only a matter of time before the belts switch, as the Headbangers look out of their depth. Thrasher looks to be having the time of his life cleaning house on two WWF legends, but the match becomes clumsy with a few mistakes. Bulldog powerslams Mosh for the titles after a messy collision, but Thrasher rightly points out that Mosh wasn't legal and the match restarts. Since when has that ever happened? Davey gets into it with a few fans and steals Old Glory off one of them before waffling Thrasher for the lazy DQ. Patriot and Vader run in to try and sell the importance of the Flag Match at the PPV. The match had serious issues with timing and neither Bret nor Bulldog brought their best for this one.
Final Rating: **

THE RAW RECAP:

Most Entertaining: Steve Austin. Almost a default award for Austin now, as his extracurricular activities still outshone the entire roster in the ring.

Least Entertaining: Brian Pillman. The angle was rather distasteful but most of the time Pillman nailed it. Tonight he was on autopilot.

Quote of the Night: "Who's next?" – Jim Ross coins Goldberg's future catchphrase to describe Steve Austin's Stunner rampage. Oddly enough, Goldberg will debut on *Nitro* next week.

Match of the Night: Owen Hart vs. The Patriot

Verdict: Not a great episode by any stretch of the imagination. The overlapping feuds and issues between various factions made it hard to maintain a solid narrative. So the WWF focused in on Steve Austin, the one guy who was too hurt to wrestle. True, he was the most popular wrestler in the company, even the business at the time, so it's not a surprising decision. Austin's rise during 1997 made him stand out as the future of the company. The difference between his promos and all the other top guys was like night and day. Bret, Shawn and Taker simply weren't cutting it on their standard promos here. In the ring the midgets almost had MOTN, only to be denied by Owen. That speaks volumes about the quality on show. Increasingly *Raw* felt like the Steve Austin Show, featuring miscellaneous others.
Rating: 37

09.20.97 - One Night Only
(Arnold Furious)
[NEC Arena, Birmingham, England]
- Hunter Hearst Helmsley def. Dude Love (***¾)
- Tiger Ali Singh def. Leif Cassidy (DUD)
- The Headbangers def. Los Boricuas (**)
- The Patriot def. Flash Funk (**)
- The Legion of Doom def. The Godwinns (*¾)
- Vader def. Owen Hart (****)
- Bret Hart def. The Undertaker (****½)
- Shawn Michaels def. The British Bulldog (****)

Rating: 93

09.22.97 by Arnold Furious

Venue: New York, NY
Taped: 09.22.97
Raw Rating: 2.35
Nitro Rating: 3.6

We're in Madison Square Garden, New York City, which means we're live. The WWF's opening shill features historic footage from the Garden, which includes notable blacklisted talent like Hulk Hogan, Randy Savage, Scott Hall, Roddy Piper and Bruno Sammartino. It's as if the WWF wanted to put over their history ahead of the politics. That's a rarity, but that's the Garden. It goes beyond political boundaries and is part of the WWF's storied history. Hosts are Vince McMahon, Jim Ross and Jerry Lawler.

Intercontinental Championship Tournament Quarter Final
Rocky Maivia vs. Ahmed Johnson
The crowd kicks off a huge "Rocky sucks" chant. This kid is over! He might go somewhere. Sgt Slaughter comes down to boot the Nation backstage. Just to further stress the importance of the tournament, Ken Shamrock has withdrawn with internal injuries and Faarooq, despite losing, has a bye! If you tried to book a tournament specifically to make a belt look weak, you couldn't do much better. Rocky does a wonderful job of selling and bumping for Ahmed. His work is so strong that Ahmed even finds himself properly over again! Rocky tests Ahmed's abilities with a floatover DDT. It is not attractive. The WWF must owe Captain Lou Albano some money or something because he strolls down to hang out at ringside. He was long past his point of usefulness by 1997. Ahmed somehow manages to bust his hand open as Lawler accuses him of being injury prone (the injury coming from a loose nail in the announce table). Rocky is outstanding here and wrestles circles around Ahmed as if to showcase his superiority, and only stopping his technical dominance to show Ahmed how to take a bump properly too. Rocky spends a while slapping Ahmed about until Johnson gets pissed off and wins with a Pearl River Plunge. A glorious showing from the Rock, who was learning at a meteoric rate. His technical counters and pinning combinations here made Ahmed look like an absolute chump, but in turn his selling made Ahmed look like a star again. As per usual Ahmed had missed time with an injury prior to this and managed to get injured, yet again, during it.
Final Rating: **½

Promo Time: Steve Austin
Austin strolls out through the crowd and points out "tonight, someone's gonna get their ass whipped". Vince's nervous reaction to Austin's music kicking in foreshadows the booking to follow.

Video Control decides to shill Lazer Tag with Special Agent Sable who shoots a defenceless Howard Finkel. We move on to *One Night Only* and stills from Shawn Michaels epic win over British Bulldog, one of the all-time great heel performances.

Promo Time: The Undertaker
Vince McMahon interviews the Undertaker about Hell in a Cell and mentions the winner gets a shot at the WWF Title at *Survivor Series*. Which rather begs the question: why didn't they just put Taker over? I'm sure Bret would have had no issue jobbing to him, Canada or not. Taker tells Shawn there's only one way out of Hell in a Cell; "over my dead body". This brings out HBK in person, with his prestigious European Championship belt, to answer. He accuses the WWF of giving him the shaft, repeating all his allegations from last week, all of which are bullshit. Shawn points out he "doesn't lay down for anybody", again insinuating that he won't do any jobs. Shawn claims he'll be one step ahead of Taker, Vince and the fans at *Badd Blood*. A better promo from Shawn than the past couple of weeks.

The Legion of Doom vs. Faarooq & Kama Mustafa
Sunny is guest ring announcer, foreshadowing her involvement with LOD, and also because the WWF has nothing else for her to do. Given her skills at burying people she might have made a decent colour commentator on jobber shows. If you're familiar with the WWF's patented New York Style, being presented here in New York, you'll recognise every spot from this match as it's a veritable powerhouse brawl. At least it's done enthusiastically as the match is less than 3-minutes long. Faarooq is basically toast so D'Lo & Rock run in for the DQ.

Ahmed Johnson runs in for the save. I wouldn't trust him, seeing as he turned heel and joined the Nation not that long ago only to flop back face when he got injured. The Nation still have a man advantage so give all three faces a shoeing.
Final Rating: ¾*

Intercontinental Championship Tournament Semi Final
Owen Hart vs. Brian Pillman
Pillman tries to squirm out of the match with a phony arm injury. Marlena is dressed significantly more whorishly this week. She's down to a leather bra and a mini-skirt. Pillman claims he broke his arm screwing Marlena in the bath last night. Owen is prepared to take the match via forfeit but Sgt. Slaughter strolls out to call bullshit on it. They don't quite get the right reactions for Sarge duping Pillman into competing, mainly because he's been portrayed as a heel in almost every segment he's been in. That's the problem with a commissioner; they switch between face and heel at a moment's notice. I'm not sure why Pillman doesn't just lie down or submit to the lock up seeing as he was prepared to forfeit the match anyway. Pillman mockingly does the little bit of wrestling that Hulk Hogan knows at barely quarter speed. It makes me laugh, but I think it is lost on the fans. They finally get going and run into each other on crossbodies, but Goldust runs in for the DQ. Owen gets hit first so he wins while Pillman bails with Marlena. Like most Attitude matches on *Raw*, there was a lot of storyline but almost no wrestling.
Final Rating: ½*

Post Match: Owen dedicates his victory to Bret so Steve Austin runs down to stomp his guts in. The cops are not far behind and Vince McMahon has to jump in the ring to stop proceedings. "What is the matter with you?" barks Vince. He reiterates that Austin should be upset at getting hurt, but he can't break the law. "Don't you know why? You're not physically able to compete. Your doctors say you're not ready. If you compete you could injure yourself for good. You could be paralysed" preaches Vince. Austin's facials on "not physically able" are great. You can sense what he's thinking of doing. "We care" says Vince. "You gotta work within the system". "This is all that I do and can't nobody tell me I ain't the best in the damn world" retorts Steve. "I feel like Cool Hand Luke, I'll work within your stupid little system… and I appreciate the fact… you can kiss my ass". STUNNER! Vince's sell is the absolute worst sell of the Stunner, ever, but what a phenomenal moment. Austin is arrested immediately, but the fans' roar of approval gives me chills and it's followed by a loud and sustained "Austin" chant. It didn't matter that both guys flubbed their lines a little before the momentous assault, as the actual act is all that's really remembered. Austin's popularity had risen and risen during 1997, but this was the point where it spilled over. Basically because all the attacks were leading to this, but everyone assumed he'd stop short of the boss. You can't beat your boss up. You just can't. Steve Austin did, and people loved him for it.

As we return Jim Ross is beside himself at Steve Austin's actions. Lawler says Austin will definitely be fired for this. JR goes on to call him a "madman". "One more look at it… BOOM!" Not that you're enjoying it, Jim. The crowd are still chanting "Austin". Bill Goldberg may have begun his famous streak the very same night, but Steve Austin not only stunned Vince McMahon here, but the whole wrestling world.

Hunter Hearst Helmsley vs. Dude Love
This is billed as Falls Count Anywhere, but that's not the Dude's bag. Lawler stops off to chat with Rhonda Shear while Hunter's music plays. Dude pops up on the Titantron and questions why he's backstage instead of "kicking some heavy duty booty". He says as pinfalls count anywhere isn't his thing, it might be Mankind's bag and brings in his own alter ego. Dude and Mankind rap back and forth and suggest someone else might like to wrestle Hunter. "CACTUS JACK, he's back". "He's alive" squeals Mankind.

Falls Count Anywhere
Hunter Hearst Helmsley vs. Cactus Jack
The crowd erupt into an "ECW" chant as Cactus brings the weapons with him. Jack's opening move is a swinging neckbreaker on the concrete. Cactus Clothesline and Jack turns to the crowd; "BANG, BANG!" Chyna is still the x-factor and she lays out Jack at ringside, turning this into a 2-on-1. They brawl into the back, which is just a set up for Cactus to use a fire extinguisher. Hunter takes a mean bump into the guardrail, knocking over the entire of one side. That provokes another meaty "ECW" chant as Hunter starts to take big bumps to sell everything. Hunter's selling is hugely underrated. I've always felt it was his leading attribute. Cactus misses his elbow, hitting a trashcan, which provides little protection. Foley, like a lunatic, hits a sunset flip off the apron. I like him inserting an actual wrestling spot into a hardcore match. Chyna interferes again, but Hunter shoves Cactus into her and she gets knocked out on the ring steps. Hunter, compassionate as ever, ignores her and carries on. Another excellent spot though. Cactus tries to lead Hunter up the ramp only to get countered into a back suplex. The vicious bumps continue as Foley seems to enjoy throwing himself back-first onto steel. Hunter pulls out a table and tries for the Pedigree but a low blow sets up a piledriver through it and Cactus gets the pin. You know what I love about this match? The way it set up *Royal Rumble 2000* years later. Because Cactus could beat Hunter when Dude Love and Mankind couldn't, it made logical sense for Mick to bring Cactus Jack back in 2000 when he needed a win against him. And that match was in the Garden too. Because of the lack of (good) hardcore matches in 1997, this gets remembered with great fondness. It's a bit brief and not as creative as it could have been but it's still one of the best TV matches of 1997. In the WWF, anyway. I reviewed this for *Best of Raw 8* in the *Complete WWF Video Guide Volume IV* and I rated it at ***½, but seen in the context of this incredible and historic show gives it an extra ¼*.
Final Rating: ***¾

Promo Time: Shawn Michaels
JR is immediately concerned that Shawn has a live mic. He's not sure he made himself clear earlier. "Undertaker, I want you to bring your dead ass out here and face me like a man". New York start chanting "Shawn is gay", which Shawn directly addresses. "Go ask your momma if Shawn is gay". Finally Undertaker strolls down, but it's a set up and Hunter jumps HIM from behind. Rick Rude and Chyna turn it into a 4-on-1 kicking from DX to the Dead Man. Taker eventually pops up and all four heels run off. You can see why everyone wanted Shawn locked inside the Hell in a Cell.

Bret Hart vs. Goldust
Bret isn't putting his title on the line because Goldust doesn't deserve a shot. Bret grabs a mic and says he's not bothered who wins Hell in a Cell. "I never was and never will be afraid of you" he says to Taker. MSG was always "Bret's House", as they appreciated the workrate freaks, so he doesn't rip on the fans like he usually does. It's a mark of respect from Bret and it's reciprocated as the fans don't hate on him like they did in most American venues. Goldust shows early fire, as he's mad

as hell about Pillman and Bret is Pillman's buddy. Bret dominates the match with his technical excellence and destroys Goldust's leg to set up the Sharpshooter. Bret's move set is by-the-numbers, but he's technically flawless so it's still good to watch. He even throws in the ringpost figure four. With Bret in charge Shawn Michaels comes out to watch. We get a great shot of him from behind, humping the European title and dodging missiles from the New Yorkers. Bret continues to dissect the leg, which is methodical and Bret is quickly becoming a relic in the new WWF, which is perhaps why Vince decided to renege on their 20 year agreement. That and the locker room animosity. Goldust mounts a comeback where he actually looks flashy because of Bret's ground attack. Bret fakes Goldust out into blocking a second rope elbow only to land on his feet and slap Goldust in the Sharpshooter. He taps immediately and Bret wins.
Final Rating: **½

Post Match: Shawn runs in and is quickly joined by Hunter before Owen and Bulldog run down, though Bulldog is not doing much running with a bad knee. Rick Rude runs down. Jim Neidhart runs down. It turns into a big heel-on-heel scrap, so the Undertaker runs down to clear the ring. The final moment being a truly epic double chokeslam on Shawn AND Bret. A really memorable way to end a fantastic episode.

THE RAW RECAP:

Most Entertaining: Mick Foley. I was tempted to go with Austin, but he wins so many of these on poor shows so on a show when everything worked, I'll go with the guy who tried the hardest.

Least Entertaining: No one deserves it.

Quote of the Night: "You can kiss my ass" – Steve Austin before laying out Vince McMahon with a historic first Stunner. The first move Vince ever took.

Match of the Night: Cactus Jack vs. Hunter Hearst Helmsley

Verdict: A phenomenal, knockout episode of *Raw*. So many memories came flooding back when I was watching this and they're all on the same show. The first ever Stunner on Vince, the three faces of Foley on the Titantron, Taker chokeslamming Bret and Shawn at the same time, and around these great moments were a series of solid wrestling matches. This is what the WWF had in their locker at the time so it makes it frustrating that the last two weeks were not at that level. This was just a great show. One of those you either remember fondly, or you missed it. I guarantee you, you've seen some footage from this show (if you're any kind of wrestling fan) because it is full of memorable and exciting moments.
Rating: 99

09.29.97 by Arnold Furious

Venue: Albany, NY
Taped: 09.23.97
Raw Rating: 2.7
Nitro Rating: 4.0

Video Control starts us off with a recap of Stone Cold Stunners on authority figures culminating in the dramatic Stunner on Vince McMahon last week. In order of sell, from best to worst, here are those ranked:

1. Jerry Lawler
(who bumped it like an active wrestler would)
2. Sgt. Slaughter
(who threw himself into it wholeheartedly)
3. Jim Ross
(who gave it a go)
4. Vince McMahon
(who struggled to understand what a bump was let alone how to take one)

Hosts are Jim Ross and Jerry Lawler with Vince McMahon already in the ring.

Promo Time: Shawn Michaels
Very strange that Vince's response to Austin's Stunner is to kick the show off by interviewing someone else. 1997 was a very different time. Shawn's DX affiliations are there for all to see as he's accompanied by Rick Rude, Triple H and Chyna. Shawn and Hunter goof around as Vince asks Rude who hired him. Rude offers his services to Vince McMahon, drawing a wry smile from the boss, compared to how irritated he looks every time Shawn sticks a pinkie finger into his ear lobe. "You can pay me now, or you will pay me later". Vince flubs his lines and calls Shawn's Taker match "the Cell in a Hell". Shawn doesn't make fun of him for it, instead opting to throw to video footage of his "garden party" attack on Taker last week. Interestingly Shawn's initial assessment of him and Hunter as a team is calling them "outlaws". HBK calls Hunter "Triple H" and he finally gets a chance to talk. He mentions issues Vince has had with the "Kliq" in the past and says he's been sitting back for a few years, while the WWF "spreads its legs like a cheap whore" for the "so-called superstars" of the WWF. Hunter claims he won't wait anymore and he'll be taking his break. This is the first time the WWF really billed Hunter as anything important to anyone, talented by association with Michaels. They continue to clown around until Sgt. Slaughter comes down to hurl gobs of spittle at Shawn, who hides behind the European Title in a remarkably juvenile display. Sarge orders Hunter to wrestle Taker tonight. Ah, the old *Raw* formula; opening interview to set up the main event. We're not done though as Bret Hart comes out to join the fun. "You crossed a line where there's no way back forever". Shawn and Hunter's mocking reaction shots are comedy gold. "What are we gonna do, it's the Hart Foundation?" asks Hunter in a sardonic tone. As far as opening *Raw* interviews go, this had its moments. DX's sheer immaturity was amusing and, in all honesty, a refreshing change compared to all the hate and anger that had been permeating the WWF in 1997. It's why people latched on to DX so quickly and so fervently. Ultimately the group would end up as babyfaces, but they were flirting with it here already.

The British Bulldog vs. Vader
There's an interesting story where Bulldog is still missing his knee brace from *One Night Only* and JR points out they're custom made so he couldn't just buy another one. Vince tries to be topical by comparing Vader to the Kodiak bear in Anthony Hopkins movie *The Edge*. Vader's star fell quite badly during 1997 so he's not considered miles above Bulldog here, but he does have a big power advantage. They run a convoluted spot where Vader basically throws himself off the top rope because Davey can't quite get his timing right to make the spot work. Davey rather makes amends by dumping Vader on the rail, showing remarkable power. As if that wasn't enough to prove himself, Davey adds in a big back suplex in the ring. Davey had that freaky power that normal people don't ever reach. Vader gets a receipt for the rail spot with his own as JR comments on

the babyface reactions Vader is getting. Davey gets squished with the Vaderbomb but Owen times his run in perfectly for the DQ. Bret follows, softening Vader up for the forthcoming Flag Match at *Badd Blood* with the ringpost figure four on the Rocky Mountain Mastodon. Patriot runs down for the unlikely save but immediately finds himself 4-on-1. It's a little disconcerting to see the WWF Champion stuck in such a midcard feeling angle as this. Bret is clearly being forced to play second fiddle to Austin, Shawn and Undertaker. The Harts bury the Americans under Maple Leafs to finish the assault.
Final Rating: **

Video Control gives us a shill for the US videotape of *One Night Only* for $35 before we move on to Ron Simmons and a brief sit down talking heads interview with him. It's a sound bites version of the Dustin Runnels/Mick Foley bits, turning a gang leader into a legitimate athlete with a troubled past. "I was mad at the world". Simmons is quite affable and the interview sheds new light on him as a man and a character. The story about his mother dying young and his dad leaving him alone puts the Faarooq character into perspective. Not only that it puts him over as a top collegiate football player. The football past gives him an angle into the Nation as it's a need for a team that works as hard as he does. This was clever business but it's a pity it arrived too late to salvage Ron's WWF career, as he was already on a bit of a downturn. Plus they didn't really build this segment up at all, just threw it out there. It missed the steady hand of Jim Ross guiding the segment too. But despite the flaws, this did more for Faarooq than any other segment in his WWF career. Damn.

Intercontinental Championship Tournament Semi Final
Faarooq vs. Ahmed Johnson
Faarooq originally lost to Ken Shamrock but was reinstated after Shamrock pulled out with an injury. How very "early UFC" of the WWF. Not that it does anything for the IC title or the tournament. As the Nation are out in force Ahmed brings back up; LOD and Shamrock. JR talks about Ahmed's hand injury from last week, where he tore it open on an exposed nail on the announce table. Shoddy workmanship! With Faarooq vs. Ahmed the fans get into a rousing chant of "Rocky sucks" as we see who the real star is in all this. Faarooq goes after the hand injury at what could politely be called a methodical pace for a 3-minute TV match. Or you could go for "lazy". Your choice. Ahmed waffles Faarooq with the ring steps, lays out the ref and that's a DQ. Another lousy match with bad booking in this tournament.
Final Rating: ¼*

Video Control takes us to part two of Agent Sable's lazer tag adventures. This time she easily beats both Headbangers, as the WWF tag champs once again getting buried. From there we head to Brian Pillman's hotel room where he's in bed with Marlena (oh, gosh!) making the same innuendo gags as before. Pillman demands that Dustin Rhodes be handcuffed to a ring post at *Badd Blood* when he wrestles Dude Love.

Goldust vs. The Sultan
Dude Love joins commentary as Vince dances with him. Lawler tries to run him down but Foley effortlessly deflects criticism of his appearance because, as Dude Love, he's brimming with self confidence. Mick knows his way around a character. The Sultan gimmick actually rumbled on into 1998 although he did nothing of note during this later part of the run and indeed is basically a TV jobber here, needing his manager the irrepressible Iron Sheik, to run interference. Vince runs through planned booking regarding the Goldust angle that was eventually aborted because Brian Pillman died. I wonder where the Dude/Goldust/Marlena angle was going if Pillman lived? It probably helped Foley to get away from what would have been a poor eventual match up or team. The match is about as by-the-numbers as you can get because nobody really cares about it. Goldust gets bored taking heat, fires up and hits a bulldog for the pin. This whole angle leaves a rather sour taste in the mouth, probably because of Pillman's death, but nevertheless I'm not keen on "wife" angles. Isn't the intensity of wrestling enough? The only one that worked for me was when Flair went after Liz and Savage saw him off, with no silly turns to ruin it.
Final Rating: *¼

Promo Time: Steve Austin
He walks right into the ring to kick off the second hour and the reaction is immense. As if Austin is actually above the entire rest of the company. He didn't even need the WWF Title, in retrospect, as he's after the owner of the company. "Get your little carcass up here" he says to Vince. "One more time" chant the crowd as Vince gets in there. "You are either a certifiable lunatic or you just don't give a damn" says Vince as he gets the mic. Vince tells Austin the violence stops right now. "If you want to fire me, fire me, because I honestly don't give a rat's ass what you do". Vince gives Austin three options; 1. Bring a certificate that he's medically cleared to wrestle. 2. That Austin signs a waiver to compete in the ring. 3. "I've got to do what I've got to do in terms of termination". Austin makes a few threats regarding his decision and goes off to think about it. Austin continues to muck about on his way out, giving Vince the double digits, causing the Chairman of the Board to get all flustered. He's more at home laughing at Rick Rude's corny jokes than getting attacked by Austin. But that's the thing: Vince was dragged out of his 80's mindset, kicking and screaming into Attitude by these few weeks.

WWF Tag Team Championship
The Headbangers (c) vs. Jesus Castillo & Jose Estrada Jr.
The Boricuas B-Team is sent out to try for the tag straps, which comes about from the Boricuas A-Team not winning the belts at *One Night Only*. I don't see what this does for the tag belts. The Headbangers have worked on a little tag team action, hitting a Midnight Express style flapjack. But then, they *should* be good at double teams as tag team champions! Boricuas wrestle in (Latino) street clothes in an attempt to get their gimmick over. It really doesn't work because Castillo looks so stupid wrestling in a shirt. It looks like he forgot to take his coat off when he got to the arena. Much like the *One Night Only* bout, the Headbangers get worked over for extensive formula heat. It doesn't get the same reactions as *One Night Only*, because Albany has seen too much formula. It's just not over and they should abandon it as soon as it gets no heat. Good workers and good teams know when to switch gears and that should happen here. But because they laid out a formula tag they have to stick to it. Unlike the majority, I actually found the *One Night Only* match to be quite dull too, but at least the crowd was hot for that. Castillo hits the rana off the top but the Godwinns run in to save the titles because they have a shot on the PPV. It really buries the Headbangers, as they needed interference to beat two virtually bottom rung scrubs like Jesus and Jose. Their title run was wrecked by atrocious booking. This is probably the worst of all the booking as it makes them look borderline incompetent as champs. There's a big difference between underdogs and jobbers.
Final Rating: ½*

Promo Time: Owen Hart
Owen debuts his "Owen 3:16"/"I just broke your neck" t-shirt here. Vince questions why Owen would provoke "that lunatic" Steve Austin. Owen has brought a riot squad with him, which is four guys in masks. Owen moves on to Faarooq and says he's a superior wrestler to him. Owen turns to Vince in order to try and drive Austin out of the WWF, pointing out Vince's father started this business and Austin is trying to ruin it. Owen plays out his scenario where Austin isn't at *Badd Blood*, Hart wins the IC title and Vince fires Austin the next night on *Raw*. One of the riot squad unmasks as Steve Austin, jumps in the ring and gives Owen a Stunner. I love how Vince McMahon sees him coming and hops out of the ring before the attack on Owen. This was yet another pointer to Austin's unparalleled popularity as he just overwhelmed the fans here. He was on a rocket ship to the stars, interjecting himself into everything.

Video Control takes us to the construction of the Hell in a Cell in an attempt to put the match over. It serves a purpose but the match itself is what sold the fans on the cage.

Triple H vs. The Undertaker
Before we even get underway Bret and Bulldog jump Taker, only for Vader and Patriot to make the save to set up that damn Flag Match. This is actually a lot smarter than you'd think. Bret just assumed Taker would beat Shawn easily in the Hell in a Cell, and wanted to soften Taker up for *Survivor Series*. Or potentially they wanted Taker to lose Hell in a Cell so Bret could wrestle Shawn, who he felt he could beat and indeed wanted to beat. DX go after Taker but he shrugs both of them off, which rather shows how strong a favourite Taker was going in to *Badd Blood*. The distractions give Hunter an opening to jump Taker, but that's short lived as Taker overpowers. Chokeslam would finish but Rick Rude comes down for the DQ. There isn't enough match to actually rate. Barely two minutes. After the match Shawn hits a superkick and they stuff Taker in a body bag, which is how the show should go off the air, but instead Taker mounts a comeback and DX high-tail it. Shawn gets wigged out by a mysterious red light coming from backstage and opts to climb the Titantron. Hunter gets Tombstoned on the stage while that's happening and we go off the air.

THE RAW RECAP:

Most Entertaining: Steve Austin. The encounters with Vince McMahon took Austin to another level and he was already more popular than the WWF Champion and all the WWF's main eventers put together. It was only a matter of time before the Austin era kicked in, and you could argue it already had.

Least Entertaining: The Headbangers. Their failure as tag champs wasn't entirely their fault but they did very little tonight to suggest they would have been good with better booking.

Quote of the Night: "Whether you'll loosen the death grip you have on your wallet remains to be seen" – Rick Rude makes fun of Vince's stinginess.

Match of the Night: The British Bulldog vs. Vader

Verdict: While on the surface this show seems to be quite poor, with the top wrestling action barely cracking **, the actual booking of the top guys worked very well. Austin's continued anti-establishment rants and attacks were thoroughly satisfying. Meanwhile Shawn and Taker remained on a collision course for the PPV, plus the Kane booking had been scaled back so his actual debut at *Badd Blood* came as a surprise. For a PPV go-home show, they managed to cover all the bases. The unfortunate death of Brian Pillman and a subsequent weak rebooked undercard ruined the PPV, but the Shawn-Taker Cell match is one for the ages.
Rating: 68

10.05.97 - Badd Blood
(James Dixon)
[Kiel Center, St. Louis, Missouri]

- Rocky Maivia, Kama Mustafa & D'Lo Brown def. The Legion of Doom (*¼)
- Max Mini & Nova def. Tarantula & Mosaic (½*)
- The Godwinns def. The Headbangers (DUD)
- Owen Hart def. Faarooq (½*)
- DOA def. Los Boricuas (*)
- Bret Hart & The British Bulldog def. Vader & The Patriot in a flag match (*½)
- Shawn Michaels def. The Undertaker in a Hell in a Cell match (*****)

Rating: 42

10.06.97 by James Dixon

Venue: Kansas City, MO
Taped: 10.06.97
Raw Rating: 3.05
Nitro Rating: 3.95

Before the opening video package (but, after Kevin Dunn's all-important fireworks and music), Vince is stood in the ring to solemnly deliver the news to the masses that Brian Pillman died in his hotel room yesterday. For the first time on *Raw*, the roster gathers on the stage and puts kayfabe aside to honour and respect the memory of a fallen comrade. Unfortunately, it would be far from the last time, and indeed a good number of those on the stage later had similar things devoted to their own honour, with all too many lives having being tragically ended far too soon. Conspicuous by their absence during the ten bell salute to the troubled but innovative genius: Shawn Michaels and Hunter Hearst Helmsley. Feuding with the Harts both on screen and off they may have been, but there is absolutely no excuse for that. Disgusting behaviour.

Promo Time: D-Generation X
Michael Cole tries to conduct the interview but DX (still unnamed mind you) are having none of it. They decide to give him an initiation into the WWF by giving him an immense wedgie. Sophomoric it might be, but seeing Cole getting humbled on international television is a delight. "That's gonna leave a mark" says Michaels. The tone becomes a little more serious as we move on to the subject of last night's epic Hell in a Cell match, which as you can see from the results above, I awarded the full *****. Michaels says he proved himself last night because he is still here and Taker is not. Last night he proved he was "the very best sports entertainer in the world today". See, that is why Vince loves him and not Bret, because Bret would never call himself that. He is a *wrestler*. Michaels refers to himself as the only icon in the WWF, saying how the term has been thrown around loosely but he is in a class of his own and "not one of those fossils". Rather, he is "the icon that can still go". It's a not so subtle dig at Hogan of course. Sycophant Hunter sticks his huge nose inside of Michaels' enabling ass, and panders to him like the true boot-licking,

glory-hound, coattail-riding suck-up that he is. Hunter: "Who is the showstopper?" "Me!" says Shawn. "Who is the main event?" says Captain Brown Nose, "Me!" says Shawn again. Michaels then puts over the Kliq as the most dominant entity in wrestling, as backstage somewhere Bret Hart and the rest of the boys are surely rolling their eyes. Technical difficulties seemingly blight *Raw* again and we are unable to show the footage from *Badd Blood* that Michaels requests, and Vince starts to get antsy on commentary. But it is all just a ruse, because footage does turn up on the 'tron, but rather than *Badd Blood* it is from the infamous "fuck you" to the business that was the Kliq Curtain Call at MSG in May 1996. It is the first time the footage has even been shown on television, as the WWF continues to push the envelope further each week and slowly remove the shroud of kayfabe, killing the business one shoot promo at a time until no one believes anything. Great call on that one, Vinny Ru. Hunter and Michaels joke around about how Helmsley "was a bad guy" and Michaels "was a good guy", as Vince turns a shade of grey along with his promotion. Let's face it though, as real as it may seem Vince is well aware of what is happening here. Hopefully no one is naive enough to think that anything ever takes place on *Raw* without Vince's say so, and if anyone did try anything, it would be cut away from instantly and the guy probably fired on the spot. This kayfabe exposing stuff from DX was no less orchestrated than Andre the Giant's heel turn or Doink's attack on Crush. Vince does sell it so well that you can't help feeling sorry for him when DX confront him at ringside and Shawn goads him by asking: "Is your dad rolling over in his grave?". He follows up with a killer Vince impression, as segment albatross Hunter nasally chimes in: "he's gonna fire us now". Oh man, if only. I am convinced Helmsley later took hormones to deepen his voice like transsexuals do when they want to sound more manly.

We cut to commercial, but return with Shawn and Hunter still berating Vince, who sits behind the announce desk and just takes it. A marked contrast to his character a few months from now. Then the Hart Foundation music hits, as Michaels mocks Vince with another killer impression: "Hit the Hart music back in the truck, they're burying me out here". Cue the Harts, and a pissed off Bret Hart. "This is what it's come down to" says Bret as Shawn dances around the ring. "You're looking at someone with no respect for anyone or anything. Shawn Michaels, you're a disgrace to professional wrestling". Michaels hams it up by pulling a big way over-the-top shocked face at Hunter. "You're nothing but a degenerate" says Bret, who then claims to know what the "HHH stands for", before throwing out some standard WWF scripted homophobia. (if you hadn't guessed already, it stands for "homo" according to the Hitman). Helmsley responds by saying; "Oh, I'm no queer". Yeah, overcompensate your manliness pal. Bret was actually really uncomfortable being forced to throw anti-gay slurs out there, but felt compelled to comply with the booking, which was actually done by Michaels in the first place. Michaels wanted Bret to throw the accusations at him because of the crowd's incessant "Shawn is gay" chants, figuring that using the heat he already generates was a smart way to go. Bret didn't like the stance or the probability that Shawn would respond in turn on television with more personal barbs about him. Previously as a heel Hart had pretty much stuck to the moral core he always had as a babyface, just with an anti-American slant. Now, he was being portrayed in a very different light. It is perhaps no coincidence that he is on the way out. Character assassination? Almost certainly. Bret tears the chortling naughty children to shreds (see Raw Recap), then claims he forced Diesel and Razor out of the WWF, which provokes belly laughs from the juveniles in the ring. Bret finishes things off by challenging Hunter to a match later tonight, and he storms off. Shawn is not finished though. "I've got two words for the Hitman: suck it!".

Tangent: And there it is, the newest addition to the quotable world of pro wrestling. I am sure many a parent and teacher were thrilled to hear young impressionable kids telling their friends to "suck it" as a playful insult. The meaning may have been lost on them, but it certainly wasn't on the older generation. At this point the WWF was still marketing itself as a kid's show too, because they are an amoral disgrace. Don't be fooled by their squeaky clean image of 2014; the only reason they reverted back to PG programming and canned the violence, language and nudity was because their reputation was in the toilet from the countless idiotic things they had done over the years and the mounting number of wrestler deaths that were becoming impossible to ignore.

Shawn goes on to reject Hart's very real jibe about money (Michaels was notoriously pissy with Hart because he earned in the region of double what he did thanks to his fat new contract), saying that while Hart may earn more he doesn't *have* more, because while he is out wrestling every night and always on the road, Michaels works once a month. "Bret Hart, you're a zero, my hero" adds Michaels to add insult to insult. Shawn closes things out by calling Hart a "paper champion" and saying that he is only in the main event of *Survivor Series* because he is working with him. That is not totally inaccurate, because Hart hasn't main evented a single show since winning the WWF Championship at *SummerSlam*. Wow, this was a long, long segment (20 minutes or so plus commercials) to open the show, and as damaging as the DX kayfabe breaking stuff is, it's undeniably fun to watch and feels so different and fresh. It was totally unheard of at the time, which was one of the reasons people starting latching on to the WWF. Bret's follow up promo was killer too, and the tension and hatred between Shawn and Hart is just suffocating, which makes it great to watch.

Lumberjack Match
The Godwinns (c) vs. The Headbangers
Peaks and valleys it is then, as we go from a tremendous opening promo to a match involving the two worst teams on the roster. To make matters worse, the Godwinns are the new tag team champions following last night's victory in a horrible match over the same opponents. The Headbangers do some crowd surfing with the lumberjacks before we get going, then Henry starts out for his team. The usual Godwinns formula follows, with Phineas coming in and the quality immediately and noticeably dropping as he lummoxes around and misses a bunch of elbows. Hank again tries to improve the quality, then Phineas comes in and does the worst splash in the history of wrestling. Why is he employed? No; why is he a CHAMPION!? The LOD have seen enough and come in with the Godwinns' slop bucket to wreak havoc, and then a brawl breaks out in the ring between all of the lumberjacks. There are no disqualifications apparently, and the Bangers score the win with a roll up. This sucked when Phineas was involved, but was almost watchable with Hank in there. Almost.
Final Rating: ½*

Miguel Perez vs. Marc Mero
This is Mero's first match in seven months after a knee injury, and the crowd give him a good response when he walks out. Well, they pop Sable in reality, but when you are Mero you take what you can get. Mero is debuting his new, inferior, look tonight, with shaven head and added bulk alongside boxing/MMA style shorts. You can see the logic behind the decision to

freshen things up, and in adding bulk he was probably hoping that Vince would notice him more and push him higher up the card, but the utter emasculation by his wife Sable really ruined any hope of that. With the change in look comes a change in ring style, with Mero shelving his exciting flying offence and high octane movement in favour of punches. Lots and lots of punches. Punches to the head, punches to the gut, punches to the neck. He has all the fists of fury bases covered. Unfortunately that now makes him one of the dullest guys to watch on the roster, and Perez hardly has the tools to make this anything other than a completely worthless glorified squash, which Mero wins with his new TKO finisher.
Final Rating: ½*

Promo Time: Jim Cornette
Jim Cornette, never one to shy from giving his opinion on anything to do with wrestling, had been letting off some stream about his frustrations with the business on the WWF's fledgling internet show *Byte This*, which he assumed no-one was even watching. This was 1997 after all, and the internet was still in its mainstream infancy. But someone was watching, and asked Jim to bring his passionate vitriol to live television. Summarising his thoughts wouldn't even begin to do justice to one of the most reality-laced, genuine and indeed accurate wrestling promos ever unleashed. And this is only the first part. In an amusing bit of trivia, this is actually the first, last and only time that Jim Cornette ever used a script for a promo. Shocked? Don't be. The script was of Cornette's own initial non-scripted promo from the internet show, and he had it put onto the teleprompter because he needed to make sure he could deliver a seven minute promo in just three allotted, but also because he had already checked the content with WWF lawyer Jerry McDevitt, and thus couldn't stray or else the WWF would be libel. Like with the epic Mick Foley interviews from earlier this year, I have transcribed the lot for your reading pleasure.

"This is Jim Cornette, and the views that I'm about to express are not necessarily those of anybody else but me. But they oughta be. And as a matter of fact, they probably are.

You know, a lot of things in the wrestling world make me cranky these days, especially the way some talent is treated and some talent is looked at by not only the promoters but some wrestling fans as well. For example, a man like Arn Anderson who just had to retire from this sport, after giving it his entire life, because of some injury he suffered. A guy like 'Nature Boy' Ric Flair, who in my opinion, is one of the greatest talents in the history of this business. Guys like Mankind, Cactus Jack, Dude Love, whatever you want to call him. Great talents in the WWF or WCW. But who gets a lot of the attention, from the wrestling fans especially? Guys like the NWO, the New World Order. You know, all the fans think these guys are so cool and so sweeeeet, and so funny. Well, as far as I'm concerned, the NWO is like a bunch of guys meeting out in the backyard in a clubhouse in a tree. They're guys who, all they have to do... They go the easiest job in the world... All they have to do is go out there and be themselves. Childish, obnoxious, adolescent guys with a case of severe arrested emotional development, and a fixation on trying to act macho.

You got a guy like Kevin Nash, 40 years old, trying to act like a teenager. Far as I'm concerned, the biggest "no-talent" in the business. He's got six moves, no mobility, and enough timing to cover-up for some of it. But what he does is he goes around and manipulates. Kevin Nash had a multi-million dollar promotional company, the WWF, push him to the moon to make him a star, and what does he do? He leaves... After he gives his word he's staying, so by the way, he's a liar too... He leaves and he goes to WCW for a big contract. Why? More on that later.

You got a guy like Scott Hall, who's a good wrestler, but "good" is about it. He's the best of the bunch. But he had the same million dollar promotional company make him a star, after being in the business 10 years without putting three asses in a seat. And what does he do? He goes to WCW for a big contract. Why? More on that later.

And then you got a guy... Syxx, 1-2-3 Kid, his name's Sean Waltman. Whatever you want to call him, as far as I'm concerned the only reason he's employed is because the other guys think he's funny when he gets drunk and throws up on himself. He has the distinction, in case you haven't noticed, of being the only guy since this "wrestling war" got started that was released from a valid contract from one company to go to the other side, which shows you how valuable he is.

You know why they're all employed? Why they're all in the spot they are today? Because of Eric Bischoff. The boss of WCW, not the NWO. Look at the credits on the PPV if you can get one for free. The idiot's name is on it. He's the boss of WCW. He works for Ted Turner. And he throws a billionaire's money around just like water, so he can have guys that he likes to hang out with. Because, even more than being a mark... Yeah, for his own face and his own voice... Eric Bischoff is a guy who's a big fan of hanging around studly guys with long hair and beards that smoke cigars and ride Harley's, so that some of that can rub off on his little pansy-ass frame. So he takes that billionaire's money, and he throws that around like water to buy guys that he can hang around with, to prove that his "johnson" is bigger than everybody else's. And that's the sole reason the NWO guys are employed.

I think, me personally, that it's about time that the wrestling fans and the promoters, all of them in this business, start recognizing guys like 'Nature Boy' Ric Flair, like Arn Anderson, like Cactus Jack. Guys who bust their ass, who work hard and have ability and have talent to get where they are. Instead of a bunch of guys that get to their spot by hanging around with the boss and sucking-up. I'm Jim Cornette, and that's my opinion."

Rocky Maivia vs. The British Bulldog
This is a strange match with both being such strong heels. It is starting to be a pleasure to watch Rocky work and see how he improves on a match by match basis. JR had obviously seen something before everyone else did, putting over Rock's ability to talk, expressing surprise that he can actually put sentences together. Vince claims the entire Nation are very articulate and educated, which shows why he is always miles behind the audience in realising something about talent. If he thinks Faarooq is articulate then he is insane. Talk changes to the Hart's wrestling a different style in America to Canada, and Lawler refutes that, saying they wrestle the same way but the fans are different. "Surely the fans are different!?" says Vince. "Don't call me Shirley!" barks JR randomly in response. Brilliant. The construction of this match is smooth and well put together, but ultimately suffers from apathy due to the all-heel nature. It makes things difficult to structure, though Bulldog takes on the babyface role, but his comebacks are met with only lukewarm responses. The match deserves a little better than that because it is a tidy encounter. It certainly feels a thousand times better having just watched the Godwinns and Marc Mero too. Surprisingly, Davey gets to go over the rising talent and future of the company, as the WWF demonstrates

that they have always been short-sighted when it comes to using talent correctly for the long term. Post match, the Nation jump in with the Harts for a brawl, as the next Hart Foundation program is set up. How it would ever happen when the WWF knew that Bret was on his way out, I have no idea. I can only assume that they expected Davey, Neidhart and Owen to stay with the company after Bret had left, with the Montreal Screwjob not yet a formulated plan and Hart still set to leave on friendly terms. Without Bret the Hart Foundation would obviously lose a lot of its lustre, but plans may have existed for the trio to continue on without him, maybe adding a new member and running Hart Foundation V.2 (much like how DX restarted without Shawn Michaels a few months from now), dropping to the midcard and using the rub gained from a successful 1997 to put guys over in 1998. It didn't turn out like that of course, and in fact Owen ended up joining the Nation is a career killing move, but that's a story for next year's book.
Final Rating: **

Promo Time: Steve Austin
Vince McMahon conducts the interview, and after the last time they were in the ring together he is understandably apprehensive. It's not exactly been a good night for Vince on camera anyway with the actions of DX, combined with the passing of Pillman and Jim Cornette opening the WWF up to a world of potential lawsuits. Vince wants answers for Austin's conduct last night at *Badd Blood*, but Austin refuses and tells Vince: "I don't care if you own the WWF or not!". Vince questions Austin not having brought his papers from the doctors clearing him to wrestle, but Austin's response is again classic, as he tells Vince "Hell I haven't been to the doctor so I ain't got no piece of paper. Jackass!" Vince doesn't bite, instead telling Austin he has papers for Austin to sign that clear him to compete but absolves the WWF of any blame if he ends up crippled. Austin says he is not dumb and won't just sign the paper right off the bat, and only will if Vince agrees to give him an IC title match with Owen Hart. Vince quickly agrees and gives him his word and offers him his hand, but this is Steve Austin we are talking about. He tells Vince to put his hand down or "wipe his ass with it" because he doesn't trust him and won't shake it. He wants a contract confirming the match or he won't sign anything. Given what occurs in a few weeks time to Bret Hart in real life, the Austin character was smart to demand things on a piece of paper, though even that didn't save the Hitman. All of a sudden Faarooq chimes in from the Titantron and tells Austin a story about "what tough is". Christ knows what the story is about though, because Faarooq is his usual indecipherable self. The gist is that the Nation want to kick his ass, which Austin naturally has no problem with. "It ain't a race thing, it ain't a colour thing, it's a me kicking your ass thing!". Damn right. To follow up, Austin torments Jerry Lawler at ringside as he is leaving, and grabs hold of the King's crown and punts it into the crowd like a football. Little things like that are what make Steve Austin the most entertaining character in the history of the business. I bet everyone who ever worked for the notoriously stingy Lawler down in Memphis got a kick out of that one too.

Backstage, Hawk cuts a rather disgusting promo comparing Owen Hart to a loogie stuck in his throat, and says it only takes one good "hawk" to get it up. Nice play on words, awful metaphor!

WWF Intercontinental Championship
Owen Hart (c) vs. Road Warrior Hawk
Before the match, Owen says he can't wait for Steve Austin to be reinstated so he can kick his ass again. I have no explanation as to why Hawk is getting an IC title shot, or where on earth Animal is. It seems so strange to see Hawk coming out alone, and this is yet another singles match against someone from the Hart Foundation for him, after a surprisingly good contest with the British Bulldog on *Friday Night's Main Event* in late August. Hawk runs through his offensive arsenal early with a gorilla press and neckbreaker, but for a change misses his charge into the corner and injures his shoulder. Owen takes over as the hideous sight of a second Godwinns appearance on *Raw* occurs, with the champions making their way down the aisle to get a better look. Owen's heart is not in this at all. He goes through the motions and works the match like a zombie, almost certainly down to grieving over former stable mate Brian Pillman. The Godwinns get involved with their famous bucket, but Hawk kicks out, and Animal shows up to even the score. Hawk goes up top, but realises his is in the wrong corner for the upcoming finish spot and gets down mid move and climbs to the opposite corner. Come on, man. Hawk hits his flying clotheslines, but Hank waffles him with a horseshoe upon landing and Owen pins him to retain. Not a good match at all.
Final Rating: ½*

Promo Time: Melanie Pillman
When an active member of the roster dies suddenly and unexpectedly, how do you the very next night go about making the best of a bad situation? Easy: you put the widow on the tube. No other sport in the world would ever think it appropriate to do so, but this is wrestling we are talking about and the WWF have a ratings war to win damn it! Remember what I said in my tangent earlier about the skewered morals of the company? They are not the first to do something so insensitive of course, and the use of real deaths as part of pro wrestling storylines can be traced back years. World Class, a company ultimately brought to ruins by the tragedy of early deaths, used to exploit those same passings on a seemingly yearly basis. Be it David or Mike Von Erich, Gino Hernandez, or even Fritz Von Erich faking a heart attack, they used every cheap trick in the book. So when Vince almost immediately probes an ashen-faced Melanie Pillman for a cause of death that absolves the WWF of any blame (suggesting Pillman may have taken too much medicine for his long-standing heart condition), I really shouldn't be surprised. And in truth I am not, but I do remain pretty much appalled. Melanie's lip furls in disgust at the line of questioning and she recounts how her young son doesn't understand why daddy isn't coming home, but her adopted daughter (whose biological mom committed suicide two years prior) screamed uncontrollably. Vince changes tact and in one of the most deplorable acts of insensitive bastardry ever witnessed on a wrestling show, questions how Melanie will support her five kids as a single parent. You can almost feel him revel in her misery behind his veneer of compassion, knowing that while the WWF will be condemned for the decision to run the piece, more importantly it will get people talking. Melanie has no answers for Vince, but she does say that something like this had been coming, could happen to anyone else, and for it to be a wakeup call for others. Sadly, no one listened. The segment finishes with Melanie giving up choking back the tears as she breaks down and declares: "I hope no one else has to die." With that Vince offers his "heartfelt" condolences and we cut to a tribute video for Pillman, which describes him as having fought a "battle with life" for 35-years.

The spot with Melanie quite rightly "won" the Wrestling Observer Newsletter end of year award for "most disgusting promotional tactic", but at least the WWF finally brought some grieving to the show. What struck me before this aired was how little actually seems to be occurring, because on the surface it just appears to be business as usual, almost like nothing ever happened. It's as if people were expecting Brian to die, and there was an air of inevitability to it all. I am sure many are upset and internally torn up, but it sure hasn't felt like a post-death show like the ones from later years when Owen Hart and Eddie Guerrero died.

The Hardy Boyz vs. The Truth Commission
Only it isn't, because the lights go out with the Hardys in the ring. "That is not on the format!" declares Lawler. Oh but it is, because it turns out to be a cue for the *Raw* debut of Kane. This is not a match but a mauling, and Kane demolishes the Hardys with ease. A double chokeslam is followed by Kane hurling Jeff from in the ring onto Matt outside and that is that for the action. Paul Bearer recaps the story of Kane, including the forgotten character trait of having only one eye thanks to the storyline fire. Bearer rambles on, and warns that Kane will tear through everyone until he gets his hands on the Undertaker.

Triple H vs. Bret Hart
So it is then that Hunter Hearst Helmsley is no more, and Hunter is now going simply by Triple H. What a stupid name. According to his book, Bret was asked to put over Helmsley a few times in 1997, including in the build up to *WrestleMania 13*, but refused because he quite rightly thought it made no sense. It didn't do much to help Hunter's perception of him as a curmudgeonly old-timer who was living in the past though, and may even have played a small part in contributing to Hunter helping to construct the Montreal Screwjob, as he was one of the chief architects. They wrestle a standard match for the first few minutes, before the extracurricular starts with the appearance of Shawn Michaels, who wanders to the ring turning to each side of the crowd and giving them frequent crotch chops and instructions to suck it. When he makes it to the ring he puts the Canadian flag up his nose and does a dance, which pisses off Owen and Anvil who head to the ring as we cut for commercial. When we return, the British Bulldog is stood with them, continuing a strange phenomenon from the evening where faction members wouldn't come out with their team but would later suddenly appear. It happened with Rick Rude at the start of the broadcast, as DX came down as a threesome and then Rude turned up at ringside during the ad break. What strange behaviour. Did everyone just miss their cue or something? Anyway back to the match, and as technically fine as it is, it suffers from the same problems as Davey-Rock earlier in that it is heel-heel and thus the crowd is quiet throughout. Looking back you can tell people within the company knew Bret was leaving, because JR begins the subtle burial job, calling Hart "too predictable". Things end up on the outside where Bret goes for the ring post figure four, only to be prevented from applying it by Chyna, who belts him with a forearm. Hart grabs her arm, but ends up getting spun into a Shawn Michaels' superkick and getting counted out. Of *course* the Kliq have to beaten him, it makes them better in real life too you see.
Final Rating: **

THE RAW RECAP:

Most Entertaining: This is the hardest it has ever been, but I will go with Jim Cornette for his immense rant against WCW and the imbeciles running the joint. Ultimately Cornette was proved to be spot on the money. There were a lot of very strong contenders tonight though, all of whom would have won it on any other show hands down.

Least Entertaining: Phineas Godwinn. I shouldn't have to explain this one anymore.

Quote of the Night: "You may have bare-backed your way to some kind of main event one pay-per-view after another, but the fact is I make more money than all three of you guys combined" - Bret Hart to Shawn Michaels, Triple H and, no not Rick Rude, but Chyna. Nice one, Bret.

Match of the Night: Rocky Maivia vs. The British Bulldog. A sign of things to come from Rocky and another solid showing from Davey Boy in a year full of fine outings from him.

Verdict: The wrestling was all pretty average, but it really didn't matter tonight because the Sportz Entertainment was off the charts. This is the best episode of *Raw* that I have seen so far, and certainly the most memorable. The show is peppered with legendary and/or historical moments at every turn, without pausing for breath. The stuff that wasn't so great was really short and built to other, better things anyway, and the important things got the time they needed and deserved. This was an example of crash television Attitude era programming at its absolute finest.
Rating: 100

10.13.97 by James Dixon

Venue: Topeka, KS
Taped: 10.07.97
Raw Rating: 2.3
Nitro Rating: 3.8

The show starts with a hype video for the Legion of Doom, outlining their rich history as one of the most dominant tag teams in wrestling in every promotion they have worked. Tonight they face the Godwinns for the tag titles, and if they lose they have vowed to retire.

Promo Time: The Hart Foundation
Vince McMahon conducts the interview and tells us that the British Bulldog is not here as he is off celebrating his birthday. I thought the WWF didn't let people have time off for anything except dying? The interview is immediately hijacked by DX on the Titantron from their locker room, with Shawn Michaels calling Bret "old" and a "curtain jerker", before showing footage of the Canadian flag tickling his brain last week. "Nobody knows Canada, like I "nose" Canada" says HBK. We quickly move on to the focal point of every DX promo from here on in: Hunter overcompensating by displaying an unhealthy obsession with his own penis. When you go on and on and on about how big it is, it ain't big. Bret rolls his eyes and shoots a disapproving look towards Vince, before challenging either of the giggling morons to a fight. After pulling more silly facials, Shawn says last time they met he beat Hart "for that stupid piece of tin" (the WWF Championship). Yeah, way to put over the company's most prestigious and important title. I get that it is part of his character, but that kind of lack of respect for a World Title would have had him beaten half to death by the rest of the locker room some years prior. Shawn says he has beaten all of the Harts anyway, but Hunter loses his cool and acts like he wants to go, before joking that he did that last week anyway and won. Shawn then turns to Hunter and for the first time coins the term D-Generation X for the group, the origins of which are disputed. There are two theories, the first from Shawn Michaels that Vince Russo came up with the name, the

second from Bret Hart who claims it was a direct response to frequent WWF basher Phil Mushnick, who referred to the company as such. Bret had been calling Shawn and Hunter "degenerates" for a few months (actually, way back at the start of the year he referred to Shawn as such), so the likelihood is that Russo heard that and Mushnick's criticisms, and all of a sudden had his "very own" great idea. Bret struggles to respond to Shawn, simply telling DX that they won't make it to *Survivor Series*. He looks world-weary, jaded and altogether unimpressed with how things are going.

Kama Mustafa vs. Owen Hart

The Nation head out immediately after the opening promo, and before the match starts DX head to ringside too, grabbing JR and Lawler's headsets and taking over on commentary. Obviously this ruins any chance the match had of being any good (which was near enough zero anyway due to Kama being involved), by spending the whole time trashing Owen and the rest of the Hart family. Shawn refers to Bret as "Mr. Charisma", and Hunter chimes in by copying him word for word, like the good little baggage carrying lapdog that he is. I mean wow, the irony of Helmsley joking about someone else lacking charisma after having ruined many a broadcast with his tedious matches and in later years endless promos, is almost too much to bear. Every word that Shawn says is met with an "oh yeah" by Hunter, with lolling tongue and furious nodding implied. DX take in a snack of bananas (because they are phallic shaped) as Lawler tries to suck up and get them to agree to be his permanent broadcast partners. Michaels shoots him down viciously, telling him he calls the shots in the WWF and asking him: "Did we pull your string and tell you to talk? Shut up!". Lawler gives up, and hands his headset to Rick Rude instead. Meanwhile in the ring, Kama is grinding away at a chinlock. Back to DX then. Hunter calls the Hart Foundation "an ancient Canadian secret", but when Michaels asks what the secret is, Helmsley can only respond that "there is none". Oh, fantastic work there Hunter, way to think on your feet. Bret gets sick of DX dicking around and makes a beeline for Shawn, but the Nation intercept and do a number on him and Neidhart. The bell rings for a no contest, with the Harts left out at ringside and Michaels taunting them. The match might as well have not even happened.
Final Rating: ½*

Mosaic & Tarantula vs. Max Mini & Nova

I think by now readers, you know how I feel about midget wrestling. However, I will concede that this match is actually pretty entertaining. The star of the piece is the supremely gifted aerialist Max Mini, who does have some remarkable counters and reversals to pretty much any move. He is innovative and different to most, and for the most part avoids silly comedy (for example, that old midget wrestling staple of biting the ref on the ass), instead keeping his humour within the context of the bout. Because of the brevity of the contest, they don't run out of things to do and start blowing stuff like they did at *Badd Blood*, and thus I have no issue with this taking place on *Raw* at all. The end sequence of dives excites the crowd, and it also amuses both me and Jerry Lawler when Nova crashes and burns, landing headfirst on the ramp with a wonderful thud. I know it is cruel to laugh because that could have been nasty, but it wasn't so I don't care! Mini finishes Mosaic with a sunset flip powerbomb, and then we get to see Nova miss his dive in slow motion.
Final Rating: **

On *Shotgun Saturday Night*, Rockabilly lost to Flash Funk thanks to an accidental trip from his manager the Honky Tonk Man. Following the loss, Jesse Jammes wearing a shirt saying "Road Dogg" on it came to the ring and told Billy that he was not a loser, and the two of them together could be money. I am not convinced he believed those words himself when he said them, but how right he turned out to be. Dogg asks Gunn if he is with him, and Honky demands an answer too. Billy responds with a guitar shot to Honky to a huge pop and the New Age Outlaws are formed, though they are yet to adopt the name. This really should have played out on *Raw* rather than *Shotgun*, but the fact it didn't shows just how little faith the WWF had in the combo prior to them making their own luck and getting over.

Flash Funk vs. Shawn Michaels

What a match this could be... but it doesn't happen because Kane comes out before Shawn's entrance. Unlike last week's attack from Kane on the Hardys, this time the ring is bathed in an annoyingly dark red light, which the WWF seem to think is a good idea but really just makes Kane's segments hard to sit through. The bell rings, for no good reason, as Kane chokeslams and Tombstones Funk to oblivion. Paul Bearer gets another promo, saying more of the same as he did last week, adding that the Undertaker will never rest in peace. Once Kane has left, Shawn Michaels heads to the ring and covers Funk, with Helmsley counting the fall, Chyna ringing the bell and Rick Rude doing the ring announcing. He is not a great choice as it turns out, because he flubs his line about Shawn being the icon of the WWF, saying a word I cannot even fathom. It sounded phonetically like "peek-on". Whatever it was, it stops Shawn and Hunter dead in their tracks and Chyna has to correct him. "Oh, I'm sorry" he says, before correcting himself. Like I said a few weeks back, Rude was not great behind the mic unless it was his own character stuff. Annoyed with himself, he grumpily demands "hit the music".

Skull & 8-Ball vs. Recon & Sniper

Arnold Furious reviewed this for one of the *Best of Raw* tapes in *The Complete WWF Video Guide Volume IV*, the irony being that it is complete shit. Arn described this as " technically mediocre, utterly heatless and devoid of creativity", which about sums it up. Vince decides to talk politics and shreds President Clinton for "getting around" and mentions how "every year I get audited, not to be vindictive". Vince is on a roll and next lays into Phil Mushnick, the aforementioned wrestling hating journalist who will be the subject of Jim Cornette's ire tonight. "He has a very high opinion of his own opinion and a very low opinion of your opinion" says Vinnie Mac. The finish of this completely worthless affair sees the Truth Commission's terrible manager Jackyl (who replaced the superior Commandant) pulling down the ropes to cause a DQ, leading to a DOA Truth brawl. Horrible.
Final Rating: DUD

Video Control shows what happened earlier between DX and the Hart Foundation, and Lawler cheekily quips that he wishes Bret Hart had grabbed Shawn Michaels by the hair and pulled it out by the roots, which is an obvious allusion to the Hartford Catfight, for which Lawler had a front row pew.

Promo Time: Steve Austin

To the next round of negotiations between Austin and Vince now, with McMahon optimistic that a deal can be struck tonight to reinstate Austin. Vince hands him a contract, but Austin refuses to sign until Vince has signed first, because he doesn't trust him as far as he can throw him. Vince puts on his old man specs and signs the papers, then Austin teases walking off before signing his part of the document. Austin tells Vince there is one thing left to do, and McMahon looks concerned, expecting a Stunner. All Austin wants is a handshake, which he gets, but he warns Vince that he could have dropped him if he wanted to. Vince takes the lack of Stunner as a sign that he can push Austin ever so slightly, and he asks for an answer regarding his actions at *Badd Blood*, where he helped Owen Hart beat Faarooq to win the vacant IC title. As if it wasn't already glaringly obvious anyway, Austin spells out that he wanted Owen to be champion so he could beat him up and get his belt back. That explanation is not good enough for Faarooq, who turns up on the stage with the rest of the Nation and rants about white picket fences and sacrifice, or some such. Austin echoes the thoughts of everyone in the building, telling Faarooq: "Basically, I didn't understand one damn word you said". Austin recognises that Faarooq is pissed off, so he calls any of the Nation to the ring to fight him. Rocky Maivia takes him up on the challenge and steams to the ring, where he is the recipient of his first of many Stunners. Recognising the danger, Austin bails through the crowd as the Nation regroup. This was good stuff again, but not quite as brilliant as last week's exchange.

Elsewhere, Sable plays Lazer Tag in a segment with Arnold Skaaland, Freddie Blassie and Max Mini. I am not making this up.

Backstage, the LOD refuse to be "like Hulk Hogan or Randy Savage" and carry on past their best if they can no longer cut it. In two months Hogan headlines *WCW Starrcade* opposite Sting, in the biggest grossing WCW pay-per-view event of all time. Just under five years from now, Hogan will be headlining *WrestleMania* with The Rock and the next month winning his 6th WWF Championship. I'm merely pointing out the facts...

Tajiri vs. Brian Christopher
Mini heavyweight Christopher is not the right opponent for Tajiri. He shows the Lawler in him right away by mockingly bowing, but once the silly character nonsense is out of the way they put together some excellent crisp sequences to start things off, which is then ruined by Tajiri going high on a spinning heel kick, and Christopher unsure whether to sell it or take over. The clue would be Tajiri selling having missed, surely? But no, Christopher chooses the wrong option and just drops down and half-heartedly holds his head. That kills the crowd a little, and Christopher taking over on offence causes them to lose any remaining interest. Why is it so difficult for the WWF to fathom what fans want from this division? They don't want to see Christopher working formula, running heat and using a generic WWF friendly style. They want action, innovation and excitement. Tajiri tries to rouse the crowd with some of his manoeuvres, which are exactly those three things, but Vince has lost interest and starts referencing Antonio Inoki, bringing up his -***** wrestler vs. Boxer match against Muhammad Ali. "That was a good investment, how much did you lose on that on?" says JR. "Speaking of good investments; there's a new Hulk Hogan movie coming out!" responds Vince. "Well, you made some money on those!" counters JR, before calling *No Holds Barred* "no profit allowed". In the ring the action continues to be far superior to the Gang Warz slugs but vastly inferior to the WCW cruiserweights, before Christopher scores a win with a roll up following a few nice sequences leading into it. Good enough for *Raw*, but it wouldn't have cut it on *Nitro*.
Final Rating: **¼

Promo Time: Jim Cornette
"I'm Jim Cornette and the views I'm about to express are my own, but as you'll see they may be yours, too. There's a man named Phil Mushnick that writes columns for the New York Post and for TV Guide. You probably never heard of Mr. Mushnick, but you should, because he's had some pretty nasty things to say about you. You see, Phil Mushnick hates pro wrestling and he's not content to just change the channel. He doesn't want you to be able to watch it either; not the WWF, WCW, ECW, nothing. And for the past several years, Mushnick has led a one-man campaign to have the wrestling industry abolished.

Recently when Ted Turner donated one billion dollars to charity, Mr. Mushnick said the world would be better served if he closed up WCW. Phil Mushnick is the man who called for and spearheaded the media and publicity barrage over the federal indictment of Vince McMahon and the WWF on steroid charges. And even though McMahon and the WWF were proven totally innocent in a federal courtroom, Mushnick ignores that fact to this day, and writes his columns as if it were a fact that they were guilty just so he can continue his one-man crusade. He even wrote a column one time about the Madison Square Garden Network firing Marv Albert, saying the Garden should cancel wrestling matches too. But Phil Mushnick not only hates wrestling, he hates wrestling fans. Here's a few things he's had to say about you and I quote:

"If not for America's lunatic fringe and the disaffected, WCW would be out of business."

"If you can tell me that you would bring an important child in your life to a pro wrestling event, I have no gripe with you because you clearly don't know right from wrong."

"And the overwhelming majority of the wrestling fans who contact me simply prove my point by flooding my mailbox with profanities, obscenities, and other acts that show them to be a distant franchised sub-culture."

Well, Mr. Mushnick, I'm a wrestling fan and a lot of the people that read the New York Post and TV Guide are wrestling fans, too. And we don't enjoy being insulted by publications we pay money to read. We don't appreciate being told we don't know how to parent our children. We don't want a pompous, self-righteous man with a grudge, sitting on top of Mount Olympus looking down his nose at us and campaigning to take away the constitutional right that every American is guaranteed, the freedom of speech, the freedom of choice, and the freedom to enjoy whatever entertainment we choose. Those are facts, Mr. Mushnick, not rumours, not suppositions, but facts. You ought to try to deal in them sometime. And I think it's time that the millions of people that you belittle as subhuman every chance you get, tell the New York Post and TV Guide what they think of you.

But if this has been going on so long, why am I mad right now? Because recently Phil Mushnick used Brian Pillman's death to call for another "outcry" against wrestling and I quote once again:

"The problem is the mainstream media don't look hard enough at pro wrestling. Imagine if middle-aged pro-baseball players dropped dead on a regular basis, this would be page one stuff and a federal inquiry would be launched."

Well Brian Pillman was a friend of mine. From the time he was born with throat cancer, he had the courage to undergo 36 different throat operations. He had the courage to withstand the punishment of pro football and 10 years as a pro wrestler. He had the courage to come back from a car wreck that shattered his ankle, and from a lot of other personal tragedies. And then one night he went to sleep in a hotel room and he died. And for you, Phil Mushnick, to use his death as an excuse for another call to action in your one man vendetta against pro wrestling is more vulgar and more obscene than anything that you've ever falsely accused the wrestling industry of being guilty of. So, on behalf of the wrestling fans, the wrestling industry, the friends and family of Brian Pillman, and anyone in this country today that denies any one man the right to force his morals and his beliefs on all of us, and take away our constitutional rights, on behalf of those people, I say GO TO HELL PHIL MUSHNICK and try to reform things down there, because we're doing just fine up here without you. I'm Jim Cornette and that's my opinion."

Hmm. Now, I absolutely loved this promo and the speed, passion and intensity with which it is delivered is a thing of beauty. I also agree with everything that Jim says, because Phil Mushnick is a disgraceful scumbag and a damn good case for some people not being allowed to have an opinion. But the timing of this was all wrong in light of Vince McMahon's own deplorable exploitation of Melanie Pillman last week. At the time Mushnick's claim of wrestlers dropping dead frequently wasn't so accurate, but in the years since that has unfortunately very much been the case, with the lifestyle imposed by the business partly to blame in some of those cases. That doesn't take away from a genuinely legendary promo from Cornette, but it does leave a slightly sour taste in the mouth when watched back years later.

Savio Vega vs. Goldust

Goldust and Marlena were supposed to have a segment last week where they renewed their wedding vows, but it was pulled immediately following the death of Brian Pillman. Pillman's passing has rather left Goldust directionless, but he is at least reunited with Marlena, for now anyway. These two have had a number of matches on *Raw*, including a surprisingly good contest last year when Goldust was IC champion, and a stinker earlier this year when Savio was in the Nation. This is sadly more akin to the latter than the first, with Savio mostly in control with his uninspired offence. He takes a time out from choking Goldust to make a pass at Terri, but sees a Goldust save coming and drills him with a nice spinning kick. Back in the ring Savio attempts a splash and hits knees, then crashes and burns on a kick attempt. Goldust looks to finish with the Curtain Call but Savio goes right over and nails another kick. The pinfall is broken up by the referee when Savio puts his feet on the ropes, and realising her man is in trouble, Marlena throws her cigar into the ring. While the ref is removing it, Goldust belts Savio with that classic wrestling foreign object, the valet's purse, and scores the win. This actually picked up significantly towards the end and was an entertaining enough slice of television wrestling.
Final Rating: *½

Triple H vs. The Patriot

Rick Rude drills the Patriot with his briefcase on his way to the ring, and Michaels declares Hunter the winner. Yes, it's another bait and switch from a company that would "never do that", and also the final appearance in the WWF for the Patriot. He suffered a triceps injury and was never brought back. Sgt. Slaughter is less than impressed with DX's antics and demands they show respect, but DX jerk off, hiding behind Shawn's European title belt to protect them from Sarge's errant spittle, and then saluting him into a crotch chop and the increasingly familiar instruction to "suck it". Sarge doesn't rise to them, instead bringing out a replacement opponent for Hunter; Ahmed Johnson. Instead of reacting with trepidation or fear, DX just laugh. Of course they do.

Triple H vs. Ahmed Johnson

This doesn't happen either because the Nation jump Ahmed before the bell, with DX hightailing it to the stage, where they take a seat and watch the action unfold with some popcorn and sodas. Ok, that is pretty amusing, especially Shawn's excitable reaction when the LOD and Ken Shamrock run out for the save. DX leave as Animal challenges the Godwinns to come out for the tag title match right now.

WWF Tag Team Championship
The Godwinns (c) vs. The Legion of Doom

Oh sure, the advertised Godwinns match goes ahead as planned! As mentioned earlier, the LOD will have to retire if they fail to procure the gold. In storyline terms the Godwinns have only held the belts for eight days, but with this being taped it is actually two in reality. In total their combined title reigns equal just over a week, but the damage to the prestige of the belts lasted a lifetime. You would think the LOD would be all guns blazing and work this match in the roughshod style they employed at their Road Warriors peak, but instead they just go through the motions. The Godwinns work over Hawk and the ref misses a hot tag to Animal, as the odds stack against the Legion of Doom. Animal gets knocked off the apron by Hank and into the steps, injuring his shoulder in the process. He has to be carted out, leaving Hawk at a 2-on-1 disadvantage. The Godwinns decide to just get themselves disqualified in order to retain the belts and cost LOD their careers, so Henry hits the Slop Drop on Earl Hebner, but of course there is no-one to make the call so the bell doesn't ring. Animal makes a Stampede Wrestling comeback and unloads with clotheslines upon his return to the ring, and then bedlam ensues, with Hank preventing a Doomsday Device and Uncle Cletus accidentally clocking HOG with a horseshoe. Phineas goes for a piledriver, but goes for it facing the wrong corner for the next spot and Animal has to shuffle him around. It is not the first time this year that Phineas has made a colossal arse of something like this. What a completely useless hunk of shit worker he is. Hawk comes off top with a clothesline on the repositioned PIG, and that is enough for the LOD to score an emotional win and lift the WWF tag titles for a second time. The Godwinns take their frustration out on poor Tony "Uncle Cletus" Anthony after the match, busting open his nose in an act of clumsiness as we go off the air. There was so much going on here that it ended up being fairly entertaining, though they did have to resort to every sympathy building trick in the book for the LOD to look in any peril.
Final Rating: **

THE RAW RECAP:

Most Entertaining: A little easier this week, but the recipient remains the same, with Jim Cornette once again blowing everyone else out of the water with his passionate promo. While DX were busy killing the business by treating it like a joke, Jim Cornette was a knight in shining armour.

Least Entertaining: Triple H. He and Shawn were all over this show, but the difference is that Shawn is a leader and an innovator, and his stuff was puerile but amusing. Hunter's was just annoying. He has far too big an opinion of himself for someone who has achieved nothing as of yet and has only had a very small handful of decent matches in his whole career to this point.

Quote of the Night: "I think Phil Mushnick is a miserable son of a bitch." - Vince McMahon. Gee, tell us how you really feel Vince.

Match of the Night: Tajiri vs. Brian Christopher. A speedy opening sequence made this stand out, even if Brian Christopher does represent everything that is wrong with the WWF light heavyweight division.

Verdict: This show never had a chance of matching up to last week's historic effort, but for a taped show it is fairly good. DX were overused and became tiresome, but there were some other solid performers around to keep the quality up, with the likes of Steve Austin and Jim Cornette excelling. Surprisingly good encounters involving Savio Vega, midgets and the Godwinns surprised me, but the unfulfilled promises of a couple of matches leaves a bitter taste.
Rating: 60

10.20.97 by James Dixon

Venue: Oklahoma City, OK
Taped: 10.20.97
Raw Rating: 2.95
Nitro Rating: 4.55

You know how you can tell that a wrestling company is on an upward swing? By the amount of signs in the crowd. The Oklahomans have gone crazy with a veritable sea of placards, and they are hot tonight.

Ken Shamrock & Ahmed Johnson
vs. Rocky Maivia & Kama Mustafa
This is a tag bout, but LOD come out with the babyfaces and the entire Nation are here en masse too, and it starts with a brawl involving everyone as Vince points out that this is not supposed to be an eight man match. It would be better if it was! Ahmed has recently flip flopped from babyface to heel and back to babyface again, resulting in no one caring about him anymore. He is still his same old sloppy self, clotheslining Rocky over the top in such a way that Maivia gets his foot caught in the ropes, and hitting his incredibly dangerous looking Michinoku Driver. For the sake of Rocky and Kama's careers, Shamrock takes over for his team for the majority of the remainder. Meanwhile DX turn up on the stage sporting a bunch of their own placards, displaying such messages as "I would rather be in Chyna", "Spank me, Vince" and "Who booked this crap!?". Back in the ring, Shamrock busts out his terrifying rana (terrifying because he looks like he is going to smack his own head every time) and his belly-to-belly, but he ends up taking the loss after Faarooq interferes with Rick Rude's briefcase. Post match, another brawl breaks out on the stage, and then the Godwinns dressed in the hillbilly equivalent of street clothes, come from under the ramp and jump LOD on the stage. A chaotic start to the show tonight!
Final Rating: *½

Backstage, Michael Cole is in the Nation of Domination's locker room, and the camera pans out reveal it has been trashed and graffitied. The not so subtle implication is that the Hart Foundation are responsible, with a large Canadian flag adorning the walls, and the tone decidedly racist. Bret Hart was not happy about being portrayed as such, but with his contract ticking down prior to his departure for WCW, this kind of thing happening against his will was becoming more and more frequent. In kayfabe world, Faarooq and the Nation are not happy about it either. Faarooq berates Vince and barks at him: "I thought you said there was no racism in the WWF? Are you a racist!?" Vince vehemently denies it: "You know I'm not!" but Faarooq is having none of it and decides to get into the ring for a rant. He cuts a vicious promo on Bret Hart, demanding that he comes out for their scheduled match right now. Faarooq accuses the WWF of being racist and tells Vince that America was built on the back of black men. Vince claims that the Harts trashing the locker room doesn't necessarily mean racism, but it is pretty obvious that it was. Faarooq loses his patience: "Oh, I get it; we're good enough to pick up after yak, we're good enough to wash your cars, we're good enough to eat the left behinds, but you can't come out here and face me like a man, can yak?", and finally the Hart Foundation respond by all heading to the ring. Instead of Bret defending himself and denying any involvement in the vandalism, they go right into the match.

Faarooq vs. Bret Hart
"I knew Bret Hart was a lot of things, but I didn't know he was a racist" says Shawn Michaels on commentary, as DX once again interject themselves in something, doing everything they can to get themselves over at the expense of everyone else's angles and matches. Bret spots him and heads outside to have a fight, and you can bet he would have been throwing potatoes if he had reached him, because relations between the two were once again at an all-time low thanks to comments Michaels made a few days earlier at a house show. Hart had tried to clear the air with Shawn what with their *Survivor Series* showdown forthcoming, telling him he had no issue putting him over. Shawn responded like a true petulant dickhead, telling Hart he appreciated that but had no intention of doing the same for him. This mark of disrespect for a champion telling someone he would pass the torch, was another thing that would have had Michaels lynched in eras past. Fortunately for the disrespectful Michaels, the Nation run defence and prevent him from being beaten, and a Nation-Harts brawl takes place at ringside. The Nation are just at war with everyone at the moment. DX leave and the match continues, but it is really just background noise to the million other things going on, and pretty soon it turns into another mass brawl. In the commotion, Steve Austin shows up through the crowd, yet another guy the Nation are feuding with, and drops Faarooq with a Stunner to a tremendous reaction from the OK faithful. Bret gets back in the ring and notices Faarooq down, but doesn't question why and instead just covers him for the win. In a rare act of unprofessionalism after the bout, Bret throws the secret wrestler hand gesture to signify that he thought the match sucked. He's not wrong.
Final Rating: *

Promo Time: Jeff Jarrett
While the announcers are having a chat prior to the next segment, a well dressed blonde gentleman makes his way to the ring. It turns out to be none other than Jeff Jarrett, last seen over in WCW just a few days ago. As is customary for Jarrett in his career it seems he has fallen out with management, and he has something to say about it. Because shooting is the new vogue thing to do on *Raw* these days, Double J gets in on the act too. He instantly launches into a tirade against WCW and Eric Bischoff for running him down on *Nitro* and burying him online because he refused to sign a new deal. Bischoff announced that he had "pulled the offer off the table", to which Jarrett responds that "the only thing you ever pulled from Jeff Jarrett was opportunity". Really? What about the whole Four

Horsemen thing? Jarrett decides he wasn't pushed because he wasn't one of Eric's "boys" and he was allowed to just float around the midcard with no upward mobility in sight, despite being one of the youngest and most talented guys the company had. This is only true to a point though, because while the nWo took over the company and everyone else was left in the dust, Jarrett's passé ring style and character hardly did him any favours. In wrestling, you make your own luck a lot of the time. If Jarrett ever really had top line potential then he would have been used in that spot eventually, but so far in his career that has never been the case. He worked and acted like someone with an upside that stopped at the midcard. In later years he would come close to cracking that glass ceiling, but left the WWF before he was given the opportunity to do so, and finally ended up on top in WCW because it was being ran by his clown buddy Vince Russo. Nepotism took Jarrett to the top, which is the exact thing he complains about occurring in WCW here. He does get in some killer lines here and there though: "you booked me with an ex-football player who can't even lock up!" he says of the hapless Steve 'Mongo' McMichael. "And his wife? She gives new meaning to the phrase "dumb blonde!"" That would be about Debra, the future Mrs. Steve Austin and in another delightful twist of irony, Jeff Jarrett's valet later in his WWF career. Jarrett lambasts Vince for snickering away, saying he left the WWF for the same reason, and while Bischoff treated him like dirt out of inexperience and/or ignorance, Vince had no excuses. Then a fan with perfect timing (and aim) throws a Ghost Face mask (the killer from the *Scream* movies), which lands right on the announce desk. Vince, instead of being irate, picks it up and hides behind it. Superb comic improv. Jarrett continues on, declaring that Vince's vision of country music star Jeff Jarrett sucked. Amen! Vince agrees: "Yeah, it may have!" he offers while beaming a smile.

Jarrett decides Vince's motivation was revenge on his father Jerry, because he was unable to put him out of business. In the best part of the segment (so far), he raves: "You booked me with a clown (Doink), a drug addict (Scott Hall), a black man who can't even speak the English language (Ahmed Johnson). Vince, you tried to bury me, and you tried to kill me off, but you didn't get the job done. I guess you figured since you didn't put my dad out of business just like you did every other wrestling promoter in the '80s, since you didn't do that, you figured the next best thing would be to kill his son off. Not only did I survive, but *I* walked out on *you*!" And he will again, getting a six figure payoff to "do the right thing" and put Chyna over for the IC title rather than taking it to WCW. It seems ludicrous in the modern era when any fan can buy an exact replica of the titles and the IC belt itself is ranked on the totem pole a grade above dirt, but in 1999 it still mattered. This is another one of those promos that seemed hard-hitting, intense and real at the time, but when you watch it back with the weight of the history that has followed since with you, it changes entirely. "From here on out, it's gonna be Jeff Jarrett's way, and if you try to stop me, fine. I'll gladly pack my bags and walk right out the door again." Prophetic words indeed.

So far so good for Jarrett who has established a new attitude that fits with the WWF's, and has buried his former boss and his current one. It's a head turner and makes people take notice. He really should have stopped there, but instead he decides to target the locker room. He says Bret Hart has been living off name recognition alone and his time has passed, which is a sentiment echoed by many of the decision makers in the WWF at the time, and with Bret about to leave, he is fair game to target. Shawn Michaels however, is not. Jarrett cuts his legs off politically right away by criticising Shawn for only working once a week, and for being reduced to pointing at his crotch and making silly signs, while sneaking in hand signals to his "boys in Atlanta". This is all pretty much accurate, but still stupid to say given the intense backstage politics rife at the time, which a savvy veteran like Jarrett must surely have known. He probably figured that since at one point he was the unofficial 6th guy in the Kliq (due to his close friendship with Sean Waltman) he could get away with it. He finishes ranting about Shawn by saying he is no longer the main event, which is pretty dumb when he just headlined the last two PPVs and is working Bret Hart for the title at *Survivor Series*. Swing and a miss, Double J. The next target of Jarrett's ire is Steve Austin, the hottest property in wrestling. Jarrett says Austin has lowered himself to saying the word ass every week in order to get noticed, but to him he will always be the Ringmaster. Jarrett is not happy with Austin's famous "Austin 3:16" merchandise either, saying how it offends him and that Austin is "ripping up the Bible to put money in (his) pocket". Again, why would you try and piss off someone who obviously was in line to be *the* man in the WWF? What Jarrett has done here, entertaining or not, is alienate the Shawn Michaels faction, the Bret Hart faction and lone wolf Steve Austin all in one fell swoop. In fact, as soon as Jarrett went through the curtain, Austin went ballistic and got in his face. It is probably where the heat and his later refusal to work with Jarrett came from. Unsurprisingly, Shawn Michaels was waiting behind the curtain to berate him too. What it all meant was that after this incredible start to his latest WWF run, he was immediately given a no hope gimmick and forced to wear Aztec attire. Politics!

Brian Christopher vs. Marc Mero

Christopher gets another foray into the heavyweight ranks, and his status as jobber to the bigger guys but star of the light heavyweight division really rather sums up Vince's attitude towards his cruisers. Vince nearly falls of his seat at the sight of Sable and gushes over her as she enters, barely even noticing that Mero is with her. The disappointing thing about this is that they could have probably done a tidy match if Mero was still the 'Wild Man', but the boxing gimmick kills everything because every match from him is now identical, as all he does it punch and punch some more. The WWF realises that, and turns the bout into a shill for Steve Austin's new baseball cap, as Lawler puts one on Sable's head in order to draw attention to it. Mero notices and gets pissed with Sable and throws the cap into the crowd as their slow-burn break-up continues. Sable had already outgrown him by now, so it was only a matter of time. Jerry Lawler gets up on the apron and tries to cause a distraction and Christopher rakes the eyes, but a piledriver is blocked by Mero punching him in the cock, and that gets the win. A punch in the cock is the finish for the babyface, even though he is acting like a heel! What is happening to this company?

Final Rating: ¾

WWF Intercontinental Championship
WWF European Championship
Owen Hart (c) vs. Shawn Michaels (c)

These guys have had some tremendous matches on *Raw* over the years, one of which Owen mentions in a promo at the start, telling Michaels that last time they met he was carted out on a stretcher. Not quite, but I appreciate the reference. Owen tells Michaels that if he is any sort of a man, he will face him one-on-one without DX or the Hart Foundation being at ringside. DX hit the stage and struggle with a microphone for an inconceivable amount of time. There is almost a joke in there somewhere; how many members of DX does it take to change a microphone? Rude eventually figures out that turning it on makes it work better, and goes into his standard promo, before introducing the "main event" of the evening. Not quite, pal. Michaels eventually comes out and indeed does come to the ring alone, meaning we might even get a match out of him this week! Shawn was probably quite apprehensive coming into this what with the real life struggles he had famously been having with Bret, but he doesn't show it in the early going and throws himself around for Owen in his usual human superball style. As we cut to commercial Shawn connects with a piledriver ON THE OUTSIDE, but when we come back Owen is in control again. That's some superman style comeback right there! John Cena would be proud. Owen continues to throw Shawn around with style before slowing things up slightly with a sleeper, which serves as a way for Michaels to mount a comeback as he escapes with a back suplex. Michaels displays some of his newfound aggression before putting on a sleeper of his own. This has been pretty strange structurally, with Owen not only getting the shine but also working the heat, but now Shawn working a heat of his own. Earlier in the show the Hart Foundation were presented as ignorant racists and Michaels and DX have acted like assholes for weeks, so who the hell do you cheer? Michaels does his usual comeback and connects with the Savage Elbow, but Owen ducks the superkick and hits the enzuigiri of doom, the same one that put Shawn out of commission two years ago. Steve Austin heads out through the crowd to a monster pop and Owen backs off in fear, only for Austin to drill the ref with a Stunner and Michaels to belt Owen with the superkick. Austin leaves and Bret charges to the ring, where he finally gets his hands on Michaels and they brawl before officials and factions break things up, rendering this a no contest. Vince can't quite fathom Austin's actions, but he already made it clear last week that he wants Owen as champion so he can beat him, so I don't see what the confusion is. Another chaotic affair on *Raw* then, but the match that preceded it was good fun.

Final Rating: ***

Backstage, the Undertaker breaks his self-imposed silence since *Badd Blood*, saying that Kane has had his mind poisoned by Paul Bearer and that he will never fight him. Anyone who witnessed their series of matches probably wishes that statement had been true.

Dude Love vs. The British Bulldog
When the lights go black as Davey is about to enter, it becomes clear that once again the WWF is going to fail to deliver on a promised match, as Kane comes down to deliver another message to Taker. Why is it always in the matches that have potential to be good and never the goddamn Godwinns? They are prime candidates to be fodder. Given that Kane has targeted Mick Foley, it is not going to be easy dismantling him, and indeed Dude puts up a fight before succumbing to a couple of chokeslams on the ramp way. Of course, the whole thing is once again ruined by the horrible red lighting that makes the whole thing impossible to actually see.

A hype video runs for a forthcoming television special called *Flashback: Survivor Series*, with the video promoting not only current WWF guys, but also WCW wrestlers Hulk Hogan, Randy Savage, Mr. Perfect, Diesel, Ric Flair, Razor Ramon and others. One segment those guys are dirt, the next they are being used to pop a rating. What a company.

Prior to the next match, Jesse Jammes and Rockabilly come through the curtain with Jammes wielding a microphone. He becomes the latest on an ever expanding list to cut an "edgy" promo, referring to Billy as "the original badass", and revealing the duo's new monikers: Bad Ass Billy Gunn and the Road Dogg. Roadie is confident, clear and concise on the microphone, something fans of the team will be well aware of now, but at the time his verbal skills were pretty much unknown. He was just that shitty country singer who droned on and on about the horrible *'With My Baby Tonight'* song prior to this. Now, he is relevant and has "attitude". For all of the numerous criticisms of Vince Russo, he unquestionably did a great job turning these guys from irrelevant nobodies prime to be cut loose, to the most entertaining tandem in the business. Dogg says that this is the start of their journey, which ends with the tag titles. At the time people scoffed, but how accurate those words proved to be.

The Headbangers vs. Bad Ass Billy Gunn & Road Dog
While they might have new names, they are not yet Outlaws and Roadie is missing a "g", but it's a start. Road Dog is sporting his new attire that he became very much associated with, donning all-black and a bandana. Gunn is in long blue tights and has his hair in a ponytail, which is somewhat different to the short tights and headband he would become more famous in. The match is nothing much due to the Outlaws getting accustomed to their new roles and the Headbangers just flat out sucking, though former babyface Road Dog takes to things a little better than Billy, who pretty much does his usual stuff. Standard formula is the order of the day, with Thrasher getting a silent hot tag and the Bangers busting out their double team stuff before Gunn absolutely decks Thrasher with the Headbangers' own boom box for the win. How the ref doesn't spot the debris is beyond me. Road Dog gets in the faces of the announcers after the match, and does everyone's new favourite pastime; shouting at Vince. "You're a freak, you're a freak and you're a faggot!" says Dog, with Lawler being the latter. A good character debut, though as noted the match was rather secondary to getting over the new look and attitude of the Outlaws.

Final Rating: *

Tajiri vs. Taka Michinoku
Sunny does her usual guest announcer spot, and announces "Tajiri Yoshihiro", whereas the on screen graphic disrespectfully tags him as "Tijiri". It's Tajiri. These two had a good match a few months back on the show, and this one starts at an immense pace with Tajiri hitting the springboard elbow right into a springboard moonsault to the outside, but he gets caught with a Taka spinning kick from the top. The pace continues with Taka hitting a dropkick, then he throws in his own springboard in the form of his always impressive big air plancha. Back inside and a seated dropkick is followed by a slam, but a lovely moonsault misses. Tajiri hits a sitout powerbomb for a near fall, and a rana gets him another two count. Tajiri goes to his famous kicks but gets caught with a knee in the corner, but Tajiri switches out of the Michinoku Driver into a German suplex. Another rana attempt from Tajiri results in a powerbomb, and Taka finishes with the Michinoku Driver. Wow. This went three minutes but the pace was just unbelievable. All action, all perfectly executed and without pausing from breath once. This is EXACTLY what the light heavyweight division should have been like, so naturally Tajiri is not even in the forthcoming tournament. Still though, what a bloody brilliant three minutes.

Final Rating: ***½

Promo Time: Jim Cornette
Part three of Jim Cornette's epic motor-mouthed venting of his frustrations, this time as he reads exerts of fan letters to Phil

Mushnick. This is not a patch on the previous two Cornette rants, as it is more akin to a call to action campaign and the start of leading a revolt rather than Jim angrily grumbling about wrestling. Cornette still gets in plenty of shots at Mushnick, and tells people to keep their cards and letters coming, and to let their opinion be heard. The WWF handily puts up the address to write to just to make this even more of an encouraged public lynching. Frankly, Mushnick deserves it.

The Godwinns vs. Skull & 8-Ball
Oh man, these are two of the worst teams ever! The Godwinns have ditched the overalls in favour of sleeveless shirts and black jeans, as the hillbilly gimmick quietly and thankfully gets pushed slightly to the side. They still suck of course, but a modicum less. All of DOA come out for this and jump the Godwinns before the bell, as a 4-on-2 beat down occurs. Hang on, shouldn't the babyfaces be the ones who are outnumbered? The Truth Commission come out to change the odds, with the Interrogator looking dominant once again. No match here then, which is a definite plus.

We close out with Mankind in a boiler room, who says he has no problems fighting Kane like the Undertaker does, and he will fight him anywhere and anyhow. Have a nice day!

THE RAW RECAP:

Most Entertaining: Jeff Jarrett. Ultimately it went nowhere because he annoyed so many people and ironically couldn't crack the WWF glass ceiling, the same thing he complained about from his WCW tenure, but this was a really good promo and showed that Jarrett could be relevant and entertaining if given the chance.

Least Entertaining: Kane. For once again ruining a match that on paper looked like it could be pretty good.

Quote of the Night: Take your pick from anything Jeff Jarrett said in his brilliant promo. Personally I enjoyed the bit about Ahmed Johnson not being able to speak English (see: every promo he has ever done), but the comments against Vince, Shawn, Austin and Bischoff were all a riot too.

Match of the Night: Tajiri vs. Taka Michinoku. Three minutes of complete fury, and another good match for Tajiri. Most fans probably don't even realise he was around in 1997, but he most certainly was, and each time he appeared he looked tremendous. Why was he not signed!?

Verdict: It's another non-stop, all-action episode of *Raw*, as the company continues its very obvious shift away from its past, with "shooting", violence, risky subjects and real life scenarios all prevalent. The Attitude Era and crash TV booking is not to everyone's tastes, mine included for the most part, but there is no doubt that *Raw* was becoming a much more vibrant and can't miss show with each passing week. Sure, not every segment is a hit, but there are enough that are to make this another show well worth your time if you want to revisit one of the WWF's most fascinating periods.
Rating: 69

10.27.97 by James Dixon

Venue: Tulsa, OK
Taped: 10.21.97
Raw Rating: 2.3

Nitro Rating: 4.55

Promo Time: The Nation of Domination
Understandably, the Nation are still pissed off about the vandalism of their locker room last week, and they want answers. Vince conducts the interview and defiantly declares: "There is no racism here in the World Wrestling Federation! We won't allow it!" Rich, coming from the man who green lighted the racist angle. Rocky gets a chance to speak, and once again his delivery is right on the money. He references his first heel promo, by declaring that "Now it *is* a black and a white thing". The Hart Foundation come out to the top of the ramp and Bret refers to the Nation as "brothers". Hmm. He goes on to say that Canada has no racial prejudice, unlike the US, and deflects the racist accusations, blaming Shawn Michaels. DX immediately appear on the screen and Michaels in incredulous. He refers to Bret and the Hart Foundation as "the grand wizard and all his KKK buddies", which is crossing a line. Hunter offers more of the same, saying Bret's first choice outfit was not a leather jacket, but a white sheet and a hood. Bret, not realising he is on camera, turns around and mouths to Owen "this is stupid". Shoot. With the Harts distracted by DX, the Nation charge and jump them, beating them down. What is the point of any of this? Bret is feuding with Shawn, the rest of the Harts are working with Team USA at *Survivor Series* and the Nation have a bout scheduled with Ken Shamrock and friends. There are no babyfaces in this program either, with the fans booing both units equally. The whole thing just goes too far, and the comments from DX are in particularly bad taste. There is no place for this nonsense in wrestling.

Goldust vs. Triple H
How many times do we need to see these guys wrestle each other this year? Their matches have ranged from abominations (*Royal Rumble*) to just plain boring (*WrestleMania*) with a few generic contests on *Raw* thrown in for good measure. Shawn Michaels joins the commentary team to give a slightly different flavour to the bout, but we have still seen it all before. It is not like either guy ever varies what they do outside of the order they do it in, so it is just like a jumbled up rehash of their previous bouts. Sorry there is one difference: Hunter points at his crotch more and asks other people to look at his crotch, which is a delightful bonus addition to his tiresome repertoire. Michaels shreds Goldust's wrestling ability, dismissing him as all punches and clotheslines, and Vince almost agrees, saying how not everyone can possess the athletic ability of Shawn. Hunter ends up taking a pasting on the outside from Marlena's wild haymakers, and Chyna jumps in and belts Goldust with Marlena's loaded purse, with Hunter hitting an academic Pedigree for the win. Goldust can hardly complain; he brought it into the ring and won the same way last week.
Final Rating: *

Promo Time: Jim Cornette
Jim is back to form this week, doing what he does best: ranting about wrestling. Thus, the segment deserves another full transcription.

"I'm Jim Cornette, and I was wondering if you are as sick as I am of guys who claim to the icon of wrestling. Hulk Hogan and Roddy Piper claim to be the icon; Shawn Michaels is the "icon that can still go"; Bret Hart would claim to be the icon if he wasn't too busy crying about being screwed by the WWF; and I guess Randy Savage is still "thinkin', thinkin'". Well, Shawn Michaels is the single most talented athlete in wrestling today inside the ring, but outside he's an adolescent, obnoxious jerk who takes his tights and goes home if he doesn't get his way.

111

Bret Hart is one of the greatest wrestlers of all time, but if he had been screwed as many times as he claims, he'd have struck oil by now. And Randy Savage is a legend, but let me ask you: how many records did Frank Sinatra sell last year?

But the pinnacle of this icon garbage came at last night's cage match between Hulk Hogan and Roddy Piper, to determine in their minds only who the real icon is. WCW had the gall to say this was the greatest cage match in history, when it was only the greatest in the three weeks since Hell In A Cell. But here you've got a 46-year old bald movie star wannabe who looks like Uncle Creepy with a good build taking on a guy with an artificial hip that hadn't wrestled a full schedule in ten years. It's a tribute to the massive egotism - in my mind - of both men and an indictment of WCW's promotional policy that this match even took place - much less in the main event - when the card was one of the best WCW was capable of having. By the ten minute mark they were sucking wind so bad, the first three rows passed out from oxygen deprivation. Would have been funny if it wasn't so sad.

Well I'm sick and damn tired of guys claiming to be the icon, especially when it usually comes from guys who didn't know when to quit. Roddy Piper was my idol when I was a teenager, but that was twenty years ago. Hulk Hogan during his best years was 50 per cent media creation, and those are long gone. This match was a slap in the face to every wrestler who takes pride in this industry. And in my mind, no one man is bigger than this sport, but if there were to be an icon it would be a guy who has incredible ability inside the ring and professionalism and maturity outside of it.

Let's leave all the petty, backstabbing "I-make-more-money-than-you" BS with the head check girl, and concentrate on talent and attitude. The Undertaker, Ric Flair and Steve Austin have never claimed to be icons, which means they're big candidates to be just that. And in a personal message to Hulk Hogan: you are a household word, but so is garbage, and it stinks when it gets old too. I'm Jim Cornette, and that's my opinion."

Earlier tonight, the WWF honoured some Oklahoma legends in a similar way to what they did in St. Louis at the *Badd Blood* pay-per-view a few weeks back. Those given credit were Jim Ross, Bill Watts, Jack and Gerry Briscoe and the great Danny Hodge. I can only assume this not being on the live broadcast was down to Kevin Dunn, who infamously wanted the *Badd Blood* honour ceremony of former NWA Champions to occur before the show aired, because "no one will know who they are".

WWF Intercontinental Championship
Owen Hart (c) vs. Ahmed Johnson
This was originally scheduled for *SummerSlam 96* at one point while Ahmed was champion, but Ahmed got... wait for it... injured and the match got changed. The roles have switched with Owen as champion, but nobody in their right mind would ever think Ahmed is winning here after Steve Austin's actions in recent weeks. Ahmed throws Owen around and then rips up the Canadian flag like an asshole, so Owen slaps him. Vince blows my mind by talking STRATEGY rather than hyping something else or busting out his clichés, commenting that riling Ahmed could be smart because it throws him off his game. We have barely got started when the Nation turn up on the ramp, though it doesn't really disadvantage either over the other, because both are Nation targets at the moment. Owen sends Ahmed into the steps and then demolishes his already injured hand with them, before choking him with the torn Maple Leaf. We cut to commercial and return to an Owen chinlock, and he continues to work over the wounded Johnson, with the Nation still observing from the ramp. Ahmed begins his Ultimate Warrior comeback and goes to his power game, but because he is dumber than Owen he gets distracted by the Nation and motions for them to hit the ring. They don't. Ahmed hits his banshee scream scissor kick and a half assed spinebuster, but Steve Austin hits the ring through the crowd and wallops Ahmed with the Stunner to cause the intentional DQ and save Owen's title. That was kind of inevitable.
Final Rating: *½

Promo Time: Mankind
Jim Ross gets in the ring for this one, as Vince jokes that he might need to give him "hazard pay". Mankind is most perturbed about what happened to Dude Love last week at the hands of Kane, and he is especially upset with "Uncle Paul", his former manager. Mankind was under the impression they had an unwritten truce having parted on good terms, but I guess he called that one wrong, huh? It actually made a lot of sense to program Mankind against Kane for his first official match, as in truth the character was pretty expendable at the time, in that a loss wouldn't hurt him. Even if it did, Foley always had both Cactus Jack and Dude Love to fall back on anyway. He was also ideal because of his superb win record against the Undertaker, and Kane dominating him and beating him would make him look even stronger going into the Taker matches. Commissioner Slaughter puts a dampener on things by rejecting Mankind's request, even after he says "please", for the sake of his own wellbeing. Mankind thinks it is a shame because he had so many awful things he wanted to do to Kane, so he decides to do them to Slaughter instead, and locks in the Mandible Claw to a huge pop. Slaughter passes out before a slew of officials make their way out, and Mankind rocks in the corner and pulls his hair out as the character regresses back into the shell of its 1996 incarnation. Great delivery as usual from Mick, and a pleasing ending. Of course, each attack on authority cheapens Steve Austin's initial ones until they eventually become a weekly occurrence, but as we have said umpteen times; that's Russo for you.

WWF Championship
Bret Hart (c) vs. Ken Shamrock
This turned out to be Bret's last "proper" match with the company on *Raw* (and indeed appearance on the show in this run), unless you choose to count the couple of half-assed bouts he had on the show post-2010. That was not Bret Hart the active wrestler, but rather Bret Hart the aged former star doing one or two of his moves, so I don't count those. If Vince wanted to take the belt off Bret before *Survivor Series* then this was his best option, and I firmly believe that Bret would have happily done the job for Shamrock, a man he helped train for his WWF career. Shamrock was not championship material, but he was as close as he would ever get in his career and his legitimate background would have been enough for him to be a perfectly acceptable caretaker title holder. Not an ideal situation by any means, but a much better option than the Montreal nonsense. The announcers stick the knife in to Bret by calling Shamrock the greatest submission wrestler in WWF history, which cannot be anything other than a dig at his opponent. Bret rolled his ankle during the fracas with the Nation earlier, obviously playing right into Shamrock's game plan which focuses on going for the ankle lock. Showing his ring smarts, Shamrock goes for it early after a judo roll, but Bret manages to make the ropes immediately. During a break in the action, Vince stops off to promote the *Flashback: Survivor Series* show airing

tomorrow night, quipping about Hulk Hogan in bad cage matches, before claiming you will see him in his prime against the Undertaker in a "classic" match. Prime!? Classic match!? What is the matter with you, Vince!? Bret takes over after a chopblock and goes to work dismantling Shamrock's leg with his usual mechanical offence, including the ring post figure four. The announcers are smart again here, quite rightly pointing out that Hart has no particular inclination to release the hold because a DQ works in his favour. They are a much better team without Lawler and his silly jokes and comments. McMahon calls Bret's offence "methodical", which is jilted Vince speak for "slow". Yes, he is old, past it and behind the times, we get it, Vince. He is also the WWF Champion and has been involved in some legendary matches over the last twelve months, but why let the facts get in the way of a good burial. Shamrock prevents Bret from using a chair and counters his Five Moves of Doom with a sweet suplex, but gets caught with a clothesline coming out of the corner and nearly locked in the Sharpshooter. Shamrock manages to muscle out and escape before it is fully on, but Bret falls into the referee and knocks him down, and thus the tap out from Shamrock's subsequent ankle lock doesn't count. Shamrock goes to revive the ref but Bret whacks him with a chair and locks on the Sharpshooter, which is the cue for Shawn Michaels to come out and leather Hart with a superkick. He then dives on top of him and gives him a pounding as revenge for last week, but an irate Shamrock recovers and snaps, taking out Shawn with a suplex and then mounting *him* with punches. Chaos! The Hart Foundation, DX and officials try and keep Shawn and Bret apart once Shamrock has been neutralised, but to no avail. They just carry on whaling away at each other! The Shamrock stuff with Michaels at the end makes it quite clear to me that Bret was always losing at *Survivor Series* whether Hart agreed to it or not, and this was a way to set up Shawn's next program. That aside, this was a decent little match and the stuff at the end was really strong. The tension between Michaels and Hart radiated through the television screen. It was palpable.
Final Rating: **½

Backstage, Bret Hart is furious and says he can't wait to finally get his hands on Shawn Michaels a *Survivor Series* and that it is going to be "the end". Quite.

The New Blackjacks vs. Bad Ass Billy Gunn & Road Dog
Vince once again rips Hulk Hogan to bits while using his name to sell tomorrow night's TV special, which is hilarious. In the ring, something resembling a match is going on, with the Blackjacks dominating. Bradshaw throws around a few big clotheslines and his team seem to have the match in complete control, but Gunn twats him in the back with a hard chair shot and Road Dog covers for the win. Well, that was super quick! Can't let the wrestling get in the way of all that talking I guess. Post match the Godwinns come down for a brawl with the Blackjacks, so the Outlaws trash the cowboys' hats. Destroying other teams' gear become something of an Outlaws tradition, like they were collecting souvenirs. Last week's recipients the Headbangers come out looking all forlorn with their broken boom box, but the Outlaws hightail it before they can get their hands on them.
Final Rating: ¾*

The announcers reveal that Sgt. Slaughter "doesn't give a damn anymore like many of the wrestlers" and has made the Kane-Mankind match official. So the message there then: if you don't get what you want from someone in a position of authority, beat them up and they will change their mind. Got it!

Promo Time: Kane
Busy double duty night for both Vince and JR tonight, with the latter getting this assignment. This lasts all of a minute, with Paul Bearer calling Mankind "a little pebble on Kane's path to destruction". He reminds the Undertaker that Kane is here to make his life a living hell, and that Kane won't stop until he gets his hands on him. It is the same promo they do every week.

Backstage, DX get the chance to offer a rebuttal to Bret Hart, and "butt" is the operative word here because instead of cutting a promo to sell the PPV, Michaels instead stands up, drops trou and moons the world, with Hunter and Chyna covering his chocolate starfish with DX signs that they accidentally on purpose move away frequently. Shawn finds the whole thing utterly hilarious and rolls around on the floor, delighted with himself, while Vince sits at ringside with pursed lips, probably wondering if things are beginning to go too far. "What's become of us!?" pleads Jim Ross.

Flash Funk vs. Mark Mero
This is another match for Mero that a year ago would have had workrate fans potentially salivating, but not so much now. Vince still does some salivating of his own, desperately lusting after Sable before lying that she is "just as nice on the inside". I wonder if he felt the same way when she sued him. Funk, who has had a fairly good year in the ring under the radar, continues to try and shine in spite of his horrible gimmick and attire, throwing himself around in a fashion reminiscent of Mero earlier in his WWF run. Mero tries to go up top to counter, but Funk boots the top rope and crotches him. They fight up top, and Mero flings Funk to the mat before connecting with a beautiful jumping springboard moonsault, but Funk escapes and connects with an equally nice spinning kick. Funk tries with a moonsault but doesn't hook the leg on the pin, and Mero goes to the cock once again, just like he did last week, landing a hard punch. For Funk, that one stings him more than most. The TKO finishes things off for Marvellous Marc, in what was easily his best display since returning.
Final Rating: **½

Promo Time: Jeff Jarrett
This is another of those quasi-shoot sit down interviews conducted by Jim Ross, and a direct follow up from last week's cutting in-ring promo. Jarrett tones it down a little after last time, unsurprisingly after the way some of the boys reacted, and speaks calmly and candidly. He talks about his past WWF run as country music singer Jeff Jarrett, which he says was Vince's vision and that it limited him in how far he could get over. It did. I was never a fan of the gimmick or Jarrett's performances in the ring when engulfed by it. How amusing too that Jarrett despite all of this talk would revert back to the character in 1998 when his NWA Aztec warrior nonsense failed to get over. WWF revisionist history rears its head by claiming Jarrett left immediately after his classic match with Shawn Michaels at *In Your House 2* to join WCW, but that just isn't true. Jarrett did leave the company after that match, but he went to Memphis for a few months before being brought back at the end of 1995 after five months away. He lasted another month and then left for WCW, and was subsequently buried by the WWF via Jesse Jammes (see: The Raw Files: 1996), but that is not brought up either. Jarrett claims that in WCW there was no ladder of opportunity and that he had his spot when he went in, and it was the same one when he left. That much is true, with WCW often criticised for not doing enough to bring new, fresh faces through to the top of the card, at a time when the WWF was doing exactly that with guys like Steve Austin, Triple H, Mankind, The Rock, Kane and numerous others as

1998 dawns. Their hand was forced due to the departure of Bret Hart and injury to Shawn Michaels mind, but the wheels were in motion for all of those guys anyway. Jarrett claims that to get pushed in WCW you had to be in Eric Bischoff's clique and that ring ability doesn't count for anything over there. Wow, watching that back years later just smacks of irony when you look at what WWE prides itself on most (look) and least (talent). He rips on WCW's live shows not being as exciting as the WWF's and then their top level roster, which is all comprised of guys in their forties. Not quite true. Sting, who was about to headline the hugely successful *Starrcade*, was 38, as was Kevin Nash. Scott Hall was closer at 39, but the Giant was only 25. Granted, Hogan, Savage and Piper were all past their, but they were still the ones drawing the house and the buys. More needed to be done to safeguard the future, sure, but if people are paying money in record numbers to see something, then it is not yet past its use by date.

The Legion of Doom vs. Savio Vega & Miguel Perez
The second *Raw* main event of the month for the Legion of Doom. The match, at under three minutes and none of it interesting, means nothing. The purpose of it is to set up a new feud between the champs and the Outlaws who are at ringside sporting the Blackjack's hats, with the pair of tealeaves nabbing LOD's shoulder pads to add to their collection. Road Dogg accidentally trips Perez, doing the same blind trip that cost Jeff Jarrett the IC title two years earlier, and Hawk gets the pin. Road Dog's overblown cartoon reaction is priceless. Both teams are pissed with the Outlaws after the match and give chase.
Final Rating: ½*

Backstage, Ahmed Johnson cuts a promo that reminds me of the Ultimate Warrior's famous "crying" promo from the early 90s. Ahmed is all dark and quiet as he calmly threatens Steve Austin, before bursting into promo flames and shouting "I'M COMING TO GET YOUUUUUUU" in a high pitched wail that could shatter glass. What a way to end!

THE RAW RECAP:

Most Entertaining: Jim Cornette. Three out of four in October for JC, who once again delivered a masterpiece of a promo, ranting and raving at a speed impossible to comprehend, without ever once losing his way.

Least Entertaining: Kane and Paul Bearer. With five months to fill between Kane's debut and his eventual *WrestleMania* showdown with the Undertaker, a lot of what occurred was just rehashing the same stuff. This was one of those nights, with Bearer saying nothing new and nothing of note.

Quote of the Night: "Oh my goodness, another bad movie! Please! Noooooooo" - Vince McMahon reacts to a fan in the crowd dressed as Hulk Hogan. Boy, Hulk was all over this show tonight.

Match of the Night: Flash Funk vs. Marc Mero. Let's give credit to Funk, one of the most underrated guys on the roster. He worked his ass off here to have an entertaining match with Mero. It was short, but that was to its benefit because it didn't stop. Bret-Shamrock was fine too, but nothing we haven't seen from Hart countless times over the years.

Verdict: The hot streak continues, despite some questionable content at the start. The edgy nature of the program was bringing out the best in some (and conversely, the worst in others), and for every underwhelming match there was a great promo or angle around the corner. So much was going on, that it was impossible to be bored by anything, making even the bad stuff seem not quite so bad. I could have lived without the ill-advised racism stuff, but great work from Jim Cornette, Jeff Jarrett and a few others make this a definite thumbs up.
Rating: 72

11.03.97 by Arnold Furious

Venue: Hershey, PA
Taped: 11.03.97
Raw Rating: 2.6
Nitro Rating: 4.0

Hosts are Jim Ross and Jim Cornette as the WWF tries to differentiate between hour one and hour two. I personally welcome the addition of Cornette, who's one of the best colour guys in the business.

Promo Time: Steve Austin
Massive pop for Austin. He's out to be interviewed by Vince McMahon. Steve's working Owen Hart on Sunday, after being out of action since Owen's piledriver at *SummerSlam*. Naturally Austin is pissed off to have missed months of action when he was at his hottest. Vince reminds us that Austin has pissed off all the Harts, the entire Nation of Domination and also Ahmed Johnson after Austin cost Ahmed the IC title last week with a Stunner. "Wham!" shouts Austin with each replay on the Titantron. Austin points out everyone who's gotten in his way has had their ass kicked. He's out to beat Owen Hart for the IC title at *SummerSlam* and anyone who stops that will face the consequences. This brings out Ahmed Johnson, looking suitably livid about the incident last week. "You keep your eye on him" yells Vince at officials, pointing at Austin. As Ahmed goes to talk the crowd get a massive "Austin" chant going. "Last week you crossed my end zone" says Ahmed before threatening to kick Austin's ass. Ahmed says he doesn't need fans, as the fans begin to chant "Ahmed sucks". Ahmed goes off on one of his trademark rants demanding a match here tonight with Steve Austin. "If anyone wants to see Ahmed Johnson get his ass whipped give me a hell yeah". HELL YEAH! Austin accepts. A fairly typical start for *Raw*, as it has come to be, two guys come out with an issue and a match is booked.

Video Control gives us the Karate Fighters holiday tournament. Carlos Cabrera vs. Tito Santana takes a turn for the weird as Santana "morphs into El Matador" and takes the win.

Light Heavyweight Championship Tournament QF
Aguila vs. Super Loco
1997 sure loved tournaments! The IC title one is barely finished before this one gets underway. Guest ring announcer is Sunny, once again, because they've still got nothing else for her to do and she's super over. Super Loco you probably know better under his Anglicised name of "Super Crazy". Aguila is one of the WWF's big hopes for the division as he's a ridiculous high flier and they've snapped him up before anyone else could. He's only 19 years old. You may know him better as Essa Rios, but Aguila was his Mexican gimmick and the one he used post-WWE. Aguila can work basic lucha stuff even if Loco is the better worker. Having said that Loco totally blows the set up for his dive, causing laughter from ringside, and Aguila hits his dive clean. Loco makes matters worse by completely missing a spin kick leaving Aguila sitting on the ropes like a jackass. Loco

improves with a rolling surfboard and they resort to telegraphing moves to avoid further botches. Loco finally nails something by hitting a cartwheel moonsault to the floor. Not to be outdone Aguila hits a picture perfect moonsault to the floor off the top. Aguila takes it with a twisting splash. The mistakes hurt the match but they perhaps set the difficulty level a little too high. If they'd nailed everything they attempted, this would have the same reputation as Taka-Sasuke.
Final Rating: **¼

Video Control takes us to JR's sit down interview with Goldust and Marlena. Originally the plan was for Marlena to turn heel, but Brian Pillman's death ruined the booking so they switched it to Goldust. The result is a bit rushed and makes little sense. Goldust spent the entirety of Marlena's absence pining for her while she just looked indifferent at times. Marlena talks for a while with Dustin sitting there looking bored. "I can't do this no more Terri". He calls the situation sickening, blames both Dusty Rhodes and Terri for ruining his life before saying he wasn't sitting at home waiting for her, he was out looking for someone who understood him. "Why, why are you doing this?" "acts" Terri. I am pleased they put an end to the cutesy family stuff with little Dakota, but neither one of them benefitted from the angles that followed. At least Dustin's weak face run was at an end, and he was on decent form here.

Video Control gives us a shill of Bret vs. Shawn, which does a handy job of capturing the hatred between them. This includes long clips from *WrestleMania XII* and interviews from *The Fab 4* tape. HBK claims he can push anyone's buttons and we get further clips of Shawn antagonising Bret lately. Bret persists that Shawn didn't deserve to win their 'Mania match, so Shawn calls him a mark. "This match was a year and a half in the making and will never, ever happen again" – Jim Ross sums it up nicely.

Ahmed Johnson vs. Steve Austin
This is supposed to happen later but Ahmed shows up early and so does… Kane. They were running a gimmick where Kane would just turn up and destroy whoever was in the ring, working his way through the company one man at a time. Ahmed doesn't back down and normally a high card guy like him, injuries or otherwise, wouldn't straight up job to a new star, but Kane was booked so strongly that Ahmed's position means very little. Chokeslam. Tombstone. Tombstone. That brings Mankind out to slap the Mandible Claw on Paul Bearer and clock Kane with a piece of metal. This was the first time Kane had shown any kind of weakness, but he sits up quickly. Mankind was getting big reactions for smacking Kane around. I know they needed Kane to go over people to set him up as a threat to the Undertaker, but I'd have been tempted to not job Foley to him.
Final Rating: N/R

Promo Time: Steve Austin
"I said Ahmed Johnson was gonna get his ass whipped and that's exactly what happened". Austin invites Ahmed to come back out here, but if he's injured he'll take on "anyone in that locker room". This brings out the Nation of Domination. Kama jumps in the ring and takes a Stunner while the LOD run out to brawl with the rest of the Nation. Austin, laughing, strolls past the carnage and heads to the back.

Promo Time: Shawn Michaels
With hour two underway, Vince McMahon, in his final appearance as *Raw*'s "voice of the WWF", and Jerry Lawler take over on commentary. Rick Rude runs the DX introduction announcing them as the "past, present and future of professional wrestling". DX bring props with them, so you know they've got a big interview planned. The best is Shawn drinking coffee, which is something almost every bad guy does in movies to show themselves as sinister (Vader will find out about this in a few weeks – stay tuned). They may not have realised what they were were doing but it works. Michael Cole is on interview duty. We get clips of Shawn interfering in the WWF Title match last week and costing Shamrock the belt. The crowd chants "Shawn is gay" so he kisses Hunter (and Chyna) and now they chant "faggot". Hunter has enough of Cole and shoves him over. Good! Shawn reels off his nicknames before playing the European Title like a guitar, Hulk Hogan style. Hunter stops off to make fun of the "Age in the Cage" main event of Halloween Havoc (Hogan vs. Piper). Shawn promises to walk naked to the ring next week and challenge Ken Shamrock. Hunter demands that Sgt. Slaughter come out here and make the match. As Slaughter starts talking, DX employ riot masks with shields on the front to protect them from the gobs of spittle. They add windscreen wipers, which gets a few laughs. This is why people liked DX, regardless of their heel status. They were funny. The more juvenile they got, the funnier they were. Slaughter demands Shawn wrestle Shamrock tonight. DX were wildly entertaining here, albeit all over the place.

Backstage: Marc Mero barges in on Sable, who's not ready despite them being up next, and hauls her out of the locker room with her tits out. No boobs were harmed during the making of this segment.

Savio Vega vs. Marc Mero
Sable has adjusted her clothing as Vince calls her "the star", ignoring Mero in the process. Mero is still slightly babyface, with Lawler choosing to barrack him, but the fans blatantly don't care for the "new" Mero, a guy with a boxing gimmick. Sable distracts to allow Mero to go low and finish with the TKO. Michael Cole stops off to interview Sable but Mero interjects to shove him away before he can ask about all the low blows.
Final Rating: ½*

Dog Collar Match
Vader vs. The British Bulldog
Bulldog brings Jim Neidhart with him, along with Doug Furnas & Phil LaFon. The dog collar rules are like strap match stipulations. Vader finds himself hugely outnumbered and takes a big Canadian beat down. Cole gets to ask Furnas & LaFon about being on Team Canada. LaFon points out he is Canadian "you idiot". Amen, Phil! Doug Furnas talks about touring the world and how he kept telling Phil how great it'd be to get to the USA and they got ignored, even when they were in a serious car crash. He offers his ass for the American fans to smooch. Neidhart tries to interfere but Vader punches him off the apron and collects the four turnbuckles. The stipulations stifled the match but the fans ignored most of it anyway. After the bell goes, in comes Steve Blackman from the crowd to make his debut and Vader makes a point of protecting him from a massive Canadian beating. Blackman looks awesome, throwing spin kicks and martial arts moves. Shame he can't talk. Vince promises he'll be "prosecuted" for invading the ring and was lucky not to get hurt. I think people could see through that one as the Harts were taking bumps for him.
Final Rating: *½

The New Age Outlaws vs. Jesus Castillo & Jose Estrada Jr
The Outlaws aren't called that yet and Road Dog is still missing his illusive second "g". They've also got no music. Road Dog

talks his way to the ring and refers to Billy as "Mr Ass" so the gimmick is coming together. The fans are silent, which shows you how early it is in their run. The crowd launch into another "faggot" chant at Billy. They promised an interview with Jeff Jarrett on this show but Vince points out they might run over so it'll be on Saturday morning instead. Jarrett being bumped off *Raw* shows you how poorly he was treated by creative on his 1997 return. Maybe Vince was resentful of how much he'd had to pay Jarrett to get him back. Especially as he'd done nothing of note while he was away. The Outlaws rather bumble through this one like the Keystone Cops and at the moment it's hard to see why they'd walked away from middling face gimmicks to be a heel team. Boricuas have their way with Road Dogg until Mr Ass comes off the top behind the ref's back to score the win.
Final Rating: ¾*

Ken Shamrock vs. Shawn Michaels
Ken had a title shot last week and rumour has it a few officials wanted Shamrock to win the title, to end the whole controversy of Bret being WWF Champion and his contract expiring. If they had done a quick switch and put Shawn over Shamrock at the December PPV, that way Bret could have left how he wanted and nobody would get screwed. Of course that never happened. Bret did tap out to Shamrock though, which made him look like a threat to all the main eventers. Shamrock starts fast and whales on Shawn before pressing him onto the rest of DX. Shawn slips out of Shamrock's further attempts to take over the match but does fall foul of a fisherman suplex. The fans actually buy into Shamrock possibly winning with that hold, which shows you how hot Ken was in 1997. His failure to win big matches turned him into a choke artist in the eyes of the fans. There's also the matter of the loud calls. There's a blatant "clothesline" call on the ropes that's audible. One of Shawn's biggest complaints about Shamrock as a worker were his audible calls. Chyna interferes to give Shawn the advantage and he sets a breakneck pace for a heel. There's something to be said for heels who bump a lot and get over by being jerks as their matches are not as boring, as heels who rely on denying the crowd fun. Like Undertaker. Or Hunter. They have some nice counters lined up and you'd think their match would have benefitted from more matches together and improved. You can see the shortfalls where something doesn't quite click. It really stands out in a Shawn Michaels match as he was so perfect 90% of the time. Ken goes after his rana but it's blocked into a sit out powerbomb. Shawn goes for the superkick but that's countered into the belly-to-belly. Another superkick is countered into the anklelock, Shawn taps out and Rick Rude jumps in to bash Shammy with the Halliburton for the DQ. Hunter Pedigrees Shamrock on the briefcase to make sure Ken doesn't go on one of his patented rampages. This is certainly a good showing from both guys and they had some interesting counters worked out. As I said earlier, more matches between them could have resulted in something special down the line. Shamrock tapping Shawn out here set up the December PPV.
Final Rating: ***

Side note: This was the final *Raw* show where Bret Hart was under contract and could have appeared. In his book he alleges the weekend before *Survivor Series* was spent both looking over contractual terms and waiting to hear from Vince McMahon. It does seem a little weird the WWF Champion isn't on the go-home show before *Survivor Series* and indeed another hint that he might not be either champion nor in the WWF for much longer.

THE RAW RECAP:

Most Entertaining: Shawn Michaels. Wonderful on the mic and way ahead of everyone else in the ring. There were times when Shawn was untouchable as a Sportz Entertainer.

Least Entertaining: Savio Vega.

Quote of the Night: "Everyone knows the Heartbreak Kid is the showstopper, the main event, the icon that can still go". – Shawn Michaels

Match of the Night: Shawn Michaels vs. Ken Shamrock

Verdict: A solid episode of *Raw*, though mostly for angles and promos rather than wrestling. In the ring there was only one worthwhile match, with Shawn and Shamrock having longer to play with than the rest to create a good bout. The light heavyweight match might have been great had they not been nervous and made a few early mistakes. It takes the gloss right off the contest. This is very much an Attitude Era show as all the best moments stemmed from talking and non-wrestling segments like Austin's promo, DX ribbing Slaughter and the shill video for Bret vs. Shawn. At least they inserted a proper main event to end the show with some wrestling.
Rating: 65

11.09.97 - Survivor Series 1997
(James Dixon)
[Molson Centre, Montreal Quebec, Canada]

- The New Age Outlaws & The Godwinns def. The Headbangers & The New Blackjacks (¼*)
- The Truth Commission def. DOA (¾*)
- The British Bulldog, Jim Neidhart, Doug Furnas & Phil LaFon def. Vader, Goldust, Marc Mero & Steve Blackman (**¼)
- Kane def. Mankind (¾*)
- The Legion of Doom, Ahmed Johnson & Ken Shamrock def. The Nation of Domination (**¼)
- Steve Austin def. Owen Hart (DUD)
- Shawn Michaels "defeated" Bret Hart (**½)

Rating: 25

11.10.97 by Arnold Furious

Venue: Ottawa, Ontario, Canada
Taped: 11.10.97
Raw Rating: 3.4
Nitro Rating: 4.4

This comes the night after the infamous Montreal Screwjob at *Survivor* Series and interestingly enough Bret Hart remains in *Raw*'s opening credits. I guess everyone was too busy to remove him, but it did lend credence to early conspiracy theories that Bret hadn't actually left the WWF. Hosts are Jim Ross and Jim Cornette, with Vince permanently removed from commentary after screwing Bret.

Promo Time: Shawn Michaels
The new champion gets himself some new theme music as DX debut their official D-Generation X tune. It's iconic. Rick Rude comes down to introduce the new champion, and milks the hell out of it. The "fat outta shape Ottawa idiots" are instructed to shut their mouths and open their eyes. The crowd erupt into a very loud "bullshit" chant before Shawn is even out here. The

champ has Hunter and Chyna in his corner. JR describes Shawn's win as a robbery and tells us Bret has left the WWF. The crowd chant "we want Bret". "Shawn Michaels beat Bret Hart in his own country, in his own finishing hold" says the champ. Shawn flubs a few lines, saying that the WWF isn't big enough for "the Heartbreak Kid and Shawn Michaels" before telling us he ran Bret off down south "with all the other dinosaurs". Shawn absorbs the hate and points out he's more talented than anyone else, which is why he's the top wrestler in the business. Once again Shawn feels the urge to slip an insult in towards the departed Bret instead of reacting to the arrival of Ken Shamrock. Way to put over your opponent at the next PPV! Shawn mockingly gives the mic to Shamrock, suggesting he should attempt to string a few words together. "We call that a sentence, Ken". Shamrock calls everyone in the ring a "disgrace to the human race" before rounding on Chyna for being man-ish. Shamrock's assertion that Rude is an "old man" is almost as harsh as the Chyna insult. He was only six years older than Shamrock. Shawn gets a rambling response, which brings out Sgt. Slaughter to announce Shamrock has a title shot, but Triple H has to wrestle him tonight. If you overlook the sheer obnoxiousness of Shawn's words, his delivery was very entertaining. Unfortunately Shamrock couldn't take the high road and was petty with his insults. The segment rather fizzled out too.

Marc Mero vs. Ahmed Johnson
Do you think they're booking Mero on *Raw* so people can see Sable? His star has badly faded since he switched ring gear after his big knee injury. His boxer persona feels like a midcard gimmick. At best. The problem with booking Mero and Ahmed is that they have the same faults. They both can't structure a match for shit and tend to do better when someone can bounce off them. Mero's bumping took a big knock when he got hurt and Ahmed's popularity is completely in the toilet after flip-flopping between face and heel in '97. Ahmed has it won clean only for Mero to go low for the DQ. Ahmed then sandbags the hell out of Mero on the TKO, resulting in the worst TKO in the history of the move. It is abysmal.
Final Rating: ½*

Video Control takes us to the Karate Fighters Arena where Dok Hendrix jobs to a midget.

Light Heavyweight Championship Tournament QF
Taka Michinoku vs. Devon Storm
Guest ring announcer is Sunny as the WWF continue to insert her to get a random pop during the evening. Brian Christopher joins commentary to add a layer of obnoxiousness that was missing without his daddy on the mic. Crowbar gets no introduction, no music and no hope. Taka flips around him before connecting on an Asai moonsault. He goes to the well off the top again but Storm TKOs him on the apron and hits a splash to the floor. Devon always seemed to throw out moves that looked painful to take but not impressive. Christopher reaches the point of insufferable on commentary after about 2-minutes of him laughing at his own jokes. Taka nails a tornado DDT, Devon responds with a release German suplex, Taka responds with a super rana. It's all very spotty. Devon hits a Death Valley Driver but misses a follow up moonsault. Superplex from Taka then a missile spinning heel kick to the ankle. Badly botched. Christopher tries to interfere and gets kicked off the apron. Storm can't take advantage of the distraction and goes down to a Michinoku Driver. Not satisfied with that, he wipes out Christopher with a plancha to really pop the crowd. You could see why people liked Taka. He hit crazy spots, didn't seem to care about his own wellbeing and always had one more wild dive lined up. The match was very spotty, but at least Taka hit, almost, all of his stuff clean.
Final Rating: *¾

Promo Time: Goldust
This is the *Raw* debut for Dustin's black face paint with the FU (forever unchained) painted on his cheeks in gold, that he had introduced last night at *Survivor Series*. Other than that he's dressed like a cross between Hugh Hefner, Wahoo McDaniel and Zsa Zsa Gabor. Goldust blames both Dusty Rhodes and Terri for telling him what to do for his entire adult life. JR challenges Goldust for walking out on his country last night, which brings out Vader, who was the guy he walked out on. "Nobody walks out on Vader" yells the Rocky Mountain Mastodon. Goldust blames a broken arm and when he doesn't give Vader a satisfactory reason for quitting on him, Vader gives him a powerbomb.

Backstage: Michael Cole reports chaos in the locker room as Blackjack Windham has been assaulted. Once again Cole is using the wrong word. One person has been knocked to the ground = ANARCHY!

Recon & Sniper vs. The Headbangers
The Truth Commission have already lost their leader, the Commandant, and now they've lost their lustre too. The DOA drive down to back up the 'Bangers, Crush making one of his final WWF appearances of this run, which causes Jackyl to get pissy and join commentary. Recon and Sniper get beaten up when it's 2-on-2 and are forced into getting heat on Thrasher. The Headbangers are quite happy to slip into lazy tag team formula, regardless of the length of the match. Their effort levels dropped off significantly after the WWF made it abundantly clear they would never be the dons of the tag division. Thrasher hot tags Mosh and then powerbombs Mosh onto Sniper for the win. The Interrogator gets pissed off and whales on the former tag champs only for the DOA to plough in there. Eventually the Truth Commission drag the big man away and leave as he attempts to take on six guys.
Final Rating: ¼*

Promo Time: Steve Austin
Austin had been getting big pops for some time, but the roof comes off when he walks out here. Michael Cole is on interview duty and Austin shoves him out of the way. "Stone Cold Steve Austin is back". Austin considers whupping Cole, but Rocky Maivia shows up to cut the IC champ off. He claims to have been the best IC champ there ever was and points out he's coming for Austin's belt. The crowd bites on it and get a big "Rocky sucks" chant going. The chemistry was there right from the beginning, though naturally in late 1997 there is a massive gulf between the two. Rock's reactions to Austin's insults are perfect though. His bug eyed staring when Austin says he sucks for example. This was too brief to go down as an all-time great segment, but it was very entertaining. A taste of things to come.

Promo Time: Steve Blackman
The Lethal Weapon comes down to chat with JR. Blackman says he did okay at *Survivor Series,* but he wasn't familiar with the rules. Jose Estrada Jr, in the ring awaiting a match, gets in Blackman's face and Los Boricuas try to put a beating on him. Like the good collection of jobbers they are, Blackman mows them down with botched kicks.

Backstage: The still unnamed New Age Outlaws admit to hospitalising Blackjack Windham and call him dumb for

117

messing with the Road Dog and Mr "A double crooked letter".

Bunkhouse Brawl
The New Age Outlaws vs. Blackjack Bradshaw
With Windham injured Bradshaw takes this solo. The old NWA staple; the Bunkhouse match, is basically just a street fight where all the guys wear jeans. Bradshaw puts a beating on both Outlaws, including a wicked big boot to Gunn's face. Bradshaw is vicious and whales on both heels with anything that isn't tied down, including the rarely used timekeeper's table. That continues until Billy gets a tornado DDT onto a chair and both Outlaws pile on for the pin. Score another duke for the Outlaws. The match was barely 2-minutes long, if that, but was entertaining. Both Outlaws took some slick bumps and Bradshaw was brutal.
Final Rating: **

Video Control takes us to a Jeff Jarrett interview where he claims the WWF got a bargain when they signed him. He says he has star potential, twelve years experience, youth, he's drug free and has no skeletons in his closet. Jarrett claims he'll be the greatest WWF Champion of all time when he wins the belt. This was recorded prior to *Survivor* Series, which explains why Jarrett says he's superior to Bret Hart and considers him a notch in his belt when he gets around to beating him. Jarrett shoots on various wrestlers but is nice about all of them… apart from Triple H, who he calls a "tag-along", which buries his WWF career before it's even underway (although to be fair, CM Punk called Triple H a "doofus" when Hunter was a McMahon and got the WWE Title out of it).

Promo Time: Butterbean
He's ringside so Michael Cole goes to interview him. He's immediately interrupted by Marc Mero who calls himself "a real boxer". "Who have you ever beaten? A few truck drivers, a few steel workers, some lousy Canadians". He calls Butterbean a nobody and promises to KO him in four rounds or less. "You are the Pillsbury Doughboy and I am Superman" rants Mero in fantastic fashion. Some surprising fried gold from Marvellous Marc here.

The Undertaker vs. Kama Mustafa
Taker plods through his stuff in an uninspiring match, which is pretty typical of these two colliding. At least Kama isn't trying to steal the urn this time. Kama gets a brief spell of hope until Taker chokeslams him. That's the cue for the lights to go out and Kane arrives. Paul Bearer says that Kane wants Taker to suffer, so he won't stroll down there and kick his ass now. Taker accuses Bearer of poisoning Kane's mind and believes there is still good in his brother. Is he cutting the Luke Skywalker promo on Darth Kane? Taker says he'll never fight Kane so he might as well join him. Instead Bearer demands a 1 on 1 contest at a later date. The match was a squash, just designed to set up a promo.
Final Rating: N/R

Ken Shamrock vs. Triple H
Sgt. Slaughter stops Shawn, Rude and Chyna from coming down and at this point it's weird seeing Hunter without Chyna in his corner. Hunter has nothing when it comes to Shamrock's offence. He just covers up and hopes he doesn't die. The crowd opts to chant "we want Bret" as Hunter takes over with a DDT. Lawler stops off to point out that Bret's WCW contract is for $3M a year. Hunter decides to get in Slaughter's face about all his buddies being banned from ringside, which leads to an absolutely terrible match at the forthcoming December PPV. Hunter reverts to form as a heel by running through boring heat on Shamrock and killing the crowd in the process. I'm not even sure if he's doing it on purpose to kill Shamrock's heat going into the PPV, as Ken can't even boss a "tag-along" let alone challenge for the WWF Title. DX's political motivation for various performances is suspect. Rick Rude walks back down, showing how serious being "banned" really is, but Sarge stops him. Hunter KOs the ref, so Shamrock taps him out with an anklelock. Chyna runs down to attack Slaughter and Shawn runs in to nail Shamrock with Rude's briefcase. The cameras don't capture the eventual pinfall as the WWF cock up the timing and finish early. Apparently it was ruled a no contest and then Shamrock pinned Shawn with Slaughter counting the fall. Not that it counts for anything in a match Shawn wasn't even in nor was it captured on TV. At the time anyway, the finish made its way onto next week's show, but like Shawn superkicking Bret after Hart ran over time a few months ago, the damage was already done.
Final Rating: *

THE RAW RECAP:

Most Entertaining: Shawn Michaels. His opening promo hit a few decent beats, albeit alongside a few flubs, and he's still awesome on the mic when he wants to be. Although, oddly enough, he was still taking shots at Bret Hart even after the Hitman was gone.

Least Entertaining: Triple H. I think James is a little harsh on Hunter, but his business killing main event disaster (in a match he should he jobbed clean in) against Shamrock was the worst thing on this show.

Quote of the Night: "Bret Hart has left the WWF" – Jim Ross

Match of the Night: It wasn't that kind of show.

Verdict: Low on wrestling, big on storylines, this was an Attitude *Raw*. It was an easy watch, but the lack of in-ring, in terms of quality at least, makes it pretty useless in the long run. You really need a mix of the work and the story to make *Raw* worthwhile. Unless the story is superb. Shawn's opening was necessary and it worked. Austin vs. the Rock on the mic was interesting and Mero's jabs at Butterbean were entertaining too. But those are three "bits". The light heavyweight tournament wasn't setting the world on fire and neither was Jeff Jarrett's lukewarm return to action. It's a show without substance. It's a show without Bret Hart, sadly, and losing the Harts takes a competitive edge off the show.
Rating: 50

11.17.97 by Arnold Furious

Venue: Cornwall, Ontario, Canada
Taped: 11.11.97
Raw Rating: 3.15
Nitro Rating: 4.12

Video Control opens with footage of the mistimed finish to *Raw* where Ken Shamrock managed to score a pin on Shawn Michaels, counted by Sgt. Slaughter. Hosts are Jim Ross and Jim Cornette.

Promo Time: Steve Austin
"If anyone wants to see Rocky Maivia get his ass whupped, gimme a hell yeah". HELL YEAH! Austin calls Rocky out and tells him he can bring whoever he wants with him. Instead

Faarooq, Kama and D'Lo Brown come down, giving Austin all of the Nation except the guy he asked for. D'Lo runs in first, eats a Stunner and Rocky sprints down to steal the IC belt and leg it to the back. "He ain't safe nowhere" says Austin to the commentators. Cornette tries to do a link but Austin comes back to say he'll be around for the whole damn show and Cornette does a fine job of sliding straight back into the shill, promoting the rest of the card. The Austin-Maivia feud was a placeholder until Austin could take the WWF title at *WrestleMania*. As far as holding feuds go, it's pretty good.

Marc Mero vs. Jerry Lawler
This is a curious booking decision, given that Lawler is a commentator and also a heel, and Mero's heel turn is in its infancy. He's slowly becoming more and more jealous of Sable's popularity. JR points out Sable has a black eye from where her horse kicked her. "Sable was riding her horse, how can you tell which one is which? I asked her age and she showed me her teeth" – Cornette. Butterbean is ringside after an altercation with Mero last week and Sable waves at him. Cornette mispronounces his name as "Butterball" and "Jellybean" to my amusement. Video Control points to a Mero victory over Brian Christopher as the reasoning for King getting this match, which makes him the de facto face for probably the first time in the WWF. The crowd hate everyone but Sable. Christopher comes out to add to the heel mix. "Kill him! Break his neck!" yells Christopher. Lawler demands a boxing match so Mero knocks him on his ass and he begs off to the ref. The crowd get bored with the stalling and chant for Sable. Brian asks Sable for her phone number. "Look, I'm sexy" he keeps yelling before giving off one of those trademark cackles. Mero gets distracted by these shenanigans, somehow mistakes a piledriver for a powerbomb, and jumps wrong for it. It's Jerry Lawler, you tool, it's his finish! Sable jumps in for the DQ, rather than see Mero lose and Mero immediately pops up and hits the TKO before blaming Sable for his loss. Sable's black eye gets the fans all worked up, suspecting Mero punched her.
Final Rating: *

Video Control takes us to footage of Bret Hart smashing up monitors after *Survivor Series*. This leads right into an interview with Vince McMahon and his black eye. JR asks him if he screwed Bret Hart. Vince responds with the famous "Bret screwed Bret" comment and JR blames Vince for orchestrating the whole thing. Vince goes off on a tangent about making a lot of decisions, some good, some bad, but he has a good batting average. Vince talks about "doing the right thing" when you leave and the "time honoured tradition" (of jobbing on your way out). He calls Bret a traditionalist and was surprised he didn't want to do business. JR mentions the 20 year contract and Vince calls Bret's decision to leave a joint decision. Vince claims Bret's move to WCW was orchestrated by him (which it was to a degree) and that Bret's contract was down to his business savvy. Vince quotes the $3M a year deal in WCW, working 125 days a year, and mentions this was all because of his help. He says the move was best for everybody. "I didn't want to lose Bret, even if it wasn't paying off from a financial standpoint". Vince says he was disappointed in Bret for punching him and claims to have "vision problems" because of it. "I allowed Bret to strike me, I hoped that he wouldn't". JR mentions legal ramifications of the punch but Vince leaves that in Bret's court. Vince talks about his desire to Bret go out the right way by losing and congratulating the winner. Vince is smug and self righteous throughout this interview, which may or may not have been intentional, but it definitely created a monster heel in McMahon. When JR asks about Vince having sympathy for Bret, Vince goes into overdrive. "I have no sympathy for Bret. None". "Bret made a very, very selfish decision. He's going to have to live with that for the rest of his life. Bret screwed Bret". This was a business changing promo as Vince had never done anything so candid. A million miles away from the standard "Vince wears a toupee" jokes that normally greeted his on camera appearances.

Los Boricuas vs. The New Age Outlaws
The Outlaws, *still* unnamed, stole a load of Boricuas' stuff earlier tonight and wear that over their normal gear to mess with their opponents. "Odelay homes" says the Road Dog. The agitated Boricuas don't follow the rules of a tag team match and the whole thing is a tornado brawl. Eventually the rest of Los Boricuas run in for the DQ. This was never a match but was specifically designed to show how chaotic the WWF had become.
Final Rating: N/R

Video Control gives us a shill package for Ken Shamrock, which includes practically every top WWF star tapping to the ankle lock.

Max Mini, Nova & Taurus vs. El Torito, Battalion & Tarantula
Sunny's job de jour is refereeing midget wrestling. As per usual the heels are all bigger. We get a bunch of head scissors and armdrags, pretty much one after another. It's at speed but it's very, very samey until Max Mini gets in there. He takes better bumps and has more innovative set ups to the same spots that everyone else does. They start running the comedy bits with Sunny when it's all cut off in mid flow; Sunny yelling "wait" at Battalion is the cue… and the lights go out. It's KANE! The midgets flee and hide behind Cornette in a bit of comedy sauce. "Ohhh, I've always liked you" says Cornette of Paul Bearer. The Headbangers run in to try and help, but both get destroyed after Kane no sells a boom box shot. Tombstone for Mosh. Tombstone for Thrasher. I think this would have been more over and memorable if Kane had Tombstoned Sunny. Nobody ever did anything like that to Sunny.
Final Rating: N/R

Video Control gives us extended footage of Hunter vs. Shamrock from last week.

Promo Time: D-Generation X
The most notable thing about this segment is the appearance of Rick Rude. Not long after *Survivor Series,* Rude decided he'd seen enough and quit for WCW, but the WWF had already taped this episode of *Raw*. So Rude appears on a taped *Raw* the same night as he appears on a live episode of *Nitro*, criticising DX and the WWF while calling the company a "sinking ship". To hammer home the point that *Nitro* is the live show, Rude shaved his moustache and appeared prior to his *Raw* taped appearance. This is also the debut of DX's psychedelic live/taped footage entrance. Shawn gets the mic and tells us "DX respects absolutely nobody". Shawn points out Ken Shamrock is one of Bret's friends and seeing as he beat Bret (and ran him out of the WWF), he's beaten all his family, he's now going to start beating up Bret's friends. Triple H gets the mic next and calls out Commissioner Slaughter. "We make the rules, not you" says Hunter and points out "we run the World Wrestling Federation". And that's a shoot, brother. As per usual Hunter talks about his dick and implies he'll nail Sarge's wife so the commish bitch slaps him. DX beats him down then haul him back up for a Pedigree. "How can you keep pointing to something that's not even there" jabs Cornette at Hunter's crotch chops. JR sells the act as "deplorable" but

the heat here was volcanic considering all they did was beat up a retired wrestler.

Light Heavyweight Championship Tournament QF
Scott Taylor vs. Eric Shelley
Shelley (spelt differently onscreen depending on whether you look at the bracket or the caption) is bald and an okay worker. Taylor is better but this is the point where the WWF ran out of talent as neither of these guys are over. I'm surprised Tajiri wasn't involved here. The match is largely ignored in favour of a Jeff Jarrett phone call where he criticises the WWF for promoting Bret Hart, a guy who doesn't even work here, and promises an in-ring *Raw* re-debut next week. Taylor and Shelley run some interesting near misses and counters at speed. A pity the WWF don't care about it at all. Taylor botches a Regal Stretch, not getting Shelley's legs tied up right. They should stick to the speedy stuff. Cornette points out this has been a solid match and also that they've been doing it a disservice by ignoring it. Refreshing! Taylor finishes with a diving DDT. A shame Taylor didn't have more charisma at this point, as he'd have been far better as Taka's foil than the irritating Brian Christopher.
Final Rating: **½

Promo Time: Marc Mero
He's back out here, disgruntled about the events from earlier. "All night this has been going on" – Cornette moans about wrestlers around the announce table. Mero refers to Sable as his property and complains of Sable being stalked by Butterbean. He calls Butterbean out and tells him if he keeps waving at Sable he'll get knocked out. In theory this was a good idea but Butterbean was a freak show attraction, not a boxer, and Mero looked like a punk for backing down from him. A shame as Mero's promo on Butterbean the week before was hugely entertaining.

Video Control takes us to part two of the Vince McMahon interview. JR asks if Vince would have Bret back after the incidents following *Survivor Series* (spitting, punching, destroying monitors). Vince calls wrestling a "strange business" and says he'd have Bret back if he apologised. He'd tell Bret "no more free shots", which insinuates Vince felt he could beat up Bret in a fair fight. It's really subtle, which is what makes it so good. Vince points out that not only did Bret sell out but he helped him do it. Vince points out that every time Bret says he didn't go to WCW for the money it hurts his credibility. When asked about regrets Vince says he "regrets Bret didn't do the right thing for the business", which again is cracking heel work. Vince claims that he had to do what he had to do for the business, for the fans and for the people he employs, whereas Bret made a mistake. Vince says he's already over it. "Bret really wasn't the best there is, the best there was and the best there ever will be. He had the opportunity to live up to that in his last match in the WWF and he failed". This interview turned out terrific for the company. Vince comes across as so detestable that the fans hate him, and it ended up giving us the biggest heel in history. It couldn't have been a more perfect set up for a feud with a top guy and it just so happened that Austin had already dropped Vince with the Stunner...

Vader vs. Goldust
This comes about because Goldust walked out on Vader's All-American team at *Survivor Series*. An infuriated Vader then powerbombed him. Goldust comes out dressed like a cross between Judy Garland, Liberace and a chess board. He's also got his arm in a sling. Goldust begs off before whipping out a hammer from his sling and knocking Vader down with it. This would be the third match tonight that didn't actually take place. This is even worse than the last two as this didn't even begin.
Final Rating: N/R

Promo Time: Sgt. Slaughter
He talks about retiring from wrestling and wearing a sports coat to become the commissioner. He points out the mixed reactions he's gotten in the role. Sarge calls Hunter scum, slime and a maggot before ordering Helmsley into the ring at the PPV to wrestle him. The crowd pop the announcement, but they wouldn't have if they knew how bad the match would be.

Rocky Maivia vs. Dude Love
Rocky wears the IC title to the ring. Rock points out he's highly intelligent and athletic and he's better than everyone else. The ego driven "The Rock" promos helped changed perception of Rocky and made him a star. Dude is back after Mick Foley threatened to leave the WWF after *Survivor Series,* but had a rethink and did the best for his family instead. If he'd gone to WCW it would have been the worst mistake of his career. But then, he knew how bad WCW was from personal experience. Rocky is still lacking in polish but a year in the WWF has seen him improve at various aspects of his game. His selling is much improved and his technical stuff is showing improvement too. It's appropriate that he headlines *Raw* against Foley, with whom he'd enjoy a fabulous feud with just a year later. They have instant chemistry with nice counters and constant work. Dude hits Sweet Shin Music and the double arm DDT, but the Nation jump in there for the DQ. Rocky aims to nail Dude with the IC strap but Steve Austin runs in for the save. Another Stunner for D'Lo! Rock slips away and takes the IC belt with him.
Final Rating: **½

THE RAW RECAP:

Most Entertaining: Vince McMahon.

Least Entertaining: Jerry Lawler.

Quote of the Night: "Bret Hart screwed Bret Hart" – Vince McMahon

Match of the Night: Rocky Maivia vs. Dude Love. If Taylor hadn't botched that Regal Stretch, this might have been a different story.

Verdict: This is a notable *Raw* for a few reasons, but the most obvious of them is the Vince McMahon interview. It was a business changing segment. Splitting the interview in half gave audiences time to digest Vince's egotistical stance and hate him all the more when he really laid it on thick in the second segment. The great thing about the interviews is that Vince just told the truth, but in big business the higher you are up the corporate ladder the more despicable you appear to be. There were subtle heel moments, and indeed Vince made for a great subtle heel in the beginning. Because in real life he's a subtle heel, not a pompous OTT crazy person like he's been portrayed on TV ever since overbooking took the character too far (somewhere around the "Higher Power" angle). Knowing where the McMahon character will go is in a way a little sad, as he's such a brilliant heel here. Because Vince believes he's right and he believes in what he's saying, his position as owner sets up a million angles in everyone's head right away. People would be thinking about what wrestlers had to deal with, negotiating with this megalomaniacal owner. It opened up the behind the scenes area and JR mentioning the internet during

their conversation made me so curious I bought a computer so I could go online. The internet opened up the business to such a degree that it completely changed. 1997 was a gateway year where the WWF became so controversial that it became unmissable TV. In the same way that WCW was a year earlier with the talent raids and the Hogan heel turn. I realise Vince Russo and DX had a lot to do with that, something the wrestling purist in me dislikes, and yet the business profited a great deal from it all. It changed everything.
Rating: 91

11.24.97 by Arnold Furious

Venue: Fayetteville, NC
Taped: 11.24.97
Raw Rating: 3.1
Nitro Rating: 3.88

Hosts are Jim Ross and Jim Cornette.

Promo Time: Shawn Michaels
DX start out by replacing Ravishing Rick Rude with "Handsome Harvey" (Wippleman). Harvey gets to do the whole Rude introduction verbatim, which he's actually pretty good at, provoking Shawn to point out how easy Rude was to replace. "That was a tough spot to fill" are his exact words before shoving Wippleman on his ass. Shawn points out they're live so he has a chance to fully address *Survivor Series* and the controversy therein. Shawn starts out taking it very seriously and seems to regret what happened to Bret Hart. Which is what he promised he'd do, to Bret's face, the night of *Survivor Series*. Shawn points out that Bret Hart is under WWF contract until 30.11.97, which is next week. "Bret Hart deserved better" says Shawn, looking thoroughly remorseful. "As God is my witness, Bret Hart and Shawn Michaels have finally had contact with each other without knowledge of the media, Vince McMahon, the internet or the underground dirt sheet writers". Keep in mind "as God is my witness". Shawn carries on to say Bret is here tonight to settle this once and for all, with a handshake or a fight. This was one hell of a teaser… but unfortunately I know what they're actually going to deliver. Considering the WWF had done nothing but talk about Bret Hart ever since *Survivor Series* it'd make sense for them to have had a payoff.

WWF Tag Team Championship
The Legion of Doom (c) vs. The New Age Outlaws
This really doesn't have the feel of a big match, as the challengers had been a big joke to this point. That's all about to end. The challengers piss LOD off pre-match by coming out wearing their stolen spikes and making fun of their age. The match was originally booked for the PPV, but the Outlaws baited LOD into demanding an early title match just so they can kick some ass. LOD put a beating on the Outlaws, getting solid pops in the process. Hawk misses in the corner to set up the heat but he's probably the last guy in the world worth working heat on because he doesn't sell worth a damn. The Outlaws are passable at working heat, as they both know all the tricks. It's just not believable on a guy like Hawk who can't or doesn't want to sell. Dogg nails Hawk with a tag belt but he kicks out of that and scores a hot tag. Animal is still great at cleaning house though and his role in this match is perfect. His flying shoulderblock misses and wipes out the ref. LOD set for the Doomsday Device only for Road Dogg to hit Animal in the spine with a chair and replacement referee Timmy White runs in to count the pin. An historic change and probably the best LOD-Outlaws tag match, as it closely adhered to standard tag team wrestling formula.
Final Rating: *¾

Video Control gives us the Karate Fighters holiday tournament where Sunny beats a midget, who hardly moves because he's staring at Sunny's tits. Just to emphasise the focus of this segment they give us a slow motion replay of Sunny's celebration. Jiggling titties, who would have thunk it?

Backstage: the Outlaws cheese it and almost hit a big white stretch limo on the way out. JR speculates that Bret Hart is in the limo.

Promo Time: Goldust
The "mental and physical invalid" was supposed to be wrestling but has a massive pink cast on his arm and comes out in a wheelchair. Goldust claims to be paraplegic and that he can't move. As Goldust is thanking the fans for their prayers and support Vader comes out here. "Oh God, no" says the supposed cripple. Vader threatens to permanently mesh Goldust into his wheelchair, which causes Goldust's nurse to throw rubbing alcohol into Vader's eyes before revealing herself to be Luna Vachon. Goldust miraculously jumps to his feet to put a beating on Vader before they skip up the ramp together. Goldust and Luna, not Goldust and Vader. The thought of Vader skipping did make me giggle though.

Promo Time: Sgt Slaughter
He claims the attack on him by DX had nothing to do with him accepting the match with Hunter. It was Hunter insulting his family. Sarge puts his hat on and is magically transformed into a wrestler again. He calls the Cobra Clutch the "most devastating move in the history of wrestling". Michael Cole, on interview duty, interjects "the Cobra Clutch???" like he's never heard of it before. Douche. Slaughter, as Commissioner, books the match to be a Boot Camp match. Sarge goes off on a military themed rant about the horrors of war including "have you ever killed a man… with your bare hands?" He suggests he might finish Hunter off permanently.

Light Heavyweight Championship Tournament QF
Brian Christopher vs. Flash Flannagan
This is the last QF match. Considering the whole division was built around Taka and Christopher, it should be obvious who goes over here. And indeed in every match in this tournament as they only built up two guys before it started. Flannigan is a big guy but he's a flier. He, like almost everyone in the tournament, is a better light heavyweight than Christopher, the mini-heavyweight. He's bland but at least he tries. Christopher is all character. All his flashy moves are used as goddamn transitions like the Stroke and a Scorpion Deathdrop. Neither of which he pins after. Naturally as he's Jerry's kid, he goes over with the Tennessee Jam.
Final Rating: *¼

Promo Time: Shawn Michaels
At the start of the show HBK cut a promo to set up this second promo. The idea being that fans would stay tuned to see if Bret Hart would actually turn up to confront Michaels. We probably should have known better. Triple H gets to talk for a bit first to take shots at Sgt. Slaughter and talk about his dick. I'm so glad we had time for that. Shawn gets the mic and introduces Bret Hart, which at the time made me mark out like hell as his music kicked in. But it's just a midget. "We all knew Bret was short on charisma, short on talent" mocks Hunter while Shawn literally falls about laughing. Short on talent? That's rich coming from

Hunter! They run a re-enactment of *Survivor Series* with Shawn Michaels slapping midget Bret in the Sharpshooter while Hunter runs his mouth. Nice work guys, way to bury a legitimate finishing move. DX slap a WCW sign on the midget's ass and kick him out of the ring. While they're laughing about it out comes Jim Neidhart. Shawn points out there's nothing between them but air and opportunity, before offering Neidhart an opportunity. Shawn's history lesson, regarding the original Hart Foundation and what happened to Anvil after they split, is riveting stuff. He asks where Davey went and Anvil replies that he's having knee surgery. "The old phoney knee injury, I know that one well" replies Shawn, practically admitting his own bullshit, before offering Neidhart a spot in DX if he wants it, later tonight. The midget stuff was obnoxious beyond belief but at least DX sold for Anvil's appearance.

Video Control gives various examples of why we should give a shit about Butterbean including his presence in a video game and a god-awful country song about him.

Ken Shamrock vs. Savio Vega

Vega has been wheeled out to put Shamrock over and further legitimise Ken's championship pedigree. Shamrock is fairly innovative here, using the beginning of a drop down to set up a crouching thrust kick. He wrestles circles around heel Savio, who's one of the dullest workers on the books. Miguel Perez runs down to make it 2-on-1 and turn the tide in Savio's favour. Shamrock eats a spot of boring heat before hitting a belly-to-belly, Hulking-up and hitting a rana. He's in the zone. Perez gets knocked off the apron and the ankle lock finishes. Just an extended squash to get Shamrock over, but Ken looked on sublime form. I persist they should have just put the belt on him when Bret was leaving. He looked like a star here.
Final Rating: **

Promo Time: Rocky Maivia

Rocky, with the IC title he stole off Austin, ignores Michael Cole's interview technique and takes over the segment. The Rock's mic keeps cutting out on him but he still gets his points across. He's the best damn Intercontinental champion there ever was. The Titantron starts flashing up a "Rocky sucks" sing-a-long and the crowd oblige. Rock sends the Nation to sort out the Titantron and Steve Austin appears in place of the message and he is in the truck, hence all the mic issues. Austin tells Rock that if his beeper goes off and it reads "3:16" he should worry. "With all this technology, is it live or is it Memorex" hints Austin. In the ring Rocky's beeper goes off, he looks down to see it reads 3:16, and turns around to see Austin behind him. Austin gets in a sneaky beat down before the Nation come back, but Austin clears them out with a chair. Rocky somehow makes it out of there with the IC belt, which shows you how much Austin actually cares about that title. Austin was entertaining as ever here but Rock's reactions made the segment.

Crush vs. Jeff Jarrett

Jarrett, with Aztec Warrior garb, has been reading his contract. It states he should get a plush locker room, a catered meal and Evian water. That's not happened. He mistakes Crush for Chainz and says he's too good to wrestle with bikers. As Crush is celebrating his forfeit victory, Kane shows up. Crush tries to put up a fight but seeing as he's on the outs Kane manhandles him. "Crush is hurt" shouts JR just as soon as the Tombstone lands, knowing full well the angle is to there to send Crush packing. An appearance on *Shotgun Saturday Night* aside, this was him done in the WWF until 2001. His departure pretty much killed off the ailing Gang Warz so that was one of the few perks of Montreal, as Crush quit and basically cited Montreal as a reason.
Final Rating: N/R

Vader vs. Shawn Michaels

Vader only has one good eye courtesy of the alcohol from earlier. It hurts his depth perception and shows how hard it must have been for Jean-Pierre Lafitte to wrestle with legitimately only one eye. Shawn introduces the newest member of DX; Jim Neidhart. This might have been quite the showdown in practically any other year where Vader was active in North America, but the booking in 1997 killed him off as a main eventer. Shawn does at least let Vader manhandle him in the early going and bumps around like a maniac. Vader even gets to duck a superkick, on his good side, before Anvil low bridges Vader and gives him a kicking with Hunter. Vader continues to mangle Shawn and should finish with a Vaderbomb but Hunter throws heel coffee in his remaining eye. Shawn superkicks the blind Vader twice for the win. Not content with that, Anvil celebrates with DX until Chyna low blows him. You can see Jim setting himself for the spot and Chyna takes her sweet time hitting it. It must suck to know you're about to get punched in the balls and you have to take it. Shawn superkicks Jim to finish the show. Lots of workers got sent packing to WCW this month. If I didn't know better I'd say that Vince was cutting loose some deadweight and piling it onto WCW's bank balance in the process. Anvil would get one more *Raw* in December, jobbing to Hunter or "doing the right thing for the business" as Vince McMahon would have it.
Final Rating: **

THE RAW RECAP:

Most Entertaining: Steve Austin and the Rock. Their segment was easily the best on the show.

Least Entertaining: Michael Cole. He kept appearing for interviews and kept ruining them with his horrible timing and bad reactions.

Quote of the Night: "I am the Hart Foundation" – Jim Neidhart.

Match of the Night: Shawn Michaels vs. Vader. And that was only 3 minutes long and full of interference. I think that sums up how good the in-ring was on this show.

Verdict: A few storyline twists and turns made this an easy show to watch but I was fuming with the way Shawn Michaels treated Bret's legacy here. It's ok to take shots at a guy but trying to kill any finishing move is just stupid and bad business. The in-ring was decidedly middling, not that anything got a chance to develop. The tag title match was the longest on the card and a historical title switch, but nothing else really sticks in the memory, not even Shawn vs. Vader.
Rating: 63

12.01.97 by James Dixon

Venue: Roanoke, VA
Taped: 11.25.97
Raw Rating: 3.0
Nitro Rating: 3.8

Promo Time: The New Age Outlaws

The new tag champions come out to brag about their title win last week, which was more akin to a hit and run than a victory.

The crowd chant "LOD" furiously, but Road Dogg refers to them as wrestling history and says they are not here because they are at home licking their wounds. He is wrong, because the LOD clad in streets and without face paint, hit the ring and run them off. Animal cuts a passionate promo full of 80's shouting and rage. Hawk is much the same, with the gist being that they won't let the Outlaws leave the building with their belts. Unusual for *Raw* to open with a midcard program rather than a top line one, but this worked nicely to progress the issue between both tandems. I have said before and I stick by it, that LOD did a tremendous and often unheralded job in "making" the Outlaws. They put them over like they never had with anyone else before.

Tonight Jeff Jarrett makes his "debut" against Ahmed Johnson, and that "ain't gonna be pretty" according to JR. It wasn't pretty at *Royal Rumble '96* when they last battled either. Also tonight, exclusive footage from *Survivor Series* of *that* finish. Far from shying away from the incident and attempting to ride out the anger felt by many fans about it, the WWF instead are embracing it and using it to pop a rating. Of course they are.

WWF Light Heavyweight Championship Tournament SF
Taka Michinoku Vs. Aguila
I have high hopes for this. JR puts his foot in his mouth right away by matter-of-factly stating "I don't think you're going to see a great deal of mat wrestling in this contest" as Taka locks on an intricate stretch, and then Aguila responds in kind with a surfboard, as Jim Cornette directly and correctly contradicts JR by saying both guys in fact *are* accomplished mat wrestlers. They run a really good dodge and fly sequence before Taka connects with his big air plancha, or his "I fear nothing move" if you are JR. They run more of the same, with misses on the outside exchanged before Aguila hits a highly impressive triple corkscrew moonsault from the top to the floor. This is far more akin to what the WWF light heavyweight division should have been like throughout; it is non-stop. Taka follows a powerbomb with a missile dropkick, before hitting the Michinoku Driver to win it. A four-minute thrill ride which was all style and no substance, but it was really fun to watch. Worth a look to see how the WWF's LHW division could and indeed *should* have been.
Final Rating: ***

Promo Time: Luna Vachon
Welcome to the disturbing side of Vince Russo's psyche. Luna is of course the new master of Goldust, or The Artist Formerly Known as Goldust, as he now is. Goldust is out with Luna, but doesn't say a word. That's because he can't say a word due to the large ball gag in his mouth, a piece of bondage equipment that compliments his choice of green pleather, a thong and a nipple shield gladiator bra. On top of all that, he has a chain around his neck and is on all fours like an obedient dog. Sportz Entertainment folks. This sure beats the hell out of legendary encounters between Steamboat and Flair in the NWA, near riots caused by Michael Hayes slamming a cage door on Kerry Von Erich's head in WCCW or the sheer size and spectacle of Andre-Hogan right here in the WWF. Wrestling hasn't evolved, it has devolved. You can hear the disdain and despair in Jim Ross and Jim Cornette's voices as they try and get this thing over, with Luna growling her way through a promo that promises "whips and chains" while Goldust spanks his own ass. To cap it off, the two have a good old tonguing session, as most viewers reach for something to throw up in. I didn't like Goldust as a babyface and preferred his infamous "machinations" from when he was a heel, but this goes way beyond that. What were they thinking!?

Four Corners Match
Chainz vs. D'Lo Brown vs. Miguel Perez vs. Recon
"Up next, we're going to have a train wreck folks!" says Cornette, clearly dreading this as much as I am. Last week Kane took out Crush with a Tombstone thus explaining his absence tonight, but the reality is he left the WWF out of disgust at the Montreal Screwjob, as he was friends with Bret Hart. All of the gangs come out with their representative, making this a potential powder keg. "Well, the hits just keep on coming" says Cornette sarcastically when Recon is announced as the Commission's rep. I agree; the Interrogator would have been preferable. This makes no sense with the tag rules that exist in a match like this, because why would you want to tag someone you hate? Similarly, why would you let someone you hate tag out to you? Cornette covers the silliness by claiming refusing a tag is a DQ, though that's the first time I have heard that one! Chainz boots Recon in the head to eliminate him, clarifying that this is indeed an elimination match. It was never made clear. Perez against D'Lo is actually not too bad because both are halfway decent, and they chop the piss out of each other before Miguel catches a lucky pin. Chainz has the match won on Miguel but Savio prevents it and that results in a four team brawl. There was an inevitability about that. JR wants clarification, and that isn't provided by the woeful Jackyl when he briefly joins the announce team because he is too big a pussy to fight. I can't be doing with that windbag. Just go away.
Final Rating: *

Promo Time: D-Generation X
Shawn is brought out in a wheelchair for this, but he still manages a few weak crotch chops. Unfortunately that is the only amusing thing about this rambling segment, which is not one for the DX highlight reel. There is a reason it never turns up when WWE shows classic DX footage or on DVD releases about the group. Hunter talks about not being scared of Sgt. Slaughter dusting off the old Boot Camp stipulation for their match at the PPV, rather than hyping his famous bout under the same rules with the Iron Sheik from 1984. Instead Hunter talks about his cock: "There's one piece of artillery that I'm not gonna use, and I'm gonna save that for your old lady; it's the big bazooka!" Yeah, great. Shawn explains his being in a wheelchair as down to the vigorous workouts he has been getting from Chyna, who has been putting him through some "hard times". Oh come on, is that the best they can come up with? Michaels finally remembers he has a match with Ken Shamrock at the PPV, and says he has been training his legs in the gym and now has an incredibly high pain tolerance. That doesn't quite make sense, at all in fact, but let's just go with it. Michaels asks Hunter to demonstrate his new pain threshold, so Hunter twists his leg right the way around a couple of times. Yes, it's a prosthetic. Because DX are incapable of putting over the threat of anyone else and instead just jerk off on their programs, JR has to do the work for them. He tries to plant the seed that Shawn is only dicking around to mask his fear of Shamrock. Nice try Jim.

The WWF shows footage of the Montreal finish, and try to put their own spin on things. I am not going over this again. A number of documentaries have been made on the subject, including one by the WWF, and it features extensively in pretty much every wrestler's book who was around when it happened. We get the promise of more footage later showing what happened between Bret and Vince.

The Rock vs. Vader
This is one of the most bizarre things I have ever seen. Just as

the match is about to start Steve Austin turns up in a black pickup truck with AC/DC's *'Back In Black'* blasting out of the stereo, while he stands on top of the car and drinks beer. Vader pounds on Rocky as we cut between the match and Austin, with the music and the red hot crowd giving this the feel of a fight taking place in a nightclub. The action is pretty good too, but it doesn't even matter because it is all background noise to the immense presence of Steve Austin. After they go back-and-forth, with plenty of interference from the Nation when the opportunity arises, we get further distraction in the form of TAFKA Goldust appearing in the aisle and belting Vader in the chops. This gives Rock the chance to hit the (not quite) People's Elbow, then Vader ups and leaves to deal with Goldie, giving Rocky the count out win. Austin doesn't budge from his perch, quite content to stand and watch things unfold before he gets his retribution at *DeGeneration X*. What a bizarre match.
Final Rating: **

Video Control gives us a Ken Shamrock highlight video in an attempt to make him appear like he has any chance of dethroning Shawn Michaels at the PPV, but nobody ever bought him as a realistic threat.

WWF Light Heavyweight Championship Tournament SF
Scott Taylor vs. Brian Christopher
Or at least, it is supposed to be, but Kane comes out instead of Christopher to dish out a beating. Taylor shows babyface heart by hitting Kane with three dropkicks and then one off the top, but Kane casually brushes them all off and treats them as a mild annoyance, before a chokeslam and Tombstone. The usual Paul Bearer promo follows. No match then, with Christopher being awarded the win via forfeit, which completely cheapens and devalues the light heavyweight title before it even exists. What horrible booking this is. Why even bother doing something if you are going to purposely undermine it?

Ahmed Johnson vs. Jeff Jarrett
This is yet another false promise from the WWF, with Jeff Jarrett refusing to wrestle due to some nonsense about contract stipulations not being met, as the man who returned with so much promise is reduced to complaining about the quality of his locker room like his is Jennifer Lopez or some other up themselves diva idiot. He does at least get in a good line about the increasingly portly Ahmed being a "water retaining idiot", but other than that his career back in the WWF is already in a definite nosedive. "I guess you *are* chickenshit" offers the ever verbose Johnson. Sgt. Slaughter comes out to tell Double J that he agrees with him and that he doesn't have to wrestle tonight, but he will be wrestling at the PPV lest he be suspended, and it will be against the Undertaker. I understand building and saving Jarrett's return match for PPV, that's fine, but the constant bait and switch promotional tactics are becoming tiresome.

Video Control shows a hype video for Sgt. Slaughter, and JR defends him being 49-years old. Remember two months ago when the company was mocking WCW for its use of Hulk Hogan and Roddy Piper? Yeah, me too...

The New Age Outlaws vs. The Headbangers
After the LOD's promise at the start of the show it is only a matter of time before they get involved in this and cause the predictable disqualification, which makes it impossible to get invested in anything that is happening. Well that, and the fact that the Headbangers suck the life out of every crowd and any match. What happens in the bout? Who cares. The story is the expected LOD run in just as the Headbangers are mounting their comeback, but they fail to get their belts back because the Outlaws outrun them. The Headbangers have a heated discussion with the LOD, quite rightly peeved for costing them the match. So, that is two forfeits and two non finishes in five matches. It's the way we are going from here on in folks.
Final Rating: ½*

Video Control shows us Jim Neidhart being a gullible idiot last week by falling for DX offering him membership in the faction, then JR promises us that Jim Cornette will "verbally assault" Marc Mero.

Promo Time: Marc Mero
Cornette cleverly belittles Mero before bringing him out, and then flat out tells him that the fans doesn't give a rat's ass about him (see Raw Recap), before sharing the widely held view that "Miss Sable" is the real star of the duo. Mero is incredulous: "Sable, have you ever done a Merosault? Have you ever been Intercontinental Champion? Who have you *ever* beaten?" For modern fans looking for a comparison to his delivery and demeanour, think Damien Sandow but more nasal. Mero claims to defy gravity and be rewriting physics books when he steps in the ring, which might have been approaching true, ish, some 18-months earlier, but certainly not now. Mero calls Sable his property and says she would be nothing without him. He then refers to Butterbean as "Butterball" so Cornette corrects him, but Mero instantly snaps back: "*It's* Butterball". His holier than thou chauvinist character is actually pretty good and his delivery snappy and just the right level of annoying. He does a boxing exhibition, with Sable wearing sparring pads that have Butterbean's face adorned on them, but he hits too hard and hurts her, then hits one shot way too hard and the pad flies off. Mero irrationally trashes Sable and tells her to pick it up and berates her for making him look bad, before ripping her to bits and telling her he is sick of looking at her. They are the modern day Randy Savage and Elizabeth, only without the charisma, ability and likeability. Cornette tells Sable to leave because "he's nuts" as the crowd boos Mero out of the building and chants for Sable. Well, Mero didn't get verbally assaulted in the segment as promised, but Sable sure did, which is a win as far as I am concerned. Mero came across as a complete asshole here, but no matter how big a dick he was it would never have advanced his own career beyond where he was at, because he was always in Sable's shadow and his actions only made her more popular. The poor guy couldn't win.

Back to Montreal then, and we see Bret spitting at Vince, then get close up footage of Bret's face while he was in the Sharpshooter. "The referee made the call that Bret gave up" say the announcers, lying through their teeth. JR thinks the footage and the lies will put an end to the controversy. Delusional.

Triple H vs. Jim Neidhart
As it turns out, this is Neidhart's last match on *Raw* for a decade, until his return in 2007 as part of a gimmick battle royal on the *Raw XV* show. Not long after this bout, he joined fellow former Hart Foundation members Davey Boy Smith and Bret Hart in WCW, where he floundered in the undercard. Someone like Neidhart had no chance of being relevant in a company as packed with talent and egos as WCW. I guess Bret helped cut him a good deal, but if the opportunity to stay with the WWF was there, he should have taken it from a purely creative standpoint. He and Owen could have formed a new Hart Foundation, or at the very least a tag team. It would have been better than working against Mongo in the opener, that's for

sure. The match is all of three minutes long and Neidhart puts in a fiery performance before succumbing to a Triple H chair shot to the back. Post match DX attack him and spray paint "WCW" on his back, but Anvil rallies on them. Eventually the numbers game takes over and he gets handcuffed to the post and beaten, only for Sgt. Slaughter and Ken Shamrock to come out and make the save. Shamrock locks Michaels in the ankle lock and he furiously taps, while Slaughter hooks the Cobra Clutch on Hunter, with Chyna held down by Anvil. The crowd loses their shit for this, forcing me to concede that maybe I am wrong about Shamrock; maybe people really did buy him as a genuine top guy. Shame that went down the toilet. And fast.
Final Rating: *½

THE RAW RECAP:

Most Entertaining: Steve Austin. It is quickly becoming predictable that Steve Austin will be the best thing on the show, but that is far from a criticism. Austin was hotter from now until his stupid heel turn in 2001 than just about anyone in the business had ever been. He didn't do much tonight, but he didn't need to in order to elicit a frenzied reaction from the crowd and a big thumbs up from this scribe.

Least Entertaining: TAFKA Goldust. Cross dressing, deviant sexual acts, ball gags and chains? No thanks.

Quote of the Night: "The fans of the World Wrestling Federation don't care if you turn blue or drop dead; that's the basic problem" - Jim Cornette puts Marc Mero in his place.

Match of the Night: Taka Michinoku vs. Aguila. This was short and sweet, with both guys just going for flash ahead of any story, but in four minutes what else can you do? Thankfully, that flash was great fun while it lasted. Taka, despite being undervalued and underutilised, has had some really good matches on the show this year.

Verdict: You can tell that this is a taped show, because other than the Austin segment and the post match stuff in the main event, there is no sense of the anything can happen feel that makes *Raw* so good at its very best. There are entertaining matches and segments, sure, and a middling show from 1997 generally trounces pretty much every show from 1994 for example, but judged against the rest of the year this is completely skip-able.
Rating: 43

12.07.97 - DeGeneration X
(Lee Maughan)
[Springfield Civic Center, Springfield, Massachusetts]

- Taka Michinoku def. Brian Christopher (***¼)
- Los Boricuas def. DOA (*½)
- Butterbean def. Marc Mero (DUD)
- The New Age Outlaws def. The Legion of Doom (*¾)
- Triple H def. Sgt. Slaughter (*)
- Jeff Jarrett def. The Undertaker (*¾)
- Steve Austin def. Rocky Maivia (**½)
- Ken Shamrock def. Shawn Michaels (**½)

Rating: 29

12.08.97 by James Dixon

Venue: Portland, ME
Taped: 12.08.97
Raw Rating: 2.7
Nitro Rating: 4.1

Tonight's hosts are Jim Ross, Michael Cole and Kevin Kelly. What kind of announce team is that!?

Promo Time: Vince McMahon
That is one hated man right there. Vince runs down Steve Austin for his recent actions, specifically last night where he apparently endangered the lives of the fans by driving his pickup truck to the ring and then using it as a weapon. Vince brings up the finish of Rock-Austin from last night's shitty PPV, where one referee tried to call for a DQ, but another counted Rock's shoulders down for the fall, and thus Vince orders Austin to defend the IC belt tonight in a rematch. Naturally this brings out Steve Austin, who does not take too kindly to being ordered around. Austin tells Vince he doesn't care who he is, so McMahon reminds him he is the boss as agents and referees surround the ring. Vince threatens consequences if Austin doesn't comply. Vince then tells off Austin for his potty mouth, leading to a funny bit where Austin keeps swearing while trying to apologise for swearing: "Hell son, I'm trying to apologise!". Austin dismisses the talk of his language and brings the discussion back to consequences, but he says he is not particularly concerned as he already beat Rock fair and square the previous night, so he will have to think about it with a couple of beers. This was a good opening segment with some fun interaction between the boss and the rebel, but unfortunately Michael Cole took it upon himself to display one of his most unlikable and annoying traits; unwanted narration during promos. "Vince is standing up to him" is an example of his insight, as if the viewer needs every tiny detail pointing out. Just shut up Cole, and let the talented people in the company do the talking. You nasal little gasbag.

The Legion of Doom vs. The Godwinns
Last night the Road Warriors came up short in their quest to retain the WWF Tag Titles from the Outlaws, thanks to interference from Hank Godwinn, thus we have this match. We have already seen it approximately a million times this year, so my apologies for not jumping for joy at the prospect. Michael Cole continues to annoy me as he overuses the word "would" in the pre match highlight package, talks more than is needed during the bout because he loves the sound of his own voice and gives constant reminders of what happened in the past rather than discussing the match in front of him. In *The Complete Video Guide Volume #IV*, Lee said there was no way Cole was the worst announcer ever. My view on that is somewhat different; frankly there is no way Cole *isn't* the worst ever. A few minutes into the bout after Animal gets sent shoulder-first into the ring steps, the lights go out and Kane makes his way to the ring! Yes! During a Godwinns match! Finally! When Kane makes it to the ring, Hawk is the only man left in there, and Kane gives him a piledriver. It is the first time he has done the move (and probably only time), and the only reason is so Hawk can no sell it like a complete fucking idiot. Kane follows with a chokeslam and the Tombstone and that keeps him down. When the lights come back on, the Outlaws jump in the ring to give the unconscious Hawk a kicking, before Animal saves with a chair. The Outlaws stay around though and hide behind the Spanish announce team until the coast is clear, so they can cut a promo.

Final Rating: N/R

Promo Time: The New Age Outlaws
Once again Cole manages to ruin this with his remarks and answers to questions that were never asked, and this time he even throws in an unfunny joke about Road Dogg. Oh will you please just go away! The Outlaws rightly point out that the WWF tag division is an embarrassment, then sing "na na na na goodbye" to the LOD, or the "OLD" as the Outlaws call them. Even *'With My Baby Tonight'* was better than this. Road Dogg decides that he and Billy have conquered tag wrestling and next they will do the same in singles, and he invites anyone "tough" to come out and fight them. Dude Love answers the call, though Cactus Jack would have been a better option.

Billy Gunn vs. Dude Love
Road Dogg sticks around on commentary and instantly puts Michael Cole to shame with his aptitude for it. Cole excels himself, getting comically overly-excited where the situation doesn't call for it: "AND HERE COMES THE BACKSLIDE" he screams. After a great deal of very little, Dude scores the clean pin following the double-arm DDT, so Dogg comes in and pulverises him with a chair. Gunn gets himself a measure of revenge by hitting a top rope legdrop onto the chair, which Dogg had placed over Dude's face. The attack is so brutal that Love has to have the stretcher job treatment, which considering it is Mick Foley, is another strong way of getting the Outlaws over. The WWF did a tremendous job turning two undercard guys who were not even slightly over into one of the hottest acts in the company. I wonder when it was exactly that they lost the ability to do that and get guys over properly.
Final Rating: ¾*

Backstage, the Rock understands Austin being indecisive about wanting to face him. He refers to himself as the "people's champion" and even throws in a cheeky early eyebrow raise. It's coming together.

Promo Time: Taka Michinoku
This is hosted by Jim Cornette, after his amusing performance in disparaging Marc Mero last week. It seems Taka has been learning English from good ol' JR, as Ross talks to him like a baby and makes him say "slobberknocker". Now in my head, there is a mental picture of Ross going around harassing talent until they say the word for him. That should have been a wwf.com online short each week. I am going of track, sorry, the point: Jerry Lawler comes out to complain about Taka's win last night, throwing in some casual racism along the way and asking Taka "do you understand?" in a "do you hear me?" kind of way, rather than because his English is poor. Cornette helpfully points out that he in fact doesn't understand what he is saying. Lawler doesn't care, and carries on berating poor Taka for his lack of English speaking, but Taka does know the phrase "you, jackass!". Lawler gets all hot but Cornette calms him down and brings out Taka's first challenger to the title: El Unico, which translates quite simply as "The One". None of the announcers know who he is, and while the ignorance of Michael Cole usually doesn't mean anything, here it is because El Unico is in fact Brian Christopher under a mask. Are we supposed to believe that management and officials hadn't ran a background check on Unico? With him never having wrestled before why would he be the number one contender? Logic DOES matter, Mr. Russo. Christopher reveals himself, then he and Lawler do a number on Taka, leaving him laying with a couple of piledrivers.

The Hart family burial continues, with the WWF tonight running a feature that details the destruction of the Hart Foundation by DX. We see Shawn Michaels beating Davey Boy Smith in England, footage again from the Montreal Screwjob and Jim Neidhart getting humbled on *Raw* two weeks ago when he thought he was joining DX. Apparently the "final chapter" of the Hart Foundation was written last night when Owen Hart attacked Shawn Michaels at the PPV. Surely that should start the feud, rather than close any books? Another hatchet job from the WWF.

Flash Funk vs. Kurrgan
The Interrogator has got a new name, removing all of his menace and intrigue. Surely they could have come up with something better than Kurrgan? Jackyl joins the commentary team to make the announcing quartet perhaps the worst ever assembled, Ross aside. In the ring the action isn't much better, with Kurrgan struggling to lock up properly. He is just so big and ridiculous though! I love him. Funk throws himself at Kurrgan and just bounces off, as Jackyl talks utter shite to the point of nauseum. Kurrgan drills Funk with a big boot and then finishes him off with his new finisher, the claw of death! JR decides that Jackyl is no longer David Koresh, and is instead Jim Jones. See my rant from a few months ago when Ross referred to Bret Hart as such, as to why that really is deeply inappropriate. Kurrgan keeps the claw applied post match until the decision gets reversed and he is disqualified, and he only releases the hold when Jackyl slaps him, following which they have a big maniacal laugh together. Swell.
Final Rating: ½*

The War Zone thankfully sees Cole and Kelly removed from the announce desk and replaced by Jerry Lawler, so the second half of the broadcast should be much more tolerable.

Promo Time: D-Generation X
Triple H brags about his victory over Sgt. Slaughter last night, which frankly is like celebrating having the stinkiest dump. That match was appalling, and Lee giving it a single snowflake was to me VASTLY overrating it. Trips puts over his manliness again because he has as severe inferiority complex due to his status as Michaels' lapdog for two years. Michaels says a lot of nothing about being the icon and about how he is still European Champion, WWF Champion and the only WWF Grand Slam winner. Well sure, if you never do a job then you will inevitably eventually end up with all the marbles. Talk turns to Owen Hart, with Shawn saying DX have destroyed the Hart Foundation and the whole family are just a lump of turd. Charming as ever. Michaels repeats himself over and over, clearly delighted to be talking about poo on the air, and he says despite having "flushed" the turd, a nugget keeps coming back up. And there folks, is the new nickname for Owen Hart, one of the finest wrestlers of his generation. Michaels says he knows Owen is not here, but calls him out and says he will be here for a fight if and when he does arrive. That should be enough for the segment with the point having being made, but DX decide to carry on eating up the TV time anyway by sitting in the ring and playing strip poker. We cut to commercial as DOA make their way to the ring for their match. Self indulgent nonsense and far too much toilet humour. Literally toilet humour. Great orators of the past must have listened to Michaels talking about bodily functions and just rolled their eyes with disdain. I know I did.

Skull & 8-Ball vs. Miguel Perez & Jose Estrada
The Gang Warz are dead, and these are the scrappy, unwanted remnants. DX move their poker game to ringside while the match goes on, which is of course more than a little

bit distracting. In this particular case it is welcomed, because let's face it, would you rather see Shawn stripping down to his pants or watch the Harris brothers wrestle? Exactly. This is the same match these guys have done a dozen times already, ending when Savio jumps in and drills one of the lumbering twins in the leg with a 2x4, and he gets pinned. Tiresome.
Final Rating: ½*

Back from commercial, and the poker game has moved back to the ring. Chyna is kicking ass, with Michaels and Hunter both shirtless and smoking cigars. JR thinks the fact that Chyna is winning is for the best, which is a strange thing for a heterosexual man to say. The game progresses and Michaels removes his trousers, as the Headbangers make their way to the ring for their match. In a foolish decision, the 'Bangers throw the poker table over and the result is a complete pasting. DX smash a glass picture over the head of Mosh before Shawn belts him repeatedly with a chair, and then Hunter powerbombs Thrasher through the poker table. The humiliation continues, with Michaels pouring liquor all over them and the duo just generally acting like complete jerks. The amount of TV time they have had is incredible, but I can never be anything than positive about a segment that ends with the utter destruction of the Headbangers. Finally, Owen Hart has seen enough and appears like a flash of lighting from the crowd, gives Shawn a quick pounding, and then bails before Hunter can fight him off. Owen's appearance in the ring is so brief, the crowd barely have chance to digest that it is him and not just some overzealous fan (this is only a few weeks after the ill-advised way they brought Steve Blackman in after all), before it is over.

Jeff Jarrett vs. Vader

This is the *Raw* "debut" of Jarrett according to JR, but it certainly isn't. Jarrett's first match back since his return was last night against the Undertaker in a drab affair at the PPV. Tonight he is supposed to work Vader, but just as the match is about to start, TAFKA Goldust turns up dressed like a raven-haired goth girl, and flashes Vader. Apparently so livid that he now cannot possibly compete, Vader heads out of the ring and chases everyone's favourite cross-dresser, getting himself counted out. So, no match at all then. I must point out too how absolutely awful Jarrett's new music it. It features a cringe-worthy quote at the start about him being a real star and then meanders in to a gentle piece of country dross. That combined with the previously mentioned horrible attire, pretty much killed him stone dead as a viable top level guy from the off. I have lost count of the number of matches that were promised but haven't happened this year.

Salvatore Sincere vs. Marc Mero

Sal is obviously well past his sell by date as a character; he positively screams "new generation" rather than Attitude. Outside of DX, is there anyone who gets as much TV time on *Raw* recently than Mero? You would think he was a main eventer. But no, his wife is. Sable doesn't come out with Mero, who cuts a promo before the match on Sal. He refers to him as a "jobber" and a "jabroni" and outs him as his real name Tom Brandi, saying he was given a stupid gimmick and he agreed to it. "Yeah, and I'm a baaaad man" says JR mockingly, in an allusion to Mero's past as the entertaining Johnny B. Badd in WCW. That Vince Russo, he loves getting in those insider terms because he thinks it is "edgy" and "cool" to expose the business and reveal its secrets to the world. It's like when Britney Spears went on a spate of flashing her beaver to cameras when she got out of cars. After years of wondering, everyone peeked and had a look, then lost all interest right away because that unknown factor was gone. Mero introduces the "new and improved" Sable, who has been forced by the controlling Mero to don a potato sack to cover up her slutty revealing outfits. Mero asks Sable to disrobe him so he can kick the butt of Brandi the jobber, but Sable instead takes off the sack to reveal an outfit that leaves nothing at all to the imagination. You can see what she had for dinner! Brandi dropkicks Mero out of the ring, and this is another lame count out after a non match. "Who's a jobber now, huh!?" shouts Brandi to no one in particular. Still you Tom, still you.

WWF Intercontinental Championship
Steve Austin (c) vs. The Rock

Austin is not dressed to wrestle and dares Vince to do something about it. Rock tells Vince to fire him. Vince doesn't, instead promising to strip Austin of the belt and award it to Rocky. Austin is nonplussed by that either, saying he has bigger fish to fry and wants the WWF Championship. Austin gives the belt to Rock and shakes his hand, then inevitably gives him a Stunner. So now both of the WWF's main singles champions didn't win their titles legitimately, and the European title will suffer a similar prestige shattering fate in a few weeks. After forfeiting the title, Austin steals the belt in the same way Rock did to him a few weeks ago, then he runs the ropes and purposely knocks Vince off the apron, much like Charlie Haas did to Lillian Garcia years later, only that one wasn't planned. The reason behind this rather shoddy title switch was apparently down to Austin refusing to put Rock over at *DeGeneration X* last night, with his reasoning being that he was already on a guaranteed journey to the WWF Title at *WrestleMania XIV*, and he felt that losing would harm his momentum. He is right, and you would never have caught the Ultimate Warrior doing jobs on the lead-up to his WWF Title win over Hulk Hogan at *WrestleMania VI* for a similar example, but at the same time it might have helped make Rock into a star even sooner. Of course it all worked out well in the end, but it was a bold move for Austin given Montreal was only a month prior. I guess the circumstances were different and Austin was more important to the WWF at this point and also wasn't heading to WCW, but still. A bit of a damp squib segment considering the three players involved, but it served the purpose of removing Austin from a division he had far outgrown and moving him on to bigger and better things.

THE RAW RECAP:

Most Entertaining: Steve Austin. Though he hardly walked it this week, because it wasn't really a vintage Stone Cold night, but rather one born out of necessity because of his refusal to do business last night. Austin was still funny though in the segment with Vince at the start with his attempts not to swear, then later on in the show closing promo, but none of it was quite up to Austin's usual high standards.

Least Entertaining: Michael Cole. The guy is just dreadful.

Quote of the Night: "Well you know, the Hart family, all of them together are like one big, huge, nasty, smelly, smoking, stinking turd" - Shawn Michaels takes the term "toilet humour" literally.

Match of the Night: None of them. Three didn't happen as scheduled, one ended as a no contest after just a couple of minutes, one was a squash where the decision was reversed and the other two were Billy Gunn-Dude Love and the gang warz redux clash, neither of which cracked a single star. Not a good night for wrestling.

Verdict: Disjointed and underwhelming, this was not a good show at all. So many of the advertised matches were messed with and didn't happen that it become very boring, very quickly. DX had too much time and spent it prattling on and messing around, and Steve Austin's segments weren't the usual home runs they have been in recent months. Not a great deal to get excited about here unfortunately. December was a difficult month for the WWF, as they tried to find and establish their new identity and shift players around. Fortunately, they do get it right eventually.
Rating: 35

12.15.97 by James Dixon

Venue: Durham, NH
Taped: 12.09.97
Raw Rating: 2.7
Nitro Rating: 4.1

Promo Time: The Undertaker

Michael Cole unfortunately hosts, and reveals that Taker will face Shawn Michaels for the WWF Championship at the *Royal Rumble* in a Casket Match. It turns out to be far more historic than anyone could have expected, as it was the match that famously put Michaels' career on hiatus for over four years. Taker says they have battled twice before and he can beat Shawn any time he wants, which doesn't really make sense given Taker didn't win either of those. How is he even the number one contender? He hasn't won on PPV in months. Taker says he has only ever lost one Casket Match and refers to *Royal Rumble '94* where it took ten men to beat him. Taker's claims are false, because he actually lost to Goldust twice at *In Your House 8* (both on the original card and the rerun two days later) and earlier this year to Vader on an MSG card in March. Taker says that DX doesn't have ten men to put him down, but there is the whole Kane issue still hanging over his head of course, and the Big Red Machine heads to the ring for the brothers' first confrontation in *Raw* since Kane's debut. Paul Bearer cuts the same promo he always does, only this time to Taker's face, as the storyline siblings engage in a seven foot stare down. Kane slaps him, but Taker turns the other cheek. As a character Taker is interesting and always over, even if he does delve frequently into the realms of silliness, but he is not a particularly brilliant orator when matched against the standards set by Steve Austin, Bret Hart, Shawn Michaels, Jim Cornette and Mick Foley already this year. He is purely gimmick, which he does well of course, but it is not always a thrill ride to watch.

Jerry Lawler vs. Taka Michinoku

"Well, this will not be a light heavyweight match up" says captain obvious Michael Cole. There he goes again, pointing out things that everyone with an IQ superior to that of a brick already knows. Taka is looking for revenge after last week's assault, though I don't see the benefits to booking the new light heavyweight champion in such an overmatched situation. He should be showcasing his skills against top flyers, not working the antithesis of that in Lawler. To their credit though, they do assemble an entertaining and logical match, with their respective styles not clashing anywhere near as much as you would probably expect them to. Lawler is a master of storytelling and building heat of course, and Taka should be able to generate sympathy easily due to his size disadvantage, but this is the wrong crowd and era for that. Lawler decides to fight fire with fire and nails a dropkick, which JR calls his first of the 90s. But it is not, because Lawler busted one out at *King of the Ring '97* specifically to mess with JR's head. Man, why do I even remember that!? Lawler goes for another one but Taka matches it, and I sure never expected to see a double dropkick spot followed by a standoff in this one! Maybe it is because of how little actual wrestling there has been on the show recently, but I am actually enjoying Lawler's old school approach to things tonight. Lawler drills Taka with the piledriver, but this is not Memphis so he misses the fist drop and gets nailed with the Michinoku Driver. It would be the win, but predictably Brian Christopher interferes to cause the DQ, only to then get schooled by Taka and then accidentally belt his daddy in the face. This turned out to be good booking in the end, with Taka getting revenge on both of the Lawlers and looking good while doing it. Lawler was respectful to him and sold for him, which helped a great deal. A lot of guys on the roster wouldn't have given him anything.
Final Rating: **½

Backstage, LOD discuss their upcoming match with DX tonight, and Hawk says the duo have never had the opportunity to wrestle against top guys like them before. This coming from the most successful team in history who have worked with everyone from Bret Hart to Hulk Hogan to Ric Flair. Opportunity indeed.

Promo Time: The Rock

Rock cuts a promo alongside his Nation of Domination teammates, at one point shushing leader Faarooq and telling him "with all due respect, the champ is talking". The seeds of a future split are sewn. Rock, the hypocrite, berates Austin for stealing his IC Title and orders him to give it back. Did he not learn from last week? Steve Austin doesn't like to be ordered to do anything! Austin comes out without the belt and calls Rock a piece of trash, which prompts a great facial. "Stop moving your mouth, I'll sew your damn lips closed" says Stone Cold. Austin says Rock is in way over his head and walks off, but Rock is not intimidated, telling Austin he has an hour to return the belt. How do you think that is going to go for him? Rock looked and acted like a genuine star here, far ahead of everyone else in the Nation and on the same level, almost, as Austin. Good segment, but it is only the first part of a bigger picture.

Dude Love vs. Road Dogg

Billy Gunn does the introduction: "Oh you didn't know? You better recognise..." Not quite, Billy. He is not a patch on his tag partner behind the stick. Is Road Dogg better in the ring though? Well, Billy and the Dude failed to crack a single snowflake last week, so it shouldn't be too hard. I am actually surprised the Dude has made this match after the stretcher job he did last week. Billy Gunn joins commentary but isn't there for long because Dogg asks him for assistance. He gets it in the form of interference on the outside, then back in the ring Road Dogg pulls of the worm! Not as overblown and ridiculous as Scotty 2 Hotty's version, but he could certainly claim to be the wrestling originator. Dude gets frustrated and "morphs" into Mankind as the match goes on, briefly putting on the Mandible Claw before pulling his hair out and unloading with other Mankind offence and rocking in the corner. The crowd doesn't seem to quite get it, as Foley flits subtly between the two. The finish is the same as last week with Dude hitting the Sweet Shin Music followed by the double arm DDT for the win, prompting Billy Gunn to attempt an attack with a chair. Dude cuts him off so Gunn bails, but Road Dogg prevents Dude from getting to him and the Outlaws double team Foley on the ramp. Gunn tries to throw him off the stage, but Dude blocks and fires back, before he gets drilled with a DDT on the stage. There is only so long you can fend off two men. The fight seems to be over, but then the Outlaws accidentally on purpose shove an

official into Dude and knock him off the stage through a table. "What did you do!?" yells a concerned referee. The Outlaws show some seemingly genuine concern, then beat the hell out of Dude some more. They really are fantastic dickhead heels, and I mean that entirely as a compliment. The match wasn't much, but the post match brawling was a lot of fun.
Final Rating: *

Mark Henry vs. The Brooklyn Brawler
Michael Cole gets a fact right! He points out that this is Henry's *Raw* debut, and from an in-ring perspective he is absolutely right. Henry made a few appearances on the program last year but never wrestled, and then he took time off prior to *Survivor Series '96* in order to heal up some injuries and actually, you know, train to wrestle. In about a decade or so he just about gets the hang of it. Steve Lombardi is always the guy who has the unfortunate task of training guys on the job, and taking bumps and bruises from all manner of muscle-bound mammoths with little aptitude for wrestling. The two had a couple of house show bouts prior to this, with other Henry victims on the live show circuit as of late including such luminaries as the Sultan (yes, he is still around) and Spellbinder, the USWA mainstay who once competed in the WWF (and I do mean *once*) as Phantasio. You already know both the result and the quality of the match, so I have nothing more to offer.
Final Rating: ¼*

Goodbye Michael Cole and Kevin Kelly, hello Jim Cornette. Talk about trading up.

Promo Time: Vince McMahon vs. Owen Hart
This should be most interesting. Vince wants words with Owen for his recent actions, not because he gives a damn about Shawn Michaels but because of his concerns for the safety of the fans, due to Owen's propensity for appearing from and leaving via the crowd as of late. "What's this all about, who do you think you are?" says Vince. Owen goes off on a tirade in response, telling Vince he owes him nothing and he is sick of the bullshit. He says Bret, Davey and Neidhart did what they had to do and now he is going to do what he has to do, which is stay in the WWF. In reality that was not a decision he wanted to make, but he was left no choice by Vince. When Bret tried to get him a job in WCW, he was threatened with legal action and told to stop being selfish and trying to ruin Owen's career. Owen had no choice but to stay put, but it was a decision that would ultimately end his life in 18-months time. Back to *Raw*, and Vince tries to dismiss Owen's anger towards him and Shawn Michaels as being about him wanting the WWF Championship, but Owen's response is vitriolic to the max: "How stupid are you? Is that what you think this is about? You think I give a damn about a worthless title, a stupid piece of leather with tin on it? This is real life Vince, this is real life. My life, my reputation, my respect, my dignity!" Well, I can't wait to buy the big upcoming PPV to see that Casket Match for the WWF Title now! Owen promises to make Shawn Michaels' life a living hell and says he "doesn't give a shit" what people call him, as Vince starts to get a little annoyed. He brings some cops into the ring to escort Owen safely away through the crowd, and warns Owen that from now on he will use the aisle like everyone else and compete like the rest of the roster. Owen stalks towards Vince and grabs him by the collar, just to prove that he can, and then leaves. As Jim Cornette rightly points out, this is the most purpose Owen has had at any point in his career. The fact that Owen is interacting with Vince proves that he was indeed set to be pushed as a top guy and potentially as the WWF's new Canadian hero, and if anything it should be Michaels-Hart at the *Royal Rumble*. Sadly Shawn Michaels put the kibosh on that because he didn't trust working with Owen after Montreal, and Steve Austin was still pissed with him about *SummerSlam* so wouldn't work with him down the line either. Owen was in a no-man's land creatively and thus his main event push stalled, stuttered and ultimately failed before it even started, with Hart's big blow off with Michaels coming on free television, before he was shunted back down to the midcard.

The Sultan vs. Tom Brandi
What is going on tonight? Henry? Lombardi? Brandi? It's the who's no one of jobberific talent. Brandi is better off without the silly Sal Sincere gimmick, but at the same time it has somewhat scooped away all of his charisma now he is just plain old Tom. Sultan hits a piledriver like it's a rest hold, then attempts some super lazy covers that Cornette berates him for, before scolding him for hot dogging. Brandi gets pulverised by his JTTS counterpart while the crowd all take the opportunity to get some popcorn and sodas, but our Tom scores a fluke win anyway, marking an incredible fall from grace for the Sultan, who was deemed good/over enough to be an IC title contender at *WrestleMania 13* earlier in the year. Post match, Marc Mero runs out and pops Brandi in the bollocks before channelling a wild hybrid of the late Brian Pillman and his own former persona Johnny B. Badd on his way backstage. I didn't realise just how entertaining Mero was in late 1997 as a character. In the ring he blew like a cheap pouty hooker, but as an entertainer he was starting to excel. Shame the talentless blonde with the whacking great tits and a willingness to exploit her body for fame, prevented him from achieving greater success.
Final Rating: ½*

Promo Time: The Rock vs. Steve Austin
With the hour up, Rocky returns to the ring and says he is pissed off that Austin hasn't returned his IC belt, and that the Nation are coming to find him. Austin appears on the big screen stood on a bridge, and in an often copied angle he throws a bunch of "useful" items into the river below such as an empty oxygen tank, a pager and a snorkel. Everyone can see where this is going, and Austin hoys the IC title into the river, telling the camera: "If he's lucky maybe he'll find it, if he doesn't maybe he'll drown, I really don't give a damn". Back in the arena, Rock's facial expressions are priceless. A great angle that really captured the Steve Austin spirit, though it has been retrospectively cheapened by the countless attempts to copy it since.

Up next is a fairly famous and notable non-kayfabed address from Vince McMahon, and he officially endorses and hypes the new look and feel of the WWF, now that the Attitude Era has got its claws buried deep inside. There is no turning back now folks.

Vince McMahon: "The Cure for the Common Show"
"It has been said that anything can happen here in the World Wrestling Federation, but now more than ever, truer words have never been spoken. This is a conscious effort on our part to "open the creative envelope", so to speak, in order to entertain you in a more contemporary manner. Even though we call ourselves "Sports Entertainment" because of the athleticism involved, the keyword in that phrase is "entertainment". The WWF extends far beyond the strict confines of sports presentation into the wide open environment of broad-based entertainment. We borrow from such program niches like soap-operas, like The Days of Our Lives or music

videos such as those on MTV, daytime talk-shows like Jerry Springer and others, cartoons like The King of The Hill on FOX, sitcoms like Seinfeld, and other widely accepted forms of television entertainment. We in the WWF think that you, the audience, are quite frankly tired of having your intelligence insulted. We also think that you're tired of the same old simplistic theory of "good guys" versus "bad guys". Surely the era of the super-hero urges you to say your prayers and take your vitamins is definitely passé. Therefore, we've embarked upon a far more innovative and contemporary creative campaign, that is far more invigorating and extemporaneous than ever before. However, due to the live nature of "Raw" and the "War Zone", we encourage some degree of parental discretion, as relates to the younger audience allowed to stay up late. Other WWF programs on USA, such as "Saturday Morning LiveWire", and "Sunday Morning Superstars", where there's a 40% increase in the younger audience obviously, however, need no such discretion. We are responsible television producers and work hard to bring you this outrageous, wacky, wonderful world known as the WWF. Through some 50 years the World Wrestling Federation has been an entertainment mainstay here in North America, and all over the world. One of the reasons for that longevity is; as the times have changed, so have we. I'm happy to say that this new vibrant, creative direction has resulted in a huge increase in television viewership, for which we thank the USA Network and TSN for allowing us to have the creative freedom, but most especially, we would like to thank you for watching. RAW and the War Zone are definitely the cure for the common show."

Jose Estrada Jr. vs. Steve Blackman
Did the Boricuas always rap their way to the ring? It is not good, and they are not over in the slightest. What has happened to all of the stars? Behind the stick this show has been excellent, but in the ring it is all jobbers, all of the time. JR decides that Steve Blackman would be a good fit for the UFC, and uses him as a segue to promote the forthcoming UFC PPV from Japan, mentioning Frank Shamrock in the process. That is still so bizarre to hear. Moments later, Blackman wins his Raw debut match with a German suplex. "This is the kind of action you are going to be seeing" says JR of an upcoming house show in Toronto. What? Unover bottom rung guys going through the motions for 2-minutes? Wow, get me a ticket to see that at once!
Final Rating: SQUASH (Not rated)

The Legion of Doom vs. Shawn Michaels & Triple H
The LOD are in something of a funk after having lost the WWF Tag Team Titles to the Outlaws and having been generally humiliated by them recently. They probably couldn't pick two tougher opponents to try and get their mojo back against than Shawn and Hunter. The opening few minutes are fairly strong, with Michaels doing his usual superb job of making his opponents look great, including taking a vicious clothesline from Hawk on the outside. Jim Cornette rips into him on commentary for his ego, saying he is the greatest athlete in WWF history, but his insistence on hot-dogging and being a jerk is his weakness. And that my friends, is a shoot. As usual in LOD matches Hawk is tasked with taking the heat, as Cornette expertly analyses the heel tactics of DX. Hell, he knows better than anyone about good tag team wrestling. DX slow things down, until Hawk powers out of a Michaels front-face lock and then both men collide. Hawk makes the tag and Animal runs through his usual energetic routine, just as the Outlaws make their way to ringside. They pull the old Giant Gonzalez chloroform trick on Hawk to send him unconscious, as Chyna levels Animal with a low blow to bring about the DQ.

Billy Gunn then shaves Hawk's mohawk and Animal gets put through a table, with DX looking on gleefully. Jim Cornette rightly points out that no one in 15-years has ever treated the Road Warriors this way. The beating continues, with Gunn and Michaels having a game of one-upmanship, with both hitting moves off the top onto the stricken Hawk, who starts foaming from the mouth. What a tremendous angle, once again putting the Outlaws over incredibly strong. It is also the birth of a union between DX and the Outlaws, which in a few months time will result in the latter duo becoming fully fledged members of the faction when HBK is forced into early retirement.
Final Rating: **

THE RAW RECAP:

Most Entertaining: Wow, tough one. I am going to give credit to the New Age Outlaws for being involved in two memorable segments that resulted in the utter destruction of three big names. This was their night; finally they had arrived as main event players. Elsewhere, there were some typically great performances from Steve Austin, the Rock, Vince McMahon and even Jerry Lawler.

Least Entertaining: Mark Henry. In a decade's time... he still sucked. But nowhere near as much as he did here. His return to WWF rings was welcomed only by apathy.

Quote of the Night: "Who do I think I am? Who the hell do you think *you* are? You think I owe you a goddamn apology? I don't owe you a goddamn thing. I'm sick and tired of trying to please everybody else around here, and the bullshit stops right now!" - Owen Hart makes his feelings perfectly clear to Vince McMahon.

Match of the Night: Taka Michinoku vs. Jerry Lawler. Another stellar performance from Taka, but the star of the bout was Jerry Lawler! His old school Memphis style match felt so different to nearly every other match on *Raw* this past few months, with the expert pacing and timing turning a potential mismatch into a really fun scrap.

Verdict: It's a glorious affair, with historical, memorable and career-making angles and interviews dotted all over the show. Other than the over abundance of jobbers in the middle of the broadcast, the in ring stuff was pretty good too. Clips from this show have been used countless times on a number of different WWE DVD releases, and you can see why. When all the pieces fall into place the WWF is a rollercoaster of excitement, and tonight they proved that.
Rating: 85

12.22.97 by James Dixon

Venue: Lowell, MA
Taped: 12.11.97
Raw Rating: 3.1
Nitro Rating: 3.5

We have a unique look for tonight's Christmas themed show, festively subtitled "Season's Beatings" by the WWF. It's a name they have used before in passing as part of the *In Your House 5* name, and ECW have used it on occasion too. As well as the Christmas theme, the WWF are also returning to the Memorial Auditorium in Lowell, a venue they have used for *Raw* tapings since 1994. Shawn Michaels and 1-2-3 Kid had a belting little match here if I recall. It was also the venue where Michaels lost his smile earlier in the year. Lowell is a fun looking venue because of the balcony surrounding it, making it very ECW in feel, and the lack of ramp way further adds to the unique experience. One of the things I dislike the most about modern wrestling is the cut and paste nature of every show and arena. It used to be that you could identify a venue and a show instantly, but now I can't tell the difference between any of the modernised arenas or a PPV from 2007 compared to one from say 2013. It's a shame, because as the old adage goes; variety is the spice of life. That is very true, and somewhere along the line WWE forgot that. Thanks, Kevin Dunn.

Promo Time: D-Generation X
DX are clad in white robes with seemingly nothing on underneath, which doesn't bode well... After last week's great job in sharing the spotlight with the New Age Outlaws for the destruction of the LOD and Michaels putting them over at the end by nodding his head in approval, this week DX are less willing to do the right thing for business, instead burying them and saying they were merely vultures and it was DX that did the work. Talk moves on to Owen Hart, and he is inevitably dismissed as little more than an afterthought. Trips won a game of rock, paper, scissors last week, so he gets the chance to take care of Owen. In other words, Owen is not considered important enough for Shawn to bother with. The crowd chant "boring" at Hunter, but they had better get used to his rambling promos, because they are going to be around for a long time yet. Trips talks about Owen whining and inevitably out come the cock references: "If you need a pacifier to suck on, come see Triple H, because I'm sure I got one for yak". What an orator. Undertaker is the next to be dismissed as a non-threat, with Michaels (quite rightly) pointing out that he didn't lose to him in either of their last PPV matches, and it won't be any different at the *Royal Rumble*. Jim Cornette tries to get over the importance of the title match by reminding fans of the stitches Shawn had to have after their last bout, and of course there was that whole Kane thing too, but there is only so much the announcers can do when the talent doesn't play ball. Shawn adds that he will never rest in peace, because he is up all night. Shagging, you see, though with guys or girls is not specified... Quite fittingly, DX look to draw a shitty segment to a close by stripping off and mooning the audience, which they do. Large Christmas themed censorship signs appear to cover their members, but the illusion of them being naked is ruined when they put their robes back on and thongs are clearly visible. Some old man in the crowd seems to like it anyway. Sgt. Slaughter comes out and ticks off Shawn for not defending his European Title in forever, to which Shawn defends himself by claiming to have been busy with the WWF Title. Of course, that brings in to question the decision to put the belt on Shawn to begin with. Slaughter says he can defend it or be stripped, Shawn runs his mouth and says he will fight anyone, and that gets him a match tonight with Triple H. DX are not happy about that at all, and they seemingly have an argument where Michaels reminds Hunter that he doesn't lay down for anybody, not even his buddy. The commentators see signs of a rift, but everyone watching surely smells a ruse. How did Slaughter not realise the potential for shenanigans?

Thrasher vs. Henry Godwinn
Michael Cole interviews Henry Godwinn on his way to the ring, who refutes claims he was outsmarted in a recent encounter with the Headbangers. He then fluffs his lines and makes himself look dumb, in a pleasing moment of irony. The match goes for just over a minute before Phineas interferes, and the hicks whip the moshers with their belts. You can imagine how thrilled I am to see this feud dragging out. They have been at it for months now, with nary a snowflake in sight. At least it was short.
Final Rating: Not rated

The WWF repeats the same angle they did a few months ago after Kane demolished Dude Love, and Mankind came to his defence, this time because of the New Age Outlaws' attack last week. Mankind is not happy that they hurt the Dude, and promises revenge on the tag champs. This would have been far cuter if it wasn't just a direct copy of the same thing from two months ago.

Video Control takes us to new footage from after last week's *Raw* went off the air, of a horny Santa in the ring letching over Sable. He complains when a child (who Santa says is a boy, but looks like a girl) sits on his lap because he is not Sable. "You're not the real Santa" says the wooden dude-looks-like-a-lady. Cue Steve Austin, who has some choice words for Santa for his treatment of the kid. He calls him out on not being the real Santa, and asks him what he asked for when he was six years old. "A Barbie doll and tiddlywinks" offers Santa. "Stand up son, let me take a good look at yak" says Austin, before drilling him with a Stunner. This should have been kept as strictly post-show fare for the live crowd, it had no place on television thanks to the corny acting from Santa and the chick dude. I guess they just wanted to get Austin on the show.

Backstage, we see footage of a door! It happens to be DX's door, and behind it Shawn and Hunter are having an argument. After that, the new WWF Attitude promo video runs. It's a superbly produced piece featuring guys like the Undertaker, Ahmed Johnson, Shawn Michaels and Steve Austin talking in sound bytes out of character. "I'm not really an athlete" (Shamrock), "This isn't real" (Shawn Michaels), "Try lacing my boots" (Steve Austin). It's almost as good as a similar video featuring Freddie Blassie, Ernie Ladd, et al. How strange that in an era which defiled tradition and long standing business practices, there would crop up something that holds such resonance.

The Rock vs. The Undertaker
These guys would go on to have a bunch of (mainly quite underwhelming) PPV matches down the years, but this is their first meeting. Taker runs through Rock at first, hitting a bunch of moves from his repertoire before Paul Bearer turns up in the aisle and Kama hits a low blow while Taker is doing the rope walk. We cut to commercial and return with Kama clotheslining Taker on the outside, as Rock takes over. More of the future Rock traits start coming through, including his famous open handed punches and the increasingly charismatic but still unnamed People's Elbow. Unfortunately Rock then borrows from a member of his extended family, one Yokozuna, and puts on an interest sapping nerve hold. At least Rock is animated and sells Taker's comeback, as opposed to Yoko who just used to sit there with his eyes half closed and sweat. Taker fights out but gets taken down with a clothesline, and a NOD distraction allows Rock to punch Taker in the nuts. That has been a popular move on *Raw* of late. Rock goes back to the nerve hold but Taker fires up again, and after an exchange he hits a Fameasser (!) when Rock puts his head down. To the more familiar with the chokeslam and Tombstone, but just as Taker is about to score the win, the lights go out and Kane heads to the ring. Couldn't they have had a finish first? They were literally seconds away! Bearer cuts the usual and then tastefully declares that Taker's parents will be celebrating the holidays with the maggots, which is enough to get Taker to lash out, and thus in turn is enough to provoke Kane into an attack.

At one point Taker looks like he might fight back for the first time, but he doesn't take the opportunity and subsequently gets a kicking from his brother. The match prior to the extra curricular was decent but nothing special, and the post match stuff all felt rather laboured and cumbersome. Unlike last week's excellent event, this show has very much felt like a taped card and everything on it so far has meandered. Hopefully the War Zone will amp things up a bit.
Final Rating: *¾

WWF European Championship
Shawn Michaels (c) vs. Triple H
This doesn't even get started, because Owen Hart ignores Vince McMahon's reprimand from last week and attacks Hunter in the aisle. We will do it again later.

Meanwhile, the New Age Outlaws have donned hard hats and are hunting for Mankind in the bowels of the arena. They think they have found him and so beat him up, but it turns out to just be some random dude. These skits continue throughout the night.

Marc Mero vs. Scott Taylor
How many consecutive weeks has Mero been on this show since he returned from injury? The deluded Mero cuts a promo before the bout, thanking his fans for braving the cold to come and see him. They chant Sable at him. Loudly. Mero acquiesces to their request and brings her out... dressed in a Rudolph costume. "You've got a nice set of antlers... are they real?" he asks while starting at the deer's tits. Mero can move and Taylor is still competing as a light heavyweight wrestler rather than a hip-hop loving entertainer, so this is pretty good for the 2-minutes it lasts before Mero puts Taylor away with the TKO. Post match Tom Brandi wants revenge for Mero outing him as his real name and killing the cartoon Sal Sincere gimmick, though really he should be thanking him. Mero injures his knee in the process, but instead of helping out her man, Sable's exhibitionist side takes over and she removes her reindeer costume to reveal a skimpy Miss Santa outfit. She is just asking for an argument now.
Final Rating: *½

8-Ball vs. Kurrgan
Oh, I bet this ends up the Hall of Shame at the back of this book. Before we even get to the delight of the action, Jackyl gets on the mic and starts one of his horrific sermon type promos, which quite simply makes everyone listening want to die. 8-Ball gets a bit of success early on, but Jackyl distracts and Kurrgan takes over with a double axehandle from the apron. He shouldn't need help to do anything, never mind beat a scrub like 8-Ball. Jackyl carries on ranting and then kills his character dead by forgetting all of the philosophical and cult elements of his gimmick and instead saying he and Kurrgan can "make a lot of money". Go and invest in the dotcom boom or something, just get the hell off my screen. Kurrgan wins with the sidewalk slam and some half-hearted brawling between the Truth Commission and the DOA breaks out, but by this point everyone is long past caring. The one positive about this? It didn't suck anywhere near as much as I expected, but then in 2-minutes flat, how could it?
Final Rating: ½*

So far we have had four matches, and if you discount the Taker-Rock match, the total wrestling in the other three makes up a grand total for 5:29 of airtime! There are two more matches left, and even when you add the running time of those to that 5:29, it still doesn't make ten minutes. That's the Russo era for yak, where everything in the ring has to be quick to get it out of the way, where every match has to have a non finish or a run in and the results no longer matter.

There sure have been a lot of recaps tonight, from earlier on the show and previous weeks of *Raw*. Did they not film enough footage or something? That's what happens when all the match times can be counted in seconds.

D'Lo Brown vs. Ken Shamrock
Shamrock starts out with some leg kicks as D'Lo goes into a fighting stance, then Shamrock scores a takedown and nearly applies the ankle lock, but D'Lo saves himself with the ropes. D'Lo gets a few shots in but Shamrock largely dominates, sticking to the basics of the game but doing them well. He drills Brown with his tidy belly-to-belly and then Shamrock taps D'Lo with his ankle lock for the super quick win. He looked good though.
Final Rating: *½

Post match, Rock turns up in the aisle and goes off on a random tangent about the Gulf crisis, before dismissing it as unimportant and a discussion for another time. It's a rare and uncharacteristic loss of concentration from one of the greatest talkers ever. Rock runs down UFC as being full of has-beens and never-was, then challenges Shamrock to a match for the IC Title at *Royal Rumble*. No one, not even Faarooq, can believe his brash over confidence.

Deep in the bowels of the building, the Outlaws finally catch up with Mankind, and a brawl ensues. Mankind holds his own for a while, until he gets locked in a walk-in freezer. "He's gonna be a Mankind-sicle" offers Cornette.

Promo Time: TAFKA Goldust & Luna
Tonight, Goldust is dressed as a Christmas tree. Obviously. Christmasdust begins to give an ultra camp reading of *The Night Before Christmas*, but he is interrupted by Santa as it starts snowing in the arena. What am I watching!? "I knew I shouldn't eat the brownies that the fans brought in!" says Cornette, equally perplexed. Goldust loses track of his reading and tells Santa to get the hell out of here, but Santa refuses to comply and belts Goldie in the back of the head with his sack and reveals himself as Vader. The instant replay shows the sack shot again, and it's a beauty!

WWF European Championship
Shawn Michaels (c) vs. Triple H
Aaaaaand, it's a ruse. They lock up, Shawn takes a big stupid bump and Hunter runs the ropes like a clown for an age, then hits the phoniest looking splash since Kamala and pins Shawn to win the belt. Hey, a clean job! JR and JC are furious at the sport being made such a mockery out of and take swipes at Michaels when he breaks down and cries after the defeat, with Cornette saying: "He always cries when we come to this town". Hunter's acceptance speech is equally hokey, as he yells "Yo Sarge, I did it!" to the watching commissioner, who has proverbial egg streaming down his face. So to recap, all three singles champions have now "won" their belts via illegitimate means, just to cheapen the prestige of all of them and make them tantamount to worthless. It's exciting though, right Russo? No one saw it coming... Just over a year later the nWo pulled the same idiotic stunt, only they did it with the WCW World Championship. It ended up being one of the catalysts for the demise of WCW. I can only assume Eric Bischoff was sat watching this and thought "that's good television", because he knows as little as Russo does about the business.

Final Rating: -***

THE RAW RECAP:

Most Entertaining: Last week was tough because the quality was so high. This week is tough because everything sucked. I was going to go with Rock for his continued improvement, but he killed it with his crappy promo. Because I can't give it to a video package (the excellent "I'm not really an athlete" Attitude promo piece), I will go with announcers Jim Ross and Jim Cornette. They seemed to share my disdain for the horrible product that was on display tonight.

Least Entertaining: DX. I am sure some reading this love them because they were the target demographic when this was new and fresh, but they are just a pair of business killing idiots on this show. Running down their opponents and burying them, dismissing the excellent work they put in last week alongside the Outlaws and then taking a big MSG sized dump on the business with that "match" at the end. What a joke.

Quote of the Night: "Is there gonna be a wrestling match in the middle of all of this? Yes, there is? Holy mackerel!" - Jim Cornette echoes the sentiments of any long time *wrestling* fan watching.

Match of the Night: The Undertaker vs. The Rock. Though by default really, and only because Rock was looking good. Taker was going through the motions, and the non finish was annoying.

Verdict: It's complete garbage. There is barely any actual wrestling, and the matches that do happen are all under 3-minutes, with the Taker-Rock exception blighted by extracurricular stuff and a lame confrontation afterwards between Taker and Kane. The usual big hitters in the segments were off their games, and Owen Hart after last week's brilliant promo was reduced to simply attacking Triple H in the aisle. To cap it all off, the main event was a joke and bastardised the business. But hey, who cares how much you have to damage the industry in order to pop a rating and win a war, right?
Rating: 20

12.29.97 by James Dixon

Venue: Long Island, NY
Taped: 12.29.97
Raw Rating: 3.6
Nitro Rating: 4.65

Thankfully we are back live after two consecutive taped shows, one of which was historic and memorable, the second of which, last week, was utterly awful. It is the last *Raw* in what has been without question the most tumultuous year for the company on record, certainly on screen anyway.

TAFKA Goldust vs. Steve Austin
Goldie continues to "express" himself, and this week he is dressed as a giant baby. You know, some people actually do that in real life; I watched a documentary on it once. They have someone take care of them, feed them and change their diapers and everything. Hands down, the damndest thing I have ever seen. In recent weeks Goldust has been using a squeaky voice with ridiculous intonation for his promos, and he does the same again here as he questions Steve Austin being the toughest S.O.B in the WWF. He wants to play dress up with Austin, and shows a pair of sexy black negligee. Oh my. Michael Cole adds to the awfulness of the segment by once again commenting on the promo as it is going on, which is a trait he has retained throughout his unbearably long tenure. This is apparently supposed to be a match, and Kevin Kelly says "Austin dressed for combat tonight", which is dumb when he is wearing jeans. There is no match happening here. Austin rips into Goldust because he sucks, and says he has a gift for him. It repels from the ceiling and Austin wrestles with the harness delivering it, but the contents remain a mystery. It turns out to be a port-a-potty, with a rudimentary sign saying "Crapper 3:16" on the front. Austin says it stinks. Well, yeah. Babydust tries to hide behind it, but Austin slams the door in his face and beats the hell out of him, then puts him in the crapper. Goldust falls out into a Stunner, and is supposed to fall back onto the toilet but the door closes behind him so it doesn't quite work. Austin puts him back on the john anyway, and then dumps the crapper on its side. You know, after Shawn Michaels' talk of dumps and nuggets a few weeks ago, I thought the literal toilet humour repertoire had been exhausted, but it seems I was wrong. Austin made it entertaining though, and Goldust was certainly game for taking a beating.

Long Island Brawl
DOA vs. Los Boricuas
You would think DOA might have added someone to their group in order to keep them on an even footing with the rest of the factions in the Gang Warz, but by this point I guess it barely matters anymore anyway. How many times do we need to see the Hispanic rappers against the generic bikers before enough is enough? Once more at least, apparently. The rules for this are that all six guys are in the ring at once, which does bring a nice level of chaos and excitement to a usually turgid bout. It starts at quite a pace, and it seems there are no DQs too because they all use chairs aplenty and just go to town on each other. The actions spills back-and-forth between the ring and the outside, and while there is not a wrestling move in sight and this is strictly brawling, it is far more akin to the kind of good old fashioned donnybrook that the Gang Warz should have been. Chainz scores the win for his team after a few minutes of non-stop action, and much to my surprise that was a lot of fun!
Final Rating: **

Promo Time: D-Generation X
Hunter tries to beg off his match with Owen Hart tonight because he dislocated his kneecap last night, allegedly. He then tells us that Shawn Michaels is not here because he is at home with a fever. He always has a fever come *Royal Rumble* season. Hunter mocks the Undertaker, which is a mistake, because the Dead Man makes his way out for a confrontation. Well, his music plays at least, but what comes to the ring is a casket and some druids. Have we gone back to 1994? "Well I can't defend myself, so I guess there is only one thing left to do: break it down!" says Hunter, as Shawn Michaels pops out of the casket. "Shenanigans" says Michael Cole. Quite. Shawn has a ramble before introducing the two newest members of DX. No, not the Outlaws, but rather Chyna's titties. The two delinquents go on to make lame jokes about her waps as the crowd groans. Shawn finally gets back to the point, briefly mentioning afterthought Owen Hart and then reminding Undertaker again that he has never beaten him. "1998 is gonna be the year of D-Generation X" says Michaels, and he is right, but he won't be involved... It seems the segment is over, but perennial DX nemesis Sgt. Slaughter wanders out to, according to Shawn, get a good look at Chyna's bazongas. DX mock him for getting fat over Christmas, but as usual he ignores them. Slaughter tells Michaels that he looks in perfect

condition to perform and that he will defend the WWF Title against Owen Hart tonight! Wow, that is much better than Hunter-Owen. Let's hope the WWF actually deliver on a match for once!

Meanwhile, there is a large wooden box on the stage. More on that later.

Kama Mustafa vs. Ken Shamrock
They did this on *Raw* once this year already! Unlike great matches such as Steamboat-Flair, Misawa-Kobashi and Rock-Austin, for which a rematch is welcomed and demanded, I have no desire to see this again. Shamrock schools Kama on the mat until interference from D'Lo turns the tide, and Kama pounds away. I don't like Shamrock having to battle hard to beat guys like Kama. He should be smashing through people like him in two minutes or less and making his ankle lock feared and deadly. Shamrock fires back and hits a clothesline which is really a fist to the face, for real, as Kevin Kelly claims the two have "similar styles". Is he even watching the same thing as me? Cheating pays no dividends for the Nation, and Kama accidentally clocks D'Lo with a savat kick and gets locked in a Fujiwara armbar transitioned into the ankle lock for the win.
Final Rating: *½

Post match, The Rock appears on the stage, having not joined his Nation teammates at ringside during the bout. He tells Shamrock he might have a lucky name, but his lucky streak is about to run out. Rock then books Faarooq against Shamrock for next week without the Nation leader's knowledge, and the look on Faarooq's face is priceless. If it were a movie, he would turn to Rock and say "Damn kid, what the fuck did you just do!?", then backhand him. Rock continues to cross a line, telling his teammates:"Kama, D'Lo, know your role. Faarooq; let's go". A power struggle between the brash upstart and the grizzled veteran is imminent. It's not quite Sammartino-Zbyszko, but it's a show of confidence in Rock from the WWF and a clear sign for Faarooq that as 1997 turns into 1998, he is on his way down the card.

From an empty arena, Vince McMahon talks directly to the camera and promises 1998 will be the most action-packed year for the WWF yet and "you ain't seen nothing yet", before wishing us all a happy new year. An unusual interlude.

Jerry Lawler & Brian Christopher
vs. Taka Michinoku & George Steele
Pre match Jerry Lawler claims Brian Christopher's real father is Jim Ross, but JR dismisses that. Steele is unadvertised, because he is Taka's mystery tag partner, and he gets a great response from the crowd when he is announced. He chases King and son out of the ring with his wild flailing goon stomp around the ring, and hell it is hard not to find him almost endearing after all these years. I was never a fan of Steele, as you may have read elsewhere, but I always enjoy the return of someone from the past. Animal eats the turnbuckles as JR questions how Taka and Steele will communicate, so the ever opportunistic Lawlers take advantage and belt Taka. Christopher beats on Taka, who fires back with a rana only to get drilled with a sick powerbomb onto his head. That looked vicious. Taka fires back and hits a moonsault but soon gets grounded again, long enough this time it turns out for King to go up top for a moonsault of his own! He chickens out, which is probably for the best. A smart old school heel like Lawler knows better than that anyway; there is no place for a flashy move like a moonsault in the arsenal of a heel, unless they are Shawn Michaels or Owen Hart. Things break down as they inevitably do, and the babyfaces get disqualified for George using an unidentified foreign object straight out of the 80s. He doesn't seem to care and chases everyone to the back. The Lawlers could have had a fun run working against surprise opponents like this, because they were entertaining doing it, clearly having fun selling and hamming it up for legends of yore. I recall an equally entertaining match in a similar vein earlier in the year against the Putskis. See, now I am trying to rack my brains to think who else on the roster they could have worked against. I guess the father and son teams would be the likes of Jeff and Jerry Jarrett, Barry Windham and Blackjack Mulligan and The Rock & Rocky Johnson... Hmm. That doesn't sound so great actually... Digressions aside, I had a lot of fun watching this, even if it was super short. It's the second pleasant surprise of the evening.
Final Rating: **

To the final hour of the show in 1997, and Jerry Lawler has managed to join the announce team fresh from his match. The New Age Outlaws come out for Road Dogg's bout with Mankind, but Dude Love appears on the big screen. He has been beaten up a bunch of times by the Outlaws so isn't going to wrestle them tonight, neither is Mankind either though because he morphs into Cactus Jack to a huge genuinely spine-tingling reaction. Cactus is still a mythical being in the WWF at this point, with only that classic MSG hardcore fight with Triple H on his résumé thus far. We are in Long Island, so Mrs. Foley's baby boy is coming home!

Road Dogg vs. Cactus Jack
Cactus heads out with Barbie and the Outlaws look terrified. The first move Cactus does is a double Mandible Claw, which I don't like. I don't think his three characters should do each other's moves, it makes them all the same. Their personalities are different, their moves should be too. Foley did that with Dude to a point, but it actually slightly damaged the act because the moves he used were so purposely lame. He makes up for the claw silliness with the Cactus Elbow from the apron because he is on a one man quest to permanently dent the ramp way, but his attempts to use Barbie on Billy lead to a violent chair to the head from Road Dogg. Ouch. Back in the ring a double arm DDT seems to have Dogg beaten, but Billy Gunn makes the match saving leap for a DQ. They brawl up the stage and into the side of the mysterious wooden box, which prompts an almighty racket. It turns out to be whoever is in the box trying to get out, via assistance from a goddamn chainsaw! Crikey. The mystery man cuts himself a door and bursts out to reveal... Chainsaw Charlie. Erm, who? It is of course the legendary Terry Funk, a man with whom Cactus Jack is synonymous after their wild death matches in Japan and ECW. He is not recognisable as Funk though, because he is wearing a pair of women's tights on his head and some dungarees over a red shirt. He looks like a psychotic version of one of the Godwinns. Funk was supposed to be brought in as himself, but he decided he wanted to be a character because, hell, it is the WWF. The idea to bring Funk in was actually Mick Foley's, but his proposal was a series of deathmatches that would have resulted in an exploding ring barbed wire deathmatch at *WrestleMania XIV*, pre recorded at Terry Funk's famous Double Cross Ranch. Vince loved the idea, but the impending Mike Tyson deal put the kibosh on the whole thing due to the WWF not wanting major mainstream coverage at *WrestleMania* and them presenting two guys getting blown up. Well, it sure would have got people talking though... Chainsaw and Cactus chase the Outlaws to the ring and the tag champs run away. No shit. Funk, the crazy old bastard, throws the

chainsaw from in the ring onto the ramp and then bounces on ropes with his crotch to celebrate. Welcome back, King Terry! Super short match, but the afters were hella fun.
Final Rating: *½

Promo Time: Sable
The WWF does its bit to further real life tensions between Sable and Sunny by putting both on the cover of Raw Magazine and making the fans decide which one they want to buy. Years later Sunny claimed the rivalry between the two was not professional but personal, stemming from some remarks Sable allegedly made about her ex-husband and father of her daughter who had been killed in a car accident. I don't buy it. Sunny is notorious for being one of the biggest bullshitters around, many times admitting that she often makes stories up for effect. On the surface, the obvious answer to why they disliked each other was because Sable was far surpassing Sunny as top female in the company, and I would imagine Sable disliked Sunny because she went around burying her to people she was close to. So, everyone. That's just my theory, but I would expect it is fairly accurate given how things behind the scenes tend to work. Back to the segment then, and slutty voyeur Sable promises to give her fans a sneak preview of the magazine tonight, which of course infuriates Marc Mero. He comes out and takes a seat, saying he is here for the show, and tells Sable he hopes she is not going to do anything to embarrass him. His brilliant delusional personality disorder shines again, as he informs Sable that no one is here to see her strip, they are here to see him wrestle. It's a statement that couldn't be further from the truth. Kevin Kelly tries to calm Mero, but he gets insulted and punched in the cock. A year ago this would be shocking, but now a non wrestler gets beaten up every week. Mero goes to drag Sable on her knees out of the ring, but Tom "jabroni" Brandi comes out for the save. This annoys the unhinged Mero, who belts him with a chair and then rips up the pictures of Sable in the magazine and shoves them in Brandi's mouth and tights. Mero is severely underrated as a dickhead heel.

A jobber's union led by the DOA head to the ring and demand that Kane come out and take a beating, because they are sick of him running roughshod over everyone on the roster. JR promises the destruction of Kane, but just as the Big Red Machine is being circled by the seven guys, the Undertaker heads to the ring. 8-on-1? Not great odds for Kane, but he seems entirely unfazed by the prospect. In a surprising turn of events, Taker doesn't lay a beating down on Kane but rather helps him clear the ring, before walking off with no confrontation between the two occurring. JR and Jerry Lawler are perplexed, but it seems fairly clear that Taker doesn't want to see his little brother beaten up and he still harbours hopes of making peace with him. On the stage, Taker looks into the camera and tells Kane he will never fight him, and then says: "I will burn in Hell before I fight you". The choice of words is important, because Taker only finally agreed to wrestle Kane after months of refusing, following being burned alive by him at Royal Rumble in a few weeks time. He didn't just suddenly change his mind, he was left with no choice. Kill or be killed and all that.

Backstage, the New Age Outlaws berate Michael Cole for asking them about the LOD when they have just been assaulted with a chainsaw. Yeah Cole, you inappropriate little toad. Speaking of which the chainsaw appears again, cutting a hole in the locker room door and causing the champions to bail. It's like a scene out of a horror film spoof.

Promo Time: Jim Cornette
After a few weeks away from the camera, Jim Cornette is back for another legendary rant, this time about the state of the wrestling business. The following could easily have been lifted from a shoot interview, and when you read the content you will probably be shocked that this went out on an episode of Raw. Trashing "sports entertainment"!? How dare he! What would the "universe" think. The sad thing is, the same rant could be plugged into Raw in the John Cena era and still be relevant and accurate, with just the acronym "TNA" replacing WCW and ECW.

"Well, the WWF has asked me to do a commentary on the state of wrestling in 1998. I guess they figure that Cornette is always good for a couple of laughs. But I'm not really gonna be too funny tonight, because you see I think the state of wrestling in 1998 STINKS. I think WCW stinks, I think the NWO stinks, I think ECW is embarrassing and I think the WWF stinks. And I'll tell you why: you don't have to go back any further than last week on Raw. You got a guy coming out dressed like a Christmas tree, you got a woman coming out dressed as a reindeer, you've got two adolescent mullet heads showing their butt cheeks on national TV and having a phony match for a championship! I think it stinks, I think it's disgusting, I think nobody has any respect for wrestling anymore. Where is wrestling? Not "sports entertainment", but wrestling?

You know just a couple of years ago I left my home in Tennessee and I moved to Connecticut, which is like trading a Hawaiian vacation for a bed in a cancer ward, to come to work for the WWF full time, the biggest wrestling promotion in the history of the planet. And I moved to Connecticut with snow on the ground seven months out of the year, real estate prices that would make Donald Trump's hair stand on end, the rudest bunch of people I have ever seen where English is a second language and traffic jams at 4 o'clock in the morning, but I think that's okay because I'm with the biggest wrestling promotion of all time, the WWF. But over the last couple of years I don't see any wrestling. They've got some great wrestlers around here, but they don't have time to wrestle because of all the falderal and the nonsense going on.

You see what the problem is, is the people running the two big promotions. One guy is a game show host wannabe from Minnesota, with phony teeth, phony hair and a phony tan, and running the WWF you got a whole office building full of Yankees from New York City who wouldn't know a wrestling match if it bit 'em! So they sit around all day listening to people on the internet, and the people on the internet wouldn't know a wristlock from a wristwatch. I don't particular care what some Yankee from New York City wants to see. I wanna see wrestling matches with wrestlers. I wanna see real old fashioned wrestling. I wanna see some people who have some respect for the traditions of the wrestling industry, have some respect for the sport of wrestling. I don't wanna see "sports entertainment" and flying donkeys all around, I think it's garbage, I think it's insulting and I think it's a shame to a fine sport like this.

Down south where I come from they know wrestling, they were brought up on it, they grew up on it and they respect it. And I think it's about time that the promoters in the wrestling industry today recognise that wrestling fans watching a wrestling program wanna see wrestlers wrestle! That's, that's easy! It's not too hard to understand if you just think about it. But the problem is, is that no one has any respect for tradition. Well I got news for yak: I got respect for tradition and I've always been associated with real good old fashioned wrestling. A sport of wrestling! Not a circus sideshow, not a cartoon show. And if nobody else is gonna bring some wrestling around here, then maybe its gonna be up to Jim Cornette. So that might be my New Year's Resolution for 1998; I might bring some tradition, I might bring some real wrestling back and clear this whole mess out, because I think it stinks. So there's my address, there's my opinion, there's my commentary. Do with it what you want, merry Christmas, bah humbug, I'm out of here."

"Amen" says Jerry Lawler, himself a staunch traditionalist. Well, at least he was until the WWF carried on paying him a bunch of money to sit and put over the ridiculous crap that Vince Russo and company were trying to peddle as wrestling. Unfortunately the Cornette promo is rather ruined by hindsight, because it led to the formation of the tiresome NWA stable, which as Jim has stated many times himself, was designed almost certainly with the intention of fucking with him. Those same Yankees in the office that Jim mentioned were the ones with the power of the pen and were not fans of old time wrestling, so set up the faction and made them as dull as possible in order to ensure they failed. What other business exists where you purposely do something to see it fail? It's a completely baffling industry.

We are about to go to a major announcement regarding Mike Tyson, but instead Sunny makes her way to the ring with that damn Raw Magazine. I guess Sable had her turn so she has to have hers. All she does is wander down the aisle and show off her centrefold, which Lawler claims is already being used as currency in prison. Fitting. Eventually. Then the Tyson announcement, which JR delivers from behind the announce desk. He reveals that the WWF are in negotiations with Tyson to participate in *WrestleMania XIV* and the crowd boo the news vociferously. Of course, the Tyson deal turned out to be a game changer for the WWF and helped them turn a corner in terms of national exposure and in the war against WCW, with the WWF not far away from defeating them for the first time in nearly two years in the ratings. I guess freeing up Bret Hart's massive contract from the wage bill was a major key to this happening, making him inadvertently responsible for two of the monumental catalysts of the phoenix like return of the WWF to the top of the wrestling tree. I bet he was thrilled.

WWF Championship
Shawn Michaels (c) vs. Owen Hart
Owen comes out to little fanfare or reaction considering he is the brother of the recently screwed Hitman and he has been absent since *Survivor Series*, but I guess that's what happens when your opponent dismisses you as a piece of shit. Owen jumps Michaels in the aisle and beats on him, with Shawn disrespecting him slightly by removing his chaps while he is supposed to be selling. He does take some meaty bumps at ringside and then on the ramp for him though, so maybe there was nothing to that. Owen continues to completely dominate Michaels as we go to commercial, and when we return Owen is still pounding him on the outside. JR gives us the unfortunate news that Triple H has wandered to the ring, as all hopes of a clean contest go out of the window. Michaels is only able to mount any offence when Chyna trips Hart, and Michaels shoves Owen off the apron and into the steel. JR puts over the bout while at the same time ripping last night's *Starrcade* main event between Sting and Hollywood Hogan, only without specifically saying it. Michaels takes over on the outside and hits a piledriver back in the ring for a near fall, and then a DDT gets the same results. We continue our trip through 80's finishers with a sleeper, but Owen fights out by sending Michaels into the corner twice and then finally escaping fully with a back suplex that leaves both men out. Owen makes his comeback with a back body drop and sends Michaels upside down in the corner as the pace begins to quicken and Michaels starts taking bigger and bigger bumps. Owen catches a number of close falls but misses a charge and takes Bret's bump, but the superkick misses and Owen hits the enzuigiri before locking on the Sharpshooter. It appears to be game over for Michaels, but Triple H swings his crutch at Owen's head, and misses like a fucking moose, then swings again and connects for the DQ. DX give Owen a beating as the show goes off the air, and thus ends the final main event run of Owen Hart's career. From here it is back to the midcard putting Hunter over every month, then a silly stint with the Nation and further demotion to the tag division, but that is all for next year's book. Still, it was nice to end this year with a match, and a pretty good one at that, which built to a hot finish and was starting to become really entertaining before Hunter stuck his enormous beak in. I guess in many ways it is the fitting end to a wild year.
Final Rating: ***

THE RAW RECAP:

Most Entertaining: There was a lot of good stuff tonight, as silly as much of it was at times, but once again I am going with Jim Cornette. His rants weren't for everyone, but what he said tonight becomes more and more true as the years go on and wrestling becomes a parody of itself with irreversible damage done. Shawn Michaels was great in the ring, but his promo was pretty average. Cactus and Chainsaw were fun too, but they were only scratching the surface tonight. I also enjoyed Steve Austin, but frankly I am amazed he only appeared at the start and nowhere else on the show. Surely there were better things for him to do than just beat up Babydust?

Least Entertaining: Triple H. Though, only because everyone else surpassed themselves tonight and didn't deserve it, whereas he cut a crappy promo and made a mess of swinging a crutch, his one spot!

Quote of the Night: "Negotiations... Wait a minute, that means Vince McMahon is probably talking to Don King! Oh my God, the world is not safe!" - Jerry Lawler. Imagine being a fly on the wall in THAT office. When you think about the two personalities involved, its remarkable that a deal was ever even struck. Perhaps Linda handled the negotiations.

Match of the Night: Owen Hart vs. Shawn Michaels. Though there were some other really entertaining bouts tonight.

Verdict: What a fun end to the year. While nothing was exceptional or legendary in the way many other segments have been on the show this year, what was on offer was consistently entertaining with not a dull or slow moment in sight. The matches were super quick, perhaps too quick, but a good main event made up for that. There were surprises, the usual dose of chaos and strong character progression, all of which makes this a definite thumbs up and a show worth revisiting.
Rating: 72

RAW RECAP SUMMARY

The following is a tally made up of the winners of the awards given at the end of each show as part of The Raw Recap.

MATCH OF THE NIGHT

1.	The British Bulldog	13
2.	Owen Hart	12
3.	Vader	8
4.	Mick Foley	7
4.	Taka Michinoku	7
6.	Shawn Michaels	6
7.	Rocky Maivia	5
8.	Steve Austin	4
8.	Bret Hart	4

The British Bulldog was almost untouchable during the first half of the year, putting on good to great matches on an almost weekly basis, usually alongside his tag partner, the ever consistent Owen Hart, who was second on the list for the third year running. The two contested the best match of the year on *Raw* and indeed ever on the show to this point opposite each other in Germany, and had other great encounters against tandems such as Furnas & LaFon, Austin & Michaels and Austin & Dude Love. It was probably the last truly great year for both, with Davey losing interest in the business after his defeat to Shawn Michaels at *One Night Only*, with Bret Hart describing him as "losing the fire in his eyes" following the loss. Owen suffered from the Montreal fallout and politics in 1998 and then tragically died in 1999. In 1997, he was superb. Vader comes in at third, as the top three is all made up of guys who were underappreciated, underutilised and underrated by the WWF. Mick Foley shone under three different guises, making the list thanks to matches from all three of Mankind, Cactus Jack and Dude Love. Taka Michinoku delivered consistently when he was allowed to shine, even in spite of the relatively lacklustre competition he was faced with most weeks. Shawn Michaels, Bret Hart and Steve Austin all would surely have placed higher if not for various injuries, whereas Rocky Maivia only started becoming really tight with his work towards the end of the year when he turned heel and became simply The Rock.

MOST ENTERTAINING

1.	Steve Austin	14
2.	Shawn Michaels	7
3.	Jim Cornette	6
3.	Mick Foley	6
5.	Bret Hart	4
6.	Vince McMahon	3
6.	Owen Hart	3

Shawn Michaels' 7 votes brings him up to a total of 30 over the course of these books, which would easily put him first overall, should that ranking table exist. But this time around, his two year winning streak was ended by the on fire Steve Austin, who doubled Michaels' tally. Every show that featured Steve Austin was generally carried by him, and even on the episodes where he didn't win the award, he was always up there. Elsewhere, Jim Cornette's superb work behind the commentary desk but more pertinently in front of the camera for his reality filled rants on the state of wrestling, garnered him much support from this office. Mick Foley entertained us with his immense interviews with JR as Mankind, his zany antics as Dude Love and his hardcore brawls as Cactus Jack. Ever dependable and reliable, Foley had a fantastic 1997.

LEAST ENTERTAINING

1.	Crush	8
1.	Triple H	8
1.	Savio Vega	8
4.	Phineas Godwinn	5
5.	Rockabilly	4

It's a three way tie at the top, with Crush heading the list, surprisingly for the first time, though he has always been in the running in previous years where he was active. Thankfully, this was his last year as a regular performer with the company, signalling a welcome end to his ponderous matches, lame martial arts and horrible promos. Brah. Savio Vega lost every ounce of charisma and fire that he had as a babyface, taking the IRS stance to heeldom: be as boring as possible. It was a stance that Hunter Hearst Helmsley already employed and for the first half of the year he was one of the most tiresomely predictable performers in the company. As the year rolled on and he was elevated up the card thanks to politics rather than talent, he improved slightly but added the less than welcome trait of an obsession with his own penis. It ruined many a promo, and combined with his obnoxious belief that he was far better than he actually ever proved, he was pretty much unbearable.

RAW RECAP SUMMARY SO FAR:

MATCH OF THE NIGHT:

1993:	Scott Steiner	8
1994:	1-2-3 Kid	7
1995:	Razor Ramon	8
1996:	Shawn Michaels	12
1997:	The British Bulldog	13

MOST ENTERTAINING:

1993:	Scott Steiner	7
1994:	Randy Savage	7
1995:	Shawn Michaels	8
1996:	Shawn Michaels	8
1997:	Steve Austin	14

LEAST ENTERTAINING:

1993:	Mr. Hughes	5
1994:	IRS	10
1995:	Kama	6
1996:	Henry Godwinn	8
1997:	Crush	8
	Triple H	8
	Savio Vega	8

THE STORY SO FAR...

11.20.95	100	01.01.96	57	05.09.94	41	09.09.96	27
10.06.97	100	07.05.93	56	02.26.96	41	12.09.96	27
09.22.97	99	02.19.96	56	03.18.96	41	10.18.93	26
01.20.97	96	04.07.97	56	07.22.96	41	07.03.95	26
11.04.96	94	07.21.97	56	06.16.97	41	06.03.96	26
11.17.97	91	05.20.96	55	05.24.93	40	01.11.93	25
06.21.93	90	10.28.96	55	05.08.95	40	01.03.94	25
05.26.97	89	07.07.97	55	12.11.95	40	10.24.94	25
12.30.96	86	03.07.94	54	05.06.96	40	07.08.96	25
12.15.97	85	05.13.96	54	11.07.94	39	07.15.96	25
06.30.97	84	07.29.96	54	09.08.97	39	04.18.94	24
05.17.93	80	08.04.97	54	05.31.93	38	05.01.95	24
08.01.94	80	11.06.95	53	12.06.93	38	03.15.93	23
02.24.97	79	05.02.94	52	05.30.94	38	04.19.93	23
01.16.95	78	04.10.95	52	01.30.95	38	10.25.93	23
03.31.97	77	10.09.95	52	03.27.95	38	03.20.95	23
06.02.97	77	10.07.96	52	08.21.95	38	02.01.93	22
12.16.96	73	11.18.96	52	10.16.95	38	05.03.93	22
03.03.97	73	09.05.97	51	12.18.95	38	12.13.93	22
04.15.96	72	04.12.93	50	10.17.94	37	12.20.93	22
06.09.97	72	10.04.93	50	09.15.97	37	11.21.94	22
10.27.97	72	01.09.95	50	02.15.93	36	01.24.94	21
12.29.97	72	01.08.96	50	06.07.93	36	05.15.95	21
01.22.96	71	03.11.96	50	09.20.93	36	05.29.95	21
04.08.96	71	08.19.96	50	10.11.93	36	07.12.93	20
08.29.97	71	01.06.97	50	09.19.94	36	09.27.93	20
04.17.95	70	11.10.97	50	06.19.95	35	11.15.93	20
10.20.97	69	03.13.95	49	12.08.97	35	02.28.94	20
03.06.95	68	05.22.95	49	05.10.93	34	09.26.94	20
09.25.95	68	05.27.96	49	11.29.93	34	12.26.94	20
03.25.96	68	11.25.96	49	08.14.21	34	10.23.95	20
04.28.97	68	02.03.97	49	09.18.95	34	12.22.97	20
05.19.97	68	03.24.97	49	02.20.95	33	02.07.94	19
09.29.97	68	09.11.95	48	07.17.95	33	04.25.94	19
01.25.93	67	01.15.96	48	03.08.93	32	08.08.94	19
06.05.95	67	04.01.96	48	01.10.94	32	10.10.94	19
07.14.97	66	05.05.97	48	08.09.93	31	04.05.93	18
10.21.96	65	11.27.95	47	05.16.94	31	06.28.93	18
11.11.96	65	05.12.97	47	06.06.94	31	05.23.94	18
11.03.97	65	03.01.93	46	09.12.94	31	06.27.94	18
03.04.96	64	07.19.93	46	01.23.95	31	10.03.94	18
03.17.97	64	10.02.95	46	04.11.94	30	08.05.96	17
08.18.97	64	10.30.95	46	07.18.94	30	07.25.94	16
07.11.94	63	06.14.93	45	10.31.94	30	01.02.95	16
11.24.97	63	11.08.93	45	09.06.96	30	01.31.94	15
07.01.96	61	02.21.94	45	01.13.97	30	04.26.93	14
09.23.96	61	11.28.94	45	08.16.93	29	06.20.94	14
01.18.93	60	07.31.95	45	11.01.93	29	07.04.94	14
07.24.95	60	12.04.95	45	12.05.94	29	02.27.95	14
02.05.96	60	09.16.96	45	04.29.96	29	03.22.93	13
06.17.96	60	08.23.93	44	06.24.96	29	12.12.94	13
04.21.97	60	01.27.97	44	12.23.96	29	12.19.94	13
10.13.97	60	06.23.97	44	07.26.93	28	01.17.94	12
10.14.96	59	11.14.94	43	12.27.93	28	02.06.95	10
08.11.97	59	06.10.96	43	03.28.94	28	04.24.95	10
11.13.95	58	03.10.97	43	04.22.96	28	07.10.95	9
01.29.96	58	07.28.97	43	08.12.96	28	06.12.95	8
09.30.96	58	12.01.97	43	12.02.96	28	04.14.97	6
02.17.97	58	02.13.97	42	02.22.93	27	08.07.95	5
08.15.94	57	08.02.93	41	04.04.94	27	03.21.94	0
04.03.95	57	09.13.93	41	06.26.95	27		

SCORE AVERAGE SO FAR...

1993: 35.3
1994: 29.0
1995: 38.2
1996: 49.5
1997: 59.6

HIGHEST RATED

1993: 90
  (06.21.93)
1994: 80
  (08.01.94)
1995: 100
  (11.20.95)
1996: 94
  (11.04.96)
1997: 100
  (10.06.97)

LOWEST RATED

1993: 13
  (03.22.93)
1994: 0
  (03.21.94)
1995: 5
  (08.07.95)
1996: 17
  (08.05.96)
1997: 6
  (04.14.97)

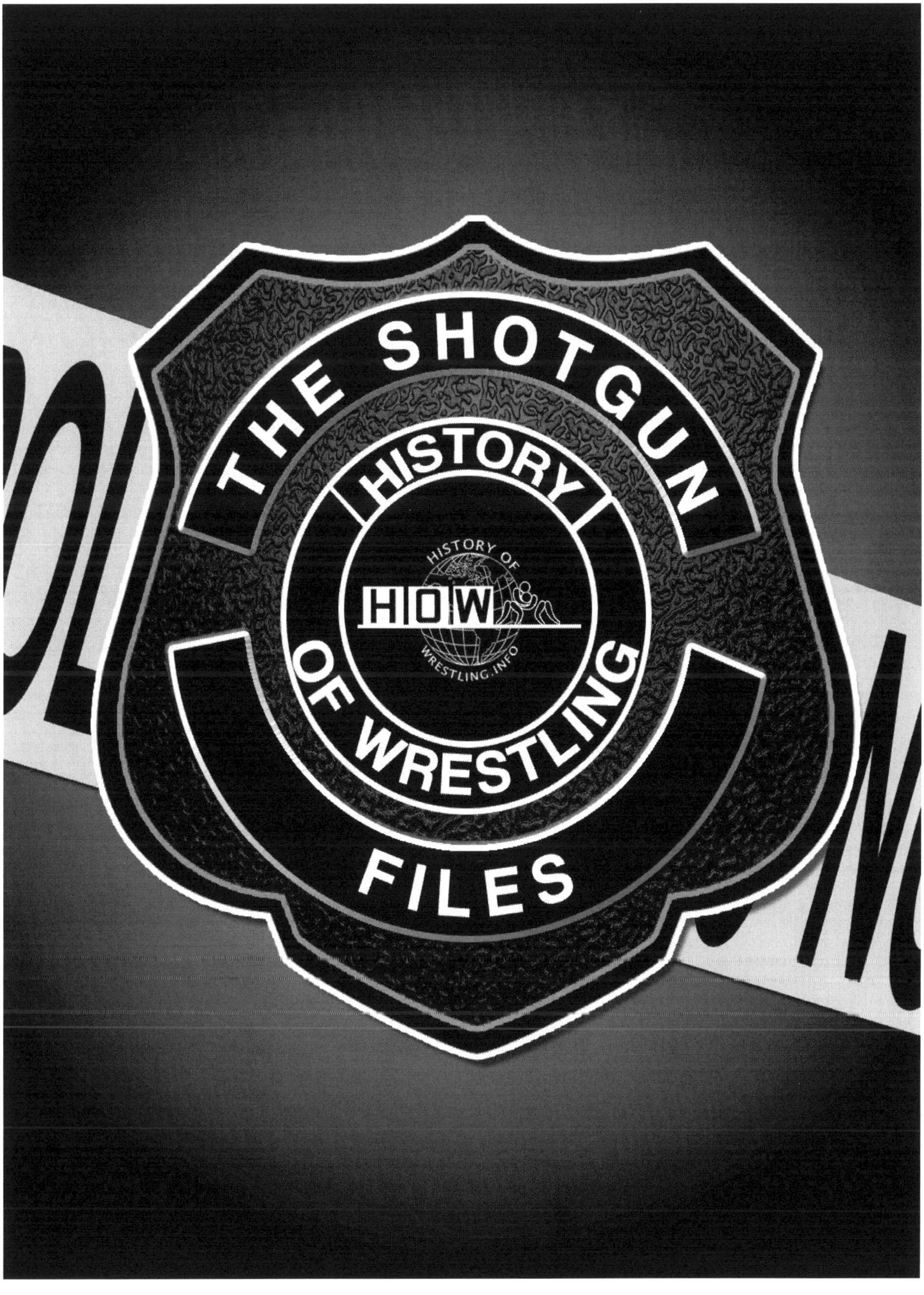
THE SHOTGUN
HISTORY
OF WRESTLING
HISTORY OF
HOW
WRESTLING.INFO
FILES

01.04.1997 - by Lee Maughan

Venue: Mirage Nightclub, New York City, NY
Taped: 01.04.97

1996 has morphed into 1997 and WCW are winning the war with *Monday Nitro*, a New World Order-powered juggernaut on wrestling's televisual landscape. ECW are continuing to make a big noise in bingo halls across the east coast, punching above their weight with a provocative product aimed squarely at an adult audience. And the WWF? They're in deep trouble. Attendance has dropped, numbers have plummeted and things are about to get *edgy*.

Welcome to the Attitude Era.

Reminiscent of the first *RAW* back in January 1993, the show kicks off on the streets of New York City. Back then, an edgy New York vibe meant gentile corporate shill Sean Mooney exposing Bobby Heenan's Les Dawson 'Cissie and Ada' tribute act. Times have changed. Here, Mary Whitehouse… sorry, I mean Bob Backlund, is protesting the perceived vulgarity on offer tonight - "There's decadence going on in there, ladies and gentlemen! There's sexual activities going on in there! There's violence! There's crime! What is this?! What is this television?! *Shotgun Saturday Night*, who's that good for?! That's a disgrace! *Shotgun Saturday Night*, should be banned! It should be banned! New York City should be banned! Matter of fact, Saturday night should be banned!" If they did ban Saturday night, Gary Lineker would cease to exist as a worthwhile entity, left to float aimlessly through the ethers of time with nothing but a replica FA Cup and a gigantic bag of Walkers crisps.

The Flying Nuns vs. The Godwinns
Quite the auspicious way to kick-start the new show, no? The Nuns are Sister Angelica and Mother Smucker, better known to you and I as Mosh and Thrasher, the Headbangers. The gimmick was all part of an elaborate angle to introduce the 'Bangers to WWF audiences, but it was dropped after this initial outing, largely owing to how touchy some Christians have a tendency to be about these things. Not that it was any great loss to professional wrestling, mind you.

Instantly the show has the feel of a underground Indy group, albeit one with million dollar production. The small but rowdy crowd are packed onto the nightclub stage, checking out the action in what looks to be about a 14x14 ring, if that, with police tape-yellow ropes, much like those that would adorn NXT rings in years to come. Now, you might be wondering why a show as edgy and as northern as one set in a New York nightclub would book a couple of hillbilly pig farmers as babyfaces here, but Todd Pettengill (yes, he's still here) rears his ugly mug to accuse them, and by association everyone from Kentucky, as inbred. And as if this show wasn't already subversive enough, who should show up at ringside but Brother Love, in his first appearance since late 1995. And wouldn't you just know it? The fans start chanting "ECW! ECW! ECW!" at all of this, which just makes no sense whatsoever.

Vince McMahon (doing commentary with Sunny) calls this match "gruelling", which it certainly is, though perhaps not quite in the way he meant it. Sister Angelica misses a legdrop off the top and Phineas begins his comeback to a resounding chorus of boos. Ah, New York. The big gag revolves around Phineas refusing to grab the Nuns' crotches on bodyslam attempts, and then Brother Love smashes him in the face with a Bible, giving Angelica the pin. Post match, Love cuts a promo full of masturbatory references and redubs the Nuns 'The Sisters of Love'. I can see why the Christians would complain about this. And not for religious reasons, either.
Final Rating: *

- Over in the VIP lounge, Backlund rails against Marlena's tits, while Vince makes sure to stress the fact that Backlund used the word "cleavage." *Edgy*!

Goldust vs. The Sultan
Neither guy gets an entrance in the traditional sense here, but they do get to stand around while a laser light show breaks out to the pulsating beat of some techno tripe. And after the transsexual tag team in the opening act, Vince now makes sure that everyone remembers Goldust's coming "in" the closet after Jerry Lawler previously demanded to know if he was a "queer". Remember when the WWF was a delightfully mom 'n' pop, family-friendly pro 'rasslin promotion full of strongmen and superheroes? Vince wonders aloud if Backlund is a "pervert" and Backlund claims he can't hear anything because he doesn't have his glasses on. The Sultan slaps on a chinlock and the crowd decides to amuse itself by chanting for the "bWo". Oddly enough, they'd get them just a few weeks later. They then decide to prove how "smart" they all are by chanting "Fatu sucks!" and "We want Raven!" The Fatu chants I get, but what does ECW have to do with any of this? The referee takes a steel chair off the Sultan (*edgy*!) then Marlena jumps up on the ring apron mid-Camel Clutch, and whips out a couple of handfuls. For some reason, that's enough to give Goldust the win. Not that I'm complaining, but did Lou Thesz ever suffer those sort of consequences? "How did you lose, Lou? DQ? Count-out? Honkers?"
Final Rating: *

Ahmed Johnson vs. Crush
As a white supremacist biker throws up his right fist in a salute of black power, I suddenly consider if the WWF could have possibly booked a worse singles match at this point and how I wish Backlund had gotten his way at the start of the show. The tag match earlier in the night may have contained twelve of the longest minutes you'll ever see, and the previous bout suffered from a despicably long rest hold that killed any flow it may have had, but they were at least competent. This is strictly amateur hour stuff, and to make matters worse, they top it off with a lousy disqualification finish when an unnamed member of the Nation of Domination (who you'd most likely recognise as D'Lo Brown) jumps in for a beat-down of Ahmed. Crush finishes the job with a disturbingly stiff chair shot to the head before Goldust and the Godwinns make the save, which allows Ahmed to stop selling, chase the Nation out of the arena, and give D'Lo a Pearl River Plunge on the hood of a car.
Final Rating: ½*

- To the Port Authority bus terminal next, where Jim Cornette collects an already-dressed Mini Vader, fresh from Mexico City and in serious need of a piss. The big gag was supposed to be that the urinals were too high for him with Cornette lifting him by the armpits, but the porcelain was already so low to the floor that the visual didn't work in the slightest, ruining the joke. The solution? They cut away from the shot just after they'd gone into the bathroom, and just had Vince *explain* the joke instead!

- And now things take a turn for the worse (that's right), as Todd Pettengill jumps in the ring to belt out that karaoke classic, *'The Macarena'*, complete with his own set of parody lyrics. 'Weird Al' Yankovic he ain't.

Mascarita Sagrada vs. Mini Vader
Or "Mascarada Sagrita" as Vince calls him. This would be the shortest match of the night (oh, har har) which is a shame, because it's the one with the most action. For anyone who's seen more than two matches with the luchador minis, you'll know that action is mostly made up of dives, huracanranas and head scissor takeovers. One of those takeovers comes from a leap off the top rope, which gets a big reaction from the crowd (who for some reason *don't* chant Rey Misterio, Jr.'s name, despite how wacky and "inside" they fancy themselves as tonight), and Mini Vader breaks out a brutal powerbomb just to mix things up. There's not much story going on though, just a natty exhibition of moves, and then Sagrada finishes it with a missile dropkick off the top.
Final Rating: **

Post-match, Cornette challenges Sagrada to a fist fight and berates Mini Vader for being such a "knucklehead", so Vader and Sagrada trip him up and strip him down to his boxers. That was so corny. In more ways than one.

THE SHOTGUN RECAP:

Most Entertaining: Mascarita Sagrada. He may have travelled all the way from Mexico, but he was just about the only guy on this show who actually brought his working boots.

Least Entertaining: Amazingly, despite this sub-60 minute show only "boasting" four matches and a crew of guys that included Phineas Godwinn, Ahmed Johnson and Crush, none of that unholy trinity scoop the award! No, the dubious honour instead goes to the Sultan for his interminably tedious chinlock on Goldust. Edgy? That hold wasn't even edgy in the 70s, never mind the 90s!

Quote of the Night: "They're virginal! Their bodies have never been touched by human hands… other than their own, of course!" - Brother Love on the Flying Nuns.

Match of the Night: Mascarita Sagrada vs. Mini Vader.

Verdict: It is terrible. The WWF's misguided "we just can't help being a complete cartoon show" version of down n' dirty, cutting-edge wrestling for the 18-30 crowd of the 90s. But damn, did it ever feel fresh. It was grimey, it was dingy, it was small… and it was *so* refreshingly different to anything the promotion had done before, or indeed, has done since. Especially when you think about WWE in the John Cena years where every single show looks the same, the same set-up, the same arenas, the same camera angles. Here was something unlike anything else you could find on TV, all wrapped up in an easily digestible hour, no matter how crappy the matches may have been.
Rating: 24

01.11.1997 - by Lee Maughan

Venue: The Official All-Star Café, New York City, NY.
Taped: 01.11.97

And we've got bad news right from the off this week as the Sisters of Love were arrested for soliciting outside the Disney store earlier today, so they're already history after debuting just last week. Bang goes that dream Flying Nuns vs. Flying Elvises match then.

Diesel vs. Marc Mero
Just to reiterate for those not paying close enough attention, this would be the second incarnation of Diesel, with Glenn Jacobs under the leather. Before the action even gets underway the differences between last week and this are obvious, as the Café, a sports bar, comes across like a somewhat more upmarket venue (as in, it's actually lit), but since the walls are curved and there's a big structural plinth in the middle of the room, the ring is very awkwardly positioned off to one side with a floating camera on a jib. Diesel goes after Sable on the outside so she shoves a cake in his face for a lame "he really takes the cake!" joke, like they basically blew their wad with last week's high calibre gag quotient. Razor Ramon soon shows up and goes after Mero, but Rocky Maivia arrives to make the save.

Back from a break, Diesel goes to work with a vertical suplex and a top rope flying clothesline. Far be it from me to underline yet again the reasons for the failure of the revived Diesel and Razor Ramon personas, but when did Kevin Nash ever vertical suplex anyone, or fly off the top rope? Obviously there were much greater problems with the gimmick than the move set, but sometimes it's the little things that need the most attention. The Nash-originated spinning sidewalk slam does however make an appearance before Mero makes a comeback with a flying head scissors and a leaping lariat. Which would be fine if not for the fact he showed absolutely no fire whatsoever before that and just took his ass-kicking. Again, it's the little things. Mero hits a tasty moonsault press but gets distracted when he spots the Honky Tonk Man of all people pursuing Sable on the outside. Diesel wallops Mero from behind with a double axehandle, and the Jackknife gives him something of a surprise win. Although, he would also go on to place highly in next week's *Royal Rumble*, so the WWF clearly had some kind of plan for the guy.
Final Rating: *½

Post match, Mero berates Sable for the loss and bails out, leaving her crying in the ring. Honky of course figures now is the best time to hit on her, so Rocky returns for his second save of the day, but that brings out Mero for a heated shoving match. "Let them go!" demand the New York crowd. I concur.

Faarooq vs. Savio Vega
Hinting at problems to come, we get the entire rap introduction of the Nation of Domination from JC Ice and Wolfie D here, but join the match in progress after commercials. Faarooq dominates (har har) in the early going until he decides to work in his electric chair bump that he always loved taking. That's pretty business-exposing if you think about it, since nobody in the promotion was doing that move unless they were specifically against Faarooq, and how dumb do you have to be to allow yourself to wind up in a position where that keeps happening to you, time and time again? I suppose the same could be said of Ric Flair's big slam off the top, but I always put that down to his own arrogance and determination to actually hit the damn thing, psychologically speaking.

Savio runs through some of his more exciting offense (back body drop, side-Russian legsweep, spinning heel kick) that would vanish following his impending heel turn (throughout the local New York feed of these shows, promos were airing for an upcoming card at Madison Square Garden that would see Savio turn on his partner that night, Ahmed Johnson, and actually side with the Nation, although there's no hint of Savio's dark side here). PG-13 soon get involved on this night of

outside interference, and Faarooq takes over with a snap suplex for two. Savio comes back with a chinbreaker but misses a charge into the corner and eats a spinebuster for the three. Pretty good back-and-forth stuff actually.
Final Rating: **½

- And now, in response to her disgruntlement with Marlena's breasts last week, it's the world premiere of Sunny's home sex tape! And if you've ever wondered about the coitus techniques of Chris Candido, Shawn Michaels or Davey Boy Smith, well, you won't find your answer here I'm afraid. No, her secret lover is none other than... Fondle Me Elmo, which is basically some guy dressed like the hottest pre-schooler's toy of 1996, Tickle Me Elmo, complete with a thong and an irritating laugh. Because what's funnier than sexualizing a *Sesame Street* Muppet aimed at infants?

- Meanwhile, Todd Pettengill is up on the stage to belt another one out in week two of his apparently ongoing series of karaoke klassics. At least it isn't another parody effort this time as he instead has the Honky Tonk Man with him for a *very* lengthy run-through of '*Honky Tonk Man*', a brand new song that Honky has trouble keeping pace with. They should have done '*Hunka Hunka Hunka Honky Love*' and just made do. You know, I never thought I'd say this, but where are the Bushwhackers when you actually need 'em? Thankfully, Rocky Maivia arrives to end the misery.

Rocky Maivia vs. Razor Ramon
And another thing; why would you knowingly book your Diesel and Razor imposters in front of an intimate, smart-ass New York crowd anyway? I mean, I say smart, they again start chanting "bWo! bWo!" just like last week, for reasons I remain unable to fathom. Back from a quick commercial, Razor dominates with some rest holds (come on man, you're doing a six minute TV match in a rowdy nightclub, ramp it up!) but Rocky fires up with dropkicks and a crossbody. Out on the floor, Honky Tonk gets a few licks in as payback for Rocky's earlier intervention on Honky's apparent attempts to make a sex tape of his own with Sable (and if you've ever been subjected to Honky's shoot interview alongside New Jack and the Iron Sheik in which all three drop their pants, bend over and pull their arse cheeks wide apart, you'll know that is something that should never ever see the light of day), and Razor goes for the Razor's Edge, escaped by Rocky and countered with a match-winning shoulderbreaker.
Final Rating: *

- Out on Times Square, Pettengill cracks a few jokes at the expense of a poor homeless man who's fallen on such hard times that he's taken to living in a cardboard box. "Look at that hobo!" he may as well have shouted. "Come on! Let's kick him to death!" Okay, Toad's lines might not have been *quite* as mean-spirited as that, drifting as they did more along the lines of "Hey, he's even got a box room for when the mother-in-law comes to stay!" And then out from the pile emerges Nikolai Volkoff! Ha! I believe Virgil moved into a plush beer crate/ tarpaulin combo crib next door to Nikolai not long after this.

- Back in the club, Vince produces a copy of *Vanity Fair* and announces that Goldust is pregnant and scheduled to give birth on next week's show. Why yes, this *is* the Attitude Era we're in.

Doug Furnas & Phil LaFon vs. The Headbangers
Time is running short now (thank goodness for all those silly skits, eh?) so this is joined in progress with a jawbreaker to Mosh from LaFon, and Thrasher crashing into Doug Furnas with a flying clothesline, but it's already time for a commercial break so you can kiss goodbye to what little flow this match has going for it. Things pick up with a snap suplex and a standing senton from LaFon to Thrasher, then all four guys get in the ring for a brawl as things completely break down... and that's it. TV time is up, and Vince promises the conclusion next week. Impossible to rate under the circumstances.

THE SHOTGUN RECAP:

Most Entertaining: Marc Mero. His psychology was as spotty as the moves he delivered, but at least those moves were exciting, and his proto-'Marvellous' face/face showdown with Rocky Maivia showed a lot of potential. A shame he blew his knee out a few weeks later, only to return a shell of his former self.

Least Entertaining: Fondle Me Elmo. An atrocious skit that just felt like it would never end.

Quote of the Night: I did consider giving it to Sunny for bamboozling Vince McMahon with her recounting of Doug Furnas' and Phil LaFon's multiple All-Asia tag team title reigns in All Japan Pro Wrestling, but I've instead gone for: "Honky Tonk man *was* looking at Razor Ramon... I don't think he's going to be looking at him after *this* match..." - Vince's apparent shoot admission that he'd finally cottoned on to what everybody else already knew - that Rick Bognar was a terrible pro wrestler.

Match of the Night: Faarooq vs. Savio Vega.

Verdict: Another largely rotten episode that still managed to fly past and leave you wanting more. The wrestling overall was pretty bad but it was short enough to never outstay its welcome, and the skits were brutally bad, albeit like a car crash you can't tear yourself away from. Yes, the New York crowd was its typically irritating self, but the different look and feel to these shows offers such a different vibe from anything else going on in wrestling in early 1997, except perhaps for ECW at the Arena, that no matter how bad the shows are, they're still masochistically entertaining.
Rating: 33

01.18.1997 - by Lee Maughan

Venue: Denim & Diamonds, San Antonio, TX.
Taped: 01.18.97

Three weeks in and there's already a change to the format, as we're out of New York and into San Antonio, with everyone in town for tomorrow's *Royal Rumble*. In another change, Sunny has been replaced with Jim Ross, so she's off line dancing with Dok Hendrix and Todd Pettengill. Line dancing? Oh, did I forget to mention Denim & Diamonds was a country and western grill? Brace yourselves for a rootin', tootin' hour folks!

Rocky Maivia vs. Hunter Hearst Helmsley
Hunter arrogantly declares this a tune-up match before his meeting with Goldust tomorrow, and basically promises to fuck Marlena once he's done. Believe it or not, this is actually the very first HHH-Rock singles match on record (hey, they had to start somewhere), and it's really rather good. Rocky has so much poise for a guy with so little experience at this point, and the only other guy I can think of in recent memory who managed to get just as good in a similarly short span of time is

probably Kurt Angle. Credit to Hunter too, who takes a typically solid ass-kicking while leading the match. Rocky runs through his basics until Helmsley hits an inverted atomic drop, and suddenly there's a python in the ring! And in true *Saturday Night's Main Event* fashion, a mid-match incident means it's time for a commercial break!

The action picks up with Jake Roberts at the announce desk, doing a wonderful job of selling the *Royal Rumble* match tomorrow. In the ring, Hunter is back in firm control, but Rocky continues to fight back with a high cross body. Helmsley fires back with a knee crusher for two, but Rocky lands a powerslam as Marlena makes her way out to ringside. A dropkick of course sends Helmsley to the floor when Goldust suddenly steps out of the shadows, and Hunter opts to flee rather than fight, giving Rocky a count-out win. Very fun stuff as it was all action-meets-angle, meaning Helmsley had no time to work in his usual chinlockery and/or other assorted tedium. Very enjoyable stuff, especially with a red hot crowd that was completely into everything here.
Final Rating: ***

- Elsewhere, Dok, Todd and Sunny run through a country-fied version of '*The Macarena*'. As if the song itself wasn't bad enough, try to imagine it drenched in backwater fiddles.

- Meanwhile, the Honky Tonk Man cheats a couple of luchadores out of their pesos over at the blackjack table.

- Back in New York, Mr. Backlund is losing his mind over morality.

Histeria & Mini Mankind vs. Venum & Mascarita Sagrada
This is actually a mixed match as Sagrada and Mankind are minis, but Venum and Histeria are full-sized luchadores. Venum is probably best known as Venum Black, having previously worked under a mask as Power Raider Rojo. Histeria you'll likely know better as Super Crazy. It's the regular luchas who start, popping the crowd with a back-and-forth sequence that concludes with Venum sending Histeria to the outside with a pair of head scissors and following with a springboard plancha. The minis follow with a sequence of their own, Sagrada landing a flying crossbody to the floor on Mini Mankind, and that's the cue for Steve Austin to hit the announce booth, which is both a blessing and a curse. He's wildly entertaining of course, rambling on about people trying to censor him because of his foul language and promising a *Royal Rumble* victory tomorrow night, but the whole thing results in a split-screen that takes the focus off the actual match. It's like someone in the production truck didn't realise that you could still *hear* Austin without the need for a close-up of his mug (or more likely, figured most people would somehow find high-flying, mask-emblazoned superhero wrestlers too dull to pay attention. Kevin Dunn, I'm looking at you). At this point, they seem to start running through some of the same spots, as often seems to happen in lucha matches owing to the wildly different psychology down Mexico way, but it's kind of hard to tell when the action is all squished into a little box at the side of the screen. Venum misses a corkscrew moonsault and Histeria lands a sitout powerbomb for the win. More good stuff here.
Final Rating: **¾

- Meanwhile, George and Adam are already at the Alamodome.

- And now for something completely different as in a total surprise, Pettengill brings out Texas legend Terry Funk, who's determined to get himself over kicking and screaming with an incredible, out-of-control promo:

"Yeah! I'm home! This is my state! This is my town! I'm in the heart of Texas, where I wanna be Pettengill! This is where I wanna be and everyone out here knows I'm a windmilling, piledriving, neck-breaking, back-breaking, bear-hugging, wrist-locking, knee-dropping, toe-holding son of a son of a gun, meaner than a rattlesnake, tougher than shoe leather, and more dangerous than a hollow-eyed scorpion, and I am ready to rumble!

Now, I wanna know what number I'm going to be in that ring. What number am I going to be? Am I going to be number 1 or am I going to be 29? To hell with number 15, I wanna walk out there with that first man. George Bush and the representatives of Texas designated me as their Texas member. I wanna start the Rumble, and I wanna end the Rumble, and I wanna start that Rumble not tomorrow night, how 'bout a one-sided rumble with you right now Pettengill? How about a rumble with you?

Well is there somebody else out there? I am looking for anybody! Where's a person that wants to rumble with me? There's not a person in the WWF that wants to rumble with me! Not a person in the WCW, those bunch of snake-sucking scumbags, they don't have an athlete enough for me! I'm looking around here, where's Vince McMahon? That Yankee BASTARD!

I realise this is live! Hey Pettengill! Give me the microphone! How about rumbling with you? Your mother's a whore! If you don't like that, why don't you rumble a little bit? You wanna rumble Pettengill? No! No you don't! Is there anybody here? Where are you Jim Ross? Where are you, you Oakie asshole! Where are you?!

Oh. Oh. Come on 'Stone Cold!' 'Stone Cold' Steve Austin! Do you wanna rumble? Do you have the guts to get in the ring? How about you? This is live! How about you? I'll lay here on the ground for you Austin! Come on! Yes! Nobody's got the guts! I'm staying out here for the rest of the show! Come on! Where's your guts Austin? I want a rumble! I wanna rumble!"

Austin finally responds to the challenge with a brief brawl into the commercial break. This was exactly the kind of segment *Shotgun* was crying out for, not that goofy karaoke shit with Pettengill the last couple of weeks.

Faarooq vs. Jesse Jammes
I guess I spoke too soon, as Pettengill joins Jammes for his latest rendition of '*With My Baby Tonight*', joy of joys. Hilariously, as well as this might play out in an actual country and western bar, Jammes' mic isn't working so nobody can hear it anyway. Brilliant. And then the WWF further endears themselves to the hometown crowd by having Faarooq squash Jammes with a spinebuster and the Dominator in around two minutes after some token offence from Jammes. I know why you'd put Faarooq over with his *Royal Rumble* showdown against Ahmed Johnson just a day away, but why would you have the country bumpkin be the one to do the honours in a hillbilly bar when so many other perfectly sacrificial guys were in town?
Final Rating: SQUASH (Not rated)

Steve Austin vs. Goldust
Goldust's on-screen graphic comes complete with the caption "What does his daddy think?" Chuckle. Once again, timing issues with the show mean this main event will only have about

four minutes before going off the air, which exactly doesn't bode well after last week. And speaking of last week, we never did see the finish to Doug Furnas & Phil LaFon vs. the Headbangers (Furnas & LaFon won), and what happened to Goldust's pregnancy anyway? Not that I particularly wanted to see such a thing, but that's such a blatant bait and switch. JR does at least address it by calling the rumours "off the mark", and Vince calls it "an attempt at a little humour." Yes, very little humour.

Austin starts by stomping his usual mudhole before Goldust fires back with a clothesline and takes over, but astonishingly, there's still a commercial break that needs to be shoehorned in. Back from that, Terry Funk returns and attacks Austin, causing the disqualification, then Faarooq, the Headbangers and the Godwinns all dive into the ring for a mini Rumble. Hunter Hearst Helmsley soon slithers out and chokes out Goldust with a pool cue, as Austin backdrops Funk into a Bud Light beer tub.

THE SHOTGUN RECAP:

Most Entertaining: How could it be anybody but Terry Funk?

Least Entertaining: Not an easy award to give out this time, but we'll go with Jesse Jammes for his microphone problems. A blessing to many no doubt, but he had his target audience right here, only for his equipment to crap out just in time for him to get his head caved in by Faarooq. Good going, Jesse!

Quote of the Night: Terry Funk's promo, as transcribed in its entirety above.

Match of the Night: Rocky Maivia vs. Hunter Hearst Helmsley.

Verdict: Good wrestling, wild brawling and crazy promos made this by far the best episode of *Shotgun* yet, and in truth, I can't imagine that status ever changing once things move back to NYC.
Rating: 73

01.25.1997 - by Lee Maughan

Venue: Webster Hall, New York City, NY.
Taped: 01.25.97

Bret Hart vs. Mankind
Owen Hart joins Vince McMahon and Sunny at the announce table for this one, tights and all even though he's not actually wrestling tonight. He and Bob Holly did lose to the Godwinns earlier in the day however. Mankind starts by crawling after a pair of go-go dancers in assless chaps until Bret makes the save and gives Mankind a pounding. Another dancer swinging around on a rope prompts Sunny to declare the scene "not for my virgin eye!"

They brawl around ringside for a while in uninspired fashion, though admittedly the guardrails are so close to the ring that it's practically impossible to do anything out there, so they head inside where Bret breaks out a snap suplex and a leg drop. Mankind's in the mood for a fight however, so they brawl up to the commentary position where Bret hits a suplex on the stage. Mankind quickly takes over and gets a legdrop for two, but Bret evades a charge and Mankind hits the deck again as we head to a commercial.

Back from that, Bret crotches Mankind on the guardrail before the annoying New York fans start chanting "HBK!" just to piss Bret off, and then wouldn't you just know it? The now-standard "bWo! bWo!" chants break out, lead by Lenny the Superfan, a/k/a Faith No More Guy, who you might recognise from many WWF and ECW front rows of the late 90s. And yes, Vladimir is stationed next to him, just as he was in Texas last week. Bret clotheslines Mankind and sends him into the steel steps, just in time to cutaway to Todd Pettengill who's found a woman in a fuzzy bra, which in his mind somehow makes her "Princess Leia." Ugh. Mankind gets a crappy double arm DDT which Bret just basically forward rolls through, then misses another charge in the corner as Bret goes into the big finishing sequence: Side-Russian legsweep, bulldog headlock, spinning neckbreaker, side backbreaker, clothesline, Sharpshooter. And then Owen jumps in for the lousy DQ finish, the plague of *Shotgun Saturday Night*. Pretty average match if all be told.
Final Rating: **¼

Savio Vega vs. Rocky Maivia
Earlier today in Madison Square Garden, Savio turned his back on tag team partner Ahmed Johnson and apparently sided with the Nation of Domination. Savio apologises for his actions, claims to really like Rocky, and promises a good, clean match. The crowd immediately start on the "Rocky sucks!" chants, and one guy has the temerity to shout "Boring!" less than a minute into it. What a tail end. And then the "bWo!" chants break out again! Who knew the Blue Meanie was such a clubhead? Faarooq and Crush arrive at ringside in time for a round of "Die Rocky, Die!" chants, and then the crowd decides it wants the Legion of Doom back. Give it a month, lads. Rocky shows the same fire he has the previous couple of weeks, but Savio keeps dragging things down with a series of trapezius holds and armbars. In fairness to the guy, he's already wrestled once today, but it's a real comedown after his energetic performance two weeks ago. Savio throws Rocky over the top to the floor and Rocky injures his knee for the count-out (the kind of finish you might expect them to run *before* the *Royal Rumble*, not after it) to cap off a truly crappy match. Savio joins Faarooq and Crush in destroying Rocky after the match, then throws up his fist in support of the Nation. Bleh.
Final Rating: ½*

- Elsewhere, Jake Roberts makes out with Revelations. I know this is late-night but do we really need bestiality on the show?

This is not for my virgin eye!

Jake Roberts vs. Salvatore Sincere
Hunter Hearst Helmsley (whose friends call him "Bob" according to his comical on-screen graphic) joins the commentary team to mock Jake's demons (and why *would* you book an alcoholic in a nightclub anyway?), and throw out a series of snappy lines. "This is the World Wrestling Federation, where the big boys don't have time to play!" he declares in a pot-shot at WCW. "Hey McMahon, that Rocky Johnson had a real good match earlier on! Good play-by-play too." Vince apologises for messing Rocky's name up before an odd discussion on New York sexuality arises - "Around here, straight's not the way to go… from what I hear." Responds McMahon, "Yes, there are some luminaries around here." Luminaries?! The crowd starts chanting "bWo" yet again, which has long since grown tiresome, and Jake finishes a routine squash with the DDT in what would actually prove to be his final televised match in the WWF.
Final Rating: SQUASH (Not rated)

- During the break, Helmsley gives poor Sal a Pedigree after declaring himself "second best", owing to his status as Intercontinental Champion. Quite the night for old Bob.

Crush vs. Sycho Sid
This might have held some intrigue if it had been 1992. Sadly it's 1997, so Sid just kicks his ass for a while until it's time for a commercial break. Well of course it is, what with time running so low yet again. Back from the break and the Nation have found their way out to ringside, giving Crush the advantage. He goes for the heart punch but Sid goozles him instead for a chokeslam. He follows that with a powerbomb but the Nation get involved, leaving Sid to grab a chair which he absolutely belts Crush with, causing the DQ. Way too long for what it was, even with time running out and the adverts eating up a good three minutes of it.
Final Rating: ½*

THE SHOTGUN RECAP:

Most Entertaining: Mankind. His match with Bret was nothing to write home about but he was still willing to get bumped around on wooden stages and steel guardrails for my viewing pleasure, plus he provided amusement with his pre and post-match pursuit of a couple of strippers.

Least Entertaining: Savio Vega by a country mile. His shifting personality work was fine, but man alive were those rest holds ever tedious.

Quote of the Night: "I know you would do anything keep Bret Hart in the World Wrestling Federation!" - Sunny adds fuel to the fire of conspiracy theorists everywhere as she address Vince McMahon after Bret "quit" the WWF last Monday on *RAW*.

Match of the Night: Bret Hart vs. Mankind. Outside of a few house show matches in England and Germany and a handful of six-man tags on *RAW* and at live events, this is actually the only high-profile in-ring meeting between Bret Hart and Mick Foley caught on film, giving it a curiosity value above its actual quality.

Verdict: Not a good show this week as everyone looked to be on autopilot after pulling double duty at MSG earlier in the day, and that Savio Vega match was interminable.
Final Rating: 22

02.01.1997 - by Lee Maughan

Venue: Mirage Nightclub, New York City, NY
Taped: 02.01.97

"Back to where it all began!" barks Vince McMahon, as if the previous four weeks have been some sort of epic journey. Out in the streets, Paul Bearer and Vader are looking through the trash for Mankind, who almost gets himself run over in the streets amidst his excitement for nightclub sex.

Ahmed Johnson vs. Vader
Vader actually ended Ahmed's undefeated streak last summer if you'll recall. Naturally, that isn't referenced here, which is a shame because it might add some colour to an otherwise bland, pointless affair. It's not bad, it's just not particularly interesting. Typical WWF big man stuff with punches, clotheslines, shoulderblocks, you know the drill. Ahmed gets a mighty spinebuster that sends Vader packing, but back from the commercial break we find Vader in control (what a surprise) with elbows and punches. Vader charges with an avalanche in the corner but hesitates on the Vaderbomb, allowing Ahmed to punt him in the gooch and land a spinning heel kick. He goes for the Pearl River Plunge but Mankind jumps in with a steel chair for the disqualification (hell, what would *Shotgun* be without a DQ to really get the party rocking?) Mankind and Vader tease accidentally nailing each other with the chair a couple of times (Mankind had belted Vader with a chair by accident on *RAW* this past week) before Ahmed takes it and runs both guys off. Average power stuff with no real point to it.
Final Rating: **

- Back in the green room, the Headbangers are busy pouring hot wax all over themselves because "this club sucks!"

Mankind vs. The British Bulldog
"Oh, what a body!" Sunny declares of Davey Boy. A pure coincidence then that Shawn Michaels has been removed from the source tape's opening credits this week, yes? Davey is playing a total babyface here as part of his ongoing angle with Owen Hart that was to see the duo split before Bret Hart's heel turn caused a cataclysmic shift in the WWF's overall direction, resulting in the formation of his new Hart Foundation stable. Mankind is still at ringside after the previous match and isn't actually prepared to wrestle, nominating Aldo Montoya as a substitute for him since he's just here to party. You can tell that from his clobber, bedecked as he is in a raggedy old coat, sweatpants and white sneakers. Oh, Mick.

Bulldog starts tearing those party clothes to shreds and kicks Mankind's ass for a while, with Mankind vainly attempting to return to the broadcast booth the whole time in a funny bit. Bulldog follows him out and backdrops him up on the stage, drawing an "ECW!" chant from the crowd. Hey, at least it's not "bWo!" again. Mankind takes a nasty leg-first spill on the stage so Bulldog goes after it. Mankind fights back and Davey really gets into the swing of things, over-selling a charging knee to the face much to my eternal delight. Mankind drops a leg across the back of Davey's head as Vader returns just in time for another commercial break.

Action resumes with Bulldog countering a piledriver into a backdrop up on the stage for another round of "ECW!" chants, but Mankind uses Davey Boy's tights for leverage to pull him into the path of Vader, who drops him across the security railing a couple of times before sending him back inside, where Mankind picks up an easy pin. Vader and Mankind then double-team Davey after the match, setting up their *WrestleMania 13* crack at Davey and Owen's tag titles, before Ahmed Johnson rushes the ring with a 2x4. Where the hell did he find that in a nightclub? Davey, not quite a babyface yet despite fist bumping a bunch of dudes in the front row during his entrance, takes umbrage at the presence of Ahmed, and the two get into a shoving match to set up a match that never happens. This was fun while it lasted though, and an interesting clash of styles that really mixed well to boot.
Final Rating: **½

Savio Vega vs. Jesse Jammes
Phineas Godwinn joins the broadcast team for this one, mainly just so he and Sunny can banter back-and-forth. I know Dennis Knight comes in for some serious stick from the scribes here at History of Wrestling, but credit where it's due - he is perfectly acceptable as the dopey bumpkin here. Savio breaks out a few more interesting moves here than he did last week, like a

crescent kick and a spinning heel kick, but he's still finding his feet as a heel and has a seeming over reliance on nerve pinches, chinlocks and chokes. Jammes does what he can to make it interesting, using a jaw buster that he actually sells himself, and rallying with mounted punches, clotheslines and a back drop. Savio manages to counter a pump handle slam attempt with a hiptoss, and finishes with another spinning heel kick. Jesse showed a lot of fire when he was on offence and Savio tried really hard to get his new heel persona across, but the majority of his offensive arsenal was a one-way ticket to snoozeville.
Final Rating: *¼

- Pettengill tries to get another interview with the Headbangers back in the green room, but Mosh gets sick and vomits all over Thrasher's face... before the 'Bangers wipe the puke up and eat it all. The WWF, ladies and germs. Lowbrow comedy at its low-browiest.

The Headbangers vs. The Godwinns
Yes, we've actually come full circle. And what a second half-hour this has been, huh? The crowd are now dead for this, but then if you will insist on booking pig farmers as babyfaces in New York nightclubs, you deserve everything you get. The Godwinns decide to work the arm as Vince decides to amuse himself by claiming Hillbilly Jim has gone duck hunting in Central Park. Back from commercial and nothing much is going on in the ring, though Vince does seem to get a zinger in on Sunny - "Well it is the flu season… and you should know!" Is that a reference to the fact she was knocking off Shawn Michaels, who had worked the *Royal Rumble* show despite being sick as a dog? Henry gets a supposed hot tag but nobody reacts to it, then all four guys spill to the floor and brawl into the crowd as the bell rings for a double DQ or a double count-out or a double something. It's never adequately explained what the actual finish is, as the show goes immediately off the air, but I guess that's better than just saying you're out of time and promising to air the finish next week despite having no intention of ever doing so.
Final Rating: *½

THE SHOTGUN RECAP:

Most Entertaining: Mankind scoops the award for the second week running as his humour really shone through in his opening skit, his comedy and his match with Davey Boy Smith.

Least Entertaining: Savio Vega becomes another two-time award winner here, and on a 60-minute show with the Godwinns too! Shameful.

Quote of the Night: "I like how this headphone feels against my missing ear!" - Mankind joins Vince and Sunny for commentary during "The Man I Call My Friend" Vader's match.

Match of the Night: Mankind also takes another consecutive award here for his match with Davey Boy Smith.

Verdict: Remember when Ahmed Johnson powerbombed D'Lo Brown on the hood of a car? Remember when Marlena got her norks out and gave the Sultan a thrill? Remember when Terry Funk went on a profanity-laced tirade at the expense of WCW and everyone in sight? In less than a month's time we've gone from that to lengthy, heatless matches with ring wizards like Savio Vega and the Godwinns, and the disturbing sight of the Headbangers blowing chunks into each other's mouths. True enough, Davey Boy was working hard and Mankind provided some wacky fun, but this show has already jumped the shark. Hell, Todd Pettengill doesn't even look like he's having much fun out there any more, and Vince McMahon has clearly given up, having already dumped his casual WWF letterman jacket in favour of a much more conservative formal suit. The end is nigh.
Rating: 21

02.08.1997 - by Lee Maughan

Venue: Penn Station, New York City, NY
Taped: 02.08.97

And with the whole *Shotgun* concept dead in the water, the WWF was unable to locate an actual nightclub for its final edition, instead setting up stall in Penn Station of all places, a public venue that resulted in the promotion being unable to make any cash back through ticket sales. Hey, maybe TNA could look into running here sometime?

Crush & Faarooq vs. The Godwinns
What an absolute armpit of an opener this promises to be. Still, if this truly is a celebration of all things *Shotgun*, one big final blowout, who better than these two cornerstones of the program? One can only hope Savio Vega is still to come. And yes, the fans are soon chanting "bWo! bWo!" as if just for old times sake. And how about a new one? "Nation sucks dick!" As all this is going down, the camera cuts to a split screen where Todd Pettengill can be found making fun of a bloke without any teeth. Really. What a jerk. And indeed, (drumroll please), Savio is here! Yay! An Irish whip and a double clothesline set up the hot tag and Phineas runs wild on both guys until Savio trips him from the outside. Phineas goes after Savio which sets him up for a charge from Crush, but he moves just in time and Crush decks Savio instead, so Phineas looks to follow with a Slop Drop but alas, Faarooq rips his head off with a clothesline to give Crush the three. Not bad given what I was expecting.
Final Rating: *½

WWF Intercontinental Title:
Hunter Hearst Helmsley (c) vs. The Undertaker
A title match! On *Shotgun*! This really IS a big final blowout! Helmsley arrives in a stretch limo, and Undertaker makes his way out through the crowd after showing up at the building in Ozzy Osbourne's *'Crazy Train'*. Time of course for a commercial break just as the match begins, but back from that comes a full replay of Helmsley jumping Undertaker to start, but Undertaker no-selling it and destroying Helmsley in the corner instead. A whip into the corner sees the referee get bumped in just the spot *Shotgun* has been crying out for all these weeks, and Helmsley bashes Undertaker with the belt as we take another commercial break! Already?!

Back again with Helmsley going to work with choking, a snapmare, a face buster and series of stomps in the corner, but Undertaker gets the best of a slugfest. Helmsley comes back off an Irish whip with a swinging neckbreaker for two, and brings the belt back into play but misses on a big swing. Undertaker grabs the belt and uses it himself for (you guessed it) the disqualification. After the match, the crowd chant for a Tombstone but Undertaker gives them a chokeslam instead. Helmsley then tries to make a dash for it but Undertaker catches him on the way up the stairs and gives him a Tombstone onto an escalator, which an unconscious Helmsley rides all the way back to the ring in the closest thing to an iconic image this wretched show ever got. Fun, energetic stuff

here.
Final Rating: **½

Savio Vega vs. Aldo Montoya
You know, if you asked me for my dream line-up before this show, as in "How do we go out with a bang on the last ever live edition of *Shotgun*?" I'd have hoped against hope that you'd book the guy with two "Least Entertaining" awards to his name against the bloke debuting on the show, with a yellow jockstrap on his head.

Savio runs through his usual, though thankfully forgoes the nerve pinching, and Aldo keeps it rolling with a hiptoss, two dropkicks to the outside and a plancha. Back in he gets two off a flying body press off the top but Savio takes control with knees to the midsection and some wicked chops. He works in his spinning heel kick in the corner and adds a delayed suplex, but soon enough he resorts to choking. In the meantime, roving reporter Pettengill has found a man named Terry who's carrying an LJN Vince McMahon action figure in his pocket. "You still have the same jacket? 1985, you were like 40 then, right?" The rapture is upon us - *Shotgun* is coming to an end, and Todd Pettengill cracked a decent joke!

Back from a commercial, Savio is firmly in control as the crowd chants "We want 2 Cold!" I do too, but Flash Funk is the best you WWF fans are going to get I'm afraid. And NOW it's time for the nerve pinch! Vince uses the dead spot to promote an upcoming Hector Camacho fight on pay-per-view, and before you know it, the Nation are brawling with the Godwinns at ringside. And you know what that means? Six-man tag team match, playa!
Final Rating: *½

The Nation of Domination vs. Aldo Montoya & The Godwinns
Back from the final mid-match commercial of the *Shotgun* era, and the Nation are busy getting heat on Aldo as Pettengill finds a woman in the crowd who wants to beat up another woman for stealing her man! "We already have midget wrestling!" decrees Todd. Back in the ring, Aldo catches Faarooq with a swinging neckbreaker after having eaten a backbreaker from Crush, and he goes for the hot tag but Savio cuts him off as the NYC crowd finally win me back over with a hearty chant of "Boring!" that even Vince himself can't ignore. Aldo actually gets a false tag, so I guess we're going all-in on this one, and the Nation give him another shit-kicking in the corner. He catches Savio with a missile dropkick off the top and it suddenly all breaks down, with Savio scoring the pin on Aldo amidst the chaos with a spinning wheel kick. The Godwinns did absolutely sod all in this, which was probably for the best.
Final Rating: *½

Back from one last commercial, and the actual purpose of the Godwinns' presence is made clear - Phineas chases the still unidentified D'Lo Brown backstage and wildly throws his slop bucket all over Pat Patterson, stationed at the Gorilla position. Given the state of his Bill Cosby-style sweater, I'd say he deserved it. He threatens to come down to ringside and make out with Sunny since she thinks its so funny.

- And finally, Pettengill catches up with Curtis Sliwa, founder of the Guardian Angels who sends out a threat to the Nation. That would equal Faarooq vs. Ray Traylor in some other far off nightmare.

THE SHOTGUN RECAP:

Most Entertaining: It's a toss-up between the Undertaker and Hunter Hearst Helmsley. Undertaker dished out the ass-kicking, but Helmsley took the ride down the escalator, so take your own pick there.

Least Entertaining: I didn't really want to single any one person out tonight, but Savio Vega *did* use that fucking nerve pinch of his again...

Quote of the Night: "Welcome to Amtrak's night train to hell! Ha ha ha!" - The Undertaker works in some corporate sponsorship in his own inimitable style.

Match of the Night: Hunter Hearst Helmsley vs. The Undertaker.

Verdict: And so to its chilling conclusion comes the WWF's month-and-a-half experiment with producing a mildly risqué yet ultimately directionless live broadcast from a dingy New York dive. In actuality, the show continued on for several more years, though under a much different make-up. The next week's show was simply a "greatest hits" from previous episodes (that's right folks, it's six sensational weeks of the *Shotgun Saturday Night* show!), while week eight saw content entirely regurgitated from the final *Superstars* taping. With *RAW* then switching to a two-hour weekly format and the cessation of all other WWF TV tapings, *Shotgun* was soon being recorded before (and occasionally after) *RAW*, a taping method that would continue with the addition of programming such as *Los Super Astros*, *Sunday Night HeAT*, *Metal*, *Jakked*, *Velocity*, *Main Event*, *NXT* and the revived *Superstars*.
Rating: 35

03.08.1997 - by Lee Maughan

Venue: Deutschlandhalle, Berlin, Germany.
Taped: 02.26.97

With the WWF only holding TV tapings for *RAW* at this point, *Shotgun Saturday Night* has started to feature matches taped on the undercard of those events. The matches on this particular edition of the show were taped prior to the *RAW* taped in Berlin, Germany, which featured the finals of the tournament to crown the WWF's first ever European Champion, which you can read about elsewhere in this book. We decided to include this episode in order to bring you the complete rundown on that historic card.

These matches also aired on *WWF Superstars*, though the version under review here specifically comes from a recording of *Shotgun Saturday Night*, despite the on-screen graphics being a mixture of both. Hosts are Jim Ross and Jim Cornette.

Ahmed Johnson vs. Leif Cassidy
And we kick things off with the perpetually injured Ahmed Johnson, here nursing a splinter-pierced bicep that had swollen up to the size of a baseball, courtesy of an errant 2x4 explosion. The man was as much a danger to himself as he was to others with his reckless ways. He starts with a nice delayed vertical suplex and a recklessly out-of-control scissors kick but misses a charge in the corner, allowing Cassidy to take over. Leif goes after the injury with an armbar takedown, removes Ahmed's protective padding and shoves him arm-first into a top turnbuckle, which is very psychologically sound and all, but he cuts a very methodical (read: dull) pace while doing

it. The tedious heat segment at least gives Cornette the opportunity to explain the problem Ahmed is facing come *WrestleMania 13* - he's in a Chicago street fight with all three members of the Nation of Domination, he's got no partners, and everyone else in the promotion is already booked. What a timely coincidence then that Chicago's own Legion of Doom have just returned to the promotion…

Ahmed soon gets as bored of taking his drubbing as everyone else is of watching, and all but rips Cassidy's head off with a clothesline. Stupidly enough, he uses his bad arm to deliver it, but I'll let him off since he at least went down selling it. A piledriver, a spinebuster, and the Pearl River Plunge finish what was either a protracted squash, or a regular outing chopped down to a much more digestible six minutes, depending on your point of view.
Final Rating: *¾

Salvatore Sincere vs. Alex Porteau
Presumably this match is being shown out of sequence and was the first thing taped on the night, because both guys get a strong reaction here despite neither meaning a whole lot to the WWF at the time, particularly Porteau. It's very much the "first guys through the curtain" response. It's fairly routine weekend TV stuff, livened up by the announcing as Cornette labels his former charge "lax" and "lackadaisical" and accuses him of "hot-dogging." Adds JR - "That's the problem with some of these youngsters, is maintaining a high level of concentration." I'm not sure what he was specifically referring to there, but after Cornette asserts the same won't be true of the Davey Boy Smith-Owen Hart match coming up later, there can be no mistake about which direction he aimed his next venomous line - "And another thing about that match James E., neither one of those men are 40-year old washed-up has-beens." I wonder how 39-year old Bret Hart felt about those kind of pot-shots? 'Pug' makes his token comeback but Sal catches him with a full Nelson slam (dubbed the "Sincerely Yours") for the pin.
Final Rating: *½

- To last Monday's *RAW* now, for a complete replay of the stunning Davey Boy Smith vs. Owen Hart European Title Tournament final, which you can read about elsewhere in this book.

Doug Furnas & Phil LaFon vs. Aldo Montoya & Bob Holly
Furnas and LaFon switch off while working some back-and-forth with Holly, who then decides to bring Montoya in for the first time… just as the action breaks away for commercials. Amusingly enough, Holly is already back in the ring when the bout picks back up. He blocks a Furnas huracanrana attempt with a tasty little powerbomb, then gets the hot tag to Aldo, whose crossbody is blocked and turned into a Doomsday Device, LaFon finishing him off with an awesome cobra suplex to a mixed reaction from a crowd that couldn't work out who the heels and faces were supposed to be. Poor Aldo was made to look like a complete geek there, but I guess that's what you get for sporting a yellow jockstrap on your face.
Final Rating: **

THE SHOTGUN RECAP:

Most Entertaining: Ignoring the Davey Boy Smith-Owen Hart match, we'll be kind and go with Ahmed Johnson for some brutal power moves.

Least Entertaining: Leif Cassidy, by far the least-motivated guy on the show.

Quote of the Night: "I don't have any empathy, sympathy, compassion or anything else for Bret Hart. He's the Rodney Dangerfield of the WWF, he's gettin' no respect 'cos now even the women think they can beat him up!" - Jim Cornette makes reference to Hart's showdown with the as-yet unnamed Chyna on this past week's episode of *RAW*.

Match of the Night: Doug Furnas & Phil LaFon vs. Aldo Montoya & Bob Holly, which again, is ignoring the replay of the superb Smith-Hart clash.

Verdict: I guess having this show tacked onto your copy of the Berlin *RAW* might make a nice souvenir if you were there, but otherwise this is just a very typical WWF weekend TV show, with nothing you need to go out of your way to see besides the Bulldog/Owen match, and you can find that in much better quality on *The Best of RAW: 15th Anniversary* and *Hart and Soul: The Hart Family Anthology* DVD sets.
Rating: 57

THE FLASHBACK FILES

WWF SUMMER FLASHBACK
WWF FLASHBACK: SURVIVOR SERIES

07.14.97 - WWF Summer Flashback
by Lee Maughan

Hosted by Vince McMahon

You may be wondering what this show is, and you could be forgiven for never having heard of it before. Part of the build to 1997's *SummerSlam*, *WWF Flashback* was a one-hour special aired on the USA Network to both hype that card, and celebrate the promotion's past, something of a rarity in those days.

1988

- Fun fact: 1988 was the first summer in WWF history. All those summers from the 50s, 60s and 70s just didn't count. It was a summer of turmoil for the promotion as 'Million Dollar Man' Ted DiBiase conspired with Andre the Giant to take over the WWF after having failed in bids to both buy and steal Hulk Hogan's title. Dubbing themselves the 'Megabucks', the treacherous twosome appeared to pay off special guest referee Jesse Ventura en route to their *SummerSlam* showdown with the Mega Powers, Hogan and then-WWF champion Randy Savage. But the Powers promised a secret weapon…

To Madison Square Garden for the eventual match and, with Hogan and Savage both in peril, corner woman Miss Elizabeth, having previously been uninvolved in shenanigans of any sort (at least, not since the WWF retroactively began ignoring her cheating freely in Savage's matches after her arrival in 1985), jumps up on the ring apron and whips off her skirt, Bucks Fizz-style, wandering up and down the apron in her bright red knickers. Andre, DiBiase, Ventura, Virgil *and* Bobby Heenan are all so stunned by this, they don't notice Hulk and 'Macho' Hulking up to make their triumphant comeback until it's too late.

- Earlier in the night, the record-breaking "greatest Intercontinental Champion of all time", the Honky Tonk Man, was dumb enough to call out anybody in the back to challenge him when his scheduled challenger, Brutus Beefcake, was put on the shelf courtesy of 'Outlaw' Ron Bass and his sharpened boot spurs. "Get me somebody out here to wrestle, I don't care who it is!" Can you say "famous last words"? Seconds later, the Ultimate Warrior was flapping his arms all over the place, swinging the belt above his head and hyperventilating against the ropes, standing tall as the new champion.

1989

- In 1989, the Berlin Wall came down as Savage and Hogan brawled in Elizabeth's hospital room. That fight actually took place in February, which I'd hardly class as "summer".

- Meanwhile, Hulk also starred in the horrendously bad action flick *No Holds Barred*, leading to co-star Tiny Lister crossing over into WWF rings *as his movie character*! Zeus would prove to be just as rotten a wrestler as Hogan was an actor, but that didn't stop *SummerSlam* '89 popping a huge pay-per-view buyrate for a tag team collision in which Hogan and Brutus Beefcake toppled Zeus and Savage.

1990

- At the Tokyo Dome, heavyweight slugger and 42-1 underdog James 'Buster' Douglas shockingly knocked out Mike Tyson to become boxing's undisputed World Champion, indirectly altering WWF history forever. What isn't mentioned here is that lifelong wrestling fan Tyson had been scheduled to referee a match between Hulk Hogan and Randy Savage on an edition of NBC's *The Main Event*, and that the WWF had been secretly negotiating at the time with Don King about some sort of Tyson vs. Hogan pay-per-view event. All talks with the Tyson camp were dropped following his loss, with Douglas taking the scheduled refereeing gig. Of course, the presence of Tyson years later generated an immeasurable amount of mainstream publicity for the promotion, spearheading its late 90s Steve Austin-led resurgence. Had Tyson already worked with the group in 1990, it's tough to guess how differently 1998 may have played out, and what the resultant grappling landscape would have looked like.

- Also in 1990, some professional wrestling happened too, as the Hart Foundation snared the WWF Tag Team Titles from Demolition in a rocking good fun best 2-out-of-3 falls match, thanks in part to an appearance from the Legion of Doom, and 'Ravishing' Rick Rude failed in his bid to capture the WWF Championship in a steel cage bout with the Ultimate Warrior. And also, Julia Roberts starred in *Pretty Woman*. Well gee, thanks for that little nugget, Vince.

1991

- With relationships making the news (an opportunity for Vince to rag on real-life chum Donald Trump for news of his affair with Marla Maples coming to light whilst still married to Ivana Zelníčková, the pair divorcing in 1992 with Maples marrying Donald the following year), Randy Savage got down on one knee and popped the question to Elizabeth. Her answer? "Oooohh yeeeaahhh!" And thus the two were married (on-screen at least, the pair had already been married for years in real life) in the ring at Madison Square Garden, a "match made in heaven" that headlined *SummerSlam* '91. All of which is another excuse for the WWF to wheel out that yacky '*Together*' song one more time.

- For fans of actual wrestling, *SummerSlam* '91 also saw a sensational Intercontinental Title match between reigning champion Mr. Perfect, and top contender Bret Hart. A classic battle, the resulting title change legitimised former tag team star Hart as a singles wrestler to be taken seriously, while Perfect's performance (he came out of secret retirement for one night to do the honours for his real-life pal) despite suffering incredible back pain from years of outrageous bumps, was a marvel.

1992

- For the first time in history, the WWF left North America for a pay-per-view extravaganza, hitting London's Wembley Stadium to the tune of around 80,000 fans, an incredible number that gave the promotion a big time feel and look, despite its rapidly declining popularity back home. The fact they pulled the attendance they did *without* Hulk Hogan on the card is a testament to just how popular this new fangled "American wrestling" was with British audiences at the time. Even Roddy Piper was on hand for the occasion to toot his bagpipes in celebration!

- With a stadium-sized show, the WWF offered a stadium-sized entrance, as the Undertaker made his arrival on the back of hearse. Sadly, the fun and games stopped once the bell rang to signal an utterly diabolical match between Undertaker and 'Ugandan Giant' Kamala.

- On the plus side, that man Bret Hart cobbled together his second classic *SummerSlam* bout in a row, carrying home country hero Davey Boy Smith to one of the greatest matches of the 1990s. More impressive than the match was the knowledge that Hart all but had to wrestle the entire match by himself, with an injured, blown up Smith, who had apparently spent most of the summer out of his mind on drugs with Jim Neidhart, completely forgetting everything he was supposed to be doing just a couple of minutes into the near-half hour outing.

1993

- Following his death from congestive heart failure, Andre the Giant was announced as the first inductee into the WWF's newly created Hall of Fame. What is it with this show? First the Hogan-Savage brawl, then the Tyson-Douglas title switch, now this… all of these things happened in February! Somebody in the WWF's production team really needs an education on what months fall within what seasons.

- By the actual summer, Yokozuna had started to make his mark on the World Wrestling Federation, breaking 'Hacksaw' Jim Duggan's ribs with a banzai drop and capturing the WWF title from Hulk Hogan at the first pay-per-view edition of the *King of the Ring*. Full of disdain for the USA, the WWF turned the xenophobia up to 11 and had Mr. Fuji challenge any American athlete to attempt to slam Yoko on July 4th aboard the USS Intrepid. The man who rose to the challenge? Former 'Narcissist' Lex Luger, reborn as the new American Hero. And then at *SummerSlam*, Luger let the entire country down by failing to wrest the title from the supposed sumo in a baffling booking decision that leaves me scratching my head to this very day.

1994

- With baseball on strike, former minor-leaguer Randy Savage began proclaiming that the WWF would "never go on strike!" Well, how could they? The wrestlers don't even have a union!

- Meanwhile, with the Undertaker still missing after his *Royal Rumble* casket collision with Yokozuna, *Naked Gun* star Leslie Nielsen is sent to crack the case in a series of comedy skits. Something smells fishy when Ted DiBiase claims to have found the 'Dead Man', and the result is a poor impersonation from independent worker Brian Lee. Paul Bearer cottons on to this much quicker than Nielsen or the WWF's crack announcing crew, and brings the real Undertaker back, completely with an updated look, for a pitiful Undertaker vs. Undertaker match at *SummerSlam* '94.

1995

- Worried that a card headlined by Diesel defending the WWF title against King Mabel is going to absolutely blow chunks, Vince McMahon (through on-screen presidential figurehead Gorilla Monsoon) scraps a planned Shawn Michaels vs. Sycho Sid Intercontinental Title bout and replaces it with Michaels defending said title against Razor Ramon in a rematch of their classic *WrestleMania X* ladder match. The match is a stunner, and evens the score after Razor won the first clash.

1996

- With the Olympic Games heading to Atlanta, the WWF latches on to the hype by releasing an amusing commercial showing various superstars shot-putting, high jumping and sprinting their way to gold medals.

- Also in 1996, 'Stone Cold' Steve Austin threatened to whip Todd Pettengill's ass, before Stunning his way to victory over Jake Roberts in the finals of the 1996 *King of the Ring* tournament. "Austin 3:16 says I just whipped your ass!"

- And finally, to *SummerSlam*, where Mankind tore it up with the Undertaker in the WWF's first ever "boiler room brawl", a somewhat unusual (and I'd say underrated) match that saw Undertaker's long-time handler Paul Bearer surprisingly turn his back on the 'Dead Man' and side with Mankind.

- Bret Hart cuts a final promo reminding everyone to check out this year's *SummerSlam* to see him win the WWF Title from the Undertaker, and a series of clips take us out, with Rocco riding on Paul Ellering's bike at Wembley Stadium, Yokozuna being so fat he breaks the top rope, 'Sensational' Sherri fainting all over Shawn Michaels and Rick Martel, Sunny skimping around, Ric Flair getting involved in Randy Savage and the Ultimate Warrior's business, the Bret Hart-Owen Hart steel cage match, the Mountie going to jail, and in one last pot shot, Dusty Rhodes jiggling about in his black and yellow polka dots.

Verdict: *WWF Summer Flashback* didn't do a lot to push 1997's *SummerSlam* event (though as a fan I'm glad I wasn't pounded over the head with constant plugs imploring me to buy it on pay-per-view), but as a rapid fire look back at some WWF history, it was a pretty fun waste of an hour. Worth seeing if you can find it, but you'll probably have a hard time tracking a copy down.

10.28.97 - WWF Flashback: Survivor Series
by Lee Maughan

Hosted by Vince McMahon.

"Survival of the fittest is a law of nature, and the basic instinct in man. At the *Survivor Series*, nature's law and man's instinct collide!"

The second (and final) instalment of the WWF's *Flashback* series, this show picks up where *WWF Summer Flashback* left off, covering the previous ten editions of the *Survivor Series* (although 1988 gets skipped over entirely for whatever reason.)

1987

- Vince calls Andre the Giant "the most recognisable and revered superstar of WWF's history", and the bullshit-o-meter is already in full swing with the claim that Hulk Hogan was the first man to attempt to follow in Andre's footsteps, as illustrated by Andre having appeared in Rob Reiner's *The Princess Bride* (1987) with that cinematic masterpiece *No Holds Barred* (1989). Ignoring Roddy Piper's role as unemployed drifter John Nada in John Carpenter's classic sci-fi satire *They Live* (1988) is one thing, but Hogan had already hit the silver screen as far back as 1982, co-starring as Thunderlips in Sylvester Stallone's tribute to over-the-top 80s excess, *Rocky III*. In fairness to Vince, Andre actually began his acting career long before Hogan ever did, way back in 1967 with *Casse-Tête Chinois Pour Le Judoka* (loosely translated as "Puzzle for the Chinese Judoka"), a French boxing movie. However both of them were trumped by Stanislaus Zbyszko's role in 1950's wrestling noir *Night and the City* and 'Super Swedish Angel' Tor Johnson, perhaps best known for his appearances in some legendarily bad flicks like Ed Wood's campy sci-fi *Plan 9 from Outer Space* (1959) and Coleman Francis' 1961 mess *The Beast of Yucca Flats*, Johnson having broken into the acting game all the way back in 1934 with *Registered Nurse* and *Kid Millions*.

Contradictorily, Vince notes that the two were destined to collide, having implied the reason was all down to butting heads over their glittering Hollywood careers, despite *WrestleMania III* taking place before either *The Princess Bride* or *No Holds Barred* had even been released. More spin follows as McMahon plays off Andre's early near fall as an actual victory, complete with slow motion footage and dubbed-in sound effects, before admitting Hogan actually retained the title.

The result in doubt however, the WWF had no choice but to bow to "worldwide fan pressure" and add a new "fall classic" to the calendar - the first *Survivor Series*, built around a team led by Hogan clashing with a team led by Andre. With Hogan's team at a 3-on-2 disadvantage, Hulk body slams the One Man Gang and King Kong Bundy out on the floor but gets counted-out in the process. Andre then finishes off Hogan's remaining team member, Bam Bam Bigelow, to claim victory. Naturally, the footage cuts away before Hogan has a chance to make his comeback.

1989

- "At the 1989 *Survivor Series*, a babyface Shawn Michaels was taking his very first steps towards superstardom" notes McMahon. Shawn rags on himself for "being a little chubby" and says "Hunter didn't like Marty and I much", but offers absolutely no context to go along with the statement.

1990

- Onto 1990 and "the most electrifying superstar of his generation", the Ultimate Warrior. A series of clips tells the whole story of the Ultimate Warriors vs. Perfect Team elimination match, and makes it all seem really rather exciting. Of course, while Warrior was otherwise considered *persona non grata* by the WWF at this point, it didn't hurt to show one of WCW's big names (Curt Hennig) doing a job.

- That's followed by some self-congratulatory back-slapping on account of the WWF offering that show for free on the Armed Forces Network during the height of the Gulf War, illustrated by a clipping from General H. Norman Schwarzkopf's book *It Doesn't Take a Hero*, reading "One day, somebody noticed that the drivers were fascinated by videotapes of American professional wrestling - Hulk Hogan versus Macho Man Randy Savage, Andre the Giant vs. Jake the Snake, and so on."

- Elsewhere, the Undertaker made his debut and "singlehandedly dismantled Dusty Rhodes' Dream Team", which wasn't quite the case but that's revisionist history for you.

- As part of an unrelated trivia contest, Owen Hart outs himself as the former Blue Blazer, declaring himself "the greatest masked wrestler to ever grace World Wrestling Federation rings, and if McMahon could have got his shtick together, I would have been the WWF Champion, and the first masked WWF Champion."

1991

- "The road down World Wrestling Federation history was dramatically altered in 1991 when legacy and change ferociously collided." Few really do grandiose hyperbole like Vince McMahon. His line about Hulk Hogan putting his "celebrity and belt on the line" is a little more perplexing. His celebrity was stake? Really? And what is this "belt" contraption anyway? Didn't Hogan actually carry a "championship title"?

In a sit-down interview, the Undertaker says Hogan "was at the top his game. He was everyone's idea of everything that was good in America, everything that was good all over the world." He takes a dig at Hogan apparently dubbing himself "The Immortal One" and says that "we've come to find out that that wasn't true", possibly in reference to the finish of this match. As the story goes, Hogan apparently played up his "neck injury" following Undertaker's steel chair assisted Tombstone piledriver with such conviction, that Undertaker for years carried guilt about hurting him, only to later learn the truth that Hogan had basically lied to him about it. One does have to ask however; when does a work stop being a work and start being a lie?

As one might suspect, all the clips from the match show Hogan getting his tail kicked, complete with crowd shots reedited at different points to make it look like they're cheering for the Undertaker, as McMahon gleefully calls Hulk's arsenal "useless." Vince also makes excuses for Ric Flair's involvement in the finish, suggesting everyone knew Undertaker had the match well in hand and was going to win anyway. And thus, Hulkamania was dead. For six days, at least.

- From *The Fab 4* series of quasi-shoot interviews, Bret Hart puts Undertaker over big time - "You know, a lot of people fail to recognise in Undertaker that he's a great technical wrestler. He does some pretty impressive stuff in there, he's very coordinated, very agile for a big guy. He's not like Sid or Diesel or some of these other guys that are giants but they lack the mobility, you're not going to get that with Undertaker. Then you're going to look at the Undertaker and you look at how bad does he want it? Maybe he doesn't want it that bad? Wrong."

- The hatchet job continues as Undertaker takes credit for ending Hulkamania - "November 19, 1991. I beat Hulk Hogan in the prime of his career. As I dropped Hulk Hogan on his head, I knew the end of Hulkamania was at hand. There's an old adage in the wrestling industry: "To be the man, you have to beat the man", well, the Undertaker beat the man when he was still somebody, when he was in his prime." I'd perhaps be remiss in not pointing out that at the time this show aired, the "past his prime nobody" 'Hollywood' Hogan was leading the New World Order as World Heavyweight Champion of the number one-rated pro wrestling organisation in North America, WCW, and just one month out from headlining WCW's biggest grossing pay-per-view event of all time, *Starrcade* '97, in a long-awaited title showdown with Sting. Just so you know.

1992

- Amazingly, 1992's coverage kicks off with the story behind the Bobby Heenan-led Ric Flair & Razor Ramon vs. Randy Savage & Mr. Perfect bout, a superb angle and a great match but a surprising inclusion given everybody involved was now part of WCW. Perhaps it was intended to show nWo members teaming with WCW guys but all it really did was serve to inadvertently hype WCW's upcoming Flair vs. Curt Hennig clash.

- More importantly, 1992 offers up the opportunity for Shawn Michaels and Bret Hart to cut promos on one another in the lead up to their Montreal meeting, all set to the backdrop of some classic clips. Bret says he never liked Shawn's cocky attitude, and that he's always been stronger than Shawn, plus close to him in speed. Shawn counters by outright suggesting that he's faster than Bret, as well as more agile, more determined and better looking, whatever that has to do with it. Bret puts over Shawn's agility before going back to the digs over his "crummy little tattoos", his earrings and his arrogance, and Shawn offers a rebuttal that he's got more will than Bret, pointing out that he beat him at *WrestleMania*. Ominously, as Bret locks in the Sharpshooter for the submission victory, Shawn declares "that'll never happen again."

1993

- In 1993, the Boston Garden "sold out in less than an hour, the capacity crowd flocked in great anticipation of the Shawn Michaels-Bret Hart showdown." In actuality, a then-suspended Shawn was an 11th hour replacement for Jerry Lawler, who was removed from the card just a few days out after being falsely accused of rape. Still, the WWF has another Hart-Michaels match to promote, so why not present it that way? Most of the clips actually centre on the angle in which Owen Hart was eliminated after accidentally colliding with Bret on the ring apron, leading to…

1994

- Ten years (actually almost eleven) after his manager Arnold Skaaland threw in the title and cost him the WWF Title, Bob Backlund finally had a shot at taking his crown back. Driven to madness by the original loss, Backlund employed Owen as his towel-wielding corner man for a submission match with Bret. A series of slow-motion clips set to a chorus of dark Italian opera illustrate the "family tragedy" of Owen convincing matriarchal Helen Hart throwing in the towel on Bret, gifting the title to Backlund. Owen's slimy crocodile tears here were a thing of beauty.

- Also in 1994, the WWF brought in *Walker, Texas Ranger* star Chuck Norris to act as the outsider enforcer for an Undertaker-Yokozuna casket match, long before Norris was a popular internet meme. The match was a stinker, playing before a largely dead crowd, but Norris did get to kick Jeff Jarrett in the tits before Undertaker got his revenge for the atrocity that was *Royal Rumble 1994*. Fun fact - Chuck Norris is the only man who can end the Undertaker's *WrestleMania* streak.

1995

- A stop in Washington, D.C. for 1995's *Survivor Series* was an opportunity for a Bill Clinton lookalike to pour popcorn down Sunny's cleavage. "He was kind of a pervert… I didn't vote for him anyway."

- More importantly, Bret Hart won his third WWF Title from Diesel in an absolutely belting match that was the best of Diesel's career to that point. Bret takes credit for "running Diesel out of the World Wrestling Federation in the first place", making sure to let everyone know that, yes, that is Kevin Nash. Can you tell there was a wrestling war on at this point?

1996

- Bret Hart makes his triumphant return to Madison Square Garden for a showdown with Steve Austin as "arguably the most celebrated superstar in WWF history." I'm not sure I'd go quite that far, but the resultant bout remains something of a forgotten classic. Vince makes sure to put 'Stone Cold' over as "just beginning." He couldn't have been more right on that one.

Verdict: Certainly it would be easy to criticise the shortcomings of this production - the subtle burial of Hulk Hogan, the refusal to really acknowledge anyone from the WWF's past as an icon besides Andre the Giant (which was pretty much company policy at the time, unless Jimmy Snuka was available), and the fact the last half hour was essentially just *The Bret Hart Show* (and in their defence, this was a vehicle designed to push the upcoming pay-per-view as much as anything else) - but overall, this was a very fun potted history of the first decade of the promotion's second regular pay-per-view extravaganza, simultaneously acting as a glancing CliffsNotes education to get newer fans up to speed, whilst also providing some breezy magazine-style nostalgia for long time Federation followers.

COLISEUM CLASSICS

WHAT THE WORLD *WAS* WATCHING

***** MATCHES

****¾ MATCHES

Owen Hart vs. The British Bulldog
Berlin, Germany   03.03.97

****½ MATCHES

**Owen Hart & The British Bulldog
vs. Shawn Michaels & Steve Austin**
Evansville, IN   05.26.97

****¼ MATCHES

**** MATCHES

***¾ MATCHES

**Owen Hart & The British Bulldog
vs. Doug Furnas & Phil LaFon**
Beaumont, TX   01.20.97

Owen Hart vs. The British Bulldog
Peoria, IL   03.31.97

Cactus Jack vs. Triple H
New York, NY   09.22.97

***½ MATCHES

Shawn Michaels vs. Mankind
Biloxi, MS   08.11.97

Tajiri vs. Taka Michinoku
Oklahoma City, OK   10.20.97

***¼ MATCHES

Owen Hart vs. Flash Funk
Nashville, TN   02.17.97

*** MATCHES

Owen Hart vs. Mankind
Albany, NY   01.06.97

*Rocky Maivia vs. Hunter Hearst Helmsley
San Antonio, TX   01.18.97

**Owen Hart & The British Bulldog
vs. Doug Furnas & Phil LaFon**
Toronto, Ontario, Canada   02.03.97

Bret Hart vs. Sycho Sid
Nashville, TN   02.17.97

Steve Austin & Shawn Michaels vs. The Legion of Doom
Huntington, WV   06.02.97

Brian Pillman vs. Mankind
Hartford, CT   06.30.97

Tajiri vs. Taka Michinoku
San Antonio, TX   07.14.97

**Steve Austin & Dude Love
vs. Owen Hart & The British Bulldog**
San Antonio, TX   07.14.97

*Jerry Lynn vs. Taka Michinoku
Chicago, IL   08.29.97

*The British Bulldog vs. Dude Love
Chicago, IL   09.05.97

Owen Hart vs. Shawn Michaels
Oklahoma City, OK   10.20.97

Ken Shamrock vs. Shawn Michaels
Hershey, PA   11.03.97

Taka Michinoku vs. Aguila
Roanoke, VA   12.01.97

Owen Hart vs. Shawn Michaels
Long Island, NY   12.29.97

HALL OF SHAME

THE WORST MATCHES OF THE YEAR

-***** MATCHES

-**** MATCHES

-*** MATCHES

Shawn Michaels vs. Triple H
Lowell, MA   12.22.97

-** MATCHES

-* MATCHES

Ahmed Johnson vs. Crush
Johannesburg, South Africa   04.14.97

DUD MATCHES

Ahmed Johnson vs. Crush
Beaumont, TX   01.27.97

Goldust vs. Crush
Toronto, Ontario, Canada   02.03.97

Goldust vs. Savio Vega
New York, NY   02.24.97

**Heavy Metal, Pentagon II & Pierroth
vs. Latin Love, Octagon & Hector Garza**
Worcester, MA   03.10.97

Hunter Hearst Helmsley vs. Jesse Jammes
Johannesburg, South Africa   04.14.97

Rocky Maivia vs. Savio Vega
Johannesburg, South Africa   04.14.97

Jesse Jammes vs. Rockabilly
Binghamton, NY   04.21.97

Tiger Ali Singh vs. Salvatore Sincere
Binghamton, NY   04.21.97

The Legion of Doom vs. Brian Pillman & Jim Neidhart
Evansville, IN   05.26.97

Faarooq vs. Goldust
Halifax, Nova Scotia, Canada   07.21.97

The Patriot vs. Hunter Hearst Helmsley vs. Savio Vega
Cincinnati, OH   09.08.97

Skull & 8-Ball vs. Recon & Sniper
Topeka, KS   10.13.97

THE BEST MATCHES SO FAR...

***** MATCHES

****¾ MATCHES
Owen Hart vs. The British Bulldog
(03.03.97)

****½ MATCHES
Doink the Clown vs. Marty Jannetty
(06.21.93)
Owen Hart & The British Bulldog
vs. Shawn Michaels & Steve Austin
(05.26.97)

****¼ MATCHES
Mr. Perfect vs. Ric Flair
(01.25.93)
Shawn Michaels vs. Marty Jannetty
(05.17.93)
Shawn Michaels vs. Marty Jannetty
(07.19.93)
Bret Hart vs. 1-2-3 Kid
(07.11.94)

**** MATCHES
*The Steiner Brothers vs. Money Inc. (Cage Match)
(08.23.93)
Razor Ramon vs. Shawn Michaels
(08.01.94)
Bret Hart vs. Jeff Jarrett
(01.16.95)
Owen Hart vs. The British Bulldog
(06.05.95)
Owen Hart vs. Shawn Michaels
(11.20.95)

***¾ MATCHES
1-2-3 Kid vs. Shawn Michaels
(12.06.93)
1-2-3 Kid vs. Owen Hart
(08.15.94)
Alundra Blayze vs. Bull Nakano
(04.03.95)
Steve Austin vs. Mankind
(11.18.96)
Owen Hart & The British Bulldog
vs. Doug Furnas & Phil LaFon
(01.20.97)
Owen Hart vs. The British Bulldog
(03.31.97)
Cactus Jack vs. Triple H
(09.22.97)

***½ MATCHES
Bret Hart vs. Fatu
(03.01.93)
Mr. Perfect vs. Doink the Clown
(05.24.93)
Steiner Brothers vs. The Quebecers
(09.13.93)
Marty Jannetty vs. 1-2-3 Kid
(10.25.93)
The Quebecers vs. The Headshrinkers
(05.02.94)
The Heavenly Bodies
vs. 1-2-3 Kid & Bob Holly
(01.16.95)
Shawn Michaels vs. The British Bulldog
(03.06.95)
Bret Hart vs. Owen Hart
(03.27.95)
Hakushi, Owen Hart & Yokozuna
vs. Bret Hart, 1-2-3 Kid & Bob Holly
(04.10.95)
Hakushi vs. 1-2-3 Kid
(11.20.95)
Raw Bowl Elimination Match
(01.01.96)
Shawn Michaels vs. 1-2-3 Kid
(03.04.96)
Shawn Michaels vs. Hunter Hearst Helmsley
(05.13.96)
Shawn Michaels & Sid
vs. The British Bulldog & Owen Hart
(11.11.96)
Shawn Michaels vs. Mankind
(08.11.97)
Tajiri vs. Taka Michinoku
(10.20.97)

***¼ MATCHES
Marty Jannetty vs. Bam Bam Bigelow
(05.31.93)
Doink the Clown vs. Marty Jannetty
(06.14.93)
Doink the Clown vs. Randy Savage
(08.02.93)
The Quebecers
vs. Marty Jannetty & 1-2-3 Kid
(01.10.94)
Alundra Blayze vs. Bull Nakano
(08.01.94)
Razor Ramon vs. Owen Hart
(01.09.95)
Bret Hart vs. Hakushi
(07.24.95)
Aja Kong & Tomoko Watanabe
vs. Alundra Blayze & Kyoko Inoue
(11.27.95)
Shawn Michaels vs. Leif Cassidy
(03.25.96)
Savio Vega vs. Goldust
(04.15.96)
Shawn Michaels vs. Marty Jannetty
(07.01.96)
Shawn Michaels vs. Owen Hart
(08.12.96)
Owen Hart vs. Flash Funk
(02.17.97)

*** MATCHES
Mr. Perfect vs. Terry Taylor
(01.18.93)
Blake Beverly vs. 1-2-3 Kid
(07.05.93)
Battle Royal
(10.04.93)
Rick Martel vs. Razor Ramon
(10.11.93)
Johnny Polo vs. Marty Jannetty
(12.27.93)
Bam Bam Bigelow vs. Sparky Plugg
(05.16.94)
Yokozuna & Owen Hart
vs. 1-2-3 Kid & Bob Holly
(04.17.95)
Owen Hart & Yokozuna
vs. Razor Ramon & Savio Vega
(07.31.95)
Marty Jannetty vs. Skip
(09.25.95)
The Undertaker vs. The British Bulldog
(09.25.95)
The British Bulldog vs. Marty Jannetty
(11.06.95)
Hakushi vs. 1-2-3 Kid
(02.05.96)
Goldust vs. Razor Ramon
(02.19.96)
Savio Vega vs. Steve Austin
(03.11.96)
Yokozuna vs. Vader
(04.08.96)
Steve Austin vs. Marc Mero
(05.20.96)
The Smoking Gunns
vs. Ahmed Johnson & Shawn Michaels
(07.22.96)
The Bodydonnas
vs. The British Bulldog & Owen Hart
(09.23.96)
Steve Austin vs. Jake Roberts
(09.30.96)
Vader & Jim Cornette
vs. Shawn Michaels & Jose Lothario
(09.30.96)
Bret Hart vs. Owen Hart
(11.25.96)
Vader vs. Steve Austin
(12.16.96)
Owen Hart vs. Mankind
(01.06.97)
*Rocky Maivia vs. Hunter Hearst Helmsley
(01.18.97)
Owen Hart & The British Bulldog
vs. Doug Furnas & Phil LaFon
(02.03.97)
Bret Hart vs. Sycho Sid
(02.17.97)
Steve Austin & Shawn Michaels
vs. The Legion of Doom
(06.02.97)
Brian Pillman vs. Mankind
(06.30.97)
Tajiri vs. Taka Michinoku
(07.14.97)
Steve Austin & Dude Love
vs. Owen Hart & The British Bulldog
(07.14.97)
*Jerry Lynn vs. Taka Michinoku
(08.29.97)
*The British Bulldog vs. Dude Love
(09.05.97)
Owen Hart vs. Shawn Michaels
(10.20.97)
Ken Shamrock vs. Shawn Michaels
(11.03.97)
Taka Michinoku vs. Aguila
(12.01.97)
Owen Hart vs. Shawn Michaels
(12.29.97)

THE WORST MATCHES SO FAR...

-***** MATCHES
The Bushwhackers vs. Damien Demento & Repo Man
(03.22.93)
The Bushwhackers vs. The Quebecers
(03.21.94)

-**** MATCHES

-*** MATCHES
Shawn Michaels vs. Triple H
(12.22.97)

-** MATCHES
Doink the Clown vs. Tony DeVito
(12.06.93)
Mabel vs. King Kong Bundy
(01.30.95)
Hunter Hearst Helmsley vs. The Stalker
(09.23.96)

-* MATCHES
Typhoon vs. Von Krus
(04.26.93)
Bastion Booger vs. Crush
(06.28.93)
Superfly Jimmy Snuka vs. Paul Van Dale
(09.27.93)
Crush vs. Tony Roy
(12.06.93)
Tatanka vs. Crush (Lumberjack Match)
06.06.94
Avatar vs. Brian Walsh
(10.23.95)
Ahmed Johnson vs. Crush
(04.14.97)

DUD MATCHES
The Undertaker vs. Damien Demento
(01.11.93)
Friar Ferguson vs. Chris Duffy
(04.12.93)
Kamala vs. Rich Myers
(05.03.93)
Crush vs. Bobby Who
(05.24.93)
Men on a Mission vs. Rich Myers & Hank Harris
(07.19.93)
Bastion Booger vs. Scott Despres
(07.19.93)
IRS vs. Scott Taylor
(10.18.93)
Men on a Mission vs. Todd Mata & Steve Greenman
(10.25.93)
Adam Bomb vs. Mark Thomas
(12.20.93)
Doink the Clown vs. Spike Gray
(12.27.93)
Crush vs. Mike Moraldo
(12.27.97)
Diesel vs. Scott Powers
(01.17.94)
Crush vs. Tony Mata
(02.07.94)
Crush vs. Ray Hudson
(03.28.94)
Typhoon vs. The Black Phantom
(06.20.94)
IRS vs. Rich Myers
(06.27.94)
Tatanka vs. Jeff Jarrett
(07.04.94)
Tatanka vs. Nikolai Volkoff
(07.25.94)
The Undertaker II vs. Butch Banks
(08.08.94)
The Bushwhackers vs. Barry Hardy & Bert Centeno
(09.12.94)
The Bushwhackers vs. Well Dunn
(12.19.94)
Henry Godwinn vs. Mike Khoury
(12.26.94)
Howard Finkel vs. Harvey Wippleman (Tuxedo Match)
(01.09.95)
Aldo Montoya vs. David Sierra
(01.30.95)
Kama vs. Jumbo Beretta
(01.30.95)
Mantaur vs. Leroy Howard
(02.06.95)
Doink the Clown vs. Bob Cook
(02.27.95)
King Kong Bundy vs. Adam Croomes & Raven Clark
(03.20.95)
Men on a Mission vs. Ben Jordan & Tony Roy
(04.03.95)
Bertha Faye vs. La Pantera Serena
(04.24.95)
Owen Hart & Yokozuna vs. Razor Ramon & Savio Vega
(08.07.95)
Tatanka & Kama vs. Savio Vega & Bob Holly
(09.18.95)
Goldust vs. The Ultimate Warrior
(05.27.96)
Savio Vega vs. Crush
(08.12.96)
The Executioner vs. Freddie Joe Floyd
(11.25.96)
Jake Roberts & Marc Mero vs. Hunter Hearst Helmsley & Billy Gunn
(12.02.96)
Ahmed Johnson vs. Crush
(01.27.97)
Goldust vs. Crush
(02.03.97)
Goldust vs. Savio Vega
(02.24.97)
Heavy Metal, Pentagon II & Pierroth vs. Latin Love, Octagon & Hector Garza
(03.10.97)
Hunter Hearst Helmsley vs. Jesse Jammes
(04.14.97)
Rocky Maivia vs. Savio Vega
(04.14.97)
Jesse Jammes vs. Rockabilly
(04.21.97)
Tiger Ali Singh vs. Salvatore Sincere
(04.21.97)
The Legion of Doom vs. Brian Pillman & Jim Neidhart
(05.26.97)
Faarooq vs. Goldust
(07.21.97)
The Patriot vs. Hunter Hearst Helmsley vs. Savio Vega
(09.08.97)
Skull & 8-Ball vs. Recon & Sniper
(10.13.97)

THE RAW AWARDS

BEST MATCH

ARNOLD FURIOUS

1. The British Bulldog vs. Owen Hart
   (03.03.97)
2. Owen Hart & The British Bulldog vs. Steve Austin & Shawn Michaels
   (05.26.97)
3. Hunter Hearst Helmsley vs. Cactus Jack
   (09.22.97)

This was an easy one to call. Owen vs. Bulldog is one of the best *Raw* matches, ever. Quite simply put: if you've not seen it you're missing out. Bulldog and Owen deserve top spot on account of how many other great TV matches they were involved in during 1997. Their match in Germany was the best thing either man did but they had a re-match in America that was pretty darn good too and both men had decent singles matches. On top of that they were the best tag team of the year and had not only a superb title match with Austin & Michaels, which is my #2 pick, but also a barnburner with Furnas & LaFon way back in January. The match with Austin & Michaels was during a brief stint in the middle of the year where both Austin and Michaels were actually fit. I imagine the entire year would have been very different if both Austin and Michaels had been fit constantly. My third choice is Hunter vs. Cactus Jack, Mick Foley's third character during 1997. It's a good old fashioned hardcore brawl with intensity and Foley's desire to self harm. Mick always brought out the savage best in Hunter and you could argue that this is the best match Hunter had until he was champion in late 1999. Of all the hardcore bouts during Attitude this one sticks out because it was early, it was clever and it was in MSG.

JAMES DIXON

1. The British Bulldog vs. Owen Hart
   (03.03.97)
2. Owen Hart & The British Bulldog vs. Steve Austin & Shawn Michaels
   (05.26.97)
3. Shawn Michaels vs. Mankind
   (08.11.97)

It didn't take place in the six months that I covered, but I could hardly overlook the best match on *Raw* to date and indeed one of the greatest in the long history of the show; Owen Hart and Davey Boy Smith put on a wrestling clinic to rival that of Davey against another of his brother-in-laws, Bret Hart, at *SummerSlam '92*. As we head balls deep into the Attitude Era, it is more than likely going to be many years before anything else comes close. One thing that *did* come close this year was a superb tag match featuring the same two guys from my number one spot, only back in their usual role of teaming up. Together they battled two all-time greats of the game, the oddball pairing of Shawn Michaels and Steve Austin. The crowd was hot, the work was smooth and the finish was satisfying, it was the best tag match in the company all year. For many years, in fact. My third choice is a rematch from a classic PPV battle in 1996 between Mankind and Shawn Michaels, though I will state that I don't enjoy either anywhere near as much as some. But still, it was a wild brawl featuring some innovative spots and plenty of excitement. The two have good chemistry together, no doubt about it.

WORST MATCH

1. The Patriot vs. Hunter Hearst Helmsley vs. Savio Vega
   (09.08.97)
2. Heavy Metal, Pentagon & Pierroth vs. Latin Lover, Octagon & Hector Garza
   (03.10.97)
3. Ahmed Johnson vs. Crush
   (01.27.97)

A badge of merit perhaps for 1997, as I didn't rate anything in negative stars. However when you're main eventing *Raw* you really need to aim higher than a DUD, which is why Patriot, Hunter and Savio claim WMOTY. A disgracefully unambitious, lazy, badly put together match. Some of my least favourite matches are three way dances because they're so hard to assemble. You need good spots, you need good cooperation and you need a good story. This match had none of that. Almost nothing involved all three men. It looked completely unplanned. It's one of the worst *Raw* main events ever. Second is the 6-man lucha-libre mess from March. With *Raw* struggling to fill its two hour run time, Vince imported an array of Mexican talent and they had difficulty translating to a US audience. I think Vince had been coerced into trying it after WCW got rave reviews for the likes of Rey Mysterio Jr. and Juventud Guerrera, but those guys were world class cruiserweights, the absolute cream of the Mexican crop. Frankly these six, while not terrible, were far from the top of the luchadore ranks. Their six man match contained too many mistakes and too much sloppy lucha action. My third choice I debated for a while, considering the LOD vs. Harts tag match that Brian Pillman ruined by himself or the Faarooq vs. Goldust match that has to be Ron Simmons' laziest outing, before settling on Ahmed vs. Crush. For starters, Crush won that match! Crush! In 1997! The booking alone is madness but the match itself is a disaster. Ahmed botched almost everything he did, while in contrast Crush tried to be really boring. And succeeded. My lasting memory remains that of Ahmed sandbagging his opponent to deliberately ruin a spot. Not the first nor last time he'd do that.

JAMES DIXON

1. Shawn Michaels vs. Triple H
   (12.22.97)
2. Crush vs. Ahmed Johnson
   (04.14.97)
3. Rocky Maivia vs. Savio Vega
   (04.14.97)

The Shawn Michaels vs. Triple H match for the European Title at the end of the year was a sad indictment of where the WWF was heading. The stable mates were forced to battle each other for the title, and instead of having a well-contest, back-and-forth match like tag partners Davey Boy Smith and Owen Hart did in the tournament final for said title, they instead made a mockery out of the belt and the business. It was hokey bullshit, with Shawn laying down for Hunter from a lock-up push down and a super gentle splash, the only two moves in the bout. Naturally, WCW thought this was great and recreated the idiocy a year later with their World Title. That snowballed and ended up killing the company down the line. Morons, everywhere. The only other match to make negative stars was the Ahmed Johnson vs. Crush match from South Africa, which was just one botch after another and went on forever. It exposed pro wrestling in many ways, as Crush frequently did, and is yet another of big Bri's blinders. On the very same show, Savio Vega and Rocky Maivia did 17-minutes of absolutely nothing, in one of the most boring matches I have ever seen. Those two had terrible chemistry.

BEST WRESTLER

ARNOLD FURIOUS

1. Owen Hart
2. The British Bulldog
3. Mick Foley

This was tough. Naturally the two most talented wrestlers in the WWF in 1997 were Shawn Michaels and Steve Austin. Without a doubt. Michaels was arguably the best wrestler in the world at the time (perhaps with the exception of Mitsuharu Misawa) and Austin the hottest. But Shawn only worked PPVs, and spent most of his TV time addressing Bret Hart in a feud that rumbled on for 11-months without a match of any kind. Meanwhile Austin picked up a serious neck injury in the middle of the year and spent the second half of it cutting non-stop promos. So the two very top guys just weren't at the races for this award. Instead I went with the ever reliable Owen Hart who, like his brother-in-law Davey Boy, was involved in the top matches on Raw this year. Their clash in Germany is the MOTY and a contender for overall MOTY including PPV matches. That's how good it is. Plus they formed an excellent tag team and had great matches all year long. They place #1 and #2 with very little in it between them. Third is Mick Foley. He had a solid, consistent year in the ring despite flitting between three different characters and being largely criticised for the standard of Dude Love's matches. I personally didn't think he was that bad as Dude, but then I have included him as a guilty pleasure to reflect the feelings of others. I thought Foley was on the cusp of something big towards the end of 1997 only to be massively overshadowed by Austin's final push to the title in early 1998. He certainly was the complete package. A terrific wrestler, albeit not in the conventional sense, a charismatic personality and a cutter of unique and brilliant promo. It took the Undertaker throwing him off the Hell in a Cell for him to finally shatter the WWF's glass ceiling and make himself a genuine title contender, but he was close here even without the massive fall.

JAMES DIXON

1. Shawn Michaels
2. The British Bulldog
3. Owen Hart

I was pretty torn on this one, but ultimately I had to go with Shawn Michaels for having the complete package of untouchable in-ring performances combined with some stellar promo work. Michaels threw himself around for all manner of opponents and made them and himself look great while doing it. He may have been a jerk, but no one would ever question his ability in the squared circle. The only reason I questioned whether to award him top spot was down to the fact he missed a significant chunk of the year through injury and sulking. Second and third spots go to the often underrated Davey Boy Smith and Owen Hart. While they are highly regarded by most, I still feel it is less than they should be. Their consistently excellent performances this year prove that. Just take a look at the star ratings guide for further proof. Elsewhere, honourable mentions go to Taka Michinoku for putting in some brilliant showings in spite of the company failing to get behind him properly, Steve Austin for his work in the first six months before he became less about the wrestling and more about the talky talk, Bret Hart for being solid but never that spectacular because of injury and Mick Foley for putting in some great showings under all three of his diverse gimmicks.

WORST WRESTLER

ARNOLD FURIOUS

1. Crush
2. Savio Vega
3. Brian Pillman

The problem with the Nation of Domination imploding and splintering into various different groups wasn't only the onset of a gang war but also that the gang leaders sucked in the ring. Faarooq was at least passable, when motivated, but as heels both Crush and Savio were phenomenally bad. Crush blows my mind as I voted him Worst Wrestler in The Raw Files: 1994 and here we are, three years later and he's still the worst wrestler in the company. At least Crush got cut loose toward the end of '97 and didn't come back until 2001, when, once again, he was the worst wrestler in the company. Savio, I feel badly for. He was a decent babyface and had a series of solid matches with Steve Austin which almost made him as a midcard star, only for the WWF to discover Austin carried Savio on his back during that feud. Savio's heel work on the other hand was abysmal. He was the shits. He's probably the most boring wrestler of 1997. Third I've reluctantly selected the horribly deteriorated Brian Pillman. He was rusty, sloppy and all over the bloody place during 1997. You could tell he wasn't in good condition, but he dosed himself up on painkillers and God knows what else to get in the ring and rushed his comeback, perhaps out of respect to the WWF who stood by and paid him big bucks during his injury, which cost him dearly. I'm really sad that Brian died, but I'm even more upset with the fact that the Monday Night War forced him back into the ring before he was ready. He wasn't an isolated incident and for years the WWF, and other companies, constantly brought back injured guys too soon and shortened their careers and indeed lives in the process.

JAMES DIXON

1. Phineas Godwinn
2. Crush
3. Savio Vega

Phineas Godwinn managed to drag down every match that he was involved in, and didn't enter a single good showing all year. Many times he just flat out exposed the business with his shocking timing, dreadful positioning and failure to grasp even the most basic concepts of wrestling psychology. One of the worst wrestlers in WWF history, no doubt about that. Crush we have seen suck for years, and he managed to live down to all expectations this year too. Whether it be as part of the Nation of Domination or leading his own Disciples of Apocalypse group, Crush was routinely one of the most boring, frustrating and insufferable guys on the show. Savio Vega went from a fiery and perfectly serviceable babyface in 1996 to a turgid and almost unwatchable heel in 1997. His run with the Nation and then as leader of Los Boricuas were equally bad. A dishonourable mention goes to Hunter Hearst Helmsley who managed to bore everyone to tears for six months before embarking upon a program with Mick Foley which started to turn things around for him. If not for Foley, Hunter would easily be on this list.

BEST PROMO

ARNOLD FURIOUS

1. Bret Screwed Bret - Vince McMahon
2. Bret Hart turns on America
3. You'll have to kill me – Steve Austin

All the top guys in the ring were also the top guys on the mic in 1997. The likes of Shawn Michaels, Bret Hart and Steve Austin suddenly became very chatty. Despite all of this the best promo of the year came from the slyly obnoxious owner of the WWF: Vince McMahon. When he cut the "Bret Hart screwed Bret Hart" promo he changed the landscape of the WWF and indeed the entire wrestling world. Everyone has been copying this ever since, including WWE who've run the same angle ad nauseum with a changing cast of characters playing the same roles. At the time it was a revolution and Vince generated volcanic, off-the-charts heat for his heel role. For the other two promo choices I've managed to include Bret, Shawn and Austin. The number two promo saw Bret denounce his American fans for turning on him at *WrestleMania 13* only to be confronted by Shawn Michaels, kick-starting a war of words that lasted until one of them left the promotion… and then carried on for a bit! Finally I've included Austin's monumental face turn promo where he told Bret Hart he would never be done with him.

JAMES DIXON

1. Steve Austin
2. Jim Cornette
3. Mankind

Once again I am choosing guys for their body of work over the year rather than for one individual promo. Steve Austin is an easy pick for number one, despite the immensely strong competition this year. Surely I don't need to explain to anyone reading this why Steve Austin is good on the mic. Number two pick Jim Cornette had all of his best moments in the space of a few months from October onwards. His promos weren't even live, but rather pre-recorded rants at the camera about everything in wrestling that pissed him off. They were captivating, and the kind of "shoot" promos that work and don't feel forced. It's a shame they ultimately led to the formation of an NWA faction in the WWF, but that wasn't the initial intention. The end result doesn't detract for the quality of the work, and I would strongly advise anyone who hasn't seen them to check them out, because much of what Jim says still applies today. Mankind takes third spot for the legendary interviews with Jim Ross which changed his career and made him into a legitimate star. I attest that they are the finest thing Mick Foley did in his entire illustrious career. There are a number of honourable mentions including Bret Hart and Shawn Michaels for the heat they generated with their promos and the venom with which they delivered their barbs against each other, Marc Mero for behind underrated behind the stick but actually really good in the role of delusional asshole misogynist and the Rock for his composed and confident delivery and some wonderful mannerisms towards the end of the year. If he had been the Rock rather than Rocky Maivia throughout 1997, he would have easily cracked the top three.

WORST PROMO

ARNOLD FURIOUS

1. Ahmed Johnson butchers two languages
2. Charred body parts - Kane
3. Special Agent Sable/Sunny's Super Soaker adverts

Ahmed Johnson isn't known for coherent promos, far from it, but when chosen for an in-ring promo in Germany his strengths completely faded away. He was denied intensity by periods of explanation from the German interviewer and the result was even more disjointed than usual. I'd have left his promo alone and let the Germans try to figure it out for themselves. That would have been more entertaining. Paul Bearer cut a vast number of samey promos during 1997 regarding his "son" and Taker's younger brother Kane. While none of them were actively bad, the sheer weight of them began to take their toll and I've picked out my least favourite; a gruelling Bearer promo where he described Kane's "charred body parts", something that was later explained away as being part of Kane's damaged psyche rather than actual charring. Part of Vince Russo's booking issues were that he'd paint himself into a corner and find some total bullshit to paint his way out again. This scenario relied entirely on Kane permanently wearing a mask and permanently covering his arm. Both have changed over the years. Finally I've gone with the WWF's super sexy product placement bits. At least the Milton Bradley Karate Fighter's tournament was entertaining. The Super Soaker and Special Agent Sable bits were a sexy chick using a product. Using sex to sell? Who would have thunk it. But these were kids toys! Questionable work from the WWF.

JAMES DIXON

1. Hunter Hearst Helmsley
2. Rick Rude
3. Savio Vega

Triple H is bad at promos, he always has been and he always will be. While in the modern era he rambles on continuously for what seems like hours without really saying anything and just RANDOMLY shouting and putting. full. stops. in. the. middle. of. sentences, in 1997 he suffered from his blue blood gimmick and delivered his interviews in a plummy accent that made him sound like a grade A prick. As part of DX he dropped some of the accent, but still had one of the most unlistenable voices in wrestling history, with the added bonus of talking about nothing but his dick, while overvaluing his own worth and sucking up to Shawn Michaels. Horrible. Rick Rude was another DXer who stunk up the stick, routinely falling over his lines and mispronouncing words. He could deliver his 80's pre match promo fine, but that never changed. Rude was unable to adapt to Attitude and was not a good fit for DX at all. I debated third spot as 90% of the Gang Warz participants could have taken it, but Savio Vega was the worst of a bad bunch. Some might argue Ahmed Johnson, but I, as usual, found every one of his promos utterly fascinating.

BEST NON-WRESTLER

ARNOLD FURIOUS

1. Jim Ross
2. Jim Cornette
3. Vince McMahon

Had Vince not been on commentary all year and just appeared towards the end as an authority figure he'd have won it hands down. As a commentator he ground at me, as an authority figure he did too, but then he was supposed to. Babyface commentators shouldn't grind at your nerves, Michael Cole. Speaking of commentators; both JR and Cornette were outstanding all year. I guess Cornette's outspoken opinions got him ousted from the spot, but he was perfect foil for Ross; both knowledgeable and a heel. The WWF went in a different direction and modified the existing Jerry Lawler to suit their Attitude needs. They tried to remove Ross too for someone more photogenic, but thankfully that doesn't happen just yet. The Ross/Cornette announce team is one of my favourites and made the second half of 1997 much easier on the ears than the first half.

JAMES DIXON

1. Jim Cornette
2. Jim Ross
3. Vince McMahon

I have nothing much to add to what Furious has already said, the only difference being I have given Cornette top spot because of the excellent promos he cut in October and again in December.

WORST NON-WRESTLER

ARNOLD FURIOUS

1. Michael Cole
2. The Honky Tonk Man
3. Uncle Cletus

Michael Cole, why must I sit through so much of your existence? In 1997 he'd not permeated the product too much but was being used sparingly on interviews. Even then he grated at my nerves and caused me a Todd Pettengill level of agitation. What's worse is facing the knowledge that he'll be a permanent fixture on WWE programming for the foreseeable future. It's a glum future indeed. Cole's many faults become glaringly obvious under the microscope, but what really jars at me is how unaware he is of his faults. He'll never improve. He doesn't understand the business. He uses words, sentences and emphasis in completely the wrong places. He looks like a smarmy douchebag. Commentators shouldn't be photogenic, they should be good. You don't need to put the camera on these guys. They're here to enhance the product, not be the product. This is something Russo never understood and apparently Kevin Dunn too as Cole continued to stink up the airwaves years after Russo's departure. To be fair, he's marginally better as a commentator than an interviewer as his stupid statements don't bring down segments, just hurt them, while his stupid questions do ruin segments. Second I've placed the Honky Tonk Man, who went through a dreadful run in 1997 searching for his protégé. This sequence of events caused Honky to join commentary and ruin entire segments by putting himself over and burying actual talent before eventually derailing the career of Billy Gunn (see: Worst Gimmick). Honky's poisonous opinions and inability to work as a mouthpiece or a manager caused him to be one of the most useless characters on TV in 1997. Slightly better was Tony Anthony's terrible Uncle Cletus gimmick, like a heel Hillbilly Jim. Fortunately the WWF realised how much the gimmick sucked and removed him from TV after a month.

JAMES DIXON

1. Michael Cole
2. Marlena
3. The Honky Tonk Man

I detest Michael Cole as a performer, and continue to be flabbergasted year after year that he remains employed by the WWE at the time of writing. He is not just bad at his job, he is terrible at it. Listening to Michael Cole worsens one's viewing experience rather than enhances it, which is the opposite to what a commentator should be doing. This was his first full year with the company, and already he had many of the unlikeable traits that make him so utterly useless. Marlena had always been a chocolate fireguard manager, but this year she added "acting" and talking to her repertoire. She was appalling at both. One segment in particular where she accepted a challenge from Brian Pillman for Goldust to fight for her services, sticks in the memory as being cringe-inducingly bad. The Honky Tonk Man comes across as a detestable asshole in shoot interviews, running down people viciously and making up story after story. In his second WWF run, he wasn't much more likeable. Bad on commentary, poor as a manager and responsible in kayfabe terms for Rockabilly, this was a bad year for the Honky Tonk Man. Thankfully WWF officials realised that and cut him loose, and it was his last extended run in any of the big leagues.

GUILTY PLEASURE

ARNOLD FURIOUS

1. The Interrogator
2. Dude Love
3. Jackyl

The Interrogator, later Kurrgan, and his impossibly huge neck, always amused me during his WWF run. I think the WWF felt he could be something special and tried like hell to get him over as such, but he was a big lummox. He was this uncoordinated mass of muscle on a gigantic frame. In any other form of entertainment he'd be a freakshow, so that's what he ended up as in the WWF. Even in the Land of the Giants this guy was too weird looking to survive. A testament to his freakish stature. I love him a lot more now thanks to *Sherlock Holmes* and his hammer fight with Robert Downey Jr, but even back in 1997 I had a soft spot for him. I've put Mick Foley's much maligned Dude Love character in second. Foley had a lot of fun, after years of hardship as Mankind and Cactus Jack, and got to show his comedic side. Dude Love's matches aren't as horrible as we've perhaps made out and I thought he was good in the role. I'm also a sucker for a common man becoming a chick magnet. It brings out the day dreamer in all of us. Say, if this guy can get the chicks and score the big win in the ring maybe any of us can. I don't remember another guy the unwashed masses had a better connection with than Mick Foley, battling the athletic superstars and coming out even. Finally I've picked Jackyl, who everyone else seems to hate but I quite like. I liked the way he spoke and yes, he was a pompous windbag but I thought that was the point. I also loved him in ECW as Cyrus, and thought he was a fantastic heel there, which might sway my opinion of the Jackyl character somewhat.

JAMES DIXON

1. Ahmed Johnson
2. The Interrogator
3. Flash Funk

Yes, I have an unhealthy level of fandom for Ahmed Johnson, I know. I realise he sucks in the ring and most people find his promos indecipherable, but I love him anyway. I have said this before, but he is so big, so unpredictable, so goddamn shiny and his promos just so off-the-wall and Warrior like, that I am secretly thrilled every time he appears on screen. Plus, I think his brief heel run in the Nation was genuinely tremendous. Honestly. The Interrogator was a beast, he almost didn't look human. He was just a big no selling machine who appeared to have a neck made of rubber. What's not to like? Flash Funk probably shouldn't be a guilty pleasure given his ability, but with that dumb jumpsuit and gimmick, I guess he has to be. I thought Flash showed, ahem, flashes of excellence this year in a couple of outings and I enjoyed his work nearly every time he appeared. I was tempted to give third spot to Marc Mero for his brilliant obnoxious prick character, but I just couldn't bring myself to.

WORST GIMMICK

ARNOLD FURIOUS

1. Rockabilly
2. Razor Ramon II
3. Leif Cassidy

How do you potentially ruin a big star name? Saddle him with the Honky Tonk Man and a ridiculous name then add in a gimmick where he is singer and guitarist who can do neither. Sorted. Billy Gunn must have loved the day he heard he was getting the hell out of this gimmick and into the New Age Outlaws. Rockabilly was death. He didn't even win! He got a push… as a jobber. Honky was so utterly useless as a manager that Rockabilly couldn't buy a win. I still have no idea why they went in this direction unless it was to deliberately sabotage Honky's push and give Billy another chance in tags. They blatantly didn't want to give the gimmick any traction from the get-go and wouldn't put him over anyone of note. I've included Razor Rick Bognar for a second year running even though he hardly appeared. I felt the gimmick was so terrible it merited mention again. The WWF agreed and got shot of him, transforming his buddy Glenn Jacobs, aka the talented one, into Kane. Leif Cassidy comes in third on account of the mysteriously long streak of TV jobber matches he managed during 1997. It actually set up Al Snow perfectly for a return run, as Cassidy was such a joke, but I'm not even sure what Cassidy was supposed to be. He was a throwback to the 70s, who wrestled like a top Indy star and wore Rockers gear half a year after Marty Jannetty had left him in singles. I think the WWF were aware that Cassidy was going nowhere but also that he had talent so he got loaned to ECW where he rebuilt his reputation and returned the WWF as a solid midcarder. Luckily for him Leif Cassidy is a distant memory.

JAMES DIXON

1. The Godwinns
2. Rockabilly
3. Rocky Maivia

Nothing is worse than hillbillies, not even Rockabillies (sorry), and Rockabilly was horrific. At least Billy Gunn had the talent to recover and end the year on a high as one half of the tag team champions, which was unthinkable at the halfway stage of the year when the abomination had first been thrust on an unsuspecting public. Rocky Maivia takes third for being so the opposite of what the Rock would become. He is just another example of the WWF clearly having no idea what they are doing when it comes to making stars, and strengthening my belief that they have lucked into nearly every major star they have ever "made" themselves, after first saddling them with a stupid gimmick. The Ringmaster? Hunter Hearst Helmsley? Mankind the Mutilator? Deacon Batista? Isaac Yankem? The list is endless, and Rocky Maivia is definitely on it.

SEGMENT/ANGLE

ARNOLD FURIOUS

1. Steve Austin gives Vince McMahon a Stunner.
2. Cactus Jack challenges Hunter in MSG.
3. Bret Hart turns heel on America, reunites with Owen

1997 is a really hard year to nail down three picks for this category. Off the top of my head I'm missing: Bret Hart quitting, ECW invading *Raw*, Rob Van Dam wrestling on *Raw*, Dude Love showing up to partner Steve Austin and the legendary "Bret screwed Bret" speech. All of that took place in the same year on the same show and didn't make my top three. Hopefully the three moments of me marking out don't need explaining as to why they're on my list. Austin hitting the Stunner on Vince for the first time was amazing TV and redefined what the era was all about. Vince going from mild-mannered commentator to being outed as the company's owner by Jim Ross in later 1996, to crazy, grapefruits walk owner of the WWF happened in about 12-months, but the moment that switched Vince's gears was the Stunner. Austin crossed a line and it opened up a whole new world. The segment on the same episode of *Raw* that followed the Stunner on Vince was Cactus Jack's return to wrestling in an MSG street fight with Triple H. All those clips of Cactus in barbed wire shown on TV during Mick's sit down interviews with JR hyped even the fans who'd never seen Cactus in ECW, WCW and Japan. So his actual arrival, unannounced, popped the hell out of New York. Finally one of the all time great heel turns; Bret turning on the US but staying babyface in Canada. The moment that sealed the deal for me was on *Raw* the week after his initial heel speech when he made up with his brother Owen. After his initial outburst you sensed the public were still willing to forgive. But palling up with Owen made sure that would never happen.

JAMES DIXON

1. ECW Raw
2. Cactus Jack in the WWF

3. Shawn Michaels loses his smile

ECW turning up on *Monday Night Raw* was an incredible moment for anyone who had been following the WWF for years, because seeing them work so closely with another company was almost unheard of, certainly in the United States and on their own show. For fans of ECW it was a major moment too, because it was a chance for the rest of the world to see what they already knew; ECW was a revolution. The ECW guys for the most part took the opportunity with both hands and I am sure created a few new fans along the way, while the remaining regular crew guys like the Godwinns, Faarooq and Savio Vega walked through their bouts at a snail's pace. The difference was night and day. Equally rewarding and surprising for long time fans of Mick Foley was the appearance of his third alter ego, Cactus Jack, in the WWF. What made it even more special was it taking place at MSG, and the fact he then tore the house down with the usually boring Hunter Hearst Helmsley was the icing on the cake. The promo to set it up and the pop when he came out were both special. Third place could have gone to various things, but the most important and surprising moment from a business perspective was Shawn Michaels "losing his smile". Not only did it catch everyone completely off guard, but it had long term ramifications as to his relationship with the rest of the locker room, and what happened with the WWF Title. Not only that, but it was captivating television, and created a new piece of wrestling terminology. Other options considered include Shawn Michaels' "Sunny days" comment, Jeff Jarrett's return and subsequent shoot promo, Vince McMahon's post *Survivor Series* "Bret screwed Bret" interview, Jim Cornette shredding Hulk Hogan, Roddy Piper, Eric Bischoff, Sean Waltman and others, Mankind's interviews with JR and pretty much everything that Steve Austin did. It was a helluva year for the WWF's much vaunted "moments".

MOST UNDERRATED BY THE WWF

ARNOLD FURIOUS

1. Vader
2. Owen Hart
3. Tajiri

Looking back it's still hard to fathom what happened to Vader. Going into 1997 he'd gotten some criticism for working stiff and his place at the top of the card was certainly in jeopardy. He took some suspect jobs in late 1996, including a clean one for Sid, and his momentum faltered. But as 1997 kicked off Vader launched himself into it like a monkey being shot into space. His performance at *Final Four* alone caused Vince McMahon to gush with praise. So what the hell happened? One must suspect political murmurings and certain individuals feeling that Vader threatened their position on the card. When Vader being stiff wasn't enough to see him demoted they accused him of being overweight. Which he was, but it shouldn't have mattered. Vader was all about being big, mean and violent. Who cares how much he weighs, as long as he can still work? And he *could*. The best big man in the business soon found himself on job duty for newcomers Ken Shamrock and Kane before sliding into a nothing feud with Goldust at the year's end. How would I have changed this? I'd have booked Vader to win at *Final Four* and carry the belt into *WrestleMania*. It would have denied Bret one of his much heralded five titles and shunted Sid into midcard obscurity, but it would have established Vader as a main event. For starters; he would have headlined 'Mania. Second I've gone with Owen Hart. Even though Owen had a much improved 1997, compared to the two years of jobbing beforehand, he was still mired in the midcard. So much so that his IC title win over Rocky Maivia was almost an upset. Who knows what might have been if he'd not injured Steve Austin? Perhaps a title run in 1998 even. Finally I've got Tajiri, who must have shit in Vince's cornflakes to not get a contract after a brilliant match with Taka Michinoku. Not only that but he wasn't even given a slot in the light heavyweight title tournament! A tournament that included such cruiserweight luminaries as Eric Shelley and Flash Flannigan. For me, not only should Tajiri have been in the tournament but he should have been in the final or at least challenged Taka soon after for the belt. They could have salvaged the division with in-ring alone.

JAMES DIXON

1. The British Bulldog
2. Vader
3. Owen Hart

Both Davey Boy and Owen Hart ranked highly in my awards for wrestler of the year, match of the year and indeed in the Raw Recap awards and the star ratings guide. Yet, they were often treated as afterthoughts by the WWF. Losing the British Bulldog was one of many saddening ramifications of Montreal, and one which often gets forgotten about. When he returned in 1999 he was a shell of his former self. Vader too had many good matches both on *Raw* and PPV, but he was again overlooked because he didn't play the political game well enough. He was a workrate dolphin amidst a sea of great whites.

RAW NEWCOMER

ARNOLD FURIOUS

1. Ken Shamrock
2. Chyna
3. Taka Michinoku

When I started to think about the contenders for this award my mind went completely blank. It's really hard to remember who debuted when, and my brain kept telling me nobody debuted in 1997. Nobody in the business at all. Oh, apart from Ken Shamrock who went straight into being a legitimate badass in the company, beat Vader in his first ever WWF match and was main eventing *Raw* (and PPVs) by the year's end. Oh yeah, and Chyna debuted in 1997. Initially as Hunter's bodyguard she was already one of the best managers in the business just a few months later, actively having storylines built around her and being devastatingly effective. It got to the point where Hunter started to look weak as a wrestler because Chyna dominated his matches so much. It was like Sable and Marc Mero, only Chyna was actually useful. If Hunter hadn't become a motor-mouth on TV and palled up with Shawn Michaels, he may have found himself shunted to the side while Chyna went on to bigger and better things too. Oh yeah, and Taka Michinoku debuted in 1997 too. One of the best cruiserweights in the world and one of the few hires that made the WWF look competitive in cruiserweight matches with the dominant WCW (who had hired the likes of Rey Mysterio Jr, Dean Malenko, Chris Benoit, Chris Jericho, Juventud Guerrera, Psicosis, Eddy Guerrero, Chavo Guerrero Jr, etc). Taka had a few barnburners on *Raw* and if the WWF had believed in actually pushing cruisers he could have broken the cruiserweight glass ceiling way before the likes of Jericho, Benoit and Eddy did in later years. I even had a fourth contender; future IC champion D'Lo Brown. It turned out 1997 produced a few talented individuals after all.

JAMES DIXON

1. Taka Michinoku
2. Ken Shamrock
3. The Legion of Doom

Taka Michinoku was exactly what the WWF's brand new light heavyweight division needed. A genuinely world class performer between the ropes, with the ability to both wow a crowd and sell a story, Taka was phenomenal. Of course the WWF didn't get behind him and by the end of the year the light heavyweight champion was working a program with semi-retired commentator Jerry Lawler. Typical. Ken Shamrock made the transition from the UFC to the WWF in style, blasting through the competition before a loss to the British Bulldog at *SummerSlam* derailed him a little and killed his aura. The WWF tried to push him as a top guy due to a lack of main event talent at the end of the year, but it was a struggle. Still, what a rookie year for the World's Most Dangerous Man. The Legion of Doom may have been around for years, but this was their first year on *Raw*, as they left the company initially in 1992 a few years before the program started. At times they stuck rigidly to their outdated formula match, but usually against inferior opponents like the Godwinns and the Headbangers. At other times they had really good matches against Steve Austin & Shawn Michaels and others, and at the end of the year put the New Age Outlaws over in tremendous fashion. I for one, was happy to see them back in the WWF.

MOST IMPROVED PERFORMER

ARNOLD FURIOUS

1. Mick Foley
2. Rocky Maivia
3. The Headbangers

I've picked Mick as number one not because he vastly improved his in-ring like Rocky or vastly improved his status in the company, like the Headbangers did (albeit briefly). No, I picked Mick because of the strides he made in 1997 as a Sportz Entertainer. A series of sit down interviews with Mankind totally changed perception of Foley as a wrestler, as a man and as a talent. After those interviews the WWF were able to mine two more separate personalities already within Mick; teenage heartthrob Dude Love and hardcore icon Cactus Jack, with Foley being kooky enough to play off both, and his current incarnation Mankind, as three separate characters. Mick's work as Dude Love and then as Cactus Jack showed WWF fans what they'd been missing. Mick wasn't just the guy who made the Undertaker into a watchable wrestler, but he was also a fun loving nutcase, addicted to pain and ambitious in the fields of title belts, deathmatches and scoring chicks. Quite the transformation considering how he ended 1996 as the one-note Mankind. Originally I'd gone for Rock as the top guy, like James has and I wouldn't argue with his pick, because his improvement in the ring was unparalleled in 1997. He went from a raw rookie grappler who hit the same moves in every match, usually in the same sequence, to a charismatic heel capable of carrying guys like Ahmed Johnson who had no interest in improving themselves. A year later he made another giant leap and became WWF Champion, but that's a story for next year's book. Thirdly I've gone with the Headbangers. They briefly became a massive asset for the company. After winning the tag team titles their confidence increased dramatically and if they'd been booked properly could have become a solid team for the WWF. But they got jobbed out a month into the reign and slid back down the card into obscurity. The increase in effort during this run was palpable and James missed the whole thing because it took place in just one month!

JAMES DIXON

1. The Rock
2. Road Dogg
3. Jerry Lawler

How can it be anyone else but the Rock? Useless at the start of the year as a hand slapping babyface with a Chihuahua on his head, by the end he was a confidence exuding badass mixing it up with Steve Austin and hanging right there with him. What an incredible turnaround. Road Dogg didn't flourish until the back end of the year either, but once he did he was a riot. His new persona was a far cry from the horrid country music singing chore that was Jesse Jammes. I have been very harsh on the King in previous *The Raw Files* releases, and rightly so I feel, but this year he was far less grating and generally much better at his job. With the freedom to speak a little more candidly and be less of a cartoon, he became a fun part of the show.

BEST TAG TEAM

ARNOLD FURIOUS

1. Owen Hart & The British Bulldog
2. Doug Furnas & Phil LaFon
3. The Legion of Doom

The tag team scene wasn't particularly vibrant during 1997. The best matches stemmed from Owen and Bulldog's title run and even then tended to be against super teams like Austin & Michaels or Austin & Foley. They were very rarely challenged in the ring by good regular teams. Furnas & LaFon are the sole exception, thus garnering second place, though their 1997 was rough. After initially getting some joy from Owen & Davey Boy, they were in a car crash and missed a chunk of the summer. When they returned and turned heel the momentum was gone and they were not the same team. By year's end they were demoted to ECW. I've thrown the LOD in at #3 not because they were particularly good but just because everyone else was pretty bad. The Outlaws only debuted towards the year's end and hadn't perfected their team. The Headbangers' brief run at the top was cut off by a lack of faith in them from the Powers That Be. The New Blackjacks were badly hindered by the presence of a washed up Barry Windham. At least the LOD turned up and looked like they belonged.

JAMES DIXON

1. Owen Hart & The British Bulldog
2. Steve Austin & Shawn Michaels
3. The Legion of Doom

Number one spot needs no explanation, as the Bulldog and Owen continue to clean up in these awards. Steve Austin and

Shawn Michaels were a team for the blink of an eye, but boy were they a good one! The Legion of Doom I have discussed in the Raw Newcomer award, and I have given them third ahead of Furnas & LaFon because they did more and were a more important part of the show.

WORST TAG TEAM

ARNOLD FURIOUS

1. The Godwinns
2. DOA (any combination)
3. Recon & Sniper

I have nothing to add to James' frequent criticisms of the Godwinns that can be found in this book (and every other book featuring matches by them) apart from to say that Hank deserved better. Henry Godwinn was a decent prospect by himself. A solid enough big man who could take a decent bump and had a fair powerhouse move set. Had he not been hampered with a hog farmer gimmick it's hard to say what might have happened to him. He may have climbed the card and become a major player in the WWF's universe. But he was saddled with a hog farmer gimmick, and a simple cousin called Phineas who couldn't work a lick. And Hillbilly Jim. The Godwinns combination of gimmick and a simplification of style made them an eyesore. I've gone with the ever popular Harris brothers in second place, though I'm willing to concede that Chainz and Crush were also terrible. Chainz was the best worker of the bunch and he played the Fake Undertaker, so that's where the bar is set. Finally we have the Truth Commission's oft used team of Recon & Sniper. A pair of "hosses" that had Jim Ross salivating at their size but everyone else snoozing at their dull matches.

JAMES DIXON

1. The Godwinns
2. Skull & 8-Ball
3. The Headbangers

How much more can I write about how much I hate cartoon scuffling' hillbillies? I will become as tiresome and predictable as they were if I keep it up. The Harris twins are lumbering and tedious in every guise, this time as the bikers Skull & 8-Ball. Name me a good match they have EVER had. There isn't one. The Headbangers take third for appearing on seemingly every show and being uninspiring on all of them. Nothing makes you reach for the remote quite like a Headbangers match.

- - -

The following is a list of the recipients of the major awards (Best Match, Worst Match, Best Wrestler and Worst Wrestler) over the course of the Raw books so far. We have awarded 3 points for first place, 2 for second and 1 for third.

BEST MATCH
1. Owen Hart   21
2. Shawn Michaels   15
3. Davey Boy Smith   13

And the rest: 1-2-3 Kid (10); Steve Austin (9); Bret Hart, Razor Ramon (8); Marty Jannetty (7); Mick Foley (5); Goldust (4); Mr. Perfect, Ric Flair, Doink the Clown, The Quebecers, Alundra Blayze, Bull Nakano, Jeff Jarrett, Yokozuna (3); Scott Steiner, Rick Steiner, Ted DiBiase, IRS, The Headshrinkers, Billy Gunn, Bart Gunn, Sycho Sid, Savio Vega, Vader, Triple H (2); Jake Roberts, Bob Holly, Hakushi (1)

WORST MATCH
1. Crush   13
2. Savio Vega   12
3. Triple H   11

And the rest: Tatanka (8); The Bushwhackers (6); Mabel, Ahmed Johnson, Howard Finkel, Harvey Wippleman (4); The Quebecers, The Patriot, Shawn Michaels The Stalker, Goldust, King Kong Bundy, Repo Man, Damien Demento, Tony DeVito, Doink the Clown (3); Nikolai Volkoff, Heavy Metal, Pentagon, Pierroth, Latin Lover, Octagon, Hector Garza, The Ultimate Warrior, Jake Roberts, Billy Gunn, Kama, Bob Holly, Bertha Faye, La Pantera Serena, Typhoon, Jimmy Snuka, Paul Van Dale, Bastion Booger (2); Rocky Maivia, The Executioner, Freddie Joe Floyd, The Undertaker, Mankind, Owen Hart, Davey Boy Smith, Bradshaw, Steve Austin, Sycho Sid, Marc Mero, Brian Walsh, Avatar, Jeff Jarrett, Tony Mata, Von Krus, The Black Phantom, Mo, Rich Myers, Hank Harris (1)

BEST WRESTLER
1. Shawn Michaels   19
2. Owen Hart   11
3. 1-2-3 Kid   6

And the rest: Bret Hart (5); Davey Boy Smith (4); Doink the Clown (3); Mr. Perfect, Marty Jannetty, Scott Steiner, Steve Austin, Goldust (2); Vader, Mick Foley (1)

WORST WRESTLER
1. Crush   13
2. Kama   6
3. Bastian Booger   5

And the rest: Tatanka, Phineas Godwinn (4); Damien Demento, IRS, The Ultimate Warrior, Razor Ramon II, Savio Vega (3); Papa Shango, Mabel, Jake Roberts, Triple H (2); Mo, Lex Luger, Mantaur, The Stalker, Henry Godwinn, Brian Pillman (1)

SHOW RANK INDEX

5* SHOWS

10.06.97	100

THE BEST SHOWS

09.22.97	99
01.20.97	96
11.17.97	91
05.26.97	89
12.15.97	85
06.30.97	84
02.24.97	79
03.31.97	77
06.02.97	77
03.03.97	73
06.09.97	72
10.27.97	72
12.29.97	72
08.29.97 (Friday Night's Main Event)	71
10.20.97	69
04.28.97	68
05.19.97	68
09.29.97	68
07.14.97	66
11.03.97	65
03.17.97	64
08.18.97	64
11.24.97	63
04.21.97	60
10.13.97	60

GOOD SHOWS

08.11.97	59
02.17.97	58
04.07.97	56
07.21.97	56
07.07.97	55
08.04.97	54
09.05.97 (Friday Night's Main Event)	51
01.06.97	50
11.10.97	50

WORTH A LOOK

02.03.97	49
03.24.97	49
05.05.97	48
05.12.97	47
01.27.97	44
06.23.97	44
03.10.97	43
07.28.97	43
12.01.97	43
02.13.97 (Thursday Raw Thursday)	42
06.16.97	41

DECIDEDLY AVERAGE SHOWS

09.08.97	39
09.15.97	37
12.08.97	35
01.13.97	30

BAD SHOWS

12.22.97	20

THE WORST SHOWS

04.14.97	6

SCORE GUIDE

100	5* Show
90-99	Unmissable viewing!
80-89	Make sure you see this
70-79	Superb
60-69	Very good
50-59	Worth watching
40-49	Good in places
30-39	More bad than good
20-29	Worthless
10-19	Really awful
0-9	I hate wrestling.